Lecture Notes in Computer Science 11341

Commenced Publication in 1973
Founding and Former Series Editors:
Gerhard Goos, Juris Hartmanis, and Jan van Leeuwen

More information about this series at http://www.springer.com/series/7409

Ryutaro Ichise · Freddy Lecue
Takahiro Kawamura · Dongyan Zhao
Stephen Muggleton · Kouji Kozaki (Eds.)

Semantic Technology

8th Joint International Conference, JIST 2018
Awaji, Japan, November 26–28, 2018
Proceedings

 Springer

Editors
Ryutaro Ichise
National Institute of Informatics
Tokyo, Japan

Freddy Lecue
Accenture Labs
Dublin, Ireland

and

Inria
Sophia Antipolis, France

Takahiro Kawamura
Japan Science and Technology Agency
Tokyo, Japan

Dongyan Zhao
Peking University
Beijing, China

Stephen Muggleton
Imperial College London
London, UK

Kouji Kozaki
Osaka University
Osaka, Japan

ISSN 0302-9743   ISSN 1611-3349   (electronic)
Lecture Notes in Computer Science
ISBN 978-3-030-04283-7   ISBN 978-3-030-04284-4   (eBook)
https://doi.org/10.1007/978-3-030-04284-4

Library of Congress Control Number: 2018961000

LNCS Sublibrary: SL3 – Information Systems and Applications, incl. Internet/Web, and HCI

This Springer imprint is published by the registered company Springer Nature Switzerland AG
The registered company address is: Gewerbestrasse 11, 6330 Cham, Switzerland

Preface

This volume constitutes the proceedings of the 8th Joint International Semantic Technology Conference (JIST 2018) held during November 26–28, 2018, in Awaji City, Hyogo, Japan. The Joint International Semantic Technology Conference (JIST) is a regional federation of semantic technology-related conferences. The mission of JIST is to bring together researchers in the semantic technology research community and other areas of semantic-related technologies to present their innovative research results or novel applications of semantic technologies. JIST 2018 was a joint effort between the JIST conference and Special Interest Group on the Semantic Web and Ontology (SIG-SWO) of Japanese Society of Artificial Intelligence (JSAI).

There were three tracks at JIST 2018 including the Research Track and two Special Session Tracks on Government Open Data and Semantic Web for Life Sciences. We had 75 submissions in total. Each submission was reviewed by at least two reviewers, and in most cases by three reviewers. The committee decided to accept 23 papers (16 for the research and seven for the special session tracks) as regular papers and six papers (four for the research and two for the special session tracks) as short papers. The topics covered a wide spectrum of semantic technologies from theoretical studies to applications of semantic technologies. In particular, many papers are related to knowledge graphs, showing the current trend in semantic technologies.

As the organizer of JIST 2018, we would like to express our sincere thanks to the Program Committee members and additional reviewers for reviewing the papers in a short period of time. We would also like to thank the sponsors and support organizations. Last but not the least, we would like to thank all the speakers, authors, and participants for their great contributions that made JIST 2018 successful.

September 2018

Ryutaro Ichise
Freddy Lecue
Takahiro Kawamura
Dongyan Zhao
Stephen Muggleton
Kouji Kozaki

Organization

General Chairs

Stephen Muggleton   Imperial College London, UK
Kouji Kozaki   Osaka University, Japan

Program Chairs

Ryutaro Ichise   National Institute of Informatics, Japan
Freddy Lecue   Accenture Labs, Ireland and Inria, France

Special Session Track Chairs

Takahiro Kawamura   Japan Science and Technology Agency, Japan
Dongyan Zhao   Peking University, China

Local Organizing Chair

Atsuko Yamaguchi   Database Center for Life Science, Japan

Poster and Demo Chairs

Hanmin Jung   KISTI, South Korea
Shinichi Nagano   Toshiba Corporation, Japan

Workshop Chairs

Marut Buranarach   NECTEC, Thailand
Ikki Omukai   National Institute of Informatics, Japan

Tutorial Chair

Naoki Fukuta   Shizuoka University, Japan

Sponsorship Chair

Takanori Ugai   Fujitsu Laboratories Ltd., Japan

Publicity Chairs

Takeshi Morita   Keio University, Japan
Guohui Xiao   Free University of Bozen-Bolzano, Italy

Program Committee

Research Track

Carlos Bobed	University of Rennes 1, France
Fernando Bobillo	University of Zaragoza, Spain
Andreas Both	DATEV eG, Germany
Marut Buranarach	NECTEC, Thailand
Gong Cheng	Nanjing University, China
Stefan Dietze	Leibniz Institute for the Social Sciences, Germany
Dejing Dou	University of Oregon, USA
Jianfeng Du	Guangdong University of Foreign Studies, China
Alessandro Faraotti	IBM, Italy
Marcelo Finger	University of São Paulo, Brazil
Armin Haller	Australian National University, Australia
Wei Hu	Nanjing University, China
Eero Hyvönen	Aalto University, Finland
Evgeny Kharlamov	University of Oxford, UK
Hong-Gee Kim	Seoul National University, South Korea
Martin Kollingbaum	University of Aberdeen, UK
Adila A. Krisnadhi	Wright State University and Universitas Indonesia, Indonesia
Juanzi Li	Tsinghua University, China
Yuan-Fang Li	Monash University, Australia
Yinglong Ma	NCEPU, China
Yue Ma	LRI-CNRS, Université Paris Sud, France
Theofilos Mailis	National and Kapodistrian University of Athens, Greece
Maria Vanina Martinez	Universidad Nacional del Sur in Bahia Blanca, Argentina
Eduardo Mena	University of Zaragoza, Spain
Riichiro Mizoguchi	Japan Advanced Institute of Science and Technology, Japan
Trina Myers	James Cook University, Australia
Jeff Z. Pan	University of Aberdeen, UK
Guilin Qi	Southeast University, China
Edelweis Rohrer	Universidad de la República, Uruguay
Tong Ruan	ECUST, China
Michele Ruta	Politecnico di Bari, Italy
Floriano Scioscia	Politecnico di Bari, Italy
Jun Shen	University of Wollongong, Australia
Giorgos Stoilos	Babylon Health, UK
Umberto Straccia	ISTI-CNR, Italy
Thepchai Supnithi	NECTEC, Thailand
Hideaki Takeda	National Institute of Informatics, Japan
Kerry Taylor	Australian National University, Australia and University of Surrey, UK
Anni-Yasmin Turhan	TU Dresden, Germany

William Van Woensel	University of Dalhousie, Canada
Shenghui Wang	OCLC Research, USA
Xin Wang	Tianjin University, China
Zhe Wang	Griffith University, Australia
Guohui Xiao	Free University of Bozen-Bolzano, Italy
Bin Xu	DCST, Tsinghua University, China
Xiaowang Zhang	Tianjin University, China
Lihua Zhao	National Institute of Advanced Industrial Science and Technology, Japan
Amal Zouaq	University of Ottawa, Canada

Special Session on Government Open Data

Session Chairs

Hideaki Takeda	National Institute of Informatics, Japan
Thepchai Supnithi	NECTEC, Thailand
Marut Buranarach	NECTEC, Thailand

PC Members

Fabiodegomes Andrade	Instituto Federal da Paraíba, Brazil
Chutiporn Anutariya	Asia Institute of Technology, Thailand
Gong Cheng	Nanjing University, China
Dongpo Deng	Industrial Technology Research Institute, Taiwan
Asanee Kawtrakul	Kasetsart University, Thailand
Ponrudee Netisopakul	KMAKE LAB, Thailand
Siraya Sitthisarn	Thaksin University, Thailand
Vilas Wuwongse	Mahidol University, Thailand

Special Session on Semantic Web for Life Sciences

Session Chairs

Lihua Zhao	National Institute of Advanced Industrial Science and Technology, Japan
Yuan-Fang Li	Monash University, Australia
Hong-Gee Kim	Seoul National University, South Korea

PC Members

Jinhyun Ahn	Jeju National University, South Korea
Ali Hasnain	Insight Centre for Data Analytics, Ireland
Ryutaro Ichise	National Institute of Informatics, Japan
Donghyuk Im	Hoseo University, South Korea
Eung-Hee Kim	Seoul National University, South Korea
Piljong Kim	Seoul National University, South Korea
Kertkeidkachorn Natthawut	National Institute of Advanced Industrial Science and Technology, Japan

Khai Nguyen	National Institute of Informatics, Japan
Kobayashi Norio	RIKEN, Japan
Dezhao Song	Thomson Reuters, USA
Honghan Wu	King's College London, UK
Atsuko Yamaguchi	Database Center for Life Science, Japan

Additional Reviewers

Tonglee Chung
Pouya Ghiasnezhad Omran
Yu Gu
Yuncheng Hua
Hyunwhan Joe
Damir Juric

Khai Nguyen
Yawei Sun
Peng Xiao
Yuji Yang
Liang Zhang

Sponsors

Platinum Sponsor

https://www.oracle.com/

Gold Sponsor

http://ontolonomy.co.jp/

Contents

Government Open Data (Special Session Track)

Semantic Web for Life Sciences (Special Session Track)

Knowledge Graphs

Knowledge Driven Intelligent Survey Systems for Linguists

Ricardo Soares[1], Elspeth Edelstein[2], Jeff Z. Pan[1(✉)], and Adam Wyner[3]

[1] Department of Computing Science, University of Aberdeen, Aberdeen, UK
jeff.z.pan@abdn.ac.uk
[2] School of Language, Literature, Music and Visual Culture, University of Aberdeen, Aberdeen, UK
[3] School of Law and Department of Computer Science, Swansea University, Swansea, UK

Abstract. In this paper, we propose Knowledge Graph (KG), an articulated underlying semantic structure, to be a semantic bridge between human and systems. To illustrate our proposal, we focus on KG based intelligent survey systems. In state of the art systems, knowledge is hardcoded or implicit in these systems, making it hard for researchers to reuse, customise, link, or transmit the structured knowledge. Furthermore, such systems do not facilitate dynamic interaction based on the semantic structure. We design and implement a knowledge-driven intelligent survey system which is based on knowledge graph, a widely used technology that facilitates sharing and querying hypotheses, survey content, results, and analyses. The approach is developed, implemented, and tested in the field of Linguistics. Syntacticians and morphologists develop theories of grammar of natural languages. To evaluate theories, they seek intuitive grammaticality (well-formedness) judgments from native speakers, which either support a theory or provide counter-evidence. Our preliminary experiments show that a knowledge graph based linguistic survey can provide more nuanced results than traditional document-based grammaticality judgment surveys by allowing for tagging and manipulation of specific linguistic variables.

Keywords: Knowledge graph · Intelligent survey system
Grammaticality judgments

1 Introduction

Scientific advances are constantly crossing new boundaries, regularly revolutionizing the limits of what we have deemed possible. Yet, in a reflection of today's scientific conduct, researchers are exposed to an incredible amount of information, which, by the traditional document-oriented workflow, carries basilar faults, as new research often comes presented in an insufficient form that does not allow its repurpose for further research nor its reproducibility. The need to evolve such methods and the relevance of Open Science has fully bloomed, as transparency,

© Springer Nature Switzerland AG 2018
R. Ichise et al. (Eds.): JIST 2018, LNCS 11341, pp. 3–18, 2018.
https://doi.org/10.1007/978-3-030-04284-4_1

re-usability and knowledge sharing [10, 11] advocates a wider stream of information to flow through the scientific community. In the era of Artificial Intelligence, this also applies to many other scenarios of human-system interactions, where a semantic bridge between human and systems is demanded.

In this paper, we propose Knowledge Graph (KG) [1, 2], an articulated underlying semantic structure [4–6], to be such a semantic bridge between human and systems. To illustrate our proposal, we focus on KG based intelligent survey systems. The advantages of the approach are that surveys are generated using the semantic information in the structure, the participants populate the structure, and survey interactions are based around specific semantic components. In addition, the approach facilitates transparency, transmission, and re-usability.

A popular approach to information gathering is *Amazon's Mechanical Turk* (MTurk)[1], a crowdsourcing platform where on-demand users do *Human Intelligence Tasks*, such as the completion of advertised surveys for a price. Another tool is SurveyMonkey[2], which allows users to develop a survey online, serve to a community, and analyse results; surveys might have if-then-else structures. More relevant to our domain, there are online Linguistic experiments, which query users for linguistic judgments.[3] As useful as these tools are, knowledge is often hard-coded or implicit in these systems, making it hard for researchers to reuse, customise, link, or transmit the knowledge. Furthermore, such systems do not easily facilitate dynamic interaction with the participant.

In our approach, we develop and deploy a novel approach to survey-based practice by building in a survey system that uses Knowledge Graphs as an articulated underlying semantic structure and which provides three different components of exposure to relevant levels of users: the participant in the survey, who answers the questions; the domain expert, who uses customises the knowledge structure to suit the problem; and the knowledge engineer, who constructs the underlying semantic structure. These will be discussed further below.

To test our survey system, we focus on an issue in Linguistics as specified by a Linguist, who provides the domain knowledge. The tool represents linguistic information about the features and syntactic relationships in sentences. The user's task in the survey is to judge a sentence acceptable or unacceptable. Given the survey results, the linguist has detailed information about the significant features and syntactic relationships. In addition, the linguist can incorporate alternative hypotheses, which are dependent patterns of features and syntactic relationships, into the system, allowing data gathering to test the alternatives. By enabling exploration of hypotheses and analysis of results into relevant components, the survey tool is a novel way to gather and analyse data.

As far as we know, this is the first effort to make use of designing an intelligent survey system based on knowledge graphs. It makes three contributions. First, it enriches existing survey systems with Knowledge Graph, while hiding technical detail from survey users and researchers. Second, it illustrates an example of

---

[1] https://www.mturk.com/.

[2] https://www.surveymonkey.com.

[3] https://www.psytoolkit.org/.

Knowledge Graph driven software engineering [3], offering a built-in semantic bridge for human and systems. And finally, it facilitates Knowledge Graph driven research management in Open Science, wherein researchers can use structured information to share knowledge and data.

The rest of the paper is organized as follows. In Sect. 2, we briefly introduce the notion of knowledge graph, some basic idea of using knowledge to facilitate scientific research and the linguistic task of grammaticality judgment. In Sect. 3, we outline the core requirements that we consider in our knowledge-driven survey systems. Section 4 introduces our design of the knowledge graph for our topic as well as the implementation of our intelligent survey system. In Sect. 5, we outline the implementation and its evaluation. Relevant existing works are reviewed in Sect. 6. Finally, we conclude with some observations and outlooks in Sect. 7.

2 Background

2.1 Knowledge Graph

A knowledge graph $\mathcal{G} = (\mathcal{D}, \mathcal{S})$ consists of a data sub-graph $\mathcal{D}$ of interconnected typed entities and their attributes as well as a schema sub-graph $\mathcal{S}$ that defines the vocabulary used to annotate entities and their properties in $\mathcal{D}$. Facts in $\mathcal{D}$ are represented as triples of the following two forms:

- *property assertion* (h, r, t), where h is the head entity, and r the property and t the tail entity; e.g., (ACMilan, playInLeague, ItalianLeague) is a property assertion.
- *class assertion* (e, rdf:type, C), where e is an entity, rdf:type is the instance-of relation from the standard W3C RDF specification and C is a class; e.g., (ACMilan, rdf:type, FootballClub) is a class assertion.

A scheme sub-graph $\mathcal{S}$ includes Class Inclusion axioms C $\sqsubseteq$ D, where C and D are class descriptions, such as the following ones: $\top \mid \bot \mid A \mid \neg C \mid C \sqcap D \mid \exists r.C \mid$ $\leq n\,r \mid\, = n\,r \mid\, \geq n\,r$, where $\top$ is the top class (representing all entities), $\bot$ is the bottom class (representing an empty set), A is a named class r, r is a property and n is a positive integer. For example, the types of River and City being disjoint can be represented as River $\sqsubseteq \neg$City, or River $\sqcap$ City $\sqsubseteq \bot$. We refer the reader to [1] for a more detailed introduction of knowledge graphs.

2.2 The Linguistic Issue: Grammaticality Judgments

In investigating syntactic phenomena, linguists require data on what is judged *grammatical* by native speakers, i.e. what syntactic forms they can and cannot use. This information may be obtained by asking speakers to provide *grammaticality judgments*, assessments of whether particular syntactic constructions are acceptable. Data of this type allows linguists to describe and define the parameters of natural language grammar as it is spoken. As such, native speaker judgments of grammaticality are especially important in the study of 'non-Standard' sentence forms which differ from a more widely used 'Standard' norm, allowing researchers to establish the extent of syntactic variation within a language.

In a traditional *grammaticality judgment task*, a native speaker *participant* is presented with a series of sentences, which they rate on a scale of acceptability defined by the *linguist*. Although linguists often seek to measure the effects of specific linguistic features or variables, judgments are made at sentence level, meaning that the reasons for speakers' judgments may be obtuse to the researcher. Clarification may be provided through follow-up discussion with participants, but this solution is not practical with large numbers of participants or surveys conducted online. Moreover, the specific variables of interest to the linguist may be obscure to the participant.

As a test case, we investigate a syntactic construction found in Scottish English, namely the use of the verbs *need, want,* or *like* followed directly by a passive participle. Such constructions contrast with the Standard use, where an auxiliary *to be* is present following the main verb.

- *The cat needs fed* (Scottish English)
- *The cat needs to be fed* (Standard English)

A number of linguistic features may affect the use of the Scottish form, especially for speakers who also allow the contrasting Standard construction. These features include the choice of the main verb (*need, want,* or *like*); whether the subject is animate (living and sentient) or inanimate; and whether the subject is definite (specific and known) or indefinite.

The above pair of sentences represent use of the main verb *need* with an animate, definite subject (*the cat*). They differ in the presence or absence of *to be*, which also constitutes a variable linguistic feature.

In our test case, *participants* were given a binary choice, mapped to the values of 0 (for *this sentence sounds strange to me*) and 1 (for *this sentence sounds good to me*).

Previous work on the Scottish form indicates *need* is the most widely used main verb with this construction, followed by *want* and then *like* [7]. Inanimate subjects may also be more frequently used with *want* and *like* in the Scottish form than in the Standard equivalent [8]. We would also expect that the Standard form is acceptable to more speakers than the Scottish form, although the reverse may be true for certain populations.

3   Requirements Analysis

In this section, we present the requirements for our knowledge driven survey system. There are three categories of requirements - on the survey system, on the linguistic domain, and on the knowledge graph design.

Scientific Survey System Requirements. These requirements constitute the skeleton of what should be expected from any survey system, representing the most basic, yet essential functions.

- SR1: The respondent should be able to read sentences and input judgments rating their grammaticality.
- SR2: The researcher should be able to query simple and complex patterns of results with respect to the Knowledge Graph structure.
- SR3: The researcher should be able to input data to the Knowledge Graph or modify the Knowledge Graph while creating surveys, without having to understand the notion of Knowledge Graph.
- SR4: The researcher should be provided with statistical evaluation with respect to the Knowledge Graph.

Linguist Domain Requirements. These are what the linguist needs for their task.

- LR1: The researcher should be able to perform linguistic variable tagging on survey sentences.
- LR2: The researcher should be able to analyse grammaticality judgments with respect to linguistic variable tags.
- LR3: The researcher should be able to test different hypothesis patterns in relation to single and multiple linguistic variables.
- LR4: The researcher should be able to obtain fine-grained results at both sentence and linguistic variable level.

Knowledge Graph Requirements. In order to make the system reusable to other subjects than Linguistics, we need to separate the basic concepts in generic survey systems from linguistic survey systems.

- KR1: The survey system knowledge graph should cover basic concepts related to the survey system.
- KR2: The linguistic feature knowledge graph should cover basic concepts needed in the linguistic surveys.

4 Design of Knowledge Graphs and System

According to the requirements, we need to have two knowledge graphs for the knowledge driven survey system: one for generic survey systems, while the other for linguistic surveys. We firstly present the schemas of the two knowledge graphs before presenting some example triples of the two knowledge graphs in Sect. 4.1. We then present our approach and design in Sect. 4.2.

4.1 Design of Knowledge Graph

Survey Ontology. The survey ontology is a general purpose survey ontology which can be extended to specific domains such as linguistics (cf. Sect. 4.2).

Firstly, we identify key classes and properties in the survey ontology. Key classes include SurveyQuestion, AnswerOption, SurveyAnswer and Hypothesis,

Participation, User, while key properties include: hasAnswerOption (connecting SurveyQuestions and AnswerOptions), hasAnswer (connecting Participation and SurveyAnswers), hasSurveyUser (connecting Participation and User), hasSurveyQuestion (connecting Participation and SurveyQuestion), and hasAnswerOptions (connecting SurveyQuestion and AnswerOptions), hasContent (connecting a survey question with its content to be defined in the domain specific ontology). Note that we use the Participation class to represent the 3-ary relation among User, SurveyQuestion and SurveyAnswer.

Secondly, we will need to specify the dependencies of the classes and properties in the survey ontology:[4]

- SurveyQuestion $\sqsubseteq \geq 1$ hasAnswerOption.AnswerOption (Each survey question has at least 1 answer option);
- SurveyQuestion $\sqsubseteq = 1$ hasSurveyContent (Each survey question has exactly 1 content);
- Participation $\sqsubseteq = 1$ hasSurveyUser.User (Each participation has exactly 1 user);
- Participation $\sqsubseteq = 1$ hasSurveyQuestion.SurveyQuestion (Each participation has exactly 1 survey question);
- Participation $\sqsubseteq = 1$ hasSurveyAnswer.SurveyAnswer (Each participation has exactly 1 survey answer).

Linguistic Feature Ontology. The survey ontology is extended with domain specific linguistic features. Firstly, we identify key classes and properties in the linguistic survey ontology. Key classes include Sentence, POS (Part of Speech), Word and Feature, while key properties include: hasPOS (connecting Sentence and POS), hasWord (connecting POS and Word), hasFeature (connecting Hypothesis/POS and Feature), hasString (connecting Sentence/POS/Word with some strings) and relatedFeature (connecting features).

Secondly, we will need to specify the dependencies of the classes and properties in the survey ontology: (See footnote 4)

- SurveyQuestion $\sqsubseteq = 1$ hasContent.Sentence (Each survey question has exactly 1 sentence);
- Sentence $\sqsubseteq \geq 1$ hasPOS.POS (Each sentence has at least 1 POS);
- POS $\sqsubseteq \geq 1$ hasWord.Word (Each POS has at least 1 Word);
- Hypothesis $\sqsubseteq \geq 1$ hasFeature.Feature (Each hypothesis has at least one feature);
- Sentence $\sqsubseteq \geq 1$ hasString (Each sentence has some string);
- POS $\sqsubseteq \geq 1$ hasString (Each POS has some string);
- Word $\sqsubseteq \geq 1$ hasString (Each word has some string).

Parts of the linguistic feature ontology are constructed by linguistic researchers: (1) by providing a list of sub-classes of Feature, such as Subject or MainVerb (Subject $\sqsubseteq$ Feature, MainVerb $\sqsubseteq$ Feature), (2) by using these sub-classes of Feature to annotate POSs in survey sentences (cf. next section).

---

[4] To save space, we do not include domain and range axioms here.

Data Sub-graph Example. To illustrate the two knowledge graphs, we consider an example survey sentence: *The cat needs fed.* For each sentence, there are two answer options: *Grammatical* and *Not grammatical.* Here are some triples related to this sentence:

- (Q1, hasContent, S1): the survey question Q1 has the sentence S1 as the content;
- (S1, hasString, '*The cat needs fed.*');
- (P1, rdf:type, POS): P1 is a POS;
- (S1, hasPOS, P1): S1 has a POS P1;
- (P1, hasString, 'The cat');
- (P1, rdf:type, Subject): P1 is annotated as an instance of Subject.

The knowledge graphs serve as a bridge between researchers and the survey system in terms of understanding the sentences, survey answers, as well as related features.

4.2 Approach and System Design

To provide a successful semantic-enabled Survey System to be of use to researchers, it is vital that the complexity of the system be obscured from them, without sacrificing the leverage provided by the KG itself - linguists are users of an ontology and not experts in ontology management. In other words, the key challenges for the design of the knowledge driven survey system are: (C1) how to embed knowledge graphs into a survey system so that knowledge graphs serve as a bridge between the system and human researchers; (C2) how to do this in a transparent way so that even the researchers who do not have a deep understanding of knowledge graph could use the system.

The challenge C2 suggests that the user interface should look similar to those of existing systems, so that users can use it without a learning curve. We call such user interface component the *Survey Component*. Challenge C1 indicates that there should be some component dealing with the mapping between elements of the Survey Component and the knowledge graphs; we call this the *Annotation Component*. Finally, we have the *Knowledge Component* to exploit knowledge graphs to provide intelligent survey services.

In what follows, we will describe these three components in detail. Figure 1 presents the architecture diagram of the three components.

Survey Component. As shown in Fig. 1, the main processes that compose the *Survey Layer* are the *Survey Creator* and the *Survey Website*. It incorporates the functionalities of a survey without any explicit knowledge. The Researcher creates the survey that is presented to the *Participant*, and the *Participant* only interacts with the survey system at this component. The researcher is provided with an access link, which sent to *Participants* in order to complete the survey. Our platform stores the *Participants'* answers on its completion. The researcher can then explore the *Survey Results*. Theoretically, existing survey systems could potentially be reused as a survey component in our architecture.

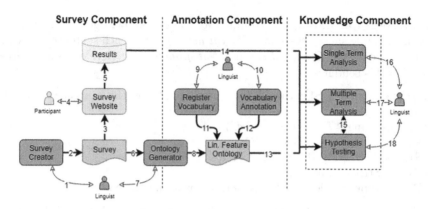

Fig. 1. Architecture diagram

Annotation Component. The main tasks of the Annotation Component including (AC1) maintaining the vocabulary (also known as terms) as *Features* in the *Linguistic Feature Ontology* and (AC2) annotating *POSs* in *Sentences* with the vocabulary (terms).

For the task of Vocabulary Registration (AC1), a user interface is needed for the researcher to add, update and remove vocabulary, including *Features* and relations. New feature vocabulary proposed by the researcher can be added as sub-classes of the *Feature* class in the *Linguistic Feature Ontology*. Similarly, the new relation vocabulary will be added as sub-properties of the *relatedFeature* in the *Linguistic Feature Ontology*.

For the task of Sentence Annotation (AC2), another user interface is needed for the researcher to annotate the *Sentences* as she sees fit with the feature and relation vocabulary. For example, given the *Sentence The cat needs fed.*, the researcher can highlight part of the *Sentence*, such as *The cat*, and then annotate it with a feature vocabulary *Subject*. Some triples will be added into the *Linguistic Feature Ontology*, as discussed in Sect. 4.1 (Fig. 2).

Knowledge Component. The main task for the Knowledge Component is to provide intelligent survey services based on knowledge graphs, including *Single Term Analysis, Multiple Term Analysis* and *Hypothesis Testing*. 'Term' here refers to feature. Thus single term analysis uses only one feature, while multiple term analysis uses more than one feature. Hypotheses can be defined on top of multiple term analysis. All these three types of survey services are based on feature vocabulary.

Single Term Analysis. This service is for the researcher to select a feature vocabulary to construct a single term query. Formally, given k sentences, n participants and the feature *term*, a single term query $Q_S(term)$ is calculated as follows:

$$\frac{\sum_{j=0}^{n} \left(\frac{\sum_{i=0}^{k} score_{ij} * appear_i(term)}{count(term)} \right)}{n} \tag{1}$$

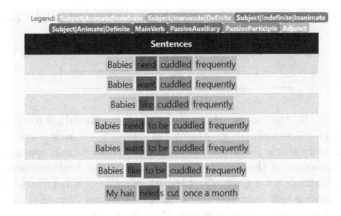

Fig. 2. Example of the annotations depicted by linguists.

where $score_{ij}$ is the score that participant j provided for sentence i, $count(term)$ is the total number of sentences containing instances of the feature $term$, $appear_i(term)$ is 1 if some instance of the $term$ appears in sentence i, otherwise 0.

Constraints can be added into single term queries. Typically, a constraint is applied on a field related to user related information, such as gender, age or location. For example, Fig. 3 illustrates a single term query $Q_S(Subject)$ with $gender = Female, 40 \leq age \leq 49$ as the constraints. The result of the query is a table, the columns of which include the two constraints, as well as all the instances of the feature *Subject*.

The constraint fields selected are *gender* - F and *age* - 40-49

Subject - The surveys have returned the following values:

#	gender	age	babies	my hair	some plants	the cat
0	F	40-49	1.00	0.33	1.00	1.00
1	F	40-49	0.83	0.33	0.33	0.50
Average	-	-	0.92	0.33	0.67	0.75

Fig. 3. Single term analysis of *subject* with two constraints.

In case there is only one instance of the feature $term$, we also compute $Q_S(\sim term)$, where $\sim$ is the Negation as Failure operator, meaning that we are looking for sentences that do not contain any instance of the given $term$. We combine the results of the two single term queries together for more insightful comparisons.

Multiple Term Analysis. This service is similar to the previous one, but with multiple terms. Formally, given k sentences, n participants and the set of feature vocabulary $term(0), \ldots, term(m)$, a multiple term query $Q_M(term(0), \ldots, term(m))$ is calculated as follows:

$$\frac{\sum_{j=0}^{n} \left(\frac{\sum_{i=0}^{k} \left(score_{ij} * \prod_{t=0}^{T} appear_i(term(t)) \right)}{count(term(1), \ldots, term(m))} \right)}{n} \tag{2}$$

where $score_{ij}$ is the score that participant j provided for sentence i, $count(term(1), \ldots, term(m))$ is the total number of sentences containing instances of every single feature within $term(0), \ldots, term(m)$, $appear_i(term(t))$ is 1 if some instance of the $term(t)$ appears in sentence i, otherwise 0. Figure 4 illustrates a multiple term query $Q_M(MainVerb, PassiveAuxiliary)$. Note that $PassiveAuxiliary$ has only one instance 'to be', thus Negation as Failure is applied by adding some columns about 'Without to be'.

MainVerb, PassiveAuxiliary – The surveys have returned the following values:

#	need+to be	need+Without to be	want+to be	want+Without to be	like+to be	like+Without to be
0	1.00	1.00	0.75	0.75	0.75	0.75
1	1.00	1.00	0.50	0.50	0.50	0.00
2	1.00	1.00	0.25	0.00	0.50	0.25
3	0.75	0.75	0.75	0.75	0.75	0.25
4	1.00	1.00	0.75	0.75	0.75	0.50
5	1.00	0.25	1.00	0.50	0.75	0.25
6	1.00	1.00	0.50	0.50	0.75	0.75
7	1.00	0.00	0.75	0.00	1.00	0.25
Average	0.97	0.75	0.66	0.47	0.72	0.38

Fig. 4. Multiple term query example: $MainVerb$ ('need', 'want', 'like') and $PassiveAuxiliary$ ('to be')

Hypothesis Testing. This service is to help the researcher to assess and register some hypotheses into the system, which could help monitor in real-time if the registered hypotheses are satisfied by the results from the participants. We consider two types of hypotheses patterns (HP1 and HP2). All hypotheses are based on multiple term queries.

(HP1) Threshold hypotheses: given a multiple term query Q_M with its two columns $MC1$ and $MC2$, and two threshold values $t1$ and $t2$, a threshold hypothesis is defined as: $H_T(MC1, MC2, t1, t2) = \neg(average(MC1) > t1) \lor (average(MC2) > t2)$. Informally, it says if $MC1$ crosses threshold $t1$, then $MC2$ should cross threshold $t2$.

(HP2) Comparator hypotheses: given a multiple term query Q_M with its two columns $MC1$ and $MC2$, and a comparator $\prec \in \{\leq, =, \geq\}$, a comparator hypothesis is defined as $H_T(MC1, MC2, \prec) = average(MC1) \prec average(MC2)$. Informally, it says $MC1$ is less ($\leq$)/equally ($=$)/more ($\geq$) acceptable than $MC2$.

5 Implementation and Evaluation

5.1 Implementation

We implemented a Web based prototype for the proposed *Knowledge Driven Survey System* in *Javascript* and *PHP*. The first functionality that is available to the *Researcher* is the building of a new Survey, using a drag-and-drop form editor (cf. Fig. 5). This incorporates the functionalities of the *formBuilder*[5] library, which is a flexible, scalable tool for survey construction. After building the desired survey structure, a *JSON* file is generated and properly adapted to be able to be received by a different library. This library, *surveyJS*[6], is a powerful survey tool which prepares the outlook of a survey from a structured *JSON* file.

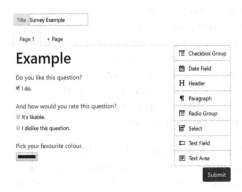

Fig. 5. Drag-and-drop interface during survey creation.

In the implementation of the Annotation Component, we allow the researcher to define a few different sets of vocabulary, so that she can have alternatives before she decides which set to use. Also, we allow the researcher to choose between annotating once only or to all the sentences containing the exact highlighted phrase. This helps significantly reducing the time needed for the researcher to annotate the sentences in the survey.

For single term queries in the Knowledge Component, in case there is only one instance of the feature *term*, we also compute $Q_S(\sim term)$, where $\sim$ is the Negation as Failure operator, meaning that we are looking for sentences that do not contain any instance of the given *term*. We combine the results of the two single term queries together for more insightful comparisons.

---

[5] https://formbuilder.online/.
[6] https://surveyjs.io/.

5.2 Case Study: Grammaticality Judgments

Experiment Setup: Evaluating SR1 and LR1. As described in Sect. 2.2, our case study examined the use, found in Scotland, of verbs such as *need, want,* or *like* followed directly by a passive participle, as compared to more Standard use of these verbs followed by an auxiliary *to be* and passive participle.

- *The cat wants fed*
- *The cat wants to be fed*

The survey was set up by a linguistic researcher with no KG background, who established a vocabulary of relevant linguistic variables: main verb (*need, want,* or *like*), subject (in)animacy, subject (in)definiteness, and presence/absence of *to be*. The researcher then input and annotated 24 sentences covering all possible combinations of these linguistic features.

Twelve respondents completed our pilot survey by rating the sentences using a binary scale. All were native speakers of English born in Scotland or Northern Ireland and currently resident in Aberdeenshire.

Results are available as a mean rating (between 0 and 1) for each of the survey sentences; each individual respondent's rating is also available. In addition, results can be calculated for specific variables that occur in more than one sentence and for combinations of variables.

Hypotheses Testing: Evaluating LR2, LR3, and LR4. The survey system has allowed examination of several hypotheses in relation to the data obtained. Multi-term analysis of the current results tells us that when *to be* is absent *need* has a higher global acceptance rate (0.90) than *want* (0.46), and *want* has a higher acceptance rate than *like* (0.31), as predicted by previous work.

On an individual sentence level, both of the sentences below, with the main verb *like*, and an animate, definite subject (*my hair*), are rejected by all speakers.

- My hair likes cut once a month
- My hair likes to be cut once a month

Many speakers accept the inanimate, indefinite subject *some plants* with *like* regardless of whether *to be* is present (.75) or absent (.50).

- Some plants like watered every day
- Some plants like to be watered every day

The higher acceptance rate for the Standard form is surprising in this instance, as it contradicts the assertion in previous work that inanimate subjects were more likely to be accepted with *like* (and *want*) in the Scottish form without *to be*.

Analysis of Results: Evaluating SR2, SR3, and SR4. As well as looking at the Scottish construction on its own, we can do more general comparison of equivalent constructions with and without *to be*. Globally, the Standard *to be* form has a higher acceptance rate (0.71) than the Scottish form without *to* *be* (0.56). Individual comparison for *need*, *want*, and *like* with and without *to be* shows the same result for each main verb (i.e. the *to be* form has a higher acceptance rate), indicating that the overall result truly represents greater global use of the Standard *to be* form, and is not down to a dispreference for the Scottish construction with a particular verb.

The hypothesis testing and analysis of results is possible through use of manual calculation based on the averaging of mean acceptance rates for each sentence. The test survey has only one value for each combination of variables, making this approach relatively straightforward. For instance, there is only one sentence with an animate, definite subject, the main verb *like*, and no auxiliary *to be*:

– *The cat likes fed*

More comprehensive data collection would involve more sentences with the same variable values and more variables. For instance, given the much higher rate of acceptance for the subject *some plants* than *my hair*, other inanimate subjects would be needed in order to establish whether there is any specific pattern pertaining to (in)animacy. With only sentence-level statistics available, these additions would complicate the manual calculations required for hypothesis testing, requiring additional researcher time, and introducing more room for human error.

Manual calculations for testing the above hypotheses on the small data set of the test survey take about twenty minutes. Annotation of linguistic variables in the survey planning stage took 5–10 min. There is therefore a considerable benefit to researchers in terms of time saved, which is likely to increase with survey complexity. Moreover, integration of hypothesis testing in the survey system allows immediate updating of results as more participants are added. Identification and annotation of linguistic variables also creates materials that can be reused for future surveys on similar linguistic constructions, thereby decreasing the time required for initial survey design and input.

5.3 Knowledge Graph Evaluation

Although our approach mainly focuses in the Linguistic Feature Ontology, it can be revised for kind of survey, given the underlying use of Knowledge Graph. Thus, it is worthwhile to apply general validation techniques to our Linguistic Feature Ontology, using the six dimensions of Ontology quality, as discussed by Poveda-Villalón [9]:

– Human understanding - how comprehensive is the ontology? The ontology uses well-known linguistic concepts, is small, and is sufficient.
– Logical consistency - is the reasoning consistent? The functionalities of the system have been exhaustingly tested. The OWL Ontology was implemented in Protegé 5.2.0 and tested with Pellet.

- Modeling issues - what is the quality of the modeling decisions? The Linguistic Feature Ontology suits the particular domain; as such, various semantic properties such as inverse relationships were not needed. Yet, this represents a modeling decision that could be reassessed.
- Ontology language specification - does the ontology comply with OWL standards? Our ontology's syntax is correct, which is supported by the implementation in Protegé.
- Real world representation - how aligned is the ontology with the application domain. The Linguistic Feature Ontology was developed with the close interaction of the Linguist researchers, ensuring a model appropriate to the domain and as fulfilling requirement KR2.
- Semantic application - is the ontology aligned with the embedding software? The Ontology supports the platform's functionalities.

6   Related Work

6.1   Intelligent Surveys

There have been attempts regarding dynamized survey systems, such as the *Dynamic Intelligent Survey Engine* (DISE) [12]. The survey platform DISE aims to implement functionalities with a focus on customers' preferences and uses a wide variety of data collection methods. As with our system, it implements a flexible approach to survey creation. In comparison to our system, the survey creation methodology is less intuitive, as the researcher builds its structure through an XML file, an approach that is successful, but after some learning curve. *DISE*'s focuses on data collection methods for a consumer-oriented domain. Most importantly, it cannot reason with knowledge. By applying semantics, we can analyse survey results at level and complexity that *DISE* does not.

6.2   Linguistic Surveys

Grammaticality judgment surveys have been developed online for a considerable time, through tools that aim to facilitate researchers in the field of Linguistics.

MiniJudge [13] attempts to complement the traditional methodology in grammaticality judgment experiments with the statistical analysis provided from modern practices. It focuses on "minimalist" experiments - small respondent groups and sets of sentences, quick surveys, and a few other constraints[7]. Although *MiniJudge* does not provide the benefits of reasoning services and is limited to two binary factors as does our approach, it has advantages in complex statistical analysis and level of research.

Other relevant tools include *WebExp* [15] and *IBEX* [16] ("Internet Based EXperiments"). *WebExp* is used in Psycholinguistics for reaction data, a feature that exploit; yet, it does not make use of a knowledge structure. *IBEX* focuses in grammaticality judgment in different tasks such as *FlashSentence*,

---

[7] See http://www.ccunix.ccu.edu.tw/~lngmyers/MJFAQ.htm.

which presents the sentence for limited time, or *DashedSentence*, presenting the sentence word-by-word or chunk-by-chunk. They do not encompass any novel analysis; in comparison of our system, they dwell entirely in the survey component, extending the capabilities of the original grammaticality judgment task.

6.3   MTurk Surveys

Two final tools are discussed, developed with the focus of running Linguist-focused tasks with the crowdsourcing platform *Amazon Mechanical Turk*. The first, *Turkolizer* [17], takes a different, domain-specific approach to individual variables, using, just like the *MiniJudge* implementation, the concept of experimental factors (a simple example is provided by *Gibson* regarding two factors with two conditions each, where sentences are defined by *Subject-Object* order, and by having two or three question words. Each combination is mapped to a sentence, and since we have two binary factors, this would represent a 4-sentence design). Myers went on to create with Chen the Web tool Worldlikeliness [14], which is focused in Topological Psycholinguistic Research. Thus, it helps researchers with cross-linguistic grammaticality judgments. The last tool is called *Turktools* [18], inspired by *Turkolizer* and it also implements its version of factorial design.

The surveys discussed do not provide the degree of freedom our knowledge-powered services offer through individual variables, as these systems hard-code the necessary variables upon survey creation. We provide a new depth of meaningful results, without big expense; a strength possible due to the Knowledge Graph that powers the present Survey System.

7   Conclusion and Outlook

In this paper, we present an inviting approach to Knowledge-driven survey systems, building a case for further interest and development on KG driven software engineering [3], in Open Science and beyond. We also investigate a new solution for Grammaticality Judgment Tasks, proving the efficiency of our system by extending our Ontology to satisfy the Linguist researcher needs. Our approach is a step forward in a field of study where semantic technologies are not yet applied, presenting with our implementations the advantages that can be retrieved.

From the application front, there is much work that can be done, in surveys based in Psycholinguistics and other application domains. Even more intriguing approaches can be developed in this field, by implementing further reasoning services, introducing the creation of properties and the disjoint sub-classes to the Linguist researcher, and the expansion of the Linguistic Feature Ontology to other relevant topics in Psycholinguistics. We also envision a modular approach which would allow our platform to extend to different application domains, linking disjoint areas semantically to our Survey Ontology.

Acknowledgement. This work was supported the EU Marie Currie K-Drive project (286348).

References

1. Pan, J.Z., Vetere, G., Manuel Gomez-Perez, J., Wu, H.: Exploiting Linked Data and Knowledge Graphs for Large Organisations. Springer, Cham (2016). https://doi.org/10.1007/978-3-319-45654-6. ISBN 978-3-319-45654-6
2. Pan, J.Z., et al. (eds.): Reasoning Web 2016. LNCS, vol. 9885. Springer, Cham (2017). https://doi.org/10.1007/978-3-319-49493-7. ISBN 978-3-319-49493-7
3. Pan, J.Z., Staab, S., Aßmann, U., Ebert, J., Zhao, Y.: Ontology-Driven Software Development. Springer, Heidelberg (2013). https://doi.org/10.1007/978-3-642-31226-7. ISBN 978-3-642-31226-7
4. Donnelly, K.: SNOMED-CT: the advanced terminology and coding system for eHealth. Stud. Health Technol. Inform. **121**, 279–290 (2006)
5. Tzitzikas, Y., et al.: Integrating heterogeneous and distributed information about marine species through a top level ontology. In: Garoufallou, E., Greenberg, J. (eds.) MTSR 2013. CCIS, vol. 390, pp. 289–301. Springer, Cham (2013). https://doi.org/10.1007/978-3-319-03437-9_29
6. Chiarcos, C., Cimiano, P., Declerck, T., McCrae, J.P.: Linguistic linked open data. Introduction and overview. In: Proceedings of the 2nd Workshop on Linked Data in Linguistics (LDL 2013): Representing and Linking Lexicons, Terminologies and Other Language Data, pp. 1–9 (2013)
7. Murray, T., Simon, B.L.: At the intersection of regional and social dialects: the case of like + past participle in American English. Am. Speech **77**(1), 32–69 (2002)
8. Edelstein, E.: This syntax needs studied. In: Zanuttini, R., Horn, L.R. (eds.) Micro-Syntactic Variation in North American English, pp. 242–268. Oxford University Press, Oxford (2014)
9. Poveda-Villalón, M., Gómez-Pérez, A., Suárez-Figueroa, M.C.: OOPS!(OntOlogy Pitfall Scanner!): an on-line tool for ontology evaluation. J. Semant. Web Inf. Syst. **10**(2), 7–34 (2014)
10. Giunchiglia, F., ChenuAbente, R.: Scientific knowledge objects v. 1. University of Trento (2009)
11. Bechhofer, S., et al.: Why linked data is not enough for scientists. Future Gener. Comput. Syst. **29**(2), 599–611 (2013)
12. Schlereth, C., Skiera, B.: DISE: dynamic intelligent survey engine. In: Diamantopoulos, A., Fritz, W., Hildebrandt, L. (eds.) Quantitative Marketing and Marketing Management, pp. 225–243. Gabler Verlag, Wiesbaden (2012)
13. Myers, J.: MiniJudge: software for minimalist experimental syntax. In: Proceedings of the 18th Conference on Computational Linguistics and Speech Processing, pp. 271–285 (2006)
14. Chen, T.Y., Myers, J.: Worldlikeness: a web-based tool for typological psycholinguistic research. Univ. Penn. Work. Pap. Linguist. **23**(1), 21–30 (2017)
15. Keller, F., Gunasekharan, S., Mayo, N., Corley, M.: Timing accuracy of web experiments: a case study using the WebExp software package. Behav. Res. Methods **41**(1), 1–12 (2009)
16. Ibex 0.3.8 Manual. http://spellout.net/latest_ibex_manual.pdf. Accessed 1 Aug 18
17. Gibson, E., Piantadosi, S., Fedorenko, K.: Using Mechanical Turk to obtain and analyze English acceptability judgments. Lang. Linguist. Compass **5**(8), 509–524 (2011)
18. Erlewine, M.Y., Kotek, H.: A streamlined approach to online linguistic surveys. Nat. Lang. Linguist. Theory **34**(2), 481–495 (2016)

More Is Better: Sequential Combinations of Knowledge Graph Embedding Approaches

Kemas Wiharja[1], Jeff Z. Pan[1(✉)], Martin Kollingbaum[1], and Yu Deng[2]

[1] Department of Computing Science, University of Aberdeen, Aberdeen, UK
jeff.z.pan@abdn.ac.uk
[2] IBM Research, New York, USA

Abstract. Constructing and maintaining large-scale good quality knowledge graphs present many challenges. Knowledge graph completion has been regarded a promising direction in the knowledge graph community. The majority of current work for knowledge graph completion approaches do not take the schema of a target knowledge graph as input. As a result, the triples generated by these approaches are not necessarily consistent with the schema of the target knowledge graph. This paper proposes to improve the correctness of knowledge graph completion based on Schema Aware Triple Classification (SATC), which enables sequential combinations of knowledge graph embedding approaches. Extensive experiments show that our proposed approaches can significantly improve the correctness of the new triples produced by knowledge graph embedding methods.

Keywords: Knowledge graph · Embedding
Schema aware triple classification
Knowledge representation and reasoning · Approximate reasoning
Artificial Intelligence

1 Introduction

The idea of representing knowledge as graphs dates back to early proposals such as semantic networks in the research of Knowledge Representation and Reasoning, which is an important branch of Artificial Intelligence. It has become popular again since Google coined the term "Knowledge Graph" and used it to improve its search engine in 2012. In general, a knowledge graph can be seen as an ontology with an entity-centric view, consisting of a set of interconnected typed entities and their attributes, as well as some schema axioms for defining the vocabulary (terminology) used in the knowledge graph [1,2]. It is often assumed that, in a knowledge graph, the size of the data (or *ABox* in description logic terminology) is much bigger than the size of the schema (or *TBox* in description logic terminology) [2,3].

© Springer Nature Switzerland AG 2018
R. Ichise et al. (Eds.): JIST 2018, LNCS 11341, pp. 19–35, 2018.
https://doi.org/10.1007/978-3-030-04284-4_2

Constructing and maintaining large-scale good quality knowledge graphs presents many challenges. At the core of them is the well-known trade-off between completeness and correctness. Most existing knowledge graph refinement approaches either focus on adding missing knowledge to the graph, i.e., completion, or on identifying wrong information in the graph, i.e., error detection.

Knowledge graph completion is sometimes also regarded as a kind of knowledge graph reasoning, or similarity reasoning [4], to be more precise, which is different from logic-based knowledge graph reasoning (cf. Sect. 2.1). Several research directions have emerged to complete a knowledge graph, such as knowledge graph embedding and rule learning. Most of them focus on multi-relational data [5], while ignoring the TBox schema and the type assertions in ABox. Link Prediction (LP) [11] is perhaps one of the most studied notions of knowledge graph completion. Given an entity and a relation, as well as the ABox of a knowledge graph, the task is to predict the missing entity in this relation. Knowledge graph embedding approaches, such as TransE [5], TransR [8], TransH [9], STransE [10] (and many others, such as [13,19,22]), complete an input knowledge graph ABox by representing the entities and their relations in a vector space, so as to learn some embedded representations of entities and relations in a knowledge graph for predicting missing entities or relationships. Rule learning approaches, such as [29,30], complete an input knowledge graph ABox by learning rules based on patterns in the ABox. The learnt rules can then be used to produce new relation assertions.

Correctness checking in knowledge graph completion often relies on the task of triple classification [12], which computes the likelihood a given triple is correct or not w.r.t. a given knowledge graph. The risk, however, is that the current notion of task classification does not usually take the schema of the target ontology into account. Therefore, the triples regarded as *correct* under this notion of triple classification might *not* be consistent with the schema of the target knowledge graph.

In this paper, we propose to improve the correctness of knowledge graph completion based on a Schema Aware Triple Classification (SATC). In general, our approach can be applied to both knowledge graph embedding and rule learning approaches mentioned above. In this paper, we will focus on the knowledge graph embedding (KGE) approaches and leave the rule learning approaches for future work. We envision two types of SATC: black-box SATC and white-box SATC approaches. The latter approaches require a tight integration of logical reasoning into KG embedding, while the former approaches do not. In this paper, we will focus on black-box SATC. The advantage of the black-box SATC approaches is that they can be applied to any KGE approaches with any KG reasoners, without having to revise the KGE algorithms. The key contributions of the paper can be summarized as follows:

1. To the best of our knowledge, this work presents the first black-box SATC approach. In order to evaluate the feasibility of this approach, we conducted several experiments with some knowledge graphs, including NELL-995 [20],

DBpedia-Politics and a knowledge graph from IBM, automatically generated based on IBM Storwize Knowledge Center articles. Our investigation shows that applying some KGE approaches, such as TransE, on NELL-995, the percentage of correct triples is less than 1% under SATC. This confirms the importance of using schema for quality assurance.

2. In our SATC approach, we propose to use the approximate reasoning to help improve the efficiency of consistency checking w.r.t. the schema.

3. We propose to use our SATC approach to support sequential combinations of the KGE approaches, by applying the KGE approaches over the union of the original graph and the correct triples from a previous iteration of KG completion. Our experiment confirms that, with the help of SATC, the KGE approaches can be run sequentially to get higher percentages of correct triples. Extensive experiments show that our proposed approaches can significantly improve the correctness of the new triples produced by the knowledge graph embedding methods; e.g., in the case of NELL-995, the improvement is over 42%.

2   Background

2.1   Knowledge Graph

More formally, we define a knowledge graph $\mathcal{G} = \mathcal{T} \cup \mathcal{A}$ consisting of two parts, $\mathcal{T}$ and $\mathcal{A}$, where $\mathcal{A}$ is the data sub-graph (or ABox) and $\mathcal{T}$ is the schema sub-graph (or TBox) [1,2]. The size of $\mathcal{T}$ is often much smaller than that of $\mathcal{A}$. Facts in the ABox are represented as triples of the following two forms:

- *Relation assertion* (h, r, t), where h is the head entity, and r the relation and t the tail entity; e.g., (ACMilan, playInLeague, ItalianLeague) is a relation assertion.
- *Type assertion* $(e, rdf:type, C)$, where e is an entity, rdf:type is the instance-of relation from the standard W3C RDF specification and C is a type; e.g., (ACMilan, rdf:type, FootballClub) is a type assertion.

A TBox includes Type Inclusion axioms $C \sqsubseteq D$, where C and D are type descriptions, such as the following ones: $\top \mid \bot \mid A \mid \neg C \mid C \sqcap D \mid \exists r.C \mid \{o\}$, where $\top$ is the top type (representing all entities), $\bot$ is the bottom type (representing an empty set), A is a named type, r is a relation, and o is an entity. For example, given the two types River and City, the disjointness of these types can be represented as River $\sqsubseteq \neg$City, or River $\sqcap$ City $\sqsubseteq \bot$.

A TBox can also include *Relation Domain axioms* Domain(r) = A, *Relation Range axioms* Range(r) = A, *Symmetric Relation axioms* Symmetric(r), *Asymmetric Relation axioms* Asymmetric(r), *Relation Inclusion axioms* r1 $\sqsubseteq$ r2 and *Relation Chain axioms* r1 $\circ$ r2 $\sqsubseteq$ r3, where r1, r2 and r3 are properties. Note that we allow multiple domains (and ranges), and the resulting domain (range) is the intersection of the individual domains (ranges).

2.2 Knowledge Graph Completion

Given a knowledge graph $\mathcal{G} = \mathcal{T} \cup \mathcal{A}$, the task of knowledge graph completion (KGC) is to produce an extension ABox $\mathcal{A}'$, of which the triples use only use types and relations from $\mathcal{T}$. The task of link prediction is a special form of KGC, in that triples in $\mathcal{A}'$ only are relation assertions only. More precisely, the task of link prediction is to predict the missing head h or the missing tail t of a triple (h, r, t). Link prediction methods often output a list of ranked entities instead of providing the best entity [14].

In this paper, we focus on knowledge graph embedding (KGE) approaches. The idea of embedding is to represent an entity as a k-dimensional vector **h** (or **t**) and defines a scoring function $f_r(\mathbf{h}, \mathbf{t})$ to measure the plausibility of the triple (h, r, t) in the embedding space. The representations of entities and relations are obtained by minimising a global loss function involving all entities and relations. Different KGE algorithms often differ in their scoring functions, transformations, and loss functions.

Triple classification (TC) is a KGC related task of searching for a relation-specific threshold σ_r to identify whether a triple (h, r, t) is plausible [12]. For doing TC, one needs to construct three datasets which are train, test and development datasets. The development dataset is considered as the golden standard. In reality, golden standards take too many efforts. Thus silver standards are often applied, which assume that the input knowledge graph itself is already of reasonable quality. This assumption is often not satisfied in real world knowledge graphs. For example, even for DBpedia, a recent version has over 25% of incorrect triples.

3 Problem Statement

We define the problem of schema aware triple classification (SATC) in this section. Firstly, we introduce the notions of schema-consistent triples.

Definition 1. *Given a knowledge graph $\mathcal{G} = \mathcal{T} \cup \mathcal{A}$, a triple (h, r, t), where h and t are entities and r is a relation in $\mathcal{G}$, (h, r, t) is a schema-consistent triple w.r.t. $\mathcal{G}$ if the extended knowledge graph $\mathcal{G} \cup (h, r, t)$ is consistent.*

From the perspective of data engineering, we further introduce the notions of correct, incorrect and unknown triples.

Definition 2. *Given a knowledge graph $\mathcal{G} = \mathcal{T} \cup \mathcal{A}$, a triple (h, r, t), where h and t are entities and r is a relation in $\mathcal{G}$, with C_h, C_t being some types of h and t resp., and D_r, R_r being the domain and range of r, (h, r, t) is a correct triple w.r.t. $\mathcal{G}$ if:*

1. the extended knowledge graph $\mathcal{G} \cup (h, r, t)$ is consistent, and
2. $C_h \equiv D_r$ and $C_t \equiv R_r$.

Definition 3. *Given a knowledge graph $\mathcal{G} = \mathcal{T} \cup \mathcal{A}$, a triple (h, r, t), where h and t are entities and r is a relation in $\mathcal{G}$, with C_h, C_t being some types of h and t resp., and D_r, R_r being the domain and range of r, (h, r, t) is an incorrect triple w.r.t. $\mathcal{G}$ if:*

1. *$\mathcal{G} \models C_h \sqcap D_r \sqsubseteq \bot$, or*
2. *$\mathcal{G} \models C_t \sqcap R_r \sqsubseteq \bot$.*

It is straight forward to see that an incorrect triple is not schema-consistent.

Lemma 1. *Given a knowledge graph $\mathcal{G} = \mathcal{T} \cup \mathcal{A}$, a triple (h, r, t), where h and t are entities and r is a relation in $\mathcal{G}$. If (h, r, t) is incorrect w.r.t. $\mathcal{G}$, then (h, r, t) is not schema-consistent w.r.t. $\mathcal{G}$.*

Definition 4. *Given a knowledge graph $\mathcal{G} = \mathcal{T} \cup \mathcal{A}$, a triple (h, r, t), where h and t are entities and r is a relation in $\mathcal{G}$, (h, r, t) is an unknown triple w.r.t. $\mathcal{G}$ if it is neither correct nor incorrect w.r.t. $\mathcal{G}$.*

Definition 5. *Let $\mathcal{G}$ be a knowledge graph, and $\mathcal{E}$ the new triples that are produced by a KGE method, the task of schema aware triple classification (SATC) is to identify the subset ζ of correct triples within $\mathcal{E}$; the percentage of correctness (PC) is defined as follows:*

$$PC = \frac{|\zeta|}{|\mathcal{E}|} * 100\% \qquad (1)$$

Given an input knowledge graph $\mathcal{G}$, our research aim is to identify the most suitable KGE methods, so as to maximise the PC for SATC.

4 Our Approach

4.1 Approximate Consistency Checking for Schema Aware Triple Classification

In this section, we will present an approach for schema aware triple classification (SATC), with the help of an approximate reasoning to address the concern of high computation complexity in ontology reasoning.

The idea behind an approximate reasoning [6,7] is to identify minimal inconsistent sub-graphs (justifications) with the help of *inconsistency justification patterns* (or IJ patterns). Obviously, it could be expensive to compute all possible justifications. Since some recent study [18] suggests type assertions are most often more correct in knowledge graphs than relation assertions, in this paper, we propose to focus on some simple inconsistency justification patterns related to relation axioms.

There are three requirements for these inconsistency justification patterns:

(R1) TBox reasoning with schema sub-graphs should be done offline.
(R2) No online reasoning is needed for dealing with data sub-graphs.
(R3) IJ patterns should help not just detect inconsistencies but also repair them.

(R1) is feasible, since knowledge graph completion algorithms only produce ABox assertions, so that the TBox parts of the IJ patterns can be computed in advance. In Table 1, IJ patterns 1–4 are about interactions among domain axioms, range axioms, relation inclusion axioms, and class disjoint axioms. IJ patterns 5–7 are about interactions among asymmetric relation axioms, symmetric relation axioms, and relation inclusion axioms. IJ pattern 8 is about irreflexive axioms. Thus, we need to run the following TBox reasoning services offline: (i) computing relation subsumptions and (ii) compute disjoint named types. Since the ABox subsets of the IJ patterns contain at most two data triples, we need to scan through the data sub-graph of a knowledge graph at most twice and no reasoning is needed during runtime. Hence, (R2) is addressed.

Table 1. Inconsistency justification patterns

ID	TBox subset of the pattern	ABox subset of the pattern
1	Domain(r) = D, D ⊓ A ⊑ ⊥	(e1, r, e2), (e1, rdf:type, A)
2	Range(r) = R, R ⊓ A ⊑ ⊥	(e1, r, e2), (e2, rdf:type, A)
3	Domain(r1) = D1, Domain(r2) = D2, r1 ⊑ r2, D1 ⊓ D2 ⊑ ⊥	(e1, r1, e2)
4	Range(r1) = R1, Range(r2) = R2, r1 ⊑ r2, R1 ⊓ R2 ⊑ ⊥	(e1, r1, e2)
5	Asymmetric(r)	(e1, r, e2), (e2, r, e1)
6	Symmetric(r1), Asymmetric(r2), r1 ⊑ r2	(e1, r1, e2)
7	Symmetric(r2), Asymmetric(r3), r1 ⊑ r2, r1 ⊑ r3	(e1, r1, e2)
8	Irreflexive(r)	(e1, r, e1)

Once an IJ pattern is detected within a target knowledge graph, one can repair it by removing the relation assertions in the pattern, i.e., the assertions in the third column in Table 1. Therefore, IJ patterns not only help us to detect logical inconsistencies but also help us to repair logical inconsistencies (R3).

4.2 Sequential Combination of Knowledge Graph Embedding Algorithms for Schema Aware Triple Classification

In this section, we will use the SATC approach to support the sequential combinations of KGE approaches, by applying a KGE over the union of the original graph and the correct triples from a previous iteration of KG completion. We incorporate the sequential combinations with an approximate reasoning for increasing the correctness of the new facts that a knowledge graph embedding approach produces. As shown in Fig. 1, the components of our approach are two knowledge graph embedding algorithms (could be the same or different) and an approximate reasoning[1].

Given an input knowledge graph, our approach works as follows. Each iteration has two steps. The first step is to run Knowledge Graph Embedding algorithm (or simply KGE) to produce new triples. In the second step, we only take the correct triples detected by the approximate reasoning and merge them with the initial KG. Unless some stopping condition (e.g., no new correct triples are produced in the current iteration) is satisfied, we will start a new iteration. Once some stopping condition is satisfied, we count the percentage of correctness (PC) of the sequential combination by using the number of correct triples and the number of new triples that we got from the executed iterations Sect. 3.

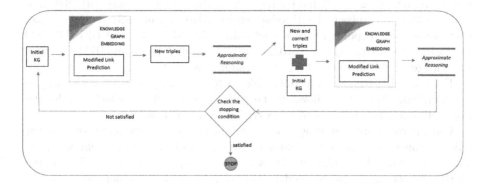

Fig. 1. Sequential combination of knowledge graph embedding (SCE) algorithms

More precisely, at the first step, given an input knowledge graph G, and a link prediction system LP, we produce the output knowledge graph G' for that iteration as follows:

1. Compute the set of recommended triples RT from LP that are above the threshold t;
2. Compute the set of new triples NT $\doteq$ RT \ G;
3. G' $\doteq$ G ∪ NT.

We will then pass G' to the approximate reasoning module. At the second step, given the set of incorrect triples IT detected by IJ patterns, the remaining new triples are NT' $\doteq$ NT \ IT. Accordingly, we can define a stopping condition as |NT'| ≤ s, where the stop threshold s is a non-negative integer. If s is set to be 0, it means that the iterations will stop when no new triples are produced in the current iteration.

---

[1] The implementation of our approach: http://github.com/bagindokemas/meOnJIST 2018.

5   Evaluation

We empirically study and evaluate our approach on three tasks: (1) Comparing the existing knowledge graph embedding approaches in terms of producing correct triples according to the schema, (2) Investigating the sequential combinations of knowledge graph embedding approaches and (3) Comparing our approximate reasoning with related justification services which was provided by some existing off-the-shelf reasoner. The first two tasks are aiming to validate the sequential combinations of knowledge graph embedding approaches meanwhile the last task is aiming to validate the approximate reasoning.

For the first and the second task, since our approach needs a KG that has a TBox and a ABox, we use these three knowledge graphs: (i) NELL-995 which is a dataset from Carnegie Mellon university containing 142,065 triples, (ii) DBpedia-Politic which is a subset of DBpedia version 2016-04 that only include triples that are related to political issue containing 352,754 triples and (iii) IBM-KG which is a knowledge graph automatically generated based on IBM Storwize Knowledge Center articles[2] dataset containing 28,982 triples.

For the third task, we are only able to test our approximate reasoning on two knowledge graphs as follows: (i) DBpedia version 2016-04 which is a dataset from DBpedia containing 17,678,218 triples, and (ii) IBM-KG.

Our approximate reasoning module consists of two components, such as the TBox scanner and the ABox scanner. We implement the TBox scanner using Java and OWLAPI [27] library. This scanner process the schema of a KG to find all the IJ patterns (as mentioned in Table 1). The ABox scanner parses all the triples on the ABox based on the IJ patterns to find the correct, incorrect, and the unknown triples.

5.1   Comparing Existing Knowledge Graph Embedding Approaches

Experimental Setup. We use this task to check which knowledge graph embedding approaches (KGE) is the best in terms of the percentage of correctness.

KGE Approaches. We used NELL-995, DBpedia-Politic, and IBM-KG as the knowledge graphs/dataset. For the KGE Approaches, we choose KB2E-TransE, STranSE, OpenKE-DistMult, and OpenKE-Complex. We chose these methods because, in their respective categories, they are the most efficient methods. We consider the top ten results from these systems for each link prediction task.

Results. Firstly, we expand a KG using a KGE approach. After that, we collect all the triples that are produced by a KGE approach and then running our schema-based inconsistency checking against the new triples. The last step of the experiment is counting the percentage of the correctness.

We can see from Table 2 that the order of the best KGE approaches in terms of the percentage of correctness is as follows: STransE, DistMult, Complex and TransE.

---

[2] https://www.ibm.com/support/knowledgecenter/en/ST3FR7.

The reason for the very good performance of STransE is in STransE, the head and tail entities are associated with their own project matrices, rather than using the same matrix for both, as in other embedding approaches.

Table 2. The comparison result of the percentage of correctness

Knowledge Graph	KB2E_TransE	STranSE	OpenKE-DistMult	OpenKe-Complex
IBM-KG	1.52%	**61.50%**	21.96%	21.59%
NELL-995	0.37%	**20.36%**	0.72%	0.67%
DBpedia-Politic	18.06%	**43.45%**	18.90%	18.90%

5.2 Investigating Sequential Combinations of KGE

Experimental Setup. Our objectives in doing this task are as follows:

- (P1). We would like to know whether running the same KGE twice sequentially will outperform than running it once (compares KGE-KGE with KGE).
- (P2). We would like to know which option is better (in terms of producing a higher percentage of correctness): running the schema-based inconsistency checking right after each run of a KGE approach (KGE-IC-KGE-IC) or running it only once in the end of a sequential combination (KGE-KGE-IC).
- (P3). We would like to know whether we can get a higher percentage of correctness (compared with all the scenarios from P1 until P2) if we combine different KGE approaches with the schema-based inconsistency checking (KGE1-IC-KGE2 or KGE2-IC-KGE1).

For the first purpose (P1), we make four scenarios as follows:

- comparing STransE-IC-STransE-IC (SE-IC-SE-IC) with STransE-IC (SE-IC)
- comparing KB2E-IC-KB2E-IC (KE-IC-KE-IC) with KB2E-IC (KE-IC)
- comparing DistMult-IC-DistMult-IC (DM-IC-DM-IC) with DistMult-IC (DM-IC)
- comparing Complex-IC-Complex-IC (CE-IC-CE-IC) with Complex-IC (CE-IC)

For the second purpose (P2), we also make four scenarios as follows:

- comparing STransE-IC-STransE-IC (SE-IC-SE-IC) with STransE-STransE-IC (SE-SE-IC)
- comparing KB2E-IC-KB2E-IC (KE-IC-KE-IC) with KB2E-KB2E-IC (KE-KE-IC)
- comparing DistMult-IC-DistMult-IC (DM-IC-DM-IC) with DistMult-Dist Mult-IC (DM-DM-IC)
- comparing Complex-IC-Complex-IC (CE-IC-CE-IC) with Complex-Complex-IC (CE-CE-IC)

For the third purpose (P3), we make twelve scenarios as follows:

- KB2E-IC-STransE-IC (KE-IC-SE-IC)
- STransE-IC-KB2E-IC (SE-IC-KE-IC)
- KB2E-IC-DistMult-IC (KE-IC-DM-IC)
- DistMult-IC-KB2E-IC (DM-IC-KE-IC)
- KB2E-IC-Complex-IC (KE-IC-CE-IC)
- Complex-IC-KB2E-IC (CE-IC-KE-IC)
- STransE-IC-DistMult-IC (SE-IC-DM-IC)
- DistMult-IC-STransE-IC (DM-IC-SE-IC)
- STransE-IC-Complex-IC (SE-IC-CE-IC)
- Complex-IC-STransE-IC (CE-IC-SE-IC)
- DistMult-IC-Complex-IC (DM-IC-CE-IC)
- Complex-IC-DistMult-IC (CE-IC-DM-IC)

KGE Approaches. We used NELL-995, DBpedia-Politic, and IBM-KG as the knowledge graphs/dataset. For the KGE Approaches, we chose KB2E-TransE, STranSE, OpenKE-DistMult, and OpenKE-Complex.

Table 3. The result for P1

ID	The PC for running KGE twice				The PC for running KGE once			
	Flow	IBM	NELL	DBP	Flow	IBM	NELL	DBP
1	SE-IC-SE-IC	**69%**	**29%**	**55.51%**	SE-IC	**61.50%**	**20.36%**	**43.45%**
2	KE-IC-KE-IC	0.86%	0.17%	17.16%	KE-IC	1.52%	0.37%	18.06%
3	DM-IC-DM-IC	22.42%	0.53%	19.25%	DM-IC	21.96%	0.72%	18.90%
4	CE-IC-CE-IC	20.95%	0.55%	19.24%	CE-IC	21.59%	0.67%	18.90%

Results. Table 3 records all the results that are related with the first purpose/P1. We could see that from all KGE approaches that we try, only STransE that have higher PC (for all KGs) if we run it twice sequentially rather than running it once. If we analyze this result deeper, we see that in the second run, all KGE approaches (except STransE), produce less correct triples compare with the first run. We continue the experiment P1 on STransE (using NELL KG) by running it for three runs sequentially (STransE-IC-StransE-IC-STransE-IC). And we got interesting fact that the percentage of correctness that we got is even higher than running STransE twice (38% against 29%). However, the number of new triples that STransE produce is decreasing on each run. In the first run, the number of new triples is 373,995. In the second run, the number of new triples is 178,654 and in the third run, the number of new triples becomes 107,587.

For the second purpose/P2, we record all the results in Table 4.

From this table we learn that for STransE, DistMult and Complex, running IC after each run produce higher PC than running IC only once because in each

Table 4. The result for P2

ID	The PC for running IC after each run				The PC for running IC only once			
	Flow	IBM	NELL	DBP	Flow	IBM	NELL	DBP
1	SE-IC-SE-IC	**69%**	**29%**	**55.51%**	SE-SE-IC	**66.44%**	**16.25%**	**43.90%**
2	KE-IC-KE-IC	0.86%	0.17%	17.16%	KE-KE-IC	1.18%	0.28%	17.31%
3	DM-IC-DM-IC	22.42%	0.53%	19.25%	DM-DM-IC	12.28%	0.22%	16.11%
4	CE-IC-CE-IC	20.95%	0.55%	19.24%	CE-CE-IC	12.38%	0.21%	16.07%

run, the number of correct triples that these approaches can feed into the next run is already high (for example in STransE, more than 20% of new triples in each run is correct). Consequently, this will increase the number of correct triples that these approaches produce in the next run.

Meanwhile for KB2E-TransE, running IC only once produce higher PC than running IC after each run, because, in each run, the number of correct triples that KB2E-TransE can feed into the next run is low (less than 1% of new triples in each run is correct). Consequently, this will decrease the number of correct triples that KB2E-TransE produces in the next run.

Table 5 records the result of the experiments for the third purpose/P3. We divide the table into three groups as follows: (1). All twelve scenarios from the third purpose/P3, (2). All the best scenarios from the first purpose/P1, (3). All the best scenarios from the second purpose/P2. Following are the lessons that we can learn from the results in Table 5:

- Different combination of KGEs (for an example: KGE1-IC-KG2-IC) with IC will produce higher PC when compared to the PC that is produced by the weakest KGE in a scenario (for an example: the weakest KGE between KGE1 and KGE2).
- The best scenario/flow from all three groups aforementioned above is SE-IC-SE-IC

5.3 Comparing Our Approximate Reasoning with Sound-and-Complete Reasoner

We compare our Approximate Reasoning approach with existing reasoners in terms of

- how many incorrect triples (in percentage) that are identified by an existing reasoner, can also be detected by our approach. For this comparison item, we collect all the justifications that are generated by a reasoner for a given knowledge graph. Then, we check whether our approach can detect all the incorrect triples that are stated in each of these explanations
- how long Approximate Reasoning takes compared to reasoning time of an existing reasoner. For this second comparison item, we need to explain first what are the processing stages for each system. In doing reasoning, every

Table 5. The result for P3

Scenarios	The percentage of correctness		
	IBM	NELL	DBP
KE-IC-SE-IC	40.72%	11.85%	30.95%
SE-IC-KE-IC	49.65%	17.34%	45.75%
KE-IC-DM-IC	11.44%	0.51%	17.93%
DM-IC-KE-IC	9.45%	0.98%	19.01%
KE-IC-CE-IC	11.40%	0.41%	17.91%
CE-IC-KE-IC	7.75%	0.87%	19.01%
SE-IC-DM-IC	55.60%	14.14%	46.29%
DM-IC-SE-IC	63.12%	16.92%	48.45%
SE-IC-CE-IC	55.65%	14.14%	46.21%
CE-IC-SE-IC	62.06%	17.15%	47.68%
DM-IC-CE-IC	22.36%	0.56%	19.20%
CE-IC-DM-IC	21.15%	0.51%	19.26%
SE-IC-SE-IC	**69%**	**29%**	**55.51%**
KE-IC	1.52%	0.37%	18.06%
DM-IC	21.96%	0.72%	18.90%
CE-IC	21.59%	0.67%	18.90%
KE-KE-IC	1.18%	0.28%	17.31%
DM-IC-DM-IC	22.42%	0.53%	19.25%
CE-IC-CE-IC	20.95%	0.55%	19.24%

existing reasoner has two steps which are the consistency checking and generating justification. Generating justification is often most costly since it needs to calculate the minimal subsets of a knowledge graph. Hence, the total of processing time for a reasoner is the consistency checking plus generating justification. Meanwhile, our approach also has two steps, which are scanning the inconsistency justification patterns (IJPs) from the TBox and then based on the IJPs, scanning the triples that conform to these IJPs in the ABox. Hence, the total processing time for our approach is the TBox scanning plus the ABox scanning. Please see Fig. 2 for the comparison of the processing stages between a reasoner and our approach.

We show the effectiveness of our approach against the consistency checking and related justification services that are provided by FACT++ 1.6.5 (run with Protege). **Dataset.** We used two datasets: (i) DBpedia version 2016-04, and (ii) IBM-KG.

Results. The comparison of the performance of the FACT++ reasoner and our Approximate Reasoning approach can be seen in Table 6.

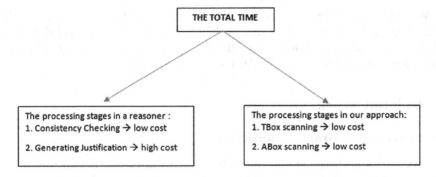

Fig. 2. The comparison of the processing stages between a reasoner and our approach.

Table 6. Comparison between pattern-based reasoning and reasoner

Dataset	Reasoner			Our approach		
	#Exp	CCT	GJT	CE	TST	AST
IBM-KG	46	1.577	4,620	100%	12.98	296.68
DBpedia	NA	NA	NA	NA	9,605	6,834.76

#Exp stands for the number of explanations that the justifications service from FACT++ generated. Each explanation consists of one or several incorrect triples. If FACT++ cannot generate the explanations (either because a KG is consistent or because we cannot run the consistency checking and justification services on a KG), we will give NA (Not Available) as the score. For DBpedia, we got an "insufficient memory" error when we tried to merge the TBox and the ABox of the DBpedia. This happened due to the sheer size of the ABox of DBpedia. Since merging the TBox and the ABox is the prerequisite of running consistency checking and justification services, hence we can not get the #Exp score for the whole DBpedia KG. CCT stands for the time that the reasoner needs to do consistency checking (in second). There are only two types of a score for CCT: the number of times and NA (Not Available). GJT stands for the time that the reasoner needs to generate the justifications (in seconds).

CE stands for coverage of the Explanations. It refers to how many of the explanations that are generated by the justification service of the reasoner, in percentage, are detected by our approach. We get the CE score by dividing the number of explanations that are detected by our approach with the number of the explanations that are generated by the reasoner. Since we do not have a number of explanation scores for the DBpedia data set, we can not count the CE score. TST stands for the time that is needed to scan the TBox part of a knowledge graph (in second). AST stands for the time that is needed to scan the ABox part of a knowledge graph (in seconds).

We observe from Table 6, that for IBM-KG, our approach is much more efficient than the consistency checking and justification service provided by the
FACT++ reasoner. Meanwhile for DBpedia, we could scan the problematic
triples less than five hours while FACT++ reasoner failed.

6   Related Work

6.1   Knowledge Graph Embedding

The idea of knowledge graph embedding is to represent an entity as a k-
dimensional vector $\mathbf{h}$ (or $\mathbf{t}$) and defines a scoring function $f_r(\mathbf{h}, \mathbf{t})$ to measure
the plausibility of the triplet (h, r, t) in the embedding space. The representa-
tions of entities and relations are obtained by minimizing a global loss function
involving all entities and relations. Different KGE algorithms often differ in their
scoring function, transformation and loss function [5, 8, 9, 12, 15–17, 28].

The above work has improved the performance of knowledge graph embedding in terms of the link prediction task but does not take into account the
correctness of the facts that they produce. Our work differs from previous work
on knowledge graph embedding as we focus on whether the new triples that are
produced by a knowledge graph embedding approach are correct respect to a
schema of a knowledge graph.

The most recent work that is very related to our work is [23]. They enhance
the existing embedding-based methods by encoding the logical consistency into
the learnt distributed representation for the knowledge graph. Their approach
enforces the new triples to be consistent in regards to the Horn theory. However,
their approach does not compute the truth degrees/the correctness level of new
triples, since according to them this technique is time-consuming.

6.2   Correctness of a Knowledge Graph

There is no specific metric to evaluate the correctness of a knowledge graph. The
closest measurements to do this are the accuracy (which is used in [21,24]) and
the percentage of consistent ABoxes [25]. Following are our explanation about
these measurements:

- The first measurement tries to validate the RDF triples in a knowledge graph
  by collecting consensus of matched triples from other knowledge graphs. Our
  work differs with this work as the latter using external information/other
  knowledge graphs to validate the triples.
- The second measurement determines the consistency of ABox regarded to a
  TBox. We could see that this work has limitation since it cannot guarantee
  soundness for inconsistency checking and justifications.

6.3   Approximate Concistency Checking

There are related work on approximate consistency checking. Meilicke et al. [24] addresses this issue but only with the DL-Lite ontology language, which is not enough for our purpose. There are also machine learning based approaches [25, 26]. However, they cannot guarantee soundness for inconsistency checking and justifications.

7   Conclusion and Future Works

In this paper, we have introduced the black-box Schema Aware Triple Classification (SATC). Extensive experiments on IBM, NELL, and DBpedia-Politic show that our approach (SE-IC-SE-IC on Table 5) can increase the level of correctness when compared to the application of single embedding-based approach (SE-IC on Table 2). We further show that from all scenarios/combinations that we can make from different knowledge graph embedding approaches, we can achieve the highest percentage of correctness by running the KGE approach that produces most correct triples followed by the approximate reasoning in a sequential manner.

The potential path for future work includes increasing the scalability of our approach and applying the sequential combinations to other approaches in the knowledge graph completion (such as the rule learning).

Acknowledgement. This work was supported by IBM Faculty Award and the EU Marie Currie K-Drive project (286348). Kemas Wiharja was also supported by the Lembaga Pengelola Dana Pendidikan (LPDP), the Ministry of Finance of Indonesia.

References

1. Pan, J.Z., Vetere, G., Gomez-Perez, J.M., Wu, H. (eds.): Exploiting Linked Data and Knowledge Graphs for Large Organisations. Springer, Cham (2017). https://doi.org/10.1007/978-3-319-45654-6. ISBN 978-3-319-45652-2
2. Pan, J.Z., et al. (eds.): Reasoning Web 2016. LNCS, vol. 9885. Springer, Cham (2017). https://doi.org/10.1007/978-3-319-49493-7
3. Paulheim, H.: Knowledge graph refinement: a survey of approaches and evaluation methods. Semant. Web J. **8**, 489–508 (2016)
4. Xiong, W., Hoang, T., Wang, W.Y.: DeepPath: a reinforcement learning method for knowledge graph reasoning. In: EMNLP (2017)
5. Bordes, A., Usunier, N., Garcia-Duran, A., Weston, J., Yakhnenko, O.: Translating embeddings for modeling multi-relational data. In: Advances in Neural Information Processing Systems 26, pp. 2787–2795. Curran Associates Inc. (2013)
6. Pan, J.Z., Thomas, E.: Approximating OWL-DL ontologies. In: AAAI 2007, pp. 1434–1439 (2007)
7. Pan, J.Z., Ren, Y., Zhao, Y.: Tractable approximate deduction for OWL. Artif. Intell. **235**, 95–155 (2016)
8. Lin, Y., Liu, Z., Sun, M., Liu, Y., Zhu, X.: Learning entity and relation embeddings for knowledge graph completion. In: Proceedings of 29th AAAI Conference on Artificial Intelligence, pp. 2181–2187 (2015)

9. Wang, Z., Zhang, J., Feng, J., Chen, Z.: Knowledge graph embedding by translating on hyperplanes. In: Proceedings of 28th AAAI Conference on Artificial Intelligence, pp. 1112–1119 (2014)

10. Nguyen, D.Q., Sirts, K., Qu, L., Johnson, M.: STransE: a novel embedding model of entities and relationships in knowledge bases. In: Proceedings Conference of the North American Chapter of the Association for Computational Linguistics: Human Language Technologies, pp. 460–466 (2016)

11. Xiao, H., Huang, M., Zhu, X.: TransG: a generative model for knowledge graph embedding. In: Proceedings of the 54th Annual Meeting of the Association for Computational Linguistics (Volume 1: Long Papers), vol. 1, pp. 2316–2325 (2016)

12. Socher, R., Chen, D., Manning, C.D., Ng, A.Y.: Reasoning with neural tensor networks for knowledge base completion. In: Proceedings of Neural Information Processing Systems, pp. 926–934 (2013)

13. Guo, S., Ding, B., Wang, Q., Wang, L., Wang, B.: Knowledge base completion via rule-enhanced relational learning. In: Chen, H., Ji, H., Sun, L., Wang, H., Qian, T., Ruan, T. (eds.) CCKS 2016. CCIS, vol. 650, pp. 219–227. Springer, Singapore (2016). https://doi.org/10.1007/978-981-10-3168-7_22

14. Du, J., Qi, K., Wan, H., Peng, B., Lu, S., Shen, Y.: Enhancing knowledge graph embedding from a logical perspective. In: Wang, Z., Turhan, A.-Y., Wang, K., Zhang, X. (eds.) JIST 2017. LNCS, vol. 10675, pp. 232–247. Springer, Cham (2017). https://doi.org/10.1007/978-3-319-70682-5_15

15. Nickel, M., Tresp, V., Kriegel, H.-P.: A three-way model for collective learning on multi-relational data. In: Proceedings of 28th International Conference on Machine Learning, pp. 809–816 (2011)

16. Jenatton, R., Roux, N.L., Bordes, A., Obozinski, G.R.: A latent factor model for highly multi-relational data. In: Proceedings of Neural Information Processing Systems, pp. 3167–3175 (2012)

17. Glorot, X., Bordes, A., Weston, J., Bengio, Y.: A semantic matching energy function for learning with multi-relational data. Mach. Learn. **94**(2), 233–259 (2014)

18. Paulheim, H., Bizer, C.: Improving the quality of linked data using statistical distributions. Int. J. Semant. Web Inf. Syst. (IJSWIS) **10**(2), 63–86 (2014)

19. Wang, Z., Zhang, J., Feng, J., Chen, Z.: Knowledge graph embedding by translating on hyperplanes. In: AAAI Conference on Artificial Intelligence (2014)

20. Mitchell, T., et al.: Never ending learning. In: AAAI Conference on Artificial Intelligence, pp. 2302–2310 (2015)

21. Liu, S., d'Aquin, M., Motta, E.: Measuring accuracy of triples in knowledge graphs. In: Gracia, J., Bond, F., McCrae, J.P., Buitelaar, P., Chiarcos, C., Hellmann, S. (eds.) LDK 2017. LNCS (LNAI), vol. 10318, pp. 343–357. Springer, Cham (2017). https://doi.org/10.1007/978-3-319-59888-8_29

22. Shi, B., Weninger, T.: Open-world knowledge graph completion. arXiv preprint arXiv:1711.03438 (2017)

23. Du, J., Qi, K., Shen, Y.: Knowledge graph embedding with logical consistency. Guangdong University of Foreign Studies (2018, unpublished paper)

24. Meilicke, C., Ruffinelli, D., Nolle, A., Paulheim, H., Stuckenschmidt, H.: Fast ABox consistency checking using incomplete reasoning and caching. In: Costantini, S., Franconi, E., Van Woensel, W., Kontchakov, R., Sadri, F., Roman, D. (eds.) RuleML+RR 2017. LNCS, vol. 10364, pp. 168–183. Springer, Cham (2017). https://doi.org/10.1007/978-3-319-61252-2_12

25. Paulheim, H., Stuckenschmidt, H.: Fast approximate A-Box consistency checking using machine learning. In: Sack, H., Blomqvist, E., d'Aquin, M., Ghidini, C., Ponzetto, S.P., Lange, C. (eds.) ESWC 2016. LNCS, vol. 9678, pp. 135–150. Springer, Cham (2016). https://doi.org/10.1007/978-3-319-34129-3_9
26. Ruffinelli, D.: Towards scalable ontological reasoning using machine learning. In: CEUR Workshop Proceedings, vol. 1875, Paper-5. RWTH (2017)
27. Horridge, M., Bechhofer, S.: The OWL API: a Java API for working with OWL 2 ontologies. In: Proceedings of the 6th International Conference on OWL: Experiences and Directions, vol. 529, pp. 49–58. CEUR-WS. org, October 2009
28. Ringsquandl, M., et al.: Event-enhanced learning for KG completion. In: Gangemi, A., et al. (eds.) ESWC 2018. LNCS, vol. 10843, pp. 541–559. Springer, Cham (2018). https://doi.org/10.1007/978-3-319-93417-4_35
29. Tran, H.D., Stepanova, D., Gad-Elrab, M.H., Lisi, F.A., Weikum, G.: Towards nonmonotonic relational learning from knowledge graphs. In: Cussens, J., Russo, A. (eds.) ILP 2016. LNCS (LNAI), vol. 10326, pp. 94–107. Springer, Cham (2017). https://doi.org/10.1007/978-3-319-63342-8_8
30. Ho, V.T., Stepanova, D., Gad-Elrab, M.H., Kharlamov, E., Weikum, G.: Rule learning from knowledge graphs guided by embedding models. In: Vrandečić, D., et al. (eds.) ISWC 2018. LNCS, vol. 11136, pp. 72–90. Springer, Cham (2018). https://doi.org/10.1007/978-3-030-00671-6_5

Knowledge Graph-Based Core Concept Identification in Learning Resources

Rubén Manrique[1]([✉]) [iD], Christian Grévisse[2] [iD], Olga Mariño[1] [iD],
and Steffen Rothkugel[2] [iD]

[1] Systems and Computing Engineering Department, School of Engineering,
Universidad de los Andes, Bogotá, Colombia
{rf.manrique,olmarino}@uniandes.edu.co
[2] Computer Science and Communications Research Unit, University of Luxembourg,
Esch-sur-Alzette, Luxembourg
{christian.grevisse,steffen.rothkugel}@uni.lu

Abstract. The automatic identification of core concepts addressed by
a learning resource is an important task in favor of organizing content
for educational purposes and for the next generation of learner support
systems. We present a set of strategies for core concept identification on
the basis of a semantic representation built using the open and available
knowledge in the so-called Knowledge Graphs (KGs). Different unsupervised weighting strategies, as well as a supervised method that operates
on the semantic representation, were implemented for core concept identification. In order to test the effectiveness of the proposed strategies,
a human-expert annotated dataset of 96 learning resources extracted
from MOOCs was built. In our experiments, we show the capacity of the
semantic representation for the core-concept identification task as well
as the superiority of the supervised method.

1 Introduction

The automatic identification of core concepts addressed by a learning resource is
an important task in favor of organizing content for educational purposes [21,23]
and for the next generation of learner support systems [15]. The coreness of a
concept is as a measure of the degree of importance of a concept explained in
the learning resource. Different concepts can be addressed and explained in a
resource; however, for those who are annotated as "core", it is expected that the
resource provides the greatest amount of relevant information. Different from
a set of terms, a concept is an unambiguous entity that is typically connected
to a semantic layer that describes the knowledge area and the relationships
among concepts. The additional information obtained from the semantic layer
that is commonly expressed in terms of an ontology has been exploited for the
development of services that support learning processes in their different stages
[7,11].

This work was partially supported by COLCIENCIAS PhD scholarship (Call 647-2014).

R. Ichise et al. (Eds.): JIST 2018, LNCS 11341, pp. 36–51, 2018.
https://doi.org/10.1007/978-3-030-04284-4_3

Much of the literature on automatic identification and annotation of core concepts has focused in specific domains described via closed ontologies and taxonomies created by human experts [5,10,21]. These closed descriptions are difficult to extend since the vocabularies vary in most cases from a community of practice to another [5]. It would be appropriate, therefore, to design strategies that operate on a common open semantic layer described by open and accessible vocabularies. This would not only allow the main concepts identified to be reused but also the strategy to extract them.

In recent years, different institutions started to publish and share their knowledge in specific domains in the form of data structured under Semantic Web standards, with the aim of promoting interconnected knowledge, reuse and discovery. The Linked Open Data (LOD) cloud is the name given to the set of interconnected datasets freely accessible on the Web and interconnected to each other under common vocabularies. From this huge space of data, KGs are particularly important since they concentrate the knowledge of multiple domains, and in general, they specify a large number of interrelationships between concepts [4,18]. DBpedia[1], YAGO[2] and Wikidata[3] are some examples of RDF datasets considered as KGs. These knowledge bases, in addition to being open and cross-domain, usually tend to be continuously updated by the community, which makes them an ideal source of knowledge to enrich different processes and systems. We hypothesize that the identification of core concepts can be facilitated by introducing the background knowledge in such KGs.

Previous work has shown applications of core concept identification in learning resources. The recent *SoLeMiO* plugin for Office allows teachers to retrieve related material that was indexed for the same set of concepts [7]. Thereby, they are supported in the authoring process to see how existing work has presented a particular topic. Apart from this help during the creation of a new resource, *SoLeMiO* also allows to enhance already existing documents by listing a set of related resources. Students benefit from this integration by being able to pinpoint related learning material, which can on one hand give additional information on a certain concept, and on the other hand present information in a different way, e.g., as a video or a gamification activity [8].

In this paper, different strategies for the automatic identification of core concepts in learning resources were implemented on top of a semantic representation built using a KG as concept space. The process starts with the extraction of concept mentions in the learning resource text. In order to identify concept mentions in a reliable, automatic and unambiguous way, we employ state of the art concept recognition and entity linking tools. Then, we propose a semantic representation by exploiting background information from the KG via different expansion strategies. Taking advantage of the graph-based structure of the semantic representation, we evaluate different concepts weighting functions. Concepts with the highest weights are selected as the core concepts of the resources. Finally,

---

[1] https://wiki.dbpedia.org.
[2] https://yago-knowledge.org.
[3] https://www.wikidata.org/wiki/Wikidata:Main_Page.

inspired by previous works [22, 23] we also use machine learning methods on a set of features extracted from the semantic representation and the learning resource structure. In order to test the effectiveness of the proposed core concept identification strategies, a human-expert annotated dataset of 96 resources extracted from Massive Open Online Courses (MOOCs) was built. Our experiments are therefore oriented to evaluate the agreement of the strategies with the human notion of coreness.

The contributions of this work can be briefly summarized as follows:

- The implementation of a semantic representation of learning resources that exploit the background knowledge present in a KG.
- A dataset of 96 learning resources extracted from MOOCs and annotated by a group of experts with their core concepts.
- The evaluation of different weighting strategies on the top of the semantic representation to score the "coreness" of a concept.
- The proposal of a set of features extracted mainly from the semantic representation as input to different supervised learning algorithms.

The remainder of this paper is organized as follows. Section 2 presents an overview of related work. Section 3 describes in general terms our proposal to identify core concepts. The semantic representation building process including the weighting strategies is presented in detail in Sect. 4. Section 5 presents the supervised approach setup and the features description. Section 6 shows the evaluation results. Finally, conclusions are presented in Sect. 7.

2   Related Work

Different works have addressed the problem of automatically pinpointing the main concepts of a learning resource. Roy et al. developed an automatic tool for annotating documents with metadata such as concepts, type of concepts, topic and the learning resource type [21]. Ontology domains are used to map lexical terms to concepts. To evaluate the importance of a concept, they analyze the frequency of its related terms. The type of concept (i.e. outcome, prerequisite, defined and used) is identified by analyzing the documents with a shallow parsing approach. They defined key verbs, sentence patterns, and rules to identify the type of concept. In more recent but similar works, [5, 10] enrich learning resources metadata with semantic concepts from a domain ontology. Using an ontology extraction algorithm named Hieron, they extract the concepts covered by the content resource with an associated weight that represents the degree of pertinence. Foster et al. [6] present a semi-supervised approach to core concept identification. They train a machine learning classifier that assigns coreness labels on the basis of a set of human-annotated features. These features include the dependence, structure and the function of the considered phrase in the text. Changuel et al. address the problem of determining an effective learning path from a corpus of Web documents via the annotation of outcome and prerequisite concepts [2]. They employ a machine-learning method to predict the class of concept on the basis of contextual and local text features. Most of the previous works have focused on strategies to identify concepts in the text and its subsequent link to a domain ontology. Different from these works we focus on the evaluation of the coreness of the concept. The concept identification and linking are carried out using state of the art tools.

Regarding learning resources representation techniques that take advantage of LOD KGs background knowledge, we only found the work done by Krieger et al. [11]. In this work, authors propose an automatic semantic description of Web Documents based on LOD concepts. The semantic description is called "fingerprint" and allows to judge if a Web resource is relevant with respect to a learning context or not. However, we do not find evidence of its use to determine core concepts or to organize learning resources.

Finally, this work is also related to weighting strategies for resources in Linked Data. Those techniques seek to rank the resources resulting from an input keyword or a SPARQL query [9,17]. Although they do not address the same problem, they also exploit the graph-based structure and use centrality measures to improve the ranking.

3   Core Concept Identification Process

Figure 1 shows the complete pipeline for the core concepts identification. The semantic representation is the main component and the source for the features employed by the supervised machine learning method. Broadly speaking, our semantic resource representation is a weighted directed graph in which nodes represent concepts, and edges represent the existence of a semantic relationship in the KG between the considered concepts. In the first module, concept mentions found in the resource text are extracted. This process takes an input text and returns a set of URIs of structured LOD concepts. Then expansion processes are applied to enrich and refine the representation. The expansion process considers the linkages that can be found in the KG to include relevant concepts. Finally, the importance of each concept is evaluated via different weighting functions that take advantage of the representation graph-based structure. For each weighting function concepts with the highest weights are selected as the core concepts of the resources. A more detailed description of the semantic representation is presented in Sect. 4.

Following the trend of related research that has opted for supervised approaches, in this paper we also use machine learning methods for the discovery of the main concepts [22,23]. However, different from such works, the set of features are extracted mostly from the semantic representation.

4   Semantic Representation

In this section, we explain the semantic representation in detail. The essential information is taken from a KG using the concepts found in the document text. A KG consists of a set of concepts/entities C and literals L that are interrelated

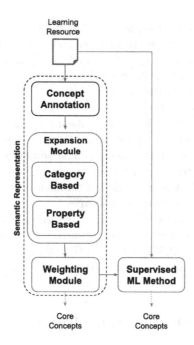

Fig. 1. Process description

through a set of properties/predicates P. Under an RDF model, KG data consists of a set of statements $S \subset C \times P \times (C \cup L)$. Each $s \in S$ is a triplet composed of a subject, a predicate, and an object/literal. Considering the above, our semantic representation follows the Definition 1.

Definition 1. *The semantic representation G_i of a learning resource r_i is a directed weighted graph $G_i = (N_i, E_i, w(r_i, c), w(r_i, e))$, where both nodes and edges have an associated weight defined by the functions $w(r_i, c) : N \rightarrow \mathbb{R}+$ and $w(r_i, e) : E \rightarrow \mathbb{R}+$. The set of nodes $N_i = \{c_1, c_2, ..., c_k\}$ are entities/concepts belonging to the space of a KG ($c_j \in C$). The node weight $w(r_i, c)$ denotes how relevant the node c is for the learning resource. A connection edge between two nodes (c_a, c_b) represents the existence of at least one statement s in the KG that links both concepts. The weight of the edge $w(r_i, e)$ denotes how strong is this linkage between the considered concepts.*

As previously mentioned, the concept annotation module (see Fig. 1) looks for concept mentions in the text (i.e. annotations) and links them to concepts in the KG. Entity linking and word sense disambiguation services such as DBpedia Spotlight[4], Aylen[5], AlchemyAPI[6], or Babelfy[7] can be employed for this task.

---

[4] https://github.com/dbpedia-spotlight/dbpedia-spotlight.
[5] https://aylien.com.
[6] https://www.ibm.com/watson/alchemy-api.html.
[7] http://babelfy.org.

It is important to emphasize that we do not perform any additional verification on the annotations discovered by the selected services. As was stated by Waitelonis et al. [24], there is no guarantee of a correct annotation via automatic services as the mentioned above, so a manual cleaning is suggested. However, in a realistic automatic scenario, a manual correction process is not feasible. In general, two main issues result of the annotation step can arise [2]: (i) *Incomplete annotation:* not all concepts present in the content are discovered. Such incompleteness might result, for example, when not all the surface forms of an entity/concept are recognized; (ii) *Incorrect annotation:* the concepts are mistakenly linked. For example, the word "Cloud" commonly used to denote a type of internet-based computing could be erroneously linked to the concept of "Cloud" in meteorology. Although the above problems are not directly addressed in this work, the expansion and weighting modules presented in the following sections can mitigate their impact in the representation.

4.1   Expansion Module

Expansion is used to enrich the representation with concepts that are not explicitly mentioned in the text or they were not identified by the annotation service. We expand the set of annotations (i.e. concepts found in the text) to new related ones following two different approaches.

- **Category-based expansion (CBE):** for each annotation, categories (or other hierarchical information about concepts in the KG) are included in the representation.
- **Property-based Expansion (PBE):** for each annotation, the representation is enriched with the concepts found by traversing some of the properties of the KG ontology.

As example consider the following definition[8] of a *Class* in the domain of computer programming:

> *"In object-oriented programming, a class is an extensible program-code-template for creating objects, providing initial values for state (member variables) and implementations of behavior (member functions or methods). In many languages, the class name is used as the name for the class (the template itself), the name for the default constructor of the class (a subroutine that creates objects), and as the type of objects generated by instantiating the class; these distinct concepts are easily conflated."*

After the concept annotation step the following set of concepts are retrieved[9]: "Constructor (object-oriented programming)", "Member variable", "Method (computer programming)", "Object (computer science)" and "Subroutine". Note

---

[8] Source: https://en.wikipedia.org/wiki/Class_(computer_programming).

[9] In this example, DBpedia was used as KG and DBpedia Spotlight as annotation service.

that even though the text is the definition of the KG concept "Class (computer programming)", it is not returned by the annotation service used. However, the concept is added via property-based expansion to the representation since it is connected to the annotations: "Member variable", "Subroutine", "Object (computer science)" and "Method (computer programming)". In the same way, concepts and categories such as "Object lifetime", "Variable (computer science)" and "Category: Programming language topics" are added to the representation.

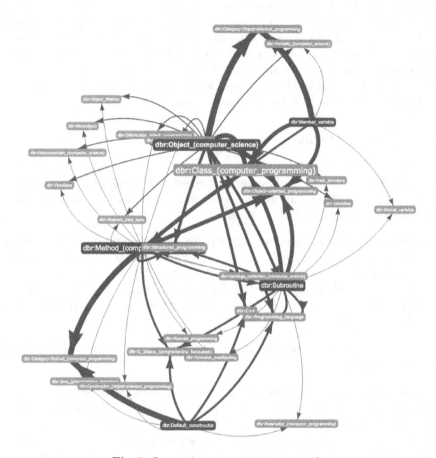

Fig. 2. Semantic representation example

The final graph representation G_i, as shown in Fig. 2, is then built using as nodes the resulting set of concepts after the expansion process. For the edge conformation, property paths[10] between every pair of nodes in the KG are returned and analyzed via SPARQL queries[11]. Basically, if a property path between two concepts is found, a directed edge in G_i is created following the direction of the

[10] https://www.w3.org/TR/sparql11-property-paths/.
[11] https://www.w3.org/TR/rdf-sparql-query/.

connection in the KG. Different property path lengths can be explored, however, following previous experimental results we limit the search to property paths of length less than or equal to 2 [15]. A normalized score that considers the number of property paths found is used as edge weight $w(r_i, e)$. In Fig. 2, red nodes are annotations while green nodes are concepts incorporated via the expansion module. The thickness of the edge indicates how strong is the link between two concepts via $w(r_i, e)$. The size of the node is proportional to the node weight $w(r_i, c)$ and it is used as an indicator of their importance in the representation. $w(r_i, c)$ is obtained in the final weighting module.

4.2   Weighting Module

This module is key in the core concept identification of the learning resource. The concepts in the representation with highest $w(r_i, c)$ are considered as the core concepts. By contrast, concepts with the lowest weight can be considered as noise in the representation. In previous work, we identified that concepts which are not related to the main topic of a learning resource tend to be infrequent in the document and/or weakly connected in the representation (i.e. few or no connections with other concepts) [14]. With the strategies presented below, such noisy concepts should have a low $w(r_i, c)$, and would therefore not be regarded as core concepts.

Concept Frequency. The most basic weighting strategy is to analyze the frequency of the concept in the representation:

$$w_{cf}(r_i, c) = f_{c,R_i} \qquad (1)$$

where f_{c,R_i} represents the number of times that c appears in the resource content plus the number of times that the concept appears in the expansion process. The problem with this strategy is that it reinforces general concepts that tend to appear frequently. Consider a set of learning resources in a structured programming course. The most basic concepts such as "variables" and "data types", which are usually explained in the first lessons, are frequently mentioned to explain more advanced concepts. Therefore, if a learning resource mentions the concept of "variable" multiple times, it does not necessarily indicate that it is one of the main concepts explained by the resource. In order to address the previous problem we propose a weighting strategy inspired by the well-known TF-IDF (term frequency-inverse document frequency) weighting scheme used in word based vector space models [20]. Thus, the proposed strategy w_{cf-idf} (Eq. 2) penalizes concepts appearing in multiple representations.

$$w_{cf-idf}(r_i, c) = w_{cf}(r_i, c) \times log \frac{M}{m_c} \qquad (2)$$

where M is the total number of learning resources and m_c is the number of learning resources with the concept c in their representation.

Discount of Expanded Concepts. In order to prevent the representation from being diverted towards frequent properties or general categories in the hierarchical structure of the KG, it is necessary to apply a discount to the new concepts incorporated via the expansion module. This problem has been previously identified in works that address a similar approach for user modeling [14,15,19]. For category-based expanded concepts the following discount is applied:

$$w_{cat}(r_i, c) = w_{cf-idf}(r_i, c) \times \frac{1}{log(SP)} \times \frac{1}{log(SC)} \tag{3}$$

where SP is the set of concepts belonging to the category and SC is the set of sub-categories in the categorical hierarchy. The idea behind this discount strategy is that categories that are too broad and generic are penalized. Similarly, for property-based expanded concepts, the following discount is applied:

$$w_{pro}(r_i, c) = w_{cf-idf}(r_i, c) \times \frac{1}{log(P)} \tag{4}$$

where P is the number of occurrences of the property in the KG from which the concept $c \in C$ is obtained.

Centrality Measures. A different weighting strategy is to exploit the structure of the graph to rank the importance of each node through different centrality measures [1]. The following centrality measures were employed:

- **Degree centrality (DE)**: The degree centrality of a node c is the relationship between the number of nodes that are connected to it and the total number of nodes.
- **Betweenness centrality (BET)**: The betweenness centrality is the fraction of shortest paths between all the possible node pairs that pass through the node of interest.
- **PageRank (PR)**: PageRank is a well-known algorithm designed to rank web pages according to incoming links. In essence PageRank is a measure that ranks important nodes on directed graphs.

For the calculation of the previous centrality measures, the NetworkX[12] library was used. The edge weights are considered for the PageRank calculation, but not for Betweenness centrality.

5   Supervised Approach

Given a pair of concept-learning resource (c, r_i), we predict whether or not c is a core concept of r_i, which is a binary classification problem. For each concept-learning resource pair (c, r_i), we calculate two types of features: text-based and graph-based features.

---

[12] https://networkx.github.io.

5.1   Text-Based Features (TF)

The first type of feature is designed to utilize textual content extracted from the learning resource (lr_{text}) and the description of the concepts in the KG (KG_{text}).

- Title. Whether c appears in the learning resource title if any.
- First-3-Sentences. Whether c appears in the first 3 sentences of lr_{text}.
- $w_{cf}(r_i, c)$ and $w_{cf-idf}(r_i, c)$. Weights that are obtained from the weighting module.
- $tf - idf$ Sim. The cosine similarity between tf-idf vectors of lr_{text} and KG_{text}. We carried out typical text processing operations for bag of words vector space models including tokenizer, stop word removal and stemming.
- TextRank. The highest normalized TextRank score among the sentences that contain the concept c. The pytextrank[13] package was used.

5.2   Graph-Based Features (GF)

These characteristics are extracted directly from the semantic representation.

- $PR(c)$. The PageRank value of the concept in the semantic representation.
- $BET(c)$. The Betweenness centrality of the concept in the semantic representation.
- $In(c)$. The number of incoming links for c.
- $Out(c)$. The number of outgoing links for c.
- $AND(c)$. The average neighbor degree of the concept c.

$$AND(c) = \frac{1}{DE(c)} \sum_{c_n \in N(c)} w(r_i, e_{(c,c_n)})DE(c_n)$$

  where $N(c)$ are the neighbors of node c, DE is the degree centrality and $w(r_i, e_{(c,c_n)})$ is the weight of the edge that links c and c_n.
- Authority and Hub. Scores obtained after the application of the HITS algorithm on semantic representation. Similar to PageRank, hub scores are used as an indicator of importance.
- GED. We employ the graph edit measure implemented in [13] to calculate the similarity between the semantic representation of the learning resource and the semantic representation obtained using as input KG_{text}.

6   Evaluation

6.1   Experimental Setup

We implemented our experimental evaluation using the following resources:

---

[13] https://github.com/ceteri/pytextrank.

- **DBpedia:** We select DBpedia 2016-10 version as KG due to its comprehensive vocabularies and its extensive relationships between concepts. Additionally, DBpedia is continuously being updated based on Wikipedia, thus enabling cross-domain modeling capabilities. The hierarchical structure of a concept is drawn from categories in DBpedia categorical system. Categories are extracted through dct:subject predicate. Similarly, the summary text extracted through dbo:abstract predicate is used as KG_{text}.

- **DBpedia Spotlight semantic annotator:** We use DBpedia Spotlight (DBS) to annotate text documents with concepts. DBpedia Spotlight allows configuring the level of annotation (precision/recall trade-off) by confidence/support parameters. The support parameter specifies the minimum number of inlinks a DBpedia resource has to have in order to be annotated, while the confidence parameter controls the topical pertinence and the contextual ambiguity to avoid incorrect annotations as much as possible [16]. Following previous results [7], we define the following configuration for DBS: support: 5, confidence: 0.35.

- **Babelfy semantic annotator:** In order to compare the influence of the quality of the semantic annotation, we also use Babelfy entity linking tool to discover concepts in the text. Unlike DBS, no special configuration was made for Babelfy and all concepts returned by the service were considered.

- **Corpus of learning resources semantic representations:** In order to calculate the inverse document frequency, we employ a set of more than 5000 video lectures from MOOCs in different domains selected mainly from the DAJEE dataset [3,12]. For each video lecture, we download the video transcripts and annotate them with the DBpedia concepts mentions using the previously mentioned semantic annotators.

- **Evaluation dataset:** A dataset of learning resources human-annotated with the core concepts was used to evaluate. We select 96 learning resources in the area of programming fundamentals. The selected resources are videos extracted from MOOCs for which an annotation process was carried out with the help of a group of domain experts. A total of seven experts participated in the annotation process. They were asked to annotate the core concepts of the resources via an online platform that showed the resources in a random way. More than 40 hours of video were reviewed by the experts. The resulting dataset, which we will call [**CCI**], contains the core concepts for which there was an agreement between the experts. Thus, in order for a concept to be included as a core concept, at least two experts had to annotate it in their respective evaluations. On average each resource was annotated by at least 3 experts and contains on average 3.8 core concept annotations. To prove our core concepts identification strategies, the video transcripts are used as input for the semantic representation construction process. Negative examples for the training of the supervised learning classifiers are randomly selected from non-core concepts in the resulting semantic representation of each learning resource in such a way that the classes remain balanced. We release the metadata such as resource titles, URLs and core concept annotations[14], yet we can not release the videos or their transcripts for copyright reasons. However, Coursera-dl and Edx-dl libraries[15] can be used to download the resources.

- **Baseline:** Like previous works, we use the concept frequency as an indicative of significance [21], therefore the weighting technique w_{cf} is used as the baseline for the unsupervised approach. It should be noted that although there are other works that address this problem, it is not possible to implement their proposals because they operate on domain descriptions (i.e. ontologies, taxonomies, knowledge bases, etc.) that are not public and are difficult to generalize to knowledge graphs.

6.2 Experimental Results

In our experiments, we compared the different weighting strategies and the machine learning method on the set of proposed features. For the machine learning method, we train three widely used binary classifiers: Naive Bayes (NB), Support Vector Machine (SVM), and Random Forest (RF). We use 250 trees for RF, a radial basis function kernel for SVM and a regularization parameter $C = 1$. We report in Table 1 the precision (P), recall (R), and F1-score (F1). The reported values are averaged in 10-fold cross-validation experiments.

Table 1. Core concept identification results via supervised approach

	DBS			Babelfy		
	P	R	F1	P	R	F1
NB	0.604	0.548	0.575	0.612	0.505	0.553
SVM	0.802	**0.702**	0.749	0.784	**0.712**	0.746
RF	**0.857**	0.687	**0.763**	**0.814**	0.697	**0.751**

Based on the reported results RF presents a better precision and F1 scores while SVM presents a better recall. Considering F1 as a comparison measure, we conclude that DBS is more appropriate as an annotation service. We noticed through a manual inspection of the different semantic representations that Babelfy presents a greater number of incorrect annotations. Naive Bayes performs the worst, which is due to the fact that the strong independence assumption does not hold for the proposed feature set.

Using the trained RF classifiers, we perform a feature analysis via the mean decrease impurity method. In descending order, the 5 most important features are: PR, AND, $tf - idf\ Sim$, w_{cf-idf}, and GED. Four of the five features can be extracted directly from the semantic representation without further processing, which demonstrates their potential for the identification of core concepts.

---

[14] https://github.com/Ruframapi/CCI.
[15] https://github.com/coursera-dl.

For the weighting strategies we report the results on [CCI] dataset in Table 2 using w_{cf}, w_{cf-idf} (with the discount for expanded concepts), DE, BET and PR as weighting strategies. For each unsupervised method, we computed results for top-k ranked concepts and for k values of 3, 5 and 10. As expected, the results show the trade-off between precision and recall with the increase of k. Small k values lead to a higher precision at the cost of a lower recall. With the increase of k, the recall also increases but the precision decreases. It is clear that the best weighting strategies are w_{cf-idf} and PR. Consistent with the results of the supervised method, better results are obtained with DBS as annotation service.

Table 2. Core concepts identification results via weighting strategies

		DBS			Babelfy		
		P@k	R@k	F1	P@k	R@k	F1
$k = 3$	w_{cf}	0.236	0.205	0.219	0.184	0.202	0.193
	w_{cf-idf}	**0.242**	0.254	0.248	**0.188**	0.198	0.193
	DE	0.185	0.171	0.178	0.151	0.161	0.156
	BET	0.194	0.203	0.198	0.171	0.201	0.185
	PR	0.239	**0.301**	**0.266**	0.183	**0.247**	**0.210**
$k = 5$	w_{cf}	0.179	0.257	0.211	0.133	0.233	0.169
	w_{cf-idf}	**0.192**	0.272	0.225	0.135	0.251	0.175
	DE	0.149	0.201	0.171	0.117	0.193	0.146
	BET	0.167	0.263	0.204	0.128	0.204	0.158
	PR	0.187	**0.351**	**0.244**	**0.146**	**0.312**	**0.199**
$k = 10$	w_{cf}	0.114	0.327	0.168	0.099	0.314	0.151
	w_{cf-idf}	**0.118**	0.373	0.179	0.113	0.332	0.169
	DE	0.085	0.281	0.131	0.094	0.268	0.139
	BET	0.096	0.332	0.149	0.101	0.277	0.148
	PR	0.116	**0.397**	**0.180**	**0.123**	**0.339**	**0.180**

Although the supervised method presents better results, the unsupervised weighting strategies are fast to calculate once the set of annotations are identified and do not require a set of training which is usually a costly process. Table 3 decomposes the total execution time into its elements: annotation, expansion, weighting and feature extraction (see Fig. 1). The supervised approach processing time for a single document is much more expensive than the non-supervised strategy since it requires an additional feature extraction process. *TextRank*, *GED* and *tf – idf Sim* are features that are time consuming but as mentioned earlier quite important for the learning phase.

We also want to emphasize that the results were obtained with a dataset in a single domain. [CCI] only considers learning resources in the area of programming fundamentals, a domain that seems to be well described in the DBpedia

Table 3. Processing times for elements of our related core concept identification strategies. It is calculated using 50 documents with 3735 words on average.

		Avg. Time (ms)
Semantic representation	*Annotation*	308
	Expansion	204
	Weighting strategies	401
Total semantic representation		913
Feature extraction		501
Total supervised approach		1414

knowledge graph. The results obtained here may vary in other domains that are not so well described in DBpedia. In general, we see the need to build a broader dataset that encompasses different fields of knowledge.

Finally, it is important to emphasize that the results obtained are based on the annotation made by automatic tools that, far from being perfect, present errors. The weighting strategies, in this case, seem adequate to rule out noise concepts due to errors in the annotation and/or off-topic concepts added in the expansion process. In none of the top-3 concepts extracted by the different weighting strategies were concepts without a high relation to the topic of the learning resource although not all were core concepts.

7   Conclusion

We presented an approach to identify core concepts in learning resources on the basis of a semantic representation built using the open and available knowledge in KGs. The semantic representation is, in essence, a directed weighted graph whose nodes represent KG concepts and edges represent the existence of a semantic relation between them. The graph construction process is driven by the expansion and weighting modules that are in charge of incorporating relevant related concepts and assigning nodes an importance score, respectively.

We explore two methods to extract core concepts. The first one extracts the concepts with greater weight from the representation through different weighting strategies. As a second strategy, we chose a supervised method based on a set of features extracted mainly from representation. With the weighting strategies and considering the top three concepts, we reach a maximum precision of 24%. In contrast, we achieved on average a precision of 85% with the supervised method using random forest classifier. Despite the superiority of the supervised method, the weighting strategies do not require a training process since they operate directly in the representation.

There are still open questions which will be addressed in future projects. Our future work will be directed to the use of KGs different from DBpedia or the combination of them. Our hypothesis is that the more sources of knowledge a more refined representation could be obtained. In the same way, we want to evaluate our core concepts identification strategies in other domains. To achieve this, it is necessary to create a more comprehensive dataset of human-annotated learning resources.

References

1. Boudin, F.: A comparison of centrality measures for graph-based keyphrase extraction. In: IJCNLP (2013)
2. Changuel, S., Labroche, N., Bouchon-Meunier, B.: Resources sequencing using automatic prerequisite-outcome annotation. ACM Trans. Intell. Syst. Technol. **6**(1), 6:1–6:30 (2015). https://doi.org/10.1145/2505349
3. Estivill-Castro, V., Limongelli, C., Lombardi, M., Marani, A.: DAJEE: a dataset of joint educational entities for information retrieval in technology enhanced learning. In: Proceedings of the 39th International ACM SIGIR Conference on Research and Development in Information Retrieval, SIGIR 2016. ACM (2016)
4. Färber, M., Ell, B., Menne, C., Rettinger, A.: A comparative survey of DBpedia, Freebase, OpenCyc, Wikidata, and YAGO. Semant. Web J., pp. 1–26, July 2015. http://www.semantic-web-journal.net/system/files/swj1141.pdf
5. Farhat, R., Jebali, B., Jemni, M.: Ontology based semantic metadata extraction system for learning objects. In: Chen, G., Kumar, V., Kinshuk, Huang, R., Kong, S.C. (eds.) Emerging Issues in Smart Learning, pp. 247–250. Springer, Berlin (2015). https://doi.org/10.1007/978-3-662-44188-6_34
6. Foster, J.M., Sultan, M.A., Devaul, H., Okoye, I., Sumner, T.: Identifying core concepts in educational resources. In: Proceedings of the 12th ACM/IEEE-CS Joint Conference on Digital Libraries. JCDL 2012, pp. 35–42. ACM, New York (2012). https://doi.org/10.1145/2232817.2232827
7. Grévisse, C., Manrique, R., Mariño, O., Rothkugel, S.: Knowledge graph-based teacher support for learning material authoring. In: Serrano, C.J., Martínez-Santos, J. (eds.) CCC 2018. CCIS, vol. 885, pp. 177–191. Springer, Cham (2018). https://doi.org/10.1007/978-3-319-98998-3_14
8. Grévisse, C., Manrique, R., Mariño, O., Rothkugel, S.: SoLeMiO: semantic integration of learning material in office. In: Proceedings of E-Learn: World Conference on E-Learning 2018. Association for the Advancement of Computing in Education (AACE) (in press)
9. Ichinose, S., Kobayashi, I., Iwazume, M., Tanaka, K.: Ranking the results of DBpedia retrieval with SPARQL query. In: Kim, W., Ding, Y., Kim, H.-G. (eds.) JIST 2013. LNCS, vol. 8388, pp. 306–319. Springer, Cham (2014). https://doi.org/10.1007/978-3-319-06826-8_23
10. Jebali, B., Farhat, R.: Ontology-based semantic metadata extraction approach. In: 2013 International Conference on Electrical Engineering and Software Applications, pp. 1–5, March 2013. https://doi.org/10.1109/ICEESA.2013.6578408
11. Krieger, K., Schneider, J., Nywelt, C., Rösner, D.: Creating semantic fingerprints for web documents. In: Proceedings of the 5th International Conference on Web Intelligence, Mining and Semantics. WIMS 2015, pp. 11:1–11:6 (2015). https://doi.org/10.1145/2797115.2797132
12. Limongelli, C., Lombardi, M., Marani, A., Taibi, D.: Enrichment of the dataset of joint educational entities with the web of data. In: 2017 IEEE 17th International Conference on Advanced Learning Technologies (ICALT), pp. 528–529 (2017)

13. Manrique, R., Cueto-Ramirez, F., Mariño, O.: Comparing graph similarity measures for semantic representations of documents. In: Serrano, C.J., Martínez-Santos, J. (eds.) CCC 2018. CCIS, vol. 885, pp. 162–176. Springer, Cham (2018). https://doi.org/10.1007/978-3-319-98998-3_13

14. Manrique, R., Herazo, O., Mariño, O.: Exploring the use of linked open data for user research interest modeling. In: Solano, A., Ordoñez, H. (eds.) CCC 2017. CCIS, vol. 735, pp. 3–16. Springer, Cham (2017). https://doi.org/10.1007/978-3-319-66562-7_1

15. Manrique, R., Mariño, O.: How does the size of a document affect linked open data user modeling strategies? In: Proceedings of the International Conference on Web Intelligence. WI 2017, pp. 1246–1252. ACM, New York (2017). https://doi.org/10.1145/3106426.3109440

16. Mendes, P.N., Jakob, M., García-Silva, A., Bizer, C.: DBpedia spotlight: shedding light on the web of documents. In: Proceedings of the 7th International Conference on Semantic Systems. I-Semantics 2011, pp. 1–8. ACM, New York (2011)

17. Mirizzi, R., Ragone, A., Di Noia, T., Di Sciascio, E.: Ranking the linked data: the case of DBpedia. In: Benatallah, B., Casati, F., Kappel, G., Rossi, G. (eds.) ICWE 2010. LNCS, vol. 6189, pp. 337–354. Springer, Heidelberg (2010). https://doi.org/10.1007/978-3-642-13911-6_23

18. Paulheim, H.: Knowledge graph refinement: a survey of approaches and evaluation methods. Semant. Web 8(3), 489–508 (2017). https://doi.org/10.3233/SW-160218

19. Piao, G., Breslin, J.G.: Analyzing aggregated semantics-enabled user modeling on Google+ and Twitter for personalized link recommendations. In: Proceedings of the 2016 Conference on User Modeling Adaptation and Personalization. UMAP 2016, pp. 105–109. ACM, New York (2016). https://doi.org/10.1145/2930238.2930278

20. Rajaraman, A., Ullman, J.D.: Mining of Massive Datasets. Cambridge University Press, New York (2011)

21. Roy, D., Sarkar, S., Ghose, S.: Automatic extraction of pedagogic metadata from learning content. Int. J. Artif. Intell. Educ. 18(2), 97–118 (2008)

22. Siehndel, P., Kawase, R., Nunes, B.P., Herder, E.: Towards automatic building of learning pathways. In: Proceedings of the 10th International Conference on Web Information Systems and Technologies, pp. 270–277 (2014). https://doi.org/10.5220/0004837602700277

23. Sultan, M.A., Bethard, S., Sumner, T.: Towards automatic identification of core concepts in educational resources. In: Proceedings of the 14th ACM/IEEE-CS Joint Conference on Digital Libraries. JCDL 2014, pp. 379–388. IEEE Press, Piscataway (2014)

24. Waitelonis, J., Exeler, C., Sack, H.: Enabled generalized vector space model to improve document retrieval. In: Proceedings of the Third NLP&DBpedia Workshop (NLP & DBpedia 2015) co-located with the 14th International Semantic Web Conference 2015 (ISWC 2015), Bethlehem, Pennsylvania, USA, 11 October 2015, pp. 33–44 (2015). http://ceur-ws.org/Vol-1581/paper4.pdf

Ranking Diagnoses for Inconsistent Knowledge Graphs by Representation Learning

Jianfeng Du$^{(\boxtimes)}$

Guangdong University of Foreign Studies, Guangzhou 510006, China
jfdu@gdufs.edu.cn

Abstract. When a knowledge graph (KG) is growing e.g. by knowledge graph completion, it might become inconsistent with the logical theory which formalizing the schema of the KG. A common approach to restoring consistency is removing a minimal set of triples from the KG, called a diagnosis of the KB. However, there can be a large number of diagnoses. It is hard to manually select the best one among these diagnoses to restore consistency. To alleviate the selection burden, this paper studies automatic methods for ranking diagnoses so that people can merely focus on top diagnoses when seeking the best one. An approach to ranking diagnoses through representation learning aka knowledge graph embedding is proposed. Given a set of diagnoses, the approach first learns the embedding of the complement set of the union of all diagnoses, then for every diagnosis, incrementally learns an embedding of the complement set of the diagnosis and employs the embedding to estimate the removal cost of the diagnosis, and finally ranks diagnoses by removal costs. To evaluate the approach, four knowledge graphs with logical theories are constructed from the four great classical masterpieces of Chinese literature. Experimental results on these datasets show that the proposed approach is significantly more effective than classical random methods in ranking the best diagnoses at top places.

1 Introduction

Knowledge graph has been widely used in knowledge representation nowadays. A knowledge graph is a directed graph with vertices labeled by entities and edges labeled by relations. It can be treated as a set of triples of the form $\langle h, r, t \rangle$, where h is the *head entity* (simply *head*), r the *relation* and t the *tail entity* (simply *tail*). To increase the expressivity of knowledge graphs, a knowledge graph is usually attached with a logical theory which formalizes the schema of the knowledge graph.

Logical consistency is a prerequisite for a meaningful knowledge graph. That is, a meaningful knowledge graph should be consistent with its attached logical theory, since everything can be entailed by the knowledge graph under the logical theory. When a knowledge graph is growing, it might become inconsistent with

© Springer Nature Switzerland AG 2018
R. Ichise et al. (Eds.): JIST 2018, LNCS 11341, pp. 52–67, 2018.
https://doi.org/10.1007/978-3-030-04284-4_4

the attached logical theory. For example, in the scenario of knowledge graph completion, new triples that are predicted by certain learning methods are added to the knowledge graph. The addition of new triples may probably render the knowledge graph inconsistent. A common approach to restoring consistency is removing a minimal set of triples from the knowledge graph, which coincides with the well-adopted minimal change principle. We simply call such a minimal set of triples a *diagnosis* of the knowledge graph wrt the attached logical theory. By viewing the logical theory as a TBox and the knowledge graph as an ABox, it can be shown from [5] that, even when the logical theory is expressed in DL-Lite$_{core}$, an extremely lightweight fragment of first-order logic, the number of diagnoses can be up to exponential in the number of triples in the knowledge graph. It is hard to manually select the best diagnosis among a large number of diagnoses. To alleviate the selection burden, it is needed to rank diagnoses so that people can merely focus on top diagnoses when seeking the best one.

It is natural to rank diagnoses by their removal costs which can be defined by truth degrees of constituent triples. A diagnosis should be ranked higher when it has a lower removal cost, namely when triples in it have lower truth degrees. Recently *representation learning* of knowledge graphs aka *knowledge graph embedding* [3,17,28] has been widely used in estimating truth degrees of triples. Knowledge graph embedding introduces distributed representations for entities and relations and encodes them into a continuous vector space, thus the truth degree of any triple can be estimated by simple numerical calculation.

We study the following two research problems in this paper:

(1) How to apply knowledge graph embedding to estimate the removal costs of diagnoses?
(2) Are methods for ranking diagnoses that are based on removal costs estimated by an embedding model more effective than classical random methods in giving the best diagnoses high ranks?

For the first research problem, we observe that the complement set of a diagnosis is a maximal subset of the knowledge graph that is consistent with the logical theory. Hence we conjecture that the complement set of a diagnosis has a stable composition state and can be used to learn an embedding model for estimating truth degrees of any triples. It follows an assumption that, if the complement set of a diagnosis is more likely to consist of true triples, it will have a more stable composition state, while the triples in the diagnosis will have lower truth degrees. Under this assumption, we propose an approach to ranking diagnoses based on embedding models. Given a set of diagnoses, the approach first learns the embedding of the complement set of the union of all diagnoses, then for every diagnosis, incrementally learns an embedding of the complement set of the diagnosis and employs the embedding to estimate the removal cost of the diagnosis, and finally ranks diagnoses in the ascending order of their removal costs, where the removal cost of a diagnosis is computed from the truth degrees of triples in the diagnosis by applying some increasing aggregation function.

For the second research problem, we need to use knowledge graphs that are attached with logical theories to evaluate our approach. In particular, the logical theory should have constraints since there is no nonempty diagnosis wrt a logical theory without constraints. Currently there is no benchmark knowledge graph coming with a logical theory that has constraints. Hence we construct four knowledge graphs and their background logical theories from a domain that we are familiar with, which is about character relationships in the four great classical masterpieces of Chinese literature, where one knowledge graph corresponds to a masterpiece. To simulate the growth of knowledge graphs, for every knowledge graph we apply an embedding based method to estimate truth degrees of new triples, and then add to the knowledge graph the top-100 unentailed triples that have the largest truth degrees and treat them as false triples in any diagnosis. We call a diagnosis *rational* if it consists of false triples only. A rational diagnosis should have a higher rank than nonrational diagnoses since it can safely be removed from the grown knowledge graph. We implement two concrete methods for our approach by respectively employing two popular embedding models TransE [3] and TransH [28]. For comparison, we also implement two classical random methods for ranking diagnoses, where one randomly ranks the whole set of given diagnoses, and the other one randomly ranks all given diagnoses and then sorts them in the ascending order of their cardinalities. Experimental results show that, compared with classical random methods, our approach significantly raises the ranks of rational diagnoses.

The main contributions of this work are two-fold:

(1) We propose knowledge graphs and logical theories from the four great classical masterpieces of Chinese literature. All the logical theories model character relationships and have constraints.
(2) We propose an embedding based approach to ranking diagnoses and empirically verify its effectiveness.

The remainder of this paper is organized as follows. Section 2 gives preliminaries on logical theory, diagnosis and knowledge graph embedding. Section 3 presents our approach to ranking diagnoses based on knowledge graph embedding. Section 4 describes our evaluation on the proposed approach. Before concluding in Sect. 6, we discuss related work in Sect. 5.

2 Preliminaries

2.1 Logical Theory and Diagnosis

First-order logic is a traditional way to knowledge representation. A logical theory expressed by first-order logic is a set of rules R of the form $\forall \boldsymbol{x} \ (\phi(\boldsymbol{x}) \rightarrow \exists \boldsymbol{y} \ \varphi(\boldsymbol{x}, \boldsymbol{y}))$, where $\phi(\boldsymbol{x})$ is a conjunction of atoms on the universally quantified variables $\boldsymbol{x}$, and $\varphi(\boldsymbol{x}, \boldsymbol{y})$ is a disjunction of atoms on both universally quantified variables $\boldsymbol{x}$ and existentially quantified variables $\boldsymbol{y}$. The part of R at the left (resp. right) of $\rightarrow$ is called the *body* (resp. *head*) of R. By body(R) (resp. head(R)) we denote the set of atoms in the body (resp. head) of R. If the head of R has no atoms, R is also called a *constraint* and the empty head is written as

$\perp$. If the head of R has a single atom without existentially quantified variables, R is also called a *datalog* rule. For brevity, in this paper we present our work with the Horn fragment of first-order logic although the proposed methods can be applied to other fragments as discussed in Sect. 3. We simply call a set of datalog rules and constraints a *Horn theory*, which may contain constants. A knowledge graph can be treated as a set of ground rules with empty bodies, or simply a set of ground atoms, by rewriting triples $\langle h, r, t \rangle$ to ground atoms $r(h, t)$, where entity-type triples of the form $\langle e, \mathsf{type}, t \rangle$ (meaning e has a type t) are also rewritten to $\mathsf{type}(e, t)$ as other triples.

A *model* of a Horn theory $\mathcal{T}$ is a set S of ground atoms such that (1) $\mathrm{body}(R)\,\theta \subseteq S$ implies $\mathrm{head}(R)\,\theta \cap S \neq \emptyset$ for any datalog rule $R \in \mathcal{T}$ and any ground substitution θ for $\mathrm{var}(R)$, and (2) $\mathrm{body}(R)\,\theta \not\subseteq S$ for any constraint $R \in \mathcal{T}$ and any ground substitution θ for $\mathrm{var}(R)$, where a *ground substitution* for a symbol maps all variables in the symbol to constants, and $\mathrm{var}(R)$ denotes the set of variables in R. By treating a knowledge graph as a set of ground rules with empty bodies, we can combine a knowledge graph and a Horn theory and simply call the union of them a *Horn KB*. A model of a Horn KB made up of a knowledge graph $\mathcal{G}$ and a Horn theory $\mathcal{T}$ is a model of $\mathcal{T}$ that contains all ground atoms in $\mathcal{G}$. A Horn KB is said to be *consistent* if it has a model. Actually a consistent Horn KB has a unique least model. A knowledge graph $\mathcal{G}$ is said to be *consistent with* a Horn theory $\mathcal{T}$ if the Horn KB $\mathcal{G} \cup \mathcal{T}$ is consistent. A triple is said to be *entailed* by a knowledge graph $\mathcal{G}$ under a Horn theory $\mathcal{T}$, or *entailed* by the Horn KB $\mathcal{G} \cup \mathcal{T}$, if the triple is in the unique least model of $\mathcal{G} \cup \mathcal{T}$. A subset S of a knowledge graph $\mathcal{G}$ is said to be a *maximal consistent subset* (an *MCS*) of $\mathcal{G}$ wrt a Horn theory $\mathcal{T}$ if $S \cup \mathcal{T}$ is consistent and for all proper supersets S' of S, $S' \cup \mathcal{T}$ is inconsistent. A subset $\mathcal{D}$ of $\mathcal{G}$ is said to be a *diagnosis* of $\mathcal{G}$ wrt $\mathcal{T}$ if the complement set of $\mathcal{D}$ namely $\mathcal{G} \backslash \mathcal{D}$ is an MCS of $\mathcal{G}$ wrt $\mathcal{T}$.

2.2   Knowledge Graph Embedding

Knowledge graph embedding encodes a knowledge graph into a continuous vector space to support a variety of prediction tasks. The translational distance models constitute a popular category of models for knowledge graph embedding. They measure the truth degree of a triple by the distance between the head and the tail, based on a translation carried out by the relation. TransE [3] is a pioneer translational distance model which defines translation directly on entity vectors. To better model 1-N, N-1 and N-N relations, most of the subsequent models define translation on projection of entity vectors. To name a few, TransH [28] defines projection on relation-specific hyperplanes, whereas TransR [17] defines projection by relation-specific matrices. All these models uniformly learn vectors by minimizing a global margin-based loss function via a loss function for triples.

The loss function for a triple $\langle h, r, t \rangle$, written $\mathsf{loss}_r(h, t)$, can be defined as $||f_r(l_h) + l_r - f_r(l_t)||_{L_1}$ or $||f_r(l_h) + l_r - f_r(l_t)||_{L_2}$, where l_x denotes $(x_1, \ldots, x_n)$ which is the vector representation for x, $||l_x||_{L_1}$ is the L1-norm of l_x defined as $\sum_{i=1}^{n} |x_i|$, $||l_x||_{L_2}$ is the L2-norm of l_x defined as $\sqrt{\sum_{i=1}^{n} x_i^2}$, and $f_r(\cdot)$ is a relation-specific projection function which maps an entity vector into another one. For example, $f_r(l_e)$ is defined as l_e in TransE, whereas it is defined as $l_e - w_r^T l_e w_r$ for w_r an r-specific normal vector in TransH.

The global margin-based loss function to be minimized is defined over the set $\mathcal{G}$ of training triples (namely positive triples) and a set $\overline{\mathcal{G}}$ of negative triples which is disjoint with $\mathcal{G}$ and constructed from $\mathcal{G}$ by randomly corrupting triples in either heads or tails. By introducing the margin γ as a hyper-parameter, the global margin-based loss function to be minimized is given by

$$\sum_{\langle h,r,t\rangle \in \mathcal{G}} \sum_{\langle h',r,t'\rangle \in \overline{\mathcal{G}}} \max(0, \gamma + \text{loss}_r(h,t) - \text{loss}_r(h',t')). \tag{1}$$

The truth degree of a triple $\langle h, r, t\rangle$ can be defined as $f(\text{loss}_r(h,t))$ for some decreasing function $f(x)$ such as e^{-x}.

3 Ranking Diagnoses by Knowledge Graph Embedding

The main problem that we address can be formalized as: given a set of diagnoses $\mathbf{D} = \{D_1, \ldots, D_n\}$ of a knowledge graph $\mathcal{G}$ wrt a Horn theory $\mathcal{T}$, estimate the set of removal costs of given diagnoses $\{c_1, \ldots, c_n\}$, where c_i denotes the removal cost of D_i for $1 \leq i \leq n$.

The key idea for solving this problem is: for every given diagnosis D_i, we learn an embedding model M_i for the complement set of D_i which is actually an MCS of $\mathcal{G}$ wrt $\mathcal{T}$, then apply the model M_i to compute the truth degrees of triples in D_i, and finally compute the removal cost c_i of D_i from the truth degrees of triples in D_i by applying some increasing aggregation function such as the sum function. This idea has a problem. That is, since embedding models are commonly learnt by stochastic gradient descent algorithms, the learnt embedding models for different diagnoses will probably converge in different local minima that vary a lot, making the truth degrees of triples in different diagnoses incomparable. To make the learnt embedding models for different diagnoses as similar as possible, we adopt an incremental learning strategy. That is, we first learn an embedding model M for the complement set of the union of all given diagnoses and then one by one learn the embedding model M_i based on M. The above idea is realized by an algorithm shown in Fig. 1.

In this algorithm, LearnEmbedding($\mathcal{G}, \mathcal{T}$) returns an embedding model of a knowledge graph $\mathcal{G}$ by taking a Horn theory $\mathcal{T}$ into account. There have been methods for enhancing representation learning with datalog rules such as [4,7, 9,10]. An efficient method which is adopted in our implementation is treating the set $\mathcal{G}^+$ of triples entailed by $\mathcal{G} \cup \mathcal{T}$ as the set of positive triples. Since $\mathcal{T}$ is a Horn theory, $\mathcal{G}^+$ is the least model of $\mathcal{G} \cup \mathcal{T}$ and can be computed as the least fix-point of $\mathcal{G}^{(t)}$, where $\mathcal{G}^{(t)} = \mathcal{G}^{(t-1)} \cup \bigcup_{R\in\mathcal{T},\text{body}(R)\theta\subseteq\mathcal{G}^{(t-1)}} \text{head}(R)\theta$ for $t > 0$, and $\mathcal{G}^{(0)} = \mathcal{G}$. For other fragments of first-order logic that have corresponding tools for entailment checking, $\mathcal{G}^+$ can also be computed, thus this method is also applicable to other logical theories in first-order logic. The method only slightly

Algorithm. `ComputeRemovalCosts`($\mathcal{G}, \mathcal{T}, \mathbf{D}$)
Input: A knowledge graph $\mathcal{G}$, a Horn theory $\mathcal{T}$, and a set of diagnoses $\mathbf{D} = \{D_1, \ldots, D_n\}$ of $\mathcal{G}$ wrt $\mathcal{T}$.
Output: The set of removal costs $\{c_1, \ldots, c_n\}$, where c_i is the removal cost of D_i.
1:   $M \leftarrow$ LearnEmbedding($\mathcal{G} \setminus \bigcup_{i=1}^n D_i, \mathcal{T}$);
2: **for** $i \in \{1, \ldots, n\}$ **do**
3:      $M_i \leftarrow$ IncrLearnEmbedding($M, \mathcal{G} \setminus D_i, \mathcal{T}$);
4:      $c_i \leftarrow$ Aggregate($\{$ComputeTruthDegree(h, r, t)$\}_{\langle h,r,t \rangle \in D_i}$);
5: **return** $\{c_1, \ldots, c_n\}$;

Fig. 1. The algorithm for estimating removal costs of given diagnoses

differs from traditional methods on altering the global margin-based loss function given by Formula (1) to

$$\sum_{\langle h,r,t \rangle \in \mathcal{G}^+} \sum_{\langle h',r,t' \rangle \in \overline{\mathcal{G}^+}} \max(0, \gamma + \text{loss}_r(h, t) - \text{loss}_r(h', t')). \tag{2}$$

Although this method is rather simple, it has been proved to be effective in improving the predictive performance of learnt models [7,9].

The remaining functions in the algorithm in Fig. 1 can be defined as follows. IncrLearnEmbedding($M, \mathcal{G}, \mathcal{T}$) is an incremental version of LearnEmbedding($\mathcal{G}, \mathcal{T}$). It only alters the original version by using M as the initial embedding model instead of randomly initializing the embedding model. ComputeTruthDegree(h, r, t) returns the truth degree of the triple $\langle h, r, t \rangle$. It is computed from the loss value of $\langle h, r, t \rangle$ namely $\text{loss}_r(h, t)$ by applying some decreasing function. In our implementation we simply define the truth degree of $\langle h, r, t \rangle$ as $e^{-\text{loss}_r(h,t)}$. Aggregate($\{v_1, \ldots, v_n\}$) is an increasing aggregation function on a set of numbers $\{v_1, \ldots, v_n\}$. In our implementation we simply define it as the sum function; i.e., we define Aggregate($\{v_1, \ldots, v_n\}$) as $\sum_{i=1}^n v_i$.

There remains a related problem on how diagnoses are computed. This problem has been well-studied since the pioneer work [20] in which a hitting set tree algorithm for computing diagnoses is proposed. Given a set $\mathcal{C}$ of sets of triples, a *hitting set* for $\mathcal{C}$ is defined as a set S of triples such that $S \cap S' \neq \emptyset$ for all sets S' in $\mathcal{C}$; intuitively, S hits every element of $\mathcal{C}$. S is further called a *minimal* hitting set for $\mathcal{C}$ if no proper subset of S is a hitting set for $\mathcal{C}$. In a following study [22] an efficient framework is proposed to enumerate all minimal hitting sets based on dualization of two kinds of minimal hitting sets. Since every diagnosis is a minimal hitting set for the set of all minimal inconsistent subsets (MISs) of the knowledge graph whereas every MIS is also a minimal hitting set for the set of diagnoses of the knowledge graph, the framework proposed in [22] can be adapted to computing diagnoses. This kind of adaptations has been verified to be highly efficient e.g. by [6]. In this work we also provide an efficient algorithm for computing diagnoses, shown in Fig. 2, which is adapted from [22] and will finish execution after a given number of (or all) diagnoses are computed. The

Algorithm. ComputeDiagnoses($\mathcal{G}$, $\mathcal{T}$, m)
Input: A knowledge graph $\mathcal{G}$, a Horn theory $\mathcal{T}$, and a number m.
Output: The set of up to m diagnoses of $\mathcal{G}$ wrt $\mathcal{T}$.
1: $n \leftarrow 0$;
2: ConstructDiagnoses($0, \emptyset$);
3: **return** $\{D_0, \ldots, D_n\}$;
Procedure ConstructDiagnoses(i, M)
Comment: This procedure reuses all symbols in the main function.
4: **if** $i = n$ **then**
5:      **if** M is inconsistent with $\mathcal{T}$ **then return**;
6:      $D_i \leftarrow \mathcal{G} \setminus$ FindMCS($M, \mathcal{G}, \mathcal{T}$);
7:      **if** $n < m - 1$ **then** $n \leftarrow n + 1$ **else return** and go to **line 3**;
8: **if** $D_i \cap M \neq \emptyset$ **then**
9:      ConstructDiagnoses($i + 1, M$)
10: **else for** each $e \in D_i$ s.t. $M \cup \{e\}$ is a minimal hitting set for $\{D_0, \ldots, D_n\}$ **do**
11:     ConstructDiagnoses($i + 1, M \cup \{e\}$);
Function FindMCS($M, \mathcal{G}, \mathcal{T}$)
Comment: Enlarges M to a maximal consistent subset of $\mathcal{G}$ wrt $\mathcal{T}$ and returns it.
12: $M' \leftarrow M$;
13: **for** each $e \in \mathcal{G} \setminus M$ **do**
14:     **if** $M' \cup \{e\}$ is consistent with $\mathcal{T}$ **then** $M' \leftarrow M' \cup \{e\}$;
15: **return** M';

Fig. 2. The algorithm for computing up to m diagnoses

setting of an upper bound for the number of output diagnoses is particularly practical because there can be exponentially many diagnoses [5] and it is too costly to compute all diagnoses for some knowledge graphs.

In a nutshell, the algorithm enumerates all minimal hitting sets (MHSs) for the set of currently generated diagnoses by depth-first search. After an MHS M for the set of currently generated diagnoses is computed, the consistency of $M \cup \mathcal{T}$ is checked. If $M \cup \mathcal{T}$ is inconsistent (line 5), it can be shown [22] that M is an MHS for the set of all diagnoses of $\mathcal{G}$ wrt $\mathcal{T}$, thus the algorithm can continue to compute another MHS for the set of currently generated diagnoses; otherwise (line 6), the algorithm computes a new diagnosis of $\mathcal{G}$ wrt $\mathcal{T}$ whose complement set is a maximal consistent subset of $\mathcal{G}$ wrt $\mathcal{T}$ and then (in lines 8–11) computes an MHS for the new set of generated diagnoses. This way guarantees that any newly computed MHS is different from previously computed ones (which means that the search of MHSs is finite and efficient) and that the set of diagnoses finally generated is complete when the input number m is set to infinity [22].

The algorithm in Fig. 2 is applicable to any other fragment of first-order logic provided that a tool for consistency or entailment checking exists for that fragment. Since entailment checking in first-order logic can be reduced to consistency checking while the execution time for consistency checks dominates the total execution time of the algorithm, we can measure the computational complexity of the algorithm by the number of consistency checks. Suppose there are N triples in $\mathcal{G}$ and there are n MHSs for the set of m computed diagnoses of $\mathcal{G}$ wrt $\mathcal{T}$, then the number consistency checks required by computing m diagnoses is under $1 + n + mN$; i.e., the time complexity measured by the number of consistency checks is $O(n + mN)$.

4   Experimental Evaluation

4.1   Experiments Setup

We focus on two concrete methods for our proposed approach, which employ the two most efficient methods for knowledge graph embedding namely TransE [3] and TransH [28], respectively, to learn embedding models. We call them the *TransE-based* method and the *TransH-based* method. To evaluate the effectiveness of our approach, we also introduce two baseline methods. One ranks all given diagnoses randomly and is called the *random* method. The other ranks all given diagnoses randomly and then sort them in the ascending order of cardinalities. This method prefers shorter diagnoses and is called the *cardinality-based random* (simply *CB-random*) method. All the above methods were implemented in Java and evaluated in the RapidMiner platform[1] for fair comparison in the same environment. In particular, the two concrete methods built on our approach were implemented in multi-threaded mode, using standard stochastic gradient descent to learn embedding models where the mini-batch size is fixed to one.

Regarding the experimental datasets, existing benchmark datasets for knowledge graph embedding do not have corresponding logical theories with constraints. It is hard to add adequate constraints to these datasets since they belong to general domains using our unfamiliar relations. Thus we constructed new knowledge graphs and the corresponding logical theories from a domain that we are familiar with. The domain is about character relationships in the four great classical masterpieces of Chinese literature, namely Dream of the Red Chamber (DRC), Journey to the West (JW), Outlaws of the Marsh (OM), and Romance of the Three Kingdoms (RTK). We collected triples on character relationships from e-books and treated them as ground truths, yielding four knowledge graphs each of which corresponds to one masterpiece. We manually constructed logical theories for these four masterpieces separately in Protege[2], a well-known ontology editor. These theories model character relationships which are originally expressed in OWL 2 QL [8], a tractable profile of OWL 2 for modeling ontologies, and then translated to Horn theories by standard transformation. As an example, a portion of the Horn theory for DRC is shown in Table 1.

The constructed knowledge graphs are consistent with their corresponding logical theories. To simulate the growth of knowledge graphs, for every knowledge graph we applied the TransE method [3] to compute loss values of new triples and added the top-100 triples to the knowledge graph that are not entailed by the

---

[1] https://www.rapidminer.com/.
[2] https://protege.stanford.edu/.

Table 1. A portion of the Horn theory for Dream of the Red Chamber (DRC)

Translated rule in first-order logic	Meaning
$\mathsf{type}(x, \mathsf{Male}) \wedge \mathsf{type}(x, \mathsf{Female}) \rightarrow \bot$	Males are not females and vise versa
$\mathsf{wife}(x, y) \rightarrow \mathsf{type}(x, \mathsf{Female})$	Wives are females
$\mathsf{wife}(x, y) \rightarrow \mathsf{family\_member}(x, y)$	Wives are family members
$\mathsf{son}(x, y) \rightarrow \mathsf{type}(x, \mathsf{Male})$	Sons are males
$\mathsf{son}(x, y) \rightarrow \mathsf{family\_member}(x, y)$	Sons are family members
$\mathsf{son}(x, x) \rightarrow \bot$	One is not a son of himself
$\mathsf{family\_member}(x, y) \rightarrow \mathsf{family\_member}(y, x)$	Family members are symmetric
$\mathsf{family\_member}(x, y) \rightarrow \mathsf{relative}(x, y)$	Family members are relatives
$\mathsf{wife}(x, y) \wedge \mathsf{son}(y, z) \rightarrow \mathsf{daughter\_in\_law}(x, z)$	Daughters in law are wives of sons
$\mathsf{daughter\_in\_law}(x, y) \rightarrow \mathsf{relative}(x, y)$	Daughters in law are relatives
$\mathsf{daughter\_in\_law}(x, x) \rightarrow \bot$	One is not a daughter in law of herself

knowledge graph under the corresponding logical theory and have the smallest loss values. Every grown knowledge graph is inconsistent with its corresponding logical theory and thus has at least one nonempty diagnosis. To set up a gold standard for ranking diagnoses, we carefully checked the added triples and made sure that all of them are false triples. We define a diagnosis as *rational* if it consists of false triples only. For an ideal method for ranking diagnoses, all rational diagnoses should be ranked at top places among all diagnoses since they can safely be removed from the grown knowledge graph. Based on this truth, we introduce two metrics from the field of Information Retrieval to evaluate a ranking method. The first metric, written $\mathrm{Rank_{min}}$, is defined as the minimum rank of all rational diagnoses in the sorted list of given diagnoses. The smaller $\mathrm{Rank_{min}}$ is, the earlier people can see rational diagnoses, thus the better the sorted list is. The second metric, written NDCG (short for Normalize Discounted Cumulative Gain), is defined as the ratio of the discounted cumulative gain (DCG) of the current sorted list to the DCG of the ideal sorted list where all rational diagnoses are ranked at top places in turn. The value of NDCG is ranged from 0 to 1. The larger NDCG is, the closer the sorted list is to the ideal one, thus the better the sorted list is. Formally, NDCG is defined as

$$\mathrm{NDCG} = \frac{\mathrm{DCG}}{\mathrm{IDCG}} = \frac{\sum_{i=1}^{n} \frac{\mathrm{rel}_i}{\log_2 i + 1}}{\sum_{i=1}^{m} \frac{1}{\log_2 i + 1}}, \tag{3}$$

where n is the number of given diagnoses, m is the number of rational diagnoses among all given diagnoses, and $\mathrm{rel}_i = 1$ if the ith diagnosis in the sorted list is rational or $\mathrm{rel}_i = 0$ otherwise.

We applied the algorithm shown in Fig. 2 to compute up to 100 diagnoses for each grown knowledge graph. The computation is efficient and was done in one second for every knowledge graph. Except for Journey to the West (JW), each of the other three datasets has less than 100 diagnoses and thus the set of computed diagnoses for it is complete. Table 2 reports the statistics about our constructed datasets and the computed diagnoses. The experimental datasets and our implemented systems are available at OpenKG.CN[3].

Table 2. Statistics about the datasets and computed diagnoses

Data	#rel	#ent	#triple	#dlog	#const	#diag	c_{min}	c_{max}	#rational	cards
DRC	48	392	380 + 100	110	107	8	3	4	1	3
JW	31	104	109 + 100	94	30	100	21	28	1	26
OM	49	156	201 + 100	111	47	9	3	5	1	3
RTK	51	123	153 + 100	142	63	96	6	16	2	6, 8

Note: #rel/#ent/#triple are respectively the number of relations/entities/triples (original+added) in the knowledge graph, #dlog/#const are respectively the number of datalog rules/constraints in the logical theory, #diag is the number of computed diagnoses, c_{min}/c_{max} are respectively the minimum/maximum cardinality of computed diagnoses, #rational is the number of rational diagnoses among all computed diagnoses, and cards is the list of cardinalities of rational diagnoses.

4.2   Experimental Results

To tune hyper-parameters in the TransE/TransH-based method, we treated the complement set of the union of all computed diagnoses as the training set. We selected the learning rate among $\{0.001, 0.005, 0.01, 0.05, 0.1\}$, the margin among $\{0.1, 0.2, 0.5, 1, 2\}$, the dimension of entity vectors among $\{20, 50, 100, 200\}$, and the dissimilarity measure as either L1-norm or L2-norm. Moreover, we used the "bern" strategy [28] for negative sampling and set the number of training rounds to 2000. Since every triple in the training set is probably true[4], we determined the optimal hyper-parameters that achieve the highest filtered Mean Reciprocal Rank (MRR) [18,25,26] by five-fold cross-validation on the training set. This way tends to make clearer the distinction between true triples and false triples.

Considering that all the four compared methods are random based, we run each of them for ten times to get the metric scores. For the TransE/TransH-based method we set the training rounds to 2000 in LearnEmbedding to learn initial embedding models and set the training rounds to 500 in IncrLearnEmbedding to incrementally learn final embedding models.

Table 3 reports comparison results of the four methods in terms of $Rank_{min}$. It can be seen that, the two embedding based methods built on our proposed approach are significantly better than at least one baseline method at the 5% significance level for all datasets, or even at the significance level 1% for some datasets. Except for JW that has more than 100 diagnoses, for other three datasets the two embedding based methods rank a rational diagnosis at the top-two place

---

[3] http://www.openkg.cn/tool/rank-diagnoses.
[4] In fact it is guaranteed true for DRC, OM and RTK, since for each of these knowledge graphs the training set is the complement set of the union of all diagnoses.

Table 3. Comparison results in terms of $Rank_{min}$

Data	Random	CB-random	TransE-based	TransH-based
DRC	3.40 ± 2.46	2.00 ± 1.05	$\mathbf{1.20 \pm 0.42^{\dagger\ddagger}}$	$1.50 \pm 0.53^{\dagger}$
JW	44.90 ± 29.15	81.40 ± 3.31	$\mathbf{42.70 \pm 19.88^{\ddagger\ddagger}}$	$48.10 \pm 21.36^{\ddagger\ddagger}$
OM	29.40 ± 25.18	2.50 ± 1.27	$\mathbf{1.00 \pm 0.00^{\dagger\dagger\ddagger\ddagger}}$	$\mathbf{1.00 \pm 0.00^{\dagger\dagger\ddagger\ddagger}}$
RTK	4.30 ± 1.95	1.80 ± 0.42	$2.00 \pm 0.00^{\dagger\dagger}$	$\mathbf{1.30 \pm 0.48^{\dagger\dagger\ddagger}}$

Note: each cell displays the mean $\pm$ std $Rank_{min}$ with the best mean in bold, which has a superscript $\dagger$ ($\dagger\dagger$) if it is significantly smaller than $Rank_{min}$ of the random method at the 5% (1%) significance level and has a superscript $\ddagger$ ($\ddagger\ddagger$) if it is significantly smaller than $Rank_{min}$ of the CB-random method at the 5% (1%) significance level.

in most cases. There are only two exceptional cases where an embedding based method gives worse results than a baseline method—one for the TransH-based method on JW, and the other for the TransE-based on RTK. But in these two cases the embedding based method is not significantly worse than the baseline method at the 5% significance level. By looking into the cardinalities of rational diagnoses (see Table 2), it can be found that rational diagnoses may not be shorter than nonrational diagnoses, hence the CB-random method is not always better than the random method e.g. on JW in which the unique rational diagnosis is longer than 73 nonrational diagnoses. However, the embedding based methods still show a good performance in ranking a rational diagnosis at the front even when it is evidently longer than many nonrational diagnoses.

Table 4. Comparison results in terms of NDCG

Data	random	CB-random	TransE-based	TransH-based
DRC	0.621 ± 0.28	0.732 ± 0.24	$\mathbf{0.926 \pm 0.16^{\dagger\dagger}}$	0.815 ± 0.19
JW	0.196 ± 0.03	0.157 ± 0.00	$\mathbf{0.199 \pm 0.05^{\ddagger}}$	$0.187 \pm 0.03^{\ddagger}$
OM	0.291 ± 0.12	0.577 ± 0.15	$\mathbf{0.879 \pm 0.02^{\dagger\dagger\ddagger\ddagger}}$	$0.848 \pm 0.02^{\dagger\dagger\ddagger\ddagger}$
RTK	0.484 ± 0.20	0.705 ± 0.16	$0.631 \pm 0.00^{\dagger}$	$\mathbf{0.889 \pm 0.18^{\dagger\dagger\ddagger}}$

Note: each cell displays the mean $\pm$ std NDCG with the best mean in bold, which has a superscript $\dagger$ ($\dagger\dagger$) if it is significantly larger than NDCG of the random method at the 5% (1%) significance level and has a superscript $\ddagger$ ($\ddagger\ddagger$) if it is significantly larger than NDCG of the CB-random method at the 5% (1%) significance level.

Table 4 reports comparison results of the four methods in terms of NDCG. It exhibits similar conclusions as Table 3. That is, except for the TransH-based method on DRC, the two embedding based methods are significantly better than at least one baseline method at the 5% (or even 1%) significance level for all datasets. Similar to comparison results in $Rank_{min}$, there are also two exceptional cases where an embedding based method gives worse results than a baseline method. But in these two cases the embedding based method is still not significantly worse than the baseline method at the 5% significance level. The embedding based methods show a much better performance than the baseline methods on OM which has two rational diagnoses where the longer one is longer than 7 nonrational diagnoses. It further shows that the embedding based methods are able to rank multiple rational diagnoses at top places even when some of them are longer than nonrational diagnoses.

As a whole, the experimental results show that the embedding based methods built on our proposed approach are significantly more effective than classical random methods in ranking rational diagnoses at top places, even for those rational diagnoses that are longer than nonrational diagnoses.

5   Related Work

This work studies the ranking of diagnoses, which depends on the ranking of triples. Since triples can be treated as ground rules with empty bodies, existing studies on ranking rules in knowledge bases (KBs) are the most related to this work. For inconsistent KBs, there have been a lot of studies for measuring the inconsistency degrees of rules, which can be used to rank rules and guide users to resolve the inconsistencies. In [24] existing methods for measuring the inconsistency degree of a KB are classified into six main categories, which are minimal inconsistent subset (MIS) based measures, maximal consistent subset (MCS) based measures, probabilistic measures, value-based measures, distance-based measures and proof-based measures. An inconsistency measure for KBs can be used to define an inconsistency measure for rules using the Shapley Inconsistency Values [12]. That is, an inconsistency measure for a rule ϕ in a KB $\mathcal{K}$ can be defined through $I(\Phi) - I(\Phi \backslash \{\phi\})$ for all subsets Φ of $\mathcal{K}$, where I is an arbitrary inconsistency measure for KBs. Existing studies for inconsistency measures mainly focus on postulates that the measures should satisfy [1] or the expressivity of the measures [24]. Seldom of them focus on the computational cost [19]. In fact, the computation of existing inconsistency measures relies on the computation of the complete set of MISs[5] or even more costly computation of certain models, making this computation hard in practice.

To reduce the computational cost for ranking rules in inconsistent KBs, some studies introduce criteria that are easier to compute to rank rules. These criteria include the impact criterion, the provenance criterion and the usage criterion. The impact criterion estimates the impact on entailments or test cases, measured by the number of impacted entailments or test cases when a rule is removed [15,16]. The provenance criterion estimates the certainty degree of a rule by exploiting provenance information, such as the reliability of the source, the reason or context for which the rule is added, and the time that the rule is created or modified [15]. The usage criterion determines how often entities in the signature of a rule are referenced in other rules [15]. These criteria are used in KB maintenance tools to assist users in debugging inconsistencies. There has not

---

[5] The computation of all MISs in a Horn KB is already intractable.

been empirical evaluation of these criteria in ranking a set of rules. The comparison between the usage of existing criteria for ranking triples and our proposed approach in terms of effectiveness in finding rational diagnoses remains an open problem in our future work.

This work employs representation learning methods to rank diagnoses, thus it is also related to the field of knowledge graph embedding. In [26] a thorough review of existing embedding models is presented. It divides existing embedding models into two main categories, namely the translational distance models and the semantic matching models. A translational distance model measures the truth degree of a triple by the distance between the head and the tail, usually after a translation carried out by the relation. Typical models in this category include TransE [3], TransH [28], TransR [17], TransD [14], KG2E [11] and TransG [30]. A semantic matching model measures truth degrees of triples by matching the latent semantics for entities and relations in their vector space. It often employs a neural network to learn the distributed representation. Typical semantic matching models include Latent Factor Model (LFM) [13], Single Layer Model (SLM) [23], Neural Tensor Network (NTN) [23], Semantic Matching Energy (SME) [2], ComplEx [25] and Analogy [18].

There are also some models that combine knowledge graph embedding with logic inference. In the work [27] and [29], datalog rules are modeled separately from embedding models and would not help to learn a more predictive distributed representation. In [7, 9, 21] several joint learning paradigms are proposed to encode the inference of implicit triples into an embedding model, where the inference is guided by propositionalized datalog rules. To avoid the costly propositionalization of datalog rules, a method for injecting lifted rules to embedding models is proposed in [4]. But the method is restricted to constant-free datalog rules made up of a single binary head atom and a single binary body atom. To make the best of soft rules that are attached with certainty degrees, a paradigm for interactively injecting soft rules to embedding models is proposed in [10]. In this work we employ a relatively simple paradigm for encoding logic inference into embedding models [7] to rank diagnosis.

For the application of embedding models, existing studies have shown promising results on applying knowledge graph embedding to link prediction [3], triple classification [23,28], relation extraction [28], etc. As far as we know, this work is the first attempt to apply knowledge graph embedding to resolving inconsistencies in growing knowledge graphs. Promising results are also achieved in our experiments for this new application.

6 Conclusions and Future Work

To resolve inconsistencies in growing knowledge graphs, we have proposed an approach to ranking diagnoses, where a diagnosis is a minimal subset of the knowledge graph whose removal can restore consistency of the knowledge graph wrt a background logical theory. Based on the truth degrees of triples estimated by an method for knowledge graph embedding, our approach will give a diagnosis a higher rank if the triples in it have lower truth degrees. To validate whether the computed ranks in our approach reflect the rationalities of diagnoses, four knowledge graphs and their corresponding background logical theories are constructed and used in our experiments. Experimental results on these datasets demonstrate that our proposed approach is significantly more effective than classical random methods in ranking rational diagnoses at top places.

Our future work can be explored in three directions. Firstly, more experiments on large datasets can be conducted to further validate our approach. Secondly, more complex embedding models can be tried to improve the performance of our approach. Finally, practical methods that exploit existing criteria for ranking triples [12,15,16,19,24] can be developed to compare with our approach in terms of the effectiveness in giving rational diagnoses high ranks.

Acknowledgements. This work was partly supported by National Natural Science Foundation of China (61375056 and 61876204), Science and Technology Program of Guangzhou (201804010496), and Scientific Research Innovation Team in Department of Education of Guangdong Province (2017KCXTD013).

References

1. Besnard, P.: Revisiting postulates for inconsistency measures. In: Fermé, E., Leite, J. (eds.) JELIA 2014. LNCS (LNAI), vol. 8761, pp. 383–396. Springer, Cham (2014). https://doi.org/10.1007/978-3-319-11558-0_27
2. Bordes, A., Glorot, X., Weston, J., Bengio, Y.: A semantic matching energy function for learning with multi-relational data - application to word-sense disambiguation. Mach. Learn. **94**(2), 233–259 (2014)
3. Bordes, A., Usunier, N., García-Durán, A., Weston, J., Yakhnenko, O.: Translating embeddings for modeling multi-relational data. In: Proceedings of the 27th Annual Conference on Neural Information Processing Systems (NIPS), pp. 2787–2795 (2013)
4. Demeester, T., Rocktäschel, T., Riedel, S.: Lifted rule injection for relation embeddings. In: Proceedings of the 2016 Conference on Empirical Methods in Natural Language Processing (EMNLP), pp. 1389–1399 (2016)
5. Du, J., Qi, G., Pan, J.Z.: Finding data tractable description logics for computing a minimum cost diagnosis based on ABox decomposition. Tsinghua Sci. Technol. **15**(6), 623–632 (2010)
6. Du, J., Qi, G., Pan, J.Z., Shen, Y.: A decomposition-based approach to OWL DL ontology diagnosis. In: Proceedings of the 23rd International Conference on Tools with Artificial Intelligence (ICTAI), pp. 659–664 (2011)
7. Du, J., Qi, K., Wan, H., Peng, B., Lu, S., Shen, Y.: Enhancing knowledge graph embedding from a logical perspective. In: Wang, Z., Turhan, A.-Y., Wang, K., Zhang, X. (eds.) JIST 2017. LNCS, vol. 10675, pp. 232–247. Springer, Cham (2017). https://doi.org/10.1007/978-3-319-70682-5_15
8. Grau, B.C., Horrocks, I., Motik, B., Parsia, B., Patel-Schneider, P.F., Sattler, U.: OWL 2: the next step for OWL. J. Web Semant. **6**(4), 309–322 (2008)
9. Guo, S., Wang, Q., Wang, L., Wang, B., Guo, L.: Jointly embedding knowledge graphs and logical rules. In: Proceedings of the 2016 Conference on Empirical Methods in Natural Language Processing (EMNLP), pp. 192–202 (2016)

10. Guo, S., Wang, Q., Wang, L., Wang, B., Guo, L.: Knowledge graph embedding with iterative guidance from soft rules. In: Proceedings of the 32nd AAAI Conference on Artificial Intelligence (AAAI), pp. 4816–4823 (2018)

11. He, S., Liu, K., Ji, G., Zhao, J.: Learning to represent knowledge graphs with Gaussian embedding. In: Proceedings of the 24th ACM International Conference on Information and Knowledge Management (CIKM), pp. 623–632 (2015)

12. Hunter, A., Konieczny, S.: On the measure of conflicts: shapley inconsistency values. Artif. Intell. **174**(14), 1007–1026 (2010)

13. Jenatton, R., Roux, N.L., Bordes, A., Obozinski, G.: A latent factor model for highly multi-relational data. In: Proceedings of the 26th Annual Conference on Neural Information Processing Systems (NIPS), pp. 3176–3184 (2012)

14. Ji, G., He, S., Xu, L., Liu, K., Zhao, J.: Knowledge graph embedding via dynamic mapping matrix. In: Proceedings of the 53rd Annual Meeting of the Association for Computational Linguistics (ACL), pp. 687–696 (2015)

15. Kalyanpur, A., Parsia, B., Sirin, E., Cuenca-Grau, B.: Repairing unsatisfiable concepts in OWL ontologies. In: Sure, Y., Domingue, J. (eds.) ESWC 2006. LNCS, vol. 4011, pp. 170–184. Springer, Heidelberg (2006). https://doi.org/10.1007/11762256_15

16. Lam, J.S.C., Sleeman, D.H., Pan, J.Z., Vasconcelos, W.W.: A fine-grained approach to resolving unsatisfiable ontologies. J. Data Semant. **10**, 62–95 (2008)

17. Lin, Y., Liu, Z., Sun, M., Liu, Y., Zhu, X.: Learning entity and relation embeddings for knowledge graph completion. In: Proceedings of the 29th AAAI Conference on Artificial Intelligence (AAAI), pp. 2181–2187 (2015)

18. Liu, H., Wu, Y., Yang, Y.: Analogical inference for multi-relational embeddings. In: Proceedings of the 34th International Conference on Machine Learning (ICML), pp. 2168–2178 (2017)

19. McAreavey, K., Liu, W., Miller, P.C.: Computational approaches to finding and measuring inconsistency in arbitrary knowledge bases. Int. J. Approx. Reason. **55**(8), 1659–1693 (2014)

20. Reiter, R.: A theory of diagnosis from first principles. Artif. Intell. **32**(1), 57–95 (1987)

21. Rocktäschel, T., Singh, S., Riedel, S.: Injecting logical background knowledge into embeddings for relation extraction. In: Proceedings of the 2015 Conference of the North American Chapter of the Association for Computational Linguistics (NAACL), pp. 1119–1129 (2015)

22. Satoh, K., Uno, T.: Enumerating minimally revised specifications using dualization. In: Washio, T., Sakurai, A., Nakajima, K., Takeda, H., Tojo, S., Yokoo, M. (eds.) JSAI 2005. LNCS (LNAI), vol. 4012, pp. 182–189. Springer, Heidelberg (2006). https://doi.org/10.1007/11780496_21

23. Socher, R., Chen, D., Manning, C.D., Ng, A.Y.: Reasoning with neural tensor networks for knowledge base completion. In: Proceedings of 27th Annual Conference on Neural Information Processing Systems (NIPS), pp. 926–934 (2013)

24. Thimm, M.: On the expressivity of inconsistency measures. Artif. Intell. **234**, 120–151 (2016)

25. Trouillon, T., Welbl, J., Riedel, S., Gaussier, É., Bouchard, G.: Complex embeddings for simple link prediction. In: Proceedings of the 33nd International Conference on Machine Learning (ICML), pp. 2071–2080 (2016)

26. Wang, Q., Mao, Z., Wang, B., Guo, L.: Knowledge graph embedding: a survey of approaches and applications. IEEE Trans. Knowl. Data Eng. **29**(12), 2724–2743 (2017)

27. Wang, Q., Wang, B., Guo, L.: Knowledge base completion using embeddings and rules. In: Proceedings of the 24th International Joint Conference on Artificial Intelligence (IJCAI), pp. 1859–1866 (2015)
28. Wang, Z., Zhang, J., Feng, J., Chen, Z.: Knowledge graph embedding by translating on hyperplanes. In: Proceedings of the 28th AAAI Conference on Artificial Intelligence (AAAI), pp. 1112–1119 (2014)
29. Wei, Z., Zhao, J., Liu, K., Qi, Z., Sun, Z., Tian, G.: Large-scale knowledge base completion: inferring via grounding network sampling over selected instances. In: Proceedings of the 24th ACM International Conference on Information and Knowledge Management (CIKM), pp. 1331–1340 (2015)
30. Xiao, H., Huang, M., Zhu, X.: TransG: a generative model for knowledge graph embedding. In: Proceedings of the 54th Annual Meeting of the Association for Computational Linguistics (ACL), pp. 992–998 (2016)

Incorporating Text into the Triple Context for Knowledge Graph Embedding

Liang Zhang$^{(\boxtimes)}$, Jun Shi, Guilin Qi$^{(\boxtimes)}$, and Weizhuo Li

School of Computer Science and Engineering, Southeast University, Nanjing, China
{lzhang,gqi}@seu.edu.cn

Abstract. Knowledge graph embedding, aiming to represent entities and relations in a knowledge graph as low-dimensional real-value vectors, has attracted the attention of a large number of researchers. However, most of the embedding methods ignore the incompleteness of the knowledge graphs and they focus on the triples themselves in the knowledge graphs. In this paper, we try to introduce the information of texts to enhance the performances based on contextual model for knowledge graph embedding. Based on the assumption of the distant supervision, the sentences in texts contains abundant semantic information of the triples in knowledge graph, so that these semantic information can be utilized to relief the incompleteness of knowledge graphs and enhance the performances of knowledge graph embedding. Compared with state-of-the-art systems, preliminary evaluation results show that our proposed method obtains the better results in Hits@10.

1 Introduction

Knowledge Graph (KG) contains many types of structured information. A typical KG usually describes knowledge as a set of triples denoted as $\{(h, r, t)\}$ that express the relations between entities. In recent years, representation learning has brought a great revolution in many application. Relatively, knowledge graph embedding, aiming to represent entities and relations in a knowledge graph as low-dimensional real-value vectors, has shown promising results on a number of prediction tasks including link prediction and attracted the attention of a large number of researchers.

Researchers have proposed a variety of models for knowledge graph embedding. Most of them can be divided into two main categories. One focus on embedding structured information in the knowledge graph, which can be further divided into the triple-based model, path-based model, and triple context model. The other models mainly consider how to incorporate the extra information like text into the knowledge graph embedding. The triple-based model does not consider extra information is that a series of models represented by TransE [1], TransR [2], TransD [3], TranSparse [4], DistMult [5] and so on. They use the distance between the head entity and the tail entity to measure the confidence of the triple.

© Springer Nature Switzerland AG 2018
R. Ichise et al. (Eds.): JIST 2018, LNCS 11341, pp. 68–76, 2018.
https://doi.org/10.1007/978-3-030-04284-4_5

The path-base model makes full use of path information in the knowledge graph. PTransE [6] extends TransE by using relational paths and combines the related vectors of the relational paths semantically to get the vector representation of paths. In [7], authors proposed a generalized combinatorial property and improved the effect of cascading queries by combining relational paths.

Besides triples and path, there are some works use triple context information for knowledge graph embedding. The GAKE [8] considers the structure of knowledge graph, it regards entity and relation as subject and uses three kinds of graph structure information. This model uses context information to predict the current subject, but it does not construct scoring function for the triple itself and does not distinguish between entity and relation, which is not conducive to embodying the nature of entity and relation. The TCE [9] has made some improvements about it. It considers two kinds of structure information, one is the neighbor context, and the other is the path context, both of the two contexts reflect various aspects of triples. The neighbor context refers to the adjacency relations of triples and the entities associated with them. These relations and entities are the most closely related parts in knowledge graph and reflect the characteristics of the target entities to a certain extent.

The above models only consider the structured information inherent in the knowledge graph. However, knowledge graphs are incomplete and may contain some noise in real scenarios. So a variety of extra information like the text has been used to supplement the semantic and further enhance the effect of the embedding model. Wang et al. firstly bring extra information into the knowledge graph embedding [10]. Their model contains three parts: a knowledge representation model, a text model, and a link model. Knowledge representation model uses an improved TransE model to learn the vector representation of entities and relations. Text model uses word2vec to train word vectors. Link model uses entity names or Wikipedia anchor text to close entities and relationships in knowledge graph. It correlates entities and relations with words in texts. DKRL [11] has expanded TransE. For each entity, the model proposes a structure-based and description-based representation, in which the structure-based representation is the entity representation in knowledge graph, the description-based representation can get the semantic information in the text. To obtain the vector of entity description, DKRL uses CBOW and RNN two encoders to encode text.

In this paper, we explore the information of texts to enhance the performance of our contextual model TCE for knowledge graph embedding. Compared with TransE and other models, the TCE model can better reflect the internal structure information of knowledge graph. So we propose a model to joint the structured information and the text information based on TCE model. The text information contains a large number of entities, and given a sentence containing two entities, the sentence usually exposes implicit features of the textual relation between the two entities. By using this feature, the entity can be used to further model the relation of the shared sentences, thus improving the knowledge graph embedding model. The results show the proposed method outperforms several state-of-the-art models in some aspects.

2   Incorporating Text into Triple Contextual Model

Actually, knowledge graphs are not complete, and the triples of them are increased by automatic or semi-automatic methods. Nevertheless, we obtain the abundant description of some entities in knowledge graph by the extra information. Facts in knowledge graph usually appear in many textual corpora. For example, each entity in Freebase [12] corresponds to a text description. Many news texts and Wikipedia articles also contain a large number of entities and relationships. These texts are very helpful to describe the relationship between entities or entities. The work presented in [13] proposes a distant supervision model for relation extraction, which includes a hypothesis. That is if two entities h and t have a relation r in the knowledge graph, the sentences that contain the two entities also usually express the relationship between them. Based on this hypothesis, this paper supplements the semantic information of knowledge graph by sentences containing entity mentions.

2.1   Problem Definition

Our goal is to train the knowledge graph and text jointly to obtain the vector of entity and relation and the vector of words in the text. The vector of entities is expressed as $\Theta_{\varepsilon} \in \mathbb{R}^{m \times k}$, the relation vector is expressed as $\Theta_{\mathcal{R}} \in \mathbb{R}^{n \times k}$, m and n respectively represent the number of entities and relationships in knowledge graphs, and k represents the dimensions of entities and relational vectors. Vector parameters of words in text are $\Theta_{\nu} \in \mathbb{R}^{|\nu| \times k}$, the text corpus is recorded as D, they consist of several sentences, $D = \{s_1, ..., s_{|D|}\}$. Every sentence is a sequence of words, marked by $s = \{w_1, ..., w_{|s|}\}$, the collection of all vocabularies in text corpus express as ν, each sentence in the text contains two mentions of entities. In this paper, we need to maximize the joint probability of knowledge graph under the condition of text. We use $\mathbf{P}$ indicate the probability to be calculated. For a knowledge graph $\mathcal{G}$, we define the following optimization objective:

$$\Theta = \arg_{\Theta} \max \mathbf{P}(\mathcal{G}|D; \Theta),$$

and the objective function is:

$$\mathbf{P} = (\mathcal{G}|D; \Theta) = \prod f(h, r, t),$$

the h represents head entity, the r represents relationship, and the t represents tail entity. Add text information to TCE model, the scoring function is defined as follows:

$$f(h, r, t) \approx \mathbf{P}(h|C_n(h); \Theta) \cdot \mathbf{P}(t|C_p(h, t), h; \Theta) \cdot \mathbf{P}(r|h, t, D; \Theta).$$

The $C_n(h)$ and the $C_p(h, t)$ represent the neighbor next and path context in TCE respectively. The neighbor context of TCE is defined as:

$$C_n(e)\{(r, t)|\forall r, t, (e, r, t) \in \mathcal{G}\},$$

r is the emission edge of entity e in the knowledge graph and t is the entity that entity e can associate with through relation r. Path context refers to the set of paths between entities in knowledge graph. In TCE, the path context of entity pair (h,t) is defined as:

$$C_p(h,t) = \{p_i = (r_1, ..., r_{l_i})|\forall r_1, ...r_{l_i}, e_1, ..., (e_{l_i-1}, r_{l_i}, t) \in \mathcal{G}\},$$

p_i is a sequence of relationships, which can be transferred from entity h to t through this relational sequence. $\mathbf{P}(r|h,t,D;\Theta)$ add the text information D into probability part. It helps to determine the relationship between entities. Specifically, the distribution of potential relationships is predicted by using h and t of referential sentences.

In order to implement the joint modeling of knowledge graph and text, it is necessary to correlate and map entities and relations with text. We use deep learning method to process the sentences and obtain the probability distribution of the relation.

2.2 The Representation Learning of Relation and Text

We assume that the sentence s contains the mention of entity h and t, and it implies the potential relation r between them in this paper. Then we need to calculate the probability distribution $\mathbf{P}(r|h,t,D;\Theta)$ of the relation r. Because the sentence s contains many words, and the length is not the same, it can not be calculated directly. Therefore, it is necessary to vectorize the words in the sentence, and then encode the whole sentence to generate a vector representation. Convolutional Neural Network (CNN) extract features of sentences and has achieved excellent results in the field of relational classification in recent years [14], so we use CNN to encode sentences. The framework of sentence processing is divided into word representation layer, feature extraction layer, and the output layer.

Word Representation Layer. The word representation layer represents each word as a vector. For a sentence s containing entity h and t, the vector $\mathbf{x}$ of each word is composed of two parts, one is the vector $\mathbf{w}$ of the word, the other is the position feature vector $\mathbf{p}$. The position feature refers to the relative position between each word and the mentions of two entities in the sentence. Such as in the sentence "[Donald John Trump] is the 45th and current President of the [United States]", the word "is" is expressed as $[1, -8]$ reference to two entities mentions, note that "is" is on the right side of entity [Donald John Trump], its distance is 1. And it is on the left side of entity [United States], so its distance is 8. Each word w in the sentence relative the position of two entities mention is represented as $[d_1, d_2]$. These two values are mapped to a k dimensional vector in the model. The location vectors $\mathbf{p} \in \mathbb{R}^{k \times 2}$ can be obtained by combining two distance vectors. A vector representation of each word can be obtained by splicing the word vector and the position feature vector, which can be defined as $\mathbf{x} = [\mathbf{w}; \mathbf{p}]$, so each sentence s is expressed as a vector sequence:

$$\mathbf{s} = \{\mathbf{x}_1, ..., \mathbf{x}_{\|s\|}\} = \{[\mathbf{w}_1; \mathbf{p}_1], ..., [\mathbf{w}_{\|s\|}; \mathbf{p}_{\|s\|}]\}.$$

Feature Extraction Layer. The feature extraction layer uses convolutional neural networks to extract sentence-level features from the output vectors of the word representation layer, which includes a convolution layer and a pooling layer. The convolution layer uses a window to slide over the vector sequence of the input sentence and combine the vectors in the window as a local feature of the sentence. The vectors in the same window are stitching together to get vectors $\mathbf{z}_i \in \mathbb{R}^{k_i}$:

$$\mathbf{z}_i = [\mathbf{x}_{i - \frac{d-1}{2}}; ...; \mathbf{x}_i; \mathbf{x}_{i + \frac{d-1}{2}}],$$

then conduct the convolution operation of combinatorial vector $\mathbf{z}_i$:

$$\mathbf{h}_i = \tanh(\mathbf{W}\mathbf{z}_i + \mathbf{b}),$$

the parameter matrix $\mathbf{W}$ is a convolution kernel and $\mathbf{b}$ is a bias vector. To further determine the most useful features in each dimension of hidden layer vectors, the maximum pooling of hidden layer vectors is performed after convolution. Assuming that the number of vectors in the hidden layer is n_h, each dimension of the output vector $\mathbf{q}$ is determined by the following way:

$$\mathbf{q}^i = \max(\mathbf{h}_1^i, ..., \mathbf{h}_{n_h}^i),$$

Output Layer. The output layer transforms the output vector of the feature extraction layer into the probability distribution of each relation. The output vector of the feature extraction layer is transformed into an n-dimensional vector by a matrix transformation:

$$\mathbf{y} = \mathbf{M}\mathbf{q},$$

Matrix $\mathbf{M}$ is a model parameter that converts $\mathbf{q}$ into n-dimensional vectors, where each dimension represents the score of each relationship. Finally, the vector $\mathbf{y}$ is input to the softmax classifier, and the probability distribution can be obtained.

2.3   Text Coding Based on Attention Mechanism

In the actual scene, a pair of entities may appear in multiple sentences, and different sentences have different effects on the prediction of the relation between entities. Because the distant supervision hypothesis is too broad, even if there is a relation r in knowledge graph, the sentence containing the mention of entities h and t does not necessarily express the relation r. Therefore, it is necessary to select the information in the sentence according to the degree of association between each sentence and the relation, then combine different sentences with different weights. We use the attention mechanism [15] to combine the semantic features of different sentences. Record the collection of sentences that contain entities h and t as $S_{(h,t)}, S_{(h,t)} = s_1, ..., s_t$. For each sentence, using CNN to encode it into a vector $\mathbf{q}$ and then input it into a fully connected layer to obtain the middle representation e of each sentence:

$$\mathbf{e}_j = \tanh(\mathbf{W}_s\mathbf{q}_j + \mathbf{b}_s),$$

The purpose of the transformation is to transform the vector dimension output from the feature extraction layer into the vector dimension of entities and relations, so as to facilitate the subsequent calculation. Then we calculate the weight of each sentence according to the vector of entity and sentence:

$$a_j = \frac{\exp((\mathbf{t} - \mathbf{h}) \cdot \mathbf{e}_j)}{\sum_{i=1}^{t} \exp(\mathbf{t} - \mathbf{h}) \cdot \mathbf{e}_i)},$$

$\mathbf{t}$-$\mathbf{h}$ is a hypothesis based on TransE $\mathbf{h} + \mathbf{r} \approx \mathbf{t}$, it used to indicate the potential relationship between h and t. Then we can get the vector representation of all sentences by summing up the vectors of each sentence:

$$\mathbf{s} = \sum_{j=1}^{t} a_j\mathbf{q}_j,$$

the output vectors are transformed into the n-dimensional vectors by the transformation matrix $\mathbf{M}$ to get the score of each relationship:

$$\mathbf{y} = \mathbf{Ms},$$

input $\mathbf{y}$ into the Softmax function to get the distribution:

$$\mathbf{P}(r|h, t, D; \Theta) = \frac{\exp(\mathbf{y}_r)}{\sum_{r' \in R} \exp(\mathbf{y}_{r'})}.$$

2.4 Model Learning

To calculate the $\mathbf{P}(r|h, t, D; \Theta)$, we use the negative sampling to approximate it:

$$\mathbf{P}(r|h, t, D; \Theta) \approx \sigma(\mathbf{y}_r) \cdot \prod_{r' \in R^-} \sigma(-\mathbf{y}_{r'}),$$

R^- represents a set of negative samples for relation r construction. Similar to the algorithm in TCE, the above formula is converted into the negative sampling logarithm and then use gradient descent to optimize the parameters.

3 Experiment

3.1 Data Set

The data set in this experiment contains two parts, the first part is the knowledge graph, the second part is the text corpus. Knowledge graph data sets are all derived from Freebase.

FB15k: FB15K is a subset of Freebase, it contains 592213 triples, which consists of 14951 entities and 1345 relations. **FB15k-237**: FB15k-237 is a subset of FB15k, which contains 310116 triples. It contains 14541 entities and 237 relations. FB15k-237 eliminates the redundant relations in FB15k. **Textual corpus**: we uses NYT10 [16], a New York Times data as the text corpus, which annotates the entities in Freebase. According to the entity pairs appearing in FB15k and FB15k-237, sentences containing these entity pairs are extracted from NYT10 as training text. For FB15k, 194,385 sentences were extracted from NYT10, and the sentences were labeled according to the relationships appearing in the knowledge graph. The sentences covered 47,103 triples, including 6,053 entities and 699 relationships. For FB15k-237, we extracts 78,978 sentences from NYT10 and annotates these sentences according to the relations existing in the knowledge graph. The annotated sentences cover 6,204 triples, including 3,000 entities and 70 relations.

3.2 Evaluation

Given a test triple $\{(h, r, t)\}$, remove the head entity h, tail entity t or relation r to form an incomplete triple, any entity e is placed in the head entity position to form a new triple $\{(e, r, t)\}$, and its score $f(e, r, t)$ is calculated by the score function. Because for each entity e can get a score $f(e, r, t)$, these entities in descending order of score get an entity sequence $L = (e_1, e_2, ..., e_m)$. We use the Hits@n as an assessment standard. It represents the ratio of the number of triples less than or equal to n of the original head entity h in the sequence L to the total number of test triples. The larger the Hits@n, the better the performance of the model. The n usually takes 10.

Based on the TCE model, we introduce some parameters about text as follows: sliding window size $d = 3$, hidden layer dimension $k_h = 230$, entity, relation and word dimension $k = k_w = 50$, position vector dimension $k_p = 5$. We use some models such as DKRL [11], TEKE [17], DESP [18], E + DistMult [19], Conv-E + DistMult [19] as contrast experiment. These models introduce text information into the knowledge graph. The experiment results are shown in Table 1. The TCE with text method has improved compared with other methods.

Table 1. The results of entity prediction on FB15k and FB15k-237

Data set	Model	Hits@10(Filtered)
FB15k	DKRL	67.4
	TEKE	73.0
	DESP	77.3
	TCE + Text	**77.5**
FB15k-237	E + DistMult	60.2
	Conv-E + DistMult	**61.1**
	TCE + Text	60.8

4 Conclusions and Future Work

We introduce the information of text to enhance the performances based on the contextual model for knowledge graph embedding. We incorporate the text information into a triple contextual model. We use CNN and attention mechanism to obtain semantic information from text and use this information to enhance the model. The experimental results show that the effectiveness of the model is higher than that of the traditional models in Hits@10.

These are several avenues for our future work. Firstly, add the extra information increased the computational complexity. Therefore, the parallel technology must be considered to further optimize the computational efficiency. Secondly, we will integrate the model with practical applications to fill a certain gap between the benchmark dataset and actual application scenarios. Finally, once the knowledge graph changes, it must retrain the model. To better satisfy the need of constantly updating knowledge graph, we must consider how to express the embedding on dynamic knowledge graph.

Acknowledgment. This work is mainly supported by the National Natural Science Foundation of China under Grant no. U1736204.

References

1. Bordes, A., Usunier, N., Garcia-Duran, A., Weston, J., Yakhnenko, O.: Translating embeddings for modeling multi-relational data. In: Advances in Neural Information Processing Systems, pp. 2787–2795 (2013)
2. Lin, Y., Liu, Z., Sun, M., Liu, Y., Zhu, X.: Learning entity and relation embeddings for knowledge graph completion. In: AAAI, vol. 15, pp. 2181–2187 (2015)
3. Ji, G., He, S., Xu, L., Liu, K., Zhao, J.: Knowledge graph embedding via dynamic mapping matrix. In: Proceedings of the 53rd Annual Meeting of the Association for Computational Linguistics and the 7th International Joint Conference on Natural Language Processing (Long Papers), vol. 1, pp. 687–696 (2015)
4. Ji, G., Liu, K., He, S., Zhao, J.: Knowledge graph completion with adaptive sparse transfer matrix. In: AAAI, pp. 985–991 (2016)
5. Yang, B., Yih, W.T., He, X., Gao, J., Deng, L.: Embedding entities and relations for learning and inference in knowledge bases. arXiv preprint arXiv:1412.6575 (2014)
6. Lin, Y., Liu, Z., Luan, H., Sun, M., Rao, S., Liu, S.: Modeling relation paths for representation learning of knowledge bases. arXiv preprint arXiv:1506.00379 (2015)
7. Guu, K., Miller, J., Liang, P.: Traversing knowledge graphs in vector space. arXiv preprint arXiv:1506.01094 (2015)
8. Feng, J., Huang, M., Yang, Y., et al.: Gake: graph aware knowledge embedding. In: Proceedings of COLING 2016, the 26th International Conference on Computational Linguistics: Technical Papers, pp. 641–651 (2016)
9. Shi, J., Gao, H., Qi, G., Zhou, Z.: Knowledge graph embedding with triple context. In: Proceedings of the 2017 ACM on Conference on Information and Knowledge Management, pp. 2299–2302. ACM (2017)
10. Wang, Z., Zhang, J., Feng, J., Chen, Z.: Knowledge graph and text jointly embedding. In: Proceedings of the 2014 Conference on Empirical Methods in Natural Language Processing (EMNLP), pp. 1591–1601 (2014)

11. Xie, R., Liu, Z., Jia, J., Luan, H., Sun, M.: Representation learning of knowledge graphs with entity descriptions. In: AAAI, pp. 2659–2665 (2016)
12. Bollacker, K., Evans, C., Paritosh, P., Sturge, T., Taylor, J.: Freebase: a collaboratively created graph database for structuring human knowledge. In: Proceedings of the 2008 ACM SIGMOD International Conference on Management of Data, pp. 1247–1250. ACM (2008)
13. Mintz, M., Bills, S., Snow, R., Jurafsky, D.: Distant supervision for relation extraction without labeled data. In: Proceedings of the Joint Conference of the 47th Annual Meeting of the ACL and the 4th International Joint Conference on Natural Language Processing of the AFNLP, vol. 2, pp. 1003–1011. Association for Computational Linguistics (2009)
14. Zeng, D., Liu, K., Chen, Y., Zhao, J.: Distant supervision for relation extraction via piecewise convolutional neural networks. In: Proceedings of the 2015 Conference on Empirical Methods in Natural Language Processing, pp. 1753–1762 (2015)
15. Bahdanau, D., Cho, K., Bengio, Y.: Neural machine translation by jointly learning to align and translate. arXiv preprint arXiv:1409.0473 (2014)
16. Riedel, S., Yao, L., McCallum, A.: Modeling relations and their mentions without labeled text. In: Balcázar, J.L., Bonchi, F., Gionis, A., Sebag, M. (eds.) ECML PKDD 2010. LNCS (LNAI), vol. 6323, pp. 148–163. Springer, Heidelberg (2010). https://doi.org/10.1007/978-3-642-15939-8_10
17. Wang, Z., Li, J.Z.: Text-enhanced representation learning for knowledge graph. In: IJCAI, pp. 1293–1299 (2016)
18. Zhong, H., Zhang, J., Wang, Z., Wan, H., Chen, Z.: Aligning knowledge and text embeddings by entity descriptions. In: Proceedings of the 2015 Conference on Empirical Methods in Natural Language Processing, pp. 267–272 (2015)
19. Toutanova, K., Chen, D., Pantel, P., Poon, H., Choudhury, P., Gamon, M.: Representing text for joint embedding of text and knowledge bases. In: Proceedings of the 2015 Conference on Empirical Methods in Natural Language Processing, pp. 1499–1509 (2015)

On Enhancing Visual Query Building over KGs Using Query Logs

Vidar Klungre[1]([✉]), Ahmet Soylu[2,3], Martin Giese[1], Arild Waaler[1], and Evgeny Kharlamov[1,4]

[1] University of Oslo, Oslo, Norway
{vidarkl,martingi,arild,evgeny.kharlamov}@ifi.uio.no
[2] Norwegian University of Science and Technology, Gøvik, Norway
ahmet.soylu@ntnu.no
[3] SINTEF Digital, Oslo, Norway
[4] University of Oxford, Oxford, UK
evgeny.kharlamov@cs.ox.ac.uk

Abstract. Knowledge Graphs have recently gained a lot of attention and have been successfully applied in both academia and industry. Since KGs may be very large: they may contain millions of entities and triples relating them to each other, to classes, and assigning them data values, it is important to provide endusers with effective tools to explore information encapsulated in KGs. In this work we present a visual query system that allows users to explore KGs by intuitively constructing tree-shaped conjunctive queries. It is known that systems of this kind suffer from the problem of information overflow: when constructing a query the users have to iteratively choose from a potentially very long list of options, sich as, entities, classes, and data values, where each such choice corresponds to an extension of the query new filters. In order to address this problem we propose an approach to substantially reduce such lists with the help of ranking and by eliminating the so-called deadends, options that yield queries with no answers over a given KG.

1 Motivation and Overview

Motivation. Knowledge Graphs (KGs) are collections of interconnected entities annotated with classes and data values, which have become powerful assets for enhancing search and are now widely used in both academia and industry. Prominent examples of large-scale knowledge graphs include Yago [31], Google's Knowledge Graph [1], that are used by search engines, and Siemens [16,17,22] and Statoil [20,21] corporate KGs.

Many existing knowledge graphs are either available as Linked Open Data, or they can be exported as RDF datasets [4] enhanced with OWL 2 ontologies [3] capturing the relevant domain background knowledge. SPARQL [12] has become the standard language for querying KGs stored as RDF datasets with OWL 2 ontologies, and an increasing number of applications offer SPARQL endpoints to access KGs. Writing SPARQL queries, however, requires some proficiency in the

© Springer Nature Switzerland AG 2018
R. Ichise et al. (Eds.): JIST 2018, LNCS 11341, pp. 77–85, 2018.
https://doi.org/10.1007/978-3-030-04284-4_6

query language and is not well-suited for the majority of users [13,33]. Thus, an important challenge that has attracted a great deal of attention in the Semantic Web community is the development of simple yet powerful query interfaces for non-expert users [2,8,10,11,26,35].

Visual Query Building. An important class of such interfaces for KGs is *visual query building* systems [28], where the users can construct queries by combining classes and properties offered by the system, and by setting constraints on classes and/or properties by selecting appropriate values offered by the system. Consider in Fig. 1a prominent example of a system for visual query building, OptiqueVQS [14,23,29,30], that we developed in tight collaboration with companies such as Statoil and Siemens. In the following example we illustrate the query formulation process in OptiqueVQS that should help the reader in understanding the mode of interaction between the users and visual query systems and will also help us to clarify challenges that we address in this work.

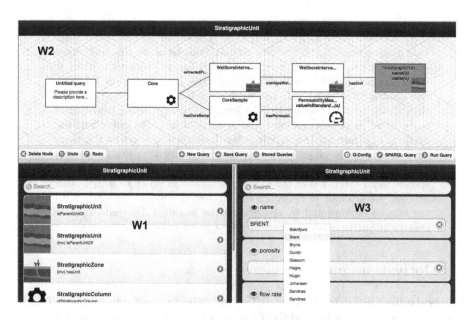

Fig. 1. Example visual query system OptiqueVQS

Example 1. In Fig. 1 one can see a real world query that was constructed by a Statoil engineer when we conducted a user study. The engineer constructed the following query:

> *Give me all the wellbore cores extracted from a wellbore interval, such that it overlaps with another wellbore interval whose stratigraphic unit is named 'BRENT', along with all the permeability measurements of their samples and the values of these measurements in standard unit.*

Now we explain OptiqueVQS in more details. The system has three main widgets: The first widget (W1 in bottom-left of Fig. 1) is menu-based and it allows the user to navigate through concepts of an ontology by selecting relationships between them. The second widget (W2 on top of Fig. 1) is diagram-based and it presents typed variables as nodes and object properties as arcs and gives an overview of the query formulated so far. The third widget (W3 in bottom-right of Fig. 1) is form-based and it presents the attributes of a selected concept for selection and projection operations.

W1 initially lists all the concepts in the ontology and a user starts formulating a query by selecting a starting concept. The concept chosen from W1 becomes the active node (i.e., pivot) and appears in W2 as a variable node. W1 then lists concept - object property pairs pertaining to the pivot, since there is now an active node. The user can continue adding more typed variables into the query by selecting a pair from W1. The selected concept-object property pair is added to the query over the pivot, and the formulated query is presented as a tree in W2. The concept from the last chosen pair automatically becomes the active node (i.e., pivot), and the active node can be changed by clicking on the corresponding variable node in W2. The user can constrain attributes (i.e., using the form elements) and/or select them for output (i.e., using the "eye" icon) through W3. The user can also refine the type of a variable node through a special multi-select form element, called "Type", in W3. (Not included in screenshot.)

To run the constructed query, the user clicks the "Run Query" button and the system allows to see sample query results and to manipulate them, e.g., to apply sorting and aggregation operations, see the widget W4 in Fig. 2. Moreover, the user can view and interact with the query in textual SPARQL mode (i.e., textual and visual modes are synchronised). In the top part of Fig. 2 one can see the SPARQL version of our example query from Fig. 1. The user can also save, modify, and load queries.   □

Information Overload Problem. An important challenge for visual query systems applied in the context of KGs is *information overload* [19,32]: a number of options for query construction that a visual query system offers to a user is comparable to the size of data over which the query is constructed. Since large scale KGs contain millions of entities, data values, and up to hundreds of classes, the number of options hampers the query construction process. Our OptiqueVQS system is not an exception and it also suffers from the information overload problem. Indeed, consider in Fig. 1, even for a small ontology the number of suggestions given in W1 for a pivot concept would require a user to scroll down in the list several times due to high number of potential concept-object property pairs and reasoning effect. The latter requires propagating concept restrictions upwards and downwards in the hierarchy and results in new concept-object property pairs for a given concept originating from its parent and child concepts [9]. The same applies to W3 not only in terms of data properties being suggested but also potential values being offered for each property. For example, the potential

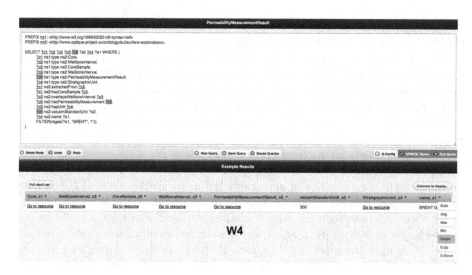

Fig. 2. Query from Example 1 in SPAQRL, presented in OptiqueVQS

values offered for the name attribute in the example is too extensive: Statoil database has several thousands of names and their variations.

Query Logs in Enhancing Query Building. In this work we propose to exploit query logs, that is, queries that the users have constructed when they used the visual query system, to enhance the query building process and reduce the information overload. Our first idea is to exploit query logs in ranking and top-k computation, that is, we show to the user only those components for query construction that occur often enough in the logs. Our second idea is to show to the user only those components for query construction that are not deadends, that is, if the user relies on any of them in query construction then the resulting query will not return empty answers over the underlying dataset. As we discuss later in the paper, deadend elimination is computationally demanding and we rely on query logs to reduce the cost of such elimination.

This is a preliminary study, we are still developing our approaches. In the following section we give more details on our ideas.

2 Our Approach and Further Directions

The main hypothesis behind our approach is that the queries over KGs that are often used by users during query construction are more important than the ones used less often or not used at all. We analyse the frequency of usage for queries and their fragments from query logs and then use the frequency to optimise suggestions of elements of KGs that we suggest to users during query construction sessions.

Queries and Query Logs. We assume that the reader is familiar with the basic notions of RDF and SPARQL, queries, databases, query evaluation and refer the reader to [3,12] for further details. In this work we consider only tree-shaped conjunctive queries over classes, object properties, data properties, entities, data values, and variables since they are supported by OptiqueVQS [29]. Given a database D and a query Q, with $ans(Q, D)$ we denote the answer set of Q over D. A query log $\mathcal{Q}$ is a set of queries. A query pattern P is a query that contains no entities or data values. Given a query Q, a query pattern for Q, denoted $p(Q)$, is Q where all entities and data values are substituted with fresh variables in such a way that the same entities are and the same values are substituted with the same variables. With $Q_1 \subseteq Q_2$ and $P_1 \subseteq P_2$ we denote that the query Q_1 is a subquery of Q_2 and that the pattern P_1 is a subquery of P_2. Finally, a *query suggestion* E is a query that consists of one atom. Then, given a query Q, with $Q \wedge E$ we denote a query obtained by extending Q with E by adding E to Q with the conjunction.

Ranking Based on Query Logs. Given a query log $\mathcal{Q}$ and a query pattern P, we define the conditional probability of P wrt to $\mathcal{Q}$ as the frequency of queries from $\mathcal{Q}$ whose patterns contain P as in Eq. (1) on the left, where $|\cdot|$ as usual denotes the cardinality of a set. Now we define how a given pattern T is 'important' for another pattern P wrt the query log $\mathcal{Q}$ as the ranking function in Eq. (1) on the right.

$$Pr(P \mid \mathcal{Q}) = \frac{|\{Q \in \mathcal{Q} \mid P \subseteq p(Q)\}|}{|\mathcal{Q}|}, \qquad r(T \mid P, \mathcal{Q}) = \frac{Pr(T \cap P \mid \mathcal{Q})}{Pr(P \mid \mathcal{Q})} \qquad (1)$$

Let Q be a query that is constructed by a user, $\mathcal{Q}$ be a query log, and E a query suggestion. Finally, we define the ranking of a suggestion E for Q wrt $\mathcal{Q}$ as the average rank of $Q \wedge E$ for patterns in $\mathcal{Q}$, that is, $r_{Q,\mathcal{Q}}(E) = \sum_{Q' \in \mathcal{Q}} r(p(Q \wedge E) \mid p(Q'), \mathcal{Q})/|\mathcal{Q}|$. In other words, the rank of a suggestion E is defined via the importance of the pattern of E to the pattern of Q wrt the query log $\mathcal{Q}$.

This approach can be further extended by incorporating the semantic distance between concepts and properties involved as a cofactor into the ranking function, so that queries from $\mathcal{Q}$ that are semantically distant from Q contribute less to the ranking. For example, Huang et al. [15] suggest a similarity measure using the depth of compared concepts and properties and their least common ancestors from the root of hierarchy to compute similarity between concepts and properties and combining them to compute similarity between triple patterns, hence queries.

Deadend Elimination Based on Query Logs. In this approach we eliminate so called *contextual deadends* [5,6,18,27,32], that is, query extensions E for a query Q such that the query $Q \wedge E$ evaluated over a given database D gives the empty set of answers. For us both Q and D form the *context* for E. Given a set of suggestions $\mathcal{E}$ and a context Q and D, a naive way to eliminiate deadends would be to go over $\mathcal{E}$, to pick $E \in \mathcal{E}$ one after another, to check whether $ans(Q \wedge E, D) = \emptyset$, and to delete from $\mathcal{E}$ all E for which it is the case. The suggestions that remain in $\mathcal{E}$ at the end of this procedure would not be deadends. A disadvantage of this approach is that such procedure requires to run $|\mathcal{E}|$ queries over D and this is computationally demanding for a large $|\mathcal{E}|$. Indeed, even when $|\mathcal{E}| = 10,000$ modern RDF backends would not be able to process that many queries in time acceptable for an interactive system, that is, in time that many users would tolerate to wait [6]. Indeed, it will take on average 15 s for such well known systems as Sesame [7][1] Stardog [25][2], and RDFox [24][3] to run that many queries. At the same time, $|\mathcal{E}| = 10,000$ can easily occur in practice, indeed, observe that DBpedia contains more that 6 million entities and many of them can be potentially relevant for being suggested, e.g., via the *linked-to* object property[4]. Even for $|\mathcal{E}| = 1,000$ the average query evaluation time is about 3 s [6] and DBpedia contains more than 2,700 data and object properties that can potentially be relevant and suggested to a user.

In order to speedup deadend elimination we propose to rely on query logs. Our idea is, given a database D and a query log $\mathcal{Q}$, to select among the queries in the log the most promising query patterns P, that is, the most frequent ones, and to pre-materialise answers $ans(P, D)$ for each Ps as databases D_P in a 'smart way' (see details below). Then, given a query Q and a set of suggestions $\mathcal{E}$ one can verify for each $E \in \mathcal{E}$ the emptiness of the answer set $ans((P \cap Q) \wedge E, D_P)$ instead of $ans(Q \wedge E, D)$ and *do not* suggest those E to the user that pass the emptiness test. One can show that this procedure is an approximation of the naive one described above, that is, there are cases when (i) $ans((P \cap Q) \wedge E, D_P) = \emptyset$, but $ans(Q \wedge E, D) \neq \emptyset$, and (ii) $ans((P \cap Q) \wedge E, D_P) \neq \emptyset$, but $ans(Q \wedge E, D) = \emptyset$. One can partially address Cases (i) by the way that D_P is materialised: one can materialise $ans(P', D)$, for P' that slightly extends P with all possible extensions at the output variable. One can show that this approach does not affect Cases (ii) and our preliminary experiments show that this also helps to significantly reduce the number of Cases (i) in practice.

Further Directions. Our current research effort is targeted towards evaluating the approaches for ranking and deadend elimination as well as towards combining and improving them. For example, the approach that we see as promising is to first compute top-k suggestions given a query partially constructed by a user and a query log, and then to eliminate the deadends among the top-k. Our preliminary evaluation of our approximate approach to deadend elimination shows

---

[1] Sesame is a widely-used Java framework for processing RDF data. It offers an easy-to-use API that can be connected to all leading RDF storage solutions.

[2] Stardog is a Java-based triple store providing reasoning support for all OWL 2 profiles as well as a SPARQL implementation.

[3] RDFox is an in-memory RDF triple store that supports shared memory parallel Datalog reasoning. It is written in C++ and comes with a Java wrapper allowing for a seamless integration with Java-based applications.

[4] https://wiki.dbpedia.org/dbpedia-version-2016-04.

that we can eliminate up to 80% of deadends using pre-materialised views that contain about 10% of the original data. This gives us a significant improvement in terms of time over the naive approach without a dramatic compromise on the quality of deadend elimination. A relevant research direction that can be potentially combined with our is on better query and ontology modifications in the context of inference-enabled SPARQL query processing [34].

3   Conclusion

The information overload is a challenging problem that is vital for the query building over large scale KGs. In this short paper we presented our preliminary work on enhancing visual query building over KGs by addressing the overload problem with the help of query logs. We presented a ranking model and an way to eliminate deadends, as well as a discussion how they can be combined and further improved. We are excited to present our work to the Semantic Web community.

Acknowledgements. This work is partially funded by EU H2020 TheyBuyForYou (780247) project, by the EPSRC projects MaSI^3, DBOnto, ED^3, and by the SIRIUS Centre, Norwegian Research Council project number 237898.

References

1. Google's KG. http://www.google.co.uk/insidesearch/features/search/knowledge.html
2. iSPARQL QBE. http://dbpedia.org/isparql/
3. W3C: OWL 2 Web Ontology Language. http://www.w3.org/TR/owl2-overview/
4. W3C: Resource Description Framework (RDF). http://www.w3.org/RDF/
5. Arenas, M., Grau, B.C., Kharlamov, E., Marciuska, S., Zheleznyakov, D.: Faceted search over ontology-enhanced RDF data. In: CIKM, pp. 939–948 (2014)
6. Arenas, M., Grau, B.C., Kharlamov, E., Marciuska, S., Zheleznyakov, D.: Faceted search over RDF-based knowledge graphs. J. Web Sem. **37–38**, 55–74 (2016)
7. Broekstra, J., Kampman, A., van Harmelen, F.: Sesame: a generic architecture for storing and querying RDF and RDF schema. In: Horrocks, I., Hendler, J. (eds.) ISWC 2002. LNCS, vol. 2342, pp. 54–68. Springer, Heidelberg (2002). https://doi.org/10.1007/3-540-48005-6_7
8. Franconi, E., Guagliardo, P., Trevisan, M., Tessaris, S.: Quelo: an ontology-driven query interface. In: DL (2011)
9. Grau, B.C., et al.: Towards query formulation, query-driven ontology extensions in OBDA systems. In: OWLED (2013)
10. Haag, F., Lohmann, S., Siek, S., Ertl, T.: Visual querying of linked data with QueryVOWL. In: Joint Proceedings of SumPre 2015 and HSWI 2014–15. CEUR-WS (2015)
11. Harabagiu, S.M., et al.: FALCON: boosting knowledge for answer engines. In: TREC (2000)
12. Harris, S., Seaborne, A.: SPARQL 1.1 query language. W3C Recommendation, 21 March 2013

13. Heim, P., Ertl, T., Ziegler, J.: Facet graphs: complex semantic querying made easy. In: Aroyo, L., et al. (eds.) ESWC 2010. LNCS, vol. 6088, pp. 288–302. Springer, Heidelberg (2010). https://doi.org/10.1007/978-3-642-13486-9_20

14. Horrocks, I., Giese, M., Kharlamov, E., Waaler, A.: Using semantic technology to tame the data variety challenge. IEEE Internet Comput. **20**(6), 62–66 (2016)

15. Huang, H., Liu, C., Zhou, X.: Computing relaxed answers on RDF databases. In: Bailey, J., Maier, D., Schewe, K.-D., Thalheim, B., Wang, X.S. (eds.) WISE 2008. LNCS, vol. 5175, pp. 163–175. Springer, Heidelberg (2008). https://doi.org/10. 1007/978-3-540-85481-4_14

16. Kharlamov, E., et al.: Enabling semantic access to static and streaming distributed data with optique: demo. In: DEBS, pp. 350–353 (2016)

17. Kharlamov, E., et al.: Ontology-based integration of streaming and static relational data with optique. In: SIGMOD, pp. 2109–2112 (2016)

18. Kharlamov, E., Giacomelli, L., Sherkhonov, E., Grau, B.C., Kostylev, E.V., Horrocks, I.: Ranking, aggregation, and reachability in faceted search with SemFacet. In: ISWC Posters & Demonstrations (2017)

19. Kharlamov, E., Giacomelli, L., Sherkhonov, E., Grau, B.C., Kostylev, E.V., Horrocks, I.: Semfacet: making hard faceted search easier. In: CIKM, pp. 2475–2478 (2017)

20. Kharlamov, E., et al.: Ontology based access to exploration data at statoil. In: Arenas, M., et al. (eds.) ISWC 2015. LNCS, vol. 9367, pp. 93–112. Springer, Cham (2015). https://doi.org/10.1007/978-3-319-25010-6_6

21. Kharlamov, E., et al.: Ontology based data access in statoil. J. Web Sem. **44**, 3–36 (2017)

22. Kharlamov, E., et al.: Semantic access to streaming and static data at siemens. J. Web Sem. **44**, 54–74 (2017)

23. Kharlamov, E., et al.: A semantic approach to polystores. In: IEEE BigData, pp. 2565–2573 (2016)

24. Motik, B., Nenov, Y., Piro, R., Horrocks, I., Olteanu, D.: Parallel materialisation of datalog programs in centralised, main-memory RDF systems. In: AAAI, pp. 129–137 (2014)

25. Pérez-Urbina, H., Rodríguez-Díaz, E., Grove, M., Konstantinidis, G., Sirin, E.: Evaluation of query rewriting approaches for OWL 2. In: Proceedings of SSWS+HPCSW (2012)

26. Russell, A., Smart, P.: NITELIGHT: a graphical editor for SPARQL queries. In: ISWC (Posters and Demos) (2008)

27. Sherkhonov, E., Grau, B.C., Kharlamov, E., Kostylev, E.V.: Semantic faceted search with aggregation and recursion. In: d'Amato, C., et al. (eds.) ISWC 2017. LNCS, vol. 10587, pp. 594–610. Springer, Cham (2017). https://doi.org/10.1007/978-3-319-68288-4_35

28. Soylu, A., Giese, M., Jimenez-Ruiz, E., Kharlamov, E., Zheleznyakov, D., Horrocks, I.: Ontology-based end-user visual query formulation: why, what, who, how, and which? Univ. Access Inf. Soc. **16**(2), 435–467 (2017)

29. Soylu, A., Giese, M., Jimenez-Ruiz, E., Vega-Gorgojo, G., Horrocks, I.: Experiencing OptiqueVQS: a multi-paradigm and ontology-based visual query system for end users. Univ. Access Inf. Soc. **15**(1), 129–152 (2016)

30. Soylu, A., et al.: OptiqueVQS: a visual query system over ontologies for industry. Semant. Web **9**(5), 627–660 (2018)

31. Suchanek, F.M., Kasneci, G., Weikum, G.: Yago: a core of semantic knowledge. In: WWW, pp. 697–706 (2007)

32. Tunkelang, D.: Faceted Search. Synthesis Lectures on Information Concepts, Retrieval, and Services. Morgan & Claypool Publishers, San Rafael (2009)
33. Wagner, A., Ladwig, G., Tran, T.: Browsing-oriented semantic faceted search. In: Hameurlain, A., Liddle, S.W., Schewe, K.-D., Zhou, X. (eds.) DEXA 2011. LNCS, vol. 6860, pp. 303–319. Springer, Heidelberg (2011). https://doi.org/10.1007/978-3-642-23088-2_22
34. Yamada, N., Yamagata, Y., Fukuta, N.: Query rewriting or ontology modification? Toward a faster approximate reasoning on LOD endpoints. IEICE Trans. Inf. Syst. **E100–D**(12), 2923–2930 (2017)
35. Zhou, Q., Wang, C., Xiong, M., Wang, H., Yu, Y.: SPARK: adapting keyword query to semantic search. In: Aberer, K., et al. (eds.) ASWC/ISWC -2007. LNCS, vol. 4825, pp. 694–707. Springer, Heidelberg (2007). https://doi.org/10.1007/978-3-540-76298-0_50

Data Management

Ontology-Based Semantic Representation of Silk Road's Caravanserais: Conceptualization of Multifaceted Links

Elham Andaroodi[1(✉)] and Frederic Andres[2]

[1] University of Tehran, Enqelab St., Tehran, Iran
andaroodi@ut.ac.ir
[2] National Institute of Informatics,
2-1-2 Hitotsubashi, Chiyoda-ku, Tokyo, Japan
andres@nii.ac.jp

Abstract. Knowledge representation and reasoning has gained relevance during the last years to improve historic architecture understanding and comparisons by developing innovative systems. This article presents research results about semantic representation of a sub set of Silk Road heritages, caravanserai. The core of the information system is an ontology-based schema to capture general and domain-based features of caravanserai by conceptualizing multifaceted links. Lexical links which are mapped from upper level sources are defined to give meaning, quotation and derivation to terms. Upper level links are proposed to give parent-child relations, part-whole relations or associative relations to building components or divisions represented as entities in terminology schema. The major contribution of the research is to conceptualize domain based links for architectural heritage. After studying different thesauruses or standards related to architectural classification or spatial reasoning, three schemas were defined as construction, services and spatial configuration. They acquire qualitative relations between building elements or divisions of a selected corpus of caravanserais. The paper concludes with technical and domain-based assessment of the ontology by publishing the ontology online in Web protégé and using the knowledge to classify 140 cases of the corpus of desert on route caravanserais of Safavid Period. Future work is to publish the RDF ontology as Linked Data.

Keywords: Ontology schema · Lexical links · Caravanserais
Architectural links · Spatial configuration

1 Introduction

In the context of cultural heritage, studies [9] about knowledge acquisition of the historical architecture have attempted to conceptualize attributes of buildings to produce machine-understandable information. Systematic recognition of a building by knowledge acquisition systems try to render it into the composing components as building elements or divisions and then to identify describable relations or semantic links between entities through an exhaustive synthesis. These relations are defined

© Springer Nature Switzerland AG 2018
R. Ichise et al. (Eds.): JIST 2018, LNCS 11341, pp. 89–103, 2018.
https://doi.org/10.1007/978-3-030-04284-4_7

based on the features of a historic building itself or its relation with the setting. Ascertaining the relations between components of a domain is a subject of ontology development in computer science [4, 13]. [13] introduces the main purpose of ontology: "Sharing common understanding of the structure of information among people or software agents". Ontological studies initially focused on a frame-based object oriented model [23] with lexical specification of concepts. Therefore, ontology designs for a domain start with taxonomy of terms and their semantics.

Further, the ontology knowledge model can be elaborated upon based on various types of relations between entities. In the domain of architecture, several kinds of relations linking architectural entities together are required to capture attributes of a built space. Initially, ontology for architecture aligns each entity as a term with its related taxonomy or thesaurus to describe a hierarchical structure, provide parental relations and disambiguate different meanings of terms. However, a lexical ontology cannot represent every attribute of a building and its spaces and is not adequate to conceptualize knowledge of architectural heritage. An architectural heritage is an immovable and tangible heritage with comprehensive attributes and multifaceted features. A building of architectural heritage is linked to its surroundings, people, technologies and evolutions, society and cultural styles. Therefore, conceptualization of a historical building in ontology knowledge model needs to specify the generic attributes of the building objects such as specialization or components (for example, different types of a vault or its material), the physical attributes (material, structure, services, etc.), and the spatial configurations of building divisions (qualitative relations, dimensions, layout, proportions, geometry, etc.). These attributes can be conceptualized in ontology-based knowledge acquisition systems by classes of interconnected links between entities.

In this process, the major question is that how visual information that has been perceived directly in a space can be analyzed as components and their relations in a building? How and ontology knowledge model can render multifaceted relations proper for architectural heritage?

As part of our research on digital documentation of cultural heritages of the Silk Road [21] (Digital Silk Roads) [17], the research has developed an ontology [1] for a type of architectural heritages of the Silk Road. It tried to capture knowledge of a specific corpus, caravanserai. Caravanserais are an important architectural heritage of the Silk Roads to shelter caravans and passengers in their distant journeys. They are located along the historical roads at an interval of a one day trip with caravans (around 36 km). Caravanserais punctuated the historical roads [14] and can be considered as the most important cultural heritage which conveys the spirit of traveling along historical roads.

This research has developed the ontology for caravanserais to enhance cultural heritage semantic annotation and knowledge bases. The main contribution of the research is to conceptualize different schemas of semantic links to represent knowledge of caravanserai architectural heritage using different upper level resources. With advances of the ontology development, this paper presents an enhancement to the ontology semantic links compared to previous work [1] with a focus on part of the schema which represents upper level and domain based relations or links, specifically generic architectural features and spatial configuration of shapes as building elements.

Ontology-based knowledge models contribute to knowledge sharing and reusing represented by a formal language. Multiple formalisms exist to cover different purposes of ontology development. Resource Description Framework [25] and the Ontology Web Language [26] are web-oriented formalisms to represent ontology. We have implemented an ontology editor with a proper interface for domain experts to formalize our ontology. The Protégé knowledge acquisition tool [24] is an open source knowledge-base-editing environment to support development of ontologies. This editor supports the construction in a frame-like fashion with classes and slots [19]. Classes can define concepts in the ontology in a taxonomic manner of subclass/superclass. Slots or properties can contain attributes or links attached to the classes. Entities are defined individually and knowledge of each is represented by attributes that are saved as properties or slots. The object-oriented model of the Protégé tool enables the entities to have multiple relations and is suitable for capturing multifaceted attributes of a built space. This paper is organized as follows: Sect. 2 introduces the ontology for Silk Road caravanserai (Onto-SRC) and its hierarchy of classes. Section 3 discusses the conceptualization of multifaceted links. Section 4 reviews the Protégé OWL/RDF implementation of the ontology schema for the selected corpus of caravanserais and the technical/content evaluation of caravanserais, specifically the advanced classification of 140 cases of the corpus. Finally, Sect. 5 concludes this paper with a discussion on a future trend, namely RDF-based publishing of the ontology for caravanserai online and moving toward Linked Data.

2 The Ontology for Silk Road Caravanserais (Onto-SRC): Upper Level Relations

Caravanserais architectural heritage exist in a wide variety of forms, components and spatial organizations. However, 3 important corpuses are identifiable as [16];

- On route caravanserais in Iran during the Safavid period (1502–1736)
- The Anatolian Khan in Turkey during the Seljuk period (1071–1299)
- The Wekalah in Cairo, Egypt, during the Mamluk sultanate (1250–1517)

Onto-SRC is developed for the corpus of desert on rout caravanserais in Safavid period. The selected corpus of this research is an important group which was studied by several scholars such as Siroux, Kleiss, Aivazian and Lebigre [16] since they share a common conceptual design with a wide variety of cases. They have coherent design which is suitable for conceptualization of common generic and specific features in an ontology system.

In modeling knowledge of a domain in an ontology it is important to amend and reuse existing ontologies; a process recommended by Noy and McGuiness [20]. The following section introduces upper level sources that are studied, analyzed and mapped to the ontology.

2.1   Review of the State of the Art

Currently there are several ontology-based terminologies, metadata or knowledge-bases with application in cultural heritage as cited by Doerr [9]. Here some of the ontologies which have similar concepts are introduced with a focus on conceptualizing the relations.

CIDOC Conceptual Reference Model. The CIDOC Conceptual Reference Model is an important ontology proposed by ICOM (International Council of Museums). It provides definitions, and a formal structure for describing concepts in cultural heritage documentation. It enables information interchange and integration in the museum community, and other places [5]. The latest version (version 6.2, as of May 2015) includes 94 classes and 168 properties. CRM can be studied through classes (entities), properties, and inheritance rules. For example a building is classified as a "Man Made object", a subclass of "Physical Man Made Thing", and another subclass of "Man Made Thing" which is categorized under "Thing". For a cultural heritage object, properties such as *"has current permanent location"*, and *"beginning (or end) is qualified by"* provide a template to give metadata-based specifications to cultural entities. General upper level relations of CIDOC CRM can be listed as *"forms part of"*, *"is composed of"*, *"has narrower term"*, *"has broader term"*, *"is component of"*, *"has component"*, *"is type of"*, *"has type"*, *"consists of"*, *"contains"*, etc. These features can be mapped with different upper level ontologies such as GOLD General Ontology for Linguistic Description or GOLD [12], under the classes such as hypernym - hyponym, or meronym – holonym.

There are examples of extensions of CRM for archeological sites to cover excavations, reconstructions and restorations. The schema is expanded to include descriptions of relic components, and the surroundings of archeological sites [11].

The classification of CIDOC CRM is general and can be mapped with a metadata-based ontology for architectural heritage. However, as it covers broad range of cultural heritage objects, such as art works or antique objects, domain-based links and generic architectural features such as material, structure or services or spatial configuration of elements and divisions are not covered. Onto-SRC is based on a terminology which has different purposes from an ontology suitable to gather metadata about a specific cultural entity such as CIDOC CRM.

Knowledge Representation of Architectural Terminology. A system of architectural knowledge can be described as a collection of structured objects identified by a precise vocabulary [8]. Blaise and Dudek have mentioned a number of research works about analyses of architectural vocabularies, and have explained the DIVA architectural vocabulary tool [3]. An important subject that is discussed in this research is similar to our challenge which is the variation of concepts for building components. Specifically, it is about how an object is named while taking into consideration the ornamental or structural differences of each case, including its evolutions and changes through time. Here the contribution of the knowledge-based model, similar to this research is clarified, and different links are provided in 3 categories: specialization, aggregation, and comparison. For each category a set of links is defined. However the links that are defined here can be compared to GOLD [12]. As part of GOLD's

"Lexical Links", antonyms, hypernyms, meronyms and synonyms are defined as either classes or properties. However, the method proposed by Blaise has considered temporal and spatial attributes of architectural objects. For example the class "quotation" includes classes and properties derivation (*has derivation*), etymology (*has alternative*) and related vocabulary (*is related to*).

Getty Vocabularies as Linked Open Data. The Getty vocabularies contain structured terminology for art, architecture, decorative arts, archival materials, visual surrogates, conservation, and bibliographic materials[1]. Currently Getty vocabularies are released as Linked Open Data[2]. It is structured and published to make it openly accessible and shareable on the Semantic Web. Each Getty vocabulary records and terms are identified by unique numeric IDs. Therefore, the vocabularies are linked to each other and share a core data structure [10].

Links or relations, which are the focus of this research, can be analyzed differently in Getty Vocabularies. Art and Architecture Thesaurus and Thesaurus of Geographic Names define a "*hierarchical relation*" and an "*associative relation*" between terms. The Union List of Artist Names includes current and historical "*associative relations*". However, metadata headings such as "*birth and death places*", "*events*", "*nationalities*" are provided for artists' names as entities. The Cultural Objects Name Authority provides different metadata headings for cultural objects such as "*work type*", "*classification*", "*creation date*", "*material*", etc. [10]. Here it is important to notice that attributes of vocabularies are provided either as a relation or as a metadata heading.

2.2 Define of Hierarchy of Classes in Onto-SRC

Classes provide meaningful way of grouping entities together. Large ontologies (e.g. SUMO upper level ontology [15]), provide a hierarchy of entities of the world (map all the WordNet Lexicon) under two classes of Abstract and Physical. For example a building is an Artifact, subclass of Object under the super-class Physical. Large generic ontologies such as SUMO need to be specialized for each domain such as architecture. In architecture, thesaurus such as AAT is an important reference of classification for our domain of study. The attributes provided by AAT for each entity as a term gives definition to the term and specifies its hierarchy under eight classes. The classes specify if the entity is an object or a person, a period of time, an activity, etc. In AAT hierarchy, a caravanserai is under the classes of public accommodation, single built works by function and built environment [10].

The research has integrated AAT hierarchy of general classes for caravanserai, with reference to its linked URI[3], with SUMO general classes as shown in Fig. 1. Therefore, the top of hierarchy of AAT which is Built Environment is a subclass of Physical attributes. Caravanserais class can have different subclasses as caravanserai by location → Persian Caravanserais → Caravanserais by Historic Period → Safavid

---

[1] http://www.getty.edu/research/tools/vocabularies/.

[2] http://www.getty.edu/research/tools/vocabularies/lod/.

[3] http://www.getty.edu/vow/AATFullDisplay?find=caravanserai&logic=AND&note=&english=
N&prev_page=1&subjectid=300007148.

Caravanserais → Caravanserais by Climate → Desert Caravanserais. Here terminology class including entities of building elements and divisions are provided as a subclass of desert caravanserais.

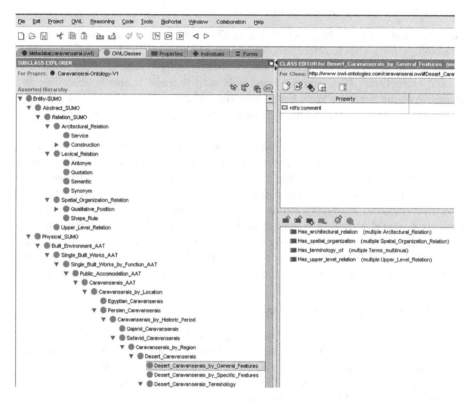

Fig. 1. Hierarchy of classes of caravanserais in Onto-SRC. Four properties of the class of generic features connect object type entities of architectural, upper level, spatial organization and lexical relations

3 Conceptualization of Multifaceted Links

Review of the state of the art shows that define of semantic links between entities for every ontology is done differently according to the scope and the purpose of the ontology development. For example a thesaurus provides associative relation or parent-child relation with links such as *is-a*, or *is-associated-with*. It is important to note that an ontology schema of links is more sophisticated than a thesaurus, as it is emphasized by Doerr "Ontologies that deal with semantics equivalent to those of data structures, contain few classes and are rich in relationships, in contrast to terminological ontologies for classifying individual items such as thesauruses [9]". An ontology knowledge model can provide a system of representing multiple relations that an entity, such as a building object, can be involved in. Therefore, the innovative approach is to extract multiple semantic links for the most generic properties.

The research has proposed four categories of relations in Onto-SRC. Four classes of links were defined under the super-class Relation as shown in Fig. 2. SUMO included the class of relations under the supper-class Abstract entities which is mapped in Onto-SRC. The four categories include:

- Domain-based links as architectural relations with subcategories as services and construction
- Upper level relations for general attributes
- Lexical relations such as synonym or semantic
- Spatial organization relations that link each building division to its qualitative position in a caravanserai.

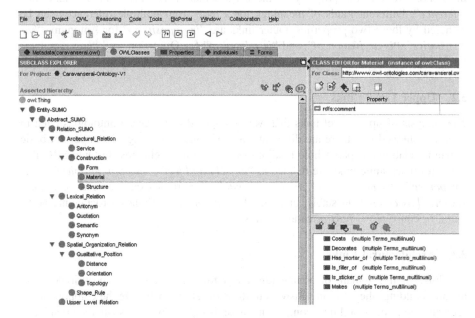

Fig. 2. Hierarchy of four classes of relations in Onto-SRC. Properties of the subclass "material" under the super class "construction", as an architectural relation is provided as *coats, decorates, has mortar of, is filler of, makes.*

It must be noted that upper level or reference ontology are not designed for the domain of architecture and a combination of these four classes of relations proposed by Onto-SRC is not available in a single ontology. One argument is to use reference ontology and try to extend it with desired attributes, similar to the cases of extension of CIDOC-CRM. However, because of the reasons discusses after the review of the state of the art in Sect. 2.1, the research tried to propose its own conceptualization of semantic links, proper for acquiring the knowledge of a terminology for caravanserais architectural heritage. For this purpose, upper level resources were used to define categories of links for each of the four classes.

3.1   Lexical Links

Ontology entities or subjects of RDF triple are defined by terms. Therefore, the first step of conceptualizing the links in an ontology is to provide linguistic descriptions to terminology. However, lexical descriptions of a historic architecture are challenging because the physical objects or conceptual entities of an architectural heritage are varied, and several questions are raised in between terminologies and knowledge-based representations [3].

In this research upper level lexical ontologies (GOLD) or terminologies of historic architecture (DIVA) are used. Initially, for each term, conventional categories of lexical relations, that mean semantic, quotation, antonym and synonym are provided and are mapped from GOLD and DIVA. Each class of lexical relation includes properties as links. For example the property of the class semantic is "*has meaning*" and "*has reference*". Different kinds of meanings for a term from multiple references can be gathered by these two properties. Other links are "*is opposite to*" for Antonym, "*has alternative*", "*is derivation of*", and "*is related to*" for Quotation, and "*has synonym*" for Synonym classes. These links are common in GOLD and DIVA.

3.2   Upper Level Links

The analysis of upper level links that were compared in reference ontologies cited in Sect. 2.1 showed that there are different ways of conceptualizing two important basic semantic relations as part-whole relations or parent-child relations. In Onto-SRC five upper level semantic links are defined as "*has child object*", "*has parent object*", "*has component*", "*is part of*", "*is associated with*". Important examples can be a caravanserai *has component* stable, or vestibule *is associate with* hashti (octagonal vestibule), or courtyard *is part of* caravanserais.

3.3   Architectural Links

The links of the domain of architecture are defined according to the attributes of a historic building; they provide answers to these questions: what are the components or specializations of a building component or division? How it is spatially organized? What is its structure? Which material is it made of? What are its services? Part of these questions can be defined by the upper level links. Other domain-based attributes are conceptualized in a schema named "Architectural Relations".

These attributes can be studied in upper level resources of classification of architectural entities in thesauruses such as AAT [10] or basic standards for Building Information Modeling (BIM) such as ASTM Uni Format II [18] or OmniClass [22]. These sources aim to classify objects or concepts related to architecture by links such as components (holonym, meronym), specializations (hypernym, hyponym), or associated concepts.

Here, two main subclasses for the physical attributes of a building are recognized: "Construction" and "Services" as listed in Table 1. The table shows a comparative analysis of Onto-SRC architectural links and upper sources such as AAT and OmniClass. Each class is discussed as follows:

Table 1. A comparison of classification of architectural knowledge and consequently extraction of domain-based links

AAT	OmniClass	Onto-SRC
Objects facet → Components → system components Subclasses: electrical systems, HVAC, infrastructural elements, protection system, plumbing and stormwater system, telecommunication system	Elements → Services Subclasses: conveying, plumbing, Heating, Ventilation, and Air Conditioning (HVAC), fire protection, electrical, communications, electronic safety and security, integrated automation, furnishings	Architectural relation → Service *warms* fireplace *warms* stable *cools* baadgir (windcathcher) *cools* Abanbar (a Persian term for traditional cistern)
Objects facet → Components → architectural elements → structural elements Subclasses: structural systems, structural assemblies, supporting elements, spanning and projecting structural elements, enclosing structural elements	Elements → Substructures Subclasses: foundations, basement constructions Element → Shells Subclasses: super structures, exterior enclosures, roofing Element → Interiors Subclasses: interior constructions, interiors, interior finishes)	Construction → Structure *has foundation* e.g. wall *has foundation* concrete limestone *encloses* wall *encloses* room *covers* cloister vault *covers* room
Materials facet → materials (substances) → materials by function Subclasses: coating, facing, filler, building material (subclasses: finishing (subclasses: flooring, roofing, siding (material)), insulation, masonry, etc.), reinforcing material, etc.)	Materials Subclasses: chemical elements, solid compounds (subclasses: mineral compounds (subclasses: sedimentary rocks, binding compounds, etc.), metallic alloys, organic compounds, synthetic compounds), liquids, gases	Material *makes* e.g. brick *makes* wall *coats* e.g. mud and straw *coats* roof *has mortar of,* e.g. wall *has mortar of* clay and chalk

Construction. The construction schema specifies what are the materials of the building components and how they are assembled together. Therefore, the subcategories can be "Structure" which describes the building system and construction process, and "Material" which focuses on the material's function.

The structure of a building can be described in 3 categories (by referring to OmniClass) as "substructure", "shell" and "interiors". Semantic links can be *"has foundation of"*, *"encloses"*, *"covers"*, *"has interior of"*, etc.

Material can be divided into different categories. For example "masonry" specifies load bearing materials (such as brick wall), "binding" defines mortars (such as chalk and clay) and "facing" represents finishing (such as mud and straw). Semantic links can be identified as *"makes"*, *"is assembled by"*; *"has mortar of"*, *"coats"*, etc.

Service. Services (in OmniClass) or systems (in AAT) provide environmental comfort in a building. Services in historical architecture work with natural sources of light, wind, water, etc. Therefore, categories of services can be "heating", "cooling", "ventilating", or "lightning". The semantic links can be defined as *"warms"*, *"cools"*, *"ventilates"*, *"lightens"*, etc.

3.4   Conceptualization of Spatial Attributes

An architectural heritage is perceived in 3 dimensional spaces. Components and building divisions are configured together according to a defined geometry or logical arrangement to form a place. Each space has qualitative attributes, such as topology or orientation, as well as quantitative features such as dimension, shape, etc. Here the Onto-SRC tries to define semantic links which describe generic spatial attributes qualitatively. Attributes those are common between the cases of the corpus (for example in every caravanserai small iwan is *in front of* room).

Qualitative Spatial Organization. In the qualitative representation, each spatial model reference is specified by the so called "non metric rulers" that measure spatial objects and their locations [6, 7]. Qualitative non metric links describe distance, orientation or topology of building divisions or components. These features were conceptualized in spatial organization relations in three categories and several properties as follows:

- Class Distance: *is adjacent to, is close to, is discrete from, is far from, and is next to.*
- Class Orientation: *is clockwise, is counterclockwise, is above of, is behind of, is below of, is in front of, and is parallel with.*
- Class Topology: *is covered by, has direct access with, has indirect access to, intersect, is around of, is aside of, is at the beginning of, is at cant of, is at side of, etc.*

For each entity of building divisions (such as an iwan, a Persian term for a covered vaulted space open on one side) or some of the building components (such as a tower), the qualitative link is specified. Examples of such links are presented in Table 2.

Table 2. Classes of qualitative spatial links and example of use

Classes of Qualitative Links *Properties*	Example of use
Distance *is adjacent to*	Room *is adjacent to* iwān
Orientation *is in front of*	Iwanche (small iwan) *is in front of* iwan
Topology *has direct access with*	Iwān *has direct access to* a courtyard Room *has direct access to* an iwānche (Persian term for small iwān)

Ontological Model of Shape Rules. Modeling the spatial organization of caravanserai by qualitative links has the ambiguity of geometry, shape, and precise location. For example a stable in a caravanserai can have different shapes under two categories of annular or non-annular. It is a question how these attributes can be conceptualized in an ontology-based system? How unique spatial organization of each case can be described in Onto-SRC?

We have shown in detail [1] the solution of this research to develop a shape grammar for selected corpus of 140 caravanserais. The shape grammar specifies how components or divisions in a specific corpus of caravanserais are placed in relation with each other with identifiable shapes and quantitative attributes. The successive shape rules are integrated with the ontology schema with the help of the morphological invariants of each rule. The shape grammar rules are formalized as part of the ontology schema under two classes of shape verification rules and function verification rules. Shape-grammar schema provided a knowledge model for describing ground floor plan layout and the geometrical organization of shape components for 140 cases of caravanserais.

4   Implementation and Assessment of Onto-SRC

The schema of Onto-SRC is implemented to represent knowledge of caravanserais in two ways: generic attributes and specific attributes. Generic attributes represent the most general to the most relevant features common to cases of the selected corpus. Later, general features of caravanserais are instantiated inside the protégé tool using four object type properties that collect instances from four schemas of ontology relations (Fig. 1). The architecture of the system is shown in Fig. 3. The initial entity is an ID which links multilingual equivalents of different terms together from terminology schema. The terms describe building divisions and elements of caravanserais. Figure 4 shows implementation of the schema to conceptualize different links for the term "principal iwan", which indicate a half covered space with the below relations:

- Upper level relations → has parent object: iwan,
- Upper level relations → is associated with: secondary iwan
- Spatial organization relations → is at center of: courtyard facade.

It is important to note that specific features of caravanserai, which is unique for each case and make spatial configuration of each caravanserai in ground floor plan different, is formalized inside the Protégé tool by implementing the shape rule schema. The schema specifies combination of rules which identify quantitative attributes of spaces of one caravanserai consisting of shapes and their configuration.

For the purpose of evaluating the ontology for caravanserais the research considered the three important stages listed below:

- Technical evaluation of the ontology file;
- Content evaluation and assessment with application for advanced classification of the specific corpus of caravanserais;
- Life time evaluation of ontology (to consider the limited period of the study).

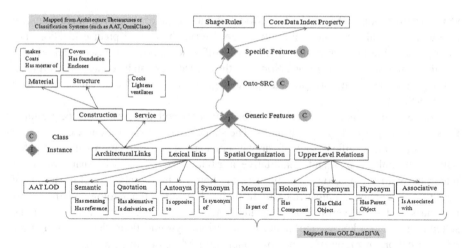

Fig. 3. Architecture of the Ontology for Silk Roads Caravanserai (Onto-SRC). Generic features of caravanserais are linked as interconnected entities of four classes of relations

The ontology is checked inside the tool by running a test and modifying the errors. The consistency of the ontology can be checked similarly. However, domain-specific ontology must be evaluated in order to reach to a consensus on the specifications between experts of the domain for the exchange and reuse of ontological information.

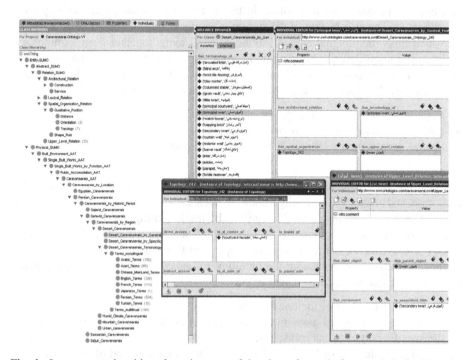

Fig. 4. Interconnected entities of one instance of the class of generic features (principal iwan).

The ontology is published online under the following URL in Web protégé:
https://webprotege.stanford.edu/#projects/6a220b23-9763-486a-95ba-406424d3f55
4/edit/Classes

The ontology is shared with expert of caravanserai heritage (most notable ones, Prof. Pierre Lebigre) for viewing and comment. There were different round of discussion the content of the ontology, and implementation of the schema by the users. For example the terminology schema is implemented to gather semantic properties for each term in Persian language. The assessment is a work in progress while the ontology is populated with newer relations between terms.

This research has proposed content based evaluation of the ontology by using the represented knowledge for advanced classification of the 140 cases of the corpus of caravanserais. The ontology represented major classification features for the cases. Morphological invariants of the features were provided and binary values of features were prepared in a relational model. The model was implemented in knowledge extraction tools such as BayesiaLab. Accordingly the research could verify six major classes and 16 subclasses of caravanserais (see Fig. 5).

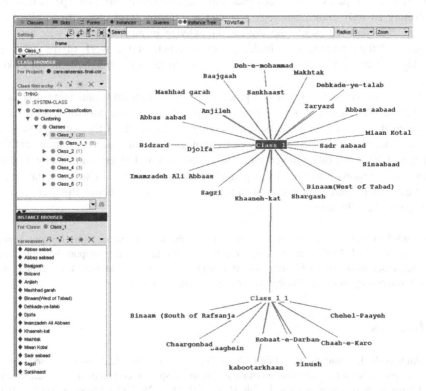

Fig. 5. Six classes and several subclasses were extracted by using a probabilistic model of BayesiaLab tool.

5 Conclusion and Future Work

The knowledge acquisition of the architectural heritage is changing undoubtedly the way historians, Archaeologists and architects comprehend and classify buildings. Informatics experts can provide support and services that will help domain experts concentrate on extracting the science of buildings rather than wrestling with barriers that keep them from manipulating/cooperating large shareable building and related datasets and from utilizing contextual data. In conclusion, we have shown that it is possible for a domain expert using the Protégé tool to create an architectural spatial domain ontology, which bodes well for the future of ontology development. As case studies, multifaceted lexical, architectural, spatial and upper level links interconnect different entities based on their various features in a caravanserai. Shape-rule schema provided a knowledge model for describing plan layout and the geometrical organization of shape components in caravanserais. Finally, the ontology featured classification attributes to compare the organization of spatial elements in a ground-floor layout of chain of caravanserais and provided an advanced way of classification. The classification of heritage buildings will have a major contribution to understanding the way architects in past centuries designed buildings and configured the space. Besides, publishing an RDF-Based ontology provides a semantic level access to architectural heritage data and represents the domain knowledge in an interwoven way between entities and their relation in a building over internet. Future work of the ontology development and publishing is required in order to meet the requirements of linked data.

Linked data refers to a set of best practices for publishing and connecting structured data on the Web, leading to the creation of a global data space containing billions of assertions the Web of Data [2]. We plan to migrate the OWL of the ontology to tools such as Vocbench to meet semantic web technologies. We also need to link the entities and their URIs with other linked data initiatives such as DBpedia and Getty Vocabularies. It is important to keep interoperability for the concept (classes) and data level (entities) and to make caravanserai ontology a core of data about the architectural heritage of the Silk Road.

Acknowledgement. We would like to commemorate the late professor, Pierre Lebigre, Emeritus Professor of ENSAPVS and Researcher at EVCAU for his constant support. We appreciate Prof. Kinji Ono from National Institute of Informatics for his ongoing advises. The Ontology has been developed by using the Protégé Knowledge Acquisition Tool.

References

1. Andaroodi, E., Andres, F., Einifar, A., Lebigre, P., Kando, N.: Ontology-based shape-grammar schema for classification of caravanserais: a specific corpus of Iranian Safavid and Ghajar open, on-route samples. J. Cult. Herit. **7**(4), 312–328 (2006). https://doi.org/10.1016/j.culher.2006.08.002
2. Berners-Lee, T.: Linked data -design issues. W3C (09/20) (2006). http://www.w3.org/DesignIssues/LinkedData.html

3. Blaise, J.Y., Dudek, I.: Terminology analysis inspires relations in a knowledge structure. In: Proceeding of TKE 2008 8th International Conference on Terminology and Knowledge Engineering, pp. 89–105 (2008)
4. Chandrasekaran, B., Josephson, J.R., Benjamins, V.R.: What are ontologies, and why do we need them? IEEE Intell. Syst. **14**(1), 20–26 (1999). https://doi.org/10.1109/5254.747902
5. CIDOC CRM (2000). http://www.cidoc-crm.org/get-last-official-release
6. Cohn, A.G., Hazarika, S.M.: Qualitative spatial representation and reasoning: an overview. Fundam. Inf. **46**(1-2), 1–29 (2001). http://dl.acm.org/citation.cfm?id=1219982.1219984
7. Cohn, A.G., Randell, D.A., Cui, Z.: Taxonomies of logically defined qualitative spatial relations. Int. J. Hum.-Comput. Stud. **43**(5-6), 831–846 (1995). https://doi.org/10.1006/ijhc.1995.1077
8. De Luca, L., Véron, P., Florenzano, M.: A generic formalism for the semantic modeling and representation of architectural elements. Vis. Comput. **23**(3), 181–205 (2007). https://doi.org/10.1007/s00371-006-0092-5
9. Doerr, M.: Ontologies for cultural heritage. In: Staab, S., Studer, R. (eds.) Handbook on Ontologies, pp. 463–486. Springer, Heidelberg (2009). https://doi.org/10.1007/978-3-540-92673-3_21
10. Getty: Art & architecture thesaurus, January 2001. www.getty.edu/research/tools/vocabularies/aat/
11. Gkrous, G.S., Nikolaidou, M.: Building digital collections for archeological sites: metadata requirements and CIDOC CRM extension. Series Advances on Information Processing and Management, vol. 2 (2011)
12. GOLD Community: General Ontology for Linguistic Description (GOLD), December 2004. http://www.linguistics-ontology.org/
13. Gruber, T.R.: A translation approach to portable ontology specifications. Knowl. Acquis. **5**(2), 199–220 (1993). https://doi.org/10.1006/knac.1993.1008. http://www.sciencedirect.com/science/article/pii/S1042814383710083
14. Hillenbrand, R.: Islamic Architecture. Edinburgh University Press, Edinburgh (2000)
15. IEEE: Suggested upper merged ontology (sumo), May 2004. www.adampease.org/OP/
16. Lebigre, P.: Caravanserais of the silk roads, towards an inventory on internet. In: Ono, K. (ed.) Proceedings of the 2001 Tokyo Symposium for Digital Silk Roads, pp. 81–89. National Institute of Informatics, Tokyo (2001)
17. NII: Digital silk road project portal, April 2006. dsr.nii.ac.jp
18. NIST UNIFORMAT II Elemental Classification for Building Specifications, Cost Estimating, and Cost Analysis, December 2007. http://www.ct.gov/dcs/lib/dcs/uniformat_ii_report.pdf
19. Noy, N.F., Hafner, C.D.: The state of the art in ontology design: a survey and comparative review. AI Mag. **18**(3), 53–74 (1997). http://dblp.unitrier.de/db/journals/aim/aim18.htmlNoyH97
20. Noy, N.F., McGuinness, D.L.: Ontology development 101: a guide to creating your first ontology. Technical report, March 2001. http://www.ksl.stanford.edu/people/dlm/papers/ontology-tutorial-noy-mcguinness-abstract.html
21. Ono, K., et al.: Progress of the digital silk roads project. Progress Inform. **1**, 93–141 (2005)
22. OmniClass Construction Classification System. http://www.omniclass.org/about/
23. Rumbaugh, J., Blaha, M., Premerlani, W., Eddy, F., Lorensen, W.: Object-oriented Modeling and Design. Prentice-Hall Inc, Upper Saddle River (1991)
24. StanfordUniv: Protégé, November 1999. protege.stanford.edu
25. W3C: resource description framework (RDF) schema specification, December 2000. https://www.w3.org/TR/2000/CR-rdf-schema-20000327/
26. W3C: Owl web ontology language 1.0 reference, December 2002. https://www.w3.org/TR/owl-ref/

Unified Access to Heterogeneous Data Sources Using an Ontology

Daniel Mercier[1]([✉]), Hyunmin Cheong[1], and Chaitanya Tapaswi[2]

[1] Autodesk Research, Toronto, ON, Canada
{daniel.mercier,hyunmin.cheong}@autodesk.com
[2] Autodesk, Pier 9, San Francisco, CA, USA
http://www.autodeskresearch.com/

Abstract. The rise of cloud computing started a transition for software applications from local to remote infrastructures. This migration created an opportunity to aggregate and consolidate analogous data content. However, this data content usually come with very different data structures and data terminologies and is usually tightly coupled to one or more applications. With these disparities and restrictions, the analogous data ends up both centrally stored but spread over several disconnected heterogeneous data sources. In this article, we present an approach to aggregate data sources using live data consolidation. The approach preserves the original data sources; and by doing so, prevents associated applications from having to migrate to a new data source. The approach uses an ontology at its core to serve as a common semantic ground between data sources and leverage its stored knowledge to expand query capabilities.

Keywords: Ontology · Databases · Aggregation · Consolidation
Standardization · Query expansion · Materials

1 Introduction

The development of Cloud technologies, remote computing infrastructures, has recently seen a steep growth due to a combination of global network coverage and higher communication speeds. Software companies are progressively moving their applications from being historically deployed locally on desktops to being deployed on these remote infrastructures. This migration provides an opportunity to aggregate data sources. The receiving data warehouses offer extreme storage capacities, resilience from redundancies, traceability over changes and connection to advanced processing pipelines. This newly aggregated data content often holds compatible and analogous data prone to consolidation. The result from consolidation is an increased availability of data on specific topics and richer data diversity.

The aggregation and consolidation of existing data sources is naturally a challenge because the sources are often historically designed, assembled, and

© Springer Nature Switzerland AG 2018
R. Ichise et al. (Eds.): JIST 2018, LNCS 11341, pp. 104–118, 2018.
https://doi.org/10.1007/978-3-030-04284-4_8

optimized for one or more specific applications; and therefore, deeply linked to these applications. A successful aggregation and consolidation of data sources would have to minimize the impact on the consuming applications and their active operations as well as avoid creating copies that could lead to synchronization issues.

Our proposed solution is to use *live data consolidation*; a method where the data aggregation happens at the time of content query to maintain the original data sources. Its core operations consist in the alignment of the data attributes and the homogenization of data structures. The unique aspect of the proposed solution is the introduction of an ontology at the core to serve as a unifying language. The architecture calls for a registry of data sources and an ontology to:

- Store the information to query each data source attribute,
- Serve as a common language to correlate attributes between data sources,
- Expand query capabilities by developing the ontology to new domains of knowledge.

In this article, we address the various considerations to generate such a solution and develop a full-service architecture. The following section goes through a background on known data aggregation and consolidation techniques; and develop the reasons for the choice of technique. Section 3 details the core operations and described a full service architecture. Finally, Sect. 4 illustrates the use of the ontology during query conversion when searching materials data sources.

2   Background on Data Aggregation

There are two primary techniques to coalesce multiple data sources: data integration and live data consolidation. The former combines multiple scattered sources into one larger source. The latter keeps the original scattered sources and only coalesces the data during content retrieval. The main difference stems from the fact that data integration is a one-off operation resulting in a new and larger data source; while live data consolidation adds operations every time a query is received to: First, convert the original query to the query format of the data sources; and second, homogenize the returned data to the requested format. Both techniques use the schema from each data source for content structure, data attributes, data types and other defining information.

2.1   Comparison Between Techniques

Data integration is appealing as a one-off operation but the decision to adopt the technique must also take into account the following considerations: The presence of a larger and more varied data content structure will have an effect on performance. The resulting data source will also likely be built using a data structure composed of a mix of attributes from the original data sources. This mixed composition will likely affect the consuming applications and require code changes inside the applications to access the new data source. Finally, if the original data sources are built from various database types, the communication protocol might also have to change. A solution to avert these issues would be to keep the original data sources along with the merged data source. But this solution is sensitive to content changes and prone to synchronization issues. In some cases, the management of copies can become far more complex and computationally intense than the initial operation to integrate the data.

On the other end, live data consolidation does not modify the original data sources; but introduces processing operations during each query for:

- Converting the query from its original format to the formats of the different data sources,
- Converting the returned data contents to the requested format,
- Cleaning the data to remove inconsistencies and data overlapping.

When compared to querying a single data source, these repeated operations add an operational time overhead. However, since each data source is independent, these operations can run in parallel. Beyond processing time, the technique is very versatile. It can easily scale up or down with the number of data sources, and it can accommodate a range of query languages and output formats. The technique is not sensitive to content changes but is sensitive to structural changes instead. For this reason, an implementation of this technique must keep track of the format in which the data is stored inside each data source. Finally, live data consolidation stands as a good intermediary solution before data integration. Its history of uses can influence the choice of attributes and data structure during data integration.

The choice between the two techniques comes down to either moving permanently to an integrated source; or keeping the original sources and incurring a processing overhead.

Both techniques have in common the need for *data standardization* to reshape and convert the extracted information into a common form; and *data cleaning* to address the issues of data overlapping and inconsistencies. Data standardization has two components: attribute matching and schema mapping.

2.2   Attribute Matching

Attribute matching is the identification and correlation of attributes between data sources. The attribute matching must consider all variations in attribute naming including homonyms, synonyms, abbreviations, abstractions, and idioms. As illustrated by recent research, effective attribute matching often goes beyond attribute names. Zhang et al. [16] addressed the relation between attributes and data types to filter out interference between data. Liu et al. [8] established a method to compute semantic similarities by considering associated properties. But most importantly, recent advances in natural language processing (NLP) using word embedding introduced robust methods for automated matching [10].

Word embedding has the capability of identifying similarities and analogies beyond lettering equivalences by encoding the semantic relationships in the Euclidean space [6]. The resulting vector-form facilitates clustering of words and idioms. The key to an effective implementation of word embedding is a domain-specific corpus composed of a consistent set of writings on a particular subject to define the initial space. Word embedding has also the capability to support multi-languages but requires for this purpose to have semantic bridges between languages with direct translations to create embedding alignment [5].

Direct attribute matching is a solution to connect two sources. But in order to support a greater number of data sources, it is more efficient to introduce a common semantic ground to bound schema attributes, e.g. Ali et al. [1] introduced the concept of a global schema in a middle-ware service to connect multiple data sources. A more powerful approach is to use an ontology, a Semantic Web technology.

2.3 Semantic Web Technologies

Research in data integration and live data consolidation frequently uses Semantic Web technologies. As envisioned by Tim Bernes-Lee et al. [3], and as formulated by the World Wide Web Consortium: "The Semantic Web provides a common framework that allows data to be shared and reused across application, enterprise, and community boundaries". Noaman et al. [11] introduced an ontology to do data integration from relational databases and assembled the final schema automatically. Zhao et al. [17] created a set of generic rules to automatically convert the data content of any SQL database, directly into the ontology as instances of ontology classes.

On *live data consolidation*, Konstantopoulos et al. [7] took the approach of federating search queries, converting the *SPARQL* queries to the query language of the Cassandra database. SPARQL is the query language for the Resource Description Framework or RDF, a popular format to store ontologies. Liu et al. [8] expanded the approach by combining multiple open-source libraries for the conversion of SPARQL to the query languages of SQL, NO-SQL, Triplestore or XML databases, and by returning the data source contents in RDF format. Ontology-Based Data Access or OBDA, [15], was developed since the mids 2000s to federate relational data sources through an ontology. OBDA focuses specifically on the query aspect. The query language uses SPARQL which is converted to SQL equivalents to retrieved content from the relational data sources. The process uses at its core a mapping between the ontology and the schema of the relational data sources. The query language is bound to the ontology taxonomy and the traversing of the ontology is limited to the capabilities of SPARQL.

3 Proposed Solution

As our data sources are deeply connected to applications, our choice of technique was primarily driven by the impact that an integrated data source would have on the associated applications. Therefore, our proposed solution is the implementation of a live data consolidation service with an ontology at its core.

3.1 Ontology for Attribute Matching

The use of an ontology, a cross-linked structure of classes and relationships, is a perfect common semantic ground for attribute matching. An ontology offers a semantic rich environment for attributes and has the advantage of situating attributes in their respective contexts. Figure 1 illustrates the basic use of an ontology for attribute matching.

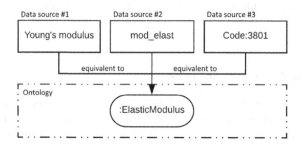

Fig. 1. Attribute matching using ontology

The capacity of an ontology to store extended knowledge adds an important feature to the live data consolidation. Beyond the attribute-bound tree of classes, the exploration of class relationships inside the ontology opens new query capabilities by connecting neighboring classes belonging to different domains of knowledge. Associations that would normally be unavailable, can now be searched with little data overhead and without affecting data sources. As an example, an attribute called 'material_type' may have a valid value called 'Water'. 'Oxygen' and 'Hydrogen' compose 'Water'. This knowledge can be added inside the ontology with a separate tree of classes for chemical atoms and the setting of two inverse relationships such as *composedOf* and *composes*. With this ontology, the user can now query for materials *composedOf* of 'Oxygen' and receive in return the data content related to 'Water'.

3.2 Description of Schema Mapping

From attribute matching, the next step is schema mapping to convert data contents between data sources. Schema mapping is fundamentally a data manipulation. The process takes data content formatted using an input schema and maps it into the format of an output schema. The complexity of the mapping operations essentially depends on the richness of the schemas, e.g. Mecca et al. [9] investigated how the mapping process changes in the presence of a richer conceptual schema.

Schema mapping uses the attribute matching, the data structure from the source schema and various additional structural connections, e.g. the association between values and units for unit conversion. The attribute matching as well as the internal connections are defined using the original schema, and often stored as metadata inside an enhanced version of the schema. Figure 2 illustrates the addition of metadata inside a JSON schema with the attribute *'ontology'* holding the ontology class matching, and the attribute *'unit'* holding the information on unit.

```
1   {
2       "property_attribute":{
3           "type": "object",
4           "ontology": [":Property_attribute_classname"],
5           "properties":{
6               "value_attribute": {
7                   "type": "number",
8                   "ontology": [":Value_attribute_classname"],
9                   "unit":{
10                      "default": "#unit_name#",
11                      "location": "./#unit_attribute#"
12                  }
13              },
14              "unit_attribute": {
15                  "type": "string",
16                  "ontology": [":Unit_attribute_classname"],
17                  "unit": "#unit_name#"
18              }
19          }
20      }
```

Fig. 2. Example of enhanced JSON schema

When describing a schema structure, the schema attributes can be split in two groups: *structural attributes* and *value-carrying attributes*. The schema mapping primarily affects structural attributes. We identified three primary transformations illustrated by Fig. 3:

- **Spreading** which flattens trees of attributes.
- **Inverting** which reverses trees of attributes. This transformation creates attribute duplicates with a parent attribute becoming a child attribute to its original child attributes.
- **Condensing** which aggregates branches of attributes into a single attribute.

Condensing was the original drive for associating single attributes to multiple ontology classes. As an example of condensing, let's consider a material with an attribute called *'young_modulus'* matched to the ontology class *:ElasticModulus*.

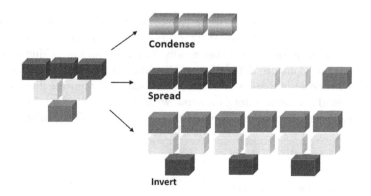

Fig. 3. Structural transformations during schema mapping

This property has two sub-properties: *'value'* attached to the ontology class *:Value*; and *'unit'* attached to the ontology class *:Unit*. The condensed version of the *'young_modulus'* branches becomes two condensed attributes:

– *'young_modulus_value'* attached to the classes: *:ElasticModulus* and *:Value*
– *'young_modulus_unit'* attached to the classes: *:ElasticModulus* and *:Unit*

This one-to-many association maintains an accurate attribute semantic significance, or attribute meaning. This is extremely useful for complex attributes with complex or composite names. For this reason, value-carrying attributes are associated to the list of ontology classes in their tree branch during schema mapping. During the development of the schema mapping engine, the presence of these associations helped identifying a few best practices for attribute matching:

1. The matching of structural attributes to ontology classes should be avoided unless there is a direct dependency with a value-carrying attributes, such as, *young_modulus* and *value*. An exhaustive matching of structural attributes reduces the chance of matching sequences of classes between schemas.
2. The order of ontology classes matched to an attribute does not affect mapping because each class is unique.

3.3 Service Architecture

Our implementation of live data consolidation takes the form of a stateless service with two primary workflows and a dedicated query language. The service acts as an agent between users and data sources as illustrated by Fig. 4.

As usual for a service, authentication and authorization protect the service and enforces access rights through user profiles. The four profiles which may interact with the service, are:

– *User* who queries data content,
– *Schema owner* who provides the necessary information about a data source and sets the mapping between the schema and the ontology,

– *Domain expert* who maintains the core ontology,
– *Administrator* who oversees users and operations.

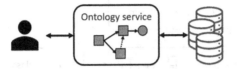

Fig. 4. Simplified view of service.

The set of service operations is tightly linked to these user profiles. While the service comes with a standard set of operations for clustering and user management, the remaining operations cover the two primary workflows for *data source registration* and *querying*.

3.4   Data Source Registration

The workflow for data source registration is designed to gather the necessary information about a new data source from its *schema owner*. The workflow is best supported by a dedicated user interface and facilitate attribute matching. Figure 5 illustrates the workflow. Upon receiving the information about a new data source in the form of its database type, location and original schema, the service immediately returns an enhanced schema with an initial attribute matching. This initial matching is currently automatically generated from lettering equivalence using Levenshtein distance function over the combination of ontology class label and previously matched attributes to that class. In the future, the implementation of word embedding should help implementing a more efficient automatic matching engine. It is worth mentioning that the service does not automatically match attributes to multiple ontology classes as this is left to the schema owner to define richer context for attributes.

During the next phase, the schema owner validates and modifies the attribute matching. To assist with the matching process, the service provides upon request the five closest alternatives to a given attribute. If the schema owner does not find an adequate match for an attribute, the service can provide the taxonomy of the ontology, the bare tree of ontology classes, with a few selected properties to aid in finding a suitable class match. If the schema owner still cannot find a match for an attribute, the schema owner may submit a request to add a new class to the ontology. Upon receiving the request, the service places the data source registration on hold, records the request and transfers the request to the domain experts in charge of curating the ontology. The domain experts in turn, may choose to add a new class or make a recommendation to the schema owner. In both cases, a notification is sent back to the schema owner to complete the registration.

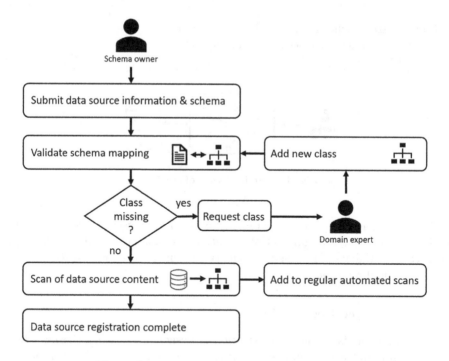

Fig. 5. Sequence during data source registration.

During attribute matching, the schema owner is also responsible for providing a set of 'equivalencies axioms'. The concept is very important to fully leverage the ontology. Some classes are outside the attribute-bound tree of classes. They are part of neighboring trees holding additional segments of knowledge; but they are not matched to attributes or connected to classes matched to attributes through relationships. These classes may still be linked to schema attributes through equivalency axioms. An equivalency axiom is illustrated by Eq. 1. It links an ontology class to a query expression recognized by the data source. These equivalency axioms are used during query conversion.

$$: Isotropic <=> \text{``}material\_structure\text{''} = 1 \qquad (1)$$

Once the service receives the final schema complemented with attribute matching, internal connections, and equivalency axioms, the service can complete the data source registration. The source general information is added to the source registry, the schema is parsed to extract operational data, and the attribute matching is modified to aggregate for each value-carrying attribute, the sequence of classes along its schema branch. Finally, for each listed equivalency axiom and value-carrying attribute, a new *individual*, an instance of an ontology class, is added to the ontology to store the necessary information in the form of individual 'data properties' to build a query for the newly registered data source.

The number of data properties depends on the type of database, and whether the individual holds information about an attribute or an equivalency axiom. The data properties may include the data type as well to check for type consistency and unit for unit conversion.

The individuals are named after their parent class names. The individuals are grouped under unique IRIs for each data source. This construction allows easy identification of the content stored inside the ontology and facilitates maintenance operations. When an attribute is attached to more than one class, its individual is attached to each of these classes and its name composed by combining class names, alphabetically sorted. The naming convention is designed for easy parsing using regular expression.

During the generation of individuals, the service creates in parallel a two-way dictionary between attributes and classes. This dictionary is used during the initial phase of query conversion from the original query language to a composition based on ontology classes. After the data source registration is complete, the newly added data source joins the pool of already available data sources and becomes available for users to query.

3.5   Query

Users have access to a query function to search the aggregated data content from the registered data sources. Figure 6 illustrates the query workflow. It hinges on the initial selection of a schema by the user. The schema sets the language for the original query and the format for the returned data content.

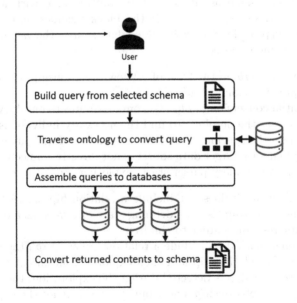

Fig. 6. Sequence during a query.

The query language is a combination of a generic query framework and a well nested declarative environment. The query framework includes logical operators (AND, OR, NOT) as well as parentheses to create groups. The nested declarative environment is generated by merging two dictionaries and adding the list of ontology relationships and associated class names. The first dictionary is the one mentioned in the previous section, extracted from the user schema between attributes and ontology classes. The second dictionary is extracted from the ontology itself with the associations between ontology class labels and ontology class names. The two dictionaries are merged by replacing any equivalent attribute/class entry inside the ontology dictionary by the one found inside the schema dictionary. Once composed, the nested declarative environment is used to do the initial conversion of the query to an intermediary form with ontology class names in place of attributes. The nested declarative environment is also used to implement an auto-complete feature to assist with early query composition and partial validation. The auto-complete feature can suggest attribute names from partially typed attributes, isolate invalid ones, check relationships, validate value types, and verify unit compatibility.

The format of a generic query is a set of logically bounded and grouped functional blocks. The query parser assumes a linguistic typology of "*subject verb object*" for the query blocks. The generic subject is assumed to be '*data*'. The '*object*' can be either be a logical expression, a numerical expression, or a string expression.

- A logical expression tests existence, and the '*object*' should be a single term,
- A string expression associates a term and a specific string with equality '=',
- A numerical expression associates a term and a value with a comparison operator =, <>, <, >, <=, >=. If the block includes unit and the unit information was provided for the intended data source, the value is converted, and the unit name removed.

In the presence of a '*verb*' in the form of a known relationship, the query parser expects a logical expression as '*object*'.

After the initial conversion of *objects* from attributes to ontology classes, the query parser accesses the ontology to find the necessary individuals to continue the conversion into the specific query language of each data source. In the case where an individual for a target data source is not directly connected to the class found as the *object*, the query parser starts exploring the ontology to find one.

- If the functional block does not include a relationship as '*verb*', the query parser assumes either an '*is*' as a defining state or a '*has*' as a defining property; and explores from parent to children.
- If the functional block does include a relationship as '*verb*', the query parser first traverses the relationship and then explores from parent to children. If an identical relationship is detected during the exploration, the query parser traverses the new relationship; and from there, continues the exploration.
- If multiple individuals are found during the exploration, the original block is converted into as many blocks as the number of found individuals.

The key to the query conversion is the effective exploration of the ontology to find individuals attached to data sources. The process can partially be driven by the SPARQL query language. However, the SPARQL language is explicit which limits lateral exploration over unknown layers of class relationships. The work of Reuter et al. [13] proposed to solve the issue by adding an additional keyword to the SPARQL language for recursive searches. Our service uses a dedicated programming language for the exploration and traversing of the ontology in place of SPARQL.

The outcome of the query conversion is a set of new queries for each of the registered data sources. If the query parser fails to compose a new query, the associated data source is excluded. Once composed, these new queries are sent to their respective data sources. The returned data content is then converted using schema mapping to the user schema. During this operation, if units are specified in both the source and destination schemas, values as well as unit names may also be converted.

The combination of attribute matching, schema mapping, operational workflows, simplified query language with the use of an ontology at the core creates an effective and functional body for the live data consolidation service.

4   Application

The aggregation of materials data sources is the original motivation for this article. Applications in Computer Aided Design, Computer Aided Manufacturing, and Computer Animation, all rely on materials data to accurately represent and simulate reality in the digital world. However, materials data is historically scattered and often application specific. The intent for building a live data consolidation service for materials data is to facilitate access to these data sources, increase the available content, and by doing so, open new research in data validation, characterization, surrogate modeling, and the discovery of new materials. The core for this implementation of the live data consolidation service is its material ontology.

4.1   Materials Ontology

The history of material ontologies is a mix of generic and dedicated approaches. One of the earliest published materials ontology, the Plinius ontology [14] focused on ceramic materials. The effort was followed by many other ontologies with diverse degrees of refinements. More recently, Premkumar et al. [12] established the Semantic LAminated Composites Knowledge management System or SLACKS, to bridge composite materials and their manufacturing processes. On the generic side, Ashino [2] established one of the earliest set of classes for materials. Cheung et al. [4] created a platform called MatOnto for materials data integration using a generic ontology to facilitate research.

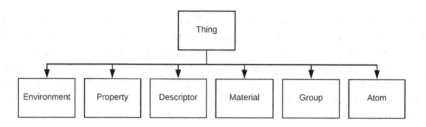

Fig. 7. Top layer of the materials ontology.

Our base ontology is inspired by the work of Ashino [2]. Ashino was one of the first to establish a well-recognized generic ontology structure to describe materials. His ontology focused on material types, families, environment and properties. While Ashino designed his ontology for direct storage of the data inside the ontology, our ontology only serves as a middleman to unify data sources. As such, Ashino's instance properties, *Object Properties* and *Datatype Properties* are data source attributes in our context and present in the ontology as standalone classes instead. The first layer of our ontology is illustrated by Fig. 7. This materials ontology before service activation has an initial set of around 50 classes. The ontology was also enhanced with the periodic table to connect materials to their chemical compositions. The periodic table adds about 120 classes and 200 individuals.

4.2   Query Examples

Here is a list of query examples for materials data.

Use of an equivalency axiom - Using the Eq. 1, and given the query:

$$query: \quad NOT \quad Isotropic \tag{2}$$

'*Isotropic*' is first replaced by the class '*:Isotropic*' and then replaced by the expression '$(material\_structure = 1)$' upon finding the equivalency axiom inside the ontology. The results are materials with '$material\_structure$' different from 1; which covers mostly composite materials, such as:

- Fiber reinforced polymers from polymer data sources,
- Reinforced concretes from construction data sources.

Traversing the ontology using class relationships - Given the query:

$$query: \quad isNamedAfter \quad Acrylate \tag{3}$$

'*Acrylate*' is converted to the class *:Acrylate* and this class is linked through the '*isNamedAfter*' relationship to four classes. Each with an equivalency axiom linking to the polymer data source:

- :AcryloNitrile with '*category* = acrylonitrile'
- :MethylMethacrylate with '*category* = methylmethacrylate'
- :PolyCyanoAcrylate with '*category* = methylmethacrylate'
- :PolyMethylMethAcrylate with '*category* = polymethylmethacrylate'

The results are the grades (commercial types) for the above categories.

Combined query capabilities - Given the query:

$$
\begin{aligned}
query: \quad Polymer \quad & AND \quad young\_modulus > 500 \quad ksi \\
& AND \quad young\_modulus < 550 \quad ksi \\
& AND \quad density > 0.2 \quad lb/in^3 \\
& AND \quad density < 0.5 \quad lb/in^3
\end{aligned} \tag{4}
$$

- '*Polymer*' becomes the class '*:Polymer*' and access the first source with the equivalency '*material_type = polymer*' and access the other source by combining children classes with the insert '*family = thermoplastic* AND *family = thermoset* AND *family = elastomer*',
- '*young_modulus*' becomes for one source '*elastic_modulus*' and for the other '*young_mod*',
- One of the source uses SI units. The young modulus is searched in '*ksi*' and the stored unit is in '*GPa*'. Therefore, the values and units are transformed during query conversion to '*GPa*' and the returned data content from that source converted back to '*ksi*'. A similar unit conversion applies to the densities.

The results are various grades (commercial types) of:

- Nylon 12
- Polyether Block amid

5   Conclusions

This article introduced an innovative and viable service architecture to access multiple heterogeneous data sources using live data consolidation. The architecture is portable and has a versatile engine for data standardization. The core of its architecture is its ontology. The ontology acts as a common language to federate data structures and attributes between data sources. The ontology also expands query capabilities with little overhead, well beyond the ones made available by the original data sources. Overall, this article illustrates the capacity for an ontology to serve as a preprocessor to connect computing resources and enhance their capabilities by leveraging its stored knowledge.

References

1. Ali, M.G.: A multidatabase system as 4-tiered client-server distributed heterogeneous database system. Int. J. Comput. Sci. Inf. Secur. **6**(2), 10–14 (2009)
2. Ashino, T.: Materials ontology: an infrastructure for exchanging materials information and knowledge. Data Sci. J. **9**, 54–61 (2010)
3. Berners-lee, T., Hendler, J., Lassila, O.: The semantic web: a new form of web content that is meaningful to computers will unleash a revolution of new possibilities. Sci. Am. **284**(5) (2001)
4. Cheung, K., Drennan, J., Hunter, J.: Towards an ontology for data-driven discovery of new materials. In: Semantic Scientific Knowledge Integration AAAI/SSS Workshop, pp. 9–14. Stanford University, Palo Alto (2008)
5. Duong, L., Kanayama, H., Ma, T., Bird, S., Cohn, T.: Multilingual training of crosslingual word embeddings. In: Proceedings of the 15th Conference of the European Chapter of the Association for Computational Linguistics, pp. 894–904 (2017)
6. Jurafsky, D., Martin, J.H.: Speech and language processing. https://web.stanford.edu/~jurafsky/slp3/
7. Konstantopoulos, S., Charalambidis, A., Mouchakis, G., Troumpoukis, A., Jakobitch, J., Karkaletsis, V.: Semantic web technologies and big data infrastructures: SPARQL federated querying of heterogeneous big data stores. In: International Semantic Web Conference (2016)
8. Liu, Z., Calve, A.L., Cretton, F., Glassey, N.: Using semantic web technologies in heterogeneous distributed database system a case study for managing energy data on mobile devices. Int. J. New Comput. Archit. Appl. **4**(2), 56–59 (2014)
9. Mecca, G., Rull, G., Santoro, D., Teniente, E.: Semantic-based mappings. In: Ng, W., Storey, V.C., Trujillo, J.C. (eds.) ER 2013. LNCS, vol. 8217, pp. 255–269. Springer, Heidelberg (2013). https://doi.org/10.1007/978-3-642-41924-9_22
10. Muzny, G., Zettlemoyer, L.S.: Automatic idiom identification in wiktionary. In: Proceedings of the 2013 Conference on Empirical Methods in Natural Language Processing, pp. 1417–1421 (2013)
11. Noaman, A., Essia, F., Salah, M.: Web services based integration tool for heterogeneous databases. Int. J. Res. Eng. Sci. **1**(3), 16–26 (2013)
12. Premkumar, V., Krishamurty, S., Wileden, J.C., Grosse, I.R.: A semantic knowledge management system for laminated composites. Adv. Eng. Inform. **28**, 91–101 (2014)
13. Reutter, J.L., Soto, A., Vrgoč, D.: Recursion in SPARQL. In: Arenas, M., et al. (eds.) ISWC 2015. LNCS, vol. 9366, pp. 19–35. Springer, Cham (2015). https://doi.org/10.1007/978-3-319-25007-6_2
14. van der Vet, P.E., Speel, P.H., Mars, N.J.: The Plinius ontology of ceramic materials. In: Proceedings of Comparison of Implemented Ontologies Workshop (1994)
15. Xiao, G., et al.: Ontology-based data access: a survey. In: Proceedings of the Twenty-Seventh International Joint Conference on Artificial Intelligence, IJCAI 2108, pp. 5511–5519 (2018)
16. Zhang, R., Wang, J., Bu, W.: Research on attribute matching method in heterogeneous databases semantic integration. J. Chem. Pharm. Res. **7**(3), 16–26 (2015)
17. Zhao, S., Qian, Q.: Ontology based heterogeneous materials database integration and semantic query. AIP Adv. **7**(10) (2017)

EmbNum: Semantic Labeling for Numerical Values with Deep Metric Learning

Phuc Nguyen[1,2(✉)], Khai Nguyen[2], Ryutaro Ichise[1,2], and Hideaki Takeda[1,2]

[1] SOKENDAI (The Graduate University for Advanced Studies),
Shonan Village, Hayama, Kanagawa, Japan
[2] National Institute of Informatics, 2-1-2 Hitotsubashi, Chiyoda-ku, Tokyo, Japan
{phucnt,nhkhai,ichise,takeda}@nii.ac.jp

Abstract. Semantic labeling for numerical values is a task of assigning semantic labels to unknown numerical attributes. The semantic labels could be numerical properties in ontologies, instances in knowledge bases, or labeled data that are manually annotated by domain experts. In this paper, we refer to semantic labeling as a retrieval setting where the label of an unknown attribute is assigned by the label of the most relevant attribute in labeled data. One of the greatest challenges is that an unknown attribute rarely has the same set of values with the similar one in the labeled data. To overcome the issue, statistical interpretation of value distribution is taken into account. However, the existing studies assume a specific form of distribution. It is not appropriate in particular to apply open data where there is no knowledge of data in advance. To address these problems, we propose a neural numerical embedding model (*EmbNum*) to learn useful representation vectors for numerical attributes without prior assumptions on the distribution of data. Then, the "semantic similarities" between the attributes are measured on these representation vectors by the Euclidean distance. Our empirical experiments on City Data and Open Data show that *EmbNum* significantly outperforms state-of-the-art methods for the task of numerical attribute semantic labeling regarding effectiveness and efficiency.

Keywords: Metric learning · Semantic labeling · Number embedding

1 Introduction

Thanks to the Open Data movement, a large number of table data resources have been published on the Web or Open Data portals. In a study of Lehmberg et al., 233 million tables were extracted from the July 2015 version of the Common Crawl[1] [11]. Additionally, Mitlohner et al. performed characteristics analysis of 200,000 tables from 232 Open Data portals [13]. These resources could be

---

[1] http://commoncrawl.org/.

© Springer Nature Switzerland AG 2018
R. Ichise et al. (Eds.): JIST 2018, LNCS 11341, pp. 119–135, 2018.
https://doi.org/10.1007/978-3-030-04284-4_9

integrated, and enabling them to be potentially useful for other applications such as table search [14,16], table extension [12], completion [2], or knowledge base construction as used in DBpedia [30], YAGO [21], Freebase [5].

However, these data resources are very heterogeneous. Each data resource is independently constructed by different people with different backgrounds, purposes, and contexts. Therefore, the use of vocabulary and schema structure might differ across various data resources. For example, one attribute uses "population" as the table header label; another table uses "number of people." Do those two attributes labels share the same meaning or different ones? As a result, the "semantic heterogeneity" may lead to the propagation of misinformation in the data integrating process.

To provide a unified view of the heterogeneous resources, one of the possible solutions is to assign a semantic label for each attribute in unknown resources. The semantic labels could be properties in ontologies, instances in knowledge bases, or labeled attributes manually annotated by domain experts. In this paper, the problem of semantic labeling is formulated as a retrieval setting where the label of an unknown attribute is assigned by the label of the most relevant attribute in labeled data. In other words, given a query as a list of values of an unknown attribute, the system will return a ranking list of the relevant labeled attributes with respect to a specific similarity metric. The label of the unknown attribute is assigned by the label of the most relevant one in the ranking list.

The most common approaches for semantic labeling use textual information, such as header labels, textual values, or table description. Previous studies [1, 6,19,26,27,30] used text-based entity linkage to search for similar concepts in knowledge bases. Then, semantic labels can be inferred by using semantic labels of matched entities in the knowledge base. However, many attributes do not have overlapping entity labels with the knowledge bases. Even if some data overlap, many attributes do not have similar labels with the entities in knowledge bases because these are expressed as numbers, IDs, codes, or abbreviations [15]. Therefore, a text-based approach cannot directly be used on these table data.

Another direction of semantic labeling uses numerical information. As mentioned in a study by Mitlohner et al., 50% of the table data taken from Open Data portals contain numerical values [13]. Prior studies [15,17,18,24] used descriptive statistics with hypothesis tests as a metric to compare the similarity of numerical attributes. However, these hypothesis tests often rely on the assumption that these attributes have to be drawn from a specific form of distribution (e.g., normal distribution or uniform distribution) or data types (e.g., continuous or discrete). Knowing the form of distributions and data types of unknown numerical attributes is a difficult challenge. As a result, a proper hypothesis test cannot be easily selected when we do not know data distribution and data type.

In recent years, there has been an increasing interest in using deep metric learning to learn similarity metric directly from data [8,20,23]. The principal advantage of this technique is an ability to learn the feature representation and the similarity metric in an end-to-end fashion. Inspired by their success and an assumption with shared meanings of numerical attributes across different data resources, we explored whether or not deep metric learning can be used to learn a metric in measuring the "semantic similarity" of numerical attributes without making any assumption on data type, or data distribution. Indeed, we used a representation network consisting of a triplet network and convolutional neural network (CNN) to learn a non-linear mapping function from numerical attributes to a transformed space. In other words, the non-linear mapping function was used as an embedding model to derive the latent features for numerical attributes. The "semantic similarity" of two numerical attributes was calculated on two extracted features using the Euclidean distance.

We also introduced an inverse transform sampling [28] to deal with the issues of varying input size of table numerical attributes. The representation network required a fixed size as the input, but the size of numerical attributes could vary from a few numerical values to thousands of them [13]. The sampling technique can capture the original distribution of numerical attributes, thereby overcoming the issue of varying the size of the input attributes. Moreover, the sampling technique also helps to speed up data processing since a small number of data values is considered instead of entire values of the attribute.

Overall, our contributions to this paper are as follows.

1. We propose a novel model called *EmbNum* to learn the representation and the similarity metric from numerical attributes. *EmbNum* is constructed by jointly learning the representation and the similarity metric from numerical attributes in an end-to-end setting.
2. We introduced an inverse transform sampling approach to handle the issue of varying the size of numerical attributes. The sampling technique can simulate the original distribution of numerical attributes.
3. We created a new dataset (Open Data) extracted from tables of Open Data portals to test semantic labeling in the open environment. The dataset is available at https://github.com/phucty/embnum.
4. We conducted benchmarks of *EmbNum* and two baseline approaches, i.e., SemanticTyper [18] and DSL [17] on the standard data, e.g., City Data [18] and real-world data, e.g., Open Data. The overall results show that using *EmbNum* achieved better performance of semantic labeling for numerical attributes on effectiveness and efficiency.

The rest of this paper is organized as follows. In Sect. 2, we discuss the related works in the task of semantic labeling for table data as well as representation learning techniques. In Sect. 3, we present the preliminaries and overall framework of our approach. Section 4 presents the details of our evaluation. Finally, we summarize the paper and discuss the future direction in Sect. 5.

2 Related Work

In this section, we present the previous approaches for semantic labeling with textual information and numerical information. Next, we will briefly present related works on representation learning.

2.1   Semantic Labeling with Textual Information:

These studies address the problem of semantic labeling for table attributes using the information on header labels and textual values [6,19,30]. The most common technique used entity linkage for mapping textual values of attributes to entities in a knowledge base. After that, the schema of entities was used to find the semantic concept for table attributes. Also, the additional textual descriptions of tables were considered in the studies of [1,26,27] which improve the performance of the labeling task. Beside textual information, numerical information should be used in other ways to build an effective integrated system.

2.2   Semantic Labeling with Numerical Information:

Several attempts have been made on using descriptive statistics with hypothesis tests as similarity metrics to compare the similarity of numerical attributes. Stonebraker et al. [24] used the Welch's t-test [10] as a similar metric to compare attributes of numerical data. SemanticTyper [18] used the Kolmogorov Skmiro test (KS test) [10] to compare the empirical distribution of numerical attributes. SemanticTyper achieved better performance than using the Welch's t-test. Pham et al. [17] (DSL) extended SemanticTyper by proposing a new similarity metric that is a combination of the KS test and two other metrics: the Mann-Whitney test (MW test) and the numeric Jaccard similarity. Their experiments showed that using the combined metric provided better results over using only a KS test. Neumaier et al. [15] created a numeric background knowledge base from DBpedia. Given an unknown numerical attribute, they used the KS test as a similarity metric to compare with each labeled attribute in the numeric background knowledge base. Overall, the similarity metrics used in these approaches are hypothesis tests which are calculated under a specific assumption about data type, and data distribution. In contrast to these approaches, we propose a neural numerical embedding model to learn a similarity metric directly from data without making any assumption about data type and data distribution.

2.3   Representation Learning

Deep metric learning has achieved considerable success in extracting useful representations of data [3,22,29]. Moreover, the features extracted with deep neural networks can be used for other tasks [23]. Florian et al. proposed a triplet network that takes an anchor, a positive sample (of the same class as the anchor), and negative sample (of a different class than an anchor) examples, to learn a mapping function to embed the anchor closer to the positive example than the negative example [20]. Herman et al. [8] proposed a method for triplet mining that selects hard examples for the learning network. It will help in training the network more efficiently. In this study, we used a representation network, which is a combination of a CNN network and triplet network, to learn a metric to measure the similarity between numerical attributes. We also introduced a sampling technique to handle the issue of varying input size of numerical attributes.

3   Approach

In this sections, we first describe the preliminary concepts (Sect. 3.1) as well as the formal definition for semantic labeling. Then, we present the overall framework in Sect. 3.2. The details explanation for each module of the framework is provided in Sects. 3.3, 3.4, and 3.5.

3.1   Preliminaries

Numerical Attributes. We call table columns as the attributes of tables. We assume that all values in one attribute have the same meaning and that shared meanings exist across tables. If all values in an attribute are numerical, we call the attribute as a numerical attribute. If not, we call it as a textual attribute. In this paper, we only consider a similarity metric between numerical attributes to infer semantic meaning. The similarity metric for a textual attribute is out of the scope of this paper. Notably, we did not tackle the problem of data scaling. For instance, if two attributes were found to have the same meaning, but they were expressed in different scales, we considered that the two attributes have a different meaning. Techniques for interpreting data scaling is left as future work.

Semantic Labeling Definition. Let $A = \{a_1, a_2, a_3, ..., a_n\}$ be a list of n numerical attributes and $Y = \{y_1, y_2, y_3, ..., y_m\}$ be a list of m semantic labels, where $m \leqslant n$. We have a data sample (a, y) with $a \in A$ and $y \in Y$ that is a pair of a numerical attribute and its semantic label. All data samples are stored in a D database.

Given an unknown attribute a_q, similarity searching is performed on all data samples in the D database with respect to specific similarity metric. The output is a ranked list of the most relevant samples. The semantic label of the top result is assigned to the label of the unknown attribute.

3.2   Overall Approach

Figure 1 depicts the workflow of the semantic labeling task with *EmbNum* which consists of two main phases: *representation learning* and *semantic labeling*.

In the *representation learning* phase, the *preprocessing* module generate samples from the original distribution of *labeled attributes*. After that, these samples are used as input for the *representation learning* module. The output of the *representation learning* is an *embedding model* which is used in the *feature extracting* module in the *semantic labeling* phase.

In the *semantic labeling* phase, *labeled attributes* also performed sampling with the *prepossessing* module and then deriving feature vectors with the *feature extracting* module. The embedding model from the previous phase is used as the feature extractor for preprocessed attributes in the feature extracting module. These feature vectors are stored in the feature *database* for future similarity comparison. Suppose we have to perform semantic labeling for an unknown

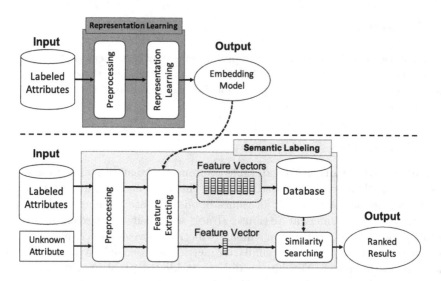

Fig. 1. The general architecture of semantic labeling with *EmbNum*

attribute, again the *preprocessing* module and *feature extracting* are performed to get the feature vector. Next, the *similarity searching* module is performed to calculate the Euclidean distance of the feature vector of the unknown attribute with all the feature vectors in the *database*. Finally, the system returns a ranking list of the most relevant attributes. The label of the top result (the most similar) is assigned to the unknown attribute.

3.3   Preprocessing Module

Because the size of numerical attributes could vary from a few to thousands of values, we use inverse transform sampling [28] to standardize the input size. This technique is chosen because it retains the original distribution of a given list of numerical values. After sampling, the list of numerical values is sorted in a specific order to leverage the capability of the CNN network to learn representations from the cumulative distribution of numerical attributes. The inverse transform sampling is described as follows.

Inverse Transform Sampling. Given a numerical attribute $a \in A$ has numerical values $V_a = \{v_1, v_2, v_3, ..., v_n\}$. We treat V_a as a discrete distribution, then the cumulative distribution function (CDF) of $v \in V_a$ is $F_{V_a}(v)$ as follows.

$$F_{V_a}(v) = P(V_a \leqslant v), v \in V_a, F_{V_a} : \mathbb{R} \to [0, 1] \tag{1}$$

$P(.)$ represents the probability of values in V_a less than or equal to v. The inverse distribution function of $F_{V_a}(.)$ takes the probability p as input and return $v \in V_a$ as follows.

$$F_{V_a}^{-1}(p) = min\{v : F_{V_a}(v) \geqslant p\}, p \in [0, 1] \tag{2}$$

We select h numbers (Sect. 4.3) from V_a with each number is the output of the inverse distribution function $F_{V_a}^{-1}(p)$ with probability $p \in \mathcal{P} = \{\frac{i}{h} | i \in \{1, 2, 3, ..., h\}\}$. For example, when $h = 100$, then $\mathcal{P} = \{0.01, 0.02, 0.03, ..., 1\}$. For each attribute $a \in A$, we have a preprocessed numerical attribute $x = \{v_1, v_2, v_3, ..., v_h\}$.

In summary, given a list of attributes $A = \{a_1, a_2, a_3, ..., a_n\}$, after preprocessing, we have a list of preprocessed attributes $X = \{x_1, x_2, x_3, ..., x_n\}$.

Sampling Analysis. In this section, we present an analysis of how well the samples of the inverse transform sampling fit with original data. We also present a comparison of the sampling results of the inverse transform sampling with the random-choice sampling technique, where a random sample was extracted from a given list of numerical values.

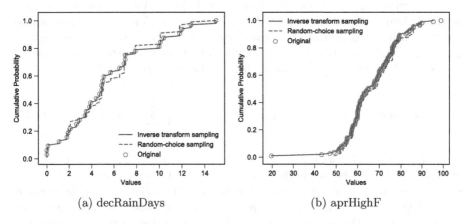

(a) decRainDays   (b) aprHighF

Fig. 2. Analysis of inverse transform sampling and random-choice sampling on the *decRainDays* property (a) and the *aprHighF* property (b) of City Data. (Color figure online)

Figure 2 depicts the sampling results of two sampling techniques on the *decRainDays* property and the *aprHighF* property of City Data. The distribution of sampling from the inverse transforms (the blue curve) clearly fit the original distribution (the red circles) better than the random-choice sampling did (the green curve). Therefore, in our experiments, we used the inverse transform sampling for preprocessing data.

3.4   Representation Learning Phase

Figure 3 depicts the architecture of representation learning phase given a list vectors $X = \{x_1, x_2, x_3, ..., x_n\}$ of n numerical attributes and their m semantic labels $Y = \{y_1, y_2, y_3, ..., y_m\}$. The blue square, and red circle indicate the semantic label y_1 and the semantic label y_2, respectively, where $y_1 \neq y_2$.

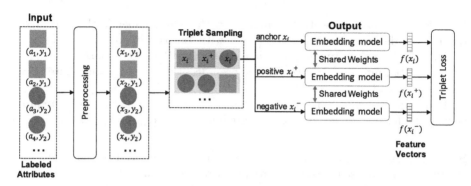

Fig. 3. Representation learning architecture (Color figure online)

We used a triplet network [20] to learn a $f(.)$ function to map a numerical attribute into an embedding space. For an input x, $f(x)$ is the output of a representation learning network to convert x into a k dimensions Euclidean space, $f(x) \in \mathbb{R}^k$. The similarity distance between two numerical attributes x_i and x_j is calculated by using the Euclidean distance between $f(x_i)$ and $f(x_j)$:

$$d_f(x_i, x_j) = d(f(x_i), f(x_j)) = ||f(x_i) - f(x_j)||_2^2 = \sqrt{\sum_{k=1}^{m}(f(x_i)_k - f(x_j)_k)^2} \quad (3)$$

A triplet (x, x^+, x^-) with $(x, x^+, x^- \in X)$ is a combination of a numerical attribute x where the semantic label is y, a similar attribute x^+ where the semantic label is y, and a dissimilar attribute x^- where the semantic label is not y. The key idea of a triplet network relies on the empirical observation that the distance between the positive pair must be less than the distance between the negative pair $d_f(x, x^+) < d_f(x, x^-)$ [20]. Then, the loss function for the triplet network is defined as follows.

$$L = max(0, \alpha + d_f(x, x^+) - d_f(x, x^-)) \quad (4)$$

where α is a hyperparameter that regularizes between positive pair distance and negative pair distance.

We utilized the hard negative sampling method [20] to select triplets for training. The hard negative sampling is a technique of choosing the closest sample to an anchor among the dissimilar attributes in a mini-batch of learning. It will help the training process to converge faster.

Embedding Model with CNN Network: Many CNN architectures have been designed to capture latent features directly from data. In this work, we used ResNet 18 [7] because it provides good accuracy and requires fewer parameters to train [4]. Its architecture used ReLU as a non-linear activation function. To normalize the distribution of each input features in each layer, we have also used batch normalization [9] after each convolution, before each ReLU activation function. Because input data were one-dimension, we modified the structure of convolutional to one-dimension on convolutional layers, batch normalization layers, and pooling layers. The output of the network is a vector with k dimensions (Sect. 4.3).

3.5   Semantic Labeling Phase

Figure 4 depicts an example of semantic labeling for an unknown attribute. Given labeled attributes and their semantic labels $\{(a_1, y_1), (a_2, y_2), (a_3, y_3), ..., (a_n, y_m)\}$, first, the data were preprocessed as $\{(x_1, y_1), (x_2, y_2), (x_3, y_3), ..., (x_n, y_m)\}$. After that, we used the mapping function $f(.)$ to map all the labeled data to embedding space $\{(f(x_1), y_1), (f(x_2), y_2), (f(x_3), y_3), ..., (f(x_n), y_m)\}$. Those data were stored in the database D for the next comparison in the semantic labeling process.

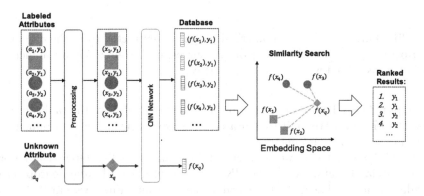

Fig. 4. Example of semantic labeling for an unknown attribute

Given an unknown attribute a_q, we performed the preprocessing to get x_q and the feature extracting to get $f(x_q)$. After that, we compared the Euclidean distance from $f(x_q)$ to each of the labeled data in D. Then we get a ranking list of the most similar attributes with $f(x_q)$. We assigned the semantic label of the top one of the ranking result to the unknown data.

4   Evaluation

In this section, we first describe benchmark datasets in Sect. 4.1 and evaluation metrics in Sect. 4.2. Next, the details about implementation of representation learning as well as the visualization of embedding features for numerical attributes are presented in Sect. 4.3. Finally, we report the experimental results of semantic labeling in terms of effectiveness and efficiency in Sect. 4.4.

4.1   Benchmark Datasets

To evaluate our proposed approach, we used two datasets i.e., City Data and Open Data. City Data is the standard data used in the previous studies [17,18]. Open Data is a newly built dataset extracted from tables of Open Data portals. All the table data were evaluated on the task of numerical attribute semantic labeling. The detailed statistics of each dataset are shown in Table 1.

Table 1. Description of City Data And Open data

	# Sources	# Labels	# Attributes	# Rows of each attribute			
				Min	Max	Median	Average
City Data	10	30	300	4	2,251	113	642.73
Open Data	10	50	500	4	186,082	467	14,659.63

The City Data [18] has 30 numerical properties extracted from the city class in DBpedia. The dataset consists of 10 sources; each source has 30 numerical attributes associated with 30 data properties.

The Open Data has 50 numerical properties extracted from the tables in five Open Data Portals. We built the dataset to test semantic labeling for numerical values in the open environment.

To build the dataset, we extracted table data from five Open Data portals, i.e., Ireland (data.gov.ie), the UK (data.gov.uk), the EU (data.europa.eu), Canada (open.canada.ca), and Australia (data.gov.au). First, we crawled CSV files from the five Open Data portals and selected files that had their sizes less than 50 MB. Then, we analyzed tables in CSV files and selected only numerical attributes. After that, we created attribute categories based on the clustering of the numerical attributes with respect to the textual similarity of column headers. We got 7,496 categories in total.

We manually evaluated these categories with two criteria: (1) The first criterion was to pick up categories with a certain frequency. By examining the collection of data, we found that high-frequency categories are often unclear on their semantics, while low-frequency categories are often unstable as data. We decided to pick up the categories with ten attributes by following the setting of City Data. (2) The second criterion was removing the categories where column headers had too general meanings such as "ID," "name," or "value."

Finally, we chose 50 categories as semantic labels; each semantic label had ten numerical attributes. Following the guideline of City Data, we also made 10 data sources by combining each numerical attributes from each category. The dataset is available at https://github.com/phucty/embnum.

4.2   Evaluation Metrics

We used the mean reciprocal rank score (MRR) to measure the effectiveness of semantic labeling. The MRR score was used in the previous studies [17,18] to measure the probability correctness of a ranking result list. To measure the efficiency of *EmbNum* over the baseline methods, we evaluated the run-time in seconds of the semantic labeling process.

4.3   Representation Learning Evaluation

We randomly divided City Data into two equal parts as 50% for learning a similarity metric, and 50% for evaluating the task of semantic labeling. The first part was used representation learning of *EmbNum*, and it had also used to learn the similarity metric for DSL. To learn the similarity metric for DSL, we followed their guideline that using logistic regression to train the similarity metrics where training samples are the pairs of numerical attributes [17].

We used PyTorch (http://pytorch.org) to implement the framework and experiments. We trained the network using stochastic gradient descent (SGD) with back-propagation, a momentum of 0.9, and a weight decay of 1E-5. We started with a learning rate of 0.01 and reduced it with a step size of 10 to finalize the model. We set the dimension of the attribute input vector h and the attribute output vector k as 100. Notice that we did not perform finding the optimal hyper-parameters of h, and k, the optimal hyper-parameter searching are left for future work. The representation learning was trained with 100 epochs. After each epoch, we evaluated the task of semantic labeling on the MRR score using the training data. We saved the learned model having the highest MRR score.

All of our experiments ran on Dell Precision 7710 with an Intel Xeon E3-1535M-CPU, 16 GB of RAM, and an NVIDIA Quadro M3000M GPU. The training time of *EmbNum* is 3,486 s while training time of DSL is 196 s. It is clear that *EmbNum* used with the deep learning approach needed more times to train the similarity metric than logistic regression with the DSL approach. However, the similarity metric is only needed to train once, and it could be applied to other domains without retraining.

Visualization of Embedding Features. Figure 5 shows the visualization of the embedding features of numerical attributes from City Data. We used t-SNE visualization [25] that projects the output features of the representation model from k dimensions into two dimensions. The left figure depicts the state before learning the representation, while the right figure depicts the state after learning. It is clear from the visualization that the distance between two similar semantic labels is close, and the distance between different semantic labels is far after the representation learning. It means the learning process has learned good representations for numerical attributes.

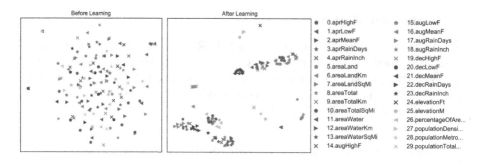

Fig. 5. t-SNE visualization [25] of City Data embedding vectors

4.4   Semantic Labeling Evaluation

This section describes the evaluation of semantic labeling in terms of effectiveness and efficiency of *EmbNum* and the two baseline approaches: SemanticTyper [18] and DSL [17].

Experimental Setting. Suppose a dataset $S = \{s_1, s_2, s_3, ..., s_d\}$ has d data sources. One data source was retained as the unknown data, and the remaining $d - 1$ data sources were used as the labeled data. We repeated this process d times, with each of the data source used exactly once as the unknown data. Additionally, we set the number of sources in the labeled data increase from one source to $d - 1$ sources to analyze the effect of increment in the number of labeled data on the performance of semantic labeling. It is noticed that we tested all possible combinations of labeled sources. We obtained the MRR scores and labeling times on $d \times (2^{d-1} - 1)$ experiments and then averaged them to produce the $d - 1$ estimations of the number of sources in the labeled data.

Table 2 depicts the experiment setting on City Data with five data sources. From 1st experiment to 15th experiment, s_1 is assigned as the unknown sources, the remaining sources are the labeled sources. The labeled data which have one source is tested in the 1st–4th experiment, whereas in the 5th–15th, more labeled sources are tested. We conducted a similar approach for the remaining experiments. Overall, we performed 75 experiments on the five sources of City Data, and 5,110 experiments on the ten sources of Open Data.

Experimental Results Regarding Effectiveness. We tested Semantic-Typer, DSL, and *EmbNum* on the semantic labeling task using the MRR score to evaluate the effectiveness. The results are shown in Table 3 and Fig. 6.

The MRR scores obtained by three methods steadily increase along with the number of labeled sources. It suggests that the more labeled sources in the database, the more accurate the assigned semantic labels are. DSL outperformed SemanticTyper because DSL uses a combined metric that includes multiple similarity features, while SemanticTyper uses only the KS test. *EmbNum* learned

Table 2. Experiment setting of semantic labeling on City Data with five data sources

Experiment	1	2	3	4	5	6	7	8	9	10	11	12	13	14	15	16	...	75
Unknown source	s_1	s_1	s_1	s_1	s_1	s_1	s_1	s_1	s_1	s_1	s_1	s_1	s_1	s_1	s_1	s_2	...	s_5
Labeled sources	s_2	s_3	s_4	s_5	s_2	s_2	s_2	s_3	s_3	s_4	s_2	s_2	s_2	s_3	s_2	s_1	...	s_1
					s_3	s_4	s_5	s_4	s_5	s_5	s_3	s_3	s_4	s_4	s_3		...	s_2
											s_4	s_5	s_5	s_5	s_4		...	s_3
															s_5		...	s_4

Table 3. Semantic Labeling in the MRR score on City Data and Open Data

Data	Method	Labeled sources								
		1	2	3	4	5	6	7	8	9
City	SemanticTyper[18]	0.816	0.861	0.878	0.890	-	-	-	-	-
	DSL[17]	0.857	0.861	0.898	0.906	-	-	-	-	-
	EmbNum	**0.867**	**0.893**	**0.905**	**0.913**	-	-	-	-	-
Open	SemanticTyper[18]	0.324	0.371	0.4070	0.425	0.444	0.456	0.464	0.468	0.471
	DSL[17]	0.538	0.566	0.584	0.597	0.606	0.614	0.620	0.626	0.631
	EmbNum	**0.554**	**0.587**	**0.609**	**0.623**	**0.632**	**0.638**	**0.644**	**0.647**	**0.651**

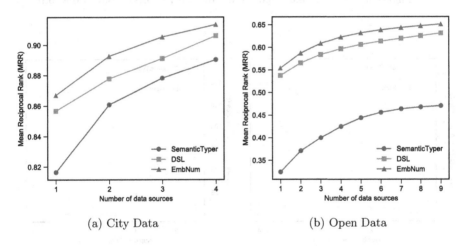

(a) City Data   (b) Open Data

Fig. 6. Semantic Labeling in the MRR score on City Data and Open Data

directly from the input without making any assumption on data type and data distribution, hence, outperformed SemanticTyper and DSL on both of datasets. The similarity metric based on a specific hypothesis test, which was used in SemanticTyper and DSL, is not optimized for semantic meanings with various data types and distributions.

To understand whether *EmbNum* does significantly outperform Semantic-Typer and DSL, we performed a paired sample t-test on the experiments of City Data and Open Data. We set the cutoff value for determining statistical significance to 0.01. The results of the paired t-test revealed that *EmbNum* significantly outperforms SemanticTyper ($p < 0.0001$) and DSL ($p = 0.0068$) on City Data. The similar results could be obtained on Open Data, where *EmbNum* significantly outperforms SemanticTyper ($p < 0.0001$) and DSL ($p < 0.0001$).

Experimental Results Regarding Efficiency. Table 4 and Fig. 7 depict the run-time of semantic labeling on SemanticTyper, DSL, and *EmbNum*.

Table 4. Run-time in seconds of semantic labeling on City Data and Open Data

Data	Method	Labeled sources								
		1	2	3	4	5	6	7	8	9
City	SemanticTyper [18]	0.3	0.4	0.4	0.5	-	-	-	-	-
	DSL [17]	1.6	3.1	4.7	6.3	-	-	-	-	-
	EmbNum	**0.1**	**0.1**	**0.2**	**0.2**	-	-	-	-	-
Open	SemanticTyper [18]	8.5	12.8	17.2	21.8	26.7	31.2	35.9	40.6	45.8
	DSL [17]	18.7	37.4	55.4	73.6	92.1	110.6	129.2	149.1	168
	EmbNum	**0.6**	**0.6**	**0.6**	**0.7**	**0.7**	**0.8**	**0.8**	**0.8**	**0.9**

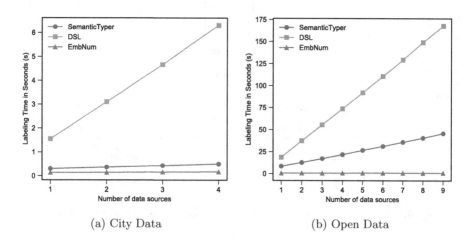

(a) City Data   (b) Open Data

Fig. 7. Run-time in seconds of semantic labeling on City Data and Open Data

The run-time of semantic labeling linearly increases with the number of labeled sources. The run-time of DSL was extremely high when the number of labeled data sources increased because three similarity metrics were needed to be performed. The run-time of SemanticTyper was less than DSL because it only used the KS test as a similarity metric. Semantic labeling with *EmbNum* is significantly faster than SemanticTyper (about 25 times), and DSL (about 92 times). *EmbNum* outperforms the baseline approaches in run-time since the similarity metric of *EmbNum* was calculated directly on extracted feature vectors instead of all original values.

5   Conclusion

In this paper, we proposed the *EmbNum* model to learn a useful representation and a similarity metric for numerical attributes. We also proposed a preprocessing method by sampling the numerical values in attributes. The experimental results of the representation learning show that the embedding model can capture good latent features from numerical attributes. In a task of semantic labeling, the performance results of *EmbNum* significantly outperforms the baseline approaches on City Data, and Open Data. Additionally, our model does not assume distribution forms of data while the baseline approaches do. As a result, *EmbNum* is more suitable to apply open data where we do not know data distribution forms in advance.

In future work, we plan to extend our work in the three directions. The first direction is to extend the similarity metric to interpret multiple scales. In this study, we assume that two numerical attributes are similar when they are expressed on the same scale. In fact, two attributes in the same meaning could be measured using different scales. For instance, the numerical attributes "human height" could be expressed in "centimeters," but they could also be expressed in "feet." The second direction is to extend the metric to interpret the hierarchical representation of numerical data. The current presentation using the Euclidean distance cannot reflect the hierarchical structure. Building a similarity metric that is hierarchy-aware can help to make a more fine-grained semantic labeling. The third direction is to detect unseen semantic labels that are not available in labeled data. Although we can use *EmbNum* as a similarity metric to cluster unseen attributes before performing the task of semantic labeling, it cannot recognize new semantic types in the labeled data. In *EmbNum*, we assign the top one semantic types of labeled data for an unknown attribute. If the unknown attribute is a new semantic type, it will return an incorrect result. In future work, we will identify the suitable threshold for the similarity metric to recognize new semantic types.

References

1. Adelfio, M.D., Samet, H.: Schema extraction for tabular data on the web. Proc. VLDB Endow. **6**(6), 421–432 (2013)
2. Ahmadov, A., Thiele, M., Eberius, J., Lehner, W., Wrembel, R.: Towards a hybrid imputation approach using web tables. In: 2015 IEEE/ACM 2nd International Symposium on Big Data Computing (BDC), pp. 21–30 (2015)

3. Bengio, Y., et al.: Learning deep architectures for AI. Found. Trends®. Mach. Learn. **2**(1), 1–127 (2009)
4. Canziani, A., Paszke, A., Culurciello, E.: An analysis of deep neural network models for practical applications. arXiv preprint arXiv:1605.07678 (2016)
5. Dong, X., et al.: Knowledge vault: a web-scale approach to probabilistic knowledge fusion. In: Proceedings of the 20th ACM SIGKDD International Conference on Knowledge Discovery and Data Mining, pp. 601–610. ACM (2014)
6. Ermilov, I., Auer, S., Stadler, C.: User-driven semantic mapping of tabular data. In: Proceedings of the 9th International Conference on Semantic Systems, pp. 105–112. ACM (2013)
7. He, K., Zhang, X., Ren, S., Sun, J.: Deep residual learning for image recognition. In: Proceedings of the IEEE Conference on Computer Vision and Pattern Recognition, pp. 770–778 (2016)
8. Hermans, A., Beyer, L., Leibe, B.: In defense of the triplet loss for person re-identification. arXiv preprint arXiv:1703.07737 (2017)
9. Ioffe, S., Szegedy, C.: Batch normalization: accelerating deep network training by reducing internal covariate shift. In: Proceedings of the 32nd International Conference on International Conference on Machine Learning, ICML 2015, vol. 37, pp. 448–456. JMLR.org (2015)
10. Lehmann, E.L., Romano, J.P.: Testing Statistical Hypotheses. Springer, Heidelberg (2006). https://doi.org/10.1007/0-387-27605-X
11. Lehmberg, O., Ritze, D., Meusel, R., Bizer, C.: A large public corpus of web tables containing time and context metadata. In: Proceedings of the 25th International Conference Companion on World Wide Web, pp. 75–76. International World Wide Web Conferences Steering Committee (2016)
12. Lehmberg, O., Ritze, D., Ristoski, P., Meusel, R., Paulheim, H., Bizer, C.: The mannheim search join engine. Web Semant.: Sci. Serv. Agents World Wide Web **35**(P3), 159–166 (2015)
13. Mitlöhner, J., Neumaier, S., Umbrich, J., Polleres, A.: Characteristics of open data CSV files. In: 2016 2nd International Conference on Open and Big Data (OBD), pp. 72–79 (2016)
14. Nargesian, F., Zhu, E., Pu, K.Q., Miller, R.J.: Table union search on open data. Proc. VLDB Endow. **11**(7), 813–825 (2018)
15. Neumaier, S., Umbrich, J., Parreira, J.X., Polleres, A.: Multi-level semantic labelling of numerical values. In: Groth, P., et al. (eds.) ISWC 2016 Part I. LNCS, vol. 9981, pp. 428–445. Springer, Cham (2016). https://doi.org/10.1007/978-3-319-46523-4_26
16. Nguyen, T.T., Nguyen, Q.V.H., Weidlich, M., Aberer, K.: Result selection and summarization for web table search. In: 2015 IEEE 31st International Conference on Data Engineering (ICDE), pp. 231–242. IEEE (2015)
17. Pham, M., Alse, S., Knoblock, C.A., Szekely, P.: Semantic labeling: a domain-independent approach. In: Groth, P., et al. (eds.) ISWC 2016 Part I. LNCS, vol. 9981, pp. 446–462. Springer, Cham (2016). https://doi.org/10.1007/978-3-319-46523-4_27
18. Ramnandan, S.K., Mittal, A., Knoblock, C.A., Szekely, P.: Assigning semantic labels to data sources. In: Gandon, F., Sabou, M., Sack, H., d'Amato, C., Cudré-Mauroux, P., Zimmermann, A. (eds.) ESWC 2015. LNCS, vol. 9088, pp. 403–417. Springer, Cham (2015). https://doi.org/10.1007/978-3-319-18818-8_25
19. Ritze, D., Lehmberg, O., Bizer, C.: Matching html tables to DBpedia. In: Proceedings of the 5th International Conference on Web Intelligence, Mining and Semantics, p. 10. ACM (2015)

20. Schroff, F., Kalenichenko, D., Philbin, J.: FaceNet: a unified embedding for face recognition and clustering. In: Proceedings of the IEEE Conference on Computer Vision and Pattern Recognition, pp. 815–823 (2015)
21. Sekhavat, Y.A., Di Paolo, F., Barbosa, D., Merialdo, P.: Knowledge base augmentation using tabular data. In: LDOW (2014)
22. Sermanet, P., Eigen, D., Zhang, X., Mathieu, M., Fergus, R., Lecun, Y.: OverFeat: integrated recognition, localization and detection using convolutional networks. In: International Conference on Learning Representations (ICLR2014), CBLS, April 2014 (2014)
23. Sharif Razavian, A., Azizpour, H., Sullivan, J., Carlsson, S.: CNN features off-the-shelf: an astounding baseline for recognition. In: Proceedings of the IEEE Conference on Computer Vision and Pattern Recognition Workshops, pp. 806–813 (2014)
24. Stonebraker, M., et al.: Data curation at scale: the data tamer system. In: CIDR (2013)
25. van der Maaten, L., Hinton, G.: Visualizing high-dimensional data using t-SNE. J. Mach. Learn. Res. 9(Nov), 2579–2605 (2008)
26. Venetis, P., et al.: Recovering semantics of tables on the web. Proc. VLDB Endow. 4(9), 528–538 (2011)
27. Wang, J., Wang, H., Wang, Z., Zhu, K.Q.: Understanding tables on the web. In: Atzeni, P., Cheung, D., Ram, S. (eds.) ER 2012. LNCS, vol. 7532, pp. 141–155. Springer, Heidelberg (2012). https://doi.org/10.1007/978-3-642-34002-4_11
28. Wikipedia contributors: Inverse transform sampling—Wikipedia, the free encyclopedia (2018). Accessed 3 July 2018
29. Zeiler, M.D., Fergus, R.: Visualizing and understanding convolutional networks. In: Fleet, D., Pajdla, T., Schiele, B., Tuytelaars, T. (eds.) ECCV 2014 Part I. LNCS, vol. 8689, pp. 818–833. Springer, Cham (2014). https://doi.org/10.1007/978-3-319-10590-1_53
30. Zhang, M., Chakrabarti, K.: Infogather+: semantic matching and annotation of numeric and time-varying attributes in web tables. In: Proceedings of the 2013 ACM SIGMOD International Conference on Management of Data, pp. 145–156. ACM (2013)

SPARQλ: A Functional Perspective on Linked Data Services

Christian Vogelgesang[⊠], Torsten Spieldenner, and René Schubotz

Saarbrücken Graduate School of Computer Science,
German Research Center for Artifical Intelligence (DFKI),
66123 Saarbrücken, Germany
{christian.vogelgesang,torsten.spieldenner,rene.schubotz}@dfki.de

Abstract. With more and more applications providing semantic data to improve interoperability, the amount of available RDF datasets is constantly increasing. The SPARQL query language is a W3C recommendation to provide query capabilities on such RDF datasets. Data integration from different RDF sources is up to now mostly task of RDF consuming clients. However, from a functional perspective, data integration boils down to a function application that consumes input data as parameters, and based on these, produces a new set of data as output. Following this notion, we introduce SPARQλ, an extension to the SPARQL 1.1 query language. SPARQλ enables dynamic injection of RDF datasets during evaluation of the query, and by this lifts SPARQL to a tool to write templates for RDF producing functions, an important step to reduce the effort to write SPARQL queries that work on data from various sources. SPARQλ is moreover suitable to directly translate to an RDF described Web service interface, which allows to lift integration of data and re-provisioning of integrated results from clients to cloud environments, and by this solving the bottleneck of RDF data integration on client side.

Keywords: SPARQL · Data integration · RDF
Functional programming

1 Introduction

The idea of the Semantic Web was to improve existing web applications by using a defined semantic datamodel called RDF [1]. In the last few years the Linked Data initiative around Tim-Berners Lee[1,2] was able to get enough traction and more and more big datasets like dbpedia[3] are available as Linked Open Data.

The hosting of Linked Data datasets is a well understood problem [23,25,26]. However, the wide range of different interface types for Linked Data datasets [28]

---

[1] https://www.w3.org/DesignIssues/LinkedData.html.
[2] https://www.w3.org/TR/ldp/.
[3] https://wiki.dbpedia.org/.

© Springer Nature Switzerland AG 2018
R. Ichise et al. (Eds.): JIST 2018, LNCS 11341, pp. 136–152, 2018.
https://doi.org/10.1007/978-3-030-04284-4_10

requires a respective range of experts to access the entirety of the data. Linked Data clients must be able to interact with these interface types.

In the past, clients were mostly data consumers that gained knowledge from RDF data to improve local applications. The trend to move more and more functionality to the cloud resulted in *prosumers* [27] that not only act as client, but also as a server by providing the own result to other clients. For this reason, prosumers face the same challenges as do data providers, and it's getting more complicated to provide a flexible, robust and scalable solutions.

One remedy from the world of Web applications is the so called *Serverless Computing* or *Functions-as-a-Service (FaaS)* [11,18]. FaaS provides concepts and frameworks for small, task-focused Web services that are usually considered as stateless functions on data. The result is an easier deployment, higher availability and scalability of the deployed services.

To our knowledge, however, there are no comparable solutions for Linked Data processing and RDF data integration. There do exist widely recognized extensions to SPARQL [4], the standard query language for RDF dataset access and processing. But like SPARQL itself, solutions like SPARQL-LD [16,17], SPARQL/Update [7], or SPARQL Microservices [21,22] only provide little means of parameterization for dynamic specification of datasets against which a query is executed.

To this extent, we add to the canon of extensions our proposal for *SPARQλ*, a SPARQL extension that is focused on flexible and dynamic integration of RDF datasets. We remove the static dataset handling and introduce the possibility to declare resource IRIs (Internationalized Resource Identifiers) of SPARQL GRAPHs in CONSTRUCT queries[4] as parameters.

Based on SPARQλ, we then define SPARQλ functions which provide a functional programming style interface and allow the definition of the dataset by parameter bindings. SPARQλ functions can either evaluate to a new, partially evaluated SPARQλ function, or to RDF data that can be used as input for other RDF consuming applications. Following the rules the of Linked Data, we also provide a self-descriptive, machine readable interface that can be created automatically by a proposed mapping.

Our contributions in this paper are:

- SPARQλ, an extended subset of SPARQL for dynamic dataset integration
- SPARQλ functions, a service definition that allows to execute a query as service invocation with a functional programming style interface
- A formal approach to generate SPARQλ functions from SPARQλ functions by partial evaluation
- SPARQλ functions as Web services with RDF-based interface description
- An implementation proposal based on FaaS-Frameworks.

In Sect. 2 we define the SPARQλ language, followed by the definition of SPARQλ functions in Sect. 3. We then present a proposal for a Web interface to expose the SPARQλ functions in Sect. 4. Section 5 explains the implementation

---

[4] https://www.w3.org/TR/2013/REC-sparql11-query-20130321/#construct.

of our prototype. Finally, we provide outlook on future work in Sect. 7 and draw a conclusion about our presented work in Sect. 8.

2   SPARQλ

In order to use SPARQL queries [4] as parameterizable functions as motivated in Sect. 1, the evaluation of a SPARQL query must support the assignment of external datasets to undistinguished variables, similar to a function in classic programming languages that binds calling parameters to local variables in the function scope.

The SPARQL 1.1 query language specification [6] requires to specify external data by dataset clauses `FROM` and `FROM NAMED` with the respective IRIs known beforehand. Commands to load external data exist in the SPARQL/Update [7] language specification, but they are not available in the standard SPARQL query language.

We for this propose *SPARQλ* as a SPARQL1.1 extension. SPARQλ extends the semantics of the `GRAPH` operator to allow on-demand fetching of specified named graphs, as well as allowing to express a `GRAPH` IRI by a variable that is bound during evaluation of the query. We restrict the query forms to the CONSTRUCT form because the SPARQL results of the `SELECT` and `ASK` forms do not produce RDF and are not suitable as an input to other RDF consuming services.

2.1   Extending the GRAPH operator

We will in the following extend the semantics of the `GRAPH` operator to allow queries like the query given in Fig. 1. The example computes the price for an offering in US-Dollar. The IRIs of the currency graph and the offering graph are not explicitly stated, but represented by variables. We will in the following refer to variables that represent `GRAPH` IRIs short as *graph variables*. A standard SPARQL 1.1 processor would iterate over all named graphs in the dataset specified beforehand for each `GRAPH` keyword, evaluate the triple pattern and unify the results.

SPARQλ changes this behavior to treat variables in `GRAPH` patterns such that they are bound to an IRI during processing, and the respective `GRAPH` is retrieved from the remote resource that is specified by the IRI. The so fetched external `GRAPH` is subsequently set as active graph, as for the original SPARQL1.1 behavior.

Loading such a requested `GRAPH` into the dataset requires calls to external endpoints, which are potentially not reachable. Following the SPARQL 1.1 specification for handling reachability, we include the `SILENT` keyword for the `GRAPH` operator to suppress errors.

We thus modify the SPARQL1.1 grammar as follows:

```
GraphGraphPattern        ::=
        'GRAPH' ( 'SILENT' )? VarOrIri GroupGraphPattern
```

```
PREFIX gr: <http://purl.org/goodrelations/v1#>
PREFIX xro: <http://purl.org/xro/ns#>
PREFIX dbpedia: <http://dbpedia.org/resource/>
PREFIX rdf: <http://www.w3.org/1999/02/22-rdf-syntax-ns#>

CONSTRUCT {
    ?s rdf:type gr:Offering ;
        gr:hasPriceSpecification _:ps .
    _:ps a gr:PriceSpecification ;
              gr:hasCurrency       dbpedia:United_States_dollar ;
              gr:hasCurrencyValue ?new_price .
}
WHERE {
   Graph ?currencyGraph {
     ?xrate xro:rate ?rate;
            xro:base dbpedia:United_States_dollar;
            xro:counter ?counter_currency .
   }
   Graph ?offering {
     ?s a gr:Offering;
         gr:hasPriceSpecification ?pspec .
     ?pspec gr:hasCurrency       ?counter_currency ;
            gr:hasCurrencyValue ?price .
   }
   BIND(?price/?rate AS ?new_price)
}
```

Fig. 1. A SPARQλ construct query to compute a price specification in US-Dollar.

We moreover modify the evaluation semantics of `GraphGraphPattern` to:

```
1    D : a dataset
2    D(G) : D a dataset with active GRAPH G (the one patterns match against)
3    D[i] : The GRAPH with IRI i in dataset D
4    P : GRAPH pattern
5
6
7    μ: a solution mapping
8    SilentOp:  boolean variable to indicate that the evaluation of
9               the corresponding GRAPH pattern is evaluated on an empty graph
10
11   Definition: Evaluation of Graph
12
13   if IRI is a GRAPH name in D
14     eval(D(G), Graph(IRI, P, SilentOp)) =
15       the result is eval(D(D[IRI]), P)
16   if IRI is not a GRAPH name in D
17     eval(D(G), Graph(IRI,P, SilentOp)) =
18       D[IRI] := FetchGraph(IRI, SilentOp)
19       the result is eval(D(D[IRI]), P)
20   eval(D(G), Graph(var, P, SilentOp)) =
21       the result is eval(D(G), Graph(μ(?var)), P, SilentOp)
22
23   where: FetchGraph(IRI, SilentOp) is the result of an executing
24         a GET request to given IRI.
25
```

2.2 Dataset Specification

The usual SPARQL dataset clauses `FROM` and `FROM NAMED` only allow for dataset specification that needs to be fixed before the execution of a query, and that requires the IRIs of the included graphs to be known beforehand. These mechanics are not suitable for dynamic dataset integration as intended for SPARQλ. We for this omit support of said dataset clauses, and instead exploit the modified semantics of GRAPH as defined in Sect. 2.1.

As soon as a GraphGraphPattern is evaluated, the respective data source as specified by a given IRI is dynamically fetched, and the respective named GRAPH is selected as scope for the GroupGraphPattern. We thus combine the specification of named GRAPH datasets as done by FROM NAMED statements in SPARQL1.1, and the selection of a named GRAPH as scope for the query based on its IRI, into one single GRAPH statement. We do not make any assumptions about the default GRAPH for a SPARQλ query, and leave interpretation of query fragments that operate outside of GraphGraphPattern to the implementation of the processor, as for usual SPARQL1.1 queries.

If the IRI in a GraphGraphPattern is not explicitly stated, but expressed by a variable, this variable may either be bound to an IRI as result of an evaluation of another part of the query, or it may work as a parameter to the query that may be specified manually when executing the query. Passing parameters to SPARQλ queries will be discussed in detail in Sects. 3 and 4.

2.3   Evaluation Strategy

If all graph variables are bound, the query can be executed as a SPARQL1.1 query. Otherwise, we partially evaluate the query and generate a new query with a pre-evaluated set of solution mappings Ω_p for evaluable subpatterns in the query. The Ω_p is stored in a placeholder object in the generated query and is used in the final evaluation.

Formally, we define the partial evaluation as follows:

Let $evaluable(P)$ be a boolean function that tests if a pattern does not contain a GraphGraphPattern with an unbound variable as argument and thus can be pre-evaluated. Let $getSubPatterns(P)$ a function that creates a list of all GroupGraphPattern in the given pattern and let $SolutionPlaceholder(P)$ be a wrapper that holds a pre-evaluated Ω_p that contains valid solution mappings. We can then perform a partial evaluation by:

```
1   partialEval(P):
2     if evaluable(P):
3       Ωp := eval(P)
4       replace(P,SolutionPlaceholder(Ωp))
5     elif P = ∅
6       return
7     else
8       for each subPat in getSubPatterns(P):
9         partialEval(subPat)
```

Furthermore, we define an extension to the SPARQL 1.1 evaluation semantic for the SolutionPlaceholder:

```
1  eval(D(G),SolutionPlaceholder)
2     = multiset of solution mappings
```

If all references to a referred graph variable are covered by the partial evaluation, the corresponding graph itself can be removed from the dataset.

In our example in Fig. 1, we have two graph variables ?offering and ?currencyGraph. If the latter variable is bound, the inner graph pattern can be fully evaluated and the graph can be removed from the dataset.

However, if ?offering is bound with an unbound ?currencyGraph, the referred graph has to be added to the dataset of the resulting query.

For some queries, there might exist equivalent patterns that allow a higher degree of partial evaluation. However, such optimizations are subject of future research.

3   SPARQλ Functions

With the modified GRAPH semantics that treat variables in GraphGraphPattern as free variables that are bound to IRIs during query executions according to Sect. 2.1, the respective dataset management strategy that dynamically fetches remote datasets as named graphs when the graph group pattern is evaluated (Sect. 2.2), and the evaluation strategy according to Sect. 2.3, we can use SPARQλ to write Lambda functions as SPARQλ CONSTRUCT query.

We for this provide a formal definition for parameterizable SPARQλ functions, and specify evaluation behavior for both fully, and partially satisfied SPARQλ functions.

3.1   Formal Definition

Let CONSTRUCT H WHERE S be a SPARQλ query with query graph pattern S. Following the definition of theSPARQL query language [6,24], we define the following sets of variables and notions for a SPARQλ query graph pattern S:

- $\mathcal{V} = \{v_i \mid v_i \in \mathbf{V}, v_i \in [a\ \text{GRAPH}\ v_i]\} \subseteq var(S)$ the set of all free variables that describe an undistiguished GRAPH IRI ("graph variables").
- $\mathcal{B} = \{(v_i, b_i) \mid v_i \in \mathcal{V}, b_i \in \mathbf{T} \cup \mathbf{B}\}$ the set of all bound graph variables in the SPARQλ query P for which holds that $\mu(v_i) = b_i$.
- We define $func(\mathbf{P}) \mapsto G$ as $SPARQλ$ function that takes a list of parameters $\mathbf{P} = \{(v_i, p_i) \mid v_i \in \mathcal{V}, p_i \in \mathbf{I}\}$ and performs a mapping $v_i \mapsto p_i$ before the query is evaluated. $func$ returns a RDF graph G by computing μ on the set of remaining free variables after parameter matching.
- We call the SPARQλ function *fully distinguished* if *after* evaluation of the query holds $\forall v_i \in \mathcal{V} : \exists (v_i, b_i) \in \mathcal{B}$, otherwise we call it *partially distinguished*.

In the following, we motivate an understanding of a SPARQλ query execution as evaluation of a *Lambda function* $\lambda \mathcal{V}.S(\mathbf{P})$ based on the notions above. The

SPARQλ query graph pattern $\mathcal{S}$ will for this take the role of encoding a function $func$:

The binding $v_i \in \mathcal{V} \mapsto p_i$ of variables to parameters in a function $\lambda \mathcal{V}.\mathcal{S}(\mathbf{P})$ is equivalent to binding the respective free variables to the provided parameter $p_i \in \mathbf{I}$, and subsequently retrieving a named graph as specified by p_i using the strategy for dataset management as specified in Sect. 2.2.

Binding GRAPH variables to actual IRIs for a SPARQλ query graph pattern $\mathcal{S}$ is then done by rewriting $\mathcal{S}$ to include BIND commands for each parameter set $(v_i, p_i) \in \mathbf{P}$ (Fig. 2):

```
1    S : the SPARQL pattern
2    V : a set of unbound graph variables in S
3    P : a set of input parameters (vi, pi)
4    BIND: the SPARQL1.1 BIND statement
5
6    Definition: bind(V,P), the
7    injection of IRI bindings into the SPARQλ
8    query:
9
10   bind(V, P) :=
11       foreach vi in V
12           S = BIND(vi, P[vi]) S
```

Fig. 2. Semantics for binding a set of Parameters $\mathbf{P}$ to graph variables $\mathcal{V}$.

We thus bind each of the unbound GRAPH IRIs to an IRI that is specified by a set of input parameters when calling the SPARQλ function.

Following this, the invocation of the SPARQλ function with all graph variables bound, which is equivalent to $|\mathcal{B}| = |\mathcal{V}|$, allows to evaluate the query as SPARQL1.1 query as described in Sect. 2.3.

3.2 Partially Evaluated Functions

After binding parameters to graph variables, and evaluating the *distinguished part* of $\mathcal{S}$, $\mathcal{S}_d$ with $evaluable(\mathcal{S}_d) = true$ (cf. Sect. 2.3), some of the graph variables in $\mathcal{S}$ may still be unbound, i.e. $|\mathcal{B}| < |\mathcal{V}|$. In this case, we consider the result of the function invocation as a partial function application which results in a SPARQλ function with the unbound graph variable list $\mathcal{V}_u$ with:

$$\mathcal{V}_u = \{v_i \mid v_i \in \mathcal{V}, \nexists (v_i, b_i) \in \mathcal{B}\},$$

which represents the list of graph variables that could not yet be bound by evaluating $\mathcal{S}_d$ during execution of the SPARQλ function.

A partial evaluation of a function thus results in a new function with a reduced set of unbound graph variables $\mathcal{V}_u$ compared to the original variable set $\mathcal{V}$. For a fully distinguished set of graph variable bindings $\mathcal{B}$, the new function computes the same results as would the original SPARQλ function on the same set $\mathcal{B}$. This follows the so-called *futamura concept* as presented by Jones et al. [19].

We by this employ the evaluation strategy for SPARQλ queries as defined in Sect. 2.3 to perform partial evaluation, in the following fashion:

① A SPARQλ query is executed with a parameter set $\mathbf{P}$ by which only a subset of graph variables is bound: $|\mathbf{P}| < |\mathcal{V}|$.

② The SPARQλ query graph pattern $\mathcal{S}$ is divided into its fully distinguished part $\mathcal{S}_d$ with `evaluable(`$\mathcal{S}_d$`)=true`, and its (partially) undistinguished part $\mathcal{S}_u$ with `evaluable(`$\mathcal{S}_u$`)=false` that contains $\mathcal{V}_u$, the remaining undistinguished variables after evaluation.

③ $\mathcal{S}_d$ is evaluated as SPARQL1.1 query fragment (cf. Sect. 2.3). The result is an updated dataset $\mathcal{D}'$ that contains the already retrieved named graphs, possibly updates to the graphs from evaluation of satisfied subqueries, and a set of solution mappings Ω_p as result of the executed subqueries: $\bigcup_{p_i \in \mathbf{P}} [\mathcal{S}_d]^D_{\sigma[p_i]} \Rightarrow (\mathcal{D}', \Omega_p)$.

④ The resulting new SPARQλ function then consists of the undistinguished query pattern $\mathcal{S}_u$, the set of remaining unbound variables $\mathcal{V}_u$, and a dataset equivalent to the dataset of the original SPARQλ function after evaluation of the distinguished query fragment, $\mathcal{D}' : \lambda\mathcal{V}.\mathcal{S} \rightarrow \lambda\mathcal{V}_u.\mathcal{S}_u$, with dataset $\mathcal{D}'$. Evaluation of $\lambda\mathcal{V}_u.\mathcal{S}_u$ has then to take into account the pre-evaluated variable mappings Ω_p as given in ③.

Figure 3 shows the remaining query after partially evaluating the example query from Fig. 1 with a bound *offering* variable, and the corresponding set of solution mappings Ω_p.

```
  ...

WHERE {
    PRE-EVALUATED-CURRENCY-GRAPH-PATTERN with Ωp

    Graph <http://currency2currency.org> {
        ?xrate xro:rate ?rate ;
               xro:base dbpedia:United_States_dollar ;
               xro:counter ?counter_currency .
    }
    BIND(?price/?rate AS ?new_price)
}
```

?s	?pspec	?counter_currency	?price
<http://offering.org/1>	_:b0	dbpedia:Euro	9.99
<http://offering.org/2>	_:b1	dbpedia:Australian_dollar	37.99

Fig. 3. Partially evaluated example query for a given ?currencyGraph variable and the precomputed set of solution mappings Ω_p.

Table 1. Defined HTTP request types to a SPARQλ functions service endpoint, expected parameters and parameter types.

HTTP method	Query string parameters	Request content type	Request message body
GET	⟨parameter⟩ (#unbound variables)	None	None
POST	None	application/x-www-form-urlencoded	URL-encoded, & -separated query parameter
POST	⟨parameter⟩ (#unbound variables) post-graph-name (exactly 1)	RDF serialization format	RDF Graph

4   SPARQλ Functions as a Web Service

Based on the definition of the SPARQλ language and SPARQλ functions, we now define the interface of SPARQλ function services and function invocations.

4.1   Interface Design and Invocation

The SPARQL 1.1 Protocol [5] defines an interface for query invocations on SPARQL 1.1 endpoints. We in the following adapt the protocol to support provisioning of graph IRI parameters and by this allow invocation of SPARQλ enpoints via HTTP requests. As SPARQλ is limited to CONSTRUCT clauses, we build on top of the SPARQL query interface definition.

The function invocation is triggered by a HTTP request to the invocation endpoint. We support three different types of requests (see Table 1): A GET request with all function parameters specified as query parameters in the IRI, a POST request with *www-form-urlencoded* body and finally a POST request that defines one additional named graph in the dataset by sending a serialized RDF graph in the request body. The name of the graph is specified by the *post-graph-name* query parameter. Binding this graph to a function parameter avoids a dynamic fetching from the given IRI.

If fetching of a graph fails and GRAPH is not used in conjunction with the SILENT keyword, the invocation endpoint has to supply an error message with the affected parameter name and the bound IRI. If the error is suppressed, the result of the fetching process is assumed as an empty graph. Other errors are handled as defined in Sect. 2.1 of the SPARQL Protocol[5].

The different types of requests are interchangeable. In the example of currency conversion (Fig. 1), the following two calls result in the same generated partially evaluated functions:

---

[5] https://www.w3.org/TR/sparql11-protocol/#query-operation.

```
Variant 1:
HTTP GET: http://example.org/function?currencyGraph=http://www.currency2currency.org
REQUEST BODY: ∅
RETURN BODY:  http://example.org/newfunction

Variant 2:
HTTP POST:     http://example.org/function
REQUEST BODY: currencyGraph=http://www.currency2currency.org
RETURN BODY:  http://example.org/newfunction
```

4.2 Describing SPARQλ Functions

As described in Sect. 1 SPARQλ function are meant to be used in Linked Data environments. For this reason, the functions have to provide a self descriptive interface, that allows the exploration of function signature, the functionality and available endpoints. SPARQλ services are for this described in terms of RDF classes as shown in Fig. 4. Figure 5 shows an example of a respective description in Turtle syntax.

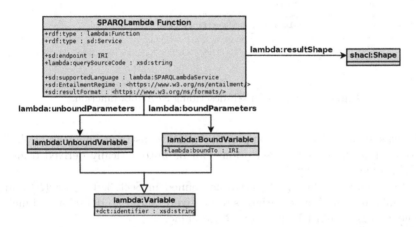

Fig. 4. Classes of a SPARQλ service description: The provided RDF describes endpoints of the function service, and the function signature in terms of parameters, and result shape in SHACL.

With *lambda:querySourceCode* the RDF description provides a link to its source code, and to the function invocation endpoint as *sd:endpoint*. The used entailment regime in basic graph pattern matching [5] is specified by *sd:Entailment Regime. sd:resultFormat* provides the used serialization format for the result graph.

The remainder of the RDF service description defines the signature of the function. Free graph variables of the SPARQλ query are exposed as *lambda: unboundParameter*. Variables that are already bound by partial evaluation are described by *lambda:boundParameter* which also contain the IRI of the graph to which they are bound. Additionally, the function can provide a constraint shape

```
1    <http://example.org/function>
2      a lambda:Function ;
3      a sd:Service ;
4
5      sd:supportedLanguage lambda:SPARQLLambdaService ;
6
7      lambda:sparqlSource <http://example.org/sparql/> ;
8      sd:endpoint <http://example.org/invocation/> ;
9
10     lambda:boundParameter _:v1;
11     lambda:unboundParameter _:v2 ;
12     lambda:resultShape _:rs1;
13
14     sd:resultFormat <http://www.w3.org/ns/formats/Turtle> ;
15     sd:EntailmentRegime <http://www.w3.org/ns/entailment/RDFS> .
16
17   _:v1 a lambda:BoundVariable ;
18       dct:identifier "currencyGraph" ;
19       lambda:boundTo <http://www.currency2currency.org/> .
20
21   _:v2 a lambda:UnboundVariable ;
22       dct:identifier "Offering" .
23
24   _:rs1 a sh:NodeShape ;
25       sh:targetClass gr:Offering ;
26       sh:property [
27         sh:path gr:hasPriceSpecification;
28         sh:class gr:PriceSpecification ;
29         sh:node _:rs2 ;
30         sh:minCount 1 .
31       ] .
32   ...
```

Fig. 5. Example of a self-describing SPARQλ function.

with *lambda:resultShape* in an appropriate RDF constraint language [2,3]. The function signature specific descriptions can be automatically derived from the SPARQλ query as follows:

Let $\lambda \mathcal{V}.\mathcal{S}$ be a SPARQλ function as defined in Sect. 3, $\mathcal{V} \subset var(\mathcal{S})$ and $\mathcal{B}$ sets of unbound and bound variables respectively, and ν an IRI minting function that generates a valid IRI from a variable name.

We then map from variable sets to the semantic parameter description by employing the following mapping rules:

$$\frac{\forall(v_i \in \mathcal{V})}{\begin{array}{l}\nu(v_i) \text{ rdf:type lambda:UnboundVariable .}\\ \nu(v_i) \text{ dct:identifier } "v_i"\hat{\ }\hat{\ }\text{xsd:String .}\end{array}} \text{ ①}$$

① All unbound variables $v_i \in \mathcal{V}$ expose there identifier that can be used to by the SPARQλ protocol to bind the parameters.

$$\frac{\forall((v_i, b_i) \in \mathcal{B})}{\begin{array}{l}\nu(v_i) \text{ rdf:type lambda:BoundVariable .}\\ \nu(v_i) \text{ dct:identifier } "v_i"\hat{\ }\hat{\ }\text{xsd:String .}\\ \nu(v_i) \text{ lambda:boundTo } b_i.\end{array}} \text{ ②}$$

② All bound variables expose there identifier and the value they are bound against.

5   Prototype Implementation

We base our prototype on the Apache Jena Framework[6], and employ the architecture shown in Fig. 6. Each SPARQλ function is provided with its own SPARQλ processor to evaluate the provided SPARQλ query, a triple store containing the local dataset and as supplementary data the potentially pre-evaluated solution mappings Ω_p.

The deployment of SPARQλ functions can be directly mapped to existing Function-as-a-Service frameworks. In our implementation, we used the OpenFaaS framework[7] due to a wide range of supported languages and a fine granular control over the deployment process itself. The FaaS Framework is responsible for the creation and management of new functions and their endpoints.

We have created an OpenFaaS environment with a Jena triple store, the SPARQλ processor and a framework for creating the function descriptions. Before starting such an environment, we specialize the environment by injecting the query and the pre-evaluated Ω_p, in case of a partially evaluated function.

SPARQλ queries are executed against the triple store by a modified Apache ARQ[8] SPARQL processor. The ARQ library provides a rich set of interfaces for customizations. For binding function parameters to graph variables, we use a predefined `QuerySolutionMap`. The `OpExecutor` interface enables users to implement custom semantics. We specialized it to implement the new graph semantic with dynamic fetching of datasets.

For the implementation of the partial evaluation, we used the `OpWalker` interface to traverse the query and find evaluable subpattern as defined in Sect. 2.3. The found patterns are evaluated, the result is serialized and the patterns are replaced by a new `PlaceholderOp` storing a GUID of the result. The evaluation of the `PlaceholderOp` is again implemented using the `OpExecutor` interface and

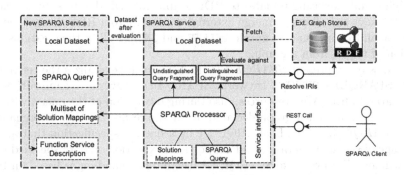

Fig. 6. Architecture of a SPARQλ function service for partial evaluation of SPARQλ queries.

---

[6] https://github.com/apache/jena/.
[7] https://github.com/openfaas/faas.
[8] https://github.com/apache/jena/tree/master/jena-arq.

a lookup to a map of all available Ω_p by this GUID is used to inject the pre-evaluated solution bindings.

Figure 6 furthermore illustrates the process of the partial evaluation. After the function invocation, the SPARQλ processor evaluates the query and creates a new SPARQLλ query, a set of Ω_p and a RDF dataset as a result. With this data, a new function is created and spawned in the FaaS framework. During the initialization process, the function description is created and made available at an endpoint.

6   Related Work

SPARQL Endpoints in the Cloud: With the ever increasing amount of data, and by this, increasing sizes of data sets, it becomes a challenging task to provide access to data efficiently and reliably [13,23]. Several works tackle the question of how to best distribute large data sets over cloud infrastructure.

Leng et al. [20] investigate RDF graph partitioning techniques to distribute the work load of SPARQL query execution over sub-graphs with their own respective SPARQL endpoints. Rietveld et al. [26] provide a novel architecture for Linked Data endpoint federation.

Rakhmawati et al. [25] provided thorough comparison of frameworks that provide SPARQL endpoint federation.

Lately, Abdelaziz et al. claimed in their survey [8] that with systems in a distributed setup often being highly specialized towards the underlying dataset, special care needs to be applied when updating datasets, a claim that we see also true for data integration over endpoints.

Data Integration with SPARQL: SPARQL 1.1 Update [7] is an official companion language of SPARQL 1.1, recommended by the W3C, and is intended for specifying and executing updates to RDF graphs in RDF datasets. Specifically, the LOAD keyword allows to merge external datasets into a RDF dataset, either in the default or in a named graph. DELETE and INSERT allow the creations and deletion of triples from a graph.

Fafalios et al. present *SPARQL-LD* [16,17], which generalizes the semantics of the SPARQL1.1 SERVICE keyword. SPARQ-LD allows to dynamically fetch RDF datasets from Web resources, also during evaluation of the query, without having to have a named graph declared under the respective URI beforehand.

C-SPARQL [12] extends SPARQL 1.1 by a dataset specification that allows the usage of streamed datasets and supports an execution on data specified by a time window. However, like SPARQL 1.1, the dataset handling is based on IRIs that are specified in query itself [15].

Daga et al. present the cloud platform *BASIL* [14]. BASIL exposes stored SPARQL queries as HTTP Web APIs, with the goal to simplify data integration and interoperation for Linked Data and RDF datasets for non RDF experts. BASIL is based on SPARQL 1.1, and contrary to SPARQλ services, it does not allow for dynamic data set bindings based on input parameters which are provided with the API call.

Michel et al. proposed to defined SPARQL microservices [21,22] to wrap arbitrary JSON-based Web APIs, and query those via SPARQL. For this, a SPARQL microservice forwards parameters that are provided with a SPARQL query to a non-RDF Web API, translates the received result of the API call into triple fragments and runs the provided query against the resulting data set. Different to our approach, the Web endpoints from which data is retrieved, are fixed after deployment of the service.

In conclusion, federation of SPARQL endpoints as discussed in [8,20,25,26] makes the importance of data integration and interoperability apparent. Even though this is topic in BASIL [14] and SPARQL Microservices [21,22], those approaches do not support dynamic data integration from federated RDF Web resources or SPARQL endpoints.

Atzori et al. [9,10] presented an approach to call external SPARQL queries as functions in SPARQL queries by introducing a generic SPARQL function *call* to call other WebAPIs as functions. As the referred functions are addressed by URI's, they can be bound to variables and then be used to describe Higher Order Functions. However, due to their more generalized approach, they do not present an interface for functions nor have a concept for partial evaluation of SPARQL functions.

SPARQL-LD [16,17] provides semantics on the SERVICE keyword similar to our specification of GRAPH, but it is lacking a formal definition that allows to perform the mapping to a lambda-function-like micro-service interface, which was our main goal in this paper. We have provided this formalism as extensions of the semantics of the GRAPH keyword instead as a matter of choice. We consider it the more fitting choice, as we load new data to our dataset, similar to how named graphs work in SPARQL1.1, rather than performing a subquery on a remote endpoint.

The purpose of SPARQL-Update is graph modification and not graph creation. It does not support the CONSTRUCT keyword to create new graphs. The LOAD keyword allows the fetching of graphs at execution time, like SPARQλ, but requires the IRIs to be known beforehand in the query definition.

7 Future Work

We see possible future work in SPARQλ by providing support of more types of datasources beyond RDF, comparable to SPARQL Microservices.

We moreover see promising work in including better handling of different RDF dataset interfaces and large datasets, as it is already offered by SPARQL-LD, in SPARQλ.

The partial evaluation of SPARQλ functions can be improved by an automatic optimization step to maximize the evaluable fragment of the query.

Multi-staged programming is another concept from functional programming, that allows to evaluate expressions to entirely new functions. This would require that the evaluation of SPARQλ functions can produce entirely new queries, not only partially evaluated functions.

8   Conclusion

We presented SPARQλ, an extension to the SPARQL 1.1 query language, that is optimized for reusable, predefined and parameterizable CONSTRUCT queries. Our modifications allow the injection of dataset sources into the query and cover possible reachability problems of external graphs.

On top of the query language, we specified a function interface for encapsulating SPARQλ queries as services with a functional programming style interface. We have formally defined the functions and respective evaluation strategies, including partial evaluation as a means to generate new SPARQλ functions with reduced parameter sets. The functions describe themselves by using a modified SPARQL service description that can be semi-automatically generated by a presented mapping from the given query. The invocation of the functions is following the notions of the SPARQL protocol, which we extended by means to provide function parameters, and purged dataset handling.

We presented an implementation proposal based on a Function-as-a-Service Framework and a customized Jena implementation that allows a flexible and scalable execution of the defined queries.

Acknowledgment. This work is supported by the Federal Ministry of Education and Research of Germany in the project Hybr-iT (Förderkennzeichen 01IS16026A).

References

1. RDF 1.1 Primer. https://www.w3.org/TR/rdf11-primer/
2. Shape Expressions Language 2.0. https://www.w3.org/TR/shex-semantics/
3. Shapes Constraint Language (SHACL). https://www.w3.org/TR/shacl/
4. SPARQL 1.1 Overview. https://www.w3.org/TR/sparql11-overview/
5. SPARQL 1.1 Protocol. https://www.w3.org/TR/sparql11-protocol/
6. SPARQL 1.1 Query Language. https://www.w3.org/TR/2013/REC-sparql11-query-20130321/
7. SPARQL 1.1 Update. https://www.w3.org/TR/sparql11-update/
8. Abdelaziz, I., Harbi, R., Khayyat, Z., Kalnis, P.: A survey and experimental comparison of distributed SPARQL engines for very large RDF data. Proc. VLDB Endow. **10**(13), 2049–2060 (2017)
9. Atzori, M.: Call: a nucleus for a web of open functions. In: Proceedings of the 2014 International Conference on Posters & Demonstrations Track, ISWC-PD 2014, vol. 1272, pp. 17–20. CEUR-WS.org, Aachen (2014)
10. Atzori, M.: Toward the web of functions: interoperable higher-order functions in SPARQL. In: Mika, P., et al. (eds.) ISWC 2014. LNCS, vol. 8797, pp. 406–421. Springer, Cham (2014). https://doi.org/10.1007/978-3-319-11915-1_26
11. Baldini, I., et al.: Serverless computing: current trends and open problems. In: Chaudhary, S., Somani, G., Buyya, R. (eds.) Research Advances in Cloud Computing, pp. 1–20. Springer, Singapore (2017). https://doi.org/10.1007/978-981-10-5026-8_1

12. Barbieri, D.F., Braga, D., Ceri, S., Valle, E.D., Grossniklaus, M.: C-SPARQL: a continuous query language for RDF data streams. Int. J. Semant. Comput. **4**(01), 3–25 (2010)
13. Buil-Aranda, C., Hogan, A., Umbrich, J., Vandenbussche, P.-Y.: SPARQL web-querying infrastructure: ready for action? In: Alani, H., et al. (eds.) ISWC 2013. LNCS, vol. 8219, pp. 277–293. Springer, Heidelberg (2013). https://doi.org/10.1007/978-3-642-41338-4_18
14. Daga, E., Panziera, L., Pedrinaci, C.: A BASILar approach for building web APIs on top of SPARQL endpoints. In: CEUR Workshop Proceedings, vol. 1359, pp. 22–32 (2015)
15. Dia, A.F., Kazi-Aoul, Z., Boly, A., Chabchoub, Y.: C-SPARQL extension for sampling RDF graphs streams. In: Pinaud, B., Guillet, F., Cremilleux, B., de Runz, C. (eds.) Advances in Knowledge Discovery and Management. SCI, vol. 732, pp. 23–40. Springer, Cham (2018). https://doi.org/10.1007/978-3-319-65406-5_2
16. Fafalios, P., Tzitzikas, Y.: SPARQL-LD: a SPARQL extension for fetching and querying linked data. In: International Semantic Web Conference (Posters & Demos) (2015)
17. Fafalios, P., Yannakis, T., Tzitzikas, Y.: Querying the web of data with SPARQL-LD. In: Fuhr, N., Kovács, L., Risse, T., Nejdl, W. (eds.) TPDL 2016. LNCS, vol. 9819, pp. 175–187. Springer, Cham (2016). https://doi.org/10.1007/978-3-319-43997-6_14
18. Fox, G.C., Ishakian, V., Muthusamy, V., Slominski, A.: Status of serverless computing and function-as-a-service (FaaS) in industry and research. arXiv preprint arXiv:1708.08028 (2017)
19. Jones, N.D., Gomard, C.K., Sestoft, P.: Partial Evaluation and Automatic Program Generation. Prentice-Hall International Series in Computer Science. Prentice Hall, New York (1993)
20. Leng, Y., Zhikui, C., Zhong, F., Li, X., Hu, Y., Yang, C.: BRGP: a balanced RDF graph partitioning algorithm for cloud storage. Concurrency Comput.: Practice Exp. **29**(14), e3896 (2017)
21. Michel, F., Faron-Zucker, C., Gandon, F.: Bridging web APIs and linked data with SPARQL micro-services. In: Gangemi, A., et al. (eds.) ESWC 2018. LNCS, vol. 11155, pp. 187–191. Springer, Cham (2018). https://doi.org/10.1007/978-3-319-98192-5_35
22. Michel, F., Zucker, C.F., Gandon, F.: SPARQL micro-services: lightweight integration of web APIs and linked data. In: Linked Data on the Web, LDOW 2018, pp. 1–10 (2018)
23. Millard, I., Glaser, H., Salvadores, M., Shadbolt, N.: Consuming multiple linked data sources: challenges and experiences (2010)
24. Pérez, J., Arenas, M., Gutierrez, C.: Semantics and complexity of SPARQL. In: Cruz, I., et al. (eds.) ISWC 2006. LNCS, vol. 4273, pp. 30–43. Springer, Heidelberg (2006). https://doi.org/10.1007/11926078_3
25. Rakhmawati, N.A., Umbrich, J., Karnstedt, M., Hasnain, A., Hausenblas, M.: A comparison of federation over SPARQL endpoints frameworks. In: Klinov, P., Mouromtsev, D. (eds.) KESW 2013. CCIS, vol. 394, pp. 132–146. Springer, Heidelberg (2013). https://doi.org/10.1007/978-3-642-41360-5_11

26. Rietveld, L., Verborgh, R., Beek, W., Vander Sande, M., Schlobach, S.: Linked data-as-a-service: the semantic web redeployed. In: Gandon, F., Sabou, M., Sack, H., d'Amato, C., Cudré-Mauroux, P., Zimmermann, A. (eds.) ESWC 2015. LNCS, vol. 9088, pp. 471–487. Springer, Cham (2015). https://doi.org/10.1007/978-3-319-18818-8_29
27. Stadtmüller, S., Speiser, S., Harth, A.: Future challenges for linked APIs. In: SALAD@ ESWC, pp. 20–27 (2013)
28. Verborgh, R., Vander Sande, M., Colpaert, P., Coppens, S., Mannens, E., Van de Walle, R.: Web-scale querying through linked data fragments. In: LDOW. Citeseer (2014)

Predicate Invention Based RDF Data Compression

Man Zhu[1]([✉]), Weixin Wu[1], Jeff Z. Pan[2], Jingyu Han[1], Pengfei Huang[3], and Qian Liu[1]

[1] School of Computer Science, Nanjing University of Posts and Telecommunications, Nanjing, China
mzhu@njupt.edu.cn
[2] Department of Computing Science, University of Aberdeen, Aberdeen, UK
[3] College of Electronic and Information Engineering, Nanjing University of Aeronautics and Astronautics, Nanjing, China

Abstract. RDF is a data representation format for schema-free structured information that is gaining speed in the context of semantic web, life science, and vice versa. With the continuing proliferation of structured data, demand for RDF compression is becoming increasingly important. In this study, we introduce a novel lossless compression technique for RDF datasets (triples), called PIC (Predicate Invention based Compression). By generating informative predicates and constructing effective mapping to original predicates, PIC only needs to store dramatically reduced number of triples with the newly created predicates, and restoring the original triples efficiently using the mapping. These predicates are automatically generated by a decomposable forward-backward procedure, which consequently supports very fast parallel bit computation. As a semantic compression method for structured data, besides the reduction of syntactic verbosity and data redundancy, we also invoke semantics in the RDF datasets. Experiments on various datasets show competitive results in terms of compression ratio.

1 Introduction

The Resource Description Framework (RDF) is gaining widespread momentum and acceptance among various fields, including science, bioinformatics, business intelligence and social networks, to mention a few [4]. For instance, Semantic-Web-style ontologies and knowledge bases with millions of facts from DBpedia [2], Probase [10], Wikidata [9] and Science Commons [11] are now publicly available. Studies like IDC's Digital Universe1 estimate that the size of the digital universe turned 1Zb (1 trillion Gb) for the first time in 2010, reached 1.8Zb just one year later in 2011 and will go beyond 35Zb in 2020. Combined with the growing size of the overall Linked Open Data cloud, with more than 30 billion triples, and of its individual datasets, with some of its hubs e.g. DBPedia exceeding 1,2 billion triples, the need of effective RDF data compression techniques is clear [8].

© Springer Nature Switzerland AG 2018
R. Ichise et al. (Eds.): JIST 2018, LNCS 11341, pp. 153–161, 2018.
https://doi.org/10.1007/978-3-030-04284-4_11

Current approaches to achieve lossless RDF document compression can be categorized into three categories, a.k.a., universal file compression techniques, RDF serialization approaches, and rule based compression methods. First of all, universal file compression techniques, such as bzip[1] and LZMA[2], can be applied on RDF document. Such approaches alter the file structure of RDF documents and can significantly reduce file size [8] without reducing file content. In RDF-3X [7], all triples are sorted lexicographically in a clustered B$^+$-tree, and all literals are replaced by ids using a mapping dictionary. Alternative RDF serializations, such as HDT serialization, lean graphs [5] and K2-triples [1] can be used to reduce file size. Such techniques preserve the structured nature of RDF documents, but they fail to utilize the semantics when compressing documents. Other approaches are based on logical compression [6,8], which can be used to reduce the number of triples in an RDF document. Our approach lies in the third category who offers a more significant reduction.

	Person	Professor	Female
Joan	1	0	1
Mike	1	1	0
Teddy	1	1	1

Fig. 1. An example of a toy RDF dataset.

In this paper, we present PIC, a predicate invention based compression method for RDF data. PIC compresses RDF triples by inventing new informative predicates instead of isolated predicates. As a result, the amount of necessary triples (constructed with the newly created predicates) to losslessly decompress the original dataset is dramatically reduced. The newly invented predicates are generated by a forward-backward procedure where very fast parallel bit computation is supported. We also define a map function to locate original predicates and restore the original dataset. To speed-up compression, we propose to use divide and conquer strategy to divide large datasets into smaller ones.

Example. To intuitively illustrate the idea, let us consider Fig. 1 for an example. Figure 1 depicts a toy RDF dataset containing 3 predicates, a.k.a. Person, Professor, and Female, and 3 instances (Joan, Mike, and Teddy). The element in the table is 1 iff the instance on its corresponding row is of the type (predicate) on the column, such as Person(Joan). There are 7 triples in this dataset, which corresponds to the number of 1s in the table. In this example, instance Joan belongs to both Person and Female, Mike belongs to both Person and Professor, and Teddy belongs to all predicates. By PIC, 3 integer labels are automatically generated after compression, whose corresponding DL (description logic, the logic foundation of semantic web) expressions are Person⊓Female (a concept of the intersection of Person and Female), Person⊓Professor, Person⊓Female⊓Professor. In

---

[1] http://www.bzip.org.
[2] http://www.7-zip.org/.

order to restore the original dataset, only Person⊓Female⊓Professor(Teddy), Person⊓ Female(Mike), and Person⊓Professor(Joan) are needed. PIC only saves the 3 integers and the indexes of the literal predicates and instances. In decompression, a mapping algorithm finds the original indexes according to these integer labels.

2   Preliminary

Resource Description Framework (RDF) is the most widely used data interchange format on the Semantic Web. Given a set of URI references $\mathcal{R}$, a set of literals $\mathcal{L}$ and a set of blank nodes $\mathcal{B}$, an RDF statement is a triple $<s, p, o>$ on $(\mathcal{R} \cup \mathcal{B}) \times \mathcal{R} \times (\mathcal{R} \cup \mathcal{L} \cup \mathcal{B})$, where s, p, o are the subject, predicate and object of the triple, respectively. An RDF document is a set of triples. An RDF document can be transformed into a 0–1 matrix M by corresponding rows to subjects, columns to predicate and object combinations, and set M_{ij} to 1 iff $<s, p, o>$ belongs to the RDF document, where s is the subject that corresponds to the i-th row, and $p - o$ combination (can roughly be understood as a predicate $\exists p.\{o\}$) corresponds to the j-th column. In this paper, we consider the matrix representation of RDF documents.

3   Approach

PIC generates predicates so that at most one triple is necessary for each subject, and by an effective mapping function the original dataset can be losslessly restored. In this section, we firstly introduce the compression and decompression algorithm, and then we discuss some speed-up techniques of PIC.

3.1   Compression

The compression algorithm is consist of a forward and a backward procedure as shown in Algorithm 1. The input of Algorithm 1 is the data matrix representation (c.f. Sect. 2) of the RDF document to be compressed. The output contains all necessary triples to be stored. In the forward procedure, we iteratively conjunct columns in bits, and cache the matrices D^i calculated in each outer iteration. The j-th column is conjunctions of columns $c_1, c_2, \ldots, c_i$ (c.f. line 3 of Algorithm 1). In D^i, an element D^i_{jk} is 1 when all elements are 1 on some set of columns of the j-th row in the original RDF data matrix, whose indexes are mapped from k by intoComp function:

intoComp. Given k the column index in D^i, and i the number of columns in the column conjunction, we iterate to find the index of columns $\{c_1, c_2, \ldots\}$ in D^i:

$$C^j_{c_i} \leq k - M < C^j_{c_i+1}$$
$$M = M + C^{j-1}_{c_i-1}$$

where c_{i-1} is the index found in the previous iteration. j initially is set to i, and is decreased by 1 in each iteration. M is set to 0 in the first iteration. When $k - M = 0$, the indexes of the rest columns are set from 0, and added by 1 each time, until all columns have been found. For example, intoComp$(0, 2) = \{0, 1\}$.

The backward procedure iteratively updates previously generated matrices D^i. The 1 elements $D^{i'}_{jk}$ in $D^{i'}$ mean that there are triples relate to subject s_j whose predicate and object combinations correspond to the set mapped from k by intoComp. Since intoComp deals with the mapping issues, we only need to store the following data in the compressed dataset:

- i: the matrix superscript, which indicates the number of columns involved in the conjunction;
- j: the row index which corresponds to the index in subjects list;
- k: the column index, together with i, encodes a set of predicate and object combinations.

Figure 2 depicts an example of Algorithm 1. During forward, the second and third matrix contains values for conjunctions of 2 columns and 3 columns. Because there are 3 columns in the original matrix, there is no need to find D^4. In the right figure, we can find a 1 in the first matrix, namely D^3, which means that there are 3 triples relate to the third subject, so a triple <3, 2, 0> is needed. Meanwhile, since the 1s on the 3rd row have been saved, there is no need to consider them in the former matrices. So D^2 is updated because intoComp(0, 3) returns $\{0, 1, 2\}$. In the same way, <2, 0, 1> and <2, 1, 0> are also stored. In the compressed dataset, only 3 triples are needed.

Algorithm 1: PIC Compression Algorithm

    Input   : data matrix D
    Output: list $\{< i, j, k >\}$
    /* forward procedure   */
1 **for** i *from 2 to* N_C **do**
2   **for** j *from 0 to* $C^i_{N_C} - 1$ **do**
3          $D^i_{\cdot j} = D_{\cdot c_1} \wedge D_{\cdot c_2} \wedge \ldots \wedge D_{\cdot c_i}$, where intoComp$(j, i) = \{c_1, c_2 \ldots, c_i\}$;
4   **if** D^i *all zero* **then**
5   break;
6 initialize empty list L;
    /* backward procedure   */
7 **foreach** D^i **do**
8      $D^{i'} = D^i$;
9   for each $D^{i+1}_{jn} \neq 0$, set $D^{i'}_{jk} = 0$ where $k \in$ intoComp(n, i);
10   add $< i, j, k >$ to L, where $D^{i'}_{jk} \neq 0$;
11 **return** L;

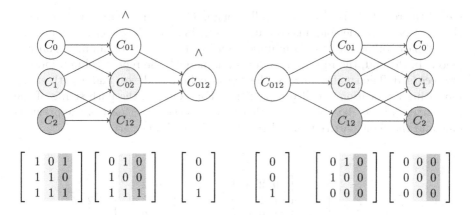

Fig. 2. An example of compression. Left and right correspond to forward and backward procedure respectively. Values of node in matrix are shown in the same color as the node.

3.2 Decompression

We briefly introduce the decompression procedure here, c.f. Algorithm 2. We take a list $<i, j, k>$ as input. Each triple decompresses to a set of triples by locating their indexes through intoComp function. R is the set of predicate-object combinations, and $\mathcal{I}_i$ is the i-th subject. Suppose R_j is the combination of p_t and o_k, then RDF triple $<\mathcal{I}_i, a, R_j>$ is transformed to $<\mathcal{I}_i, p_t, o_k>$.

Algorithm 2: PIC Decompression Algorithm

   Input   : list $\{< i, j, k >\}$
   Output: D'
1 **foreach** $< i, j, k > \in \{< i, j, k >\}$ **do**
2 | $R = \{\mathcal{R}_j\}$, where j $\in$ intoComp(k, j);
3 | store RDF triple $< \mathcal{I}_i$, a, $R_j >$, where $R_j \in R$;

3.3 Speeding-Up Strategy

In order to evidently reduce the column conjunctions, we adopt a partition and merge procedure. The objective of this procedure is to divide the RDF data matrix into a set of independent partitions, where the number of columns in each partition is decreased.

As depicted in Fig. 3, given an RDF data matrix, affixed with a first row indicating the original index of the property column, this procedure reorder its columns and recursively divide the matrix horizontally in the middle, until the size of the resulted matrices are small enough. The column reordering scheme is that first part are the columns containing both 1s and 0s in upper and blow, the second part containing 1s only in upper, and the third part containing 1s only in below. In the end, the repeated columns are merged, the repeat column indexes are recorded. The smaller matrix, the repeat column indexes, and a path string indicating its location is called a partition. For example, the path string of the left partition is "0" because the smaller matrix is the upper part of the previous one, and the right partition is "1" because it is the lower part.

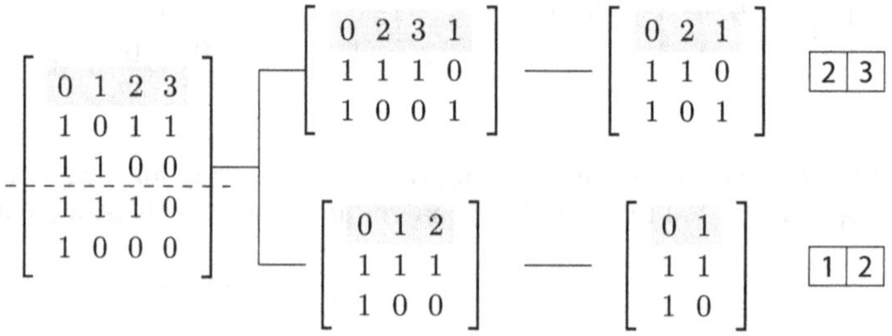

Fig. 3. An example of data partition.

When compressing the data partitions, the decompression slightly differs. Assume the matrix in the partition is M, $M - 1$ is the matrix whose path string equals to M's eliminating the last character, $last(M)$ is short for the last character of M's path string, and rows is the number of rows in the original matrix. Then the first row index of M is:

$$loc(M) = \begin{cases} loc(M - 1) & \text{if } last(M) \text{ is } 0 \\ loc(M - 1) + \lceil \tfrac{1}{2}\text{offset}(M - 1) \rceil & \text{if } last(M) \text{ is } 1 \end{cases}$$

where

$$\text{offset}(M) = \begin{cases} \lceil \tfrac{1}{2}\text{offset}(M - 1) \rceil & \text{if } last(M) \text{ is } 0 \\ \lfloor \tfrac{1}{2}\text{offset}(M - 1) \rfloor & \text{if } last(M) \text{ is } 1 \end{cases}$$

and offset("") $=$ #rows, $loc($""$) = 0$. Besides, here are some other speed-up strategies for compression:

– In some D^i, if the number of columns containing 1 is less than $i + 1$, the forward procedure can pre-terminate.
– In some D^i, if the numbers in a column are all 0, this column can be dropped out of consideration in the following-up conjunction calculations.
– We use different stop criterion in finding matrix partitions, since the calculations of bit conjunction are pretty cheap, there is no need to have trivial matrices.

4   Preliminary Evaluation

This section shows preliminary evaluations of the compression performed by our system. Our experiment is conducted on several linked open datasets of varying sizes (cf Table 1). The smallest dataset consists of 130 K triples while the largest dataset consists of one million triples.

Table 1. Dataset statistics (the first 3 columns) and compression ratio γ (the last 2 columns). LOG stands for the logical linked data compression approach [6].

Dataset	#triples (K)	#predicate-object	size (M)	#triples (PIC)	#triples (LOG)	γ (PIC)	γ (LOG)
Dog food	130	77,064	20.7	12.7 K	106.6 K	12.3%	82.0%
CN 2012	137	41,770	17.9	14.6 K	58.9 K	10.7%	43.0%
ArchiveHub	431	204,360	71.7	51.4 K	306.0 K	12.0%	71.0%
Jamendo	1047	485,443	143.0	335.9 K	858.5 K	32.1%	82.0%

Table 2. Compressed size for various RDF datasets. LOG stands for the logical linked data compression approach [6].

Dataset	Size (PIC-head)	Size (PIC-triples)	Size (PIC+bzip2)	Size (LOG+bzip2)
Dog food	4.4 M	649 K	1330.0 K	1492 K
CN 2012	1.1 M	492 K	226.6 K	296 K
ArchiveHub	11.7 MB	1.81 MB	2.3 MB	1.9 MB
Jamendo	26.7 M	4.86 M	5.6 MB	5.6 MB

The comparisons are mainly based on two metrics: compression ratio and running time. The compression ratio, γ is defined as the ratio of the number of triples in compressed dataset to that in uncompressed dataset [6]. Besides the compression ratio, we also measure time it takes to perform full compression and full decompression.

Now we firstly discuss the stop criterion of the data partition algorithm. Then, we report the experimental results in terms of compression ratio and running time compared to the logical linked data compression approach [6]. We compress the resulting datasets (in N-Triples format) by bzip2, which is one of the best universal compressors [3].

To find data partitions, we use 2 thresholds. One threshold controls the maximum number of rows each partition has, and the other dominates the number of columns of each partition. Specifically, on these 4 datasets, we first iterate to find partitions of no more than 400 rows. Then for each dataset, different threshold of columns are adopted according to the running time. The thresholds are 25, 30, 27, and 25 on DogFood, CN 2012, ArchiveHub, and Jamendo respectively.

From Table 2 we can find that: (1) the data reduction of PIC is significant, which is due to the discovery of expressive predicates; (2) PIC gets better results on DogFood and CN 2012, but not on ArchiveHub. In ArchiveHub, there are lots of isolated triples, which are not connected with others. However, the benefit of PIC is shrinking multiple triples related to the same subject into at most one triple, which cannot be done on ArchiveHub and Jamendo; (3) it is interesting that on DogFood and CN 2012, the numbers of triples after compression by LOG and PIC show reverse tendency. LOG needs significantly less triples for CN 2012 compared to DogFood, but PIC is the opposite. As mentioned above, PIC is not good at handle single isolated triples, which can be handled by LOG using subsumption axioms. (4) the size of head in PIC is large because we only draw namespaces in RDF data instead of striving to compress texts by lexical methods, since this is not our concern at the moment.

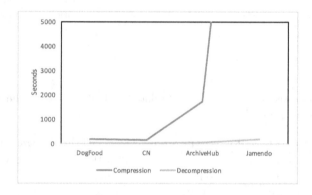

Fig. 4. Running time of compression and decompression by PIC.

Figure 4 shows the comparison between total time required for compression and the full decompression. In general, the compression time increases with the increase in triple size. However, the compression time is influenced by number of predicate-object triples, which is shown by the compression time of Dog Food and CN 2012. Decompression is faster by several order of magnitudes compared to the compression.

5   Discussion

This paper has presented PIC, a predicate invention based RDF compression method. As our experiments have shown, PIC outperforms other methods on dense datasets in terms of compression ratio and compressed size. These datasets contain multiple triples with a same subject, which are transformed into one triple at most by PIC. As a result, we can find that the data reduction is significant from experimental results. For other datasets having sparse data, PIC is not effective enough. In terms of running time, PIC is efficient during decompression, but is still not efficient enough for compression.

Our future work includes two parts: (1) PIC needs further improvements on the running time of compression; (2) We will find more intelligent way to partition the RDF data matrix, and use PIC to compress dense partitions.

Acknowledgement. This work is partially funded by the National Science Foundation of China under grant 61602260 and 61702279.

References

1. Álvarez García, S., Brisaboa, N.R., Fernández, J.D., Martínez-Prieto, M.A.: Compressed k2-triples for full-in-memory RDF engines. In: AMCIS (2011)
2. Auer, S., Bizer, C., Kobilarov, G., Lehmann, J., Cyganiak, R., Ives, Z.: DBpedia: a nucleus for a web of open data. In: Proceedings of the ISWC 2007/ASWC 2007, pp. 722–735 (2007)
3. Fernández, J.D., Gutiérrez, C., Martínez-Prieto, M.A.: RDF compression: basic approaches. In: Proceedings of the WWW 2010, pp. 1091–1092 (2010)
4. Hammoud, M., Rabbou, D.A., Nouri, R., Beheshti, S., Sakr, S.: DREAM: distributed RDF engine with adaptive query planner and minimal communication. In: Proceedings of the VLDB 2015, pp. 654–665 (2015)
5. Iannone, L., Palmisano, I., Redavid, D.: Optimizing RDF storage removing redundancies: an algorithm. In: Ali, M., Esposito, F. (eds.) IEA/AIE 2005. LNCS (LNAI), vol. 3533, pp. 732–742. Springer, Heidelberg (2005). https://doi.org/10.1007/11504894_101
6. Joshi, A.K., Hitzler, P., Dong, G.: Logical linked data compression. In: Cimiano, P., Corcho, O., Presutti, V., Hollink, L., Rudolph, S. (eds.) ESWC 2013. LNCS, vol. 7882, pp. 170–184. Springer, Heidelberg (2013). https://doi.org/10.1007/978-3-642-38288-8_12
7. Neumann, T., Weikum, G.: RDF-3X: a RISC-style engine for RDF. Proc. VLDB Endow. **1**(1), 647–659 (2008)
8. Pan, J.Z., Pérez, J.M.G., Ren, Y., Wu, H., Wang, H., Zhu, M.: Graph pattern based RDF data compression. In: Supnithi, T., Yamaguchi, T., Pan, J.Z., Wuwongse, V., Buranarach, M. (eds.) JIST 2014. LNCS, vol. 8943, pp. 239–256. Springer, Cham (2015). https://doi.org/10.1007/978-3-319-15615-6_18
9. Vrandečić, D.: Wikidata: a new platform for collaborative data collection. In: Proceedings of the WWW 2012, pp. 1063–1064 (2012)
10. Wu, W., Li, H., Wang, H., Zhu, K.Q.: Probase: a probabilistic taxonomy for text understanding. In: Proceedings of the SIGMOD 2012, pp. 481–492 (2012)
11. Yuan, P., Liu, P., Wu, B., Jin, H., Zhang, W., Liu, L.: TripleBit: a fast and compact system for large scale RDF data. PVLDB **6**(7), 517–528 (2013)

Question Answering and NLP

Question Answering and IR

A Marker Passing Approach to Winograd Schemas

Johannes Fähndrich[✉], Sabine Weber, and Hannes Kanthak

Technische Universität Berlin, Berlin, Germany
Johannes.Faehndirch@dai-labor.de
https://www.fahndrich.de

Abstract. This paper approaches a solution of Winograd Schemas with
a marker passing algorithm which operates on an automatically generated semantic graph. The semantic graph contains common sense facts
from data sources form the semantic web like domain ontologies e.g.
from Linked Open Data (LOD), WordNet, Wikidata, and ConceptNet.
Out of those facts, a semantic decomposition algorithm selects relevant
facts for the concepts used in the Winograd Schema and adds them
to the semantic graph. Markers are propagated through the graph and
used to identify an answer to the Winograd Schema. Depending on the
encoded knowledge in the graph (connectionist view of world knowledge)
and the information encoded on the marker (for symbolic reasoning) our
approach selects the answers. With this selection, the marker passing
approach is able to beat the state-of-the-art approach by about 12%.

Keywords: Semantic web · LOD · Winograd Schema
Common sense reasoning · Symbolic connectionist AI

1 Introduction

Artificial Intelligence (AI) helps to solve ever more complex problems. The use of
increasingly sophisticated software enables us to automate many tedious tasks,
perform better research and grasp a better understanding of the world, e.g.,
playing Go [30], or fighting cancer [9]. But *"Despite all these developments, the
promises of strong artificial intelligence set forth in the 1960s have not been
fulfilled."* [31, p. 7], meaning that AI is not able to understand natural language
[33], construct plans on dynamic domains [12], or do common sense reasoning like
humans [27]. These second kinds of problems are solved by a so-called "strong
AI" [25][1]. A strong AI is able to learn new problem-solving skills in new domains.
The adaption to new domains is one of the differences to special purpose AI
where a chess AI is, e.g., unable to drive a car.

One of the reasons for human intelligence might be the ability to think. Having a language to formulate thoughts, meaning and ideas, helps us to handle

---

[1] *Strong AI* (sometimes called *full AI* or *hard AI*) [14, p. 260] refers to a human level
intelligence.

© Springer Nature Switzerland AG 2018
R. Ichise et al. (Eds.): JIST 2018, LNCS 11341, pp. 165–181, 2018.
https://doi.org/10.1007/978-3-030-04284-4_12

unknown situations with adaptiveness and dynamic behavior. Part of the capacity to think is reasoning, which does not always "obey the rules of classical logic" but gives us our common sense [11]. The foundation for a language to think is a representation of meaning. Consequently, research in AI analyzes how methods from mathematics, linguistics, psychology, philosophy and computer science can be used to create machines with the ability to represent meaning.

A main source of world knowledge is the semantic web consisting of multiple ontologies which are created and maintained by multiple organizations [32]. Collecting knowledge from the semantic web and merging it into one representation can be seen as a first step to reasoning on with the LOD which includes Information sources like DBPedia [2] or Freebase or YAGO [1].

The use of world knowledge in common sense reasoning has multiple applications [15]. One application is to answer commonsense reasoning questions like the test questions called Winograd Schemas. The *Commonsense Reasoning - Winograd Schema Challenge (WSC)*[2] tests the best approaches solving Winograd Schemas.

This paper describes our approach to solving Winograd Schemas: Using knowledge extracted form the Semantic Web to create an connections representation of facts. This connectionist representation is then used for pragmatic inference. For the evaluation, we will use the Common-sense Reasoning Winograd Challenge dataset.

In the following we will use the example Winograd Schema, as an running example:

"The trophy would not fit in the brown suitcase because it was too big (small). What was too big (small)?" Answer 0: **the trophy** Answer 1: **the suitcase**

In this example the answer changes depending of the used adjective: big (the trophy) or small (the suitcase).

2   State-of-the-Art

The Winograd Schema Challenge was first proposed in the year 2011 by Hector Levesque [16] as a test for machine intelligence as an alternative to the Turing Test. On the first glance, the Winograd Schema Challenge seems like a task in anaphora resolution. However, rather than to be solvable with only grammatical and semantic relations, it requires world knowledge and common sense reasoning. This section will look at the newest AI approaches to solve Winograd Schemas and describe the available data sets.

2.1   Related Work

After the initial Winograd Schema Challenge described by Levesque [16], multiple approaches to solving Winograd Schemas where published. The result of

---

[2] http://commonsensereasoning.org/winograd.html last visited on 30.07.2018.

our analysis of related work is shown in Fig. 1. One of the first approaches by Rahman and Ng [23] combines eight different methods, e.g., using the Google search engine and comparing the number of results.

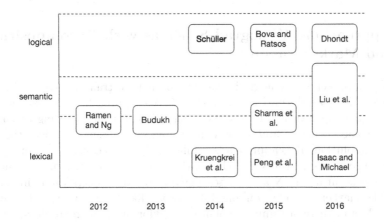

Fig. 1. Classification of state-of-the-art in time.

Starting in 2015 a new era of approaches were introduced by Sharma et al. [26]. They developed an approach which combines existing methods for knowledge collection and extends them with a semantic parser. Also in 2015 Sharma et al. [22] used statistical methods with the focus on sentence predicates. Since the statistical analysis of Winograd Schema evades the challenge of common sense reasoning a change in the competition dataset was needed.

After the rules for the construction of Winograd Schemas have been changed with the suggestions of Levesque et al. [16], approaches building solely on statistical analysis are no longer capable of mastering the challenge. After this change, the first official Common Sense Reasoning Winograd Schema Challenge organized by the New York University was conducted. With the improved data set, the results of the known approaches dropped to the extent that the best result in 2016 was as low as 58%, with a random score of 48% [6]. One of the most promising approaches in 2016 was Liu et al. which reached in 2017 Liu et al. [17] a result of 61.7%. No other results are reported by [8] or [24].

2.2   Data Set

In this section, we will describe the data set on which we evaluate our approach. There has been a multitude of Winograd data sets over the last few years.

Rahman and Ng [23] present a manually created data set of 941 sentences. This data set had the caveat of being solvable without common sense reasoning.

The most recent Winograd Schema dataset is based on the work of Morgenstern et al. [19]. It contains 60 Winograd Schemas and is more difficult than the others because the example schemas have been selected with the criteria to not be solvable by statistics. This focus on difficult schemas has been done to ensure that the approaches explicitly do not use a black box or statistical models to approximate answers. This dataset has been used at the IJCAI 2016 in the last official Winograd Schema Challenge and therefore will be used in this work.

3 Approaching Winograd Schemas with Decomposition and Marker Passing

The best approach on Winograd Schemas so far is to train an Artificial Neural Network (ANN) as shown by Liu et al. [17]. We approach Winograd Schemas with a similar approach in two parts: First, automatically creating a semantic graph for each schema, and second, using marker passing to select the right pronoun resolution. This approach is similar to ANNs because a network is used to encode semantic features and the markers describe activation. Each node is activated like in an ANN and passes markers to the concepts it is in relation with. The markers encode symbolic information like the activation of a node in the graph, and therefore simulate neural behavior but with more detail then in an ANN like in [17]. This section describes how the semantic graph is built and how the marker passing is configured in our approach.

3.1 Decomposing

The first phase collects all information available and creates a semantic graph, which forms the knowledge base for this approach. This collection of connectionist information is called Decomposition. A Decomposition is a process of looking up a concept in the given information sources. As shown in Fig. 2 the input of the decomposition is a set of information sources like WordNet, Wikipedia or domain ontologies, which then are used to build semantic graphs[3].

The lookup of a concept is done by collecting all semantic relations known to the concepts. These relations could be, e.g., synonyms, hypernyms or meronyms. The semantic relations are completed with the concepts making up the definition of a concept, e.g., as described in WordNet. If an added concept was not present in the graph before the concepts will be decomposed iteratively until a termination criterion is met. The termination criteria were selected to be the iteration depth of two since the graph becomes intractable afterward.

This resulting semantic graph is domain specific and depends on the concepts which are decomposed. The decomposition is the process of looking up a given word in the given resources and adding all found concepts and relations to the resulting graph.

Depending on the decomposed concepts, the resulting graph consists of different concepts. This has been proven to be useful for different problems, e.g., semantic distance measures [10]. The questions for the decomposition is now on

---

[3] `git@gitlab.tubit.tu-berlin.de:johannes_faehndrich/semantic-decomposition.git` for access please contact the author.

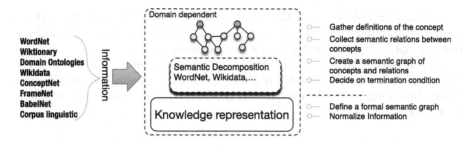

Fig. 2. Abstract description of the semantic decomposition to automatically create a semantic graph.

which concepts to decompose regarding Winograd Schemas. The next subsection will explain how we created the knowledge graph which is used by the marker passing.

Decomposing Winograd Schemas. At first, each word of the Winograd Schema (WGS) is decomposed, and the resulting graphs are merged. This graph forms the basis of semantic information, the facts we know about the words used in the WGS. This first decomposition thus contains all semantic information available to our approach, including synonyms, antonyms, meronyms, hypo- and hypernyms of each word. Depending on the information sources connected to the decomposition, additional concepts and relations can be part of this graph.

The result of decomposing of the word "suitcase" in our example is shown in Fig. 3:

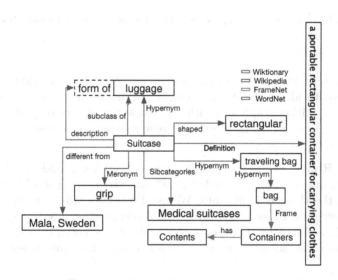

Fig. 3. Example decomposition of the word suitcase. (Color figure online)

In Fig. 3 the colors denote the source of information. The node of the graph represent concepts, and the edges the relations between them. The decomposition contains not only semantic but also syntactic information.

Now it is time to add other information which is already contained in the WGS. The next sections will describe how syntactic, semantic roles and Named Entity Recognition (NER) information is added. We start out with syntactic information.

Syntax. The syntactic information contains the information which constructs sentences out of words. Without syntax the word order would not matter, inflection is ignored, and references cannot be followed. Adding syntactic information is done by using a state of the art NLP library called CoreNLP[4]. CoreNLP [18] has been chosen because of its performance on English texts regarding grammatical analysis like Part-of-Speech (POS) and Named Entity Recognition (NER) tagging as well as basic dependency identification. Figure 4 shows one example output of the CoreNLP framework for a dependency analysis of our example sentence. Here the colors describe the different POS, and the arrows describe the syntactic relations between the words. These nodes and edges are added to our decomposition graph, which includes syntactic information into the purely semantic result of the decomposition.

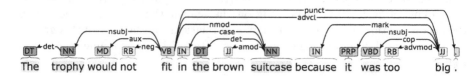

Fig. 4. CoreNLP output of a dependency tree for our example phrase. (Color figure online)

The syntactic analysis creates an abstract syntax tree with additional nodes and relations to all words of the WGS. Those nodes and relations are added to the decomposition graph and with that allow the marker to pass over them. Enabling our approach to take syntactic relations into the count.

Semantic Roles. Semantic role labeling analyses verbs and annotates roles involved. In our example the verb "to fit" has two roles: The object which is fitting and the thing it is fits into. We use PropBank[5] to determine semantic roles. We integrate those as edges into the decomposition graph. Especially for the resolution of Winograd Schemas, those roles are essential because Winograd Schemas are those border cases where the assignment of roles is ambiguous. If

---

[4] https://stanfordnlp.github.io/CoreNLP/ last visited 12.08.2018.
[5] https://propbank.github.io/ last visited 12.08.2018.

the program assigning semantic roles can guess right here, the battle is mostly won: In many cases, this would create a direct connection between the ambiguous pronoun and one of the answer candidates.

NER. If semantic decomposition is applied to names, information enters the semantic graph that is not helpful for the resolution of the Winograd Schema (e.g., etymological information about the names of people mentioned in the sentence). This makes it necessary to recognize names entities and exclude them from the decomposition. Rather than the named entity itself the assigned named entity tag is decomposed, e.g., "Person". This leads to more semantically useful links in the graph, adding qualities of people or organizations linked to the names, which can, in turn, lead to meaningful connections to other parts of the graph.

The resulting graph decomposes all words which are not stop words and connects them to the given answers. A simplification of this graph is shown in Fig. 5.

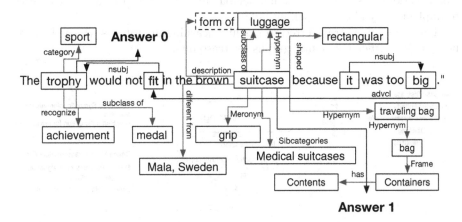

Fig. 5. Example decomposition graph of a Winograd Schema.

Figure 5 simplifies the decomposition for the ease of understanding. This graph is extended with syntactic edges discussed in the next section.

If no information source of the decomposition contains information about a given concept, the graph only contains the concept it self. If a concept has additionally no syntactic relations to the rest of the graph, the concept is not connected to the graph.

3.2   Marker Passing

Marker passing is the generalization of spreading activation [5] which models how semantic memory [4, 28] is used for reasoning in humans. One theory about reasoning in humans claims that humans think in concepts in a connectionist way [13]. Concepts are abstract representations of things, meaning less detailed, a model of which properties we remember if we think of something. This something could be e.g. a *dog*, or *love*, but in all cases it contains connections to other concepts, like *legs* or *feelings*. But a concept is abstract because it is a model of the real dog. It contains relevant information, not every hair of the dog, not every moment of feeling we had, but only those relevant. The connectionist part, is that the concept is connected to other concepts, with relations. A relation could be e.g. *has* as in a *dog* has four *legs*, or e.g. *is-a* as *love* is a *choice* or *feeling*. Those connections are part of the meaning of the concepts. Thus if we connect a dog with *hurt* or *fear* the meaning of *dog* is different then if we connect it with *protection* or *puppies*. Therefore, the meaning of concepts is subjective. But meaning is not only subjective but also context dependent [20,21]. Context dependent means that regarding the current situation, the meaning of concepts changes. Good examples are ambiguous words like *bank*, where we get money or where we sit on our surfboard. The concepts and how they are connected, is given by the decomposition. Thus the semantic graph shows what was learned. The questions answered by the marker passing is: how can this graph be used to implement symbolic reasoning [3,29]?

This principle is transferred to machine learning algorithms which then can be used on artificial semantic graphs for reasoning.

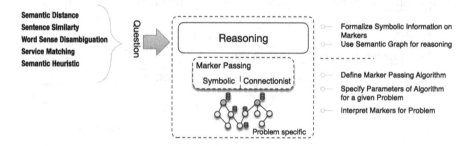

Fig. 6. Reasoning on semantic graphs.

The basic idea is that markers are placed on concepts of interest in a semantic graph, and are passed over the edges connecting the concepts to other concepts. This creates a marker distribution over the graph. Such an algorithm is quite general and can be adapted to many applications. In this work we adapt it to the solution of WGSs. The markers include application-specific information like an activation level or an edge history over which the marker traveled so far. Additional application-specific properties of the algorithm are encoded in the configuration of the marker passing. Those properties could be the placement of the initial markers, or when an concept is being regarded as active. This application specificness is shown in Fig. 6: the marker passing is specialized by a questions we want to answer. For the Winograd Schemas, this question is:

What is the right resolution of the ambiguous pronoun? After configuring the marker passing, the marker passing algorithm then passes markers from their start location to connected nodes, regarding those application specific rules.

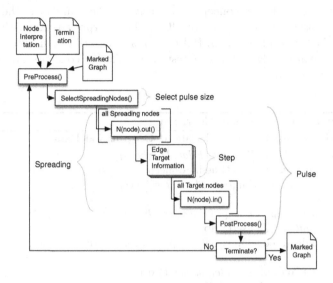

Fig. 7. Marker Passing Algorithm

Figure 7 shows the abstract marker passing algorithm. The main loop (called a Pulse) is executed until a termination condition is met. Each Pulse consists of selecting the active nodes, which pass their markers, the passing of the markers to neighboring nodes and the integration of the nodes into those neighbors.

The generic marker passing algorithm has variation points which allow specialization for different areas of application. These parameters are dependent on each other. Simple examples of such variation points are the *selectActiveConcepts* function, the *terminationCondition* and the *markers*: Here the *selectActiveConcepts* function needs to interpret the *markers* to decide if a concept is active or not. These examples show that the variation points can inter-depend. The needed variation points of the marker passing are the following:

Active Concept: is a concept which has markers on it.
Passing Concept: is a concept which has been selected by the activation function to pass markers in the next pulse.
Data: describes the marker and with that the information available to the marked node.
Pulse size: selecting which nodes pass markers.
In-Function: describes how the node handles incoming markers.
Out-Function and After-Send: describe how the nodes pass markers and what happens on the node after passing them.

Edge-Function: describes how the edges handle markers passed over them.
Termination Condition: describes when to stop the passing of markers.
Pre- and Post-Adjustment: describes what happens before and after a pulse.

In this way, the relevant concepts can receive markers, and after the algorithm has finished passing markers, the result can be interpreted. Algorithm 1 shows a more detailed view of the main Pulse loop, and describes our extension of the spreading activation algorithm of Crestani [5]. Active concepts are defined by getActiveConcepts().

Algorithm 1 Marker Passing Algorithm

Name: MarkerPassing **Input:** NodeData M **Output:**NodeData

1: $pulse_{out}$ = new Map<Concept,$(Edge, Markers)^*$ >();
2: **for all** sourceConcept $\in$ getPassingConcepts(M) **do**
3: 　 $pulse_{out}$.addAll(outFuntion(M, sourceConcept));
4: **end for**
5: $pulse_{in}$ = new Map<Concept,$(Edge, Markers)^*$ >();
6: **for all** $e \in pulse_{out}.keyset()$ **do**
7: 　 $pulse_{in}$.addAll(edgeFunction(M,e,$pulse_{out}.get(e)$));
8: **end for**
9: **for all** targetConcept $\in pulse_{in}.keyset()$ **do**
10: 　 M = inFunction(M, targetConcept, $pulse_{in}$.get(targetConcept));
11: **end for**
12: **for all** sourceConcept $\in$ getPassingConcepts(M) **do**
13: 　 M = afterSend(M, sourceConcept);
14: **end for**
15: **return** M

In the abstract representation of the marker passing algorithm in Fig. 7 the inputs are parts of the specification of the marker passing algorithm. In the more concrete pseudo code, in Algorithm 1 the input is a data type called "NodeData" which describes a graph created by the semantic decomposition with markers on the nodes. As input this markers are the start markers, and as output this is the resulting graph with its marker distribution. Now lets look at what the algorithm does step by step:

Line 2–4: All passing concepts activate their out-function and the result to the current pulse stored in the variable $pulse_{out}$. This is the input for the edge functions of the appropriate relations of the next step.

Line 5–9: Each marker passed by the current pulse is given to the appropriate relation it is passed to, and this relation activates its edge-function. The result of the edge-function is added to the pulse which is used as input for the in-functions of the targets of this relations.

Line 10–12: The concepts which are targets of the relations passing markers are given the markers passed to them and activate their in-function.

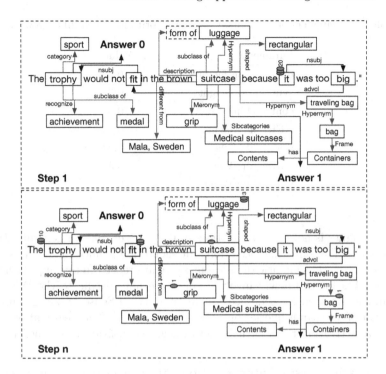

Fig. 8. Marker passing Example.

Line 13–15: The after-send-function is activated to fix the markers on the source concepts if needed.

In our running example we can see in Fig. 8 Step 1 that the initial markers have been placed at the pronoun. With each pulse the markers pass over the edges to other concepts, until they reach e.g. the position of step n in Fig. 8.

The Step n could be one outcome of the marker passing which then needs interpretation. How the markers are interpreted is subject of the next section.

This algorithm is used to perform inference on the graphs created by the Winograd Schema. The specialization of the algorithm passes markers over all edges, weighted by edge specific weights. The parameters are chosen like in the experiment regarding a semantic similarity measure [10]. These parameters let the markers pass through the graph and propagate like measuring a semantic similarity. This lets the markers pass through, e.g., big, fit and trophy, to select an answer. The parameters specialized for this experiment with Winograd Schemas are shown in Table 1.

The parameters in Table 1 have been established in experiments where each parameter has been analyzed, and an selection has been made depending on the expressibility of the edges. The other link weights propagate markers as a factor on the activation described on the marker. With the additional links (Semantic roles, NER, Syntax, ...) new weights had to be introduced. The selection of those

Table 1. Parameters of the marker passing algorithms which differ from [10].

Parameter	Value
degradation factor (negative)	0.05
syntaxLinkWeight	0.5
contrastLinkWeight	−0.5
NERLinkWeight	0.3
roleLinkWeight	−0.94
vnRoleLinkWeight	0.3
vnRoleLinkWeight	0.3

new link weights is not an optimization on the test set, but an general setup of the approach. The same has been done for semantic distance in [10], where the weights of a general semantic distance measure are reused in our approach here. Those weights for the newly involved edges are not specific to the WSC but, e.g., can also be used for sentence similarity or Word Sense Disambiguation or the relaxation of search queries on knowledge bases [7]. The degradation factor of negative activation reduces the effect of negative activation in general.

Marker Passing Result Interpretation. After the marker passing has terminated moving markers on the semantic graph, it is time to interpret the result. The interpretation of the marker distribution on the semantic graph depends on the problem solved. For our example application of the Winograd Schemas, we count the amount of markers set on each answer. We then select the answer with the most total amount of activation on all markers. This maximal activation represents a mix of semantic and syntactic distances. The distance is measured, because each time a concept is activated, its markers are split up between multiple edges. Passing the markers to multiple edges, means that ever less activation is carried on markers with each puls. This reduction of activation results in an abstract distance measure.

Here multiple interpretations have been tested: maximal average activation, maximal peak activation, the maximal sum of activation over the history of a concepts activation. The best performing interpretation was to use the marker activation divided through the total activation on all answers.

4   Evaluation

We evaluated our approach on the Winograd Schema Challenge[6]. For this evaluation, we have used parameters of the marker passing which have been learned for semantic similarity [10]. Those parameters are not specialized to the data

---

[6] https://cs.nyu.edu/faculty/davise/papers/WinogradSchemas/WSCollection.xml
last visited 12.08.2018.

set. Other parameters have been specialized, e.g., the decomposition depth, or the start marker allocation. Smaller experiments have shown that the placement of markers on the pronoun instead on the answer possibilities performs better in solving the WSC. The results of our experiments compared to the state-of-the-art are shown in Table 2 [17].

Table 2. Approaches and their performance in 2016 Winograd Schema Challenge [17, Table 4], and the result of Liu et al. [17].

Approach	Result
Our Approach	74%
Liu et al. [17]	62%
Quan Liu	58%
Nikos Isaak	48%
Patrick Dhondt	45%
Denis Robert	32%

These results show that the inference on the semantic and syntactic graph can distinguish the ambiguous pronouns. Furthermore, the interpretation of the markers lets us evaluate the ratio of the amount of activation placed on each answer possibility, which gives us insight into the confidence of our approach.

The evaluation has been done in multiple smaller experiments. The different components have been evaluated to their impact to the result. As an example the placement of the start markers. The start marker placement could be on the pronoun or an the answers. Putting the start markers on the answers, which have multiple edges in the graph, spreads the markers across the graph. This spread is caused by multiple use of the answers e.g. names and the on average high edge count of the answer nodes. This spread of markers can be reduced by placing the markers on the ambiguous pronoun, which in average has less edges then an answer node. Because the markers did not have to find the e.g. one edge connecting the pronoun to the sentence, the graph was not flooded with markers, resulting an better performance then placing start markers on the answers.

Another example of an additional experiment is the investigation of the influence of the different information sources. Regarding the Winograd Schema challenge using only WordNet, Wiktionary and Wikidata worked best.

The use of syntactic relations, in addition to the semantic relations of the decomposition connects many concepts (especially the pronoun) to the rest of the sentence. These additional relations increase the performance of the approach significantly.

5   Conclusion

The paper presents our unsupervised approach to solving Winograd Schemas. Our approach includes two parts: Part one is connectionist, where resources like

Wikipedia or WordNet are used to collect semantic information about the words used and build up a semantic graph. The second part is a symbolic one, where marker passing is used to traverse the created semantic and syntactic graph. The combination of symbolic and connectionist approaches allows the approach to be adapted to multiple problems. The experiments in this paper show that it is possible to use this approach to beat the state-of-the-art in the Winograd Schema Challenge. Some of the wrongly answered schemas have properties in common. One example is the following schemas:

- Mark heard **Steve's** feet going down the ladder. The door of the shop closed after him. He ran to look out the window.
- So Mark slept. It was daylight when he woke with **Warren's** hand upon his shoulder.
- Papa looked down at the **children's faces**, so puzzled and sad now. It was bad enough that they had to be denied so many things because he couldn't afford them.

All of those schemas have a "s" in one of the answers. The apostrophe seems to confuse the syntactic analysis and the decomposition independent of the being singular or plural. On a positive note, our approach is able to handle multiple sentences, handle multi word answers like "life and soul" like in:

- Lionel is holding captive a scientist, **Dr. Vardi**, who has invented a device that turns animals invisible; Lionel plans to use it on Geoffrey and send him to steal nuclear material from an army vault.
- I sat there feeling rather like a chappie I'd once read about in a book, who murdered another cove and hid the body under the dining-room table, and then had to be the **life and soul** of a **dinner party**, with it there all the time.

Additionally our approach still performs well if more than two answer possibilities are part of the schema. Here 67% of the schemas with three or more answers have been solved successfully.

5.1 Future Work

The here presented approach combines prior knowledge in the form of a knowledge source like the LOD, Wikipedia or WordNet with a reasoning algorithm extending modern ANN. Since the marker passing can be configured to use weights in relations, which changes the marker distribution on the graph, the weights can be learned. This learning of weights would specialize the resulting algorithm to the given problem, and most likely reduce its generality. With this loss in generality, the results would be as specific as the results produced by black box ANN approaches.

Another drawback of our approach is the dependence of the marker passing on the decomposition. Thus if the performance of the approach is not as expected, it might at first be unclear if a faulty decomposition or a misconfigured marker massing is the cause. Solving such development problems needs experience on which data sources contain which kind of information so that the decomposition can be changed to fit the needs of the problem. Additionally, the developer needs a sufficient understanding of the marker massing, and the effect of a change in parameters have on the result. During the design of the algorithm, the needed information in the decomposition can be estimated, and with that information, the needed data sources can be specified. Based on the available information in the semantic graph the marker passing can be specified.

It can be argued that the use of knowledge sources which are open to public debate include unverified information. This unverified information can lead the algorithm to be biased towards beliefs of the authors of such knowledge sources. Furthermore is the amount of knowledge sources in which a piece of information has been stated of interest to the decomposition since we do not yet identify and remove duplicate information.

Additionally, we do not use the full extent of the knowledge available, since the multi-lingual information, presented, e.g., in Wikidata is neglected. The extension to use multi-lingual information of all Wikipedia, BabelNet, and Wikidata is part of future work.

References

1. Arenas, M., Grau, B.C., Kharlamov, E., Marciuška, Š., Zheleznyakov, D.: Faceted search over RDF-based knowledge graphs. Web. Semant.: Sci. Serv. Agents World Wide Web **37–38**, 55–74 (2016). https://doi.org/10.1016/j.websem.2015.12.002. http://www.sciencedirect.com/science/article/pii/S1570826815001432

2. Auer, S., Bizer, C., Kobilarov, G., Lehmann, J., Cyganiak, R., Ives, Z.: DBpedia: a nucleus for a web of open data. In: Aberer, K., et al. (eds.) ISWC 2007, ASWC 2007. LNCS, vol. 4825, pp. 722–735. Springer, Heidelberg (2007). https://doi.org/10.1007/978-3-540-76298-0_52. (Chapter 52)

3. Austin, J.: Distributed associative memories for high-speed symbolic reasoning. Fuzzy Sets Syst. **82**(2), 223–233 (1996). https://doi.org/10.1016/0165-0114(95)00258-8. http://eprints.whiterose.ac.uk/1871/1/austinj18.pdf

4. Collins, A., Quillian, R.: Retrieval time from semantic memory. J. Verbal Learn. Verbal Behav. **8**(2), 240–247 (1968). https://doi.org/10.1016/S0022-5371(69)80069-1. http://linkinghub.elsevier.com/retrieve/pii/S0022537169800691

5. Crestani, F.: Application of spreading activation techniques in information retrieval. Artif. Intell. Rev. **11**(6), 453–482 (1997). https://doi.org/10.1023/A:1006569829653

6. Davis, E., Morgenstern, L., Ortiz, C.: The first Winograd schema challenge at IJCAI-16. AI Mag. **38**(3), 97–98 (2017). https://doi.org/10.1609/aimag.v38i4.2734. https://dblp.org/rec/journals/aim/DavisMO17

7. Ecke, A., Peñaloza, R., Turhan, A.Y.: Similarity-based relaxed instance queries. J. Appl. Logic **13**(1), 480–508 (2015). https://doi.org/10.1016/j.jal.2015.01.002. http://www.sciencedirect.com/science/article/pii/S1570868315000038Workshop on Weighted Logics for AI - 2013

8. Emami, A., Trischler, A., Suleman, K., Cheung, J.C.K.: A generalized knowledge hunting framework for the Winograd schema challenge. In: NAACL-HLT (2018). https://dblp.org/rec/conf/naacl/EmamiTSC18

9. Esteva, A., et al.: Dermatologist-level classification of skin cancer with deep neural networks. Nature **542**(7639), 115–118 (2017). https://doi.org/10.1038/nature21056. http://www.nature.com/doifinder/10.1038/nature21056

10. Fähndrich, J., Weber, S., Ahrndt, S.: Design and use of a semantic similarity measure for interoperability among agents. In: Klusch, M., Unland, R., Shehory, O., Pokahr, A., Ahrndt, S. (eds.) Multiagent System Technologies, vol. 9872, pp. 41–57. Springer, Cham (2016). https://doi.org/10.1007/978-3-319-45889-2_4

11. Furbach, U., Schon, C.: Commonsense reasoning meets theorem proving. In: Klusch, M., Unland, R., Shehory, O., Pokahr, A., Ahrndt, S. (eds.) Multiagent System Technologies. LNCS, vol. 9872, pp. 3–17. Springer, Cham (2016). https://doi.org/10.1007/978-3-319-45889-2_1

12. Ghallab, M., Nau, D., Traverso, P.: The actor's view of automated planning and acting: a position paper. Artif. Intell. **208**, 1–17 (2014). https://doi.org/10.1016/j.artint.2013.11.002. http://linkinghub.elsevier.com/retrieve/pii/S0004370213001173

13. Jones, M.N., Willits, J., Dennis, S.: Models of Semantic Memory, Models of Semantic Memory, vol. 1. Oxford University Press, Oxford (2015). https://doi.org/10.1093/oxfordhb/9780199957996.013.11

14. Kurzweil, R.: The Singularity is Near. Gerald Duckworth & Co, London (2005)

15. Lecue, F.: Applying machine reasoning and learning in real world applications. In: Pan, J.Z., et al. (eds.) Reasoning Web 2016. LNCS, vol. 9885, pp. 241–257. Springer, Cham (2017). https://doi.org/10.1007/978-3-319-49493-7_7

16. Levesque, H., Davis, E., Morgenstern, L.: The Winograd schema challenge. In: Proceedings of the Thirteenth International Conference on Principles of Knowledge Representation and Reasoning, vol. 46, pp. 552–561 (2011)

17. Liu, Q., Jiang, H., Ling, Z.H., Zhu, X., Wei, S., Hu, Y.: Combing context and commonsense knowledge through neural networks for solving Winograd schema problems. Assoc. Adv. Artif. Intell. (2017). http://dblp.org/rec/journals/corr/LiuJLZWH16

18. Manning, C., Surdeanu, M., Bauer, J., Finkel, J., Bethard, S., McClosky, D.: The stanford CoreNLP natural language processing toolkit. In: ACL (2014). http://dblp.org/rec/conf/acl/ManningSBFBM14

19. Morgenstern, L., Davis, E., Ortiz Jr, C.: Planning, executing, and evaluating the Winograd schema challenge. AI Mag. (2016). https://dblp.org/rec/journals/aim/MorgensternDO16

20. Neely, J.H.: Semantic priming and retrieval from lexical memory: roles of inhibitionless spreading activation and limited-capacity attention. J. Exp. Psychol.: Gen. **106**(3), 226–254 (1977)

21. Pace-Sigge, M.: Spreading Activation Lexical Priming and the Semantic Web. Early Psycholinguistic Theories, Corpus Linguistics and AI Applications. Springer, Cham (2018). https://doi.org/10.1007/978-3-319-90719-2

22. Peng, H., Khashabi, D., Roth, D.: Solving hard coreference problems. In: Annual Conference of the North American Chapter of the Association for Computational Linguistics: Human Language Technologies (2015). http://dblp.org/rec/conf/naacl/PengKR15

23. Rahman, A., Ng, V.: Resolving complex cases of definite pronouns: the Winograd schema challenge. In: Proceedings of the 2012 Joint Conference on Empirical Methods in Natural Language Processing and Computational Natural Language Learning, pp. 777–789 (2012)

24. Richard-Bollans, A., Álvarez, L.G., Cohn, A.G.: The role of pragmatics in solving the Winograd schema challenge. In: COMMONSENSE (2017). https://dblp.org/rec/conf/commonsense/Richard-Bollans17

25. Searle, J.: Minds, brains, and programs. Behav. Brain Sci. **3**(3), 417–424 (1980). https://doi.org/10.1017/S0140525X00005756. http://www.journals.cambridge.org/abstract_S0140525X00005756

26. Sharma, A., Vo, N.H., Aditya, S., Baral, C.: Towards addressing the Winograd schema challenge-building and using a semantic parser and a knowledge hunting module. In: International Joint Conference on Artificial Intelligence, pp. 1319–1325 (2015)

27. Shastri, L., Ajjanagadde, V.: From simple associations to systematic reasoning: a connectionist representation of rules, variables and dynamic bindings using temporal synchrony. Behav. Brain Sci. **16**(03), 417–451 (2010). https://doi.org/10.1017/S0140525X00030910. http://www.journals.cambridge.org/abstract_S0140525X00030910

28. Smith, E., Shoben, E., Rips, L.: Structure and process in semantic memory: a featural model for semantic decisions. Psychol. Rev. **81**(3), 214–241 (1974). https://doi.org/10.1037/h0036351

29. Sun, R.: A connectionist model for commonsense reasoning incorporating rules and similarities. Knowl. Acquis. **4**(3), 293–321 (1992). https://doi.org/10.1016/1042-8143(92)90020-2

30. Wang, F.Y., et al.: Where does AlphaGo go: from church-turing thesis to AlphaGo thesis and beyond. IEEE/CAA J. Autom. Sin. **3**(2), 113–120 (2016). https://doi.org/10.1109/JAS.2016.7471613

31. de Winter, J., Dodou, D.: Why the Fitts list has persisted throughout the history of function allocation. Cognit. Technol. Work. **16**, 1–11 (2014). https://doi.org/10.1007/s10111-011-0188-1. http://dx.doi.org/10.1007/s10111-011-0188-1

32. Yamaguchi, A., Kozaki, K., Yamamoto, Y., Masuya, H., Kobayashi, N.: Semantic graph analysis for federated LOD surfing in life sciences. JIST **10675**(5), 268–276 (2017). https://doi.org/10.1007/978-3-319-70682-5-18

33. Yampolskiy, R.: AI-complete, AI-hard, or AI-easy - classification of problems in AI. In: Twenty-third Midwest Artificial Intelligence and Cognitive Science Conference, pp. 94–101 (2012). http://ceur-ws.org/Vol-841/submission_3.pdf

Leveraging Part-of-Speech Tagging for Sentiment Analysis in Short Texts and Regular Texts

Wai-Howe Khong[1], Lay-Ki Soon[1,2(✉)], Hui-Ngo Goh[1],
and Su-Cheng Haw[1]

[1] Faculty of Computing and Informatics, Multimedia University,
Cyberjaya, Malaysia
`soon.layki@monash.edu`
[2] School of Information Technology, Monash University Malaysia,
Subang Jaya, Malaysia

Abstract. Sentiment analysis has been approached from a spectrum of methodologies, including statistical learning using labelled corpus and rule-based approach where rules may be constructed based on the observations on the lexicons as well as the output from natural language processing tools. In this paper, the experiments to transform labelled datasets by using NLP tools and subsequently performing sentiment analysis via statistical learning algorithms are detailed. In addition to the common data pre-processing prior to sentiment analysis, we represent the tokens in the datasets using Part-Of-Speech (POS) tags. The aim of the experiments is to investigate the impact of POS tags on sentiment analysis, particularly on both short texts and regular texts. The experimental results on short texts show that the combination of adjective and adverb predicts the sentiment of short texts the best. While noun is generally deemed to be neutral in sentiment polarity, the experimental results show that it helps to increase the accuracy of sentiment analysis on regular texts. Besides, the role of negation analysis in the datasets has also been investigated and reported based on the experimental results obtained.

Keywords: Part-of-speech tagging · Sentiment analaysis

1 Introduction

Sentiment analysis is a study of human opinions towards entities, where the entities can be products, services, places, politicians, events or issues [6, 11, 12]. Sentiment analysis also known as opinion mining, which mainly focuses on determining opinions into the polarities of positive or negative [6, 11]. Identifying opinions as either positive or negative is essential in decision making. Sentiment analysis has gathered tremendous attentions in both research and commercial venues. The emergence of sentiment analysis is not only due to the advantages it offers, but also very much motivated by the humongous data made available on the Internet. There are basically two categories of data which can be used for sentiment analysis, namely short texts and regular texts. Short texts refer to texts that are typically written and published short, such as

R. Ichise et al. (Eds.): JIST 2018, LNCS 11341, pp. 182–197, 2018.
https://doi.org/10.1007/978-3-030-04284-4_13

short-messages-service (SMS) over mobile phones and tweet on Twitter. On the other hand, regular texts refer to longer texts, such as product reviews, emails, and news articles. In this paper, we have included both short texts, particularly tweets and also regular texts, particularly online product reviews in the experiments.

This paper explores, investigates and analyzes the significance of Part-of-Speech (POS) tagging in representing texts for sentiment analysis. The POS-represented texts are then sent to statistical learning for predicting the polarity of the sentiment. Similar study has shown that POS, especially adjectives are sufficiently discriminative in predicting the sentiment polarity [9]. However, our experiments prove that in addition to adjective, other POS such as adverb and noun can be useful in improving the results. First, the impact of different POS tags, such as adjectives, adverbs, verbs and nouns in the representation of texts for sentiment analysis were investigated. The impact of these different POS tags are also analyzed when applied to short texts and regular texts.

This paper is organized as follows. Section 2 presents the related work. Section 3 details our methodology, including the extensive data pre-processing while Sect. 4 explains the experimental dataset. Experimental results are presented and analyzed in Sect. 5. Finally, the paper is concluded in Sect. 6. In this paper, the terms features and aspect are used interchangeably as they refer to the same thing contextually.

2   Related Work

Sentiment analysis has been explored by different paradigms of study. One of the most popular methods is statistical learning where machine learning algorithms, such as Naïve Bayes, Maximum Entropy, and Support Vector Machines (SVM) have been applied on labeled corpus in order to predict the polarity of unlabeled opinions [12]. Statistical learning approach is often chosen for its speed and accuracy in sentiment analysis. However, between the mentioned machine learning techniques, SVM tends to perform better and Naïve Bayes tends to perform worst although the differences are insignificant. It was mentioned that machine learning algorithm is not suitable for word level opinion extraction because the semantics within a word is not enough for a machine learning classifier [10, 12].

On the other hand, natural language processing (NLP) approach were proposed in multiple different approaches. Feature-based opinion summarization was one of the earliest technique proposed that has a significant contribution to the NLP approaches [6]. Later, double propagation approach [14] was proposed which exploit the opinion and opinion target relationship using dependency parser. By using a seed set of opinion lexicons it is able to extends its list of opinion words and identify its target and outperforms models like CRF and KN06 [8].

Rule based approach [13] is a technique that exploits common-sense knowledge and sentence dependency trees. It is one of the techniques that outperforms previous NLP techniques when it comes to identify implicit aspect and explicit aspect extraction from opinionated texts [16]. For twitter dataset however, feature based and tree kernel based model [1] outperforms unigram models and proven that through feature-based approach, the most important features are those that combine the prior polarity of words and their parts-of-speech tag. They too conclude that sentiment analysis on Twitter data does not have a lot of difference compared to other genres.

As of present, there are research works that take certain POS as opinionated words like adjectives only into account [4, 6, 7, 14], some research does not discriminate [3, 17] as they believe that opinionated words can occur in other POS such as verbs and nouns. However, no research has been conducted to leverage the effectiveness of different combination of POS. It was mentioned that verbs like "recommend, fluctuate, worsen etc." do contain opinion polarity and should not be ignored [17]. Hence, the goal of this paper is to explore the accuracy of different combination of Part-of-Speech (POS) using Natural Language approach.

3   Methodology

In order to perform sentiment classification based on different combination of part-of-speech (POS), the data were pre-processed the data, which includes cleaning and transforming the dataset. POS Tagging was first performed, followed by Word Sense Disambiguation (WSD), sentiment tagging and lastly negation conversion. After data pre-processing, sentiment classification is performed on the review and tweets, which are represented in different combinations of POS. Figure 1 outlines the general flow of data pre-processing before sentiment classification. Each steps is explained in the subsequent sub-sections.

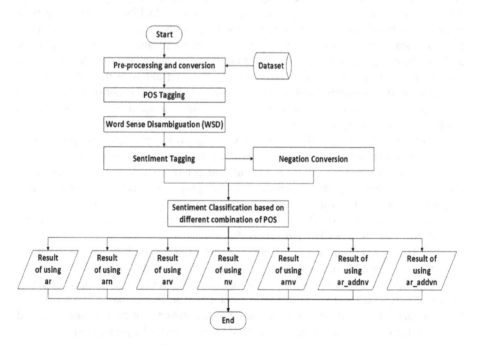

Fig. 1. Data pre-processing steps.

3.1 Data Pre-processing and Conversion

Convert HTML Codes and Unicode. Some of these data contain symbols that uses HTML codes and Unicode for example: HTML code like ">" that refers to ">" and "<" that refers to "<"; Unicode like "\u2018" which means single open quote. These HTML codes and Unicode were replaced accordingly. This step is necessary for us to convert emoticons into words.

URL Removal. Any links or URLs which starts with "http" were removed from the tweets. Replacing it with a representative token however will increase unnecessary frequency in a single token.

Removal of Hashtag and Twitter ID Sign. For the Twitter dataset, hashtags and Twitter ID will not be removed as they pose important part-of-speech for later analysis. Hashtag contains important information as it is a type of metadata tag used on social network and microblogging services to simplify the searching of similar theme or contents, while Twitter ID contains usernames of companies and products. Instead of removing them completely, the Twitter ID sign ("@") and hashtag sign ("#") which represent the Twitter ID and hashtag respectively were removed, for example "#IOS, @Microsoft" become "IOS, Microsoft".

Emoticon Conversion. Emoticons were converted to what they mean in word form. For example, ":)" was converted to "happy", "T_T" was converted to "cry". There are altogether 186 emoticons converted.

Abbreviation Conversion. Abbreviations will be converted into their full words, for example "lol" will be changed into "laughing out loud". There are a total of 388 sets of abbreviations used in these conversion.

Colon Removal. The colon symbol in tweets will be removed due to some bugs with the WSD tool that is unable to completely process tweets that contain colon.

Spell Checking. Most typo in the dataset were corrected with a spell checker tool[1] that utilizes Levenshtein Distance, the edit distance is set to 2.

3.2 Part-of-Speech Tagging

Part-of-speech (POS) tagging was then applied to the processed datasets from Sect. 3.1. In this step, TreeTagger[2] was used. TreeTagger is a tool for annotating text with POS and lemma information. It was developed by Helmut Schmid in the TC project at the Institute for Computational Linguistics of the University of Stuttgart. It has higher accuracy when tagging noun and verbs, followed by Stanford POS Tagger [5, 15].

---

[1] http://norvig.com/spell-correct.html.

[2] http://www.cis.uni-muenchen.de/ ~ schmid/tools/TreeTagger.

3.3 Word Sense Disambiguation and SentiWordnet

After the step in Sect. 3.2, the POS-tagged datasets will go through Word Sense Disambiguation (WSD) using a WSD tool for Wordnet[3]. WSD is the process of identifying the sense of a polysemic word. It usually uses WordNet as a reference sense inventory for English, which is a computational lexicon that encodes concepts as synonym sets. Every word after WSD will be changed, for example:

"living" -> "living#a#3", where "#a" (adjective) is the POS and "#3" (the third meaning of the adjective word, "living" in WordNet) is the word sense in WordNet. For words that does not contain sense, or not included in WordNet but contains POS will be converted to, "living#a" instead where "#a" is the POS of the word "living". If the POS and word sense of a word is undetermined, it will be ignored.

3.4 Sentiment Tagging

Next, sentiment tags will be assigned to every word based on SentiWordNet [2]. SentitWordNet is a lexical resource based on the well-known WordNet for opinion mining. SentiWordNet assigns a weighted score to each synset (the basic item of information in WordNet and it represents a "concept" that is unambiguous) of WordNet.

For the weighted sentiment on SentiWordNet, sentiment with the largest weight and with the matched POS attached to the word sense were taken into account. For example, given a row in SentiWordNet as follows:

$$\text{"a 0.5   0.125   living#3"}$$

It indicates that "a" is the part-of-speech of the word (living), "0.5" is the positive weight and "0.125" is the negative weight and "living#3" is the word sense. Since "0.5" is more than "0.125", the word will be considered as positive and vice versa. In case of same weight, it will be tagged as neutral. For the word however, it will be changed from "living#3" to "living#a#3" where "a" is the POS adverb of this word to match the output after WSD. For words that are not included in SentiWordNet like "tweeting" and "cannot", they were checked against a compiled list of opinion lexicon [6] to determine the sentiment polarity of a word. The words were then tagged as p, g or n respectively, where p represent positive, g represents negative and n represents neutral. Table 1 depicts the process flow of converting an original tweet to sentiment tagged output (as explained from Sects. 3.1 to 3.4).

3.5 Negation Conversion

By tagging opinion on word level, sentence structure is not being taken into consideration. Some sentences with negation like "no" and "not" will have the opposite sentiment, such as, "not bad, not as good". By applying negation conversion, it will

---

[3] http://maraca.d.umn.edu/allwords/allwords.html.

Table 1. Process flow of converting raw tweet to sentiment-tagged tweet.

Process	Tweet
Original tweet (input)	RT @MN2NOVA: Love ios5 Easter eggs. Pull down from middle top to bottom and see what pulls down. Awesome little feature! #ios5 @apple
Pre-processing and conversion	retweet MN2NOVA Love ios5 Easter eggs. Pull down from middle top to bottom and see what pulls down. Awesome little feature! ios5 apple
POS tagging	retweet/NP MN2NOVA/NP Love/NP ios5/NP Easter/NP eggs/NNS./SENT Pull/VV down/RB from/IN middle/JJ top/NN to/TO bottom/VV and/CC see/VV what/WP pulls/VVZ down/RP./SENT Awesome/JJ little/JJ feature/NN!/SENT ios5/JJ apple/NN
Word sense disambiguation	retweet MN2NOVA Love ios5 Easter egg#n#3. Pull down#r#1 from#r middle#a#1 top#n#9 to bottom and see what pulls down#r#2. Awesome#a#1 little#a#1 feature#n#1 ios5#a apple#n#2
Sentiment tagging (output)	retweet#n mn2nova#n love#p ios5#n easter#n egg#n. #n pull#n down#n from#n middle#n top#n to#n bottom#n and#n see#n what#n pulls#n down#n. #n awesome#p little#g feature#n ios5#n apple#n

reflect a more accurate sentiment for the sentence as a whole. Negation conversion is done by detecting any opinionated words that is near to the negation. Dependency structure was not used to detect the subject of negation. If there is any opinionated words around the negation, before or after the negation word, our algorithm (as shown in Figs. 2 and 3) will attempt to change it to the opposite sentiment.

Figure 2 shows the start and end point of negation conversion and whether to convert the negation word's sentiment polarity into neutral sentiment. The input will first go into node 1, which will be resumed in Fig. 3 and the result from Fig. 3 will return via node 2 or node 3. Figure 3 depicts the algorithm to detect if an opinionated word occurs before or after the negation and then reverse the opinionated word's sentiment polarity. If negation words are not present in the input or there is no opinionated words before or after the negation, it will exit at node 2 and proceed to the next input. If it detect an opinionated word, it will try to change the opinionated word's sentiment polarity and the output will exit via node 3.

By analyzing both datasets for short texts (tweets) and regular texts (online reviews), a huge amount of the word "be" was being tagged as "positive" based on SentiWordNet. As the word actually does not hold any sentiment in the sentence structure, a sample set was produced by ignoring the word "be" when it comes to negation conversion. Hypothetically, by reversing the subject sentiment based on the negated word, the negated word should be changed to neutral as it already serves its purpose, negating the subject. Based on these hypothesis, several different variations of negation conversion were generated to find the one that represents a more accurate dataset, which include:

Negation Conversion. Any opinionated words around the negation, before or after the negation will be changed to its opposite sentiment.

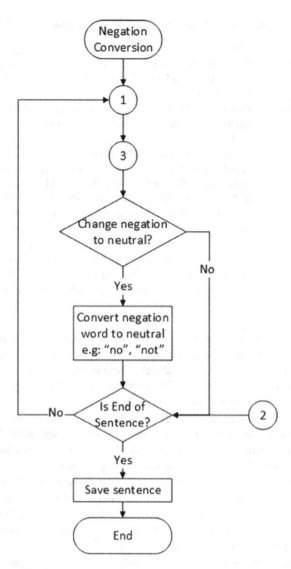

Fig. 2. Flowchart of negation conversion (first part).

Negation Conversion Excluding "be". Same as above but ignore the word "be" if it is being tagged as positive.

Negation Conversion Neutral Negation. Any opinionated words around the negation, before or after the negation will be changed and the negation word itself will be set to neutral. For example, negation words like "no" and "not" will be convert to neutral sentiment instead of its original sentiment.

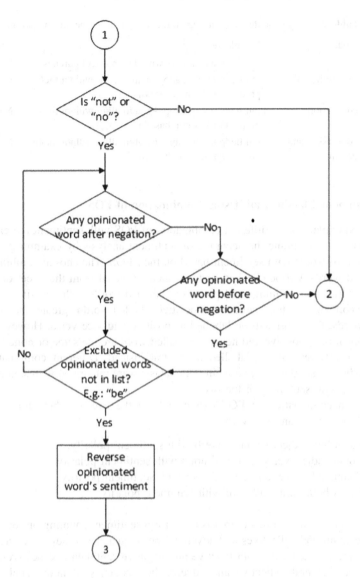

Fig. 3. Flowchart of negation conversion (second part).

Negation Conversion Neutral Negation Excluding "be". Same as above but ignore the word "be" if it is being tagged as positive.

Table 2 shows a sample tweet from the dataset with the application of negation conversion. The algorithm searches three words ahead of the negation for an opinionated word. If there is none, it will search three words before the negation. The default mode does not perform negation conversion while negation conversion converts the sentiment of the word "happy" into negative. As for negation conversion with neutral negation, the negation will be converted to neutral as it has altered its target opinion.

Table 2. Sample sentence after negation conversion and neutral negation.

Negation mode	Sample sentence	Sentiment
Raw text	I am not happy at all with the product I purchased	Negative
Default after sentiment tagging	i#n be#p not#g happy#p at#n all#n with#n the#n product#n i#n purchase#n	Positive
Negation conversion	i#n be#p not#g happy#g at#n all#n with#n the#n product#n i#n purchase#n	Negative
Negation conversion and neutral negation	i#n be#p not#n happy#g at#n all#n with#n the#n product#n i#n purchase#n	Neutral

3.6 Sentiment Classification Using Combination of POS

This section explains how different combination of POS with sentiment are extracted. The purpose is to examine the accuracy of sentiment analysis by examining different combination of words with sentiment based on their POS. The chosen combination of POS tagged words will be checked first and then extracted from the tweet or review. After the extraction, the number of positively labelled words with negatively labelled words are compared. If the frequency of positive labelled word is greater than negative labelled words, the tweet will be labelled as positive and vice versa. However, if the frequencies of both positive and negative labelled word are the same or none has been identified, the tweet will be labelled as neutral instead. Different combinations of adverbs, adjectives, nouns and verbs in both dataset were integrated with sentiments to derive the general sentiment of the tweet.

Here is a combination of POS extracted from the tweets, where a = adjective, r = adverb, n = noun and v = verb:

ar. Counts both adjective and adverb with sentiment polarity.
arn. Counts adjective, adverb and noun with sentiment polarity.
arv. Counts adjective, adverb and verb with sentiment polarity.
nv. Counts both noun and verb with sentiment polarity.

ar_addnv. The motive of this output is to perform sentiment counting on reviews that does not contain both adjectives and adverbs. The frequencies of adjective and adverb in a tweet are counted with both positive and negative sentiments respectively. If the count is zero for both adjective and adverb, the frequency of noun labels will be checked. If it is still 0, the frequency of verbs will be checked. Finally, if it manage to find either one, it will stop counting and will decide on the sentiment of the tweet. For example, a tweet contains two positive nouns and two negative verbs. First, it will count the adjective and adverb, which will return a zero for the sentiment-labelled words. Then it will count for noun that have sentiment polarity and it will return two positive count. Since it is able to get a count on noun, it will not count the sentiment labelled verbs. In the end, the result will be two positive count, which will then label this tweet as positive.

ar_addvn. Same as the above but with different arrangement, if the count of both adjective and adverb is 0, then the frequencies of verbs will be checked first, followed by noun.

arnv. Counts adjective, adverb, noun and verb with sentiment polarity at the same time. The difference between this and the first two is that all four POS with labelled sentiment will be counted at the same time, while the formal ones will look into adjective and adverb first then into a different priority of noun and verb. For example, if a tweet contains one positive labelled adjective, one negative labelled adverb, no noun and two negative labelled verbs, all these sentiment-labelled POS will be counted at the same time without any particular order. Finally, the tweet will be labelled negative, if the numbers of negative labelled POS is larger than positive labelled POS. Section 5 discusses and compares the results of experiments performed on the output of this section.

Table 3 shows an example of sentiment counting using combination of POS tagging.

Table 3. An example of sentiment counting in different POS combination (including "be", without negation conversion).

Raw text	Is at the apple store waiting for a poorly iMac to be seen by a genius. Hopefully this will be painless. Not too bad in here.		
Word sense disambiguation	be#v#1 at#r the apple#n#1 store#n#3 waiting for#r a poorly#r#1 iMac#a to be#v#1 seen by#r#1 a genius#n#5. Hopefully#r#1 this will#v#3 be#v#1 painless#a#2. Not#r#1 too#r#1 bad#a#1 in#r#1 here#r#3.		
Sentiment tagging	be#p at#n the#n apple#n store#n waiting#n for#n a#n poorly#g imac#n to#n be#p seen#n by#n a#n genius#p. #n hopefully#p this#n will#n be#p painless#g. #n not#g too#p bad#g in#n here#n. #n		
Output	*Positive words*	*Negative words*	*Sentiment*
ar	Hopefully#r#1, too#r#1	poorly#r#1 painless#a#2, Not#r#1, bad#a#1	Negative
arn	Hopefully#r#1, too#r#1, genius#n#5	poorly#r#1 painless#a#2, Not#r#1, bad#a#1	Negative
arv	be#v#1, Hopefully#r#1, too#r#1, be#v#1	poorly#r#1 painless#a#2, Not#r#1, bad#a#1	Neutral
nv	be#v#1, genius#n#5, be#v#1		Positive
ar_addnv	Hopefully#r#1, too#r#1	poorly#r#1 painless#a#2, Not#r#1, bad#a#1	Negative
ar_addvn	Hopefully#r#1, too#r#1	poorly#r#1 painless#a#2, Not#r#1, bad#a#1	Negative
arvn	be#v#1, genius#n#5, Hopefully#r#1, too#r#1, be#v#1	poorly#r#1 painless#a#2, Not#r#1, bad#a#1	Positive

4 Experimental Dataset

To evaluate the impact of POS-tagging in sentiment analysis, two types of datasets were used for the experiments. The Twitter dataset downloaded from Sanders Analytics[4]. It consists of 5,113 tweets. Amongst those tweets, 1,689 of them are being labelled as "irrelevant". For example, some irrelevant tweets consists of words in foreign languages, URL only or Unicode characters that appears as "???". All these tweets will not be included in the experiments, which left us with 3,424 tweets with sentiment of either positive, negative or neutral. The tweets focus on four main topics, namely Apple, Microsoft, Google and Twitter itself. Table 4 shows a breakdown of the tweets. The sentiments of the dataset were manually labelled.

Table 4. Breakdown of Twitter dataset.

Tweet sentiment/company TwEETS	Positive tweets	Negative tweets	Neutral tweets	Total company tweets
Apple tweets	164	316	523	1003
Google tweets	202	57	579	838
Microsoft tweets	91	132	641	864
Twitter tweets	62	67	590	719
Total tweets with sentiment	519	572	2333	3424
Total irrelevant tweets				**1689**
Total tweets in dataset				**5113**

For regular texts, online reviews dataset on laptop has been obtained from SemEval-2015 Task 12: Aspect Based Sentiment Analysis[5]. It consists of 1,739 sentences that are pre-labelled. For the purpose of our experiments, the sentences are grouped into reviews according to the review IDs given in the dataset. The overall sentiment polarity of a review is based on the frequency of the sentiments labelled on each sentence, where sentiment counting was applied on the sentences in a review. It results in a total of 277 reviews with 167 positive review, 98 negative reviews and 12 neutral reviews. Table 5 shows the breakdown of the reviews.

Table 5. Breakdown of laptop review.

Laptop reviews	Positive	Negative	Neutral	Total
Sentiment polarity count	167	98	12	277

---

[4] http://www.sananalytics.com/lab/twitter-sentiment/.

[5] http://alt.qcri.org/semeval2015/task12/.

5   Results and Discussion

5.1   Results from Twitter Dataset

Based on the evaluation from Sect. 3.6, as observed from the results in Table 6, the combination of adjective and adverb POS provides the best result across all variations of negation conversion, followed by the combination of noun and verb. Negation conversion with neutral negation for adjective and adverb POS provide the best result by a very small margin compared to the other variations. Due to Tweets being short in nature, its sentence structure are more straight-forward. Hence, the difference is rather insignificant when it comes to negation conversion. However, it is harder to determine the sentiments of the tweets because the sentence consists of incoherent text, hashtags that combine words without punctuation and expressions through words. For instance, "haaaaa", "hmmmm", "ha ha ha very funny (in a sarcastic tone)". Furthermore, excluding the word "be" and neutralize negated words has an insignificance impact on the overall sentiment for a single tweet.

Table 6. Accuracy of negation conversion variations for Twitter dataset in percentage.

Negation conversion variation/POS sentiment	ar_addvn	ar_addnv	ar	arv	arn	nv	arnv
Without Negation Conversion	47.78	48.31	55.40	49.27	52.92	53.18	47.61
Negation Conversion	47.58	48.04	55.08	49.01	52.60	53.62	47.25
Negation Conversion and exclude "be"	47.25	47.69	54.79	49.39	52.10	52.80	47.43
Negation Conversion with neutral negation	47.11	47.55	**55.43**	49.33	52.63	53.62	47.28
Negation Conversion with neutral negation and exclude "be"	46.73	47.17	55.40	48.77	52.66	52.80	46.82

An example is shown in Table 7, SentiWordNet determines that any words that are "be#v#1" are considered positive while words like "plain#a#2" and "simple#a#2" are tagged as negative but contextually it should be considered as positive. The word "like#r" was originally a positive word but was converted to negative due to negation (not#r#1) appearing in the tweet's last sentence. The outcome shows that negation conversion including the word "be" with or without neutral negation produce the most accurate result for tweets, and it also paints an inaccurate outcome from tagging each words with their own sentiment without prior contextual knowledge.

Table 7. Sample of including "be" to determine the sentiment of a single tweet.

Raw text	Plain and simple, it (laptop) runs great and loads fast. Easy to carry, can be taken anywhere, can be hooked up to printers, headsets. Love that it doesn't take up space like a regular computer
Word sense disambiguated tweet	**plain#a#2** and **simple#a#1** it laptop#a run#n#2 **great#a#3** and load#n#8 fast#r#1. **easy#a#3** to carry can#v#2 **be#v#1** take anywhere#r#1 can#v#2 **be#v#1** hook up#r#4 to printer#n#2 headset#n#1. **love** that it do **not#r#1** take up#r#1 space#n#1 **like#r** a regular#a#1 computer#n#1
Sentiment tagged tweet	**plain#g** and#n simple#g it#n laptop#n run#n **great#p** and#n load#n fast#n. #n **easy#p** to#n carry#n can#n **be#p** take#n anywhere#n can#n **be#p** hook#n up#n to#n printer#n headset#n. #n **love#p** that#n it#n do#n **not#g** take#n up#n space#n **like#g** a#n regular#n computer#n. #n
Annotated result	Positive
Negation conversion and exclude "be"	**Negative**
Words tagged as positive	great#a#3 easy#a#3 love
Words tagged as negative	plain#a#2 simple#a#1 like#r not#r#1
Negation conversion (include "be")	**Positive**
Words tagged as positive	great#a#3 easy#a#3 love be#v#1
Words tagged as negative	plain#a#2 simple#a#1 like#r not#r#1
Negation conversion (include "be") neutral negation (don't count negation words like no and not)	**Positive**
Words tagged as positive	great#a#3 easy#a#3 love be#v#1
Words tagged as negative	plain#a#2 simple#a#1 like#r
Negation conversion neutral negation (don't count negation words like no and not) and exclude "be"	**Neutral**
Words tagged as positive	great#a#3 easy#a#3 love
Words tagged as negative	plain#a#2 simple#a#1 like#r

5.2 Results from Laptop Reviews

Sentiment classification based on POS seems to produce a better result for review as observed from Table 8. Its overall result is much higher compared to Twitter dataset due to more well-structured sentences and coherent text. The combination of adjective, adverb and noun POS however has the best overall result compared to the other POS combination. Negation conversion and exclude "be" produce the best result for the combination of adjective, adverb and noun POS, which is 71.12%. This is surprising as noun are usually thought to be neutral while most opinionated words normally come from either adjective, adverb or verb. This combination also shows that noun will have a positive impact to sentiment classification if it is taken into account in addition to adjective and adverb.

Table 8. Accuracy of negation conversion variations for laptop reviews in percentage

Negation conversion variation/POS sentiment	ar_addvn	ar_addnv	ar	arv	arn	nv	arnv
Without negation conversion	67.51	67.87	67.15	68.23	69.31	57.76	68.59
Negation conversion	68.23	68.23	67.51	68.23	70.76	58.84	69.31
Negation conversion and exclude "be"	68.59	68.95	68.23	64.98	71.12	58.12	65.70
Negation conversion with neutral negation	62.45	62.82	62.09	61.01	65.70	58.12	62.82
Negation conversion with neutral negation and exclude "be"	63.90	63.90	63.18	61.37	67.15	58.84	63.90

The better result from the *arn* combination did pique our interest. Hence, in order to identify the number of opinionated noun, an analysis has been done on the laptop review and found that out of 1,091 unique noun, 170 of them were opinionated, which amounts to 15.58% of the unique nouns identified. In terms of occurrences however, it sums up to 4,460 of total nouns, of which 391 were opinionated, which is 8.7668% of the total noun. On the other hand, the Twitter dataset contains a total of 3,154 unique nouns where 338 of them are opinionated, placing it at 10.71%. The amount may not be significant but it does contribute to a better accuracy when it comes to sentiment classification for laptop reviews. However, due to the feature of microblog like hashtags and Internet language in tweets, some nouns are not recognized TreeTagger. This is the major contributing factor for the lower accuracy rating when noun is taken into account compared to the higher accuracy of laptop review. Table 9 shows the noun counts in each dataset while Table 10 shows sample nouns that are opinionated.

Table 9. Total noun and opinionated noun in each dataset.

Dataset	Laptop review	Twitter
Total noun	4460	11267
Total unique noun	1091	3154
Opinionated noun	391	846
Unique opinionated noun	180	338
Percentage of unique opinionated noun over total unique noun	15.58%	10.71%

Table 10. A sample list of opinionated nouns that appears in laptop review.

Nouns	Problem	Love	Trouble	Error	Nightmare
Total occurrences in the review	34	5	5	5	4
Sentiment	Negative	Positive	Negative	Negative	Negative

6   Conclusion and Future Work

Sentiment classification based on POS can produce a better result for regular texts but falls short when it comes to short texts. Negation rules should not be overlooked while performing sentiment analysis on both reviews. At the meantime, POS like noun does have a positive impact on sentiment classification due to well-constructed sentences which enable WSD to clearly define the sense of the words. This proves that opinions will appear in other POS and should be taken into consideration when performing sentiment classification. For future work, a combination of the current processes with more grammatical rules or dependency structure will be explored, estimated to provide a better understanding and accurate results for sentiment analysis, particularly for online reviews. However, for short texts, using a natural language processing tool catered for short messages appears to be a better alternative compared to the standard tools for normal text and reviews.

References

1. Agarwal, A., Xie, B., Vovsha, I., Rambow, O., Passonneau, R.: Sentiment analysis of Twitter data. In: Proceedings of the Workshop on Languages in Social Media, pp. 30–38. Association for Computational Linguistics, June 2011
2. Baccianella, S., Esuli, A., Sebastiani, F.: SentiWordNet 3.0: an enhanced lexical resource for sentiment analysis and opinion mining. In: LREC, vol. 10, pp. 2200–2204, May 2010
3. Brody, S., Elhadad, N.: An unsupervised aspect-sentiment model for online reviews. In: Human Language Technologies: The 2010 Annual Conference of the North American Chapter of the Association for Computational Linguistics, pp. 804–812. Association for Computational Linguistics, June 2010
4. Fei, G., Liu, B., Hsu, M., Castellanos, M., Ghosh, R.: A dictionary-based approach to identifying aspects im-plied by adjectives for opinion mining. In: 24th International Conference on Computational Linguistics, p. 309, December 2012
5. Giesbrecht, E., Evert, S.: Is part-of-speech tagging a solved task? An evaluation of POS taggers for the German web as corpus. In: Proceedings of the Fifth Web as Corpus Workshop, pp. 27–35, September 2009
6. Hu, M., Liu, B.: Mining and summarizing customer reviews. In: Proceedings of the Tenth ACM SIGKDD International Conference on Knowledge Discovery and Data Mining, pp. 168–177. ACM, August 2004
7. Jin, H., Huang, M., Zhu, X.: Sentiment analysis with multi-source product reviews. In: Huang, D.-S., Jiang, C., Bevilacqua, V., Figueroa, J.C. (eds.) ICIC 2012. LNCS, vol. 7389, pp. 301–308. Springer, Heidelberg (2012). https://doi.org/10.1007/978-3-642-31588-6_39

8. Kanayama, H., Nasukawa, T.: Fully automatic lexicon expansion for domain-oriented sentiment analysis. In: Proceedings of the 2006 Conference on Empirical Methods in Natural Language Processing, pp. 355–363. Association for Computational Linguistics, July 2006
9. Khong, W.H., Soon, L.K., Goh, H.N.: A comparative study of statistical and natural language processing techniques for sentiment analysis. Jurnal Teknologi **77**(18), 155–161 (2015)
10. Ku, L.W., Liang, Y.T., Chen, H.H.: Opinion extraction, summarization and tracking in news and blog corpora. In: AAAI Spring Symposium: Computational Approaches to Analyzing Weblogs, vol. 100107, March 2006
11. Liu, B.: Sentiment Analysis and Opinion Mining. Synth. Lect. Hum. Lang. Technol. **5**(1), 1–167 (2012)
12. Pang, B., Lee, L., Vaithyanathan, S.: Thumbs up? Sentiment classification using machine learning techniques. In: Proceedings of the ACL-02 Conference on Empirical Methods in Natural Language Processing, vol. 10. Association for Computational Linguistics (2002)
13. Poria, S., Cambria, E., Ku, L.W., Gui, C., Gelbukh, A.: A rule-based approach to aspect extraction from product reviews. In: Proceedings of the Second Workshop on Natural Language Processing for Social Media (SocialNLP), pp. 28–37, August 2014
14. Qiu, G., Liu, B., Bu, J., Chen, C.: Opinion word expansion and target extraction through double propagation. Comput. Linguist. **37**(1), 9–27 (2011)
15. Tian, Y., Lo, D.: A comparative study on the effectiveness of part-of-speech tagging techniques on bug reports. In: 2015 IEEE 22nd International Conference on Software Analysis, Evolution and Reengineering (SANER), pp. 570–574. IEEE, March 2015
16. Zhang, Y., Zhu, W.: Extracting implicit features in online customer reviews for opinion mining. In: Proceedings of the 22nd International Conference on World Wide Web Companion, pp. 103–104. International World Wide Web Conferences Steering Committee, May 2013
17. Zhao, W.X., Jiang, J., Yan, H., Li, X.: Jointly modeling aspects and opinions with a MaxEnt-LDA hybrid. In: Proceedings of the 2010 Conference on Empirical Methods in Natural Language Processing, pp. 56–65. Association for Computational Linguistics, October 2010

A Methodology for a Criminal Law and Procedure Ontology for Legal Question Answering

Biralatei Fawei[1], Jeff Z. Pan[1(✉)], Martin Kollingbaum[1], and Adam Z. Wyner[2]

[1] Department of Computing Science, University of Aberdeen, Aberdeen, UK
jeff.z.pan@abdn.ac.uk
[2] Department of Computer Science, School of Law, Swansea University,
Swansea, UK

Abstract. The Internet and the development of the semantic web have created the opportunity to provide structured legal data on the web. However, most legal information is in text. It is difficult to automatically determine the right natural language answer about the law to a given natural language question. One approach is to develop systems of legal ontologies and rules. Our example ontology represents semantic information about USA criminal law and procedure as well as the applicable legal rules. The purpose of the ontology is to provide reasoning support to an legal question answering tool that determines entailment between a pair of texts, one known as the Background information (Bg) and the other Question statement (Q), whether Bg entails Q based on the application of the law. The key contribution of this paper is a clear and well-structured methodology that serves to develop such criminal law ontologies and rules (CLOR).

Keywords: Ontology · Legal rules · Bar examination

1 Introduction

To develop question answering systems, ontologies can be used to develop domain-specific semantic information. However, capturing human-created semantic information from text for automated processing is not a linear process. In this paper, we consider legal reasoning such as from legal facts and rules to legal determinations as found in legal cases. Our ultimate aim is to (semi or fully) automate the process of judging legal case. We take a legal ontology along with rules to be core elements in this process as the link all the necessary legal elements of a case and support automated reasoning. However, making ontologies and rules is a difficult endeavour. To facilitate this, our main contribution is an engineering methodology for criminal legal ontologies and rules (CLOR).

We organise the analysis around a textual entailment task to question–answering as it is used in the US Bar exam [5], our benchmark of choice. More

© Springer Nature Switzerland AG 2018
R. Ichise et al. (Eds.): JIST 2018, LNCS 11341, pp. 198–214, 2018.
https://doi.org/10.1007/978-3-030-04284-4_14

formally, we can state that given a theory text T and hypothesis text H, we can determine whether or not from T one can infer H [1,2]. A range of approaches can be applied to the textual entailment task, e.g. machine learning, lexical information as well syntactic and semantic dependencies. However, these techniques lack the sort of legal knowledge and reasoning required to determine and explain entailment in the text representing bar examination questions.

The original bar exam questions are organized in the form of background information (Bg), which is the theory T, and multiple-choice question statements (Q), each of which we take as an hypotheses H. The objective is to select the correct H, given T. That is, given the background information, one must either accept or reject each multiple-choice question statement based on the application of the law[1] For the purposes of this paper, we illustrate the issue with one Bg and Q example pair (See Table 1). The question is, from the information in Bg, can one infer an answer (indicated here with Q).

Table 1. Sample bar examination criminal law question (adapted).

Bg	After being fired from his job, Mel drank almost a quart of vodka and decided to ride the bus home. While on the bus, he saw a briefcase he mistakenly thought was his own, and began struggling with the passenger carrying the briefcase. Mel knocked the passenger to the floor, took the briefcase, and fled. Mel was arrested and charged with robbery. The mistake of Mel negated the required specific intent
Q	Mel should be acquitted

An ontology and rule set for criminal law and procedure is large, complex, and evolving. Our contribution develops an interesting and relevant fragment, which can be developed further. In addition, an important research contribution is our incremental methodology for the criminal legal ontology and rule (CLOR) development, wherein we start with some initial ontology and rules and build upon them to account for further bar examination questions. The idea is that within this process, we come to identify specific or repeated patterns of legal reasoning, which then lead towards further generalization and application of legal rules. This is demonstrated later, where an initial system is developed on the basis of a limited set of data, then applied to further examples which had not be considered in the initial system.

The current paper builds on [4], which provided an initial criminal law ontology along with SWRL rules to draw inferences; we provided preliminary results from an initial experiment. In addition, the approach used NLP techniques to extract textual information from the source text. However, that paper did not have a clearly articulated methodology which be useful for further development

---

[1] See [3] for further discussion of the full dataset and the manipulations on it.

of the ontology and rules. The novelty of this paper is the description of articulated methodology for ontology and rule construction, further development of the ontology and rules, and some further evaluation of the quality of the ontology.

The rest of the paper is organized as follows. Section 2 discusses legal ontologies, and closely related works. Section 3, describes the criminal law and procedure ontology. The methodology applied in constructing the ontology is explained in Sect. 4. Section 5 presents the Semantic Web Rule Language and legal rules; an illustration of how the rules are applied to ontological information is in Sect. 6. Section 7 outlines how the ontology was evaluated. We conclude with some discussion in Sect. 8.

2   Related Work

Osathitporn et al. [14] describe an ontology for Thai criminal legal code with concepts about crime, justification, and criminal impunity. It aims to help users to understand and interpret the legal elements of criminal law. However, the focus of the ontology as well as its structural and hierarchical organization differs from an ontology for legal question answering. Bak et al. [13] describe an ontology as well as rules that capture and represent the relationship existing between legal actors and their different roles in money laundering crime. It includes relational information about companies, entities, people, and actions. Ceci and Gangemi [19] present an OWL2-DL ontology library that describes the interpretation a judge makes of the law in providing a judgment while engaged in a legal reasoning process to adjudicate a case. This approach is based on a theoretical model and some specific patterns that use some newly introduced features of OWL2. This approach delivers meaningful legal semantics while the link to the source document is strongly maintained (that is, fragments of the legal texts). Gangemi et al. [21] describe how new legal decision support systems can be created by exploiting existing legal ontologies. Legal ontology design patterns were proposed in [20], wherein they applied conceptual ontology design patterns (CODePs). However, this work differs from legal question answering in which legal rules need to be applied to facts extracted from legal text to reason with to determine an answer.

Several ontology development methodologies have been proposed. However, these different methodologies have not delivered a complete ontology development standard as in software engineering. Suárez-Figueroa et al. [36] present the NeOn ontology development methodology. NeOn is a scenario-based approach that applies a different insight into existing ontology construction methodologies. However, this approach does not specify a particular workflow for the ontology development, rather it recognizes nine scenarios for collaborative ontology construction, re-engineering, alignment, and so on. De Nicola and Missikoff [37] proposed the Unified Process for ONtology (UPON Lite), an ontology construction methodology that depends on an incremental process to enhance the role of end users without requiring any specific ontology expertise at the heart of the process. The approach is established with an ordered set of six steps. Each step displays a complete and independent artefact that is immediately available to end users, which serves as an input to the subsequent step. This whole process reduces the role of ontology engineers.

An overview of ontology design patterns was presented in [28] exploring how ontologies are constructed in the legal domain. Current approaches on ontology development can be categorized as either "top-down" or "bottom-up". The manual development of ontologies from scratch by a knowledge engineer and with the support of domain experts is known as the top-down approach [29], which is later used to annotate existing documents. When an ontology is extracted by automatic mappings or extraction rules or by machine learning from vital data sources [29], then this is regarded as a bottom-up approach. Much of the research works on legal data harmonization, applying a standardized formal language to express legal knowledge, its metadata, and its axiomatization. With respect to a top-down approach, Hoekstra et al. [9] present the Legal Knowledge Interchange Format (LKIF), an alternative schema that can be seen as an extension of MetaLex. It is more expressive than OWL and includes LKIF rules that support axiomatization. Related, Athan et al. [30] propose the LegalRuleML language that is an extension of the XML based markup language known as RuleML. It can be applied for expressing and inferencing over legal knowledge. In addition, Gandon et al. [31] proposed an extension of the LegalRuleML that supports modeling of normative rules. There has not been an instantiation of LKIF and LegalRuleML at scale or used for formalizing or annotating the content of a legal corpora either automatically or manually. Also, different theoretical approaches have argued that laws can be formally defined and reasoned with by applying non-classical logics like defeasible logic or deontic logic, of which their application involves the manual encoding of some specific parts of a legislative document, that may not scale to a full legal corpus [32, 33].

3   Ontology of Criminal Law and Procedure

The goal of the legal ontology is to design a terminological knowledge base and a rule base for legal reasoning. For the terminological knowledge base, we establish terminological relationships like subclass, is-part-of and so on. In our process, the schematic information is translated into an RDF [26] or OWL format to make it machine-processable.[2] The rule base represents legal rules for reasoning about the elements of crime and the statutory information. The Semantic Web Rule Language (SWRL) is used to express the rules, which makes use of the vocabulary of the OWL ontology in order to consistently reason. CLOR is expressed in the $\mathcal{ALCH(D)}$ description logic, with about 90 classes and 130 properties.

Methodologically, we work with a limited set of questions (16 questions and with multiple choices answers, yielding 64 question answer pairs), which are extracted from a larger corpus of 400 questions [4]. The purpose is to engineer solutions and incrementally augment them for more complete coverage of the data. Furthermore, we manually extract legal knowledge from domain experts,

---

[2] The OWL file is available upon request.

bar examination preparatory materials, and some law textbooks [6,10,11,16]. The purpose of the manual process is to ensure a proper consultation with domain experts. Moreover, the manual method of ontology development is more precise and accurate compared to an automatic information retrieval or machine learning techniques, which do not provide sufficient level of accuracy [19,22] especially for legal text. The manual process allows us to maintain a reference to the model and close to the process of legal reasoning. Where possible, existing legal [9,12–15] and common-sense ontologies were reused [17,18].

4   Methodology

In this section, we present our methodology, first with some general points, then with more specific considerations. This methodology consists of 18 steps that lead to the creation of a legal ontology and a corresponding set of rules. We selected source material about criminal law and legal procedures from exam preparation material [6,11,16,27], information from domain experts, and twelve randomly selected bar exam questions (questions 7, 15, 61, 66, 76, 98, 101, 102, 103, 107, 115 and 117) from a set of 200 questions [5]. The bar exam questions come with an answer key, which constitutes the benchmark for our methodology.

The selected questions contain criminal law and procedural notions such as: acquit, robbery, larceny, felony murder, arson, drug dealing and motion moving in criminal procedure. The idea is to ensure that all the information necessary for applying the law are extracted and represented in the ontology. That means, we systematically analyse the questions in order to identify and extract concepts, properties and relationships relevant for applying the legal rules for making legal decisions.

Due to the challenging nature of ontology and rule authoring [7,25], we decompose the analysis into a series of simpler *competency questions* (CQ) [7,8], each of which is aimed at collecting some specific information and can be used to ensure quality control of the knowledge base [23,24]. The domain expert seeks to answer the questions with respect to the corpus of bar exam questions and answers. These questions play a crucial part in the knowledge acquisition phase of the ontology development life cycle, as they describe the requirements of the intended ontology (see sample competency questions in Table 2). Next, we created a methodology consisting of 18 steps (see Fig. 1). Some steps process the text in order to provide material for further analysis, e.g. *Select all nouns*. Other steps filter or process information, e.g. *Identify relevant nouns* (given some notion of relevance) and *Identify atomic and definable classes* (given some notions of *atomic* and *definable*), and yet other steps further select information in response to particular *competency questions*. Thus, for each step, we process or seek to identify specific information from the bar exam question material and extract it into an ontology.

Steps 1 and 2: We identified and created competency questions relevant for extracting necessary information from the textbooks describing law and procedures [6,11,16,27]. For example, the relevant information for competency questions 1, 2, and 3 above could be retrieved from these textbooks:

Table 2. Sample competency question.

1	What are the elements of robbery?
2	Under what conditions should x be convicted?
3	Under what conditions should x be acquitted?
4	What are the differences between robbery and X (such as theft)?
5	What are the similarities between robbery and X (such as theft)?
6	What element(s) of robbery is necessary?
7	What element(s) of robbery is sufficient?
8	What elements(s) of robbery is optional?
9	What are the defenses for robbery?
10	What are the penalties for robbery?
11	What is the sentencing for robbery?

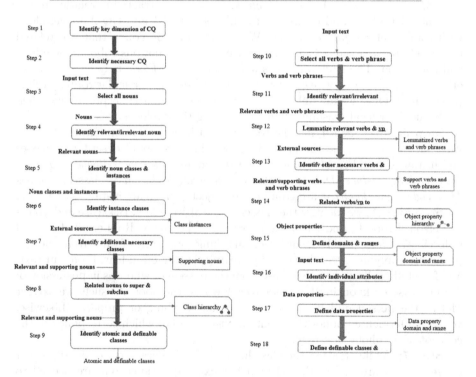

Fig. 1. Ontology design procedure

1. The elements of robbery are: "property is taken from the person or presence of the owner; and the taking is accomplished with the application of physical force or putting the owner in fear. A threat of harm will suffice" [6,16].
2. To convict someone, the crime has at least three elements: criminal act (actus reus), criminal intent (mens rea), and occurrence = act + intent [11].

Using the *competency questions* and other elements of our methodology, we extract legal concepts from these texts for our ontology.

Step 3: We start by identifying and collecting all the nouns in a particular bar exam question (question 7) without minding their relationships, the overlap between them, the characteristic attributes of the nouns or whether the nouns should be in a class or not. We want to know the elements of a crime which we would like to reason with. Hence, the following nouns were identified and collected from the bar exam question text (see Table 1) - *Job, Mel, Quart, Vodka, Bus, Home, Briefcase, Passenger, Floor, Robbery, Threat, Intoxication, Mistake, Defense, Voluntary action*, and *Intent* are extracted in relation to the elements of robbery and elements of crime as in CQ 1 and CQ 2 above along with some useful legal key terms.

Step 4: We separate the relevant nouns from the irrelevant ones (see Fig. 1). The relevant nouns *Mel, Vodka, Briefcase, Passenger, Robbery, Threat, Intoxication, Mistake, Defense, Voluntary-action, Intent* are extracted in relation to the elements of robbery and elements of crime as in CQ 1 and CQ 2 above, along with some useful legal key terms. We are looking for nouns that are related to the selected questions CQ 1–3 which bear on the notions robbery, acquittal and conviction. The irrelevant ones *Job, Bus, Home, Floor* may be relevant to other crimes, but are not relevant to reason with in this particular robbery crime (question 7). Once we are able to identify all the relevant concepts, we can then apply them for legal reasoning while discarding the irrelevant ones.

Step 5: After identifying the relevant and irrelevant nouns, from the relevant ones we determine the type of nouns which we could describe as classes and instances (see Fig. 1). We identified the nouns *Passenger, Robbery, Threat, Intoxication, Mistake, Defense, Voluntary-action*, and *Intent* as classes, whereas *Mel, Vodka* and *Briefcase* are ground level objects, which are instances of a class.

Step 6: Here, we identify the classes of the objects Mel, Briefcase and Vodka as Person, Property and Alcoholic-beverage, respectively. Robbery is described as forcible stealing [16]. It means a person taking something of value from another person by applying force, threat or by putting the person in fear. From our text, Mel forcefully collected the briefcase from the passenger who was in possession of the briefcase by knocking the passenger down on the floor. As such, we extract Mel as the person and briefcase as the valuable thing or property. Likewise, vodka is a fermented liquor that contains ethyl alcohol which corresponds to the concept of Alcoholic beverage.

Step 7: While creating the class hierarchy, it is necessary to identify other classes, which are not in the selected bar exam questions, but are needed to create clear class hierarchies (see Fig. 1). For example, classes such as *Person, Alcoholic-beverage, Crime, Felony, Controlled-material* and so on are created as conceptual "covers" of the particular terms in our examples. More generally, the task is to classify a set of named entities in the texts as persons, organizations, locations, quantities, times, and so on. Here, Mel is a name of a person and, therefore, a Person concept. Alcoholic beverages like liquor are controlled materials, therefore, we create the Controlled-Material class as a superclass of the Alcoholic-beverage class, and define vodka as an instance of this class.

Step 8: In creating the class hierarchy, the class Robbery is a subclass of Felony (R ⊑ F) and Felony a subclass of Crime (F ⊑ C) (see Fig. 2). Furthermore, has-committed-robbery (HCR ⊑ J), should_be_acquitted (SBA ⊑ J), and should-be-convicted (SBC ⊑ J) are subclasses of the Judgement class, and Alcoholic-beverage is a subclass of Controlled-material (AB ⊑ CM).

Step 9: The above identified concepts are classified into atomic and defined classes. Atomic classes have no definitions and are used types of instances. These are self-explanatory concepts and cannot be derived using other classes or properties. For example, *Mel* is a person and so Mel is a member of the *Person* class. Definable classes can be defined by using other classes and properties. For example, an *Offense* is defined as consisting of both *a guilty act* and *a guilty mind*. Often definable classes do not have direct instances; instead, objects can be classified as their instances by reasoning. Here, the definable classes are *has-committed-robbery, should-be-acquitted, and should-be-convicted*. In order to define the definable classes, we need to use properties (cf. the next steps).

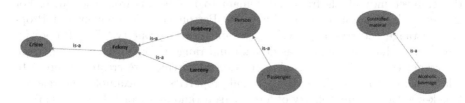

Fig. 2. Fragments of our legal ontology

Step 10: For object property identification, we start by identifying and extracting all the main verbs in the text (see Fig. 1). We do not consider verb phrases – a verb together with objects. Such objects are related to subjects in the ontology as below. For example, from the text we identify *being fired, decide to ride, carrying, knocked, took, was charged with, and negated required*.

Step 11: Amongst the extracted verbs, we determine the relevant ones by identifying the ones that link the identified nouns together in our earlier concept identification phase. The ones that do not link the selected concepts are the irrelevant ones. Here, in relation to our example text in Table 1 and the element of robbery and crime as in CQ 1 and CQ 2 above, the following verbs are relevant: *carrying, knocked, took, was charged with, and negated required*. They link together the concepts identified earlier. These relations are helpful in defining the elements of robbery and crime in which criminal law and procedural rules can be applied. Furthermore, verb phrases such as "being fired", "decide to ride" and some others are irrelevant since they do not link the extracted concepts together.

Step 12: The relevant verbs extracted are lemmatised to eliminate inflectional forms except the "to be" verbs. For example, from the extracted relations, we have *carry, knock, take, be charge with*, and *negate require*. We keep compound verbs, which are those together with selected prepositions.

Step 13: Other verbs that may be useful and necessary for linking some of the relevant concepts are identified in order to answer our competency question, for example, *forced* and *in-possession-of*.

Step 14: The retrieved verbs are then related into super and sub-property relations, thereby creating the object-property hierarchy. It is important to point out that due to the peculiarity of legal text, verbs that define a unary relationship are classified as classes. Such class names may also appear as a relation where that verb describes a binary or n-relationship. For example, the main verb *arrested* in the text *Mel was arrested* describes a unary relationship. To solve this peculiarity, the verb *arrested* is identified as a class in its base form. This means we have *Arrested* as a class. However, in a case of binary relationship, for example, *Mel was arrested for robbery*, the main verb *arrestedFor* is treated as a relation linking Mel to robbery as *Mel was arrested for robbery*. As such, the verb assumes a class position when it defines a unary relationship and an object property when it defines a binary relationship.

Step 15: We define domains and ranges of the identified relations as well as the characteristics as a way of restricting the relation. Since, object properties connect individuals from the domain to individuals from the range. For example, the relation carry-property has Person class as domain and Property as range ($\exists$carry-property.$\top \sqsubseteq$ Person, $\exists$carry-property$^-$.$\top \sqsubseteq$ Property); force-person has Person class as domain and range ($\exists$force-person.$\top \sqsubseteq$ Person, $\exists$force-person$^-$.$\top \sqsubseteq$ Person). Also, relation hierarchies are created in order to relate them into superproperties and subproperties. For example, the relation knock-person is a subproperty of force-person (knock-person $\sqsubseteq$ force_person).

Step 16: In same way, we identify datatype properties. These are the properties that links individuals to datatypes. Here, we identify drink-volume as datatype property.

Step 17: From the datatype properties, we identify the respective domains and ranges. For example, the domain and range of the datatype property drink-volume are Person ($\exists$drink-volume.$\top \sqsubseteq$ Person) and xsd:string ($\exists$drink-volume$^-$.$\top \sqsubseteq$ xsd:string) respectively.

Step 18: Here, we define the definable classes, which can be defined using OWL axioms or SWRL rules (cf. Sect. 5). Rules are often more intuitive to construct. Similar to definable classes, there are definable properties too, which can be defined using SWRL rules (cf. Sect. 5).

5   Legal Rule Acquisition and Representation

Rules can be used to define definable classes and properties. In our case, we captured criminal law and procedure rules from bar examination preparatory material [6, 10, 11, 16] and in consultation with domain experts. The expression of legal rules in SWRL is not a simple task and requires interpreting and formalising the source text.

The acquired rules were then expressed in the Semantic Web Rule Language (SWRL), which makes use of the vocabulary defined in our OWL ontology. The rules may be triggered in either a forward or backward chaining fashion. The essence is to ensure a consistent way of reasoning in order to exploit both the ontology and rules to draw inferences. SWRL rules are in the form of Datalog, where the predicates are OWL classes or properties. Moreover, rules may interact with OWL axioms, such as domain and range axioms for properties. For example, given the legal rule:

$$own\_property(?x, ?pr) \land decide\_to\_steal(?y, ?pr) \land take\_property(?y, ?pr)$$
$$\land differentFrom(?x, ?y) \rightarrow has\_committed\_larceny(?y)$$

The proeprty $own\_property$ has a domain of Person ($\exists own\_property.\top \sqsubseteq$ Person) and a range of Property ($\exists own\_property^-.\top \sqsubseteq$ Property) as defined in the ontology. They add implicit constraints on variable $?x$ and $?pr$, which must be instances of Person and Property, respectively.

All atoms in the premises need to be satisfied for the rule to be triggered. For example, for the crime of robbery, suppose P1 is *taking*, P2 is *by force*, P3 *use of weapon*, and P4 *robbery*. Suppose we have the legal rule (simplified by removing the variables): P1 ∧ P2 ∧ P3 → P4. Assuming that we have only P2 and P3 hold in the knowledge base, then we cannot assert that robbery. The fact that there was an application of force on someone and the presences of a weapon does not constitute a robbery, since taking is not involved. Martin and Storey [11] describe the elements of robbery as "theft by force or putting or seeking to put any person in fear of force." Therefore, the elements: theft and force are the main focus and must be explicitly defined in the rule. The extracted and transformed robbery rule from [11,16] and *Panel Law art 160* in relation to our ontological concepts and properties is given as:

$$in\_possession\_of(?y, ?pr) \land force\_person(?x, ?y) \land take\_property(?x, ?pr)$$
$$\land differentFrom(?x, ?y) \rightarrow has\_committed(?x, robbery).$$

Due to domain and range axioms, the variables $?x$ and $?y$ are instances of the Person class while "$?pr$" is an instance of the Property class. The rule can be read as:

If person $?y$ is in possession of property pr and person $?x$ forced $?y$ and take property $?pr$ and $?x$ is different from $?y$ then $?x$ has committed robbery.

Also, Martin and Storey describe the elements of crime as "*actus reus + mens rea = offense*" [11] – the concurrence of the two elements *actus reus* and *mens rea*. We translate these elements into rules, where an *offense* is:

$$has\_committed(?x, ?y) \land has\_intent(?x, ?i) \rightarrow guilty\_of\_offense(?x)$$

Here, due to the domain and range axioms from the ontology, $?x$ is an instance of the Person class, $?y$ is an instance of the Crime class, and $?i$ is an instance of the Intention class. The atom *has_committed(?x, ?y)* corresponds to the *actus reus* and *has_intent(?x, ?i)* to *mens rea* as the elements of crime. The rule can be read as:

"If person $?x$ has committed a crime $?y$ and person $?x$ had intention $?i$ to commit a crime $?y$, then person $?x$ is guilty of an offense".

A more complex example enables reasoning to acquittal. Note the chaining of rules between conclusions and premises, where the conclusion of rule (a) is a premise of rule (c), and the conclusion of rule (c) is a premise of rule (d).

(a) $carry\_property(?x, ?p) \land Property(?p) \rightarrow in\_possession\_of(?x, ?p)$

(b) $has\_committed(?x, ?r) \land negate\_required(?m, ?i) \land Intent(?i) \rightarrow did\_not\_intend(?x, ?r)$

(c) $force\_person(?x, ?y) \land take\_property(?x, ?p) \land in\_possession\_of(?y, ?p) \land charge\_with(?x, ?r) \land differentFrom(?x, ?y) \rightarrow has\_committed(?x, ?r)$

(d) $has\_committed(?x, ?r) \land did\_not\_intend(?x, ?r) \land Crime(?r) \rightarrow should\_be\_acquitted\_of(?x, ?r)$

The importance of using this approach is that legal rules defined are reusable and the whole process could lead to generalization of the rules. Some rules could be applicable to other legal subdomains. In addition, having a clear rule set will be helpful to automate legal rule development process in future.

6   Application of the CLOR

To understand the dependencies between the rules, we tested each of the rules individually with a populated ontology. Our queries are formulated in the Semantic Query-Enhanced Web Rule Language (SQWRL), which is based on SWRL and provides SQL-like operators for querying information from OWL ontologies. We assumed the following ABox assertions.

> $carry\_property(passenger, briefcase)$, $take\_property(Mel, briefcase)$, $knock\_person(Mel, passenger)$, $Crime(robbery)$, $perform\_bymistake(Mel, robbery)$, $Intention(intent)$, $differentFrom(Mel, passenger)$

from the example question in Table 1. In effect, the SQWRL queries enable assessment of the ontology relative to the competency questions as well as the relevant to rule firing.

We have the following queries for the ontology:

– The query $in\_possession\_of(?x, ?r) \rightarrow sqwrl : select(?x, ?r)$ is used in querying the possession rule (a) and the output is *(?x=passenger, ?r=briefcase)*.
– The query $has\_committed(?x, ?r) \rightarrow sqwrl : select(?x, ?r)$ is used for querying the robbery rule (c) and the output is *(?x=Mel, ?r= robbery)*;
– The query $did\_not\_intend(?x, ?r) \rightarrow sqwrl : select(?x, ?r)$ for querying the did not intend to commit rule (b) and the output is *(?x=Mel, ?r=robbery)*;
– The query $should\_be\_acquitted(?x, ?r) \rightarrow sqwrl : select(?x, ?r)$ for the acquit rule in (d) and the output is *(?x=Mel, ?r=robbery)*.

However, to be sure that the rules satisfy the dependencies in sequence to arrive at the final conclusion, we altered the ABox fact *carry_property(passenger, briefcase)* in the ontology. Then we executed the same queries and examine the output, which did not generate any results. In addition, we altered the fact *knock_person(Mel, passenger)*, leaving all others intact. As a result, the query

$$in\_possession\_of(?x, ?r) \rightarrow sqwrl : select(?x, ?r)$$

returned *(?x=passenger, ?r=briefcase)*, while the rest did not generate any results. Also, we kept all facts intact and altered *perform_bymistake(Mel, robbery)*. In executing the queries, we observed that the last two queries did not generate any result. Finally, we also tested the situation where we had all facts intact and altered *Crime(robbery)* fact. We observed that all rules work as usual, due to the fact that the Crime class is the range of has_committed, thus even if we do not have *Crime(robbery)* explicitly stated, it is entailed by the ontology. This shows that the dependencies amongst the rules were executed in the right order.

7   Ontology Evaluation

While the criminal law and procedure ontology and rule sets are still under development, we evaluated them in three ways: task-based, competency questions, and ontology evaluation tools. We note that while the results in Table 3 is incrementally better than previously reported, this has been done in the context of a systematic and transparent methodology. The advantage now is that in error analysis, we can trace the problem to a particular part of the methodology and revised that component, then rerun and test. We should emphasise that CLOR was developed on 12 multiple choice questions out of 16, which constitute the training data (results below), then applied to 4 new questions (for a 30 % increase of data), which constitute the testing data, as they had not been included amongst the questions used to develop the ontology. Of the 4 testing data, CLOR accounted for three, while CLOR required slight modifications to take the fourth question into account. This demonstrates that our iterative approach to the development of CLOR is feasible.

Firstly, we took a task-based approach, assessing the performance of CLOR with respect to benchmark answers to the bar examination questions. A semantic interpretation is said to be accurate if it produces the correct answer based on the question with respect to the application of the law. We present a preliminary experimental results from 16 MBE questions, each with four possible answers, constituting a total of 64 question-answer pairs. CLOR was evaluated against our previous work [4]. See evaluation result in Table 3. Secondly, we evaluated the system against our competency questions in the development stage. The ontology is evaluated with respect to how its concepts match with the respective terms in the competency questions. Here, we want to ascertain the completeness of the ontology in relation to the competency questions and whether the ontology answers the list of previously formed competency questions or not.

Table 3. Evaluation results

Index	Previous work	CLOR
True positive	15.0	16.0
False positive	16.0	16.0
True negative	32.0	32.0
False negative	1.0	0.0
Precision	0.48	0.5
Recall	0.93	1.0
Accuracy	0.73	0.75
F-measure	0.63	0.66

Finally, we used several ontology evaluation tools. To ensure the ontology is consistent and its general qualities are sustained, we applied the Pellet reasoner and the OntOlogy Pitfall Scanner (OOPS) [34, 35]. The ontology is consistent. The OOPS is a web based evaluation tool for evaluating OWL ontologies. Its evaluation is mainly based on structural and lexical patterns that recognize pitfalls in ontologies. Currently, the tool contains 41 pitfalls in its catalogue, which are applied worldwide in different domains. OOPS evaluates an OWL ontology against its catalogue of common mistakes in ontology design and creates a single issue in Github with the respective summary of the detected pitfalls with an extended explanation for more information. Each of the OOPS pitfalls are evaluated into three categories based on its impact on the ontology:

(a) Critical means that the pitfall needs to be corrected else it may affect the consistency and applicability of the ontology, amongst others.
(b) Important means that it is not critical in terms of functionality of the ontology but it is important that the pitfall is corrected.
(c) Minor means that it does not impose any problem. However, for better organization and user friendliness, it is important make correction.

Not all the pitfalls in [34] are relevant for evaluating our ontology. Moreover, some of these pitfalls depend on the domain being modeled while others on the specific requirements or use case of the ontology.

Our criminal law and procedure ontology was evaluated against the 41 pitfalls in OOPS (see evaluation result in Fig. 3). The evaluation is to ensure that our ontology is free from the critical and important pitfalls. On evaluating our ontology we observed that critical pitfalls polysemous elements are not present in the ontology as well as synonymous classes. Other pitfalls like "is" relations, equivalent properties, specialization of too many hierarchies and primitive and defined classes are not misused. Also, the naming criteria is consistent and so on. However, it returned an evaluation report of 3 minor pitfalls as shown in Fig. 3) (P04, P08, and P13). P04 is about creating unconnected ontology elements, P08 is missing annotations while P13 is about inverse relations not explicitly declared. At this initial evaluation, these pitfalls appear to be irrelevant, since the construction of the ontology is still in progress.

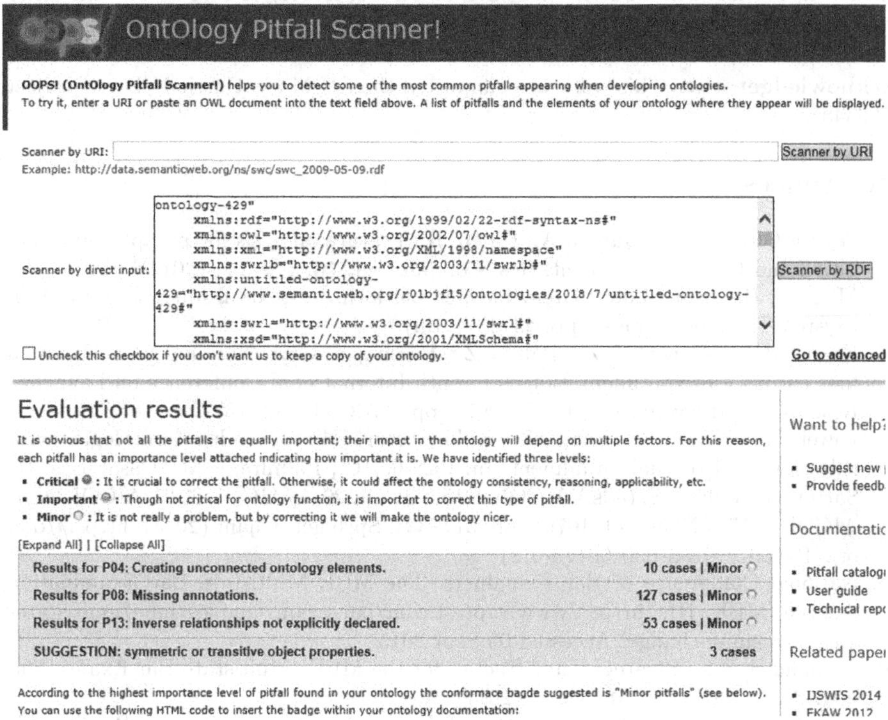

Fig. 3. OOPS evaluation summary

8   Conclusion

We have developed a methodology for a criminal law ontology in OWL with legal rules in SWRL to infer conclusions. The resulting CLOR ontology represents legal concepts and the relations among those concepts in criminal law and procedure. As far as we know, this is the first fine-grained methodology for constructing legal OWL ontologies with SWRL rules. We envision that such methodology can be applied to other domains and applications of textual entailments, such as fake news detection [38]. However, it is important to emphasize that the system does not address a range of challenging issues such as defeasible reasoning complex compound nouns, polysemy, legal named entity recognition, and implicit information in legal text. In the future, NLP techniques will be adopted to automate our methodology. Ontology learning techniques [39,40] might be used to learn further OWL axioms, which can be used together with

SWRL rules. Due to the uncertainties introduced by NLP and ontology learning techniques, we will consider some uncertainty/fuzzy extensions of OWL [41] and SWRL [42] in our future work. We will develop a Legal NER system to serve in identifying legal named entities such as Judge, Barrister and so on and other issues such as scalability for wider coverage.

Acknowledgement. This work was supported the EU Marie Currie K-Drive project (286348).

References

1. Segura-Olivares, A., Garcia, A., Calvo, H.: Feature analysis for paraphrase recognition and textual entailment. Res. Comput. Sci. **70**, 119–144 (2013)
2. Magnini, B., et al.: The excitement open platform for textual inferences. In: ACL (System Demonstrations), pp. 43–48 (2014)
3. Fawei, B.J., Wyner, A.Z., Pan, J.Z.: Passing a USA National Bar Exam: a first corpus for experimentation. In: Tenth International Conference on Language Resources and Evaluation, LREC 2016, pp. 3373–3378 (2016)
4. Fawei, B., Wyner, A., Pan, J.Z., Kollingbaum, M.: Using legal ontologies with rules for legal textual entailment. In: Pagallo, U., Palmirani, M., Casanovas, P., Sartor, G., Villata, S. (eds.) AICOL 2015, AICOL 2016, AICOL 2016, AICOL 2017, AICOL 2017. LNCS, vol. 10791, pp. 317–324. Springer, Cham (2018). https://doi.org/10.1007/978-3-030-00178-0_21
5. National Conference of Bar Examiners: The MBE Multistate Bar Examination Sample MBE III. http://www.kaptest.com/bar-exam/courses/mbe/multistate-bar-exam-mbe-change. Accessed 05 Sept 2015
6. Emmanuel, S.L.: Strategies and Tactics for the MBE (Multistate Bar Exam), 2nd edn. Wolters Kluwer, Maryland (2011)
7. Ren, Y., Parvizi, A., Mellish, C., Pan, J.Z., van Deemter, K., Stevens, R.: Towards competency question-driven ontology authoring. In: Presutti, V., d'Amato, C., Gandon, F., d'Aquin, M., Staab, S., Tordai, A. (eds.) ESWC 2014. LNCS, vol. 8465, pp. 752–767. Springer, Cham (2014). https://doi.org/10.1007/978-3-319-07443-6_50
8. Dennis, M., van Deemter, K., Dell'Aglio, D., Pan, J.Z.: Computing authoring tests from competency questions: experimental validation. In: d'Amato, C., et al. (eds.) ISWC 2017. LNCS, vol. 10587, pp. 243–259. Springer, Cham (2017). https://doi.org/10.1007/978-3-319-68288-4_15
9. Hoekstra, R., Breuker, J., Di Bello, M., Boer, A.: The LKIF core ontology of basic legal concepts. LOAIT **321**, 43–63 (2007)
10. Herring, J.: Criminal Law: Text, Cases, and Materials. Oxford University Press USA, New York (2014)
11. Martin, J., Storey, T.: Unlocking criminal law, 4th edn. Routledge, New York (2013)
12. Breuker, J.: The construction and use of ontologies of criminal law in the eCourt European project. In: Proceedings of Means of Electronic Communication in Court Administration, pp. 15–40 (2003)
13. Bak, J., Cybulka, J., Jedrzejek, C.: Ontological modeling of a class of linked economic crimes. In: Nguyen, N.T. (ed.) Transactions on Computational Collective Intelligence IX. LNCS, vol. 7770, pp. 98–123. Springer, Heidelberg (2013). https://doi.org/10.1007/978-3-642-36815-8_5

14. Osathitporn, P., Soonthornphisaj, N., Vatanawood, W.: A scheme of criminal law knowledge acquisition using ontology. In: 2017 18th IEEE/ACIS International Conference on Software Engineering, Artificial Intelligence, Networking and Parallel/Distributed Computing (SNPD), pp. 29–34. IEEE (2017)

15. Breuker, J., Elhag, A., Petkov, E., Winkels, R.: Ontologies for legal information serving and knowledge management. In: Legal Knowledge and Information Systems, Jurix 2002: The Fifteenth Annual Conference, pp. 1–10 (2002)

16. New York State Board of Law Examiners: Course Materials for the New York Law Course and New York Law Examination. https://www.newyorklawcourse.org/CourseMaterials/NewYorkCourseMaterials.pdf. Accessed 15 July 2018

17. Davis, E., Marcus, G.: Commonsense reasoning and commonsense knowledge in artificial intelligence. Commun. ACM **58**(9), 92–103 (2015)

18. Liu, H., Singh, P.: ConceptNet - a practical commonsense reasoning tool-kit. BT Technol. J. **22**(4), 211–226 (2004)

19. Ceci, M., Gangemi, A.: An OWL ontology library representing judicial interpretations. Semant. Web **7**(3), 229–253 (2016)

20. Gangemi, A.: Introducing pattern-based design for legal ontologies. In: Law, Ontologies and the Semantic Web, pp. 53–71 (2009)

21. Gangemi, A., Sagri, M.-T., Tiscornia, D.: A constructive framework for legal ontologies. In: Benjamins, V.R., Casanovas, P., Breuker, J., Gangemi, A. (eds.) Law and the Semantic Web. LNCS (LNAI), vol. 3369, pp. 97–124. Springer, Heidelberg (2005). https://doi.org/10.1007/978-3-540-32253-5_7

22. Maxwell, K.T., Schafer, B.: Concept and context in legal information retrieval. JURIX, pp. 63–72 (2008)

23. Pan, J.Z., Vetere, G., Gomez-Perez, J.M., Wu, H.: Exploiting Linked Data and Knowledge Graphs for Large Organisations. Springer, Cham (2016). https://doi.org/10.1007/978-3-319-45654-6. ISBN 978-3-319-45652-2

24. Pan, J.Z., et al.: Reasoning Web: Logical Foundation of Knowledge Graph Construction and Querying Answering. Springer, Cham (2017). https://doi.org/10.1007/978-3-319-49493-7

25. Bezerra, C., Freitas, F., Santana, F.: Evaluating ontologies with competency questions. In: WI-IAT, pp. 284–285 (2013)

26. Pan, J.Z.: Resource description framework. In: Staab, S., Studer, R. (eds.) Handbook on Ontologies, pp. 71–90. Springer, Heidelberg (2009). https://doi.org/10.1007/978-3-540-92673-3_3

27. Clarkson, K.W., Miller, R.L., Cross, F.B.: Business Law: Text and Cases: Legal, Ethical, Global, and Corporate Environment. Cengage Learning, Mason (2010)

28. Gangemi, A.: Design patterns for legal ontology constructions. LOAIT **2007**, 65–85 (2007)

29. Golbreich, C., Horrocks, I.: The OBO to OWL mapping, GO to OWL 1.1. In: Proceedings of the OWLED 2007 Workshop on OWL: Experiences and Directions. Citeseer (2007)

30. Athan, T., Boley, H., Governatori, G., Palmirani, M., Paschke, A., Wyner, A.: OASIS legalRuleML. In: Proceedings of the Fourteenth International Conference on Artificial Intelligence and Law, pp. 3–12. ACM (2013)

31. Gandon, F., Governatori, G., Villata, S.: Normative requirements as linked data. In: The 30th International Conference on Legal Knowledge and Information Systems. JURIX (2017)

32. Moens, M.F., Spyns, P.: Norm modifications in defeasible logic. In: Legal Knowledge and Information Systems: JURIX 2005: The Eighteenth Annual Conference, vol. 134, no. 13. IOS Press (2005)

33. Navarro, P.E., Rodríguez, J.L.: Deontic Logic and Legal Systems. Cambridge University Press, Cambridge (2014)
34. Poveda-Villalón, M., Gómez-Pérez, A., Suárez-Figueroa, M.C.: OOPS! (ontology pitfall scanner!): an on-line tool for ontology evaluation. IJSWIS **10**(2), 7–34 (2014)
35. Poveda-Villalón, M., Suárez-Figueroa, M.C.: OOPS!-ontology pitfalls scanner! Ontology Engineering Group, Universidad Politécnica de Madrid (2012)
36. Suárez-Figueroa, M.C., Gómez-Pérez, A., Fernández-López, M.: The NeOn methodology for ontology engineering. In: Suárez-Figueroa, M.C., Gómez-Pérez, A., Motta, E., Gangemi, A. (eds.) Ontology Engineering in a Networked World, pp. 9–34. Springer, Heidelberg (2012). https://doi.org/10.1007/978-3-642-24794-1_2
37. De Nicola, A., Missikoff, M.: A lightweight methodology for rapid ontology engineering. Commun. ACM **59**(3), 79–86 (2016)
38. Pan, J.Z., Pavlova, S., Li, C., Li, N., Li, Y., Liu, J.: Content based fake news detection using knowledge graphs. In: Vrandečić, D., et al. (eds.) ISWC 2018, vol. 11136. Springer, Cham (2018). https://doi.org/10.1007/978-3-030-00671-6_39
39. Maedche, A., Staab, S.: Ontology learning for the semantic web. IEEE Intell. Syst. **16**(2), 72–79 (2001)
40. Zhu, M., Gao, Z., Pan, J.Z., Zhao, Y., Xu, Y., Quan, Z.: TBox Learning from Incomplete Data by Inference in BelNet+. Knowl. Based Syst. **75**, 30–40 (2015)
41. Stoilos, G., Stamou, G., Pan, J.Z., Tzouvaras, V., Horrocks, I.: Reasoning with very expressive fuzzy description logics. JAIR **30**, 273–320 (2007)
42. Pan, J.Z., Stoilos, G., Stamou, G., Tzouvaras, V., Horrocks, I.: f-SWRL: a fuzzy extension of SWRL. In: Spaccapietra, S., Aberer, K., Cudré-Mauroux, P. (eds.) Journal on Data Semantics VI. LNCS, vol. 4090, pp. 28–46. Springer, Heidelberg (2006). https://doi.org/10.1007/11803034_2

A Quantitative Evaluation of Natural Language Question Interpretation for Question Answering Systems

Takuto Asakura[1]([✉]), Jin-Dong Kim[3], Yasunori Yamamoto[3], Yuka Tateisi[4], and Toshihisa Takagi[2]

[1] Department of Informatics, SOKENDAI, Tokyo, Japan
asakura@nii.ac.jp
[2] Department of Bioinformatics and Systems Biology, The University of Tokyo, Tokyo, Japan
tt@bs.s.u-tokyo.ac.jp
[3] Database Center for Life Science, Chiba, Japan
{jdkim,yy}@dbcls.rois.ac.jp
[4] National Bioscience Database Center, Tokyo, Japan
tateisi@biosciencedbc.jp

Abstract. Systematic benchmark evaluation plays an important role in the process of improving technologies for Question Answering (QA) systems. While currently there are a number of existing evaluation methods for natural language (NL) QA systems, most of them consider only the final answers, limiting their utility within a black box style evaluation. Herein, we propose a subdivided evaluation approach to enable finer-grained evaluation of QA systems, and present an evaluation tool which targets the NL question (NLQ) interpretation step, an initial step of a QA pipeline. The results of experiments using two public benchmark datasets suggest that we can get a deeper insight about the performance of a QA system using the proposed approach, which should provide a better guidance for improving the systems, than using black box style approaches.

1 Introduction

Recently, Linked Data (LD) has been recognized as an emerging standard for the integration of databases and the number of RDF Knowledge Bases (RKBs) is rapidly increasing [4,16,27]. While SPARQL is recognized as a standard tool for treating RKBs, authoring queries in SPARQL is not so easy especially for non-technicians [10]. For this reason, systems that allow users to search RKBs through NL questions (NLQs), the so-called Question Answering (QA) systems, are recognized as being highly useful. In particular, QA systems generating SPARQL queries from NLQs are called Semantic QA (SQA) systems (the exact definition is available in a study by Höffner [11]).

© Springer Nature Switzerland AG 2018
R. Ichise et al. (Eds.): JIST 2018, LNCS 11341, pp. 215–231, 2018.
https://doi.org/10.1007/978-3-030-04284-4_15

Benchmarking evaluations play an important role in improving SQA systems. While there are a number of existing evaluation methods, these methods essentially evaluate only the final answers per input NLQs [17]. However, since SQA systems have to involve various processes (e.g., parsing NLQs and finding URIs of entities), evaluations with only the final answers will not highlight the reasons why the results of the evaluations are unexpected. This limitation is considerably inconvenient for developers who are trying to improve their systems.

With this observation in mind, we propose a new evaluation method for SQA systems with which we aim to provide subdivided evaluation results rather than checking only the final answers. One of the possible evaluation directions is to focus on how valid logical expressions can be generated from the input NLQs. In other words, evaluations on the NLQ interpreter, a module of SQA systems, are useful. As a similar attempt, Ben Abacha et al. analyzed the false cases of their SQA system and classified them into (1) errors associated with the answer type and (2) errors associated with relation extraction [2]. Herein, we employ this approach to evaluate NLQ interpreters and present a calculation scheme for quantitative evaluation. The method has been implemented for evaluating a module of OKBQA, a highly generalized SQA framework (see Sect. 2.2), and it is available at https://github.com/wtsnjp/eval_tgm. This program will be the first module of the subdivided evaluation framework for the entire SQA system.

2   Benchmark Datasets and SQA Systems

2.1   Datasets

There are several famous benchmarks for QA systems, e.g., WEBQUESTIONS [3], SIMPLEQUESTIONS [5] and BIOASQ [1]. Although such datasets contain thousands of question–answer pairs, which are also annotated with some other information, these are not suitable for our purpose because nothing that expresses the logical structures of the questions is contained in these datasets.

One of the formal languages or logical expressions is λ-Calculi, and FREE917 [6] has 917 pairs of NLQs and corresponding λ-Calculuses. However, using SPARQL as a logical expression is much more reasonable for our tasks. This is because questions that can be annotated with SPARQL clearly lie in the scope of the SQA systems, and both SPARQL queries or some similar expressions collected from datasets and those generated by SQA systems can be treated in exactly the same way (e.g., both SPARQL queries out of databases and generated SPARQL queries can be parsed by the same parser). For these reasons, two datasets comprising pairs of NLQs and SPARQL queries are chosen to be the benchmark datasets for our evaluation.

QALD. As one of the most well-known evaluation tasks, QALD[1] [7,17,22–24,26] contains a number of questions annotated with equivalent SPARQL queries (Table 1). Some of the datasets (e.g., those named `multilingual`) contain not only English questions but also questions in several other languages;

---

[1] https://qald.sebastianwalter.org/.

however, we used only the English questions. The questions in the datasets that do not contain SPARQL queries (i.e., hybrid datasets from QALD-4–7) are annotated with pseudo queries instead. These are quite similar to SPARQL queries but can contain free text as the node of the triples, which makes the triple patterns of the pseudo queries different from those of the actual queries. Therefore, these datasets are inappropriate for our evaluation.

Practically, datacube from QALD-6 and largescale-test from QALD-7 are also inappropriate for our purpose. The SPARQL queries in the former datasets comprise a lot of extended syntaxes; thus, it is difficult for us to treat them as valid SPARQL queries. The latter dataset has 2 million questions, but this dataset is mechanically generated by an algorithm using the questions available in the training dataset. Thus, largescale-test contains a large number of similar questions; hence, we have chosen to skip the dataset in our evaluation.

Moreover, although each newer dataset is not a proper superset of the dataset for the previous tasks, many questions appear multiple times throughout the datasets. Using the same questions more than once can cause bias in the evaluation results; hence, such occurrences should be avoided.

Due to these reasons, quite a few questions were discarded from our evaluations, but we could still obtain a reasonable number of questions annotated with appropriate SPARQL queries. The exact number of questions used for our experiments and some of the basic analyses conducted on them will be presented in Sect. 4.

LC-QuAD. Largescale Complex Question Answering Dataset (LC-QuAD)[2] [21] is a newer dataset that also contains 5,000 pairs of questions in English and SPARQL queries. This dataset is for machine learning-based QA approaches. It is also useful for our evaluation owing to its size and complexity. Unlike the largescale-test dataset from QALD-7, LC-QuAD was carefully created to exclude questions that are similar to each other.

2.2   The SQA Framework: OKBQA

The Open Knowledge Base and Question-Answering (OKBQA)[3] community has been developing the OKBQA framework by modularizing general SQA systems so that each module can be developed independently by experts in each of the related technologies [12,13]. Hence the framework share the same goal with our evaluation method. The main part of the framework or the SQA workflow comprises the following modules (Fig. 1).

– **Template Generation Modules (TGMs)** take an NLQ (q) as their input and return a list of SPARQL templates $T(q)$, which are pairs of template queries and sets of slots (τ_i, S_i). Here, a template query, τ_i, is similar to a SPARQL query, but all components of its triples are unbounded variables, and the set of slots S_i holds the descriptions of the variables. Generally, SPARQL

---

[2] https://figshare.com/projects/LC-QuAD/21812.
[3] http://www.okbqa.org/.

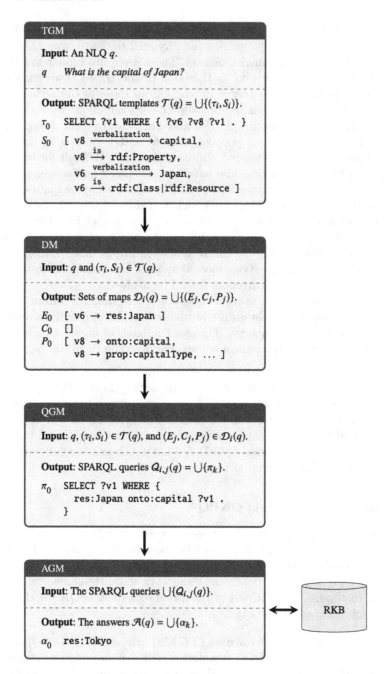

Fig. 1. The workflow of the OKBQA framework with the example outputs for the question "What is the capital of Japan?" The prefixes used in this figure are summarized in Table 3. Only the essences of the inputs or outputs of each module are shown here; hence, the actual APIs allow for attaching additional information to the inputs. For instance, many components of the outputs are annotated with a score so that AGMs will be able to select or filter the candidate SPARQL queries.

Table 1. Overview of datasets provided by QALD. The rightmost column shows whether each dataset was used for our experiments (see Sect. 2.1 for detailed reasons).

Challenge	Dataset	Size	Question (en)	SPARQL query	Used
QALD-1	dbpedia-{train,test}	100	✓	✓	✓
	musicbrainz-{train,test}	100	✓	✓	✓
QALD-2	dbpedia-{train,test}	200	✓	✓	✓
	musicbrainz-{train,test}	200	✓	✓	✓
	participants-challenge	7	✓	✓	✓
QALD-3	esdbpedia-{train,test}	100	✓	✓	✓
	dbpedia-{train,test}	199	✓	✓	✓
	musicbrainz-{train,test}	199	✓	✓	✓
QALD-4	multilingual-{train,test}	250	✓	✓	✓
	biomedical-{train,test}	50	✓	✓	✓
	hybrid-{train,test}	35	✓		
QALD-5	multilingual-{train,test}	350	✓	✓	✓
	hybrid-{train,test}	50	✓		
QALD-6	multilingual-{train,test}	450	✓	✓	✓
	hybrid-{train,test}	75	✓		
	datacube-{train,test}	150	✓	✓	
QALD-7	multilingual-{train,test}	314	✓	✓	✓
	hybrid-{train,test}	150	✓		
	largescale-train	100	✓	✓	✓
	largescale-test	2M	✓	✓	
	en-wikidata-{train,test}	150	✓	✓	✓

templates represent the semantic structures of the questions [25]. Therefore, typical TGMs create them by using some NLP techniques.

- **Disambiguation Modules (DMs)** receive a SPARQL template $(\tau_i, S_i) \in \mathcal{T}(q)$ and identify resources corresponding to each of the slots in S_i. More specifically, a result of DMs $\mathcal{D}_i$ is a set of three tuples (E_j, C_j, P_j), where each tuple is a list of slots to URIs mappings for entities, classes, and properties, respectively. Normally, DMs require RKB-dependent information in addition to their input from TGMs.
- **Query Generation Modules (QGMs)** generate actual SPARQL queries $\mathcal{Q}_{i,j}(q)$ based on a template $((\tau_i, S_i) \in \mathcal{T}(q))$ and three tuples of mappings $(E_j, C_j, P_j) \in \mathcal{D}_i(q)$. This module tends to generate many SPARQL queries for each input template.
- **Answer Generation Modules (AGMs)** query all specified RKBs using SPARQL queries generated by a QGM and return the list of final answers $\mathcal{A}(q)$ for the question q. The role of this module is not only collecting results from RKBs but also selecting and filtering the input SPARQL queries.

Because of this modular architecture, the users of the SQA system can freely choose the exact implementation to execute as each module in the SQA workflow, and for easing the collaboration, every module implementation has REST services to exchange their inputs/outputs. It is worth noting that the framework is particularly useful for our subdivided evaluations because it is helpful to clarify that the scopes of the evaluations and the evaluators developed for each module can be easily applied to multiple implementations.

Now, we can clearly declare the objective of this study, which is to define and develop an evaluation for the TGMs of the OKBQA framework. Currently, there are two TGM implementations for English QA: Rocknrole and LODQA. We evaluated both using our evaluation method.

Rocknrole. Rocknrole[4] [25] is a rule-based TGM implementation. The approach of this implementation is quite simple: first, the input question is parsed by the general natural language (NL) parser included in Stanford CoreNLP [18] and then converted to a SPARQL template query using predefined rules (e.g., the node *who* is renamed to AGENT). Because of its SPARQL templates generation scheme, the quality and coverage of the output are dependent on the rules.

LODQA. Linked Open Data Question-Answering (LODQA)[5] [8,14] is one of the SQA systems that generate SPARQL queries. LODQA has a modular architecture that resembles the OKBQA framework, and one of the modules of the system called *Graphicator* can be used as a TGM implementation solely by adjusting the output to conform to the TGM specification. The backend for deep relation extraction of the system is Enju [19], a state-of-the-art HPSG-based English parser. Then, a graph conversion algorithm involving tasks such as entity recognition and graph simplification is executed.

3   Methods

Figure 2 shows the overview of the calculation scheme in our evaluator. The detailed information about each process is described in this section.

3.1   Preparation

Before using the pairs of the NLQs and SPARQL queries from the datasets of QALD and LC-QuAD, two simple processes were required to be applied to these queries for cleaning purposes. First, due to the existence of duplicate questions in both datasets, it was necessary to remove those duplicate questions from the input of the evaluator. Duplicate NLQs that were paired with different SPARQL queries existed in the QALD datasets, and thus, the queries from the newer datasets may be more effective compared with those contained in the older ones. Consequently, the pairs from the newer datasets were selected in such cases. Second, the SPARQL queries from both datasets included extended syntaxes of

---

[4] http://repository.okbqa.org/components/21.

[5] http://lodqa.org/.

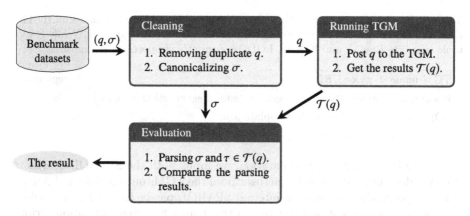

Fig. 2. The calculation scheme of the evaluation. The inputs of our evaluator are pairs of the NLQs and corresponding SPARQL queries (q, σ). After executing all the processes, the evaluator outputs the evaluation results for the TGM.

Virtuoso,[6] so many of these queries did not satisfy the specification of SPARQL 1.1,[7] which may cause parse failure of the queries. To avoid such trivial errors, these invalid queries were modified to conform to the official specification before the evaluation. This process was performed in an ad-hoc manner: we made the modification using regular expressions in our formatter scripts to create the input data files (Fig. 3).

```
A ... SELECT DISTINCT (?h1 - ?h2) WHERE ...
  → ... SELECT DISTINCT ((?h1 - ?h2) AS ?tgm_eval_result) WHERE ...
B ... SELECT COUNT (DISTINCT ?uri) WHERE ...
  → ... SELECT (COUNT (DISTINCT ?uri) AS ?tgm_eval_result) WHERE ...
```

Fig. 3. Examples of the substitutions to modify the SPARQL queries containing extended syntaxes. Here, the names of variables added by our scripts have prefix `tgm_eval_` to avoid any name confliction.

After filtering and modification, the remaining NLQs constituted our benchmark datasets. These datasets were then fed to the two TGMs and the outputs were retrieved through their REST services (Table 2). As a result, we obtained the pairs of NLQs and corresponding SPARQL queries (q, σ) from the datasets as well as the pairs of template queries and sets of slots $\mathcal{T}(q) = (\tau, S)$ from the two TGMs. As mentioned in Sect. 2.2, the specification of theOKBQA framework allows TGMs to output multiple SPARQL templates for an NLQ, but both Rocknrole and LODQA currently output at most one template. Hence, we did not consider the cases of multiple TGM outputs from an input for our experiments.

---

[6] https://virtuoso.openlinksw.com/.
[7] https://www.w3.org/TR/sparql11-query/.

Table 2. The REST services of the TGMs. When users send POST requests on HTTP, the services will run the TGM internally and return the results to users. While Rocknrole supports English and Korean, LODQA currently supports only English.

TGM name	Service URL	Languages
Rocknrole	http://ws.okbqa.org:1515/templategeneration/rocknrole	en, ko
LODQA	http://lodqa.org/template.json	en

As the last step for our preparation, we input both the SPARQL queries σ from the datasets and template queries τ from the TGMs outputs into a SPARQL parser. Specifically, we used an internal SPARQL parser from RDFLib[8] solely because it is convenient and fast to call this parser from our evaluation scripts written in Python. The parser outputs the internal expressions of the parsed SPARQL queries, similar to SPARQL syntax expressions or SPARQL Algebra, and we can easily extract the logical structure of the SPARQL queries, e.g., the triple patterns and the length of the answers from such queries. Technically, the parser must be initialized with a few namespace mappings (Table 3) because some of the SPARQL queries in the datasets do not have an explicit declaration of the prefixes.

Table 3. The namespace mappings used to initialized the internal SPARQL parser of RDFLib in our experiments. Since our evaluation for TGMs does not check any particular resource, the exact URIs shown here is not so important.

Prefix	Partial URIs string
dc	http://purl.org/dc/elements/1.1/
foaf	http://xmlns.com/foaf/0.1/
obo	http://purl.obolibrary.org/obo/
onto	http://dbpedia.org/ontology/
owl	http://www.w3.org/2002/07/owl
prop	http://dbpedia.org/property/
rdf	http://www.w3.org/1999/02/22-rdf-syntax-ns
reds	http://www.w3.org/2000/01/rdf-schema
res	http://dbpedia.org/resource/
xsd	http://www.w3.org/2001/XMLSchema

3.2 Evaluation

The goal of our evaluation is to judge the qualities of the outputs of TGMs independently from the other part of the SQA systems (namely, DMs, QGMs, and

---

[8] https://rdflib.readthedocs.io/en/stable/.

AGMs). For this reason, we leave the analyses on the sets of slots S and comparing graph similarity to another step, which will follow the TGMs evaluation (see Sect. 5.3). Thus, our method focus on foundational analyses particularly on the template queries τ.

To achieve our goal for subdivided evaluation, we established six evaluation criteria based on three aspects: (1) robustness of a TGM, (2) validity of query types and the ranges (i.e., lengths and offsets) expressed in template queries, and (3) accuracy of the graph patterns in template queries. For each aspect, two actual evaluation criteria have been developed, as listed in Table 4. Our evaluator is implemented to check every output of a TGM via a comparison with the corresponding queries from the benchmark dataset to verify whether any of the six criteria are met. If an output clears all the criteria, it is determined to be *good*.

Table 4. Overview of the evaluation criteria. Our evaluator checks every output of a TGM to evaluate whether the output has any problem when compared with each criterion in the exact order shown here. If errors are found, the error that is found first is considered. For details of each criteria, see Sect. 3.2.

No.	Evaluation criteria	Aspects	Level
1	TGM failure	Robustness	Critical
2	Syntax	Robustness	Critical
3	Question type	Query types and ranges	Critical
4	Disconnected target	Graph patterns	Critical
5	Wrong range	Query types and ranges	Notice
6	Disconnected triple	Graph patterns	Notice

For the convenience of the developers of TGMs, we also categorized the criteria into two severity levels: *critical* and *notice*. The difference between the two levels is related to the impact on the general evaluation criteria, e.g., recall and precision, which are widely used for evaluation in information systems, e.g., QALD campaign [17]:

$$\text{Recall}(q) = \frac{\text{Number of correct system answers for } q}{\text{Number of gold standard answers for } q},$$

$$\text{Precision}(q) = \frac{\text{Number of correct system answers for } q}{\text{Number of system answers for } q}.$$

For instance, if a SPARQL template, $\mathcal{T}(q)$, is judged to have a critical error, it means there is no chance of a correct answer, regardless of the performance of other modules. Additionally, the contribution of the template for precision and recall will be zero. On the contrary, if a $\mathcal{T}(q)$ is determined to have a notice problem, it means there is still a chance for obtaining correct answers, irrespective of how low this chance is. Thus, its contribution to precision and recall may not be zero.

Robustness. The first two steps for our evaluation are related to the robustness of the TGMs. We call it a *TGM failure* error if the status code of the HTTP response from the REST service is not 200, which means that somehow the TGM did not return normal results (e.g., a kind of internal error was raised for the input). If the REST service would have returned a SPARQL template, $\mathcal{T}(q)$, the parsing result of the template query τ would have been checked for the next step. As explained in Sect. 2.2, a valid template query is also valid as a SPARQL query. Therefore, a template query for which the parsing result is "syntax error" has *syntactic problems*. Since both the problems concerning the criteria explained here will make it difficult to follow the steps of the framework, these problems are classified into *critical* errors.

Query Types and Ranges. Generally, NLQs, which can be treated as the inputs of SQA systems, are roughly categorized into the following question types [1,11].

- **Yes/no questions** are questions that can be answered simply as "*yes*" or "*no*" (e.g., "Are there drugs that target the Protein kinase Cβ type?"). These questions can be converted directly to SPARQL queries using the ASK form, i.e., the so-called ask queries.
- **Factoid questions** require one or more entities as their answers (e.g., "Which drugs have no side-effects?"). The aim of these questions can be easily reached by the most common SPARQL queries using the SELECT form, namely select queries. Sometimes, the questions that require more than one answer are distinguished from this category (often referred to as "list questions"), but we did not separate that category from factoid questions because it is a trivial matter for SPARQL queries.
- **Summary questions** are questions that are not categorized into any of the previous types (e.g., "Why do people fall in love?"). The questions typically require text as the answers; therefore, the questions belonging to this class are out of the scope of SPARQL queries.

In summary, an input NLQ of an SQA system is basically classified into yes/no questions or factoid questions, which can be easily detected by checking the type of the annotated SPARQL query. Using this idea, we determined whether TGMs can accurately recognize the question types by comparing the parsing results of the dataset SPARQL queries σ and the template queries τ: in the case wherein one of the queries is an ask query and the other is not and vice versa, we judged that the TGM failed to recognize the *question type* of the NLQ. This error is *critical* because incorrect types of queries always return the wrong type of answers.

Focusing on the factoid questions, it is worth considering more detailed classification among them. There are some questions, e.g., "Who are the four youngest MVP basketball players?" wherein the number of answers have important meanings. Moreover, the positions or the offsets of the answers (i.e., the positions in the sorted lists of answer candidates) are important in some questions, e.g., a SPARQL query corresponding to a question such as "What is the largest country in the world?" should consider the first entity from the (sorted) candidate entities while it is desirable for a SPARQL query to consider the second question "What is the second highest mountain on Earth?" Herein, we refer to these questions as **range-specified factoid questions**. The ranges of the answers, a pair of length l and starting position s, can be expressed in a SPARQL query by adding clauses, such as "LIMIT l OFFSET $(s - 1)$." Thus, we checked every template query τ that correctly recognized the original question as a factoid question (if and if only one of the queries σ and τ was not an ask query) and had the appropriate range specification in the query again using the parsing result of both the σ and τ queries. If a range (l, s) explicitly appeared in the SPARQL query σ and either one of the lengths and starting positions in the template query τ were different from l and s, respectively, the template was judged to have *wrong range* for the answers. Since adding the range annotations to template queries is an optional behavior of TGM to increase the precision, this criterion is rightfully categorized to *notice*.

Graph Patterns. The basic structures of SPARQL queries (select queries in a precise sense) can briefly be expressed as follows [15].

SELECT ⟨*result description*⟩ WHERE ⟨*graph patterns*⟩,

where the part ⟨*graph patterns*⟩ is a set of triple patterns and ⟨*result description*⟩ is an enumeration of the variables requested to be solved by the queried RDF store, possibly with some arithmetic operators. Herein, we simply call these variables "target variables."

For each template query that has the form of select queries, we checked whether all target variables appeared in the ⟨*graph patterns*⟩. If there were target variables that did not exist in the ⟨*graph patterns*⟩, then an alert was generated as a *disconnected target* error (Fig. 4A, B). This is one of the *critical* errors because the queries having this problem will retrieve nothing for those targets.

```
A SELECT ?v4 WHERE { ?v1 ?v2 ?v3 . }
B SELECT (COUNT(?v1) AS ?v1_count) WHERE { ?v1 ?v2 ?v3 . }
C SELECT ?v1 WHERE { ?v1 ?v2 ?v3 . ?v3 ?v4 ?v5 . ?v6 ?v7 ?v8 . }
```

Fig. 4. Examples of template queries. A. The target variable ?v4 is a disconnected target because it does not appear in the graph patterns. B. The target variable ?v1_count does not appear in the graph patterns, but the variable is bound as the number of ?v1 and ?v1 appears in the patterns "?v1 ?v2 ?v3." Therefore, this template query does not have any problem. C. This query has a disconnected triple: while the first two triples in the graph patterns have a connection to the target variable ?v1, the last triple does not.

The last criterion of our evaluation is related to another kind of analysis on ⟨*graph patterns*⟩. If there are triple patterns that are disconnected from any target, this can be a cause of reducing the meaningful results from the final answers for nothing. Thus, our evaluator found template queries having those triples that were highly unnecessary, which were considered as *disconnected triple notifications* (Fig. 4C).

4   Results

After removing the duplicate NLQs from the datasets, we obtained 1,011 pairs of NLQs and SPARQL queries from the QALD datasets and 4,977 pairs from LC-QuAD (Fig. 5). For the datasets pertaining to QALD and LC-QuAD, the ratio of yes/no questions was 8.4% and 7.4%, respectively. In contrast, 7.0% of the factoid questions from QALD are range-specified, which are useful to check the existence of the *wrong range* criterion, but there are no range-specified factoid questions in LC-QuAD. All pairs were entered into our evaluator, and every NLQ in them was successfully sent to the REST services of the TGMs. Likewise, every query in the pairs was parsed by the SPARQL parser in RDFLib without any issues owing to the normalization adopted in our formatter.

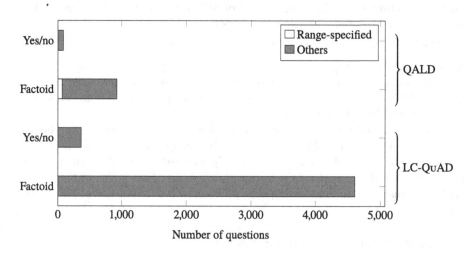

Fig. 5. Sizes of the datasets used in our experiments. The datasets from QALD contain 85 yes/no questions and 926 factoid questions, 65 of which were range-specified. On the contrary, the dataset from LC-QuAD comprises 368 yes/no questions and 4,609 factoid questions, none of which had a range specification.

Table 5 summarizes the problems of TGM outputs we found through evaluation using the whole datasets (5,988 questions in total). These problems are classified into the six criteria, as defined earlier. Overall, 9.9% of the SPARQL templates produced by Rocknrole had *critical* errors and 48.7% of these were alerted to have *notice* problems. Similarly, 7.8% of the templates generated by LODQA had *critical* errors and 1.1% of these were alerted to have *notice* problems (Fig. 6).

Table 5. Number of the problematic SPARQL templates from the two TGM for each of the evaluation criteria (DC represents the term "disconnected").

TGM name	TGM failure	Syntax	Question type	DC target	Wrong range	DC triple
Rocknrole	0	0	262	330	28	2,898
LODQA	1	18	446	0	64	0

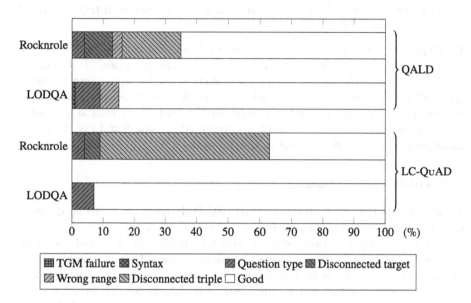

Fig. 6. Ratios of the problematic SPARQL templates from the two TGMs for all evaluation criteria. The dark segments ■ represent the ratios for the *critical* criteria, and the lighter segments □ show those for the *notice* criteria.

5 Discussions

5.1 Qualitative Evaluation of the TGMs

Rocknrole. Since Rocknrole is a rule-based NLQ interpreter, the coverage of the system is dependent on the rules. According to our evaluation results, we determined that (1) this TGM covers both the question types, i.e., yes/no questions and factoid questions, which are possibly assigned to SQA systems, (2) the system is also able to add range specification to the template queries, and (3) the system, however, often fails to generate good SPARQL templates. It is worth noting that Rocknrole can perfectly recognize yes/no questions in our experiments, but it judged 4.7% of the factoid questions as yes/no questions throughout all the datasets used herein. In addition, the TGM failed to add appropriate range specification to its outputs for nearly half of the range-specified factoid questions (45.2%) in the QALD datasets. Note that this level of insight into the performance of the TGM is something that could only be achieved through the subdivided evaluation proposed in this study.

One possible way to improve Rocknrole to prevent the occurrence of errors, particularly the *question-type*, *disconnected target*, and *wrong range* errors, is to add predefined rules to decrease the error rates. For this purpose, the false cases dumped by our evaluator will be useful. Furthermore, Rocknrole can only enhance the system to remove disconnected triples so that such triples will not decrease the values of recalls.

LODQA. As for the TGM provided by LODQA, the evaluation shows that (1) it does not distinguish the yes/no- and factoid-type questions, (2) it does not produce range specification to the template queries, and (3) it, however, produces good SPARQL templates more stably than Rocknrole. Since the system does not cover yes/no questions and range-specified factoid questions, the number of *question-type* and *wrong range* problems presented in Table 5 and Fig. 6 are only those problems that are included in the datasets.

5.2 Quality of the Datasets

Figure 5 shows that the questions in the QALD datasets are richer in diversity than those in LC-QuAD. In fact, LC-QuAD is not sufficiently diverse to be used solely for our evaluation because it contains no range-specified factoid questions.

The size of both the datasets seems sufficiently large for our evaluation task because we were able to find at least one case for each of the criteria. Nevertheless, the larger the size is, the better the dataset for our evaluation. In this regard, LC-QuAD has an advantage. The generation process of LC-QuAD is quite unique: the NLQ in the dataset is transformed from SPARQL queries, which is completely opposite to the generation processes of the other well-known datasets, including QALD [21]. As the translations from SPARQL queries to NLQs were conducted using specific question templates called "normalized natural question templates," if the variety of the templates is increased, the dataset will be more useful for our evaluation.

5.3 Unsuitable Evaluation Criteria

Several methods have been proposed to determine the similarity degrees or distances among SPARQL queries [9,15], which seems to be useful for evaluating SQA systems. Although this may also be true for evaluating the whole OKBQA framework, these methods are not appropriate for our evaluation because our evaluation currently focuses on only TGMs. First, most aforementioned measurements cannot be applied to SPARQL queries that do not contain URIs. Second, comparing or measuring the similarity between the graph patterns of the SPARQL queries without resource annotations seems meaningless because one semantic structure of a question can generally be expressed in several forms of SPARQL queries.

Another possible criterion is the expected type of the answer, namely the type or class of the target variable in the template queries. However, this is also not appropriate for our evaluation because template queries do not contain any URI. We thus reserve this for the evaluation of other modules, which follow a TGM in a QA workflow.

5.4 Limitations, Possible Extensions, and Future Work

Both TGM implementations currently do not generate more than one SPARQL template for an NLQ, whereas the specification of the OKBQA framework allows TGM to generate multiple templates for an input. For this reason, currently, we simply took the first template from the result lists, the length of which is always one, returned by TGMs; however, this behavior is required to be changed for TGMs that generate more than one templates for an NLQ. We think we can always take standard approaches which are broadly understood. For example, we can count positives/negatives and evaluate the performance in terms of precision and recall.

Though we evaluated only two TGMs for our experiments, our methods and implementation can be easily applied to other TGM implementations by merely specifying the URL of the REST service. Other datasets from QALD and LC-QuAD can also be used for the evaluation. Our evaluation is not specialized for English questions; thus, if applicable TGMs and datasets are provided, these TGM can also be tested for other languages. Furthermore, our evaluation methods can possibly be applied not only to TGM in the OKBQA framework but also to every SQA system that generates SPARQL queries because the methods are solely based on the results of a general SPARQL parser. The results in such cases will demonstrate the performance of the functions corresponding to the TGM of the systems, which will be helpful in improving the systems as well.

Finally, for future research, defining and developing similar subdivided, systematic, and semantic evaluations of the other modules of the OKBQA framework will also be interesting. Evaluation methods optimized for more complex questions than our current corpus, such as those discussed by Talmor et al. [20], should also be implemented. Simultaneously, these evaluations will be helpful in improving the ability of the entire SQA system.

6 Conclusions

Herein, we proposed a systematic semantic evaluation for TGMs, which are a type of subdivided modules of SQA systems. Our evaluation results for the two publicly available TGMs revealed that in comparison with existing methods, the new evaluation method can extract and provide much more detailed information on their performance. Specifically, the limitations and the problems of the TGMs were detected; these are hoped to be fixed in the future. The information from our evaluator will be useful for addressing this issue.

Improvement of SQA systems is important for expanding the use of LD, and this paper showed that the presented evaluation method has a good potential to play an important role for advancing the technology. Therefore, it will be worth to extend the approach to other modules of SQA systems, and even to other SQA frameworks, which is remained as a prospective future work.

References

1. Balikas, G., Krithara, A., Partalas, I., Paliouras, G.: BioASQ: a challenge on large-scale biomedical semantic indexing and question answering. In: Multimodal Retrieval in the Medical Domain, pp. 26–39 (2015)
2. Ben Abacha, A., Zweigenbaum, P.: Medical question answering: translating medical questions into SPARQL queries. In: Proceedings of the 2nd ACM SIGHIT International Health Informatics Symposium, pp. 41–50 (2012)
3. Berant, J., Chou, A., Frostig, R., Liang, P.: Semantic parsing on freebase from question-answer pairs. In: Proceedings of EMNLP, pp. 1533–1544 (2013)
4. Bizer, C., Heath, T., Berners-Lee, T.: Linked data-the story so far. Int. J. Semant. Web Inf. Syst. **5**(3), 1–22 (2009)
5. Trivedi, P., Maheshwari, G., Dubey, M., Lehmann, J.: LC-QuAD: a corpus for complex question answering over knowledge graphs. In: d'Amato, C., et al. (eds.) ISWC 2017. LNCS, vol. 10588, pp. 210–218. Springer, Cham (2017). https://doi.org/10.1007/978-3-319-68204-4_22
6. Cai, Q., Yates, A.: Large-scale semantic parsing via schema matching and lexicon extension. In: Proceedings of the 51st Annual Meeting of the Association for Computational Linguistics, Long Papers, vol. 1, pp. 423–433 (2013)
7. Cimiano, P., Lopez, V., Unger, C., Cabrio, E., Ngonga Ngomo, A.-C., Walter, S.: Multilingual question answering over linked data (QALD-3): lab overview. In: Forner, P., Müller, H., Paredes, R., Rosso, P., Stein, B. (eds.) CLEF 2013. LNCS, vol. 8138, pp. 321–332. Springer, Heidelberg (2013). https://doi.org/10.1007/978-3-642-40802-1_30
8. Cohen, K.B., Kim, J.-D.: Evaluation of SPARQL query generation from natural language questions. In: Proceedings of the Joint Workshop on NLP&LOD and SWAIE, pp. 3–7 (2013)
9. Dividino, R.Q., Gröner, G.: Which of the following SPARQL queries are Similar? Why? In: Proceedings of the First International Conference on Linked Data for Information Extraction, pp. 2–13 (2013)
10. Harris, S., Seaborne, A., Prud'hommeaux, E.: SPARQL 1.1 query language. W3C Recomm. **21**(10) (2013)
11. Höffner, K.: Survey on challenges of question answering in the semantic web. Semant. Web **8**(6), 895–920 (2017)
12. Kim, J.-D.: OKBQA framework towards an open collaboration for development of natural language question-answering systems over knowledge bases. In: International Semantic Web Conference 2017 (2017)
13. Kim, J.-D., Choi, G., Kim, J.-U., Kim, E.-K., Choi, K.-S.: The open framework for developing knowledge base and question answering system. In: Proceedings of the 26th International Conference on Computational Linguistics, pp. 161–165 (2016)
14. Kim, J.-D., Cohen, K.B.: Natural language query processing for SPARQL generation: a prototype system for SNOMED CT. In: Proceedings of BioLINK SIG 2013, pp. 32–38 (2013)

15. Le, W., Kementsietsidis, A., Duan, S., Li, F.: Scalable multi-query optimization for SPARQL. In: 2012 IEEE 28th International Conference on Data Engineering (ICDE), pp. 666–677 (2012)
16. Lehmann, J.: DBpedia-a large-scale, multilingual knowledge base extracted from Wikipedia. Semant. Web **6**(2), 167–195 (2015)
17. Lopez, V., Unger, C., Cimiano, P., Motta, E.: Evaluating question answering over linked data. Web Semant.: Sci., Serv. Agents World Wide Web **21**, 3–13 (2013)
18. Manning, C.D.: The Stanford CoreNLP natural language processing toolkit. In: Proceedings of 52nd Annual Meeting of the Association for Computational Linguistics: System Demonstrations, pp. 55–60 (2014)
19. Miyao, Y., Tsujii, J.: Feature forest models for probabilistic HPSG parsing. Comput. Linguist. **34**(1), 35–80 (2008)
20. Talmor, A., Berant, J.: The web as a knowledge-base for answering complex questions. In: Proceedings of the 2018 Conference of the North American Chapter of the Association for Computational Linguistics: Human Language Technologies, vol. 1, pp. 641–651 (2018)
21. Trivedi, P., Maheshwari, G., Dubey, M., Lehmann, J.: LC-QuAD: a corpus for complex question answering over knowledge graphs. In: International Semantic Web Conference 2017, pp. 210–218 (2017)
22. Unger, C., Ngomo, A.-C.N., Cabrio, E.: 6th open challenge on question answering over linked data (QALD-6). In: Sack, H., Dietze, S., Tordai, A., Lange, C. (eds.) SemWebEval 2016. CCIS, vol. 641, pp. 171–177. Springer, Cham (2016). https://doi.org/10.1007/978-3-319-46565-4_13
23. Unger, C.: Question answering over linked data (QALD-4). In: Working Notes for CLEF 2014 Conference, pp. 1172–1180 (2014)
24. Unger, C.: Question answering over linked data (QALD-5). In: Working Notes of CLEF 2015 - Conference and Labs of the Evaluation Forum (2015)
25. Unger, C.: Template-based question answering over RDF data. In: Proceedings of the 21st International Conference on World Wide Web, pp. 639–648 (2012)
26. Usbeck, R., Ngomo, A.-C.N., Haarmann, B., Krithara, A., Röder, M., Napolitano, G.: 7th open challenge on question answering over linked data (QALD-7). In: Dragoni, M., Solanki, M., Blomqvist, E. (eds.) SemWebEval 2017. CCIS, vol. 769, pp. 59–69. Springer, Cham (2017). https://doi.org/10.1007/978-3-319-69146-6_6
27. Vrandečić, D.: Wikidata: a new platform for collaborative data collection. In: Proceedings of the 21st International Conference on World Wide Web, pp. 1063–1064 (2012)

Ontology and Reasoning

DeFind: A Protege Plugin for Computing Concept Definitions in $\mathcal{EL}$ Ontologies

Denis Ponomaryov[1,2]($^{(\boxtimes)}$) and Stepan Yakovenko[2]

[1] Institute of Mathematics, Novosibirsk State University, Novosibirsk, Russia
[2] Institute of Informatics Systems, Novosibirsk State University, Novosibirsk, Russia
ponom@iis.nsk.su, stiv.yakovenko@gmail.com

Abstract. We introduce an extension to the Protégé ontology editor, which allows for discovering concept definitions, which are not explicitly present in axioms, but are logically implied by an ontology. The plugin supports ontologies formulated in the Description Logic $\mathcal{EL}$, which underpins the OWL 2 EL profile of the Web Ontology Language and despite its limited expressiveness captures most of the biomedical ontologies published on the Web. The developed tool allows to verify whether a concept can be defined using a vocabulary of interest specified by a user. In particular, it allows to decide whether some vocabulary items cabe omitted in a formulation of a complex concept. The corresponding definitions are presented to the user and are provided with explanations generated by an ontology reasoner.

1 Introduction

The development and application of large terminological systems pose new challenges for ontology engineering and automated reasoning tools. A question which becomes evidently important in the context of large ontologies is whether their content and logical consequences are easy to comprehend. To address this problem, a number of visualization and explanation tools has been integrated into ontology editing environments such as, e.g., visualization and explanation services implemented for the Protégé ontology editor. It is common that an expert exploring an ontology encounters concepts, which are formulated in a vocabulary she is not familiar with. More generally, only a certain part of an ontology vocabulary may be familiar to an expert, while the remaining part may be not. When a formulation of some concept employs vocabulary items unknown to an expert, typically she would like to know whether this concept can be reformulated in the familiar vocabulary. To give a simplified example, suppose an ontology of cuisines contains axiom $Dumplings \sqcap Entree \sqsubseteq Gnocci$ (stating that $Dumplings$ being $Entree$ are $Gnocci$) together with concept inclusions $Gnocci \sqsubseteq Dumplings$ and $Dumplings \sqsubseteq Entree$. Assume an expert is familiar with concepts $Entree$ and

The research was supported by the Russian Science Foundation, grant No. 17-11-01166. Implementation was supported by the Siberian Branch of the Russian Academy of Sciences (Block 36.1 of the Program for Basic Scientific Research II.1).

R. Ichise et al. (Eds.): JIST 2018, LNCS 11341, pp. 235–243, 2018.
https://doi.org/10.1007/978-3-030-04284-4_16

Gnocci and she encounters the concept *Dumplings* ⊓ *Entree* mentioned in the ontology. First, one may notice that this concept can be simplified, i.e., it is equivalent to *Dumplings* wrt the ontology, due to the inclusions above. Second, the ontology entails that *Dumplings* and *Gnocci* are equivalent, thus, the original concept can be reformulated as *Gnocci* (or as *Gnocci* ⊓ *Entree*) in the vocabulary known to the user.

In this paper, we introduce DeFind, an extension to the Protégé ontology editor, which allows to find concept definitions in a user specified vocabulary consisting of concept and relations names from an input ontology. In particular, it allows to verify whether some concept or relation names can be omitted in a formulation of a (complex) concept. To the best of our knowledge, this is the first implementation of these reasoning services as a part of an ontology editing tool. Specifically, for a given ontology $\mathcal{O}$, vocabulary Σ, and a concept C of interest, DeFind computes definitions of C wrt $\mathcal{O}$ in Σ, i.e. concepts $\{D_1, \dots, D_n\}$ (whenever they exist) such that D_i contains symbols only from Σ and $\mathcal{O} \models C \equiv D_i$, for all $i = 1, \dots, n$. DeFind supports ontologies formulated in the Description Logic $\mathcal{EL}$, which allows for building concepts using conjunction and existential restriction, and includes built-in concepts such as $\bot$ and $\top$. For example, it is possible to state in $\mathcal{EL}$ that some concepts are disjoint (e.g., *Entree* ⊓ *Dessert* ⊑ $\bot$), specify subsumption relationship between concepts (*Dumplings* ⊓ *Entree* ⊑ *Gnocci*) or domains of relations ($\exists hasIngredient.\top \sqsubseteq Food$), and use existential restriction to specify relationships of other kinds (e.g., *Salad* ⊑ $\exists hasDressing.\top$, $\exists hasIngredient.Meat \sqsubseteq NonVegeterianFood$). The expressive features of $\mathcal{EL}$ although limited (e.g., negation/disjunction of concepts is not allowed), are sufficient to capture a great variety of ontologies. Most of the biomedical ontologies published on the Web fall within the formalism of $\mathcal{EL}$, which underpins the OWL 2 EL profile of the Web Ontology Language.

2   Techniques

In the Description Logic $\mathcal{EL}$, concepts are built using a countably infinite alphabet of *roles names* N_r and *concept names* N_c, with two distinguished concepts $\bot, \top \in N_c$. The notion of *concept* is defined inductively: any element of N_c is a concept and if C, D are concepts and $r \in N_r$ is a role then $C \sqcap D$ and $\exists r.C$ are concepts. A *concept inclusion* is an expression of the form $C \sqsubseteq D$, where C, D are concepts. A *concept equivalence* is a expression $C \equiv D$. An *ontology* is a finite set of concept inclusions and equivalences (called *axioms*). A *signature* is a subset of $N_r \cup N_c \setminus \{\bot, \top\}$. The signature of a concept C, denoted as $\text{sig}(C)$, is the set of role and concept names (excluding $\bot$ and $\top$), which occur in C. The signature of a concept inclusion or ontology is defined similarly. Semantics is defined by using the notion of interpretation, which is a pair $\mathcal{I} = \langle \Delta, \cdot^{\mathcal{I}} \rangle$, where Δ is a universe and $\cdot^{\mathcal{I}}$ is a function which maps every concept name from N_c to a subset of Δ such that $(\bot)^{\mathcal{I}} = \varnothing$, $(\top)^{\mathcal{I}} = \Delta$, and every role name to a subset of $\Delta \times \Delta$. This function is extended to arbitrary concepts by setting $(C \sqcap D)^{\mathcal{I}} = C^{\mathcal{I}} \cap D^{\mathcal{I}}$ and $(\exists r.C)^{\mathcal{I}} = \{x \in \Delta \mid \exists y \ \langle x, y \rangle \in r^{\mathcal{I}} \text{ and } \ y \in C^{\mathcal{I}}\}$.

An interpretation $\mathcal{I}$ is a model of a concept inclusion $C \sqsubseteq D$ (written as $\mathcal{I} \models C \sqsubseteq D$) if $C^{\mathcal{I}} \subseteq D^{\mathcal{I}}$. Similarly, $\mathcal{I} \models C \equiv D$ if $C^{\mathcal{I}} = D^{\mathcal{I}}$. An interpretation is a model of an ontology $\mathcal{O}$ if it is a model of every axiom of $\mathcal{O}$. An ontology $\mathcal{O}$ *entails* a concept inclusion $C \sqsubseteq D$ (written as $\mathcal{O} \models C \sqsubseteq D$) if $\mathcal{I} \models \mathcal{O}$ yields $\mathcal{I} \models C \sqsubseteq D$, for any interpretation $\mathcal{I}$.

Let Σ be a signature. We say that a concept C is Σ-*definable* wrt an ontology $\mathcal{O}$ if $\mathcal{O} \models C \equiv D$, where $\mathtt{sig}\,(D) \subseteq \Sigma$. The concept D is called Σ-*definition* of C (wrt ontology $\mathcal{O}$). For example, the concept *Dumplings* $\sqcap$ *Entree* is Σ-definable wrt the ontology from the introduction, where $\Sigma = \{Gnocci\}$. It is known that in $\mathcal{EL}$ a concept C is Σ-definable wrt an ontology $\mathcal{O}$ iff it holds $\mathcal{O} \cup \mathcal{O}^* \models C \sqsubseteq C^*$, where $\mathcal{O}^*$ and C^* are "copies" of $\mathcal{O}$ and C, respectively, obtained by an injective renaming of all non-Σ-symbols into "fresh" ones, not occurring in $\mathcal{O}$ and C. Indeed, if $\mathcal{O} \models C \equiv D$, for some concept D, with $\mathtt{sig}\,(D) \subseteq \Sigma$, then it holds $\mathcal{O} \models C \sqsubseteq D$ and $\mathcal{O}^* \models D \sqsubseteq C^*$, which means $\mathcal{O} \cup \mathcal{O}^* \models C \sqsubseteq C^*$. The converse can be proved constructively by computing the corresponding concept D from a proof of the inclusion $C \sqsubseteq C^*$ from $\mathcal{O} \cup \mathcal{O}^*$; we provide a justification below. Various proof systems have been proposed for the Description Logic $\mathcal{EL}$ in the literature. For example, it follows from the results in [1] that the following set of inference rules is sound and complete for entailment of concept inclusions $C \sqsubseteq D$ from an ontology $\mathcal{O}$, where C and D occur in the axioms of $\mathcal{O}$:

$$\mathsf{R}_0 \; \overline{C \sqsubseteq C} \qquad \mathsf{R}_\top \; \overline{C \sqsubseteq \top} \qquad \mathsf{R}_\bot \; \overline{\bot \sqsubseteq C} \qquad \mathsf{R}_\sqsubseteq \; \frac{C \sqsubseteq E}{C \sqsubseteq F} \; E \bowtie F \in \mathcal{O}, \; \bowtie \, \in \{\sqsubseteq, \equiv\}$$

$$\mathsf{R}_\sqcap^- \; \frac{C \sqsubseteq E_1 \sqcap E_2}{C \sqsubseteq E_1 \; C \sqsubseteq E_2} \qquad \mathsf{R}_\sqcap^+ \; \frac{C \sqsubseteq E_1 \; C \sqsubseteq E_2}{C \sqsubseteq E_1 \sqcap E_2} \; E_1 \sqcap E_2 \text{ occurs in } \mathcal{O}$$

$$\mathsf{R}_\exists^\bot \; \frac{C \sqsubseteq \exists r.E \; E \sqsubseteq \bot}{C \sqsubseteq \bot} \qquad \mathsf{R}_\exists \; \frac{C \sqsubseteq \exists r.E \; E \sqsubseteq F}{C \sqsubseteq \exists r.F} \; \exists r.F \text{ occurs in } \mathcal{O}$$

Fig. 1. Basic inference rules for reasoning in $\mathcal{EL}$

An *inference* is a triple $\langle$rule name, premises, conclusion$\rangle$ of the form $\langle \mathsf{R}, \{\varphi_1, .., \varphi_n\}, \psi \rangle$, where $n \geqslant 0$ and ψ is obtained by an inference rule R with premises $\varphi_1, \ldots, \varphi_n$. A *proof* of a concept inclusion ψ (from an ontology $\mathcal{O}$) is a set of inferences $\{\iota_1, \ldots, \iota_n\}$, where $n \geqslant 1$, such that ψ is the conclusion of ι_n and for all $k = 1, \ldots, n$ and any axiom φ, if φ is a premise of ι_k, then there is a unique $j < k$ such that φ is the conclusion of ι_j and if φ is the conclusion of ι_k and $k \neq n$ then there is $l > k$ such that φ is a premise of ι_l. Observe that due to the injective renaming of non Σ-symbols it holds $\mathtt{sig}\,(\mathcal{O}) \cap \mathtt{sig}\,(\mathcal{O}^*) \subseteq \Sigma$ and whenever a concept C occurs in ontology $\mathcal{O}$, we have $\mathtt{sig}\,(C) \subseteq \mathtt{sig}\,(\mathcal{O})$ and hence, $\mathtt{sig}\,(C^*) \subseteq \mathtt{sig}\,(\mathcal{O}^*)$. If there is a concept D such that $\mathtt{sig}\,(D) \subseteq \Sigma$ and $\mathcal{O} \cup \mathcal{O}^* \models \{C \sqsubseteq D, \; D \sqsubseteq C^*\}$ (in which case D is called *interpolant* for $C \sqsubseteq C^*$) then due to the renaming it holds that $\mathcal{O} \models \{C \sqsubseteq D, D \sqsubseteq C\}$ and thus, $\mathcal{O} \models C \equiv D$, i.e., D is a definition of concept C in signature Σ.

Theorem 1. *Let Σ be a signature, $\mathcal{O}_1, \mathcal{O}_2$ ontologies and C_1, C_2 concepts such that $\mathrm{sig}\,(\mathcal{O}_1) \cap \mathrm{sig}\,(\mathcal{O}_2) \subseteq \Sigma$ and C_i occurs in $\mathcal{O}_i$, for $i = 1, 2$. If $\mathcal{O}_1 \cup \mathcal{O}_2 \models C_1 \sqsubseteq C_2$ then there exists a concept D such that $\mathrm{sig}\,(D) \subseteq \Sigma$ and $\mathcal{O}_1 \cup \mathcal{O}_2 \models \{C_1 \sqsubseteq D,\ D \sqsubseteq C_2\}$.*

Proof. We note the following property (referred to as $\star$), which immediately follows from the definition of the inference rules: if there is a proof of a concept inclusion $C \sqsubseteq E$ from an ontology $\mathcal{O}$ then either it is obtained by one of the rules $\mathsf{R_\top}, \mathsf{R_\bot}, \mathsf{R_\exists^\bot}$, or E occurs in C or $\mathcal{O}$. We use induction on the number of inferences in a proof $\langle \iota_i, \ldots, \iota_n \rangle$ of a concept inclusion $\varphi = C_1 \sqsubseteq C_2$ from $\mathcal{O}_1 \cup \mathcal{O}_2$. For $n = 1$, if φ is obtained by $\mathsf{R_0}$ or $\mathsf{R_\top}$ then $\mathrm{sig}\,(C_2) \subseteq \Sigma$ and thus, C_2 is an interpolant for φ. If it is obtained by $\mathsf{R_\bot}$, then $\bot$ is an interpolant. For the induction step, if φ is obtained by $\mathsf{R_\exists^\bot}$ then $\bot$ is an interpolant. If the rule is $\mathsf{R_\sqcap^+}$ then by the induction assumption there is an interpolant D_i for each premise $C \sqsubseteq E_i$, $i = 1, 2$, and hence, $D_1 \sqcap D_2$ is an interpolant for φ. If the rule is $\mathsf{R_\sqsubseteq}$ then $E \bowtie F \in \mathcal{O}_1 \cup \mathcal{O}_2$, for some $i = 1, 2$, where $\bowtie \in \{\sqsubseteq, \equiv\}$. If $i = 1$ then it follows from $\mathrm{sig}\,(F) \subseteq \mathrm{sig}\,(\mathcal{O}_2)$ that $\mathrm{sig}\,(F) \subseteq \Sigma$ and thus, F is an interpolant for φ. If $i = 2$ then $\mathrm{sig}\,(E) \subseteq \mathrm{sig}\,(\mathcal{O}_2)$, thus by the induction assumption there is an interpolant for $C \sqsubseteq E$, which is an interpolant for φ. If the rule is $\mathsf{R_\sqcap^-}$, consider its premise $C \sqsubseteq E_1 \sqcap E_2$; w.l.o.g we assume that $\varphi = C \sqsubseteq E_1$. It follows from $(\star)$ that $\mathrm{sig}\,(E_1 \sqcap E_2) \subseteq \mathrm{sig}\,(\mathcal{O}_i)$, for some $i = 1, 2$. If $i = 2$, then there is an interpolant for $C \sqsubseteq E_1 \sqcap E_2$, which is an interpolant for φ. If $i = 1$ then $\mathrm{sig}\,(E_1) \subseteq \mathrm{sig}\,(\mathcal{O}_2)$ yields $\mathrm{sig}\,(E_1) \subseteq \Sigma$ and hence, E_1 is an interpolant for φ. Finally, if the rule is $\mathsf{R_\exists}$ then it follows from $(\star)$ that $\mathrm{sig}\,(\exists r.E) \subseteq \mathrm{sig}\,(\mathcal{O}_i)$, for some $i = 1, 2$. If $i = 2$ then there is an interpolant for $C \sqsubseteq \exists r.E$, which is an interpolant for φ. If $i = 1$ then it follows from the condition $\mathrm{sig}\,(\exists r.F) \subseteq \mathrm{sig}\,(\mathcal{O}_2)$ that $r \in \Sigma$ and by the induction assumption there is an interpolant D for $E \sqsubseteq F$. Then $\exists r.D$ is an interpolant for φ.   □

The proof of the theorem gives an idea of a recursive algorithm for computing interpolants and hence, concept definitions, by traversing proofs of $C \sqsubseteq C^*$ from the union $\mathcal{O} \sqcup \mathcal{O}^*$. In general, there can exist several proofs and each of them can yield a different definition of the concept C. Although the idea is simple, its implementation is not straightforward. First, it requires an ontology reasoner, which is not only able to decide entailment of concept inclusions from an ontology, but supports proof tracing, i.e., provides proofs as certificates for entailment. Second, the method presented by Theorem 1 has to rely on a proof system implemented by a reasoner. DeFind employs ELK [1], which is a highly optimized reasoner for the Description Logic $\mathcal{EL}$ and its extensions. The add-ons to ELK, which provide proof tracing and explanation services, employ the set of inference rules given in Fig. 2. Showing a direct analogue of Theorem 1 for this proof system is not straightforward, since (in contrast to the rules from Fig. 1) there exist proofs, from which an interpolant can not be directly computed. However, it can be shown that there always exists (at least a single) proof, which is appropriate for computing interpolants and hence, concept definitions.

DeFind implements a recursive procedure, which traverses proofs obtained by using the tracing service for ELK reasoner. Proofs are built for the entailment

$$S_0 \;\overline{\;C \sqsubseteq C\;} \qquad S_\top \;\overline{\;C \sqsubseteq \top\;} \qquad S_\bot \;\overline{\;\bot \sqsubseteq C\;} \qquad S_{ax} \;\overline{\;C \sqsubseteq E\;}\; C \sqsubseteq E \in \mathcal{O}$$

$$S_\sqsubseteq \;\frac{C_0 \sqsubseteq C_1 \dots C_{n-1} \sqsubseteq C_n}{C_0 \sqsubseteq C_n} \qquad S_\equiv \;\frac{}{C_j \sqsubseteq C_k}\; C_i \equiv C_{i+1} \in \mathcal{O},\; 0 \leqslant i < n,\; 0 \leqslant j,k \leqslant n$$

$$S_\sqcap^- \;\overline{\;C_1 \sqcap \dots \sqcap C_n \sqsubseteq C_i\;} \qquad S_\sqcap^+ \;\frac{C \sqsubseteq E_1 \;\dots\; C \sqsubseteq E_n}{C \sqsubseteq E_1 \sqcap \dots \sqcap E_n}$$

$$S_\exists^\bot \;\overline{\;\exists r.\bot \sqsubseteq \bot\;} \qquad S_\exists \;\frac{C \sqsubseteq E}{\exists r.C \sqsubseteq \exists r.E}$$

Fig. 2. Inference rules used by the proof tracing service for ELK reasoner

$\mathcal{O} \cup \mathcal{O}^* \models C \sqsubseteq C^*$, where $\mathcal{O}^*$ and C^* are "copies" (of a given ontology $\mathcal{O}$ and concept C) constructed wrt a specified signature Σ. The procedure applies recursively the rules below to compute a label expression $L(\varphi)$ for every concept inclusion φ appearing as the conclusion of an inference and outputs a label computed for $C \sqsubseteq C^*$. Whenever there are several proofs for the same φ, each of them is traversed. A *label* is a concept formulated in an extension of $\mathcal{EL}$ with disjunction $\sqcup$ (denoted as $\mathcal{EL}_\sqcup$) and a distinguished "empty" concept ϵ, for which the following holds: $\epsilon \sqcap D = \epsilon$, $\epsilon \sqcup D = D$, $\exists r.\epsilon = \epsilon$, and $\exists r.(D \sqcup E) = \exists r.D \sqcup \exists r.E$, for any concepts D, E and role r. By using the latter equation, the notion of Disjunctive Normal Form of a $\mathcal{EL}_\sqcup$-concept is naturally defined. We say that a label expression is *empty* if it equals ϵ. Initially the label of every conclusion appearing in a proof is assumed to be empty. Each rule below is provided with a name and gives a label to the conclusion φ of an inference being visited during proof traversal, depending on the type of the inference rule and the labels of its premises. We use the notations from Fig. 2 for the premises of each inference rule mentioned below:

($L_\bot$) rule is $S_\bot \Rightarrow L(\varphi) := L(\varphi) \sqcup \bot$
(L_Σ) rule is one of $S_0, S_\top, S_{ax}, S_\equiv, S_\sqcap^-, S_\exists^\bot$, $\varphi = C \sqsubseteq E$, and $\mathbf{sig}(E) \subseteq \Sigma \Rightarrow$
    $L(\varphi) := L(\varphi) \sqcup E$
($L_\sqsubseteq$) rule is $S_\sqsubseteq \Rightarrow L(\varphi) := L(\varphi) \sqcup \bigsqcup_{i=1,\dots,n} L(C_{i-1} \sqsubseteq C_i)$
($L_\sqcap^+$) rule is $S_\sqcap^+ \Rightarrow L(\varphi) := L(\varphi) \sqcup \sqcap_{i=1,\dots,n} L(C \sqsubseteq E_i)$
($L_\exists$) rule is $S_\exists$ and $r \in \Sigma \Rightarrow L(\varphi) := L(\varphi) \sqcup \exists r.L(C \sqsubseteq E)$.

Theorem 2. *Let Σ be a signature, $\mathcal{O}$ ontology, and C a concept occurring in $\mathcal{O}$. The concept C is Σ-definable wrt $\mathcal{O}$ iff the procedure returns a non-empty $\mathcal{EL}_\sqcup$-expression $L(C \sqsubseteq C^*)$. Every conjunct from the Disjunctive Normal Form of $L(C \sqsubseteq C^*)$ is a $\mathcal{EL}$-concept and it is a Σ-definition of C wrt $\mathcal{O}$.*

3   Complexity of Definitions

We now estimate the size and the number of definitions computed by DeFind. The above mentioned procedure recursively computes labels for conclusions of inferences appearing in proofs. Under the assumption that every proof is computed in polynomial time in the size of an input ontology $\mathcal{O}$ (which is true when using the ELK reasoner), the size of every proof is polynomially bounded by the size of $\mathcal{O}$. For any conclusion, the label is computed once, when traversing a single proof. The rules $(L_\perp)$, (L_Σ) give a label concept from a conclusion of some inference and hence, its size is bounded by the size of $\mathcal{O}$. Every other rule of the procedure gives a label, which is obtained as a combination (under $\sqcup$, $\sqcap$, or $\exists r.$, with $r \in \mathrm{sig}\,(\mathcal{O})$) of k expressions computed at the previous steps of the recursion, where $k \geqslant 1$ is the number of premises of an inference rule and hence, k is bounded by the size of the proof. In particular, the rules $L_\sqsubseteq$, $L_\sqcap^+$ give a label, which is at most k times longer than the labels of the premises of $S_\sqsubseteq$, $S_\sqcap^+$. Therefore, the size of any label computed from a single proof is at most exponential in the size of the ontology. Since every proof is polynomially bounded, there are at most exponentially many proofs for any conclusion and hence, the output of the procedure has at most exponential size. By Theorem 2, every conjunct from the DNF of the output label is a definition and therefore, the upper bound on the number of definitions computed by DeFind is double exponential in the size of the ontology. To estimate the size of the computed definitions one can w.l.o.g. assume that every rule of the procedure gives a label in DNF and show the following by induction. Every conjunct from a label obtained by some rule of the procedure is either a concept from a conclusion of an inference from a proof, or a combination (under $\sqcup$, $\sqcap$, or $\exists r.$) of conjuncts from the labels computed at the previous steps. Therefore, the size of every definition is at most exponential in the size of the input ontology. We now show that these bound are tight by giving an example of an ontology $\mathcal{O}$, concept C, and a signature Σ such that there is a double exponential number of shortest Σ-definitions of C wrt $\mathcal{O}$, where every definition has size exponential in the size of $\mathcal{O}$. Let $\Sigma = \{r, s, D_1, D_2\}$, $C = A_0$, and for $n \geqslant 1$, let $\mathcal{O}$ consist of axioms: $A_0 \equiv \exists r.A_1 \sqcap \exists s.A_1, \ldots,$ $A_{n-1} \equiv \exists r.A_n \sqcap \exists s.A_n$, $A_n \equiv D_1$, $A_n \equiv D_2$. Observe that $\mathcal{O} \models A_n \equiv D_1 \sqcup D_2$, hence, $\mathcal{O} \models A_{n-1} \equiv \exists r.(D_1 \sqcup D_2) \sqcap \exists s.(D_1 \sqcup D_2)$. Converting this expression into DNF gives four Σ-definitions of A_{n-1} wrt $\mathcal{O}$, i.e., concepts $\exists r.D_i \sqcap \exists s.D_j$, where $i, j = 1, 2$. Similarly, A_0 is equivalent wrt $\mathcal{O}$ to a $\mathcal{EL}_\sqcup$-concept, which has 2^n occurrences of $D_1 \sqcup D_2$. Converting this concept into DNF gives a double exponential number of Σ-definitions of A_0 wrt $\mathcal{O}$ and it can be shown that no shorter Σ-definitions exist.

4   Features of DeFind

DeFind (available at https://github.com/stiv-yakovenko/defind) requires the ELK reasoner [1] and proof explanation plugin [2] for Protégé. The interface of DeFind is given in Fig. 3. The screenshot shows Σ-definitions of concept $\exists r.A_1 \sqcap \exists s.A_1$ computed by DeFind wrt ontology $\mathcal{O}$ and signature Σ from the previous section for $n = 1$. The user can input a complex concept in the Manchester OWL Syntax into the field "Class expression" or drag-and-drop a concept name from the class hierarchy of the ontology. To specify concept and role names for the target signature, one can drag-and-drop items from the class or object property hierarchy. One can simultaneously add all role names from the ontology into the target signature by pressing "Add all Object Properties" button. Selecting "doesn't include symbols" option sets the target signature to consist of all those concept an role names from the ontology, which are not listed in the "Target signature" field. On pressing "Compute definitions", the corresponding Σ-definitions are computed (or a notification is shown if no definition exists). On pressing the question mark at the right-hand side of a definition, an explanation is shown, why it corresponds to the specified class expression: the Protégé proof explanation plugin is called to visualize a proof (see, e.g., Fig. 5 in [2]) of the equivalence of the class expression to the concept computed by DeFind.

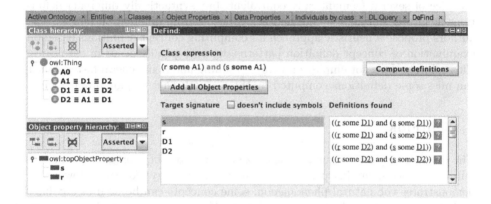

Fig. 3. Interface of DeFind in the Protégé ontology editor

5   Related Work

In [3], a similar approach is implemented to compute concept definitions from tableaux proofs in the Description Logic $\mathcal{ALC}$ and its extensions. The authors provide a constructive proof of an analogue of Theorem 1 and derive an algorithm, which computes a definition of at most double exponential size, whenever there exists one in a target signature. This bound is tight and is one exponential larger than the size of the shortest definitions in $\mathcal{EL}$. It is known that general tableaux methods, when applied to $\mathcal{EL}$, provide exponentially longer proofs than the ones obtained in the proof systems from this paper. It should be noted that the algorithm from [3] computes a single definition from a proof, whereas DeFind computes several definitions, the number of which is bounded by a double exponential in the size of the ontology. DeFind explores all proofs provided by a reasoner and traversing a single proof can potentially give several definitions for a concept of interest. In [4], the authors propose an algorithm, which finds a single concept definition in a signature of interest wrt a normalised

$\mathcal{EL}$-ontology. The algorithm computes an algebraic representation of an ontology as a canonical model provided with an information on how each element of the model is obtained. Essentially, it implements the two features, which are required for computing concept definitions, i.e., ontology reasoning and proof tracing. In contrast, DeFind relies on external reasoning and proof tracing services. The question whether it suffices to compute a single concept definition strongly depends on application. For instance, the method from [3] is employed in [5] to compute query reformulations. In [6], checking for existence of a concept definition (or computing a single one) is used for ontology decomposition. In both applications, the quality of the obtained result is strongly related to the form of a computed definition. On the other hand, it is argued in [7] that having multiple definitions is helpful in the context of ontology alignment, since having a choice of several (semantically equivalent, but syntactically different) definitions facilitates finding matches between concepts from different ontologies. The authors propose a heuristic approach for computing concept definitions based on examination of concept definition patterns, which typically occur in ontologies. This solution does not employ ontology reasoning and is in general faster, but it can miss some definitions computed by the methods that employ proof tracing.

6   Outlook

The exponential lower bound for the size and number of shortest concept definitions is shown in this paper by an artificial ontology example. However it demonstrates the natural phenomenon: some concepts can be used as auxiliary ones in ontology to make definitions shorter. If one asks whether there is a definition, which does not contain certain concept or role names, then one may get a positive answer, but the obtained definition may be long and not easy to comprehend. It is to be understood whether a significant increase of definition size can happen in real-world ontologies. Further, it may be important to develop techniques that help to automatically suggest extensions of the target signature, when a blow-up is unavoidable. One of the primary goals of further implementation is to support other language features of OWL 2 EL profile of the Web Ontology Language, e.g., inclusion and composition of roles. These features are particularly interesting, because on one hand they are frequently used in ontologies and on the other hand, Theorem 1 is no longer true for $\mathcal{EL}$ extended with these features. Finally, there is a room for optimizations for DeFind. If the plugin is used extensively to compute definitions of the same concept wrt different signatures then it makes sense to implement optimizations proposed in [4], which employ incremental reasoning to reduce computation overhead, when only a small part of the input is changed.

References

1. Kazakov, Y., Krötzsch, M., Simancik, F.: The incredible ELK - from polynomial procedures to efficient reasoning with $\mathcal{EL}$ ontologies. J. Autom. Reason. **53**(1), 1–61 (2014)
2. Kazakov, Y., Klinov, P., Stupnikov, A.: Towards reusable explanation services in protege. In: Artale, A., Glimm, B., Kontchakov, R. (eds.) Proceedings of the 30th International Workshop on Description Logics, CEUR Workshop Proceedings, Montpellier, France, 18–21 July 2017, vol. 1879. CEUR-WS.org (2017)
3. ten Cate, B., Franconi, E., Seylan, I.: Beth definability in expressive description logics. J. Artif. Intell. Res. **48**, 347–414 (2013)
4. Ponomaryov, D.K., Vlasov, D.: Concept definability and interpolation in enriched models of $\mathcal{EL}$ -tboxes. In: Eiter, T., Glimm, B., Kazakov, Y., Krötzsch, M. (eds.) Informal Proceedings of the 26th International Workshop on Description Logics, CEUR Workshop Proceedings, Ulm, Germany, 23–26 July 2013, vol. 1014, pp. 898–916. CEUR-WS.org (2013)
5. Franconi, E., Kerhet, V., Ngo, N.: Exact query reformulation over databases with first-order and description logics ontologies. J. Artif. Intell. Res. **48**, 885–922 (2013)
6. Konev, B., Lutz, C., Ponomaryov, D.K., Wolter, F.: Decomposing description logic ontologies. In: Lin, F., Sattler, U., Truszczynski, M. (eds.) Principles of Knowledge Representation and Reasoning: Proceedings of the Twelfth International Conference, KR 2010, Toronto, Ontario, Canada, 9–13 May 2010. AAAI Press (2010)
7. Geleta, D., Payne, T.R., Tamma, V., Wolter, F.: Computing minimal definition signatures in description logic ontologies. Technical report, University of Liverpool (2016)

A Graph-Based Method for Interactive Mapping Revision

Weizhuo Li[1,2]($\boxtimes$), Songmao Zhang[2], Guilin Qi[1], Xuefeng Fu[3], and Qiu Ji[4]

[1] School of Computer Science and Engineering, Southeast University, Nanjing, China
liweizhuo@amss.ac.cn, gqi@seu.edu.cn
[2] Academy of Mathematics and Systems Science, Chinese Academy of Sciences,
Beijing, China
smzhang@math.ac.cn
[3] School of Information Engineering, Nanchang Institute of Technology,
Nanchang, China
fxf@nit.edu.cn
[4] School of Modern Posts and Institute of Modern Posts,
Nanjing University of Posts and Telecommunications, Nanjing, China
qiuji@njupt.edu.cn

Abstract. Discovering semantic relations between heterogeneous ontologies is one of the key research topics in the Semantic Web. As the matching strategies adopted are largely heuristic, wrong mappings often exist in alignments generated by ontology matching systems. The mainstream methods for mapping revision deal with logical inconsistencies, so erroneous mappings not causing an inconsistency may be left out. Therefore, manual validations from domain experts are required. In this paper, we propose a graph-based method for interactive mapping revision with the purpose of reducing manual efforts as much as possible. Source ontologies are encoded into an integrated graph, where its mapping arcs are obtained by transforming mappings and will be evaluated by the expert. We specify the decision space for mapping revision and the corresponding operations that can be applied in the graph. After a human decision is made in each interaction, the mappings entailed by the manually confirmed ones are automatically approved. Conversely, those that would entail the rejected mappings or make the graph incoherent are declined. The whole update process modeled in the decision space can be done in polynomial time. Moreover, we define an impact function based on the integrated graph to identify the most influential mappings that will be displayed to the expert. In this way, the efforts of manual evaluation could be reduced further. The experiment on real-world ontology alignments shows that our method can save more decisions made by the expert than other revisions in most cases.

1 Introduction

Ontologies aim to model domain conceptualizations for sharing and reusing knowledge on the Semantic Web. Discovering semantic relations between heterogeneous ontologies is one of the key research topics in ontology matching

© Springer Nature Switzerland AG 2018
R. Ichise et al. (Eds.): JIST 2018, LNCS 11341, pp. 244–261, 2018.
https://doi.org/10.1007/978-3-030-04284-4_17

community, and many promising approaches have been developed for producing ontology mappings in (semi-) automatic ways [1]. Most of the matching systems adopt heuristic strategies, and thus wrong mappings often exist in the generated alignments, which have negative impacts on many applications on the Semantic Web such as terminological reasoning, data transformation and query answering [2]. Mapping revision, which plays an important role in ontology matching, is proposed to target this problem [3].

Up to now, the mainstream methods depend on eliminating inconsistencies among ontologies and mappings to improve the quality of alignments. Such mappings are referred to as incoherent as they yield unsatisfiable concepts and roles in source ontologies [2]. In these works, mappings are interpreted as sets of axioms in description logics (DL), their variants, or restricted logic programmings, and logical reasoners are applied to detect the inconsistency (see Alcomo [2], LogMap [4] and AMLR [5] for example). At the repair stage, some local or global strategies are adopted to remove some mappings so as to regain the consistency. Alternatively, there exist works that consider the uncertainty of mappings and model mapping revision as an optimization problem where probabilistic reasoning techniques are applied to solve the conflicts, as exemplified by ContraBovemRufum [6] and ELog [7].

Although existing mapping revision methods are effective in maintaining the consistency of mappings with source ontologies, they suffer from two limitations. Firstly, logical unsatisfiability is caused by erroneous mappings across ontologies, but not all wrong mappings will lead to unsatisfiability. Such mappings are often reserved by the revision systems in the final alignments. Generally, the detection of incoherent mappings depends on the presence of disjointness axioms. When there are fewer or none such axioms specified in source ontologies, the effectiveness of mapping revision will be affected. Secondly, after the incoherence detection that often identifies hundreds or thousands of minimal incoherence preserving subalignments (MIPSs) [2] for large and complex domain ontologies, tracking down the true negatives in MIPSs remains a challenge. To address it, heuristic principles are instantiated including consistency and conservativity principle, minimal change principle, and many others [2,8,9], whereas the accuracy and completeness are not guaranteed. This calls for manual revisions with domain expertise.

Interactive methods have been proposed for mapping revision by providing more information for human to make better decisions [10–13] or to reduce the number of human decisions in the interaction with the support of distributed description logics (DDL) [14]. On the other hand, in the research of ontology quality assurance, an interactive ontology revision theory was developed by Nikitina et al. in [15]. The notion of decision space was proposed and it was proved to be capable of reducing the cost of required reasoning operations during the interactive revision iterations for DL ontologies. Inspired by [15], we propose a graph-based method in this paper for interactive mapping revision.

Specifically, we focus on repairing incoherent mappings among DL-Lite ontologies. In our previous studies [16,17], we show that the mapping revision process for DL-Lite ontologies can be reduced to operations on a directed graph without losing any information in polynomial time. Based on this, in our interactive revision model, firstly source ontologies are encoded into an integrated graph, where its mapping arcs are obtained by transforming mappings to be evaluated by the expert. We specify the decision space for mapping revision and the corresponding operations that can be applied in the integrated graph. After a decision is made by the expert in each interaction, the mapping arcs in the graph will be updated automatically. For every mapping confirmed manually, we identify mappings that can be entailed as correct ones whereas mappings in conflict with the evaluated mapping are discarded. On the other hand, for every mapping declined manually, we identify mappings that can entail it and recognize them as incorrect ones. The whole update process modeled in decision space can be finished in polynomial time (e.g., $O(n^3)$) that is lower than the one in [15]. Moreover, we define an impact function based on the integrated graph so as to show the most influential mapping to human in each interaction.

The contribution of our study is summarized as follows.

1. We propose a graph-based method for interactive mapping revision, where mapping arcs can be updated in an automated way according to the human decision in polynomial time. To further reduce the number of human decisions, we design an impact function based on the graph so as to ask for human opinions solely for the most influential mappings.
2. We have implemented our algorithms and evaluated on validating real-world alignments across ontologies. The empirical results show that for most cases our method can save more human decisions than other interactive revisions.

The rest of this paper is organized as follows. Section 2 presents the theoretical preliminaries of DL-Lite, interactive ontology revision, and incoherent ontology mappings. Our interactive mapping revision method is described in Sect. 3 with formalizations and algorithms, which are evaluated in Sect. 4 against other interactive revisions. Related works are introduced in Sect. 5, followed by a conclusion in Sect. 6.

2   Preliminaries

2.1   DL-Lite

We start with the introduction of DL-Lite$_{core}$, which is the core language for DL-Lite [18]. DL-Lite$_{core}$ has pairwise disjoint sets of concepts, roles and individuals, where concepts and roles are further partitioned. In our convention, A denotes an atomic concept, P an atomic role, B a basic concept, Q a basic role, C a general concept, and R a general role. Moreover, $\bot$ denotes the bottom concept. Syntactically, the DL-Lite$_{core}$ concepts and roles are defined as follows: (1) $C :=B|\neg B$, (2) $B := A|\exists Q$, (3) $Q := P|P^-$, and (4) $R := Q|\neg Q$. An axiom is an expression taking one of the following forms: (1) the concept inclusion axiom $B \sqsubseteq C$, (2) the role inclusion axiom $Q \sqsubseteq R$, (3) the functionality axiom

$funct(Q)$, (4) the concept membership axiom $A(a)$, where a is an individual, or (5) the role membership axiom $P(a, b)$, where a and b are individuals. In DL-Lite_{core}, an ontology $O = \langle \mathcal{T}, \mathcal{A} \rangle$ consists of a TBox $\mathcal{T}$ and an ABox $\mathcal{A}$, where $\mathcal{T}$ is a finite set of concept inclusion axioms and $\mathcal{A}$ a finite set of membership axioms of concepts and roles. Further, DL-$\text{Lite}_{\mathcal{R}}$ extends DL-Lite_{core} with role inclusion axioms and DL-$\text{Lite}_{\mathcal{F}}$ allows for functionality axioms based on DL-Lite_{core}.

The semantics of the DL-Lite logics is based on the general first-order interpretation [18]. The satisfaction of an axiom F in an interpretation $\mathcal{I} = \langle \Delta^{\mathcal{I}}, \cdot^{\mathcal{I}} \rangle$, denoted as $\mathcal{I} \models F$, is defined as follows: (1) $\mathcal{I} \models B \sqsubseteq C$ iff $B^{\mathcal{I}} \subseteq C^{\mathcal{I}}$; (2) $\mathcal{I} \models Q \sqsubseteq R$ iff $Q^{\mathcal{I}} \subseteq R^{\mathcal{I}}$; (3) $\mathcal{I} \models \text{Funct}(Q)$ iff $Q^{\mathcal{I}}$ is functional; (4) $\mathcal{I} \models A(a)$ iff $a^{\mathcal{I}} \in A^{\mathcal{I}}$; (5) $\mathcal{I} \models P(a, b)$ iff $(a^{\mathcal{I}}, b^{\mathcal{I}}) \in P^{\mathcal{I}}$. An ontology O is consistent iff there exists an interpretation $\mathcal{I}$ such that for every axiom $F \in O$, $\mathcal{I} \models F$ holds. Such an interpretation is called a model of O. If axiom F is satisfied by all the models of ontology O, we can also write $O \models F$. Satisfiability of concepts and roles is specified in the following definition, which leads to the coherence of ontology.

Definition 1 [18] *(Unsatisfiability and Incoherence). Let O be a DL-Lite ontology. A concept C (role R) in O is unsatisfiable iff $O \models C \sqsubseteq \bot$ ($O \models R \sqsubseteq \bot$) holds. Ontology O is incoherent iff there exists at least one unsatisfiable concept or role in O.*

2.2 Ontology Revision State and Decision Space

In [15], revision state and decision space are the two key notions for interactive ontology revision, which could significantly reduce the cost of required reasoning operations.

Definition 2 [15] *(Revision State). A revision state is defined as a tuple $(\mathcal{O}, \mathcal{O}^{\models}, \mathcal{O}^{\not\models})$ of ontologies, where $\mathcal{O}^{\models} \subseteq \mathcal{O}$, $\mathcal{O}^{\not\models} \subseteq \mathcal{O}$ and $\mathcal{O}^{\not\models} \cap \mathcal{O} = \emptyset$. A revision state is complete if $\mathcal{O} = \mathcal{O}^{\models} \cup \mathcal{O}^{\not\models}$.*

An incomplete revision state $(\mathcal{O}, \mathcal{O}^{\models}, \mathcal{O}^{\not\models})$ can be refined by evaluating a further axiom $F \in (\mathcal{O} \backslash (\mathcal{O}^{\models} \cup \mathcal{O}^{\not\models})$, obtaining $(\mathcal{O}, \mathcal{O}^{\models} \cup \{F\}, \mathcal{O}^{\not\models})$ or $(\mathcal{O}, \mathcal{O}^{\models}, \mathcal{O}^{\not\models} \cup \{F\})$.

Revision state $(\mathcal{O}, \mathcal{O}^{\models}, \mathcal{O}^{\not\models})$ is consistent if there exists no $F \in \mathcal{O}^{\not\models}$ such that $\mathcal{O}^{\models} \models F$. The revision closure $\text{clos}(\mathcal{O}, \mathcal{O}^{\models}, \mathcal{O}^{\not\models})$ of $(\mathcal{O}, \mathcal{O}^{\models}, \mathcal{O}^{\not\models})$ is $(\mathcal{O}, \mathcal{O}_c^{\models}, \mathcal{O}_c^{\not\models})$, where $\mathcal{O}_c^{\models} = \{F \in \mathcal{O} | \mathcal{O}^{\models} \models F\}$ and $\mathcal{O}_c^{\not\models} = \{F \in \mathcal{O} | \mathcal{O}^{\models} \cup \{F\} \models F'$ for some $F' \in \mathcal{O}^{\not\models}\}$.

As computing the closure of a revision state is expensive, Nikitina et al. introduced the notion of decision space that could significantly reduce the cost of computing the closure upon elementary revisions.

Definition 3 [15] *(Decision Space). Given a revision state $(\mathcal{O}, \mathcal{O}^{\models}, \mathcal{O}^{\not\models})$ with $\mathcal{O}^{\not\models} \neq \emptyset$, the according decision space $\mathbb{D}_{(\mathcal{O}, \mathcal{O}^{\models}, \mathcal{O}^{\not\models})} = (\mathcal{O}^?, \mathcal{E}, \mathcal{C})$ contains the set $\mathcal{O}^? = \mathcal{O} \backslash (\{F | \mathcal{O}^{\models} \models F\} \cup \{F | \mathcal{O}^{\models} \cup \{F\} \models F', F' \in \mathcal{O}^{\not\models}\})$ of unevaluated axioms and two binary relations, $\mathcal{E}$ (entails) and $\mathcal{C}$ (conflicts) defined by $F \mathcal{E} F'$ iff $\mathcal{O}^{\models} \cup \{F\} \models F'$ and $F \mathcal{C} F'$ iff $\mathcal{O}^{\models} \cup \{F, F'\} \models F''$ for some $F'' \in \mathcal{O}^{\not\models}$.*

The following lemma shows that computing the whole closure of a revision state w.r.t evaluated axiom F can be reduced to the operations on the decision space.

Lemma 1 [15]. *Given* $\mathbb{D}_{(\mathcal{O},\mathcal{O}^\vDash,\mathcal{O}^\nvDash)} = (\mathcal{O}^?, \mathcal{E}, \mathcal{C})$ *for a revision state* $(\mathcal{O}, \mathcal{O}^\vDash, \mathcal{O}^\nvDash)$ *such that* $(\mathcal{O}, \mathcal{O}^\vDash, \mathcal{O}^\nvDash) = clos(\mathcal{O}, \mathcal{O}^\vDash, \mathcal{O}^\nvDash)$ *with* $\mathcal{O}^\nvDash \neq \emptyset$ *and* $F \in \mathcal{O}^?$, *then*

1. $clos(\mathcal{O}, \mathcal{O}^\vDash, \mathcal{O}^\nvDash) = (\mathcal{O}, \mathcal{O}^\vDash \cup \uparrow F, \mathcal{O}^\nvDash \cup \wr F)$.
2. $clos(\mathcal{O}, \mathcal{O}^\vDash, \mathcal{O}^\nvDash) = (\mathcal{O}, \mathcal{O}^\vDash, \mathcal{O}^\nvDash \cup \downarrow F)$.

where $\uparrow F = \{F' | F \mathcal{E} F'\}$, $\downarrow F = \{F' | F' \mathcal{E} F\}$ *and* $\wr F = \{F | F \mathcal{C} F'\}$.

2.3   Ontology Mappings and Their Incoherence

We define ontology mappings in the same way as the ontology matching community do [3]. To focus on revising mappings, the ontologies to be matched are assumed to be consistent and coherent. A set of mappings, often identified by one matching system or algorithm, is also called an alignment.

Definition 4 [3] *(Ontology Mapping). Let* O_i *and* O_j *be two DL-Lite ontologies. A mapping is a 4-tuple* (e_i, e_j, r, n), *where* e_i *and* e_j *are two elements, i.e., concepts, roles, or individuals, from* O_i *and* O_j, *respectively,* $r \in \{\sqsubseteq, \sqsupseteq, \equiv\}$ *is a relation holding between* e_i *and* e_j, *and* n *is a weight in the range* $[0, 1]$.

When the weights are ignored, the mappings together with their source ontologies can be seen as a DL-Lite ontology. Such an ontology can be incoherent due to the introduction of the mappings across source ontologies.

Definition 5 [2] *(Mapping Incoherence). Given two DL-Lite ontologies* O_i *and* O_j *and the set of their mappings* $\mathcal{M}$, $\mathcal{M}$ *is incoherent with regard to* O_i *and* O_j *if there exists at least one concept* C_k *or role* R_k, $k \in \{i, j\}$, *such that it is satisfiable in* O_k *but unsatisfiable in* $O_i \cup O_j \cup \mathcal{M}$ *where the weights of mappings are ignored. Otherwise* $\mathcal{M}$ *is coherent.*

Example 1. *Ontologies* O_1 *and* O_2 *describe the domain of the conference management systems, whose axioms are listed as follows:*

$$Meta - Review_1 \sqsubseteq Review_1 \qquad \exists hasName_1^- \sqsubseteq Conference_1$$
$$Conference_1 \sqsubseteq \neg Regular\_Author_1$$
$$Author\_of\_paper_2 \sqsubseteq Author_2 \qquad \exists hasname_2^- \sqsubseteq Author_2$$

Their alignment $\mathcal{M}$ *consists of the following mappings:*

$$m_1 = (Regular\_Author_1, Author_2, \equiv, 0.8)$$
$$m_2 = (Regular\_Author_1, Author\_of\_paper_2, \sqsupseteq, 0.7)$$
$$m_3 = (\exists hasName_1^-, \exists hasname_2^-, \equiv, 0.8)$$
$$m_4 = (Review_1, Reviewing\_event_2, \equiv, 0.6)$$
$$m_5 = (Meta - Review_1, Reviewing\_event_2, \sqsupseteq, 0.7)$$

According to Definition 5, the roles hasName$_1$ *and* hasname$_2$ *are unsatisfiable in* $O_1 \cup O_2 \cup \mathcal{M}$ *because the two anonymous concepts in* m_3 *are subsumed by disjoint concepts. Both* $O_1 \cup O_2 \cup \mathcal{M} \models \exists$hasname$_2^- \sqsubseteq \neg$Regular_ Author$_1$ *and* $O_1 \cup O_2 \cup \mathcal{M} \models \exists$hasname$_2^- \sqsubseteq$ Regular_ Author$_1$ *hold, so* $O_1 \cup O_2 \cup \mathcal{M} \models \exists$hasname$_2^- \sqsubseteq \bot$. *This means that* $\exists$hasname$_2^-$ *is unsatisfiable. Thus* $\mathcal{M}$ *is incoherent.*

In DL-Lite, the concept and role membership axioms asserted in ABox can solely take the form of $A(a)$ or $P(a,b)$ where A is an atomic concept and P an atomic role. This does not cause any unsatisfiability, thus in the remainder of the paper, we only consider the TBox of DL-Lite ontology.

3   The Interactive Mapping Revision Based on Graph

In this section, we first present a formal model of interactive mapping revision, and then recall the graph-based method in our previous study for representing DL-Lite ontologies and their mappings. Based on these, we model the interactive mapping revision process in the graph and present corresponding algorithms.

3.1   A Formal Model of Interactive Mapping Revision

Ontology matching systems often adopt heuristic matching strategies, resulting in the frequent existence of wrong mappings in alignments. Domain experts are required to play a role so as to ensure the correctness of mappings before actually applying them. For a given mapping, its evaluation status is labeled as "unknown" by default. For decisions made by experts, they can be modeled as a function that assigns to each mapping a value from the set {correct, incorrect}. After the evaluation, mappings are divided into two disjoint sets: the set of correct mappings $\mathcal{M}^\models$ and the set of incorrect mappings $\mathcal{M}^{\not\models}$.

Inspired by [15], we specify interactive mapping revision as the process to estimate the unlabeled mappings step by step until none mappings are "unknown", which is equipped with reasoning-based techniques in order to reduce the decisions made by human. Algorithm 1 is a general framework for interactive mapping revision. With ontologies O_1, O_2 and their mappings $\mathcal{M}$ as input, Step 1 initiates the correct mapping set $\mathcal{M}^\models$ and incorrect mapping set $\mathcal{M}^{\not\models}$ with empty set. When an expert confirms the selected mapping m, reasoning-based techniques are executed w.r.t m, i.e., mappings causing unsatisfiability together with $O_1 \cup O_2 \cup \{m\}$ are added to $\mathcal{M}^{\not\models}$ whereas mappings entailed by $O_1 \cup O_2 \cup \{m\}$ are added to $\mathcal{M}^\models$. On the other hand, when m is declined by the expert, mappings that can entail m are added to $\mathcal{M}^{\not\models}$. Mappings labeled by $\mathcal{M}^\models$ or $\mathcal{M}^{\not\models}$ by reasoning no longer need to ask for human decisions. The whole interactive process will not be terminated until all mappings are labeled.

Algorithm 1. Interactive Mapping Revision.

Input: Two ontologies O_1 and O_2, and their mappings $\mathcal{M}$.
Output: Correct mapping set $\mathcal{M}^{\models}$.

1   $\mathcal{M}^{\models} \leftarrow \emptyset$, $\mathcal{M}^{\not\models} \leftarrow \emptyset$;
2   **while** $\mathcal{M}^{\models} \cup \mathcal{M}^{\not\models} \neq \mathcal{M}$ **do**
3   Choose $m \in (\mathcal{M} \setminus (\mathcal{M}^{\models} \cup \mathcal{M}^{\not\models}))$;
4   **if** *expert confirms* m **then**
5         $(\mathcal{M}^{\models}, \mathcal{M}^{\not\models}) \leftarrow$ Reasoning$(O_1, O_2, \mathcal{M}, \mathcal{M}^{\models} \cup \{m\}, \mathcal{M}^{\not\models})$;
6   **else**
7         $(\mathcal{M}^{\models}, \mathcal{M}^{\not\models}) \leftarrow$ Reasoning$(O_1, O_2, \mathcal{M}, \mathcal{M}^{\models}, \mathcal{M}^{\not\models} \cup \{m\})$;

8   **return** $\mathcal{M}^{\models}$;

Example 2 *(Example 1 cont'd). When an expert confirms mapping* $m_1 = (Regular\_ Author_1, Author_2, \equiv, 0.8)$, *by reasoning* $m_3 = (\exists hasName_1^-, \exists hasname_2^-, \equiv, 0.8)$ *shall be added to* $\mathcal{M}^{\not\models}$. *Conversely, expert confirming mapping* m_3 *will lead* m_1 *to be added to* $\mathcal{M}^{\not\models}$.

Note that the key of Algorithm 1 is the reasoning-based technique in line 5 and line 7. In addition, an appropriate sequence of given mappings can also reduce the number of decisions made by an expert. Our graph-based algorithms presented subsequently are designed to address these two issues.

3.2 Constructing Graphs to Represent Ontology and Their Mappings

According to the works in [16,17,19], DL-Lite ontologies and their mappings can be encoded into a directed graph without any loss of information. Concretely, we first construct two subgraphs $\mathcal{G}_{T_i} = (N_i, E_i)$ and $\mathcal{G}_{T_j} = (N_j, E_j)$ for ontologies O_i and O_j, respectively, in which $N_k (k \in \{i, j\})$ represents the concepts or roles of ontologies, and $E_k (k \in \{i, j\})$ represents the inclusion relationships among them. Then, we transform their mappings $\mathcal{M}$ into mapping arcs for connecting two subgraphs. The constructed graph about ontologies O_i, O_j and $\mathcal{M}$, called the integrated graph, is denoted as $\mathcal{G} = (N, E \cup E_{\mathcal{M}})$. Here, $N = N_i \cup N_j$ and $E = E_i \cup E_j$ are the union of the nodes and arcs in subgraphs $\mathcal{G}_{T_i}$ and $\mathcal{G}_{T_j}$. $E_{\mathcal{M}}$ represents a set of mapping arcs, that are bridges linking those nodes across $\mathcal{G}_{T_i}$ and $\mathcal{G}_{T_j}$.

In a directed graph, the transitive closure of a graph $\mathcal{G} = (N, E)$ is a graph (N, E^*) such that there is an arc $\langle s, t \rangle$ in E^* iff there exists a directed path from node s to t in $\mathcal{G}$.

Theorem 1 [17]. *Let* $\mathcal{G} = (N, E \cup E_{\mathcal{M}})$ *be an integrated graph constructed from DL-Lite ontologies* O_i, O_j *and their mappings* $\mathcal{M}$, *and* $\mathcal{G}^* = (N, (E \cup E_{\mathcal{M}})^*)$ *be the transitive closure of* $\mathcal{G}$. *Let* S_i *be a basic concept (or role) in* O_i *and* S_j *a general concept (or role) in* O_j. $O_i \cup O_j \cup \mathcal{M} \models S_i \sqsubseteq S_j$ *iff arc* $\langle S_i, S_j \rangle$ $\in (E \cup E_{\mathcal{M}})^*$.

Theorem 1 indicates that the entailments between the concepts (roles) can be reduced to the graph reachability problem. Based on this, we can detect unsatisfiable concepts or roles in the graph, as shown in the following definition.

Definition 6 [17] *(Path-Unsatisfiability). Let $\mathcal{G} = (N, E \cup E_{\mathcal{M}})$ be the integrated graph constructed from two DL-Lite ontologies O_i and O_j and their mappings $\mathcal{M}$. A node $S \in N$ is path-unsatisfiable if there exist two paths in $\mathcal{G}$ starting from S and ending with node S' and node $\neg S'$, respectively. Graph $\mathcal{G}$ is incoherent iff there exists at least one path-unsatisfiable node in $\mathcal{G}$.*

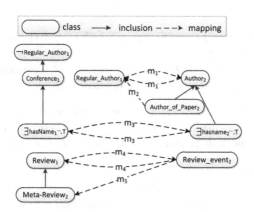

Fig. 1. The integrated graph constructed from ontologies and mappings in Example 1

Example 3 *(Example 1 cont'd). Figure 1 shows an integrated graph constructed from the ontologies and their mappings in Example 1. One can see that the nodes $\exists hasName_1^-$ and $\exists hasname_2^-$ are path-unsatisfiable in $O_1 \cup O_2 \cup \mathcal{M}$ because there exist two paths starting from them to node Regular_ Author$_1$ and node $\neg$Regular_ Author$_1$, respectively.*

3.3   Interactive Mapping Revision in the Graph

In parallel with the revision state and decision space proposed in [15] for interactive ontology revision, we define counterparts as follows for interactive mapping revision based on graph. For convenience, arcs α, β and γ represent three different arcs in the constructed graph.

Definition 7 *(Graph-based Revision State). A graph-based revision state is defined as a tuple $(E \cup E_{\mathcal{M}}, E^{\models}, E^{\not\models})$ of arcs in the graph $\mathcal{G} = (N, E \cup E_{\mathcal{M}})$ with $E^{\models} \subseteq E \cup E_{\mathcal{M}}$, $E^{\not\models} \subseteq E_{\mathcal{M}}$ and $E^{\models} \cap E^{\not\models} = \emptyset$. A graph-based revision state is complete, if $E \cup E_{\mathcal{M}} = E^{\models} \cup E^{\not\models}$. The closure of a graph-based revision state is denoted by $clos(E \cup E_{\mathcal{M}}, E^{\models}, E^{\not\models}) = (E \cup E_{\mathcal{M}}, E_c^{\models}, E_c^{\not\models})$ with $E_c^{\models} = \{\alpha \in E \cup E_{\mathcal{M}} | \alpha \in (E^{\models})^*\}$ and $E_c^{\not\models} = \{\alpha \in E_{\mathcal{M}} | \beta \in (E^{\models} \cup \{\alpha\})^*$ and $\beta \in E^{\not\models}\}$.*

Definition 8 *(Graph-based Decision Space). Given a graph-based revision state* $(E \cup E_{\mathcal{M}}, E^{\vDash}, E^{\nvDash})$ *with* $E^{\nvDash} \neq \emptyset$, *the graph-based decision space* $\mathbb{D}_{(E \cup E_{\mathcal{M}}, E^{\vDash}, E^{\nvDash})} = (E^?_{\mathcal{M}}, \mathcal{E}, \mathcal{C})$ *contains the set* $E^?_{\mathcal{M}} = (E \cup E_{\mathcal{M}}) \backslash (E^{\vDash}_c \cup E^{\nvDash}_c)$ *of unevaluated mapping arcs and two binary relations,* $\mathcal{E}$ *(entails) and* $\mathcal{C}$ *(conflicts) defined by* $\alpha \mathcal{E} \beta$ *iff* $\beta \in (E^{\vDash} \cup \{\alpha\})^*$ *and* $\alpha \mathcal{C} \beta$ *iff* $\gamma \in (E^{\vDash} \cup \{\alpha, \beta\})^*$ *for some* $\gamma \in E^{\nvDash}$.

Considering the requirement that $E^{\nvDash} \neq \emptyset$, we can add a special kind of arcs $\{\langle S_k, \neg S_k \rangle\}$ $(S_k \in N, \neg S_k \in N)$ to check the graph's incoherence, where S_k corresponds to a concept or role in DL-Lite ontologies. The operations about $\mathcal{E}$ and $\mathcal{C}$ in $(E^?_{\mathcal{M}}, \mathcal{E}, \mathcal{C})$ w.r.t mappings can be reduced to the reachability of two nodes as follows.

1. Given two arcs α, β and $\beta = \langle S_i, S_j \rangle$, $\alpha \mathcal{E} \beta$ iff $E^{\vDash} \cup \{\alpha\}$ contains at least one path from node S_i to S_j.
2. Given two arcs α, β, $\alpha \mathcal{C} \beta$ iff $E^{\vDash} \cup \{\alpha, \beta\}$ contains at least one path from node S_i to S_j, where $\langle S_i, S_j \rangle$ is an arc that belongs to $E^{\nvDash}$.

We denote $\uparrow \alpha = \{\beta | \alpha \mathcal{E} \beta\}$, $\downarrow \alpha = \{\beta | \beta \mathcal{E} \alpha\}$ and $\wr \alpha = \{\beta | \alpha \mathcal{C} \beta\}$, representing all the arcs that α can entail, the arcs that entail α, and the arcs conflict with α. We can obtain following properties of the integrated graph.

Proposition 1. *Let* $\mathcal{G} = (N, E \cup E_{\mathcal{M}})$ *be the integrated graph constructed from DL-Lite ontologies* O_i, O_j *and their mappings* $\mathcal{M}$. *Let* $\mathbb{D}_{(E \cup E_{\mathcal{M}}, E^{\vDash}, E^{\nvDash})} = (E^?_{\mathcal{M}}, \mathcal{E}, \mathcal{C})$ *be the decision space w.r.t* $\mathcal{G}$. *Assume that* α *is a mapping arc which needs to be evaluated by an expert. The following hold:*

1. *If expert confirms* α, $clos(E \cup E_{\mathcal{M}}, E^{\vDash} \cup \{\alpha\}, E^{\nvDash}) = (E \cup E_{\mathcal{M}}, E^{\vDash} \cup \uparrow \alpha, E^{\nvDash} \cup \wr \alpha)$
2. *If expert declines* α, $clos(E \cup E_{\mathcal{M}}, E^{\vDash}, E^{\nvDash} \cup \{\alpha\}) = (E \cup E_{\mathcal{M}}, E^{\vDash}, E^{\nvDash} \cup \downarrow \alpha)$.

Proof. (Sketch) With Lemma 1, it can infer that $clos(\mathcal{O}, \mathcal{O}^{\vDash} \cup \{\alpha\}, \mathcal{O}^{\nvDash}) = (\mathcal{O}, \mathcal{O}^{\vDash} \cup \uparrow \alpha, \mathcal{O}^{\nvDash} \cup \wr \alpha)$ and $clos(\mathcal{O}, \mathcal{O}^{\vDash}, \mathcal{O}^{\nvDash} \cup \{\alpha\}) = (\mathcal{O}, \mathcal{O}^{\vDash}, \mathcal{O}^{\nvDash} \cup \downarrow \alpha)$. According to Theorem 1, we can obtain $clos(E \cup E_{\mathcal{M}}, E^{\vDash} \cup \{\alpha\}, E^{\nvDash}) = clos(\mathcal{O}, \mathcal{O}^{\vDash} \cup \{\alpha\}, \mathcal{O}^{\nvDash})$ and $clos(E \cup E_{\mathcal{M}}, E^{\vDash}, E^{\nvDash} \cup \{\alpha\}) = clos(\mathcal{O}, \mathcal{O}^{\vDash}, \mathcal{O}^{\nvDash} \cup \{\alpha\})$. Since the calculation of the relations $\mathcal{E}$ and $\mathcal{C}$ has been reduced to the graph reachability problem in the constructed graph, so $(E \cup E_{\mathcal{M}}, E^{\vDash} \cup \uparrow \alpha, E^{\nvDash} \cup \wr \alpha) = (\mathcal{O}, \mathcal{O}^{\vDash} \cup \uparrow \alpha, \mathcal{O}^{\nvDash} \cup \wr \alpha)$ and $(E \cup E_{\mathcal{M}}, E^{\vDash}, E^{\nvDash} \cup \downarrow \alpha) = (\mathcal{O}, \mathcal{O}^{\vDash}, \mathcal{O}^{\nvDash} \cup \downarrow \alpha)$. Therefore, Proposition 1 holds.

Proposition 2. *For the decision space* $\mathbb{D}_{(E \cup E_{\mathcal{M}}, E^{\vDash}, E^{\nvDash})} = (E^?_{\mathcal{M}}, \mathcal{E}, \mathcal{C})$ *w.r.t* $\mathcal{G}$, *the following hold:*

P1: Relation $\mathcal{E}$ *is reflexive and transitive.*
P2: Relation $\mathcal{C}$ *is symmetric.*
P3: $\alpha \mathcal{E} \beta$ *and* $\alpha \mathcal{C} \beta$ *do not hold at the same time in* $\mathbb{D}_{(E \cup E_{\mathcal{M}}, E^{\vDash}, E^{\nvDash})}$.

Proof. For P1, due to $\alpha \in (E^\models \cup \{\alpha\})$, $\mathcal{E}$ is reflexive. Given $\beta \in (E^\models \cup \{\alpha\})^*$ and $\gamma \in (E^\models \cup \{\beta\})^*$, we can easily obtain that $\gamma \in (E^\models \cup \{\alpha\})^*$ according to the closure property of the graph. For P2, relation $\mathcal{C}$ is symmetric according to Definition 8. For P3, we can prove it by contradiction. If $\alpha\mathcal{E}\beta$ and $\alpha\mathcal{C}\beta$ hold at the same time, then $\beta \in (E^\models \cup \{\alpha\})^*$ and $\gamma \in (E^\models \cup \{\alpha, \beta\})^*$ for some $\gamma \in E^\nvDash$. Therefore, $\gamma \in (E^\models \cup \{\alpha\})^*$ holds. This contradicts with that α cannot be in $E_\mathcal{M}^?$ according to Definition 7.

As the operations of the decision space are implemented in the integrated graph, $\mathcal{E}$ and $\mathcal{C}$ w.r.t mapping arcs can be implemented in polynomial time, whose complexity can be bound in $O(n^3)$ [20].

Now we address the problem of how to find an appropriate sequence of the given mappings so as to further reduce the number of expert's decisions. We define the impact function as follows to measure the influence of a mapping in terms of how many mappings are in entailment or conflicting relationships with this mapping. In each interaction, the most influential mapping is shown to the expert for his/her decision. Note that if a mapping specifies an equivalence correspondence between two concepts across ontologies, we represent it by two mapping arcs and add up their impacts.

Definition 9 *(Impact Function). Let $(E \cup E_\mathcal{M}, E^\models, E^\nvDash)$ be a graph-based revision state and Let $\mathbb{D}_{(E \cup E_\mathcal{M}, E^\models, E^\nvDash)} = (E_\mathcal{M}^?, \mathcal{E}, \mathcal{C})$ be the graph-based decision space. For mapping arc α, its approval impact, decline impact and impact are computed as follows.*

1. $impact^+(\alpha) = map(\uparrow \alpha) + map(\wr \alpha)$
2. $impact^-(\alpha) = map(\downarrow \alpha)$
3. $impact(\alpha) = max(impact^+(\alpha), impact^-(\alpha))$

where $map(\cdot)$ represents the number of the entailed arcs belonging to $E_\mathcal{M}$.

Algorithm 2 presents the graph-based framework for interactive mapping revision. Concretely, we firstly employ the construction rules designed in [17] to encode ontologies into an integrated graph and obtain the mapping arcs from mappings. Then, we initiate the revision state and decision space in Steps 4–5. Steps 6–13 are a concrete realization of an interactive mapping revision: in each interaction, a mapping arc m_0 with the largest impact is selected for an expert to make a decision. If an expert confirms m_0, the decision space is updated based on the confirmed m_0 by Algorithm 3; otherwise, the decision space is updated based on the declined m_0 by Algorithm 4. When the correctness of all mappings is decided, either manually or by reasoning. Step 14 transforms confirmed mapping arcs into the format of mappings. Note that there may be multiple mapping arcs with the largest impact value. We can refine the selection according to the weights of mappings, i.e., if the impact of mapping arcs comes from approval impacts, the one with the highest weight is selected; otherwise the lowest weight.

Algorithm 2. Graph-based Framework for Interactive Mapping Revision.

Input: Two DL-Lite ontologies O_i and O_j, and mappings $\mathcal{M}$.

Output: The repaired mapping $\mathcal{M}'$.

1   Construct two sub-graphs $\mathcal{G}_i = (N_i, E_i)$ and $\mathcal{G}_j = (N_j, E_j)$ of ontologies O_i and O_j according to six construction rules for ontologies in [17];

2   Transform mappings $\mathcal{M}$ into mapping arcs $E_{\mathcal{M}}$ according to six mapping rules in [17];

3   Initial an integrated graph $\mathcal{G} = (N, E)$, where $N = N_i \cup N_j$ and $E = E_i \cup E_j$;

4   $E^{\models} \leftarrow E$, $E^{\not\models} \leftarrow \{\langle S_k, \neg S_k \rangle\}$ $(S_k \in N, \neg S_k \in N)$, $E^?_{\mathcal{M}} \leftarrow E_{\mathcal{M}}$;

5   $\mathbb{D}_{(E \cup E_{\mathcal{M}}, E^{\models}, E^{\not\models})} = (E^?_{\mathcal{M}}, \mathcal{E}, \mathcal{C})$;

6   **while** $E^?_{\mathcal{M}} \neq \emptyset$ **do**

7   **for** *each mapping arc* $m \in E^?_{\mathcal{M}}$ **do**

8   Calculate the impact(m);

9      $m_0 \longleftarrow$ Select one mapping arc with the largest impact;

10   **if** *expert confirms* m_0 **then**

11        $\mathbb{D}_{(E \cup E_{\mathcal{M}}, E^{\models}, E^{\not\models})} \leftarrow$ UDS-C$(\mathbb{D}_{(E \cup E_{\mathcal{M}}, E^{\models}, E^{\not\models})}, m_0, E^?_{\mathcal{M}})$;

12   **else**

13        $\mathbb{D}_{(E \cup E_{\mathcal{M}}, E^{\models}, E^{\not\models})} \leftarrow$ UDS-D$(\mathbb{D}_{(E \cup E_{\mathcal{M}}, E^{\models}, E^{\not\models})}, m_0, E^?_{\mathcal{M}})$;

14   $\mathcal{M}' \longleftarrow$ TransformSoucreMappings$(E^{\models} \cap E_{\mathcal{M}})$;

15   **return** $\mathcal{M}'$;

Table 1. The intermediate results for Example 1 in each interaction of Algorithm 2

Iteration	Selected mapping in $E^?_{\mathcal{M}}$	Expert decision	Entailed mappings	Unlabeled mappings
1	**impact$(m_1) = 3$** impact$(m_2) = 2$, impact$(m_3) = 2$ impact$(m_4) = 2$, impact$(m_5) = 2$	Confirm	m_2, m_3	m_4, m_5
2	**impact$(m_4) = 2$**, impact$(m_5) = 2$	Decline	m_5	None

Example 4 *(Example 1 cont'd). Table 1 summarizes the intermediate results for Example 1 in each interaction of Algorithm 2. The second column lists the mappings with their impacts and shows the selected one in bold. The third column shows the expert's decision of the selected mapping, and the last two columns list the entailed mappings and left mappings in each loop. For five mappings in Example 1, two are evaluated by human whereas the others are automatically decided by our algorithms, and the final correct mappings are $m_1 = $ (Regular_ Author$_1$, Author$_2$, $\equiv$, 0.8) and $m_2 = $ (Regular_ Author$_1$, Author_ of_ paper$_2$, $\sqsupseteq$, 0.7).*

Algorithm 3. UDS-C($\mathbb{D}_{(E \cup E_\mathcal{M}, E^\models, E^{\not\models})}, \alpha, E^?_{\mathcal{M},}$).

Input: The decision space $\mathbb{D}_{(E \cup E_\mathcal{M}, E^\models, E^{\not\models})}$, confirmed mapping arc α.

Output: The updated decision space $\mathbb{D}_{(E \cup E_\mathcal{M}, E^\models \cup \uparrow \alpha, E^{\not\models} \cup \imath \alpha)} = (E^?_\mathcal{M}, \mathcal{E}, \mathcal{C})$.

1   $E^\models \leftarrow E^\models \cup \{\alpha\}$;

2   **for** *each mapping arc* $\beta \in (E \cup E_\mathcal{M}) \setminus (E^\models \cup E^{\not\models})$ **do**

3   **if** $\beta \in (E^\models \cup \{\alpha\})^*$ **then**

4        $E^\models \leftarrow E^\models \cup \{\beta\}$;

5   **for** *each mapping arc* $\gamma \in E^{\not\models}$ **do**

6   **if** $\gamma \in (E^\models \cup \{\alpha, \beta\})^*$ *or there exists an aligned path-unsatisfiable node*
         w.r.t an integrated graph $\mathcal{G}' = (N, E^\models \cup \{\alpha, \beta\})$ **then**

7          $E^{\not\models} \leftarrow E^{\not\models} \cup \{\beta\}$;

8   $E^?_\mathcal{M} \leftarrow E_\mathcal{M} \setminus (E^\models \cup E^{\not\models})$;

9   **return** $(E^?_\mathcal{M}, \mathcal{E}, \mathcal{C})$;

Algorithm 4. UDS-D($\mathbb{D}_{(E \cup E_\mathcal{M}, E^\models, E^{\not\models})}, \alpha, E^?_\mathcal{M}$).

Input: The decision space $\mathbb{D}_{(E \cup E_\mathcal{M}, E^\models, E^{\not\models})}$, declined mapping arc α.

Output: The updated decision space $\mathbb{D}_{(E \cup E_\mathcal{M}, E^\models, E^{\not\models} \cup \imath \alpha)} = (E^?_\mathcal{M}, \mathcal{E}, \mathcal{C})$.

1   $E^{\not\models} \leftarrow E^{\not\models} \cup \{\alpha\}$;

2   **for** *each mapping arc* $\beta \in (E \cup E_\mathcal{M}) \setminus (E^\models \cup E^{\not\models})$ **do**

3   **if** $\beta \in (E^\models \cup \{\alpha\})^*$ **then**

4        $E^{\not\models} \leftarrow E^{\not\models} \cup \{\beta\}$;

5   $E^?_\mathcal{M} \leftarrow E_\mathcal{M} \setminus (E^\models \cup E^{\not\models})$;

6   **return** $(E^?_\mathcal{M}, \mathcal{E}, \mathcal{C})$;

---

4   Experiment

In this section, we present the experimental results of our method. Our algorithms were implemented with the OWLAPI[1], a tool for managing OWL ontologies. We compared our method with the method proposed by Meilicke et al. proposed in [14]. To our knowledge, it is the only interactive mapping revision work that can save human decisions. Concretely, we have implemented a total of four systems for comparison.

1. **1:1-Repair** manually repairs mappings with 1:1 constraint where no automated reasoning is applied. When an expert accepts a mapping, all the mappings sharing concepts with this mapping will be treated as declined ones [2]. **1:1-Repair** is used as the baseline in our experiment.
2. **DDL-Repair** employs distributed description logics (DDL) to detect and propagate implications of expert decisions on the correctness of mappings, as proposed by Meilicke et al. in [14].

---

[1] http://owlapi.sourceforge.net/.

3. **Graph-Repair1** implements our algorithms with impact function proposed by Meilicke et al. in [14].
4. **Graph-Repair2** implements our algorithms with impact function defined in Definition 9.

For the sake of fairness, we require that the expert must evaluate alignments with 1:1-Repair first, and maintain the same decisions for other repair systems. All the experiments were performed on a desktop computer with Intel Core i7-2600 and 32 GB RAM in Java 1.8. Source codes of our system together with the data sets and results can be downloaded at https://github.com/liweizhuo001/SAOR. A technical report with more details of our algorithms and system can also be downloaded in the same address.

For repair tasks, we selected Conference Track from OAEI[2] (Ontology Alignment Evaluation Initiative) in our experiments, which is an annual campaign for evaluating ontology matching systems that attracts many participants all over the world. The other ontologies were not employed because not all of them provide reference alignment or it may require strong expertise. The alignments are automatically generated between all pairs of conference ontologies by applying the matching system HMatch [21] and ASMOV [22]. In contrast to the majority of existing systems limited to the discovery of "≡" mapping precisely, HMatch can generate lots of 1:n mappings and ASMOV is additionally capable of finding "⊑" and "⊒" relations with few inconsistency cases. It is suitable for us to compare repair systems and analyze their inherent properties.

In order to measure the repair performance, we count up the number of confirm and decline of the expert, which are represented by "Appd" and "Rej" in the following tables. The efficiency of manual revision (denoted as *Saved*) can be revealed by the fraction of mappings without manual evaluation. Moreover, we utilize the number of correct mappings (denoted as *Corr*) to evaluate the quality of repair. Given a alignment $\mathcal{M}$, a reference alignment $\mathcal{R}$ and the number of confirm "Appd" and decline "Rej" of the expert, the formulas about *Saved* and *Corr* are defined as follows.

$$Saved = 1 - \frac{|Appd| + |Rej|}{|\mathcal{M}|} \qquad Corr = |Appd \cap \mathcal{R}|$$

Table 2 lists the evaluation result of twenty-one alignments across ontologies generated by HMatch. Overall, all the reasoning-based revision methods can keep most correct mappings and significantly save the decisions made by expert. In terms of the efficiency of manual revision, our two graph-based methods are better than DDL-Repair, which achieve the best results in ten and nine out of twenty-one repair tasks, respectively, but DDL-Repair only achieve the five out of twenty-one. The main reason is that our graph-based method models the entailment process when expert declined mappings, which may be suitable for alignments generated by 1:n matchers. Nevertheless, it may lead to some correct mappings removed indirectly such as cmt-edas alignment repaired by the graph

---

[2] http://oaei.ontologymatching.org/.

Table 2. The evaluation result of alignments generated by HMatch

Repair Task	$|\mathcal{M}|$	MIPS	1:1-Repair			DDL-Repair			Graph-Repair1			Graph-Repair2		
			Appd/Rej	Corr	Saved	Appd/Rej	Corr	Saved	Appd/Rej	Corr	Saved	Appd/Rej	Corr	Saved
cmt-Conference	24	16	10/9	7	20.8%	9/9	6	25.0%	9/9	6	25.0%	9/6	7	37.5%
cmt-confOf	13	10	6/7	5	0.0%	5/4	4	30.8%	5/3	4	38.5%	5/4	4	30.8%
cmt-edas	22	20	9/11	9	9.1%	8/4	8	45.5%	7/4	7	50%	7/5	7	45.5%
cmt-ekaw	29	28	10/19	7	0.0%	9/11	6	31.0%	9/11	6	31.0%	9/11	6	31.0%
cmt-iasted	9	2	5/4	4	0.0%	5/4	4	0.0%	5/4	4	0.0%	5/4	4	0.0%
cmt-sigkdd	20	16	10/8	9	10.0%	10/7	9	15%	10/7	9	15%	10/4	9	30.0%
Conference-confOf	25	18	9/16	8	0.0%	7/13	7	20.0%	7/13	7	20.0%	7/10	6	30.0%
Conference-edas	38	32	10/26	6	5.3%	8/19	6	28.9%	7/19	5	31.6%	8/18	5	31.6%
Conference-ekaw	43	26	20/12	14	25.6%	20/17	14	14.0%	19/14	14	23.3%	18/13	12	27.9%
Conference-iasted	13	0	6/7	5	0.0%	6/7	5	0.0%	6/7	5	0.0%	6/7	5	0.0%
Conference-sigkdd	27	4	9/8	8	37.0%	9/17	8	3.7%	9/16	8	7.4%	9/17	8	3.7%
confOf-edas	29	19	16/13	12	0.0%	13/8	10	27.6%	13/8	10	27.6%	13/9	10	24.1%
confOf-ekaw	26	13	14/11	13	3.8%	12/7	11	26.9%	12/7	11	26.9%	12/6	11	30.8%
confOf-iasted	8	0	4/4	4	0.0%	4/4	4	0.0%	4/4	4	0.0%	4/4	4	0.0%
confOf-sigkdd	11	8	4/7	4	0.0%	4/4	4	27.3%	4/4	4	27.3%	4/4	4	27.3%
edas-ekaw	49	50	16/29	14	8.2%	14/19	12	32.7%	12/17	10	40.8%	11/16	10	44.9%
edas-iasted	16	7	10/5	7	6.3%	10/5	7	6.3%	10/5	7	6.3%	10/7	7	0.0%
edas-sigkdd	28	19	8/12	7	28.6%	8/12	7	28.6%	7/12	6	32.1%	8/12	7	28.6%
ekaw-iasted	7	0	6/1	6	0.0%	6/1	6	0.0%	6/1	6	0.0%	6/1	6	0.0%
ekaw-sigkdd	21	16	7/10	7	19.0%	7/7	7	33.3%	7/7	7	33.3%	7/8	7	28.6%
iasted-sigkdd	34	6	15/18	13	2.9%	15/16	13	8.8%	15/16	13	8.8%	15/17	13	5.9%

methods. Note that the impact function proposed in DDL-Repair also has a positive effect on our graph-based method in some repair tasks such as cmt-confOf alignment repaired by Graph-Repair1. It makes sense to combine these two impact functions for selecting mappings, we leave this issue for future work.

Table 3 lists the evaluation result of the alignments generated by ASMOV. Compared the alignments generated by HMatch, there exist few MIPSs [2] that cause concepts or roles unsatisfiable because ASMOV has corrected the

Table 3. The evaluation result of alignments generated by ASMOV

Repair Task	$|\mathcal{M}|$	MIPS	1:1-Repair			DDL-Repair			Graph-Repair1			Graph-Repair2		
			Appd/Rej	Corr	Saved	Appd/Rej	Corr	Saved	Appd/Rej	Corr	Saved	Appd/Rej	Corr	Saved
cmt-Conference	16	0	8/8	7	0.0%	8/8	7	0.0%	8/8	7	0.0%	8/8	7	0.0%
cmt-confOf	9	0	5/4	4	0.0%	5/4	4	0.0%	5/4	4	0.0%	5/4	4	0.0%
cmt-edas	15	6	8/7	8	0.0%	7/6	7	13.3%	7/6	7	13.3%	5/6	5	26.7%
cmt-ekaw	15	0	7/8	6	0.0%	7/8	6	0.0%	7/8	6	0.0%	7/8	6	0.0%
cmt-iasted	15	0	4/11	3	0.0%	4/11	3	0.0%	4/11	3	0.0%	4/11	3	0.0%
cmt-sigkdd	17	0	9/8	7	0.0%	9/8	7	0.0%	9/8	7	0.0%	9/8	7	0.0%
Conference-confOf	24	0	9/15	8	0.0%	9/15	8	0.0%	9/15	8	0.0%	9/15	8	0.0%
Conference-edas	25	6	9/16	6	0.0%	9/14	6	8.0%	9/14	6	8.0%	9/14	6	8.0%
Conference-ekaw	27	2	15/12	11	0.0%	14/12	10	3.7%	14/12	10	3.7%	14/12	10	3.7%
Conference-iasted	29	0	6/23	5	0.0%	6/23	5	0.0%	6/23	5	0.0%	6/23	5	0.0%
Conference-sigkdd	30	0	14/16	10	0.0%	14/16	10	0.0%	14/16	10	0.0%	14/16	10	0.0%
confOf-edas	21	2	10/11	9	0.0%	10/11	9	0.0%	10/11	9	0.0%	10/11	9	0.0%
confOf-ekaw	23	7	15/18	14	0.0%	13/8	12	8.7%	13/8	12	8.7%	13/7	12	13.0%
confOf-iasted	32	3	8/24	7	0.0%	8/24	7	0.0%	8/24	7	0.0%	8/24	7	0.0%
confOf-sigkdd	14	5	4/10	4	0.0%	4/8	4	14.3%	4/8	4	14.3%	4/8	4	14.3%
edas-ekaw	36	9	14/22	12	0.0%	12/22	10	5.6%	12/22	10	5.6%	11/21	9	11.1%
edas-iasted	39	2	13/26	10	0.0%	12/26	9	2.6%	12/26	9	2.6%	12/26	9	2.6%
edas-sigkdd	24	0	10/14	9	0.0%	10/14	9	0.0%	10/14	9	0.0%	10/14	9	0.0%
ekaw-iasted	45	0	12/33	8	0.0%	12/33	8	0.0%	12/33	8	0.0%	12/33	8	0.0%
ekaw-sigkdd	28	2	9/19	7	0.0%	9/19	7	0.0%	9/19	7	0.0%	9/18	7	3.6%
iasted-sigkdd	35	0	15/20	12	0.0%	15/20	12	0.0%	15/20	12	0.0%	15/20	12	0.0%

alignment by anti-patterns before its final delivery [22], which weakens the efficiency of reasoning-based revision methods. Of note, reasoning-based methods may not be effective for all alignments including incoherent mappings because all the mappings in MIPSs could be wrong such as confOf-iasted alignment. Benefited from our defined impact function, Graph-Repair2 achieve the best results in eight out of twenty-one repair tasks. Compared with a static impact function in [14], our impact function is dynamic one that could be adaptive according to the current state of decision space. It is suitable for improving the correctness of repair results such as confOf-ekaw alignment repaired by Graph-Repair2.

5   Related Work

This work is closely related to the work presented in [15]. In [15], the authors developed an interactive ontology revision theory and introduced the notion of decision space to reduce the cost of required reasoning operations during the interactive revision iterations for DL ontologies. We adapt this notion and define a graph-based decision space, which is used for mapping revision. However, the time complexity of algorithms in [15] for updating the decision space is high (e.g., $O(n^5)$). In contrast, the complexity of mapping revision can be bounded in $O(n^3)$ [20], which may be more suitable for repairing the mappings among large and complex domain ontologies. More importantly, we designed a new impact function based on graph tailored for mapping revision, which does not need to learn the validity ratio of ranking function given in [15].

Meilicke et al. employed DDL to detect and propagate implications of expert decisions on the correctness of mappings [14]. With the reasoning support of DDL, the number of decisions made by the expert were reduced. Its main limitation is that the detection of inconsistencies in a mapping relies on the presence of disjointness axioms. In addition, there exists no entailment process when a declined decision made by expert. Relatively, our method models this process by graph-based algorithms, which can relief the deficiency of disjointness axioms. Moreover, compared with a static ranked function of mappings proposed in their method, we propose a dynamic adaptive function based on graph for selecting mappings, which is helpful to save expert's decision further.

ContentMap aims at helping users understand and evaluate the semantic consequences of the integration, so that it focuses on the visualization of consequences and user guidance in case of difficult evaluation decisions [10]. The key of repair framework is based on the notion of deductive difference, which not only can detect some obvious inconsistencies, but also can describe any unintended entailments. Nevertheless, the minimization of the manual and computational effort is not considered in it [15].

Recently, Jiménez-Ruiz et al. [11] modeled the mapping revision as the negotiation among muti-agents, in which conservatively principle [9] was employed for measuring limiting logical violations among mappings. In addition, Euzenat observed the restriction of the communication-based repair methods, and proposed some techniques to improve existing adaptation operators [12]. Both these works are novel, repairing alignments based on agent communication in limited scenarios.

Other interactive techniques applied in ontologies can be conceivably applied to mapping revision (e.g. query strategy [23], employing meta information [24]). Both of them employed the idea based on dynamic adjustment to refresh prior-probability. Incorporating these ideas into our method is one direction left for our future work.

6 Conclusions

In this paper, we proposed a method based on a graph to reduce manual evaluation for interactive mapping revision. We first encoded ontologies into an integrated graph and mappings into the mapping arcs. After a decision was made by the expert in each interaction, the mapping arcs were automatically updated in polynomial time. Moreover, we defined an impact function based on the integrated graph to measure the influence of mappings, so that every time the mapping that had the largest impact on others gets to be displayed to the expert. In this way, the manual efforts could be minimized and the automated reasoning prevails. We implemented the algorithms and the evaluation on real-world ontologies indicated that our method was effective in saving human decisions and outperformed the method proposed by Meilicke et al. in most cases.

The revised ontologies in the interaction theory proposed in [15] are more expressive than DL-Lite. Comparatively, we intend to extend our previous study on graph-based mapping revision to an interactive revision model. Graphs can provide a better interpretability of the revision process and proposed operations are efficient for DL-Lite ontologies. For future work, the extensions shall include validating mappings across expressive ontologies and catering for new scenarios such as networks of ontologies [25].

Acknowledgements. We thank the anonymous reviewers for their comments. This work was partially supported by the National Key Research and Development Program of China under grant 2016YFB1000902, the NSFC grants U1736204, 61621003, 61762063, 61602259, the Natural Science Foundation of Jiangxi 20171BAB202024, the fund from JiangXi Educational Committee GJJ170991.

References

1. Otero-Cerdeira, L., Rodríguez-Martínez, F.J., Gómez-Rodríguez, A.: Ontology matching: a literature review. Expert Syst. Appl. **42**(2), 949–971 (2015)
2. Meilicke, C.: Alignment incoherence in ontology matching. Ph.D. thesis, Universitätsbibliothek Mannheim (2011)
3. Euzenat, J., Shvaiko, P.: Ontology Matching. Springer, Heidelberg (2013). https://doi.org/10.1007/978-3-642-38721-0
4. Jiménez-Ruiz, E., Cuenca Grau, B.: LogMap: logic-based and scalable ontology matching. In: Aroyo, L., et al. (eds.) ISWC 2011. LNCS, vol. 7031, pp. 273–288. Springer, Heidelberg (2011). https://doi.org/10.1007/978-3-642-25073-6_18

5. Santos, E., Faria, D., Pesquita, C., Couto, F.M.: Ontology alignment repair through modularization and confidence-based heuristics. PloS ONE **10**(12), 1–19 (2015)
6. Castano, S., Ferrara, A., Lorusso, D., Näth, T.H., Möller, R.: Mapping validation by probabilistic reasoning. In: Bechhofer, S., Hauswirth, M., Hoffmann, J., Koubarakis, M. (eds.) ESWC 2008. LNCS, vol. 5021, pp. 170–184. Springer, Heidelberg (2008). https://doi.org/10.1007/978-3-540-68234-9_15
7. Noessner, J., Niepert, M.: ELOG: a probabilistic reasoner for OWL EL. In: Rudolph, S., Gutierrez, C. (eds.) RR 2011. LNCS, vol. 6902, pp. 281–286. Springer, Heidelberg (2011). https://doi.org/10.1007/978-3-642-23580-1_25
8. Qi, G., Ji, Q., Haase, P.: A conflict-based operator for mapping revision. In: Bernstein, A., et al. (eds.) ISWC 2009. LNCS, vol. 5823, pp. 521–536. Springer, Heidelberg (2009). https://doi.org/10.1007/978-3-642-04930-9_33
9. Solimando, A., Jiménez-Ruiz, E., Guerrini, G.: Minimizing conservativity violations in ontology alignments: algorithms and evaluation. Knowl. Inf. Syst. **51**(3), 775–819 (2017)
10. Jiménez-Ruiz, E., Cuenca Grau, B., Horrocks, I., Berlanga, R.: Ontology integration using mappings: towards getting the right logical consequences. In: Aroyo, L., et al. (eds.) ESWC 2009. LNCS, vol. 5554, pp. 173–187. Springer, Heidelberg (2009). https://doi.org/10.1007/978-3-642-02121-3_16
11. Jiménez-Ruiz, E., Payne, T.R., Solimando, A., Tamma, V.A.M.: Limiting logical violations in ontology alignnment through negotiation. In: KR, pp. 217–226. AAAI Press (2016)
12. Euzenat, J.: Interaction-based ontology alignment repair with expansion and relaxation. In: IJCAI, pp. 185–191. AAAI Press (2017)
13. Dragisic, Z., Ivanova, V., Lambrix, P., Faria, D., Jiménez-Ruiz, E., Pesquita, C.: User validation in ontology alignment. In: Groth, P., et al. (eds.) ISWC 2016. LNCS, vol. 9981, pp. 200–217. Springer, Cham (2016). https://doi.org/10.1007/978-3-319-46523-4_13
14. Meilicke, C., Stuckenschmidt, H., Tamilin, A.: Supporting manual mapping revision using logical reasoning. In: AAAI, pp. 1213–1218. AAAI Press (2008)
15. Nikitina, N., Rudolph, S., Glimm, B.: Interactive ontology revision. J. Web Semant. **12**, 118–130 (2012)
16. Fu, X., Qi, G., Zhang, Y., Zhou, Z.: Graph-based approaches to debugging and revision of terminologies in DL-Lite. Knowl.-Based Syst. **100**, 1–12 (2016)
17. Li, W., Zhang, S., Qi, G.: A graph-based approach for resolving incoherent ontology mappings. Web Intell. **16**(1), 15–35 (2018)
18. Calvanese, D., De Giacomo, G., Lemho, D., Lenzerini, M., Rosati, R.: DL-Lite: tractable description logics for ontologies. In: AAAI, pp. 602–607. AAAI Press (2005)
19. Lembo, D., Santarelli, V., Savo, D.F.: Graph-based ontology classification in OWL 2 QL. In: Cimiano, P., Corcho, O., Presutti, V., Hollink, L., Rudolph, S. (eds.) ESWC 2013. LNCS, vol. 7882, pp. 320–334. Springer, Heidelberg (2013). https://doi.org/10.1007/978-3-642-38288-8_22
20. Even, S.: Graph Algorithms. Cambridge University Press, Cambridge (2011)
21. Castano, S., Ferrara, A., Montanelli, S.: Dealing with matching variability of semantic web data using contexts. In: Pernici, B. (ed.) CAiSE 2010. LNCS, vol. 6051, pp. 194–208. Springer, Heidelberg (2010). https://doi.org/10.1007/978-3-642-13094-6_16
22. Jean-Mary, Y.R., Shironoshita, E.P., Kabuka, M.R.: Ontology matching with semantic verification. J. Web Semant. **7**(3), 235–251 (2009)

23. Shchekotykhin, K., Friedrich, G.: Query strategy for sequential ontology debugging. In: Patel-Schneider, P.F., et al. (eds.) ISWC 2010. LNCS, vol. 6496, pp. 696–712. Springer, Heidelberg (2010). https://doi.org/10.1007/978-3-642-17746-0_44
24. Rodler, P., Shchekotykhin, K., Fleiss, P., Friedrich, G.: RIO: minimizing user interaction in ontology debugging. In: Faber, W., Lembo, D. (eds.) RR 2013. LNCS, vol. 7994, pp. 153–167. Springer, Heidelberg (2013). https://doi.org/10.1007/978-3-642-39666-3_12
25. Euzenat, J.: Revision in networks of ontologies. Artif. Intell. **228**, 195–216 (2015)

Automatic Ontology Development from Semi-structured Data in Web-Portal: Towards Ontology of Thai Rice Knowledge

Taneth Ruangrajitpakorn[1,2](✉), Rachada Kongkachandra[1], Pokpong Songmuang[1], and Thepchai Supnithi[2]

[1] Department of Computer Science, Faculty of Science and Technology, Thammasat University, Pathumthani, Thailand
taneth.rua@nectec.or.th
[2] Language and Semantic Technology Laboratory, NECTEC, Pathumthani, Thailand

Abstract. Heavyweight ontology is difficult to develop even for experienced ontology engineer, but it is required for semantic based computer software as core knowledge. Most of existing automated ontology development methods however focuses on lightweight ontology, taxonomy-instance extraction. This work presents a method to automatically construct relation-heavy ontology from semi-structured web content providing deep knowledge in specific domain. Classes, instances and hierarchical relation are derived from the category content from the web. Relations are extracted based on frequent expression details. Templates of relation and its range are extracted from common content with partial difference. Similar contexts are grouped with similarity and form as relation to attach to ontology classes. The case study of this work is Thai rice knowledge including rice variety, disease, weed and pest provided in website from responsible government. The complete ontology is used as core knowledge for personalised web service. The service assists in filter content in summary that matched to users' information. Courtesy to the generated relation-heavy ontology, it is able to recommend relevant chained concepts to users based on semantic relation. From evaluation from an expert, the generated ontology obtained about 97% accuracy.

Keywords: Ontology learning · Knowledge extraction
Pattern-based detection · Textual template · Semi-structured content

1 Introduction

Ontology in information science is defined as a formal, explicit specification of a shared conceptualization [1]. Ontologies are a representation of concepts and their relations as a knowledge base for human interoperability or human-machine knowledge transfer. Ontology as knowledge representation has been used in many modern applications that require semantics or logical inference. The direct usage of ontology is such as a core information for semantic web in a specific domain [2–4] and knowledge based recommender system. Otherwise, it can be applied into several other application

© Springer Nature Switzerland AG 2018
R. Ichise et al. (Eds.): JIST 2018, LNCS 11341, pp. 262–276, 2018.
https://doi.org/10.1007/978-3-030-04284-4_18

fields to help in their endeavours such as machine translation, document classification, and query expansion. Most in-used famous ontologies such as WordNet [5] and Gene ontology [6] are manually developed and maintained since manually crafted ontologies can guarantee highest accuracy and usability for complex knowledge with a lot of tacit.

In fact, an ontology can be categorised into two main degrees of expressiveness, i.e. lightweight ontology and heavyweight ontology (or full fledge ontology). The lightweight ontology (LWO) is an ontology with restricted expressiveness [7], such as taxonomies. LWOs are sufficient for a task that requires hierarchical grouping such as query expansion or document classification. LWOs are easier to develop, and they are preferred to cover a wider range of concepts with an automatic learning technique. On the other hand, heavyweight ontology (HWO) contains richer structure which consists both hierarchical relation and additional relationships between concepts [8]. The concepts are more deeply related and become more logically informative. HWOs are required for ontology-based applications that need logical inference and insight understanding of domain knowledge such as question-answering, semantic search and expert system. HWOs apparently are harder to develop since they need both explicit and tacit knowledge.

Ontologies can be created with several methods including manual design, automatic learning, or a combination of them. Despite being assured in quality, manual design method becomes less favourable since it is expensive in terms of cost and time-consuming and requires ontology engineer specialists to work with domain experts. In the information era, automatic learning method gains more learning sources. However, most of the existing automatic learning methods tend to learning an LWO from text documents, for example [9] applies biologically inspired neural network (BINN) in combination with text mining to learn LWO in health domain, and ASIUM [10] uses agglomerative clustering for discovering taxonomy relations from texts. For HWO learning, Yago [11] proposes a method to capture concepts and relations from Wikipeida with help from WordNet; however, its focus is on the structural information such as details given in an infobox.

In this work, we aim to create a heavyweight ontology from a semi-structure text provided in a domain-specific web-portal providing insight-level information to users. Frequently used lexical patterns are extracted as a template to distinguish between concepts and data. As a case study, this work applies on rice knowledge provided by Rice Department, Ministry of Agriculture and Cooperatives, Thailand. Moreover, to prove usability of the automatically created ontology, it is used as a core knowledge base for a personalised web. The rest of this paper is organised as follows. Section 2 describes background knowledge including ontology and its development. Section 3 presents a proposed method for constructing a heavyweight ontology from semi-structured web-based text. In Sect. 4, usage of the generated ontology as a core knowledge representation for a dynamic web is explained. Section 5 provides experiment setting, results and discussion. Last, Sect. 6 gives conclusions of this paper and a list of possible future works.

2 Ontology and Its Development Methods

2.1 Ontology and Its Expressiveness

In information science, ontology representation is a formal model of concepts in a domain. The most referred definition was mentioned as "An ontology is a formal, explicit specification of a shared conceptualization" by Studer et al. [1]. It includes relevant entities and relations connected to form representation of facts from observation and realisation. In ontology, the relevant entities are organised as concept and relation. The foremost component of an ontology is a hierarchy structure of concepts to form relation of generalization/specialization [12]. Not only that, an ontology also involves in extension relations to define relationship between entities that reflect ground truth.

An ontology can be categorised into types in many aspects. For its expressiveness, ontology is divided into two categories, i.e. lightweight ontology (LWO) and heavyweight ontology (HWO). LWO is an ontology with a low degree in expressiveness, and is mostly composed with hierarchical relation of concepts. The main component of LWO is taxonomy with a little relation. The clear advantages of LWO are larger in scope and much easier to craft and interpret. On the other hand, HWO is an ontology with rich expression, namely many extended relations. It provides a deeper definition of entities as semantic level. HWOs thus are difficult to craft even for experienced users [13]. Usages of HWOs are for a system that requires knowledge as a core such as expert system.

In general, developing ontology involves in conceptualising and assigning relations to concepts. A common representation of conceptualisation is in a form of a triple. A triple is a set of three entities codifying a statement about semantic data in the form of subject– predicate–object expressions. In ontology, predicate stands for relation, and subject is treated as domain of a relation while object is a range of relation. In fact, defining entities manually to develop an ontology is a tedious task and time-consuming. In development regardless of LWO or HWO, an ontology editor in the market can help ontology engineer to skip in annotating the triple or formatting their ontology. Moreover, several research projects have been reported to automatically construct ontologies.

2.2 Ontology Development: Manual and Automated Approach

In ontology development, there are mainly two approaches. The first and more general approach is a manual development. This approach basically requires an ontology engineer to conceptualise relevant entities and model a structure of concepts into an ontology. Facts from knowledge ground truth are analysed in consideration to represent both explicit knowledge and tacit knowledge on the selected domain. There are guidelines to craft an ontology [8, 12] to help in the task. Unfortunately, the task is tedious and error-prone even for the experienced ontology developers. However, most of the man-crafted ontologies tend to be HWOs with careful design to serve as knowledge base for computer systems and complex knowledge interoperation.

In the era of information, another approach becomes more viable as to develop ontology from existing information. There have been reports for a successful automatic ontology development called ontology learning. Ontology learning refers to a computational process extracting ontological elements from textual source, such as semi-structured HTML and unstructured documents, and building ontology from them. The methods to learn an ontology can be categorised into several approaches. We summarised the methods and their specification in Table 1.

The existing ontology learning methods mostly focused on hierarchical structure development. Despite being backbone of ontology, a hierarchy part is not the only informative element part of ontology, and most of them result in a lightweight ontology manner. Although they can be a good starter to enrich more extension relations towards full-fledge ontology, the difficult and tedious tasks in linking concepts still remains. On the other hand, HWO learning is less researched. YAGO method is interesting in terms of applying existing large content source and hierarchy reference such as WordNet. However, it focused on structured part of content, and such contents are rare especially in specific domains. This work thus aims to handle semi-structured web contents to automatically develop a relation-heavy ontology suitable as knowledge base for intelligent system.

3   Methodology

This work aims to extract knowledge from semi-structured information given in a knowledge-providing portal web. From observation, a knowledge-providing portal web usually displays their details in a semi-structured format which uses a closed set of words to identify ones' specification. Additionally, the web commonly aligns items in taxonomy of things for browsing, and this can be a good starter for hierarchical structure.

To form a usable ontology, the main components to collect are concepts, relations and instances. Each component is handled separately with different methods and is combined in the last process. An overview of the proposed method is sketched in Fig. 1. In this study, we focus on a case of a Thai rice knowledge web portal [19] from Rice Department, Ministry of Agriculture and Cooperatives, Thailand.

3.1   Ontology Model

Based on ontology standard, the current knowledge representation is the Web Ontology Language (OWL). OWL, an extended version of RDFS, is a semantic web language able to express rich and complex knowledge about things, category of things, and relations between things in formal computational logic-based structure. In this work, the standard is exploited to represent the extracted data. In ontology, conceptual objects (in both physical and abstract) are considered as entities, and an entity is related to one another with a relation. According to RDFS, basic relations are exemplified in Table 2.

Aside from the basic relations, additional relations can be generated to inform specific relations among entities discussed in Sect. 3.3.

Table 1. Existing automatic ontology development methods

Name	Technique	Source type	Specification
Sabou et al. [14]	– Syntactic parser	Unstructured document	– LWO with few relation – Apply a syntactic dependency parser to discover the dependency relations between words to form hierarchy – Detect prepositional phrase (in) for part-of relation
Cimiano et al. [15]	– Syntactic parser – Clustering	Unstructured document	– LWO, focused on hierarchy tree – Apply Formal Concept Analysis to discover inherent relationships between objects through a set of common attributes
Text2Onto [16]	– RTF, TF-IDF – WordNet – Linguistic heuristics rules	Unstructured document	– Learn concepts using RTF, TFIDF, Entropy and the C value/NC value method – Apply WordNet for hierarchy – Apply patterns matching technique for part-of relation
Karoui et al. [17]	– Clustering	Semi-structured web content	– LWO, focused on hierarchy – Apply divisive clustering to group similar words into hierarchical clusters
OntoMiner [18]	– Data mining – Promotion rules	Semi-structured web content	– LWO, focused on hierarchy with instances and synonym labelling – Use web-crawler to define taxonomy of pages – Use data-mining to define labels as instances
Reimer et al. [9]	– Biological inspired neural network (BINN)	Unstructured document	– LWO, focused on hierarchy tree – Apply biologically inspired neural network (BINN) in combination with text mining to define concept hierarchy
ASIUM [10]	– Clustering	Unstructured document	– LWO, focused on hierarchy tree – Use agglomerative clustering to define concepts and taxonomy relations
Yago [11]	– Pattern matching rules – WordNet	Structured content in Wikipedia	– HWO with large amount of facts – Detect concepts from Web structure – Apply WordNet to define taxonomy and synonym – Use predefined rules to extract relation and range of relation

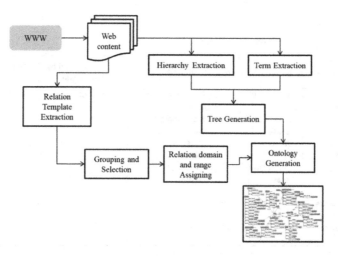

Fig. 1. An overview of processes.

Table 2. Basic relations in ontology development

Relation name	Description
SUBCLASSOF	Specific kind of
TYPE	Instance of
MEAN	Same entity (synonym relation)
FOUNDIN	Reference

3.2   Extraction of Concepts and Hierarchy Relation

As manual design, the very first process in ontology development is to realise concepts and a representative group of concepts to form a hierarchical relation. In a knowledge-providing portal web, there is at least a page with categorisation to provide link to each detailed page. Each detailed page represents a concept and contains its many details. Hence, we extract the category system as concepts with an initial hierarchical structure. Please be reminded that the categorisation in a knowledge providing web page is usually acyclic graph, and can be comfortably used as a base for hierarchy. The category system can be given in a tree format or a table format.

Each extracted concept is served as an entity being candidate for a class. The given hierarchy is to form SUBCLASSOF relation among them while leaf concepts are formed a TYPE relation to its parent class. Please consider an example (English-translated) given in Fig. 2.

From Fig. 2, the page shows details about rice disease given in a table form. The title of the page is taken as a top concept. The table separates the disease into category based on cause of disease. The head row of the table shows types of disease cause separated in column while each of remaining links in each column is a name of rice disease. For this case, a top class is Rice_Disease. There are five classes related to Rice_Disease with SUBCLASSOF relation while each of diseases is related with

Rice Disease

Group by cause of disease

Fungal Disease	Bacterial Disease	Viral Disease	Disease Caused by Nematode	Unknown Cause Disease
- Rice Blast Disease - Dirty Panicle Disease - Sheath Blight Disease - Brown Spot Disease - Sheath Rot Disease - Bakanae Disease - Leaf Scald Disease - Narrow Brown Spot Disease	- Bacterial Blight Disease - Orange Leaf Disease - Bacterial Leaf Streak Disease - Yellow Dwarf Disease	- Rice Ragged Stunt Disease - Rice Tungro Disease - Grassy Stunt Disease - Gall Dwarf Disease	- Root-knot Disease	- Red Stripe Disease

Fig. 2. Hierarchy extraction example.

TYPE relation to its parent. A result of this process is a hierarchical tree of concepts. These concepts will be used to as an ontological range for other relations in the later process.

3.3   Extraction of Additional Relations and Data

A crucial component in a heavyweight ontology is properties of a concept. There can be many details given in texts. From observation, same types of detail are commonly expressed similarly with certain clue words or pattern of words. This can be used to denote a property of an ontology class if the detail is given to several concepts under the same class. In this process, we want to find properties and concept range of properties from text.

Details of each page from leaf classes in the same category are segmented based on a line. With a collection of lines, a template of content is extracted to detect common part and unique part of content. A common part can be detected with the same textual expression from several class entities while the difference is treated as a unique part. The common part is extracted for property name while the unique part is for assigning range of concept or data type for part-of (object property) and attribute-of (data property) relation, respectively.

From the content, each line will be compared to perform/non-greedy matching/on same strings as a common context. The found common context is treated as a common part and the difference is replaced with placeholder $\{x^n\}$. The $\{x\}$ of the same context is kept to find the range of a relation. To match a common part, at least two words in the same position must be exactly identical. For example, please see Fig. 3.

From the pages of three different rice varieties, there are details given in each box in Fig. 3. The details are expressed about specification of each variety. Text over the box is a name of rice variety. From the example, the three pages contain the similar content such as Average Productivity – $\{X\}$ Kg./Rai. This indicates that the average

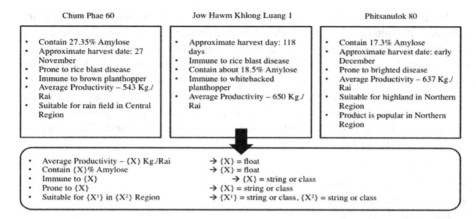

Fig. 3. An example of additional relation extraction.

productivity is a common detail for rice variety, and it should be a property of the class. The {X} part is where the different information is given, and the variation of such information is a specification for each rice variety.

It is possible that the context may contain typos or omit some words. Thus, the extracted templates are a list of candidate relations. A text similarity is applied to handle typos issue using overlap coefficient given in (1) [20]. Equation (1) is to calculate similarity of strings by dividing the size of the intersection by the smaller of the size of the two string sets. The conditions for grouping templates are more than 0.8 similarity score, and a unique part must be the same data type. Once grouping, the representative term of the grouping is selected according to the most frequently occurred template.

$$SIM\_score = overlap(X, Y) = \frac{|X \cap Y|}{\min(|X|, |Y|)} \tag{1}$$

Next step is to handle a unique part. A unique part can be strings, numbers or a combination of those. The template group containing numbers is to be assigned with attribute-of relation, and a range of relation is for float or integer data type. For those with strings, a unique part is checked with the class in a hierarchy previously developed. If they are matched, the relation is established as part-of property, and the range is referred to the designated class. Else, its range will be assigned as a string data type as same as the part with a combination of strings and numbers.

3.4 Composing Ontology

From the previous processes, hierarchy tree and property relation are developed. In this part, those two components are composed together to form an ontology. For tree part, they are attached directly to the root node. Property part however is required to approve before connecting to classes in the tree. Since the previous process collects all common parts as candidates, criteria are applied to prune improper relation that may occur in a text.

Initially, a leaf class level is handled. The criteria to attach found properties to the class are either the frequency of relation is more than five times or more than 50% of all classes in the same categories. The criteria are designed to prevent outlier expression to be included. In the leaf level, range of relation is specifically defined as detected from the text. For other class level, relations given in leaf classes are collected. However, range of relation is assigned with the data type or parent class of the referred classes. For ontology generation, we applied data from rice knowledge [19] provided by Rice Department, Ministry of Agriculture and Cooperatives, Thailand. The scope of extraction covers the followings.

- Farming Type (1 page)
- Rice Variety (139 pages)
- Rice Disease (18 pages)
- Rice Pest (35 pages)
- Weed in Rice Field (24 pages)
- Rice_Anatomy (1 page)

With the proposed method, six trees under root node are obtained. Generated hierarchical level and list of properties (English-translated from Thai) were assigned as given in Table 2. Since there are excessive numbers of TYPE relations, we only provide counted number in the table. In details, TYPE in class rice variety is specie of rice such as RD1, Chum_Phae_60 and Phitsanulok_80. An entity in TYPE level (leaf concept) contains specified details following the given relations. For example, Chum_Phae_60 obtains ontological relation details as shown in Fig. 4.

Chum_Phae_60 TYPE **Common_Rice**
Chum_Phae_60 has_Average Productivity –Kg./Rai {564}
Chum_Phae_60 has_Contain % Amylose {*27.35*}
Chum_Phae_60 has_Immune to **Brown_Plant_Hopper**
Chum_Phae_60 has_Immune to **Green_Rice_Leafhopper**
Chum_Phae_60 has_Immune to **Whitebacked_Hopper**
Chum_Phae_60 has_Prone to **Rice_Blast_Disease**
Chum_Phae_60 has_Suitable for **Rain_based_Field**
Chum_Phae_60 has_Suitable in Region {*North-Eastern*}
Chum_Phae_60 has_Estimated_Harvest_Date: {*27_November*}
Chum_Phae_60 has_Sensitivity_to_Sunlight: {*Sensitive*}
Chum_Phae_60 has_Size_of_Grain HieghtXWidthXDepth:c.m. {10.2X 2.7X 2.1}

Fig. 4. Ontological detail of Chum_Phae_60 class.

4   Using Generated Ontology for Personalised Web

To make use of the generated ontology, we exploit it as a core knowledge base to personalised web to assist Thai rice farmers. Since the original web-portal aims to provide knowledge in depth and various directions, it is more suitable to academics scholar or experts to browse through the content with correct keyword in mind. However, Thai rice farmers who aim for practical knowledge and scope to their own related need may find the content in the original website to be excessive and not direct to their need. We thus develop the personalised web using the developed ontology to provide only summarised content matching to users' profile.

The personalised web is split into two parts. The first part is for users to provide general and harmless information. The information includes farm location (in region), farm environment (e.g. plain land, high land or low land) and accessible water source (e.g. rain based or Irrigation). These details are designed to match for ontology class for retrieval once all questions are filled. The second part is a retrieving. Details of concepts that match to the answers are retrieved based on ontology category; hence, the results are contents for browsing that relate to users' setting. In retrieving, answers from users play as criteria to reach leaf classes of each tree. Retrieved classes are grouped together based on tree category to prevent mixing content types.

For result of matching, the personalised web is designed to display two different outcomes that are (1) direct result and (2) connected result. The former is a list of information from ontology classes directly matched to users' input. The results are as follows.

- rice variety suited for given field type, region and water resource type
- rice disease prevalent for given field type and region
- pest prevalent in region and often invaded or given field type and region
- weed prevalent to given field type

By matching to ontology schema, the web is able to filter only contents for individuals.

The latter output is connected result. Unlike direct result, relations defined in ontology as given in Table 3 are more exploited. Relations such as 'Immune to {**Rice_Disease**} and Prone to {**Rice_Disease**} of domain class Rice_Variety' and 'Prevalent in Region of domain class Rice_Disease' are used to provide a list of rice varieties that immune to diseases prevalent in a specific region. Not only that, for each class matched to the condition, details stored as attribute-of relation are also displayed in a table to inform summarised characteristic of the selected item. An example of a user interface of a connected result type is demonstrated in Fig. 5.

Table 3. Details of generated ontology

Tree	SubClassOf	Property
Rice_Farming_Type	– Highland – Plain – Rain_based_field – Irrigated_based_field – Flood_land – Deep_water_land	– A/o → description {*datatype:string*}
Rice_Variety	– Common_Rice (68 types) – Glutinous_Rice (58 types) – Barley (5 types) – Wheat (3 types) – Japanese_Rice (3 types)	– A/o → Average Productivity –Kg./Rai {*datatype:float*} – A/o → Contain % Amylose {*datatype:float*} – P/o → Immune to {**Rice_Pest**} – P/o → Prone to { **Rice_Pest**} – P/o → Immune to {**Rice_Disease**} – P/o → Prone to { **Rice_Disease**} – P/o → Suitable for {**Rice_Farming_Type**}

(continued)

Table 3. (*continued*)

Tree	SubClassOf	Property
		– A/o → Suitable in Region {*datatype:string*} – A/o → Estimated_Harvest_Date: {*datatype: string*} – A/o → Estimated_Harvest_Day: {*datatype: string*} – A/o → *Sensitivity_to_Sunlight: {*datatype: string*} (This relation is not literally translated since wording in Thai is descriptive. The technical translation is photosensitive or non-photosensitive.) – A/o →Size_of_Grain HieghtXWidthXDepth: {*datatype:string*} c.m.
Rice_Disease	– Fungal_Disease (8 types) – Viral_Disease (4 types) – Bacterial_Disease (4 types) – Disease_Caused_by_Nematode (1 type) – Unknown_Cause_Disease (1 type)	– A/o → Scientific_Name: {*datatype:string*} – P/o → Often_Attack_to {**Rice_Farming_Type**} – P/o → Effect to {**Rice_Anatomy**} – A/o → Prevalent in Region: {*datatype:string*}
Rice_Pest	– Rice_Pest_in_Field (19 types)	– A/o → Scientific_Name: {*datatype:string*} – A/o → Prevalent in Region: {*datatype:string*} – P/o → Found_Often_in: {**Rice_Farming_Type**} – P/o → Damage_to {**Rice_Anatomy**}
	– Rice_Pest_in_Granary (21 types)	– A/o → Scientific_Name: {*datatype:string*} – A/o → Damage_Description: {*datatype: string*}
Weed_in_Rice_Field		– A/o → Scientific_Name: {*datatype:string*} – P/o → Found_Often_in: {**Rice_Farming_Type**}
Rice_Anatomy	(7 types)	

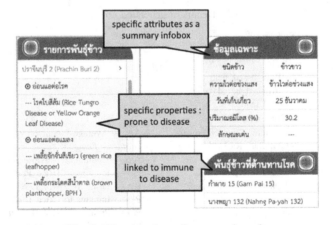

Fig. 5. User interface of connected result.

The two output types are designed to serve different objectives. The direct result aims for users who want to learn available options in general for their personal conditions. On the other hand, the connected type focuses more for those who work on rice farm in practical and require suggestions.

5   Evaluations and Discussions

To evaluate the accuracy of an ontology, its given facts and some ground truth are required to be compared. However, there is currently no computer-based process that can handle the task. Thus, we relied on manual evaluation. We presented all leaf classes from the generated ontology in a triple form to an expert to examine their accuracy. To prevent insufficient or different background knowledge involving in judgment, we also provide the source learnt by our ontology as a reference. Facts were counted as accurate if they were in truth statement. The evaluated result is given in Table 4.

Table 4. Details of generated ontology and accuracy result

Relation	Number of facts	Accuracy
SubClassOf	18	100
Type	204	100
Immune_to_Rice_Disease	88	92.04545455
Prone_to_Rice_Disease	76	93.42105263
Immune_to_Rice_Pest	91	96.7032967
Prone_to_Rice_Pest	72	94.44444444
Prevalent_in_Region	30	100
Estimated_Harvest_Date	69	94.20289855
Average_Productivity_Kg./Rai	137	97.81021898
Contain_%_Amylose	118	100
Effect_to_Rice_Anatomy	18	83.33333333
Sensitivity_to_Sunlight	135	100

The evaluation result shows promising accuracy. The best ones are SubClassOf, Type, Prevalent_in_Region, Contain_%_Amylose and Sensitivity_to_Sunlight. In fact, SubClassOf and Type relation are self-guaranteed since these relations were directly imitated from the given tree structure of the source. However, although the expert returned all accuracy for 'Prevalent_in_Region' relation, he also mentioned that the expressed regions were correct based on reference, but they were not in a hierarchy. This was because the source does not provide a page about Thai regions; hence, there was no source to learn for Thai region hierarchy relation. For the incorrect facts, we analysed them and grouped into two cases. The first case is a partial missing content. This case is caused from the extra expression adding to the part for unique detail. This causes a range of relation from leaf class to miss some informative detail. For example, the range of 'Prone_to_Rice_Pest' relation is supposed to only be a name of rice pest, but the source content expresses extra content to the pest such Brown Plant Hopper in Pitsanulok Province (province of Thailand). From asking the expert, he mentioned that the sub-specie of the insect from the area is slightly different from the rest; hence, stating only brown plant hopper is not sufficient and results as incorrect fact. From the process, the sub-specie is not a class in the ontology. Moreover, the extra expression although was extracted to candidate list but was grouped with other similar relation candidates since the frequency was low. The partial missing content was about 92% from all incorrect facts. The second case is a wholly missing range of relation. This is about ontology class containing a relation but a range of a relation is not given. From examining, the cause was from the different data type of source and system-assigned data type. For example, a data type of 'Estimated_Harvest_Day' is assigned to integer, but some of the content expresses in descriptive expression such as 'about three months'. This descriptive expression although semantically refers to 'about 90 days' and is understandable to human, but current method cannot handle it automatically and requires manual post-edition.

Furthermore, the expert also mentioned missing relations for 26 facts. These cases belong to classes under Rice_Variety. We found that the missing facts are given in a context entirely different from the usual expression, and did not satisfy the criterion to create a relation template. As an example, Suitable_in_{X}_Region is a usual expression, but there is a case that the expression alternates to '{X} region is the best to plant for this variety'. For these cases, the proposed method cannot detect these sole expressions for property. It still remains as a limitation to handle single different expression in knowledge extraction.

6   Conclusion and Future Work

This paper presents an automated method to develop a heavyweight ontology from semi-structured web content. The focused ontological elements include taxonomy trees and relations of concepts in triple form. Classes and their hierarchy are extracted from the notation provided in the contents such as a table and category tree. For detecting relations, templates of contents are derived from similar text expressions in provided details. The common part is extracted as a relation role while the different part is treated as possible range of relation. String similarity is applied to group typos and slightly different expression into the same relation. Once hierarchy tree and relations are created, they are combined using predefined criteria to form a complete ontology. The case study in this work is Thai rice knowledge provided in Thai language. The generated ontology is exploited as core knowledge for personalised web to prove its usability. The personalised web provides a service to filter contents in summary according to personal profile from users. With the generated relation-heavy ontology, a service to recommend relevant content based on semantic inference is available. From evaluation, the generated ontology obtained average of 97% accuracy from the generate fact from manual examining. However, an evaluator also pointed out the missing facts from extraction for 26 cases. In overall, the proposed method shows promising in automatic extraction of relation-heavy ontology. The current limitation is that it cannot extract an ontological relation with solely occurred expression and semantic similar expression without assistance from other semantic sources.

References

1. Studer, R., Benjamins, R., Fensel, D.: Knowledge engineering: principles and methods. Data Knowl. Eng. **25**(1–2), 161–198 (1998)
2. Swartout, W., Tate, A.: Ontologies. IEEE Intell. Syst. **14**(1), 18–19 (1999)
3. Uschold, M.: Ontologies and semantics for seamless connectivity. SIGMOD Rec. **33**(4), 58–64 (2004)
4. Smith, B.: Beyond concepts: ontology as reality representation. In: Varzi, A.C., Vieu, L. (eds.) Formal Ontology in Information Systems – Proceedings of the Third International Conference (FOIS 2004), pp. 73–85. IOS Press, Amsterdam (2004)
5. Miller, G.: WordNet: An electronic Lexical Database. MIT Press, Cambridge (1998)
6. Ashburner, M., et al.: Gene ontology: tool for the unification of biology. Nat. Genet. **25**(1), 25–29 (2000)
7. Davies, J.: Lightweight ontologies. In: Poli, R., Healy, M., Kameas, A. (eds.) Theory and Applications of Ontology: Computer Applications, pp. 197–229. Springer, Dordrecht (2010). https://doi.org/10.1007/978-90-481-8847-5_9
8. Mizoguchi, R.: Tutorial on ontological engineering—part 1: introduction to ontological engineering. New Gener. Comput. **21**(4), 365–384 (2003)
9. Reimer, U., Maier, E., Streit, S., Diggelmann, T., Hoffleisch, M.: Learning a lightweight ontology for semantic retrieval in patient-centered information systems. Int. J. Knowl. Manag. **7**(3), 11–26 (2011)
10. Faure, D., Nédellec, C.: Knowledge acquisition of predicate argument structures from technical texts using machine learning: the system ASIUM. In: Fensel, D., Studer, R. (eds.) EKAW 1999. LNCS (LNAI), vol. 1621, pp. 329–334. Springer, Heidelberg (1999). https://doi.org/10.1007/3-540-48775-1_22
11. Suchanek, F., Kasneci, G., Weikum, G.; Yago: a core of semantic knowledge. In: Proceedings of the 16th International Conference on World Wide Web, pp. 697–706 (2004)
12. Gruber, T.R.: Towards principles for the design of ontologies used for knowledge sharing. In: Guarino, N., Poli, R. (eds.) Formal Ontology in Conceptual Analysis and Knowledge Representation. Kluwer Academic Publishers, Deventer (1993)
13. Rector, A., et al.: OWL pizzas: practical experience of teaching OWL-DL: common errors & common patterns. In: Motta, E., Shadbolt, N.R., Stutt, A., Gibbins, N. (eds.) EKAW 2004. LNCS, vol. 3257, pp. 63–81. Springer, Heidelberg (2004). https://doi.org/10.1007/978-3-540-30202-5_5
14. Sabou, M., Wroe, C., Goble, C., Mishne, G.: Learning domain ontologies for web service descriptions: an experiment in bioinformatics. In: Proceedings of the 14th International World Wide Web Conference (WWW 2005), Chiba, Japan (2005)
15. Cimiano, P., Hotho, A., Staab, S.: Learning concept hierarchies from text corpora using formal concept analysis. JAIR – J. AI Res. **24**, 305–339 (2005)
16. Cimiano, P., Völker, J.: Text2Onto. In: Montoyo, A., Muńoz, R., Métais, E. (eds.) NLDB 2005. LNCS, vol. 3513, pp. 227–238. Springer, Heidelberg (2005). https://doi.org/10.1007/11428817_21
17. Karoui, L., Aufaure, M., Bennacer, N.: Ontology discovery from web pages: application to tourism. In: Proceedings of ECML/PKDD 2004: Knowledge Discovery and Ontologies (KDO 2004) (2004)

18. Davulcu, H., Vadrevu, S., Nagarajan, S., Ramakrishnan, I.: OntoMiner: bootstrapping and populating ontologies from domain specific web sites. IEEE Intell. Syst. **18**(5), 24–33 (2003)
19. Thai. http://www.brrd.in.th/rkb/. Accessed 12 Aug 2016
20. Vijaymeena, M., Kavitha, K.: A survey on similarity measures in text mining. Mach. Learn. Appl.: Int. J. (MLAIJ) **3**(1), 19–28 (2016)

Semantic Diagnostics of Smart Factories

Ognjen Savković[1], Evgeny Kharlamov[2,3]([✉]), Martin Ringsquandl[4,5],
Guohui Xiao[1], Gulnar Mehdi[4,6], Elem Güzel Kalayc[1], Werner Nutt[1],
and Ian Horrocks[2]

[1] Free University of Bozen-Bolzano, Bolzano, Italy
[2] University of Oxford, Oxford, UK
evgeny.kharlamov@cs.ox.ac.uk
[3] University of Oslo, Oslo, Norway
[4] Siemens AG, Corporate Technology, Munich, Germany
[5] Ludwig-Maximilians University, Munich, Germany
[6] Technical University of Munich, Munich, Germany

Abstract. Smart factories are one of the biggest trends in modern manufacturing, also known as Industry 4.0. They reach a new level of process automation and make heavy use of sensors in manufactoring equipment, which brings new challenges to monitoring and diagnostics at smart factories. We propose to address the challenges with a novel rule-based monitoring and diagnostics language that relies on ontologies and reasoning and allows one to write diagnostic tasks at a high level of abstraction. We show that our approach speeds up the diagnostic routine of engineers at Siemens: they can formulate and deploy diagnostic tasks in factories faster than with existing Siemens data-driven solutions. Moreover we show that our diagnostic language, despite the built-in reasoning, allows for efficient execution of diagnostic tasks over large volumes of industrial data. Finally, we implemented our ideas in a prototypical diagnostic system for smart factories.

1 Introduction

1.1 Diagnostics of Smart Factories

The new level of automation brings new challenges to monitoring and diagnostics at smart factories, which is vital for maximising the equipment's up-time and minimising its maintenance and operating costs [38]. At Siemens and other large companies such diagnostics typically rely on *rule-based* systems that allow diagnostic engineers to create and deploy complex diagnostic rule sets over a factory's equipment. Patterns of sensor measurements that are encoded in a rule set help to detect abnormalities during equipment run time. These patterns are then combined with sophisticated analytical models as well as models of physical aspects of equipment such as thermodynamics and energy efficacy in order to compute a factory's key performance indicators (KPIs), and analyse and optimise its overall performance.

© Springer Nature Switzerland AG 2018
R. Ichise et al. (Eds.): JIST 2018, LNCS 11341, pp. 277–294, 2018.
https://doi.org/10.1007/978-3-030-04284-4_19

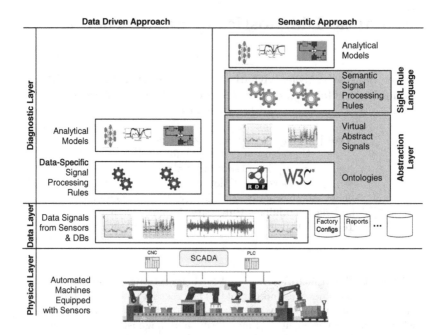

Fig. 1. Two approaches to diagnostics for an automated factory with signal-processing rules: data driven (commonly used in practice nowadays) and semantics driven (our proposal). Both approaches rely on the same data: sensor signals as well as factory configurations, reports, etc.

An important class of industrial diagnostic rules that are commonly used at Siemens are *signal processing rules* (SPRs). SPRs allow one to filter, aggregate, combine, and compare *signals*, i.e., time-stamped measurement values, coming from sensors installed in equipment, and trigger error or notification messages when a certain criterion has been met. Thus, sensors report temperature, pressure, vibration and other relevant parameters of equipment and SPRs process this data and issue alerts whenever a certain pattern is detected.

We summarise such SPR-based diagnostics of a smart factory in Fig. 1, which has three layers. At the *physical layer* there is the actual factory controlled by Supervisory control and data acquisition (SCADA) systems such as Programmable logic controllers (PLCs) and Computer numerical controllers (CNCs) that generate signal data. The *data layer* consists of two parts: *master data* that contains factory engineering specifications, results of previous diagnostic tasks, and diagnostic event data, and *operational data* that contains recorded signals from sensors installed in manufacturing equipment. The *diagnostic layer* consists of SPRs and analytical models. At the diagnostic layer of the figure we distinguish between the data driven and the semantic approach. We now discuss these approaches in detail.

1.2   Challenges with Existing Diagnostic Approaches

SPRs that are currently offered in most existing diagnostic systems and used at Siemens are highly *data dependent*: *(i)* data about specific characteristics like speed, capacity, and identifiers of individual sensors and pieces of equipment are explicitly encoded in SPRs and *(ii)* the schema of such data is reflected in the SPRs. As a result, for a typical simple factory diagnostic task an engineer has to write up to hundreds of SPRs with hundreds of sensor tags, component codes, sensor and threshold values and equipment configs and design data.

For example, a simple Siemens automated conveyor has up to hundreds of consecutive operations on a manufactured component. Each operation is performed in a separate automated module or machine. Such machines have from tens to hundreds of different sensors, that measure physical characteristics of the produced components and the environment. Thus, a small automated conveyor at Siemens has from several hundreds to more than a thousand sensors. As a result, for a typical simple factory diagnostic task an engineer has to write up to hundreds of SPRs with hundreds of sensor tags, component codes, sensor and threshold values and equipment configs and design data. Consider the following diagnostic task that detects whether the manufacturing complies with the expected quality:

All produced components satisfy the quality criterion of staying compact when a certain amount force is applied in a particular direction.

Informally, this diagnostic task requires to make sure that: *(i)* the number of produced components that failed the force test is not trending up over two production cycles. Further, we also need to consider other technical aspects when doing the check. In particular, we should consider: *(ii)* only time intervals when non-test products are produced and *(iii)* when the quality test is performed for different products. Each of the above tasks can be checked by analysing the equipment sensors.

For instance, consider step *(i)*. Let us assume that the force test involves sensors PRS_01, PRS_02, PRS_03 and PRS_04, that measure the bending or breaking of the component when a certain amount of force is applied to them. Then, the following data dependent SPR, written in a syntax similar to the one of Siemens SPRs, can be used perform the task. The SPR checks whether the average values of the sensors indicate that the flexing is greater than the allowed value (2200 mm) and that the number of components having such flexing is trending up over a certain period of time (55 sec):

$$\$HighScrap = avg\{PRS\_01, PRS\_02, PRS\_03, PRS\_04\} : value(>, 2200mm) \quad \&\&$$
$$trending(avg\{PRS\_01, PRS\_02, PRS\_03, PRS\_04\}, 'up') : duration(>, 55sec) \tag{1}$$

Similarly, one can write such data-dependent SPRs for tasks *(ii)* and *(iii)*.

In order to express all quality checks one has to write around 400 SPRs, some of which are as in the running example. Many of these SPRs differ only on specific sensor identifiers, their number and the threshold values. For example, another quality test (that applies a test force from a different angle) may have five sensors with ids PRS_X01, PRS_X02, PRS_X03, PRS_X05 and PRS_X05, a different threshold value and time period. Thus, the rules for that test would be like the ones above, but with these new sensor ids and threshold values.

At a higher level, if we consider different conveyors we may have that one conveyor has three such quality tests while another conveyor has five. Since the parameters of such rules as well as even their number are characteristics of a particular conveyor, it is desirable to abstract them away from the SPR rules and to automatically instantiate them only at run time.

Indeed, this is desirable since such data dependency of SPRs poses significant challenges for diagnostic engineers in *(i)* authoring, and then *(ii)* reuse, and *(iii)* maintenance of SPRs. These challenges are common for large enterprises and Siemens is not an exception. Indeed, *authoring* such rules is time consuming and error prone, e.g., while aggregating signals from drilling machines in a conveying line one has to find all machines among the relevant ones in the line and ensure that *all* the relevant signals are included in the aggregation while other signals, e.g., packaging related signals, are not included. Finding this information is hard, since relevant data is scattered across multiple databases. As a result, of the overall time that a Siemens engineer spends on diagnostics up to 80% is devoted to rule authoring where the major part of this time is devoted to data access and integration [26]. *Reuse* of such rules is limited since they are too specific for concrete equipment and in many cases it is easier to write a new rule set than to understand and adapt an existing one. Consequently, over the years Siemens has acquired a huge library of SPRs with more than 200,000 rules and it constantly grows. Finally, *maintenance* of such SPRs is also challenging and requires significant manual work, since the semantics behind them is limited.

1.3   Semantic Diagnostics and Our Contributions

Semantic technologies can help in addressing the challenges with authoring, reuse, and maintenance of SPRs. An *ontology* can be used to abstractly represent sensors and background knowledge about a factory and its equipment, including locations of sensors, structure and characteristics of conveyors. Then, in the spirit of *Ontology Based Data Access* (OBDA) [32], the ontology can be 'connected' to the data about the actual conveyors and machines, their sensors and signals with the help of declarative *mapping specifications*. OBDA has recently attracted a lot of attention by the research community: a solid theory has been developed, e.g. [10], and a number of mature systems have been implemented, e.g. [8,9,13,15,16,23]. Moreover, OBDA has been successfully applied in several industrial applications, e.g. [11,19,20,22,24].

Adopting OBDA for rule-based diagnostics at Siemens, however, requires a rule based language for SPRs that enjoys the following features:

(i) Signal orientation: The language should treat signals as first-class citizens and allow for their manipulation: to filter, aggregate, combine, and compare signals;

(ii) Expressiveness: The language should capture most of the features of the Siemens rule language used for diagnostics;

(iii) Usability: The language should be simple and concise enough so that the engineers can significantly save time in specifying diagnostic tasks;

(iv) Efficiency: The language should allow for efficient execution of diagnostic tasks.

To the best of our knowledge no rule language exists that fulfills all these requirements (see details in Sect. 4).

In this work we propose to extend the traditional data-driven approach to diagnostics with an OBDA layer and a new rule language to what we call *Semantic Rule-based Diagnostics*. Our approach is schematically depicted in Fig. 1 (top-right). To this end we propose the language *SDRL* (Semantic Diagnostic Rule Language) for SPRs that satisfies the four requirements above. Our language allows one to write SPRs for complex diagnostic tasks in an abstract fashion and to exploit both ontological vocabulary and queries over ontologies to identify relevant sensors and data values. We designed the language in such a way that, on the one hand, it captures the main signal processing features required by Siemens diagnostic engineers and, on the other hand, it has good computational properties. In particular, *SDRL* allows for rewriting [10] of diagnostic rule sets written over OWL 2 QL ontologies (that are the W3C standard for OBDA) into multiple data-dependent rule sets with the help of ontologies and OBDA mappings. This rewriting allows one to exploit standard infrastructure, including the one of Siemens, for processing data-dependent SPRs.

We implemented *SDRL* and a prototypical Semantic Rule-based Diagnostic system. We deployed our implementation at Siemens over a simulated smart factory and evaluated the deployment with encouraging results. In particular, we conducted a study of the efficiency of our solution in processing diagnostic tasks over manufacturing signals in a controlled environment. Currently, our deployment is not included in the production processes, it is a prototype that we plan to evaluate and improve further before it can be used in production.

This work significantly extends our previous publications [25,28,29]: Here we *(i)* non-trivially extended *SDRL* with two novel operators: one that allows for completeness-aware aggregates, and another, the loop operator, that allows for iteration, *(ii)* developed a new use case of automated manufacturing that includes a set of diagnostic tasks and real Siemens data, *(iii)* simulated a large-scale data set of transactional and master data and conducted a new backend evaluation, *(iv)* improved and deployed our system over a Siemens smart factory.

2   Signal Processing Language *SDRL*

In this section we introduce our signal processing language *SDRL*. It has three components: *(i)* Basic signals that come from sensors; *(ii)* *Knowledge Bases* (KBs) that capture background knowledge of equipment and signals as well as concrete characteristics of the equipment that undergoing diagnostics; and *(iii)* Signal processing expressions that manipulate basic signals using mathematical functions and queries over KBs.

$C =$	Concept C contains
Q	all signal ids returned by Q evaluated over the KB.
$\alpha \circ C_1$	one signal s' for each signal s_1 in C_1 with $f_{s'} = \alpha \circ f_{s_1}$.
$C_1 \circ C_2$	one signal s' for each signal s_1 in C_1 and each signal s_2 in C_2 with $f_{s'} = f_{s_1} \circ f_{s_2}$.
$C_1 : value(\odot, \alpha)$	one signal s' for each signal s in C_1 with $f_{s'}(t) = \alpha \odot f_s(t)$ if $f_s(t) \odot \alpha$ at time point t; otherwise $f_{s'}(t) = \perp$.
$C_1 : duration(\odot, t')$	one signal s' for each signal s in C_1 with $f_{s'}(t) = f_s(t)$ if exists on an interval I s.t.: f_s is defined I, $t \in I$ and $size(I) \odot t'$; otherwise $f_{s'}(t) = \perp$.
$\{s_1, \ldots, s_m\}$	all enumerated signal $\{s_1, \ldots, s_m\}$.
$C = \text{agg } C_1$	one signal s' with $f_{s'}(t) = \text{agg}_{s \in C_1} f_s(t)$, that is, s' is obtained from all signals in C_1 by applying the aggregate agg at each time point t.
$C = \text{agg}_{incompl} C_1$	one signal s' with $f_{s'}(t) = \text{agg}_{incompl \; s \in C_1} f_s(t)$, that is, s' is obtained from all signals in C_1 by applying the "incompleteness tolerant" aggregate at each time point t.
$C_1 : align \; C_2$	a signal s_1 from C_1 if: exists a signal s_2 from C_2 that is *aligned* with s_1, i.e., for each interval I_1 where f_{s_1} is defined there is an interval I_2 where f_{s_2} is defined s.t. I_1 *aligns* with I_2.
$C_1 : trend(direct)$	one signal s' for each signal s in C_1 with $f_{s'}(t) = f_s(t)$ if exists an interval I around t s.t.: f_s is defined I, and f_s is an increasing (decreasing) function on I for *direct=up* (*=down* resp.)

Fig. 2. Meaning of signal processing expressions. For the interval I, $size(I)$ is its size. For intervals I_1, I_2 the *alignment* is: "I_1 *within* I_2" if $I_1 \subseteq I_2$; "I_1 *after*[t] I_2" if all points of I_2 are after I_1 and the start of I_2 is within the end of I_1 plus period t; "I_1 *before*[t] I_2" if "I_2 *start*[t] I_1".

Signals. In our setting, a *signal* is a first-class citizen. A signal s is a pair (o_s, f_s) of a *sensor id* o_s and a *signal function* f_s defined on $\mathbb{R}$ to $\mathbb{R} \cup \{\perp\}$, where $\perp$ denotes the absence of a value. A *basic signal* is a signal whose value is obtained from a single sensor (e.g., in a quality check module) for different time points. In practice, it may happen that a signal has a period without identified values. Also, such periods are obtained when combining and manipulating basic signals. We say that a signal s is *defined* on a real interval I if it has a value for each point of the interval, i.e., $\perp \notin f_s(I)$. For technical reasons we introduce the *undefined* signal function $f_\perp$ that maps all reals to $\perp$. In practice, signals are typically step functions over time intervals, since they correspond to sensor values delivered with some frequency. In our model, we assume that we are given a finite set of basic signals $\mathcal{S} = \{s_1, \ldots, s_n\}$.

Knowledge Bases and Queries. A Knowledge Base $\mathcal{K}$ is a pair of an *ontology* $\mathcal{O}$ and a *data set* $\mathcal{A}$. An *ontology* describes background knowledge of an application domain in a formal language. We refer the reader to [10] for detailed definitions of ontologies. In our setting we consider ontologies that describe general characteristics of equipment, which includes partonomy of its components, characteristics and locations of its sensors, etc. As an example consider the following ontological expression that says that P2ConveyorMotorPower is a kind of PowerSensor:

$$\text{SubClassOf}(\text{P2ConveyorMotorPower} \quad \text{PowerSensor}). \tag{2}$$

Data sets of KBs consist of *data assertions* enumerating concrete sensors, components, and their connections. The following assertions say that the sensors PRS_01, PRS_02, PRS_03 and PRS_04 are all sensors in quality test module 1:

$$\begin{aligned}
&\text{ClassAssertion}(\text{PressurePointQualityTest1} \quad \text{PRS\_01}), \\
&\text{ClassAssertion}(\text{PressurePointQualityTest1} \quad \text{PRS\_02}), \\
&\text{ClassAssertion}(\text{PressurePointQualityTest1} \quad \text{PRS\_03}), \\
&\text{ClassAssertion}(\text{PressurePointQualityTest1} \quad \text{PRS\_04}).
\end{aligned} \tag{3}$$

In order to enjoy the favourable semantic and computational characteristics of OBDA, we consider the well-studied ontology language OWL 2 QL, that allows one to express subclass (resp. sub-property) axioms between classes and projections of properties (resp. between properties). We refer the reader to [10] for details on OWL 2 QL.

To query KBs we rely on conjunctive queries (CQs) and certain answer semantics, that have been extensively studied for OWL 2 QL KBs and proved to be tractable [10]. For example, the following CQ returns all sensor ids of motors for product 'p2' in conveyor Y:

$$\begin{aligned}
\text{P2ConveyorMotorCurrent}(X) \leftarrow\ &\text{VoltageSensor}(X), \text{locatedIn}(X, Y), \text{Conveyor}(Y), \quad (4) \\
&\text{involvedInProcess}(Y, Z), \text{assignedToProduct}(Z, \text{'p2'})
\end{aligned}$$

The unary/binary predicates in the query body are concepts/roles defined in the KB.

Signal Processing Expressions. We introduce signal expressions that filter and manipulate basic signals and create new more complex signals. Intuitively, in our language we group signals in ontological concepts (also called classes) and signal expression are defined at the level of concepts. Then, a *signal processing expression* is recursively defined as follows:

$$\begin{aligned}
C \quad = \quad &Q &&|\ \{s_1, \dots, s_m\} &&| \\
&\alpha \circ C_2 &&|\ C_1 \circ C_2 &&| \\
&\textbf{agg}\ C_1 &&|\ \textbf{agg}_{incompl}\ C_1 &&| \\
&C_1 : value(\odot, \alpha) &&|\ C_1 : duration(\odot, t) &&| \\
&C_1 : align\ C_2 &&|\ C_1 : trend(direction),
\end{aligned}$$

where Q is a concept or a CQ with one output variable, $s_1, s_2, \ldots$ are basic signals, $\circ \in \{+, -, \times, /\}$, $\mathsf{agg} \in \{\mathsf{min}, \mathsf{max}, \mathsf{avg}, \mathsf{sum}\}$, $\alpha \in \mathbb{R}$, $\odot \in \{=, \neq, <, >, \leq, \geq\}$, t is a period, and also $align \in \{within, after[t], before[t]\}$ and $direction \in \{\mathsf{up}, \mathsf{down}\}$.

The formal meaning of signal processing expressions is defined in Fig. 2. In order to get the mathematics right, we assume that $c \circ \bot = \bot \circ c = \bot$ and $c \odot \bot = \bot \odot c = false$ for $c \in \mathbb{R}$, and make analogous assumptions for aggregate functions. If the value of a signal function at a time point is not defined with these rules, then we set it as $\bot$.

Since sensor data is not always available (e.g., one of the five temperature sensors may be broken), we introduce aggregate operators $\mathsf{agg}_{incompl}$ that are tolerant when a value is missing. To do so we adjust the semantics of arithmetics to ignore missing values. For example, the average value of the set $\{3, 5, \bot\}$ under incompleteness tolerant semantics is 4. For the other aggregates, we proceed similarly.

Example 1. The data-driven rules to determine a quality test as in Eq. (1) from the running example can be expressed in *SDRL* as follows:

$$\mathsf{HighScrapPeriodQA1} = \mathsf{avg}_{incompl}\ \mathsf{PressurePointQualityTest1}:$$
$$value(>, MaxPressureQualityThreshold1):$$
$$trend('up') : duration(>, CycleTime1). \tag{5}$$

Here, $\mathsf{PressurePointQualityTest1}$ is the concept defined in Eq. (3). For brevity, we do not introduce a new concept for each expression but we just concatenate them with the symbol ":" (interpreting it as left-association). Constants *MaxPressureQualityThreshold1* and *CycleTime1* are parameters of the quality test, and they are instantiated from the conveyor configuration when the expressions are evaluated.

On top of signal expressions we introduce for-rules that allow for an even more effective representation of signals. In particular, a *for-rule* is a rule of the form:

$$for\ \mathsf{\$Var}\ in\ \mathsf{B}\ \{\ rule[\mathsf{\$Var}]\ \}$$

where $\mathsf{\$Var}$ is a variable, B is a atomic concept from ontology and $rule[\mathsf{\$Var}]$ is a signal expression parametrized with $\mathsf{\$Var}$. For example, the following for-rule defines several quality checks:

$$for\ \mathsf{\$X}\ in\ \mathsf{QAids}\{$$
$$\mathsf{HighScrapPeriodQA\$X} = \mathsf{avg}_{incompl}\ \mathsf{PressurePointQualityTest\$X}:$$
$$value(>, MaxPressureQualityThreshold\$X):$$
$$trend('up') : duration(>, CycleTime\$X)\} \tag{6}$$

Here, QAids is an ontological concept that contains ids of quality tests and $X is a variable that takes values from QAids. Assume that QAids contains the three ids. Then the above loop will run three times and execute one rule after each loop, where new concepts HighScrapPeriodQA$X will be defined and instantiated for each $X.

Similarly to rule (6), we can define rules for steps *(ii)* and *(iii)* for our initial example (see Eqs. (9) and (8) below). To complete the example, we only mention that the concept names MaxProducedQuantityUp and NotTestProduct encode signals for steps *(ii)* and *(iii)* respectively.

Diagnostic Programs and Messages. We now show how to use signal expressions to compose diagnostic programs and to create alert messages. In the following we will consider *well-formed* sets of signal expressions, that is, sets where each concept is defined at most once and where definitions of new concepts are assumed to be acyclic: if C_1 is used to define C_2 (directly or indirectly) then C_1 cannot be defined (directly or indirectly) using C_1. Note that, in case we have for-rules, such a check can be done only at run-time when the ontology instantiates the atomic concepts.

A *diagnostic program* (or simply *program*) Π is a tuple $(\mathcal{S}, \mathcal{K}, \mathcal{M})$, where $\mathcal{S}$ is a set of basic signals, $\mathcal{K}$ a KB, $\mathcal{M}$ a set of well-formed signal processing expressions such that each concept that is defined in $\mathcal{M}$ does not appear in $\mathcal{K}$.

Example 2. The program for our running example $\Pi = (\mathcal{S}, \mathcal{K}, \mathcal{M})$ has the following components: sensor set $\mathcal{S} = \{\text{PRS\_01}, \text{PRS\_02}, \text{PRS\_03}, \text{PRS\_04}\}$, KB $\mathcal{K}$, consisting of the axioms from Eq. (2) and (3), and expression set $\mathcal{M}$, consisting of the expressions in Eq. (5), and in Eqs. (9) and (8) in Fig. 5.

On top of diagnostic programs Π, *SDRL* allows one to define *message rules* that report the current status of a system. A *message rule* is a rule of the following form, where C is a concept from $\mathcal{K}$ and m is a (text) message:

$$\text{msg}(m) = C.$$

For example, we can encode our running example with the following rule:

$$\text{msg}(\textit{"HighScrapPeriod"}) = \text{HighScrapPeriodQA1} : \textit{within}$$
$$\text{MaxProducedQuantityUp} : \textit{within} \ \text{NotTestProduct} \,.$$
$$(7)$$

Now we are ready to define the semantics of the rules, expression and programs.

Semantics of *SDRL*. We now define how to determine whether a program Π fires a rule r. To this end, we extend the first-order interpretations that are used to define the semantics of OWL 2 KBs. In OWL 2, a first-class citizen is an object o, and an interpretation defines whether $C(o)$ is true or not for particular concept

C. In our scenario, the domain of objects is a domain of sensor ids (basic ids or ids defined by expressions). Thus, each object o also has an assigned function f_o that represents the signal value of that object. Observe that o can also be an id of a conveyor component that does not have signal function. At the moment, (since it is not crucial for this study and it simplifies the formalism) we also assign the undefined signal $f_\perp$ to such (non-signal) objects.

Formally, now an *interpretation* $\mathcal{I}$ is a pair $(\mathcal{I}_{FOL}, \mathcal{I}_S)$, where $\mathcal{I}_{FOL}$ interprets objects and their relationships (like in OWL 2) and $\mathcal{I}_S$—signals. First, we define how $\mathcal{I}$ interprets basic signals. Given a set of signals for an interpretation $\mathcal{I}$: $\mathcal{S}^{\mathcal{I}} = \{s_1^{\mathcal{I}}, \ldots, s_n^{\mathcal{I}}\}$ s.t. $\mathcal{I}_{FOL}$ 'returns' the signal id, $s^{\mathcal{I}_{FOL}} = o_s$ and $\mathcal{I}_S$ 'returns' the signal itself, $s^{\mathcal{I}_S} = s$.

Now we define how $\mathcal{I}$ interprets KBs. The interpretation of a KB $\mathcal{K}^{\mathcal{I}}$ extends the notion of first-order logic interpretation as follows: $\mathcal{K}^{\mathcal{I}_{FOL}}$ is a first-order logic interpretation $\mathcal{K}$, and $\mathcal{K}^{\mathcal{I}_S}$ is defined for objects, concepts and roles following $\mathcal{S}^{\mathcal{I}}$. That is, for each object o we define $o^{\mathcal{I}_S}$ as s if o is the id of s from $\mathcal{S}$; otherwise $(o, f_\perp)$. Then, for a concept A we define $A^{\mathcal{I}_S} = \{s^{\mathcal{I}_S} \mid o_s^{\mathcal{I}_{FOL}} \in A^{\mathcal{I}_{FOL}}\}$. Similarly, we define $\cdot^{\mathcal{I}_S}$ for roles.

Finally, we are ready to define $\mathcal{I}$ for signal expressions and we do it recursively following the definitions in Fig. 2. We now illustrate some of them. For example, if $C = \{s_1, \ldots, s_m\}$, then $C^{\mathcal{I}} = \{s_1^{\mathcal{I}}, \ldots, s_m^{\mathcal{I}}\}$; if $C = Q$ then $C^{\mathcal{I}_{FOL}} = Q^{\mathcal{I}_{FOL}}$ where $Q^{\mathcal{I}_{FOL}}$ is the evaluation of Q over $\mathcal{I}_{FOL}$ and $C^{\mathcal{I}_S} = \{s \mid o_s^{\mathcal{I}_{FOL}} \in Q^{\mathcal{I}_{FOL}}\}$, provided that $\mathcal{I}_{FOL}$ is a model of $\mathcal{K}$. Otherwise we define $C^{\mathcal{I}} = \emptyset$. Similarly, we define the interpretation of the other expressions.

Firing a Message. Let Π be a program and '$r : message(m) = C$' a message rule. We say that Π *fires* message r if *for each* interpretation $\mathcal{I} = (\mathcal{I}_{FOL}, \mathcal{I}_S)$ of Π it holds $C^{\mathcal{I}_{FOL}} \neq \emptyset$, that is, the concept that fires r is not empty. Our programs and rules enjoy the *canonical* model property, that is, each program has a unique (Herbrand) interpretation [5], which is minimal and can be constructed starting from basic signals and ontology by following signal expressions. In [33], we showed how to encode *SDRL* programs into metric Datalog programs with functional symbols. This result yields uniqueness of the (Herbrand) interpretation.

Thus, one can verify whether $C^{\mathcal{I}_{FOL}} \neq \emptyset$ based only on the canonical model. This implies that one can evaluate *SDRL* programs and expressions in a bottom-up fashion. We now illustrate this approach on our running example.

Example 3. Consider our running program Π from Example 2 and its canonical interpretation $\mathcal{I}_\Pi$. First, for each query Q in $\mathcal{M}$ we evaluate Q over KB $\mathcal{K}$ by computing $Q^{\mathcal{I}_\Pi}$. That, for example, populates atomic concept P2ConveyorMotorCurrent. Then, other atomic concepts are populated, e.g., QAids, and this allows to populate atomic concepts in for-loops, such as PressurePointQualityTest\$$X$. In the next step, we evaluate the expressions in $\mathcal{M}$ following the dependency graph of definitions. In our running example, we start by evaluation the expression from Eq. (6), again in a bottom-up fashion. In

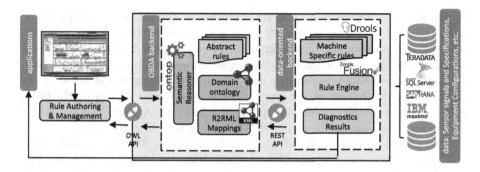

Fig. 3. Architecture of our semantic rule-based diagnostics system.

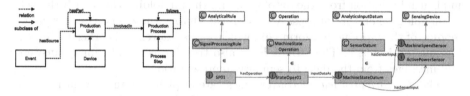

Fig. 4. Left: several concepts from the manufacturing ontology and their relation via object properties and the subclass relation; Right: example of manufacturing master data.

the final step, if there is at least one signal that satisfies the body of a message rule, e.g., (7), the message is fired.

3 Siemens Implementation and Evaluation

We first review the implementation of our system and its deployment at Siemens, then present the evaluation of the system over real Siemens data that we scaled.

3.1 System Implementation

We implemented our ideas in a prototypical semantic rule-based diagnostics system that allows one to author *SDRL* diagnostic programs, to execute them, and to visualise the results of execution. Our system is mostly implemented in Java and organised in four essential layers (see Fig. 3) that we discuss next: *applications, OBDA backend, data-oriented backend,* and *data.*

At the *application* layer, the system offers user-oriented modules that allow engineers to author, store, and load diagnostic programs by formulating sets of SPRs in *SDRL* and sensor retrieving queries. These modules are embedded in the Siemens analytical toolkit and include an SPR editor, a monitoring dashboard, and a semantic Wiki that allows among other features to visualize signals and messages (triggered by programs), and to track the deployment of SPRs in equipment. The formulation of SPRs is guided by the domain ontology stored in the system; in Fig. 4 we present several concepts from our manufacturing ontology and an example of master manufacturing data. Diagnostic programs formulated at the application layer are converted into XML-based specifications and sent to the OBDA backend, which returns the messages and materialized semantic signals, that is, signals over the ontological terms. We rely on the OWL API to communicate between the application and OBDA layers and the REST API to communicate between the OBDA and the data oriented layers.

The *OBDA backend* layer takes care of transforming SPRs written in *SDRL* into either SPRs written in the Siemens data-driven rule language or SQL. This transformation has two steps: rewriting of programs and queries with the help of ontologies (at this step, both programs and queries are enriched with the implicit information from the ontology), and then unfolding them with the help of mappings. For this purpose we extended Ontop, the query transformation module of the Optique platform [26], which we had developed earlier within the Optique project [13]. The OBDA layer also transforms signals, query answers, and messages from the data to semantic representation.

The *data-oriented backend* layer takes care of planning and executing data-driven rules and queries received from the OBDA layer. If the received rules are in the Siemens SPR language then the rule executor instantiates them with concrete sensors extracted with queries and passes them to Drools Fusion, [1] i.e., the engine used by Siemens. If the received rules are in SQL then it plans the execution order and executes them together with the other queries. Later in Sect. 3.2 we evaluate the efficiency of our system assuming the SQL case.

Finally, at the *data* layer we store the relevant data: master manufacturing data such as equipment specifications, historical information about diagnostics and services that were performed in the factory, previously detected events and the raw sensor signals.

We deployed our Semantic Rule-Based Diagnostics system on the real data from a Siemens smart factory with 1500 production machines and 70 conveying lines. In this deployment we rely on Teradata to store signals; MS SQL Server for manufacturing configurations of machines in the factory; SAP HANA for purchase data, material consumption and spare-part information; and IBM Maximo for data about maintenance and repair tasks incident reports, stock information, component history, defect information etc. For rule processing, we connected our system to the Siemens deployment of Drools Fusion. An important aspect of the deployment was the development of a diagnostic ontology and mappings. Our ontology was inspired by the *(i)* Siemens Technical System Ontology (TSO) and W3C Semantic Sensor Network Ontology (SSN) and *(ii)* the international standards IEC 81346 and ISO/TS 16952-10. The development of the ontology was a joint effort of domain experts from Siemens business units together with a specialist from Siemens Corporate Technology. Our ontology consists of four modules and it is expressed in OWL 2 QL. In order to connect the ontology to the data, we introduced 376 TriplesMaps using the R2RML language.

---

[1] http://drools.jboss.org/drools-fusion.html.

Diagnostics Task T_1: "Verify that all conveyors involved in the production of the product P2 are ready and operating well."

$$\mathsf{msg}(\textit{"ConveyorsNotReady"}) = min_{incompl}\ \mathsf{P2ConveyorMotorPower}:$$
$$value(<, \textit{ConveyorMotorMinPower})$$

In other words, if the minimal power consumed by conveyors motors is below the threshold a message is fired.

Diagnostic Task T_2: "Check if product variants are the same for all units.":

$$\mathsf{msg}(\textit{"ProductsIncompatible"}) = max\ \mathsf{ComponentSensor} - min\ \mathsf{ComponentSensor}: value(\neq, 0)$$

Diagnostics Task T_3: "Assert that after the material supply has been turned on, the conveyor has been working for a given period of time and then got turned off.":

$$\mathsf{msg}(\textit{"StartUpFailure"}) = \mathsf{SupplyStationEnergyConsumption}: value(>, \textit{idlevalueStation}):$$
$$after[10s]:$$
$$\mathsf{MaterialConveyorEnergyConsumption}: value(<, \textit{idlevalueConveyor})$$

Diagnostics Task T_4: "Verify that all quality tests has been passed.":
We do it in three steps. First we select only those time periods where new components have been produced (quantity is trending up) and these were not test products.

$$\mathsf{MaxProducedQuantityUp} = max\ \mathsf{ProducedQuantity}: \textit{trend('up')} \tag{8}$$
$$\mathsf{NotTestProduct} = \mathsf{ProducedProduct}: value(\neq, \textit{TestProduct}) \tag{9}$$

Then, we check each of the quality tests with ids from QAids with the rule (6).
Finally, for each such test we are only interested in the time intervals when the quality test occurred within time on non-test product and the quantity of product was increasing:

$$\textit{for}\ \$Y\ \textit{in}\ \mathsf{QAids}\ \{$$
$$\mathsf{msg}(\textit{"HighScrapPeriod"}) = \mathsf{HighScrapPeriodQA}\$Y: \textit{within}$$
$$\mathsf{MaxProducedQuantityUp}\$Y: \textit{within}$$
$$\mathsf{NotTestProduct}\}$$

Fig. 5. Signal processing rules that evaluate performance in a Siemens smart factory.

3.2 Performance Evaluation

In this experiment, we evaluate how well our SQL translation approach scales. To this end we have prepared diagnostic tasks, corresponding data, and verified firing of messages using a standard relational database engine PostgreSQL.

The data comes from a smart factory that produces switches for electrical circuits in batches. We took data from one moving conveyor belt that carries the workpieces from start to end and contains in total ten Siemens custom-built production machines connected to the conveyor. When the conveyor is active, the raw materials such as plates and wires are inserted in the machines that carry out different mounting, assembly, and welding tasks using the materials. The concrete sequence of steps that the machines do depend on the product variant. Each

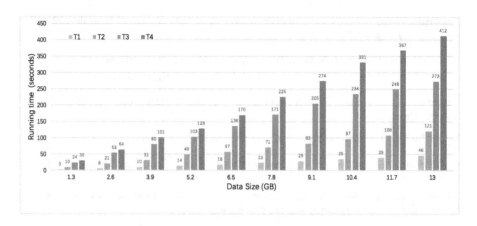

Fig. 6. Performance evaluation results for the Smart Factory use case.

machine is controlled by a Siemens Programming-logic controller (PLC) that has physical and soft-sensors attached: 36 sensors in total per machine. Moreover, one of the machines is equipped with a special type of sensors that are needed for the QA (quality assessment) tests and they report so-called force/displacement measurements. We gathered transaction data from 15 days of the conveyor's run. In this period of time each machine generated around 325 MB of data. In order to evaluate the scalability, we scaled the data up to 40 conveyors. This gave us 10 datasets with 4 to 40 conveyors each.

We prepared four manufacturing diagnosis tasks T_1 to T_4. These tasks are representative in the sense that they cover different aspects during a manufacturing process and they are of different levels of complexity. These tasks are formulated as signal processing rules in Fig. 5. Note that the tasks check for failures by asking negative questions, that is, the check whether something that should *not* hold actually occurs.

We conducted the experiments on an HP Proliant server with 2 Intel Xeon X5690 Processors (each with 12 logical cores at 3.47 GHz), 106 GB of RAM. The data is stored in a PostgreSQL v9.6 database. The rewritten SQL queries for these tasks are up to 263 lines long, showing that our approach has a good level of abstraction. The running times are provided in Fig. 6. We observe that query evaluation scales well. Specifically, the running time grows linearly with respect to the data size. The most challenging query T4 over 40 conveyors can be answered in 7 min.

4   Related Work, Lessons Learned and Future Work

Related Work. Existing semantic streaming languages, such as SPARQL$_{stream}$ [12], STARQL [26] and C-SPARQL [6], are different from our work, since we propose *(i)* a rule diagnostic language and *(ii)* focus on temporal properties of signals, which are not naturally representable in those languages. Extension of ontologies with analytical and temporal concepts, e.g., [3,4] that allow for temporal operators in queries and ontologies are different from our work, since they use temporal logics (e.g., LTL) which is not adequate for our case since sensor data are organised based on intervals, e.g. $[0s, 10s]$. OBDA preserving extensions of ontological rules with analytical operations, e.g., [21,26] allow one to define analytical functions on concepts, e.g. avg C, in an OBDA setting, however, differently from us, they do not consider the temporal dimension of the rules. Our work is related to the well-studied Metric Temporal Logic [27]. In particular, we use a non-trivial extension of the non-recursive Datalog language $\text{Datalog}_{\text{nr}}\text{MTL}$, which is suitable for an OBDA scenario. $\text{Datalog}_{\text{nr}}\text{MTL}$ has been introduced in [7], where the authors conduct a theoretical and experimental study investigating the computational characteristics of the language. They show how query answering over a program in $\text{Datalog}_{\text{nr}}\text{MTL}$ can be rewritten into the problem of query answering in SQL (so-called FO-rewriting, see [10]). Following similar principles, we define how to rewrite our *SDRL* language into SQL and show that such rewriting performs reasonably well on sensor data.

Lessons Learned. In this paper we showcase an application of semantic technologies to diagnostics of smart factories. We focused on the advantages and feasibility of the ontology-based solution for diagnostic rule formulation and execution. To this end we studied and described a diagnostic use-case at Siemens. Based on the insights gained, we reported limitations of existing Siemens and ontology-based solutions to factory diagnostics. In order to address the limitations we proposed the signal processing rule language *SDRL* that extends the one we investigated earlier [28], studied its formal properties, implemented, and integrated it in an ontology-based system, which we deployed at Siemens. The main lesson we learned is that our system can handle relatively complex diagnostic tasks over realistic-size smart factories. We have also conducted a preliminary user evaluation with five engineers from a Siemens smart factory with encouraging results, while a formal usability study is our future work. In particular, the fact that our example diagnostic tasks in Fig. 5 take two to five lines when written in *SDRL*, more than 250 lines in SQL, and a similar number of lines in the Siemens data-driven diagnostic language was very impressive and encouraging to Siemens diagnostic engineers. Based on these results we believe that our semantic solution would be of great help at Siemens and other companies that specialize in equipment monitoring and diagnostics: it will allow diagnostic engineers to focus more on analyzing the diagnostic output rather than on the data understanding and gathering that they have to do nowadays for authoring data-driven diagnostic rules.

Future Work. We are in the process of preparing a deployment of our system in the Siemens remote diagnostic system to further evaluate the usability and impact. An important future work for us is to allow engineers an easy way to explore both the manufacturing ontology and the semantic diagnostic rules –

the catalog of such rules grows and one should be able efficiently and effectively explore them in order to avoid rule duplications. In particular we plant to explore some of our earlier developed techniques to query and explore semantic data and ontologies [1,2,17,18,34–37]. Finally, there is a strong need in good tooling to relate the manufacturing ontology to the underlying Siemens relational data and plan to explore some of our earlier techniques for ontology and mapping bootstrapping [14,30,31].

Acknowledgments. This research is supported by the EPSRC projects MaSI[3], DBOnto, ED[3], and by the SIRIUS Centre, Norwegian Research Council project number 237898. Also it is partially supported by the Free University of Bozen-Bolzano projects QUEST, ROBAST and QUADRO.

References

1. Arenas, M., Grau, B.C., Kharlamov, E., Marciuska, S., Zheleznyakov, D.: Faceted search over ontology-enhanced RDF data. In: CIKM, pp. 939–948 (2014)
2. Arenas, M., Grau, B.C., Kharlamov, E., Marciuska, S., Zheleznyakov, D.: Faceted search over RDF-based knowledge graphs. J. Web Semant. **37–38**, 55–74 (2016)
3. Artale, A., Kontchakov, R., Ryzhikov, V., Zakharyaschev, M.: The complexity of clausal fragments of LTL. In: McMillan, K., Middeldorp, A., Voronkov, A. (eds.) LPAR 2013. LNCS, vol. 8312, pp. 35–52. Springer, Heidelberg (2013). https://doi.org/10.1007/978-3-642-45221-5_3
4. Artale, A., Kontchakov, R., Wolter, F., Zakharyaschev, M.: Temporal description logic for ontology-based data access. In: IJCAI 2013, pp. 711–717 (2013)
5. Baader, F., Calvanese, D., McGuinness, D.L., Nardi, D., Patel-Schneider, P.F. (eds.): The Description Logic Handbook: Theory, Implementation, and Applications. Cambridge University Press, New York (2003)
6. Barbieri, D.F., Braga, D., Ceri, S., Valle, E.D., Grossniklaus, M.: C-SPARQL: a continuous query language for RDF data streams. Int. J. Semant. Comput. **4**(1), 3–25 (2010)
7. Brandt, S., Kalaycı, E.G., Kontchakov, R., Ryzhikov, V., Xiao, G., Zakharyaschev, M.: Ontology-based data access with a Horn fragment of metric temporal logic. In: AAAI (2017)
8. Calvanese, D., et al.: Ontop: answering SPARQL queries over relational databases. Semant. Web **8**(3), 471–487 (2017)
9. Calvanese, D., et al.: The MASTRO system for ontology-based data access. Semant. Web **2**(1), 43–53 (2011)
10. Calvanese, D., De Giacomo, G., Lembo, D., Lenzerini, M., Rosati, R.: Tractable reasoning and efficient query answering in description logics: the DL-Lite family. JAR **39**(3), 385–429 (2007)
11. Charron, B., Hirate, Y., Purcell, D., Rezk, M.: Extracting semantic information for e-commerce. In: Groth, P., et al. (eds.) ISWC 2016. LNCS, vol. 9982, pp. 273–290. Springer, Cham (2016). https://doi.org/10.1007/978-3-319-46547-0_27
12. Corcho, O., Calbimonte, J.P., Jeung, H., Aberer, K.: Enabling query technologies for the semantic sensor web. Int. J. Semant. Web Inf. Syst. **8**(1), 43–63 (2012)
13. Horrocks, I., Giese, M., Kharlamov, E., Waaler, A.: Using semantic technology to tame the data variety challenge. IEEE Internet Comput. **20**(6), 62–66 (2016)

14. Jiménez-Ruiz, E., et al.: BOOTOX: practical mapping of RDBs to OWL 2. In: Arenas, M., et al. (eds.) ISWC 2015. LNCS, vol. 9367, pp. 113–132. Springer, Cham (2015). https://doi.org/10.1007/978-3-319-25010-6_7

15. Kharlamov, E., et al.: Enabling semantic access to static and streaming distributed data with optique: demo. In: DEBS, pp. 350–353 (2016)

16. Kharlamov, E., et al.: Ontology-based integration of streaming and static relational data with optique. In: SIGMOD, pp. 2109–2112 (2016)

17. Kharlamov, E., Giacomelli, L., Sherkhonov, E., Grau, B.C., Kostylev, E.V., Horrocks, I.: Ranking, aggregation, and reachability in faceted search with semfacet. In: ISWC Posters & Demonstrations (2017)

18. Kharlamov, E., Giacomelli, L., Sherkhonov, E., Grau, B.C., Kostylev, E.V., Horrocks, I.: SemFacet: making hard faceted search easier. In: CIKM, pp. 2475–2478 (2017)

19. Kharlamov, E., et al.: Ontology based access to exploration data at statoil. In: ISWC, pp. 93–112 (2015)

20. Kharlamov, E., et al.: Ontology based data access in statoil. J. Web Semant. **44**, 3–36 (2017)

21. Kharlamov, E., et al.: Optique: towards OBDA systems for industry. In: Cimiano, P., Fernández, M., Lopez, V., Schlobach, S., Völker, J. (eds.) ESWC 2013. LNCS, vol. 7955, pp. 125–140. Springer, Heidelberg (2013). https://doi.org/10.1007/978-3-642-41242-4_11

22. Kharlamov, E., et al.: Semantic access to streaming and static data at Siemens. J. Web Semant. **44**, 54–74 (2017)

23. Kharlamov, E., et al.: A semantic approach to polystores. In: IEEE BigData, pp. 2565–2573 (2016)

24. Kharlamov, E., et al.: Diagnostics of trains with semantic diagnostics rules. In: Riguzzi, F., Bellodi, E., Zese, R. (eds.) ILP 2018. LNCS (LNAI), vol. 11105, pp. 54–71. Springer, Cham (2018). https://doi.org/10.1007/978-3-319-99960-9_4

25. Kharlamov, E., et al.: Semantic rules for machine diagnostics: execution and management. In: CIKM, pp. 2131–2134 (2017)

26. Kharlamov, E., et al.: How semantic technologies can enhance data access at siemens energy. ISWC 2014. LNCS, vol. 8796, pp. 601–619. Springer, Cham (2014). https://doi.org/10.1007/978-3-319-11964-9_38

27. Koymans, R.: Specifying real-time properties with metric temporal logic. Real-Time Syst. **2**(4), 255–299 (1990)

28. Mehdi, G., et al.: Semantic rule-based equipment diagnostics. In: d'Amato, C., et al. (eds.) ISWC 2017. LNCS, vol. 10588, pp. 314–333. Springer, Cham (2017). https://doi.org/10.1007/978-3-319-68204-4_29

29. Mehdi, G., et al.: SemDia: semantic rule-based equipment diagnostics tool. In: CIKM, pp. 2507–2510 (2017)

30. Pinkel, C., et al.: RODI: benchmarking relational-to-ontology mapping generation quality. Semant. Web **9**(1), 25–52 (2018)

31. Pinkel, C., et al.: IncMap: a journey towards ontology-based data integration. In: BTW, DBIS, pp. 145–164 (2017)

32. Poggi, A., Lembo, D., Calvanese, D., De Giacomo, G., Lenzerini, M., Rosati, R.: Linking data to ontologies. J. Data Semant. **10**, 133–173 (2008)

33. Savkovic, O., et al.: Theoretical characterization of signal diagnostic processing language. In: Description Logic Workshop (DL 2018), pp. 1–11 (2018)

34. Sherkhonov, E., Cuenca Grau, B., Kharlamov, E., Kostylev, E.V.: Semantic faceted search with aggregation and recursion. In: d'Amato, C., et al. (eds.) ISWC 2017. LNCS, vol. 10587, pp. 594–610. Springer, Cham (2017). https://doi.org/10.1007/978-3-319-68288-4_35

35. Soylu, A., Giese, M., Jiménez-Ruiz, E., Kharlamov, E., Zheleznyakov, D., Horrocks, I.: Ontology-based end-user visual query formulation: why, what, who, how, and which? Univers. Access Inf. Soc. **16**(2), 435–467 (2017)

36. Soylu, A., et al.: Querying industrial stream-temporal data: an ontology-based visual approach. JAISE **9**(1), 77–95 (2017)

37. Soylu, A., et al.: OptiqueVQS: a visual query system over ontologies for industry. Semant. Web **9**(5), 627–660 (2018)

38. Vachtsevanos, G., Lewis, F.L., Roemer, M., Hess, A., Wu, B.: Intelligent Fault Diagnosis and Prognosis for Engineering Systems. Wiley, Hoboken (2006)

Making Complex Ontologies End User Accessible via Ontology Projections

Ahmet Soylu[1,2(✉)] and Evgeny Kharlamov[3,4]

[1] Norwegian University of Science and Technology, Gjøvik, Norway
ahmet.soylu@ntnu.no
[2] SINTEF Digital, Oslo, Norway
[3] University of Oxford, Oxford, UK
evgeny.kharlamov@cs.ox.ac.uk
[4] University of Oslo, Oslo, Norway
evgeny.kharlamov@ifi.uio.no

Abstract. Ontologies are a powerful mechanism to structure domains of interest. They have successfully been applied in medical domain, industry and other important areas. Despite the simplicity of ontological vocabularies that consist of classes and properties, ontologies can relate elements of the vocabulary with the help of axioms in a very non-trivial way. Thus, the relationship between classes and properties can become hardly accessible by end users thus affecting the practical value of ontologies. Indeed, it is essential for end users to be able to navigate or browse through an ontology, to get a big picture of what classes there are and what they have in common in terms of other related classes and properties. This helps end users in effectively performing various knowledge engineering tasks such as querying and domain exploration. To this end, in this short paper, we describe an approach to project OWL 2 ontologies into graphs and show how to leverage this approach in practical systems for visual query formulation and faceted search that we tested in various scenarios.

1 Introduction

Ontologies are a powerful mechanism to structure domains of interest. They have successfully been applied in medical domain [21], industry [9,14–18] and other important areas [11,12,19,24,25]. Particularly, OWL 2 ontologies [7] have been key for constructing semantic knowledge graphs. A knowledge graph describes real world entities and their interrelations [37]. They have been used both in academia, such as Yago [4] and DBpedia [22], and in industry such as Google's Knowledge Graph, Facebook's Graph Search, and Microsoft's Satori. Semantic knowledge graphs are typically stored or exported as RDF datasets, which allow for storing sparse and diverse data in an extensible and adaptable way [35]. Semantics of such datasets are typically encoded in OWL 2 ontologies.

Despite the simplicity of ontological vocabularies that consist of classes and properties, ontologies can relate elements of the vocabulary with the help of axioms in a very non-trivial way. Thus, the relationship between classes and

© Springer Nature Switzerland AG 2018
R. Ichise et al. (Eds.): JIST 2018, LNCS 11341, pp. 295–303, 2018.
https://doi.org/10.1007/978-3-030-04284-4_20

properties can become hardly accessible by end users thus affecting the practical value of ontologies. Indeed, it is essential for end users to be able to navigate or browse through an ontology, to get a big picture of what classes are there, what they have in common in terms of other related classes and properties [10,23]. This helps end users in effectively performing various knowledge engineering tasks such as querying and domain exploration, e.g., via query by navigation [30,34].

In order to help end users to query and explore ontologies, in this short paper, we describe an approach to project OWL 2 ontologies into graphs and show how to leverage this approach in practical systems for visual query formulation and faceted search that we tested in various scenarios. In particular, we implemented this approach in two semantic tools, namely OptiqueVQS [33] for visual query formulation and SemFacet [1,2,13,28] for faceted search and evaluated under different use cases.

The rest of the paper is structured as follows. Section 2 presents our graph projection approach from ontologies, while Sect. 3 presents the tools using our approach. Finally, Sect. 5 concludes the paper.

2   Graph Projection

Our goal for graph projection is, given an ontology, to create a directed labelled graph, called navigation graph [2], whose nodes correspond to the named classes and datatypes in the ontology and edges between nodes to the object properties and datatype properties. Let C_1, C_2, and C_3 be classes, r_1, r_2, and r_3 object properties, d_1 a datatype property, i_1 and i_2 individuals, and dt_1 a data type. First, each class and datatype in the ontology is translated to a node in the navigation graph. Then we add edges of the form $r_1(C_1, C_2)$ and $d_1(C_1, dt_1)$ derived from the axioms of the ontology. The types of axioms resulting in an edge are presented with examples in the followings using description logic (DL) [3].

Ontologies have a propagative effect on the amount of information to be presented. This case is considered in two forms, namely the top-down and bottom-up propagation of property restrictions [6,30]. The first form emerges from the fact that, in an ontology, explicit restrictions attached to a class are inherited by its subclasses. The second form is rooted from the fact that the interpretation of an OWL class also includes the interpretations of all its subclasses. Therefore, for a given class, it may also make sense to derive edges from the (potential) object and datatype properties of its subclasses and superclasses.

2.1   Edges Through Object Properties

Domains and Ranges: Domain and range axioms using named classes are translated to an edge. For example, axioms given in Ex. 1 map to edge $r_1(C_1, C_2)$.

$$\exists r_1.\top \sqsubseteq C_1 \text{ and } \top \sqsubseteq \forall r_1.C_2 \tag{1}$$

$$\exists r_1.\top \sqsubseteq C_1 \text{ and } \top \sqsubseteq \forall r_1.(C_2 \sqcup C_3) \tag{2}$$

If a complex class expression, formed through intersection ($\sqcap$) or union ($\sqcup$), appears as a domain and/or range, then an edge is created for each pair of domain and range classes. For example, axioms given in Ex. 2 map to edges $r_1(C_1, C_2)$ and $r_1(C_1, C_3)$.

Object Property Restrictions: Object property restrictions used in class descriptions, formed through existential quantification ($\exists$), universal quantification ($\forall$), individual value restriction, max ($\geq$), min ($\leq$), and exactly ($=$), are mapped to edges. For example, axioms given in Ex. 3 to 5 map to $r_1(C_1, C_2)$. Note that in Ex. 5, there is a complex class expression on the left-hand-side.

$$C_1 \sqsubseteq \exists r_1.C_2 \tag{3}$$

$$C_1 \equiv \leq_n r_1.C_2 \tag{4}$$

$$\forall r_1.C_1 \sqsubseteq C_2 \tag{5}$$

Axioms given in Ex. 6 include an individual value restriction and an edge is created with the type of individual, that is $r_1(C_1, C_2)$.

$$C_1 \sqsubseteq \exists r_1.\{i_1\} \text{, and } i_1 : C_2 \tag{6}$$

Axiom given in Ex. 7 includes a complex class expression. In this case, an edge is created for each named class, that is $r_1(C_1, C_2)$ and $r_1(C_1, C_3)$.

$$C_1 \sqsubseteq \exists r_1.(C_2 \sqcup C_3) \tag{7}$$

Given an enumeration of individuals, an edge is created for each individual's type. For example, axioms given in Ex. 8 map to two edges, that is $r_1(C_1, C_2)$ and $r_1(C_1, C_3)$.

$$C_1 \sqsubseteq \exists r_1.\{i_1\} \sqcup \{i_2\} \text{, } i_1 : C_2 \text{, and } i_2 : C_3 \tag{8}$$

Inverse Properties: Given an edge in the navigation graph such as $r_1(C_1, C_2)$ and an inverse property axiom for the corresponding object property such as given in Ex. 9, a new edge is created for the inverse property, that is $r_{\bar{1}}(C_2, C_1)$.

$$r_1 \equiv r_{\bar{1}} \tag{9}$$

Role Chains: Given two edges $r_1(C_1, C_2)$ and $r_2(C_2, C_3)$ in the navigation graph, and a role chain axiom between r_1, r_2, r_3 such as given in Ex. 10, a new edge is created for $r3$, that is $r_3(C_1, C_3)$.

$$r_1 \circ r_2 \sqsubseteq r_3 \tag{10}$$

Top-Down Propagation: Given an edge $r_1(C_1, C_2)$ in the navigation graph and a subclass axiom such as as given in Ex. 11, a new edge is added to the graph, that is $r_1(C_3, C_2)$. Similar edges could be created for subproperties.

$$C_3 \sqsubseteq C_1 \tag{11}$$

Bottom-Up Propagation: Given an edge $r_1(C_1, C_2)$ in the navigation graph and a subclass class axiom such as given in Ex. 12, a new edge is added to the graph, that is $r_1(C_3, C_2)$. Similar edges could be created for superproperties.

$$C_1 \sqsubseteq C_3 \tag{12}$$

2.2 Edges Through Datatype Properties

Domains and Ranges: Domain and range axioms using datatype properties are translated to an edge. For example, axioms given in Ex. 13 map to an edge, that is $d_1(C_1, dt_1)$.

$$\exists d_1.DatatypeLiteral \sqsubseteq C_1 \text{ and } \top \sqsubseteq \forall r_1.dt_1 \tag{13}$$

Datatype Property Restrictions: Datatype property restrictions, formed through existential quantification ($\exists$), universal quantification ($\forall$), max ($\geq$), min ($\leq$), exactly ($=$), and value are mapped to edges. For example, axiom given in Ex. 14 maps to $d_1(C_1, dt_1)$.

$$C_1 \sqsubseteq \exists d_1.dt_1 \tag{14}$$

Top-Down Propagation: Given an edge $d_1(C_1, dt_1)$ in the navigation graph and a subclass axiom such as as given in Ex. 15, a new edge is added to the graph, that is $d_1(C_2, dt_1)$. Similar edges could be created for subproperties.

$$C_2 \sqsubseteq C_1 \tag{15}$$

Bottom-Up Propagation: Given an edge $d_1(C_1, dt_1)$ in the navigation graph and a subclass class axiom such as given in Ex. 16, a new edge is added to the graph, that is $d_1(C_3, dt_1)$. Similar edges could be created for superproperties.

$$C_1 \sqsubseteq C_3 \tag{16}$$

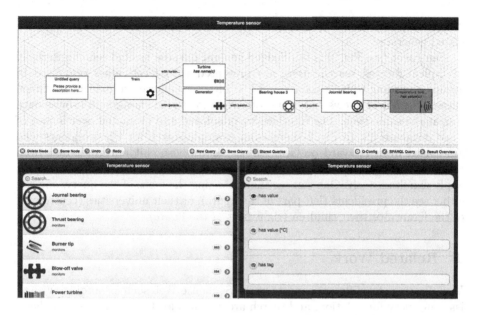

Fig. 1. OptiqueVQS over a use case provided by Siemens.

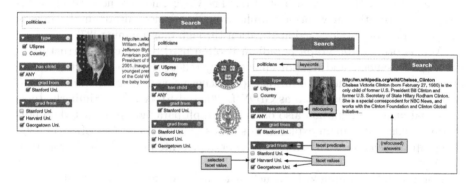

Fig. 2. SemFacet over Yago knowledge graph.

3 Applications

Variants of this approach have been implemented and evaluated in OptiqueVQS [33], a visual query formulation tool, and SemFacet [2], a faceted search tool. Both interfaces support tree-shaped conjunctive queries.

OptiqueVQS (see Fig. 1) is a visual query system. It allows users to navigate the conceptual space and each traversal from a class to another adds a typed variable-node and object property connecting it to the query graph. OptiqueVQS was deployed and evaluated in different use cases, including Siemens' case for sensor data [32], Statoil's case for oil and gas [33], and on generic datasets [31]. In Fig. 1, there is an example query asking for all trains with a turbine named

"Bearing Assembly" and their journal bearing temperature readings in the associated generator.

SemFacet (see Fig. 2) is full-fledged general-purpose faceted search interface. In typical faceted search, users are presented with facet-values organised in groups according to facet-names and it is often not allowed to navigate between classes. SemFacet allows end users to navigate between classes and browse data sets at the same time. The interface was deployed and evaluated over a slice of Yago database [2]. In Fig. 2 there is an example search for US presidents who graduated from Harvard or Georgetown, and whose children graduated from Stanford. All this conditions are combined conjunctively and their constraints apply simultaneously. One can see that changing the focus of the query, one can either see the presidents (left part of the figure), or their universities (centre part of the figure), or their children (right part of the figure).

4   Related Work

Visualisations for different aspects of the Semantic Web such as ontology visualisation, query formulation, and search are relevant for the work presented here, since they mainly require end users to examine and interact with the elements of a given ontology. However, to best of our knowledge, non of the existing works deal with projecting navigation graphs from ontologies, although the inverse exists such as for ontology axiomatization through diagramming [27].

Among others [10], graph paradigm is often used to depict the structure of ontological elements and relationships as they reflect the interconnected nature of ontology classes. There are various approaches using graphs for ontology visualisation and exploration such as GrOWL [20] and KC-Viz [26]. Similarly, tools for visual query formulation also often use graph paradigm to depict the information needs and domain exploration such as gFacet [8] and NITELIGHT [29]. In a graph based approach, classes are often represented as nodes and properties as edges.

Non-graph based approaches, such as form-based, still use a navigation approach for browsing through ontology classes. Examples include Rhizomer [5], a faceted search tool, and PepeSearch [36], a form-based query formulation tool. Typically, form-based approaches are meant to operate on a single class level; however, as in the case of Rhizomer and PepeSearch, navigation between classes is an essential instrument.

OptiqueVQS and SemFacet represent these two different paradigms, that is graph-based and form-based respectively. In OptiqueVQS, the navigation graph is used to explore domain, while a constrained tree-shaped representation is used for query visualisation instead of a graph for usability purposes, while SemFacet allows navigation between classes and employs form elements rather than graphical visualisations. We refer interested readers to related publications [2,33] on these tools for end user and performance experiments, which present positive evidence for the usefulness of our approach.

5   Conclusions

In this paper, we presented an approach, together with two example applications, for navigating OWL 2 ontologies by projecting them into graphs through harvesting a set of axioms. We consider two major challenges to be addressed for the future work. First challenge is to enable users to navigate distant classes that are not directly connected but are multiple edges away. We call this non-local navigation, which could be useful for navigating large class networks. Second challenge, concerns the information overflow during the query formulation and ontology exploration due to large number of ontology elements; we aim to develop mechanism for adaptively filtering down ontology elements.

Acknowledgements. This work is partially funded by EU H2020 TheyBuyForYou (780247) project. This research is supported by the EPSRC projects MaSI[3], DBOnto, ED[3], and by the SIRIUS Centre, Norwegian Research Council project number 237898.

References

1. Arenas, M., Grau, B.C., Kharlamov, E., Marciuska, S., Zheleznyakov, D.: Faceted search over ontology-enhanced RDF data. In: CIKM, pp. 939–948 (2014)
2. Arenas, M., Grau, B.C., Kharlamov, E., Marciuska, S., Zheleznyakov, D.: Faceted search over RDF-based knowledge graphs. J. Web Semant. **37–38**, 55–74 (2016)
3. Baader, F., Calvanese, D., McGuinness, D.L., Nardi, D., Patel-Schneider, P.F. (eds.): The Description Logic Handbook: Theory, Implementation, and Applications. Cambridge University Press, New York (2003)
4. Biega, J., Kuzey, E., Suchanek, F.M.: Inside YAGO2s: a transparent information extraction architecture. In: Proceedings of the 22nd International Conference on World Wide Web (WWW 2013), pp. 325–328. ACM (2013)
5. Brunetti, J.M., García, R., Auer, S.: From overview to facets and pivoting for interactive exploration of semantic web data. Int. J. Semant. Web Inf. Syst. **9**(1), 1–20 (2013)
6. Grau, B.C., et al.: Towards query formulation, query-driven ontology extensions in OBDA systems. In: Proceedings of the 10th International Workshop on OWL: Experiences and Directions (OWLED 2013), CEUR Workshop Proceedings, vol. 1080. CEUR-WS.org (2013)
7. Grau, B.C., Horrocks, I., Motik, B., Parsia, B., Patel-Schneider, P., Sattler, U.: OWL 2: The next step for OWL. J. Web Semant. **6**(4), 309–322 (2008)
8. Heim, P., Ertl, T., Ziegler, J.: Facet graphs: complex semantic querying made easy. In: Aroyo, L., et al. (eds.) ESWC 2010. LNCS, vol. 6088, pp. 288–302. Springer, Heidelberg (2010). https://doi.org/10.1007/978-3-642-13486-9_20
9. Horrocks, I., Giese, M., Kharlamov, E., Waaler, A.: Using semantic technology to tame the data variety challenge. IEEE Internet Comput. **20**(6), 62–66 (2016)
10. Katifori, A., Halatsis, C., Lepouras, G., Vassilakis, C., Giannopoulou, E.G.: Ontology visualization methods - a survey. ACM Comput. Surv. **39**(4), 10 (2007)
11. Kharlamov, E., et al.: Enabling semantic access to static and streaming distributed data with optique: demo. In: DEBS, pp. 350–353 (2016)
12. Kharlamov, E., et al.: Ontology-based integration of streaming and static relational data with optique. In: SIGMOD, pp. 2109–2112 (2016)

13. Kharlamov, E., Giacomelli, L., Sherkhonov, E., Grau, B.C., Kostylev, E.V., Horrocks, I.: Ranking, aggregation, and reachability in faceted search with semfacet. In: ISWC Posters & Demonstrations (2017)
14. Kharlamov, E.E., et al.: Ontology based access to exploration data at statoil. In: Arenas, M., et al. (eds.) ISWC 2015. LNCS, vol. 9367, pp. 93–112. Springer, Cham (2015). https://doi.org/10.1007/978-3-319-25010-6_6
15. Kharlamov, E., et al.: Ontology based data access in statoil. J. Web Semant. **44**, 3–36 (2017)
16. Kharlamov, E., et al.: Semantic access to streaming and static data at Siemens. J. Web Semant. **44**, 54–74 (2017)
17. Kharlamov, E., et al.: A semantic approach to polystores. In: IEEE BigData, pp. 2565–2573 (2016)
18. Kharlamov, E., et al.: Diagnostics of trains with semantic diagnostics rules. In: Riguzzi, F., Bellodi, E., Zese, R. (eds.) ILP 2018. LNCS (LNAI), vol. 11105, pp. 54–71. Springer, Cham (2018). https://doi.org/10.1007/978-3-319-99960-9_4
19. Kharlamov, E., et al.: Semantic rules for machine diagnostics: execution and management. In: CIKM, pp. 2131–2134 (2017)
20. Krivov, S., Williams, R., Villa, F.: GrOWL: a tool for visualization and editing of OWL ontologies. J. Web Semant. **5**(2), 54–57 (2007)
21. Lee, D., Cornet, R., Lau, F.Y., de Keizer, N.: A survey of SNOMED CT implementations. J. Biomed. Inf. **46**(1), 87–96 (2013)
22. Lehmann, J., et al.: DBpedia - a large-scale, multilingual knowledge base extracted from Wikipedia. Semant. Web **6**(2), 167–195 (2015)
23. Lohmann, S., Negru, S., Haag, F., Ertl, T.: Visualizing ontologies with VOWL. Semant. Web **7**(4), 399–419 (2016)
24. Mehdi, G., et al.: Semantic rule-based equipment diagnostics. In: d'Amato, C., et al. (eds.) ISWC 2017. LNCS, vol. 10588, pp. 314–333. Springer, Cham (2017). https://doi.org/10.1007/978-3-319-68204-4_29
25. Mehdi, G., et al.: SemDia: semantic rule-based equipment diagnostics tool. In: CIKM, pp. 2507–2510 (2017)
26. Motta, E., et al.: A novel approach to visualizing and navigating ontologies. In: Aroyo, L., et al. (eds.) ISWC 2011. LNCS, vol. 7031, pp. 470–486. Springer, Heidelberg (2011). https://doi.org/10.1007/978-3-642-25073-6_30
27. Sarker, M.K., Krisnadhi, A.A., Hitzler, P.: OWLAx: a Protege plugin to support ontology axiomatization through diagramming. In: Proceedings of the Posters & Demonstrations Track co-located with 15th International Semantic Web Conference (ISWC 2016), CEUR Workshop Proceedings, vol. 1690. CEUR-WS.org (2016)
28. Sherkhonov, E., Cuenca Grau, B., Kharlamov, E., Kostylev, E.V.: Semantic faceted search with aggregation and recursion. In: d'Amato, C., et al. (eds.) ISWC 2017. LNCS, vol. 10587, pp. 594–610. Springer, Cham (2017). https://doi.org/10.1007/978-3-319-68288-4_35
29. Smart, P.R., Russell, A., Braines, D., Kalfoglou, Y., Bao, J., Shadbolt, N.R.: A visual approach to semantic query design using a web-based graphical query designer. In: Gangemi, A., Euzenat, J. (eds.) EKAW 2008. LNCS (LNAI), vol. 5268, pp. 275–291. Springer, Heidelberg (2008). https://doi.org/10.1007/978-3-540-87696-0_25
30. Soylu, A., Giese, M., Jiménez-Ruiz, E., Kharlamov, E., Zheleznyakov, D., Horrocks, I.: Ontology-based end-user visual query formulation: why, what, who, how, and which? Univers. Access Inf. Soc. **16**(2), 435–467 (2017)

31. Soylu, A., Giese, M., Jiménez-Ruiz, E., Vega-Gorgojo, G., Horrocks, I.: Experiencing OptiqueVQS: a multi-paradigm and ontology-based visual query system for end users. Univers. Access Inf. Soc. **15**(1), 129–152 (2016)
32. Soylu, A., et al.: Querying industrial stream-temporal data: an ontology-based visual approach. J. Ambient Intell. Smart Environ. **9**(1), 77–95 (2017)
33. Soylu, A., et al.: OptiqueVQS: a visual query system over ontologies for industry. Semant. Web **9**(5), 627–660 (2018)
34. Soylu, A., Mödritscher, F., Causmaecker, P.D.: Ubiquitous web navigation through harvesting embedded semantic data: a mobile scenario. Integr. Comput.-Aided Eng. **19**(1), 93–109 (2012)
35. Suchanek, F.M., Weikum, G.: Knowledge bases in the age of big data analytics. PVLDB **7**(13), 1713–1714 (2014)
36. Vega-Gorgojo, G., Giese, M., Heggestøyl, S., Soylu, A., Waaler, A.: PepeSearch: semantic data for the masses. PLoS One **11**(3), e0151573 (2016)
37. Yan, J., Wang, C., Cheng, W., Gao, M., Zhou, A.: A retrospective of knowledge graphs. Front. Comput. Sci. **12**(1), 55–74 (2018)

Government Open Data
(Special Session Track)

Publication of Statistical Linked Open Data in Japan

Junichi Matsuda[1]([⊠]), Akie Mizutani[1], Yu Asano[1], Dan Yamamoto[1],
Hideaki Takeda[2], Ikki Ohmukai[2], Fumihiro Kato[2], Seiji Koide[3],
Hiromu Harada[4], and Shoki Nishimura[4]

[1] Hitachi, Ltd., Tokyo, Japan
{junichi.matsuda.ru, akie.mizutani.kj,
yu.asano.ko, dan.yamamoto.vx}@hitachi.com
[2] National Institute of Informatics, Tokyo, Japan
{takeda, i2k, fumi}@nii.ac.jp
[3] Ontolonomy, LLC, Tokyo, Japan
koide@ontolonomy.co.jp
[4] National Statistics Center, Tokyo, Japan
{hharada, snishimura}@nstac.go.jp

Abstract. The Japanese Statistics Center began publishing a statistical linked open data (LOD) site in 2016. The data currently consists of approximately 1.3 billion triples. The publication of statistical data as LOD enables datasets and categorizations to be clarified. This allows users not only to search objective data easily, but also to combine the data with other domestic or international data. This paper first introduces a design policy for LOD and a method for representing geographic areas. Then, it explains the method used to query the LOD by using SPARQL or GeoSPARQL, and provides one example application.

Keywords: Statistics · Linked open data · RDF Data Cube Vocabulary
SPARQL · GeoSPARQL

1 Introduction

The Japanese Statistics Bureau and the Japanese National Statistics Center publish approximately 600 kinds of government statistics on a one-stop portal site called e-Stat [1]. The main statistics are published as linked open data (LOD). The LOD site was first published in 2016, and the data is being continually expanded [2]. Publishing the statistical data as LOD allows datasets and categorizations to be clarified. This allows users not only to search objective data easily, but also to combine the data with other domestic or international data.

Nine statistics such as a population census, economic census, and labor force survey are published as LOD. The data consists of approximately 1.3 billion triples, which represent approximately 110 million observations. This is one of the largest collections of statistical LOD in the world [3]. The site also provides an endpoint for SPARQL, which also supports GeoSPARQL [4].

© Springer Nature Switzerland AG 2018
R. Ichise et al. (Eds.): JIST 2018, LNCS 11341, pp. 307–319, 2018.
https://doi.org/10.1007/978-3-030-04284-4_21

The national statistics institutes of Italy, Ireland, Greece, Scotland, and the UK, along with Japan, have begun to provide their statistical data to the public by using linked open data technologies [5–9]. These institutes use the RDF Data Cube Vocabulary [10], which is a World Wide Web (W3C) recommendation standard for the representation of statistical data as LOD. This vocabulary is intended to allow multi-dimensional data to be published in such a way that the data is linked to related data. This contributes to the automation of processes such as filtering, aggregating, and integrating multi-dimensional data.

In this paper, we will introduce the statistical LOD that has been published in Japan. The following section (Sect. 2), introduces the design policy for this LOD, and Sect. 3 describes the methods used to represent geographic areas, which might change as a result of the absorption or abolishment of administrative divisions. The final section (Sect. 4) introduces methods for querying the LOD by using SPARQL and GeoSPARQL, and an example application.

2 Generation of Statistical LOD

Once statistical LOD has been generated, users can easily process data, such as by filtering, aggregating, and integrating the data. This contributes to the advancement of the utilization of statistical data. This section describes a design policy for statistical data in Japan.

The statistical LOD can be generated by converting existing statistical data in a relational database, Excel, or CSV to a resource description framework (RDF). The LOD is connected to other LOD. The RDF represents a target data by using three components (a triple). A triple consists of a subject, a predicate, and an object. For example, the data "The population of Tokyo is 13.5 million" can be represented by a triple whose subject is "Tokyo", whose predicate is "population", and whose object is "13.5 million". In the RDF, concepts such as "Tokyo" and "population" can be represented by using a uniform resource identifier (URI). Even if the data is included in different tables, the data can be linked by using the same URI. By generating statistical LOD, users are able to process statistical data without needing to consider differences in tables or vocabulary.

From the perspective of promoting the utilization of statistical data inside and outside Japan, statistical LOD is generated in accordance with the following basic policy.

(a) Use of International Standards

We use the RDF Data Cube Vocabulary. By using RDF Data Cube Vocabulary, each set of multi-dimensional data is expressed based on the following components.

(A) The dimension and its value (to identify the observation)
(B) The measure (the phenomenon being observed)
(C) The attribute (to qualify and interpret the observed value)

We also give naming rules for URIs. These rules take the following into account.

(1) Uniqueness: Use of own domain (http://data.e-stat.go.jp/) in the URI
(2) Immutableness: Use of establishment year in the URI for changeable items
(3) Consistency: Use of unified naming rules for all items

The following table shows some examples of these naming rules. In each name, parts enclosed in double quotation marks are placeholders and will be replaced, in practice, with an appropriate value. We use "crossDomain" for "Government Statistical Code", which appears in multiple government statistics. The names of some items that will not be revised every survey year, such as gender, do not include the placeholder "Establishment Year" (Table 1).

Table 1. Examples of naming rules for items of statistical LOD

Item	Naming rule and example	
Measures	Naming rule	http://data.e-stat.go.jp/lod/ontology/measure/ "Measure Name"
	Example	http://data.e-stat.go.jp/lod/ontology/measure/population
Dimensions	Naming rule	http://data.e-stat.go.jp/lod/ontology/"Government Statistical Code"/dimension/"Establishment Year"/"Dimension Name"
	Example	http://data.e-stat.go.jp/lod/ontology/g00200521/dimension/2010/familyType
Attributes	Naming rule	http://data.e-stat.go.jp/lod/ontology/attribute/"Attribute Name"
	Example	http://data.e-stat.go.jp/lod/ontology/attribute/unitMeasure
Value of dimension (code)	Naming rule	http://data.e-stat.go.jp/lod/ontology/"Statistics Name"/code/ "Establishment Year"/"Dimension Name"-"Value of Dimension"
	Example	http://data.e-stat.go.jp/lod/ontology/crossDomain/code/sex-male

Figure 1 shows an example expression of an observation of the population of 0-year-old girls in Hokkaido. The dimension gender is defined as "cd-dimension:sex". Other dimensions, measures, values of dimensions, attributes, and values of attributes are defined in the same way. Lines 4 to 9 contain the dimension data, lines 10 and 11 contain the attribute data, and line 13 contains the observation.

(b) Use of Unified Vocabulary

For this statistical LOD, great importance is placed on linkage with external data from other organizations, such as statistics institutes in other countries, Japanese ministries and administrative divisions, and private organizations. Therefore, standard vocabularies are taken into account. This data linkage advances the utilization of the data.

```
1:<http://data.e-stat.go.jp/lod/dataset/populationCensus/d0003041389/
obs6LT45KX3MPJN7AT2WKCMYXDLQCUTIDOJ>
2:    a qb:Observation;
3:    #Dimensions
4:    cd-dimension:age  cd-code:age-0;
5:    cd-dimension:nationality  cd-code:nationality-japan;
6:    sdmx-dimension:refArea  sac:C01000-19700401;
7:    cd-dimension:sex  cd-code:sex-female;
8:    cd-dimension:timePeriod  "2015"^^<http://www.w3.org/2001/XMLSchema#gYear>;
9:    #Attributes
10:   estat-attribute:unitMeasure  estat-attribute-code:unitMeasure-person;
11:   estat-attribute:unitMult  estat-attribute-code:unitMult-0;
12:   #Observation
13:   estat-measure:population " 17102"^^<http://www.w3.org/2001/XMLSchema#decimal>.
```

Fig. 1. RDF expression showing the number of 0-year-old girls in Hokkaido

When a standard vocabulary exists, we use it as-is. When a standard vocabulary does not exist, we define new vocabulary by taking into account linkage with other vocabulary. If a vocabulary is related to other vocabulary, we define the relationships among them. Actually, relationships are defined among the vocabulary used for statistical LOD by the Italian National Institute of Statistics (Istat) [6], the Statistical Data and Metadata Exchange (SDMX) [11], and RDF + SDMX [12]. For example, the above dimension "sex" is linked to three items as shown in Fig. 2. A property, "dcterms:relation", which was originally defined by Dublin Core [13], is used to link corresponding properties. In consideration of linkage with external vocabularies, codes are defined by using the Simple Knowledge Organization System (SKOS) [14]. For linkage among codes, we use "skos:closeMatch". Prefixes such as "skos" and "dcterms" are abbreviations of namespaces, and are listed in Appendix A.

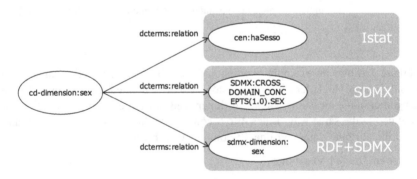

Fig. 2. Linking the dimension "sex" to existing vocabularies

3 Definitions of Geographic Areas Handled in Statistics

3.1 Geographic Areas Handled in Statistics

Each statistical data is related to the following three types of geographic areas [15]:

(1) Administrative divisions

Japanese administrative divisions consist of two layers: prefectural-level divisions and municipal divisions. Most statistical data is organized by administrative division. The entire country is divided into 47 prefectural divisions, and each prefectural division is further divided into municipal divisions. Approximately two thousand municipal divisions exist in Japan.

The Japanese Statistics Bureau has a standardized codelist, the Standard Area Codes for Statistical Use, which enables each division to be uniquely identified. Every code is represented as a five-digit number, where the first two digits identify a specific prefectural division and the remaining three digits represent a specific municipal division located within the prefectural division. For example, Shinjuku Ward in Tokyo is coded as "13104", which consists of Tokyo's code, "13", and Shinjuku Ward's code, "104".

(2) Small areas:

Small areas are subdivisions of a municipal division. Frequently-used statistical data, such as census data, is generated for small areas as well as for administrative divisions. Several codelists, which are defined in each statistics and not standardized, exist to uniquely identify each small area.

(3) Grid squares:

Grid squares are portions of the country which are defined by using a grid of longitudinal and latitudinal lines. Frequently-used statistical data, such as census data, is also generated for grid squares. Table 2 shows three levels of grid squares used in Japanese statistics.

Table 2. Grid squares used in Japanese statistics

Third level grid squares (base level)	Divide Japan into equal parts measuring 2/3 degree of latitude by 1 degree of longitude. Divide one of the parts into 80 equal parts in latitude and longitude directions. Approximately 1 km square, 386,877 grid squares exist for Japan
Fourth level grid squares	Divide third level grid square in half in latitude and longitude directions
Fifth level grid squares	Divide fourth level grid square in half in latitude and longitude directions

3.2   Brief Description of Absorption and Abolishment of Municipal Divisions

The implication of each geographic area, in regard to attributes including city classification and borders, changes with time by passing through events such as: absorption, abolishment, separation, establishment of new municipalities, division into several municipalities, name change, boundary change, and shift to a designated city. Figure 3 shows the case of Kawaguchi-City (standard area code: 11203) as an example of absorption and abolishment of city and district municipalities. The city absorbed the neighboring Hatogaya-City (standard area code: 11226) on October 11, 2011. The implication of "Kawaguchi-City" changed at the time. Specifically, attributes, such as borders, changed.

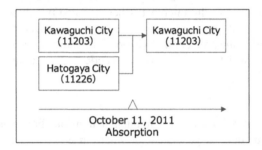

Fig. 3. Example of the absorption and abolishment of municipal divisions

The geographic areas referenced by statistical tables are actually snapshots of areas at a certain point in time or during a finite time period. The population and the number of households of "Kawaguchi-City" are included in both the population censuses in 2010 and 2015. However, "Kawaguchi-City" in 2010 and "Kawaguchi-City" in 2015 are not the same.

Because the above standard area codes themselves do not include the concept of time, they are insufficient to express areas as snapshots. In the example above, using only the code 11203, we cannot distinguish between "Kawaguchi-City" in 2010 and that in 2015 after absorbing "Hatogaya-City." Such an absorption has a big influence on a change of population and the number of households. Therefore, being unable to distinguish between data before and after absorption will pose a problem when we use statistical data.

At first, in view of the above, we defined a system of standard area codes with the notion of time period (hereafter called "temporal standard area codes") to identify an area at a certain period of time by expanding the conventional area codes. The temporal standard area codes are provided by connecting conventional standard area codes and the date when events such as absorption were enforced with a hyphen (-). The temporal standard area code is valid until the next event. In the example above, "Kawaguchi-City" at the time of the population census in 2010 is expressed as 11203-20010401. The city at the time of the population census in 2015, after the admission merger on October 11, 2011, is expressed as 11203-20111011.

To achieve our LOD-enabled statistical data format, we adopted the policy in which we consider the temporal standard area codes as core resources and link them to the relevant information regarding areas (as snapshots) during the period. Each observation in our dataset can refer to the temporal standard area code as a value of dimension such as "sdmx-dimension:refArea".

In addition, we made conventional standard area codes without period (hereafter called "plain standard area codes") LOD-enabled so that the users can use them as pointers to the standard area codes with period. It enables users to refer to each area by one stop without considering period. Plain standard area codes are useful for the users who only know the existing standard area codes to obtain information from our statistical LOD. Figure 4 shows an example of the LOD-enabled temporal standard area codes and plain standard area codes, both of which are described with namespace prefix "sac".

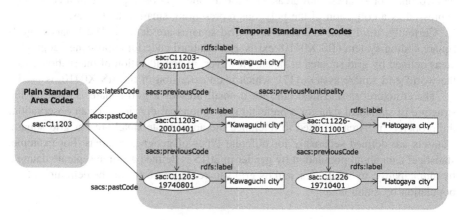

Fig. 4. Example of LOD-enabled temporal standard area code and plain standard area code

3.3 Definition of Small Areas and Grid Squares

Each small area and grid square is defined as a polygon, which represents an area that has a unique code. The polygons are defined according to the standards of the Open Geospatial Consortium (OGC) [16]. The zoning of each small area is determined by the relevant municipalities. Some areas contain smaller areas that belong to different municipal divisions, and some municipal divisions include enclaves that are physically separated from the rest of the division. These areas are represented as follows (Fig. 5).

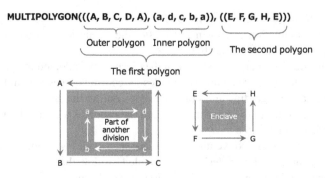

Fig. 5. Definition of polygons

Each municipal division is subdivided into small areas. Therefore, each small area is linked to the corresponding municipality in the LOD. There are two kinds of small areas: smallest-unit areas (individual neighborhoods) and collections of smallest-unit areas (areas of a municipal division that contain multiple neighborhoods). Polygons are defined only for smallest-unit areas, because a collection of smallest-unit areas can be expressed as a collection of the polygons representing smallest-unit areas.

Currently, third level and forth level grid squares are defined. The Japanese grid-square coding system (JIS X0410) exists as a standard code for expressing geographic areas defined by grid squares in Japan. However, in consideration of international use, the world grid square system [17], which is an extension of the JIS X0410, is used.

The structure of statistical data for a small area or a grid square is same as the structure of statistical data for a prefectural or municipal division. For an observation, the property "refArea" is used to reference the appropriate small area or grid square. Datasets are defined separately for different types of geographic areas. For example, statistical data about population by gender in 2015 is defined as three separate datasets by municipality, by small area, and by grid square. Figure 6 shows the definition of the population by small area.

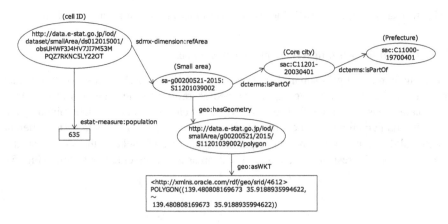

Fig. 6. Example definition of population data by small area

4 Applications

4.1 SPARQL Endpoint

A SPARQL endpoint is provided for accessing the statistical LOD [18]. After some
statistical data has been converted into LOD, users can access data in a batch by
specifying dimensions or measures. Figure 7 is an example of a SPARQL query for
searching data for a combination of two statistics. This query refers to the number of
over 85 years-old and the number of elderly nursing facilities by area. Figure 8 shows a
visual representation of the search results. Tokyo (C13000) has a lower number of
elderly nursing facilities considering the number of elderly people, compared to the
ratios for other prefectures.

```
SELECT  ?area_code ?population ?numberOfFacilities
WHERE {
  ?area_code sacs:administrativeClass sacs:Prefecture .
  ?o1 estat-measure:population ?population ;
      cd-dimension:sex cd-code:sex-all ;
      cd-dimension:age cd-code:age-over85 ;
      sdmx-dimension:refArea ?area_code .
  ?o2 sdmx-measure:obsValue ?numberOfFacilities ;
      cd-dimension:timePeriod "2014"^^xsd:gYear ;
      g00200502-dimension:indicator g00200502-code:indicator-J230121 ;
      sdmx-dimension:refArea ?area_code . }
```

Fig. 7. Example of a SPARQL query

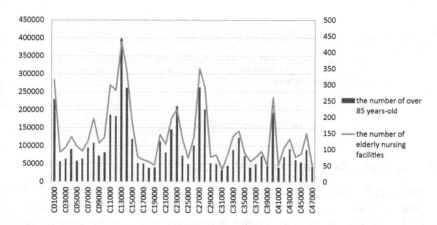

Fig. 8. Example of the visual representation of the results of a SPARQL query

4.2   GeoSPARQL Search

The statistical LOD supports GeoSPARQL for searching geographic data. Although some countries are in the process of preparing geographic data, no other country currently provides endpoints that support GeoSPARQL [19–21].

By using the function provided by GeoSPARQL, SPARQL queries that include latitude and longitude can be used to search geographic areas. Figure 9 shows an example of a query that references the statistical data (such as the area code, survey year, and population) for the geographic area that includes the coordinate 139.48°E, 35.92°N. The results of such a query can be used, for example, to survey the population of an area in order to formulate a plan for opening a shop.

```
select  ?area ?year ?population
where {
       ?s estat-measure:population ?population ;
          cd-dimension:timePeriod ?year ;
          cd-dimension:sex cd-code:sex-all ;
          cd-dimension:age cd-code:age-10-14 ;
          sdmx-dimension:refArea ?area .
       ?area <http://www.opengis.net/ont/geosparql#hasGeometry> ?polygon .
       ?polygon geo:asWKT ?geom .
       FILTER (ogcf:sfContains(?geom, "POINT(139.48 35.92)"^^geo:wktLiteral)) .
}
```

Fig. 9. Example query for searching the population of an area that includes a particular point

Furthermore, users can use a sophisticated function for issuing queries by using extended functions of Oracle databases [22]. For example, the size (area) of a certain geographic area can be calculated based on the polygon data as shown in Fig. 10.

```
select (orageo:area(?geom, "unit=SQ_M") as ?area)
where {
       <http://data.e-stat.go.jp/lod/smallArea/g00200521/2015/S11201039002>
            <http://www.opengis.net/ont/geosparql#hasGeometry> ?polygon .
       ?polygon geo:asWKT ?geom .
}
```

Fig. 10. Example query for calculating area

4.3   An Application that Uses GeoSPARQL

A sample application that uses GeoSPARQL is provided as shown in Fig. 11. Users can filter datasets and dimensions of observations by selecting an area on the map. GeoSPARQL is used to acquire information about the prefectural division, municipal division, small area, and grid square that correspond to the selected area on the map.

Because only small areas and grid squares are currently defined as polygons, the function returns small areas and grid squares as the result, based on the latitude and longitude acquired from the pointer on the map. In the LOD, each small area is linked to the temporal standard area code that includes the small area. Furthermore, each temporal standard area code is linked to the temporal standard area codes of any higher-level geographic areas, such as the municipal or prefectural division. The higher-level geographic areas therefore can be acquired based on a small area.

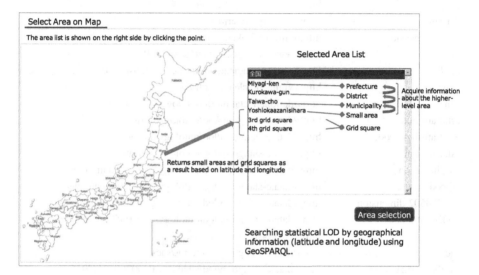

Fig. 11. Illustrative image of an application that shows a list of geographic areas corresponding to a selected location on the map

5   Conclusions

This paper introduces the statistical LOD used in Japan, with a focus on definitions of vocabulary and geographic areas.

In order to promote the utilization of statistics both inside and outside Japan, activities to further unify the vocabulary and the structure used to express statistical data will continue to be important in the future. These activities will improve the ease with which statistical data from multiple countries can be compared, and will increase the number of ways such data can be applied.

Maintenance of geographic data helps with data visualization and with the development of useful applications. We expect that this data will be used to generate new applications in the future.

However, there is also a high possibility that the number of triples will rapidly increase with the introduction of grid squares. Further solutions for quickly searching data and for effectively creating triples will be necessary.

Appendix

A. List of prefixes and namespaces.

Prefix	Namespace
skos	http://www.w3.org/2004/02/skos/core#
rdfs	http://www.w3.org/2000/01/rdf-schema#
xsd	http://www.w3.org/2001/XMLSchema#
qb	http://purl.org/linked-data/cube#
dcterms	http://purl.org/dc/terms/
sdmx-dimension	http://purl.org/linked-data/sdmx/2009/dimension#
geo	http://www.opengis.net/ont/geosparql#
ogcf	http://www.opengis.net/def/function/geosparql/
orageo	http://xmlns.oracle.com/rdf/geo/
cen	http://datiopen.istat.it/odi/ontologia/censimento/
estat-attribute	http://data.e-stat.go.jp/lod/ontology/attribute/
estat-attribute-code	http://data.e-stat.go.jp/lod/ontology/attribute/code/
estat-measure	http://data.e-stat.go.jp/lod/ontology/measure/
cd-dimension	http://data.e-stat.go.jp/lod/ontology/crossDomain/dimension/
cd-code	http://data.e-stat.go.jp/lod/ontology/crossDomain/code/
g00200502-dimension	http://data.e-stat.go.jp/lod/ontology/g00200502/dimension/
g00200502-code	http://data.e-stat.go.jp/lod/ontology/g00200502/code/
sac	http://data.e-stat.go.jp/lod/sac/
sacs	http://data.e-stat.go.jp/lod/terms/sacs#
sa-g00200521-2015	http://data.e-stat.go.jp/lod/smallArea/g00200521/2015/

References

1. Portal Site of Official Statistics of Japan. http://www.e-stat.go.jp/en. Accessed 24 Sept 2018
2. Statistical LOD of Japan. http://data.e-stat.go.jp/lodw/en. Accessed 24 Sept 2018
3. Asano, Y., Takeyoshi, Y., Matsuda, J., Nishimura, S.: Publication of statistical linked open data in Japan. In: 4th International Workshop on Semantic Statistics (2016). http://ceur-ws.org/Vol-1654/article-01.pdf
4. Open Geospatial Consortium: OGC GeoSPARQL - A Geographic Query Language for RDF Data. Version 1.0 (2012). http://www.opengis.net/doc/IS/geosparql/1.0
5. Statistical LOD of the Italian National Institute of Statistics (Istat). http://datiopen.istat.it/index.php?language=eng. Accessed 24 Sept 2018
6. Scotland's official statistics SPARQL endpoint. http://statistics.gov.scot/sparqls. Accessed 24 Sept 2018
7. Central Statistics Office of Ireland SPARQL endpoint. http://data.cso.ie/sparql. Accessed 24 Sept 2018
8. Office for National Statistics in the UK SPARQL endpoint. http://statistics.data.gov.uk/sparql. Accessed 24 Sept 2018

9. Linked Open Statistical Data in Greece SPARQL endpoint. http://linked-statistics.gr/sparql. Accessed 24 Sept 2018
10. Cyganiak, R., Reynolds, D. (eds.): The RDF Data Cube Vocabulary. W3C Recommendation. World Wide Web Consortium, 16 January 2014. http://www.w3.org/TR/vocab-data-cube/. Accessed 24 Sept 2018
11. SDMX Global Registry. https://registry.sdmx.org/. Accessed 24 Sept 2018
12. RDF + SDMX. http://purl.org/linked-data/sdmx/2009/code. Accessed 24 Sept 2018
13. Dublin Core. http://dublincore.org/documents/dcmi-terms/. Accessed 24 Sept 2018
14. Miles, A., Bechhofer, S.: SKOS Simple Knowledge Organization System Namespace Document - HTML Variant. W3C Recommendation, World Wide Web Consortium, 18 August 2009. https://www.w3.org/2009/08/skos-reference/skos.html. Accessed 24 Sept 2018
15. Yamamoto, D., et al.: Geographic area representations in statistical linked open data of Japan. In: 5th International Workshop on Semantic Statistics (2017). http://semstats.org/2017/ceur/ceur-ws/article-09.pdf
16. OpenGIS implementation specification for geographic information - simple feature access - part 1: common architecture (2010). http://www.opengeospatial.org/standards/sfa
17. World grid square codes. https://www.fttsus.jp/worldgrids/en/top-en/. Accessed 24 Sept 2018
18. SPARQL endpoint for accessing the statistical LOD of Japan. https://data.e-stat.go.jp/lod/sparql/. Accessed 24 Sept 2018
19. Cavin, L., Roberts, B.: Open data with statistics.gov.scot. In: Webinar Series Government Linked Data Infrastructures (2018). https://www.dropbox.com/s/ticd89szm0kdvpm/scotland.pdf?dl=0
20. Aracri, R., Corcione, G., Pagano, A., Pizzo, P., Scannapieco, M., Tosco, L.: Highlighting the added-value of Statistical Linked Open Data. In: New Techniques and Technologies for Statistics 2017 (2017). http://nt17.pg2.at/data/abstracts/abstract_110.html
21. Migacz, M.: Investigation of linked open data technologies for purposes of publishing georeferenced statistical data. In: Workshop on Integrating Geospatial and Statistical Standards (2017). https://www.unece.org/fileadmin/DAM/stats/documents/ece/ces/ge.58/2017/mtg3/S3_MIGACZ_MIGACZ_LOD.pdf
22. Oracle Spatial and Graph RDF Semantic Graph Developer's Guide. https://docs.oracle.com/database/121/RDFRM/sem-match-spatial.htm#RDFRM400. Accessed 24 Sept 2018

Building the Core Vocabulary of Crop Names to Integrate the Vocabularies by Multiple Government Agencies

Sungmin Joo[1]([✉]), Hideaki Takeda[1], Akane Takezaki[2], and Tomokazu Yoshida[2]

[1] National Institute of Informatics, 2-1-2 Hitotsubashi, Chiyoda-ku, Tokyo, Japan
{joo,takeda}@nii.ac.jp
[2] National Agriculture and Food Research Organization, 1-31-1, Kannondai,
Tsukuba, Ibaraki, Japan
{akane,jones}@affrc.go.jp

Abstract. Since agriculture is the oldest industry in our society and the basis of our life and economics, knowledge of crops as product of agriculture is also old and spread all over the society. As a result, the names of crops are messy and sometimes inconsistent. It is problematic in the digital and Internet era since interoperability is not assured. In this paper, we proposes Crop Vocabulary (CVO) as the core vocabulary of crop names to solve interoperability and machine-readability on crop names. There are many vocabularies about crops by various food chain stakeholders. Here we picked up three vocabularies issued by Japanese government with respect to food security, namely the Agricultural chemical use reference, the Agricultural chemical residue reference, and the Food composition database, since food security is the primary concern of all food chain stakeholders including farmers and consumers. As the result of comparative analysis of these vocabularies, we defined the concept of crop as the botanical information such as the scientific name of species with additional information such as edible parts, cultivation methods and usage. According to the definition, we investigated these three vocabularies and identified 1,249 crops with unique names. The element of CVO contains the information about the crop itself such as synonym, English name and scientific name as well as links to names in the above-mentioned vocabularies and other external vocabularies such as Wikipedia, AGROVOC and NCBI Taxonomy. We develop web-based API for CVO and an application for the farm management as an example. The value of CVO as a core vocabulary in the field of agriculture is identified by compatibility with existing vocabularies and its usefulness is demonstrated by web services applications developed based on CVO.

Keywords: Crop vocabulary · Agriculture · Open data
Agronomic sciences · Knowledge representation · Core vocabulary
Vocabulary management

© Springer Nature Switzerland AG 2018
R. Ichise et al. (Eds.): JIST 2018, LNCS 11341, pp. 320–335, 2018.
https://doi.org/10.1007/978-3-030-04284-4_22

1   Introduction

Recently, the dissemination of ICT-based systems in agriculture has contributed greatly to the automation of production and distribution of agricultural products. The deployment of sensor networks and farm management systems enables the automation of crop cultivation and harvest as well as data analysis to forecast production and the decision of plans. It is not only applicable for the production phase but also for distribution and sales phases. The utilization of management systems enables more accurate inventory management and forecasting of demand based on data. So far diverse ICT systems are introduced at each step of the food chain from the production site to the consumers.

Although crops are primary elements of the food chain, there is a serious diversity of names of crops. For example, the names of crops may differ among regions, cultivation method or edible parts in the harvesting phase. The stakeholders of the food chain often use their own names for crops according to their interest on crops. Some are interested in crops for harvesting, some for distribution, some for food safety, and so on. Every stakeholder may have their own standard for naming crops. Then ICT systems introduced into individual steps of the food chain may use different standards. It makes information sharing among systems difficult, i.e., the consistent management of information on crops in the food chain is far to reach because of lack of the standard of crop names throughout the food chain. For example, traceability of food is of interest in the society because of social demand. But it is not easy without such a standard for crop names.

In this paper, we analyze the existing vocabularies issued by the Japanese government agencies to manage crops and propose the Crop Vocabulary (CVO), a core vocabulary of crop names with a logical structure compatible with the those of individual vocabularies. Its value as a core vocabulary in the field of agriculture is identified by compatibility with existing vocabularies and its usefulness is demonstrated by web services applications developed based on CVO. Finally, we discuss the future direction of improvement of the vocabulary and international interoperability.

2   Existing Vocabularies in the Field of Agriculture in Japan

The government has different interests on the agriculture, e.g., as the domestic economic sector, as land preservation, as regional development. One of the top interests for agriculture by the Government is safety of food that is directly related to people's health problems. For the sake, the Government has long been established regulations and standards to keep produced crops safe and secure. It should be noted that keeping crops safe and secure is not realized by the regulations and standards in the production of crops, Rather other phases like distribution, processing and consumption of crops should be also taken into account. The main competent administrative agency for agriculture in Japan is the Ministry of Agriculture, Forestry and Fisheries (MAFF). But the health issue is under the jurisdiction of the Ministry of Health, Labor and Welfare (MHLW). On the other hand, the scientific knowledge for nutrition is provided by he Ministry of Education, Culture, Sports, Science and Technology (MEXT). There are more agencies to commit crop issues, e.g., the Custom under Ministry of Finance controls regulation and statistics of crop import and export. We picked up and examined the standards by the former three agencies because they are closely related to crop safety and security. The points for examination is (1) how crops are identified, (2) how the structure is like, and (3) how much it is machine-readable.

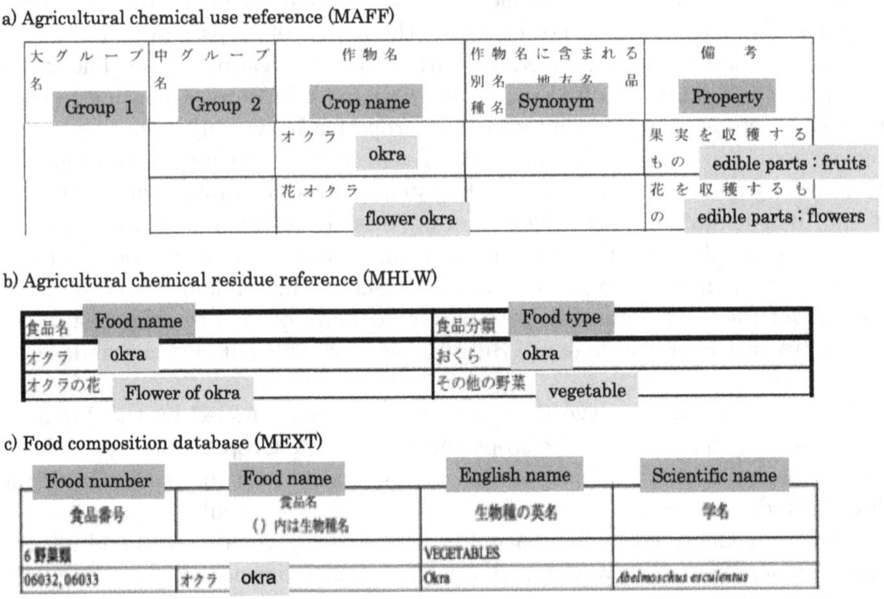

a) Agricultural chemical use reference (MAFF)

大グループ名 Group 1	中グループ名 Group 2	作物名 Crop name	作物名に含まれる別名 地方名 品種名 Synonym	備考 Property
		オクラ okra		果実を収穫するもの edible parts : fruits
		花オクラ flower okra		花を収穫するもの edible parts : flowers

b) Agricultural chemical residue reference (MHLW)

食品名 Food name		食品分類 Food type	
オクラ okra		おくら okra	
オクラの花 Flower of okra		その他の野菜 vegetable	

c) Food composition database (MEXT)

Food number 食品番号	Food name 食品名 ()内は生物種名	English name 生物種の英名	Scientific name 学名
6 野菜類		VEGETABLES	
06032, 06033	オクラ okra	Okra	*Abelmoschus esculentus*

Fig. 1. Three vocabularies in the field of agriculture in Japan.

2.1 Existing Vocabularies

As mentioned above, we picked up three major agricultural vocabularies issued by government agencies in Japan. These three vocabularies were issued by different departments for the purpose of managing agricultural chemicals, safety, and nutrition, respectively.

Agricultural Chemical Use Reference. The Agricultural chemical use reference [1] (hereinafter called ACUR) is a vocabulary containing the crops for which agricultural chemicals should be registered, which is issued by the Ministry of Agriculture, Forestry and Fisheries(MAFF). It contains are 893 crops and each crop has two group names, related names and information on notes. It should be noted that a crop is not identical to a botanical species. For example, *okra* and *flower okra* that are botanically the same crop have different names according to the edible parts (Fig. 1-a). It is issued in a PDF format and can be downloaded from the Ministry of Agriculture, Forestry and Fisheries website[1]. ACUR, which contains information on agricultural chemicals, is at the most important position for the production of crops and is also a vocabulary that is often referred to in the preparation of related materials.

Agricultural Chemical Residue Reference. The Agricultural chemical residue reference [2] (hereinafter called ACRR) is a vocabulary issued by the Ministry of Health, Labor and Welfare(MHLW) and contains information on the standard for agricultural chemical residues. Its information entry items include the names and categories of foods and the latest version contains 1,179 crops. As with the Agricultural chemical use reference, crops are divided into edible parts and the names and categories are often different from each other as with the examples shown in Fig. 1-b. It is issued in a PDF format and can be downloaded from the Ministry of Health, Labor and Welfare website[2].

Food Composition Database. The Food composition database [3] (hereinafter called FCD) is a vocabulary issued by the Ministry of Education, Culture, Sports, Science and Technology(MEXT). It is a document that defines food compositions for the health and nutrition management of the people. Cooking methods and nutrients according to edible parts can be identified through unique food numbers and the names of the crops are contained collectively in a separate table. A total of 625 crop names are contained along with their food numbers, English names and scientific names (Fig. 1-c). It can be downloaded from the Ministry of Education website[3] and is published in an Excel format.

2.2 Problems with Existing Vocabularies

The existing vocabularies described in the previous section have some problems to be solved for use in ICT systems. These problems should be improved for the vocabularies to be used as data as they are obstructive factors against system utilization and interoperability.

Consistency of Names. Because the three vocabularies were prepared by different issuing institutions for different purposes, there are names with different expressions for the same crops in some cases. For instance, the roots of wasabi

---

[1] http://www.maff.go.jp.

[2] https://www.mhlw.go.jp.

[3] http://www.mext.go.jp.

are listed as *wasabi (root)* in ACUR and as *roots of wasabi* in ACRR. The flower of okra used as food is written as *flower okra* in ACUR and as *flower of okra* in ACRR. On the other hand, the food composition databases contains only *wasabi* and *okra*, respectively. Since this problem is an obstacle to data sharing among ICT systems, the corresponding relations of individual crops should be defined to control the names so that they can be treated as the same crops for the interoperability of the food chain.

Definition with Cultivation Methods. In the case of some crops in the existing vocabularies, the cultivation methods have been included in naming them. For example, ACUR and ACRR use the cultivation method for *wasabi* as water culture. However, since *wasabi* is sometimes cultivated in the field, it is difficult to identify in the field whether the agricultural chemicals should be applied identically to water culture in such cases. Since it is an issue considered sensitively by farmers as it is related to agricultural chemicals, the names of crops with cultivation environments should be considered seriously to prevent ambiguous applications.

Inclusion of Cultivar Names. In Japan, cultivar names are often used as crop names. Since cultivar names are not contained in the existing vocabularies in many cases, it is difficult to grasp relations with other crops. In such cases, the relations should be inferable using information on botanical classification but the existing vocabularies do not contain such information. Therefore, responses for cultivar names are necessary.

2.3   Evaluation as Open Data

The Japanese government has pursued the Electronic administration open data strategy from 2012 in order to improve credibility, promote public participation and activate the economy and administration, and established the following basic principles [4].

- The government should disclose public data actively.
- Disclose the public data in machine-readable forms.
- Promote utilization of public data both for for-profit and for non-profit.
- Increase the achievements steadily by starting with pubic data that can be disclosed easily.

  This policy adopts the basic principles of free use of public data and machine-readability, and targets the data owned by the government[4]. It also includes the purpose of promoting the development of statistics or related services by distributing the data in machine-readable forms and allowing secondary processing.
  The existing vocabularies in the field of agriculture mentioned in the previous section are also subject to the Japanese government's open data strategy. They

---

[4] Excluding some safety assurance related information.

are already accessible by anyone through the Internet, i.e., they can be downloadable from the sites of the agencies. However, the data now available have a lot of drawbacks as open data. First, ACUR and ACRR are issued in the form of PDF so that they are hardly machine-processable. It is simply not because they are PDF rather than the structured form like Excel or CSV, but also the structure inside is designed just for human so that it is very difficult to extract information about individual entries in these vocabularies. In the case of ACUR, since the names and meanings of the entities are dependent on their hierarchical structure, interpretation of any part of the data should be done with data about their upper classification. Although FCD is distributed in an Excel format, since the number of rows containing information varies depending on crops, manual corrections are necessary eventually. Thus the machine-readability of these vocabularies are quite low so that each vocabulary should be processed again if ICT systems may use them. The situation is not only unfit with the basic principles of the policies related to open data promoted by the Japanese government, but also it is an obstacle to disseminate ICT-based technologies rapidly in the field of agriculture.

2.4   Discussion

Currently two of the vocabularies are not distributed in the machine-readable form. They should of course be provided in the machine-readable form. But it is not enough. The above three vocabularies have two major problems as those for agricultural ICT systems besides simple machine-readability. One is lack of interoperability among them and the other is opaqueness of their structures. The former means that there are no clear rules for sharing names of crops either because of notation rules or conceptulization for crops. We need sharing of crops names under the clear notation rules and conceptulization for crop. The latter means that the opaque structures are obstructive against data sharing among ICT systems. Opaque structures yield uncertainty in the transfer of meanings of vocabularies one to the other, i.e., interoperability among the structured vocabularies is decreased seriously.

It should be noted that the individual vocabularies were constructed based on their purposes so that it is not an appropriate way to integrate different expressions for the same crop into one and remove other expressions. The semantic relations should be defined in such cases. Corresponding names should be organized to treat them as synonyms and vocabulary systems should be constructed in the structure where related information items are linked in order to enable consistent information processing in the individual systems.

The existing vocabularies are not provided as open data in distribution. We had meetings with persons in charge in various departments that provide vocabularies, but most of them lacked understanding of open data and structuring of data. In addition, there are many fields where the existing vocabularies are applied. If the data structures of the existing vocabularies are changed into machine-readable structures, the guidance of relevant institutions and local organizations will become necessary so that considerable time and efforts will be necessary until the entire data structures are changed. Therefore, we realized that we need data that processed the existing vocabularies in a form that conform to the conditions of open data as an alternative.

3   Crop Vocabulary (CVO): A Core Vocabulary of Crop Names for Interoperability

In the previous chapters, we examined the problems of the existing vocabularies with respect to the interoperability for ICT systems and open data. Therefore, in this study, we set the following tasks as the specifications for core vocabulary of crops.

- Machine-readable data structure
- Compatibility with existing vocabularies
- Making existing vocabularies into open data.

We propose CVO as a core vocabulary that conforms to the above specifications.

3.1   The Structuralization of Crops

First, we collected the names of crops used in the cultivation and distribution phases of crops in Japan. The main sources are the above-mentioned three vocabularies. Crops there are mostly distinguished in the species level. But ACUR and ACRR contain crops that are categorized as cultivar. Some fruit trees are only described as cultivar names since there are many interspecific hybrids. We decided to separate cultivars from crops in order to clarify the concept of crop. As a result, ACUR, ACRR, FCD contain 893,1179, 625 names of crops respectively. On the other hand, we collected 30,202 cultivar names including hybrids separately. We also investigated the crop names and their usage in various situations through interviews with key players in the food chain such as farmers, the agricultural chemical association, distribution management organizations and JA (Japan Agricultural cooperatives). Finally we fixed the characteristics of individual crops to collected terms and to define the names of crops.

We defined the concept of crops as follows;

1. A crop is basically identified as a species.
2. A crop is sometimes identified with modifier(s). A modifier is either edible part, cultivation method or usage.
3. A crop with modifier(s) has ISA relationship to the crop without modifiers that share the same species.

Basic Information of Crops. Crops are primarily identified as a species. So far, a crop concept provides a representative name (Katakana in Japanese) and synonyms including name variations by Hiragana and Kanji characters as well as a scientific name and its common name in Japanese, and its common name in English.

Definition by Edible Part. Although crops are generally identified by their species, some names also refer to their parts. For example, in the case of *okra*, ACUR indicates *edible parts: fruits* in its reference so that *okra* means the fruit of okra. In the other land, *flower okra* is provided separately to denote harvesting flowers as a different crop from the *okra* as a fruit. Interestingly *flower okra* is labeled as *flower of okra* in ACRR so that they can be recognized as different crops. Meanwhile, FCD defines *okra* as a food regardless of edible parts. In this case, okra should be defined based on edible parts and the relationship with okra as a species of plants should be also defined. Therefore, in our approach, the name of crops related to the edible parts is denoted as *crop name (edible part)*. *Flower okra* and *flower of okra* in ACUR and ACCR are now unified and denoted as *okra (flower)*. Names in the existing vocabularies are described as synonyms to secure compatibility.

Definition by Cultivation Methods. There are cases where crops, which are the same species botanically, become different crops because of cultivation methods. *Wasabi* is the name of species (Eutrema japonicum) generally but in some vocabularies, *wasabi* means a crop harvested using water culture since it is the major cultivation method. Then the problem arises because the wasabi cultivated in the field is excluded and no names for it. Therefore, in our approach, the crop names are defined as *water-grown wasabi* and *farm-grown wasabi*. In addition, since diverse parts of *wasabi* such as roots, leaves and stems are used, *water-grown wasabi* and *farm-grown wasabi* are respectively divided further by classification based on edible parts.

Definition by Usage. Since some crops should be applied with different agricultural chemicals, cultivation methods and distribution methods according to their uses, they should be defined by use. For example, *flax* is classified into that for food and that for fibers and *sorghum* is classified into that for feed and that for food to have different crop names.

Hierarchical Structure of Crops. In our approach, we use modifiers such as edible parts, cultivation methods and usage to define the names of crops. Since crops are processed and managed as food after harvest, they need to be associated with generic names. Therefore, crop names of upper concepts are necessary and these crop names should be generic names. Therefore, we provide generic names for crops wherever crops with modifiers are defined. For example, *okra(fruit)* and *okra(flower)* are narrower concepts of *okra* as a generic name. In addition, the upper concept of *water-grown wasabi* and *farm-grown wasabi* is the generic name *wasabi*. The introduction of generic names as such is useful for integration with media that address general information on crops or external resources that use botanical information.

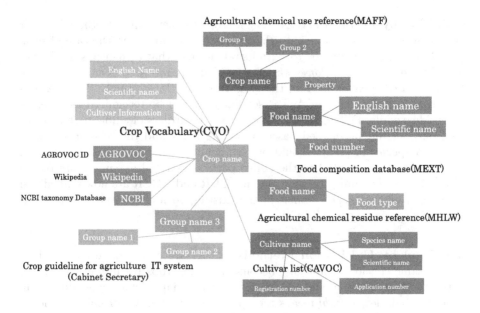

Fig. 2. Interoperability between CVO and vocabularies.

3.2 The Basic Structure of CVO

By the above policy, we built a vocabulary called CVO. CVO was built on the basis of the three vocabularies (ACUR, ACCR, and FCD) issued by the government agencies in Japan. It contains 1,249 unique crop concepts and each crop concept describes its names, information as species, and hierarchical relationship to others. Since the interoperability of crop names is the primary mission for CVO, we also includes links to names in various vocabularies. As analyzed in Chap. 2, ACUR, ACCR and FCO are not available machine-readable online resources. We also rebuilt them as online resources separately and link the corresponding names between CVO and them. As mentioned in Chap. 3, Cultivars are separated from crop but they are important in particular for agriculture chemical usage. We built the Cultivar Database separately and made links between cultivars and crops in CVO.

In addition, there are diverse resources related to crops and foods both at home and abroad. Integration with these resources enables securing interoperability between systems along with international interoperability and the utilization of diverse information. First, we investigated and linked from CVO to Wikipedia and the Names of crops in the Crop guideline for agriculture IT system issued by the Cabinet Secretary, Japan. Representative international resources related to crops include AGROVOC(a portmanteau of agriculture and vocabulary)[5] and the Taxonomy database of NCBI[6]. We found the relations with crop

---

[5] http://aims.fao.org/vest-registry/vocabularies/agrovoc.
[6] https://www.ncbi.nlm.nih.gov/taxonomy.

names in CVO to use AGROVOC items and IDs in taxonomy database. Since the resources in these vocabularies are mostly species, we linked them to the generic names of crops. But we also add these links to the lower crops (crops with modifiers) for convenience (Fig. 2).

4 Web Services Based on CVO

CVO is hosted on CAVOC (Common Agricultural VOCabulary)[7], and it is publicly available along with the existing vocabularies about crops. This chapter describes data available with CVO and Web services and applications based on CVO.

4.1 Namespace of Crop Name

CAVOC allows browsing and searching crop names in CVO. A crop name has a unique URI with the defined namespace for CVO. Each URI is structured in the form of http://cavoc.org/cvo/ns/1/namespace and crops with modifiers are expressed in a hierarchical structure. Figure 3 is an example of the URL of *okra(fruit)*. The crop name, species name, English name, synonym, scientific name and hierarchy are indicated as basic information of the crop. There are links to the existing vocabularies and external information resources. The window on the right shows a list of crops included in CVO for browsing. Each URI has data written in Turtle so that Turtle is output when URI is accessed with ttl extension. This format provides convenience both for people and for systems to get information from one URI.

In addition, it also provides URIs in the same form for existing vocabularies in ACUR, ACRR, FCD and the Crop guideline for agriculture IT system. Figure 4 is an example of *okra* which is contained in ACUR. The crop name, group name and basic information on properties, which are information items of this vocabulary and a link to the corresponding item of CVO are indicated. Again, Turtle type data are also supported. This improves the machine-readability of these vocabularies, i.e., the system can use the information of each vocabulary through linking between the URIs in each vocabulary and those in CVO,

Although the URIs provided by CAVOC includes Japanese characters in their components, information associated to them can be shown in English. So CVO is usable as a crop vocabulary in English. Since the vocabularies issued Japanese government agencies do not support English, the English page of the CVO only displays only the links to the information of AGROVOC and NCBI which are serving in English as outgoing links.

4.2 Version History

Based on the above design policy, we have built CVO that is the core vocabulary of crops. CVO is now available at CAVOC. On October 19, 2017, a public version containing 1,188 items was released. The latest version, 1.52, contains 1,249

---

[7] http://www.cavoc.org.

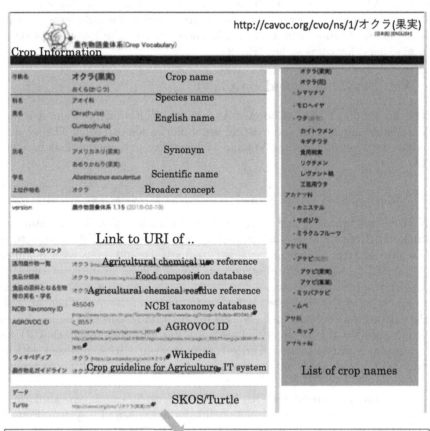

Fig. 3. The namespace of *okra(fruit)* of CVO.

Fig. 4. The namespace of *okra* of Agricultural chemical use reference.

items. The addition of crop names and the checking of the identifying of contained crops have been continued. The update history to date is shown in Table 1. CVO data and the existing vocabularies are provided in machine-readable forms and related services and applications are also provided. The content of the foregoing is described in the next chapter.

4.3 Data Sharing

CAVOC provides namespaces for CVO and the existing vocabularies, and each namespace provides data for the relevant items in Turtle formats. In addition, data on all items are provided in Turtle and CSV formats[8]. The structures of the existing vocabularies were converted to make it easier for system vendors to utilize and different character codes were unified into UTF-8 to help the data analysis and system development in the agricultural field.

---

[8] Excluding the Crop guideline for agriculture IT system by the Cabinet Secretary, Japan.

Table 1. Listing of the history of CVO version changes

Version	Date initiated	Terms
1.52	2018-05-02	1,249
1.15	2018-02-19	1,191
1.12	2018-01-10	1,191
1.05	2017-11-16	1,187
1.00	2017-10-19	1,188
0.91	2017-09-14	1,198

4.4 APIs

Because CVO defines the relationship with other vocabularies, it can be used as a mapping table. Through CVO, information of the vocabularies can be used in an integrated way, i.e., vocabulary translation from one to another is easily realized with CVO. CAVOC provides an API for vocabulary translation and information retrieval so that any system can use it. For example, one can start from a crop name in ACUR and obtain the corresponding crop names in CVO, then obtain the scientific name and the English name in CVO, and further obtain the corresponding crop name in FCD.

4.5 Applications

The food supply chains consist of various steps and stakeholders like crop production, food processing and retail so that sharing of data maintained at steps of the chains is preferable but difficult because of lack of common standards for data [6]. Suppose that a new farmer is choosing crops for the next season. The analysis of data about agricultural products throughout the food systems may be useful to choose best crops with respect to crop productivity and profitability, but it is not easy for them to obtain such data.

We developed the crop reference tool for MAFF vegetable statistics using CVO as a standard vocabulary. MAFF has performed various kinds of surveys on agricultural products at different steps of the food chain to provide information for planning, and evaluation of agricultural policy [7]. The main data sources in the tool are "Statistics on production and shipment of vegetable", "Statistical survey on farm management and economy" and "Statistical survey on prices in agriculture" published by MAFF. In the tool, since crops in these statistics are aligned to crops in CVO and data from the statistics are integrated, users can easily access the integrated information for the individual crops by selecting crop names. Figure 5 shows statistical surveys on *welsh onion*, and vegetables to represent its narrower meaning such as *green onion, white onion, welsh onion harvested in summer* and *welsh onion harvested in spring*. This integrated information helps new farmers to assume economic activity, necessary resources and production when *welsh onion* is cultivated.

Step 1) Select CVO crop name

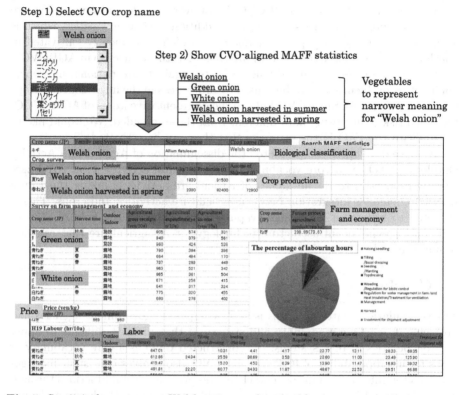

Fig. 5. Statistical surveys on *Welsh onion*, and vegetables to represent its narrower meaning in crop reference tool.

5 Discussion and Future Work

While constructing CVO, we investigated the relationships between diverse crop names. In the course of the investigation, we found that various crop names, cultivar names and local cultivar names are used together without distinction and also found that some crops with different names are the same crops indeed. Furthermore cultivation methods associated to crop names are sometimes different among regions. These problems are obstructive factors against consistent management of the food chains. So we have basically solved these problems by defining CVO, but we understand that there are still more diversity of information depending on expertise and localities, which is not covered by CVO. We will continue the work by revising the contents through opinion exchanges with experts.

This study targets the vocabularies used in the agricultural field in Japan. Therefore, CVO was built by focusing on crops mainly grown in Japan, and some crop names are not compatible with international vocabularies such as AGROVOC. For example, *wasabi*, one of the representative crops cultivated in Japan, is a crop different from *horseradish* and is harvested through a different cultivation processes. In AGROVOC, however, *wasabi* and *horseradish* are treated as synonyms of the same crop. In addition, although *Perilla*[9], which is a representative crop of Japan and *Egoma*[10], which is frequently cultivated in South Korea, are different crops, they are treated as the same crop in AGROVOC so that they may become an obstructive factor against international interoperability. This problem seems to be caused by differences in the importance of crops in different countries. Since CVO links to the representative items of AGROVOC, there is a risk of acquiring data different from those intended. We would like to discuss with the FAO in the future so that they can be corrected.

We have developed and promoted the dissemination of Agricultural Activity Ontology (AAO) as a core vocabulary of agricultural activity [8,9]. AAO uses *crop* as properties to define names of agriculture activity. Linking the values with CVO enables integration between agriculture activities and crops. This is expected to become a knowledge graph that is a base of the field of agriculture and become an infrastructure technology for AI agriculture that can link comprehensively.

6   Conclusion

The vocabularies related to crops issued by Japanese government agencies had problems in machine-readability and structures that make it difficult to apply the vocabularies to ICT systems. We constructed CVO as a core vocabulary of crops for interoperability of ICT systems. CVO also enables consistent management of crop information in the food chain and provides useful functions through links to external information media. In addition, we have developed and published the existing vocabularies for crop names as machine-readable formats to encourage the government to publish them as open and structured data such as linked data. We believe that the work contributes to establish the infrastructure for automation of Japanese agriculture and AI agriculture where standards in different steps in the food chain are seamlessly used through the core vocabulary.

Acknowledgement. This work was supported by Council for Science, Technology and Innovation (CSTI), Cross-ministerial Strategic Innovation Promotion Program (SIP), "Technologies for creating next-generation agriculture, forestry and fisheries" (funding agency: Bio-oriented Technology Research Advancement Institution, NARO).

References

1. Ministry of Agriculture, Forestry and Fisheries (MAFF), Japan: Agricultural chemical use reference. https://www.acis.famic.go.jp/shinsei/3986/3986beppyou1.pdf. Accessed 20 July 2018. (in japanese)
2. Ministry of Health, Labor and Welfare (MHLW), Japan: Agricultural chemical residue reference. http://www.mhlw.go.jp/file/06-Seisakujouhou-11130500-Shokuhinanzenbu/0000159254.pdf. Accessed 20 July 2018. (in japanese)

---

[9] Scientific name: Perilla frutescens (var. crispa).
[10] Scientific name: Perilla frutescens (var. frutescens).

3. Ministry of Education, Culture, Sports, Science and Technology (MEXT), Japan: Food composition database. http://www.mext.go.jp/component/a_menu/science/detail/__icsFiles/afieldfile/2017/06/22/1365334-1-0321r2.xlsx. Accessed 20 July 2018. (in japanese)
4. Ministry of Internal Affairs and Communications (MIC), Japan: Electronic administration open data strategy. http://www.kantei.go.jp/jp/singi/it2/pdf/120704_siryou2.pdf. Accessed 20 July 2018. (in japanese)
5. Cabinet Secretariat, Japan: Crop guideline for agriculture IT system. http://www.kantei.go.jp/jp/singi/it2/senmon_bunka/shiryo/170310gl1_besshi.xlsx. Accessed 20 July 2018. (in japanese)
6. Verhoosel, J., van Bekkum, M., Verwaart, T.: Semantic interoperability for data analysis in the food supply chain. Int. J. Food Syst. Dyn. 9(1), 101–111 (2018)
7. Ministry of Internal Affairs and Communications (MIC), Japan: Statistics Bureau. http://www.stat.go.jp/english/data/nenkan/1431-08e.html. Accessed 20 July 2018
8. Joo, S., Koide, S., Takeda, H., Horyu, D., Takezaki, A., Yoshida, T.: Agriculture activity ontology: an ontology for core vocabulary of agriculture activity. In: International Semantic Web Conference (Posters & Demos) (2016)
9. Joo, S., Koide, S., Takeda, H., Horyu, D., Takezaki, A., Yoshida, T.: Designing of ontology for domain vocabulary on agriculture activity ontology (AAO) and a lesson learned. In: Li, Y.-F., et al. (eds.) JIST 2016. LNCS, vol. 10055, pp. 32–46. Springer, Cham (2016). https://doi.org/10.1007/978-3-319-50112-3_3

IMI: A Common Vocabulary Framework for Open Government Data

Fumihiro Kato[1]([⊠])[iD], Hideaki Takeda[1][iD], Shuichi Tashiro[2], Kenji Hiramoto[3], and Yuzo Matsuzawa[4]

[1] National Institute of Informatics, Tokyo, Japan
{fumi,takeda}@nii.ac.jp
[2] Information-technology Promotion Agency, Tokyo, Japan
tashiro@ipa.go.jp
[3] Ministry of Economy, Trade and Industry, Tokyo, Japan
hiramoto-kenji@meti.go.jp
[4] Indigo, Tokyo, Japan
yuzo@indigo.co.jp
http://www.nii.ac.jp

Abstract. Making meanings of terms used in government systems exchangeable is important to enhance semantic interoperability between systems and promote use of open government data. IMI is an interoperability framework for digital government and open government data in Japan. The IMI common vocabulary framework which is a part of IMI since 2013 aims to provide a mechanism for sharing meanings of terms and relationships between terms to enhance interoperability. This paper describes the current status of the IMI common vocabulary framework to share our experiences and knowledge from the development in five years. At first we illustrate the IMI common vocabulary and its core vocabulary which includes a basic set of terms used in data or referred from existing data to share meanings. Then we describe specifications of components in the common vocabulary framework like data exchange formats, notations and a package system. As the IMI common vocabulary has been already used in various areas, we also introduce its deployment support and real use cases of the common vocabulary framework.

Keywords: Semantic interoperability · Common vocabulary
Open government data · Linked Open Data

1 Introduction

In May 2017, the Japanese government published the new Japan's IT strategy plan titled "Declaration to Be the Most Advanced IT Nation Basic Plan for the Advancement of Public and Private Sector Data Utilization" [1] under the "Basic Act on the Advancement of Public and Private Sector Data Utilization" enacted in December 2016. The purpose of this plan is to promote smooth data distribution beyond data owners in order to create new services and innovation

© Springer Nature Switzerland AG 2018
R. Ichise et al. (Eds.): JIST 2018, LNCS 11341, pp. 336–351, 2018.
https://doi.org/10.1007/978-3-030-04284-4_23

and reform administration and industry based on data. Publishing open data by local public entities was arbitrary before the basic act. However, according to the basic act and plan, government agencies and prefectural governments must publish their data openly to promote the utilization.

Data standardization is a key to promote open data and its utilization. Data standardization means not only data format but also vocabulary, code, characters and so on. If they are not interchangeable, the interpretation of contents of data will be different. For instance, if "101-8430" is in the "tel" column of a CSV file, a user can guess that it is a telephone number but a system needs a dictionary to understand the relationship between "telephone number" and "tel" explicitly. Another dataset may have "101-8430" in the "contact" column. Then can a user think it is a telephone number, too? Actually "101-8430" is also a valid postal code so that a system needs to know the meaning of the "contact" in the dataset and relationships with other terms. Such reference dictionary is needed to share vocabulary to represent data in the same format.

The IMI (Infrastructure for Multilayer Interoperability) [2] is a part of the government's action plan for the development of an open usage environment in the electronic administration field to share and utilize information by standardizing characters and terms used in data. IMI consists of a common vocabulary framework which is a mechanism for sharing the vocabulary commonly used for datasets and a character information infrastructure which is a mechanism for handling characters requiring administration. This paper describes the common vocabulary framework that has been developed since 2013.

2   Common Vocabulary

A common vocabulary forms the heart of the IMI common vocabulary framework. It is a set of terms which are representative notations of shared concepts in Japanese. A shared concept is either a class concept or a property concept and has a structure to denote a meaning. Representing words in documents and labels in datasets as shared concepts increases data and communication interoperability among Japanese government systems.

NIEM (National Information Exchange Model) [4] (Sect. 7) in the United States is one of our reference models to develop the IMI common vocabulary framework. We have learned from NIEM that there are two types of common vocabulary: core and domain. The core vocabulary is a set of terms used across domains such as person, name and organization. Both the NIEM and the IMI common vocabulary framework maintain the core vocabulary by top down.

A domain vocabulary is a set of terms that are commonly used within each field like finance or environment. A domain vocabulary inherits the core vocabulary to define terms in the domain. NIEM has a formal process to create and manage a domain vocabulary. All NIEM domains are led by a domain steward which is responsible for the domain's model content, governance and maintenance. On the other hand, a domain vocabulary does not exist in the IMI common vocabulary framework yet as it is difficult to formalize the process to make a domain vocabulary available in the Japanese government.

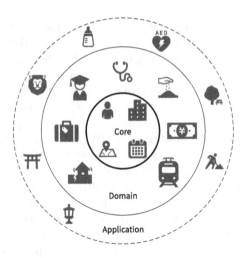

Fig. 1. IMI common vocabulary

An application vocabulary is a set of terms that the core vocabulary and domain vocabularies do not cover. The core vocabulary focuses on basic terms only and is sometimes insufficient to describe a real dataset. Therefore we provide a way to define an application vocabulary which includes original terms inheriting the core vocabulary by a creator of a dataset. We suppose some application vocabularies in the same field will be organized into a domain vocabulary in the future by identifying common terms among them. Figure 1 illustrates the three tier structure of the IMI common vocabulary.

3   Design of Core Vocabulary

This section introduces the design of the IMI common vocabulary with the core vocabulary version 2.4.1 [3] which is the latest version as of Aug. 2018.

3.1   Class and Property

The IMI core vocabulary is a fundamental part of the IMI common vocabulary and is a set of terms used in all social activities such as name, address and organization. Terms include classes and properties. A class has one or more combinable properties. Properties have literals or are associated with other classes. The core vocabulary version 2.4.1 defines 63 class concepts and 266 property concepts.

The most important design decision for the common vocabulary is to use a Japanese identifier to define a term. In regular vocabulary designs, an English identifier is used to define a term. However, because the common vocabulary aims to make a dictionary to exchange representations of Japanese words, being closed in the Japanese language is more effective so that we do not need to take care of the difference between languages. For instance, the "イベント型 (Event)" class

Fig. 2. IMI Core Vocabulary: Person class

is to express an event including a business, educational or entertaining activity held at the specified time and location. This meaning of the "Event" is a widely used in the Japanese government while there is a problem to say just "Event" in English. As an English label is prepared for each term, this paper describes both a Japanese identifier and its English label for English readers.

Figure 2 is an excerpt from the " 人型 (Person)" class of the core vocabulary. The " 人型 (Person)" class has " 性別 (gender)" and " 氏名 (name)" properties. The value type of the " 性別 (gender)" property is a string, and the value type of the " 氏名 (name)" property is the " 氏名 (Name)" class. If a value type is a sort of literal like a string, it should assign datatypes of XML Schema [5]. On the other hand, it has a hierarchical structure if the value type is a class because the class has further properties. The " 氏名 (Name)" class has the " 姓名 (full name)" property and the " 姓名ローマ字表記 (full name in Romaji)" property.

A property can specify the number of occurrences for its value. The occurrence of the " 性別 (gender)" property in the " 人型 (Person)" class is 0 to 1. The number of occurrences of most properties in the core vocabulary is set to 0..n because of flexibility unless the number constraint of occurrences is necessary.

3.2   Class Hierarchy

The class inheritance mechanism in the common vocabulary is as follows. A new class is defined by inheriting one of existing classes in the common vocabulary. It inherits properties from ancestor classes and can add more properties. The common vocabulary does not allow to delete inherited properties from ancestor classes. The core vocabulary uses this inheritance mechanism to define a class. Also when creating a new vocabulary like domain vocabulary or application vocabulary, we request to define a class by inheriting a class of the core vocabulary to keep interoperability of classes.

Figure 3 shows an excerpt of the class hierarchy of the " 人型 (Person)" class and its surroundings in the core vocabulary as an example. A dotted arrow indicates an inheritance relation. The " 概念型 (Concept)" class is defined as the base class of all classes in the core vocabulary. The " 事物型 (Thing)" class

Fig. 3. Excerpt of IMI Core Vocabulary Hierarchy

derived from the "概念型 (Concept)" class represents identifiable things. Classes to represent substantial entities inherit the "事物型 (Thing)" class and add specific properties for classes. For instance, both the "人型 (Person)" class and the "組織型 (Organization)" class in the core vocabulary inherit the "実体型 (Entity)" class, the "事物型 (Thing)" class and the "概念型 (Concept)" class. The "場所型 (Location)" class and the "住所型 (Address)" class also inherit the "事物型 (Thing)" class and the "概念型 (Concept)" class. There are also special classes for representing IDs, codes, restrictions and others as siblings of the "事物型 (Thing)" class. More detailed descriptions of classes are in Table 1.

3.3 History of Core Vocabulary

The IMI core vocabulary version 2.0 as a trial was publicly released in April 2014 while version 1.x had been developed internally. After this release, we exchanged opinions with people in charge of similar projects namely NIEM and ISA[2]. Also we demonstrated and discussed to collect comments from governments, vendors and users widely to revise the core vocabulary to improve the design and arrange terms. We would like to share a knowledge from the brief history of the core vocabulary as an example of a vocabulary development.

The version 2.1 was also released as a trial version. The base class was changed from the "基本型 (Base)" class to the "事物 (Thing)" class. The reason of this change was aligned to the OWL ontology language which was often used for vocabulary definitions. Also we changed to use datatypes of XML Schema simply instead of our own data types like text and boolean with structures because the hierarchy became deep and it was hard to use.

The version 2.2 was released as the first official version. Properties were separated from classes and became the first-class citizens like RDF while each property had been defined in each class before. For instance, the "名称 (name)"

Table 1. Class description in Fig. 3

class	English	description
概念型	Concept	base class of all classes
事物型	Thing	class to represent an identifiable thing with properties like identification and textual expression
ID型	Identifier	special class to represent an identifier with properties like identification value
制約型	Restriction	special class to express a constraint condition, which is the super class of specific constraint like range constraint
場所型	Location	class to express a place with properties like name of place geographical identifier, address, geographical coordinates
住所型	Address	class that represents an address with properties like zip code, prefecture and city.
実体型	Entity	convenient class for abstracting organization and person
組織型	Organization	class to represent an organization with properties like representative, establishment date, contact address
人型	Person	class to represent a person with properties like as name, birth date and age.

property had been defined in both the " 組織 (Organization)" class and the " 施設 (Facility)" class, but it was generalized from and associated to them. Another big change was classes related to geospatial information. The " 地点型 (Point)" class was changed to the " 地物型 (Feature)" class based on opinions from GIS community. And the relation of geographic classes namely " 場所型 (Location)", " 地物型 (Feature)" and " 施設型 (Facility)" was re-arranged. In addition, coordinates were adapted not only to points but also to lines and area.

The " 単位コード型 (Unit code)" class was added in the version 2.3 to describe numerical values with units like weight. We also added the " 関与型 (Participation)" class to express related people and organizations and the " 活動型 (Activity)" class to express the activities of people and organizations. The version 2.3.1 had no design change but added English labels and explanations for oversea collaborations. The version 2.3.2 was only the change of the IMI domain from imi.ipa.go.jp to imi.go.jp. This issue is described in Sect. 4.5.

The change in the version 2.4 was that common properties in descendant classes of the " 事物 (Thing)" class like "ID (identification)", " 表記 (textual expression)", " 参照 (reference)" and " 画像 (image)" were aggregated into the " 事物 (Thing)" class for convenience. This was a big design change because the " 事物 (Thing)" class had been designed as the top abstract class without properties. Also a new class called the " 概念型 (Concept)" class was introduced as the new base class to arrange the class hierarchy. New classes like the " 文書型 (Document)" class, the " サービス型 (Service)" class and the " 制約型 (Restriction)" class were also added. The " 文書型 (Document)" class expresses document information by using compatible properties with Dublin Core Metadata Element Set [6]. The " サービス型 (Service)" class represents services in administration like childcare. Services and events were often subject to limited usage and duration, therefore we also added classes to describe restrictions such as the " 範囲制約型 (Range restriction)" class and " 期間制約型 (Period restriction)" class.

One of important changes of the current version 2.4.1 is that the " メタデータ (metadata)" property is introduced into the " 概念型 (Concept)" class to describe provenance information for instance. Also two category properties namely " 種別 (category)" and " 種別コード (category code)" are aggregated into the " 概念型 (Concept)" class as these are used in all of classes.

4 Specifications

A set of specifications are prepared to implement the common vocabulary framework. Data exchange formats and the Structured Item Name Notation are string representations to describe data with vocabularies. DMD is a package mechanism to exchange a data model on vocabulary usage. IMI Vocabulary Notation is a notation to define a vocabulary and a data model. Specifications are language independent and used for developing a non-Japanese common vocabulary.

4.1 Data Exchange Format

The IMI common vocabulary and its data structure discussed in the previous sections are the abstract specification. Then we need to represent a concrete dataset with the IMI common vocabulary in a digital format to handle with computers. The IMI common vocabulary framework provides three formats: XML, RDF and JSON. We assume that XML is used for strict data exchanges between systems in the digital government while RDF and JSON are used for data exchanges on the Internet like open government data. The schema files of the core vocabulary for XML and RDF are published on the IMI web site [2]. There is no JSON Schema file for the JSON format now. JSON is actually implemented as JSON-LD which is a serialization format of RDF so that the schema file of RDF should be referred for JSON. A JSON-LD context document for the core vocabulary is also provided on the web site so that a dataset in the JSON format can refer to the context document to expand terms of the core vocabulary. The following example is a JSON representation of Fig. 2.

```
{ "@context": "https://imi.go.jp/ns/core/context.jsonld",
  "@id": "https://example.org/person1",
  "@type": "人型",
  "氏名": {
    "姓名": "葛飾 北斎",
    "姓名ローマ字表記": "Hokusai Katsushika" } }
```

4.2 Structured Item Name Notation

As the common vocabulary has a hierarchical structure, there is a demand to represent a hierarchical structure as a single string. For instance, using the common vocabulary for field names in the header part of a tabular format like CSV or Excel is one of popular requirements for open government data. The purpose of the Structured Item Name Notation is to provide a notation to describe a term with its hierarchical structure. Therefore it is not allowed to omit intermediate terms in a string of Structured Item Name Notation, while XPath [7] aims to indicate specific nodes in an XML document and allows such omission.

The basic structure of the Structured Item Name Notation consists of one class to indicate the starting node of the structure and arbitrary properties separated by the character '>' to follow nodes from the starting node. The fragment of Fig. 2 is represented by the following combination of strings.

人型 > 氏名 > 姓名
人型 > 氏名 > 姓名ローマ字表記

The first string means that " 人型 (Person)" is the class of the starting node and has the " 氏名 (name of Person)" property which has a node with the " 姓名 (full name)" property. If the same property is used in each string within the same node, it is interpreted as the node via the property is the same instance. In this example, the " 氏名 (name of Person)" property is the same so that the node via the " 氏名 (name of Person)" property is the same as shown in Fig. 2).

The common vocabulary often allows to use the same property multiple times to distinguish nodes via properties. For this reason, a user can specify a property with a group name in a pair of square brackets like " 氏名[本名] (name of Person[real name])" or " 氏名[ペンネーム] (name of Person[pen name])" in order to distinguish multiple nodes via the same property as well as to aggregate properties in the same group to the same node.

4.3   Data Model Description

The core vocabulary is designed with general versatility to cover a wide variety of use cases. The " 人型 (Person)" class has 25 properties, however, many of them are not always needed to construct a specific dataset. The " 住所 (address)" property is important to describe residents while it is not necessary to represent creators of art works. On the other hand, the " 姓名 (name)" property is expected once in the former, but a plurality of the " 姓名 (name)" property are commonplace like real names and pen names in the latter.

DMD (Data Model Description) is a package system to enable a data creator to construct and share a data model for a specific purpose. This is similar to IEPD (Information Exchange Package Document) in NIEM. 11 DMD packages are currently shared at the IMI website [8]. A data model is defined in the IMI Vocabulary Notation (Sect. 4.4) by picking necessary terms up from the core vocabulary and defining their own application vocabulary if needed.

A DMD package must include one or more mapping files to associate each term in a data model with each representative label. A representative label is an item name of data when creating a DMD in many cases. A data model fragment corresponding to a label is specified by Structured Item Name Notation. In the following example, the "defaultVocab" attribute indicates to use the core vocabulary, and the "name" is associated with "人型 >氏名 >姓名". A mapping file can be used separately from a DMD package and point to corresponding a data model with a URL of a DMD package.

```
{ "defaultVocab": "http://imi.go.jp/ns/core/2",
  "mapping": { "name": "人型 > 氏名 > 姓名" } }
```

The benefit of DMD is reusability of data models. A data creator can reuse a data model to save time by avoiding to make yet another data models. If there is a DMD package for public facilities, a data creator generates a public facility dataset with the DMD tools described in Sect. 5.1. In addition, by developing applications according to the data model specified by DMD, the applications can handle all data according to the DMD. It implies that other public facility data published using the same DMD is compatible with applications supporting the DMD.

4.4   IMI Vocabulary Notation

IMI Vocabulary Notation is a unique machine readable format to describe definitions of terms of a common vocabulary and a data model of DMD. It is a neutral notation apart from the existing exchange formats. We need to maintain definitions of terms and schema files for supported data exchange formats described in Sect. 4.1 without committing specific formats. The core vocabulary is defined with the IMI Vocabulary Notation since the version 2.4[1]. It uses Structured Item Name Notation to describe the fragment of the structure. The following example is excerpt of " 人型 (Person)" class in version 2.4.1.

```
#name@en "Person"
#description@en "A class term to express information of a person."
class ic:人型 {@ic:実体型} ;

#description@en "The full name (family and given name)."
set ic:人型>ic:氏名 {0..n} ;
```

The basic structure of the IMI Vocabulary Notation is a pair of a directive and its value. The directives started with '#' are metadata of the class just after them. The line 1 describes the English name of the class and the line 2 describes the English description of the class. The line 3 is the class declaration. The " ic:人型 (Person)" class is defined to extend the " ic:実体型 (Entity)" class. The prefix ic is used for the core vocabulary. The lines 5 shows the English description of the following property. The line 6 means the " ic:氏名 (name of Person)" property is associated with the " ic:人型 (Person)" class which is declared most near before.

---

[1] Until the core vocabulary version 2.3.2, the definition of the vocabulary was managed in a tabular format.

4.5   Discussion on Specifications

The major issue at specifications is differences between XML and RDF. Including a version number in the namespace is important for XML since it is used to identify a set of XML elements. On the contrary, it is better not to change the namespace as much as possible to maintain compatibility in RDF because all of terms are totally changed in RDF if the namespace is updated with the version. As a result, we have decided to prepare two namespaces for the core vocabulary since version 2.2. XML uses a namespace with version numbers and RDF uses a version less namespace though having two namespaces sometime confuses users.

The another issue is constraints in each format. XML has a tree structure and the order of properties is important while RDF has no order for properties. A user needs to write the " 姓名ローマ字表記 (full name in Romaji)" property after the " 姓名 (full name)" property in XML.

Ather namespace problem was a domain change. At the beginning of IMI, the imi.ipa.go.jp domain under IPA was used since IMI was started as a project of the Ministry of Economy, Trade and Industry and IPA. Then IMI became a large project and needed to use the imi.go.jp domain to show the service name only for the long-term stability since version 2.3.2. It caused a problem that existing open data was isolated from new data as the namespace was a part of the core vocabulary URI. Some users have inherited both old and new classes to keep their data compatibility after the change [9]. Vocabulary designers need to consider the persistence of namespaces carefully at the initial stage.

Another topic that we have encountered is the HTTPS transition which is one of the major issues in Semantic Web and Linked Open Data fields. Government web sites are recently demanded to use HTTPS to guarantees confidentiality, authenticity and integrity. The problem of this transition is that a URI of http scheme is totally different from a URI of https scheme even the rest parts of both URIs are the same [10]. The consensus of this issue is to keep using http scheme for existing identifiers and set the infrastructure to upgrade quietly to https [11]. In fact this solution or similar methods are widely used for RDF Vocabularies so that existing applications need no changes. IMI also uses this solution now.

GeoJSON is our next target of data exchange formats as it is a commonly used JSON format for geographic information. As we mentioned in Sect. 3.3, geographic classes in the core vocabulary are changed to align to geographic information. GeoJSON-LD [12] might be a bridge as IMI JSON uses JSON-LD.

5   Deployment Support

This section describes support systems to help users to apply the common vocabulary framework to their datasets.

5.1   Tools

One of the Important issues for the operation of the common vocabulary framework is to support users to create and use vocabularies and DMDs. In the common vocabulary framework, we have developed support tools and databases

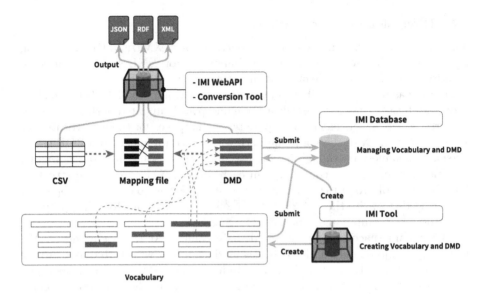

Fig. 4. IMI project

(Fig. 4). The tool "Data model from table" supports DMD creation and utilization includes more than 150 DMDs [13]. The tool provides a tabular format template corresponding to each DMD package. A user can create and upload a dataset in the given tabular format in order to convert to XML and RDF formats according to the targeted DMD package without knowledge of DMD.

The tool supports not only to create a DMD package from the scratch but also to modify a third party package. Users can find an existing package which matches to their needs, modify it to add missing properties and publish as a new package. We encourage a user to re-use DMD packages openly on the tool. Also the IMI database is under development for registering and searching DMDs, application vocabularies and codes. It will help users to reuse resources of the common vocabulary framework.

5.2   Partnership and Public Draft

The IMI partnership system is established to cooperate with organizations using the common vocabulary framework to conduct their vocabulary development and data maintenance. 12 organizations are IMI partners as of August 2018. Government offices are treated equivalent to partners by default.

Each IMI partner works on constructing datasets with the common vocabulary framework like organizing item names in existing datasets, creating an application vocabulary or mapping item names to the core and application vocabulary. An IMI partner can publish a result of these processes at the common vocabulary framework site as a public draft. The objective of a public draft is to share basic knowledge acquired from processes to keep interoperability. We review each public draft to share comments after receiving from each partner.

A public draft has two types. One is a list of item names and mappings to common vocabularies. Another is a draft of an application vocabulary. A unique namespace is assigned to each public draft so that a partner can define their own terms freely with the namespace. Public drafts help to construct an application vocabulary as well as a domain vocabulary in future.

5.3 Deployment Issues

One of the major deployment issues is how to apply codes for datasets because many datasets refer to codes to classify data. The common vocabulary framework provides a way to describe codes with the " コード型 (Code) class and the " コードリスト型 (Codelist)" class. However, it does not provide actual contents of codes as they are often managed and copyrighted by external organizations.

We have received requests to share codes in the form of the common vocabulary framework to refer from datasets seamlessly. Therefore we consider to provide lists and samples of popular codes. We also consider building cooperative relationships with organizations managing existing codes. We have already worked with National Statistics Center to provide area codes for national statistics by using the " コード型 (Code)" class in Statistical LOD of Japan [14].

As the IMI database has a feature to create and share codes, it should be used to not only publish existing codes in the form of the common vocabulary framework but also create and share new codes in future.

6 In Use

We promote to use the common vocabulary framework widely in the society to get feedbacks. This section introduces current use cases by government offices.

6.1 Corporate Information

Corporate Information [15] (Hojin Information in Japanese) is a web site operated mainly by the Ministry of Economy, Trade and Industry under the IT strategy [1]. It provides corporate basic and activity information of about 4 million Japanese legal entities. Corporate basic information includes corporate number and corporate name, and corporate activity information includes contract and award information with ministries and agencies. Corporate Information is published under Government of Japan Standard Terms of Use [16] which is compatible with Creative Commons Attribution 4.0 International License.

Corporate Information is developed based on RDF to provide the SPARQL endpoint. The application vocabulary for Corporate Information extends the core vocabulary version 2.4. It defines the" 法人基本情報型 (Corporate Basic Information)" class derived from the " 法人型 (Corporation)" class in the core vocabulary to add properties such as shareholders and settlement information and business contents. It also defines the "法人活動情報型 (Corporate Activity Information)" class which inherits the "法人基本情報型 (Corporate Basic Information)" class and adds properties like certification numbers and dates. The following excerpt in turtle shows an example of the "調達型 (Procurement)" class derived from "法人活動情報型". It describes that Toyota Motor Corp. has had a lease contract of fuel cell vehicles with Ministry of Environment in 2017. The "hj" prefix indicates the application vocabulary for Corporate Information.

```
ext:1180301018771_2017_調達情報_環境省_20171215_001018 a hj:調達型;
    ic:名称 [ ic:表記 "トヨタ自動車株式会社" ];
    ic:ID [ ic:識別値 "1180301018771" ];
    ic:住所 [ ic:表記 "東京都文京区後楽１−４−１８" ];
    hj:対象 "平成２９年度普通乗用自動車（燃料電池自動車）の賃貸借" ;
    hj:公表組織 [ ic:名称 [ ic:表記 "環境省" ] ;
        ic:ID [ ic:識別値 "1000012110001" ] ] .
```

The application vocabulary has been also fed back to the common vocabulary framework as the public draft PD2342 "Vocabulary of Corporate Information" [17]. In addition, the data model used in Corporate Information is published as Corporate Basic Information DMD and Corporate Activity Information DMD [8]. The vocabulary and DMDs make third parties easier to create datasets and applications related to Corporate Information. At least four web sites have already used data of Corporate Information. For instance, the corporate analysis web application [18] by Fujitsu Laboratories collects and arranges various datasets related to corporations to show their own visualization and analysis.

6.2 Prefecture and Municipality

Saitama prefectural government has established a working group in 2016 to publish open datasets in common formats from all 58 municipalities in Saitama Prefecture [19]. As of August 2018, 46 organizations of them have already published their datasets openly. The number of the common formats is limited to 10. The common formats support public facility and event calendar for instance. Each common format has mapping relationships from item names to the common vocabulary in a tabular format. Such item names and mappings are provided as public drafts on the common vocabulary web site and Saitama prefecture uses the namespaces of public drafts. Each municipality creates open datasets based on common formats. And these datasets are aggregated in the open data portal site of Saitama Prefecture. Saitama prefectural government converts them into RDF datasets with the core vocabulary and vocabularies for common formats to provide their SPARQL endpoint. Therefore a user can do a single query to datasets across municipalities in Saitama Prefecture.

Also several municipalities have already provided SPARQL endpoints and RDF files with the IMI common vocabulary as part of open data publishing. City of Osaka has published a SPARQL endpoint from March 2016 [20]. Currently available data are public facilities, evacuation centers, public relations and event information. City of Kyoto has released a SPARQL endpoint including facility information and metadata of datasets registered at their open data portal from January 2017 [21]. City of Kobe has provided a SPARQL endpoint for event information from April 2017 [22]. City of Kobe has also opened an official event site "KOBE Today" by using the SPARQL Endpoint.

Opendata.cc by B Inc. [23] is an aggregated SPARQL endpoint to collect RDF datasets by local public entities. The application 5star opendatamap uses Opendata.cc to mix and display location information described with the common vocabulary. This is the effect to use the same data structure, vocabulary and API.

7 Related Work

As opportunities for global data exchanges are increasing, it is necessary to consider semantic interoperability with overseas. This section shows three related activities outside of Japan. NIEM and ISA^2 have already worked with IMI to create trial mappings among their data models [24]. And Schema.org is widely used for the data on the web.

NIEM [4] is a common model for information sharing promoted by the Federal Government of the United States since 2005. At first the Department of Homeland Security and the Department of Justice has worked together on the basis of the Global Justice XML Data Model (GJXDM). After that other departments has joined to the project. NIEM version 4.1 has been released as of August 2018. NIEM plays a common dictionary at the system level and is supposed to be used by referring from individual systems. In NIEM's model, NIEM Core is a common vocabulary used by administrative agencies such as people, places and organizations. NIEM Domains are common vocabularies for each field such as agriculture, biometrics and immigration. NIEM depends on XML Schema to define a vocabulary but also uses UML Profile [25] as abstract representation. JSON representation based on JSON-LD is also provided since version 4.0. IEPD is a package to group XML Schema files to exchange information in NIEM. IMI has been influenced by many parts of NIEM like the information model, vocabulary and IEPD. NIEM has already prepared domain vocabularies well while IMI has no concrete domain vocabulary. IMI includes application vocabularies by bottom up instead of domain vocabularies.

The European Commission has established the ISA programme since 2010 and the current ISA^2 programme since 2016 under the Directorate-General of Informatics to ensure interoperability among administration, business and citizens in Europe. The ISA^2 programme supports the development of frameworks, strategies and structures for interoperability. Joinup [26] is the platform for information sharing in ISA^2. SEMIC (Semantic Interoperability Community) in Joinup is the actual activities to study and develop data standards for interoperability. The data model of ISA^2 consists of three layers: core data models, domain data models, and information exchange data models. Core data models and domain data models are corresponding with NIEM Core and Domains. Information exchange data models is similar to IEPD in NIEM. Six vocabularies such as Person, Registered Organization and Location are defined as the core vocabularies in the core data models layer. A core vocabulary provides its conceptual model based on UML, schema files for XML and RDF and its JSON-LD context file. An interesting point is that the namespaces of core vocabularies applies the w3 domain instead of their own domain to provide more stable URIs. For instance, the namespace of Core Person Vocabulary is http://www.w3.org/ns/person#Person. About domain vocabularies in the domain data models layer, there is only EU Budget Vocabulary which is an RDF vocabulary for the EU Budget as of July 2018.

Schema.org [27] is one of the most attracted common vocabulary of structured data used on the Web. Schema.org has been developed since 2011 by four major search companies, Google, Microsoft, Yahoo and Yandex. The discussion place has been moved to Schema.org Community Group [28] from 2015, however, the final decision is still done by the Steering Committee that consists of representatives of the search engine companies and experts with high contributions. Schema.org suggests web developers to publish structured data with the Schema.org vocabulary to improve search results. The vocabulary is written in English. The data model is looser than other vocabularies as a class allows multiple inheritance and a property allows to specify more than one domain and range. In fact a property can be used in any class regardless of its definition while the common vocabulary framework only adopts multiple domain of properties. Another interesting point is the relationship between the core vocabulary and extended vocabularies. The vocabulary at http://schema.org is all core vocabulary. And a vocabulary used by a community can be published as an extended vocabulary. There are two types of extended vocabulary: an extension hosted by Schema.org and an extension operated by an external organization. The former has an official review after submitting to Schema.org. An extension passed the review is received a subdomain of Schema.org to provide information of the extension. For instance, the bibliographic extension has http://bib.schema.org. The namespace of this type of extended vocabulary is the same as the core vocabulary. The latter is to publish the extension outside of schema.org and link it to the core vocabulary. For example, GS1 Web Vocabulary [29] is an external extended vocabulary of products. The idea of the expansion also affects the common vocabulary framework as application vocabularies.

8 Conclusion

The IMI common vocabulary framework has designed the common vocabulary and constructed the core vocabulary to cover basic needs of terms. And application vocabularies and use cases of the common vocabulary have come out. Under the "Basic Act on the Advancement of Public and Private Sector Data Utilization" law, a wider range of application cases will increase in the future. We hope that more vocabularies will be shared in both bottom-up and top-down.

References

1. Declaration to Be the World's Most Advanced IT Nation Basic Plan for the Advancement of Public and Private Sector Data Utilization (2017). https://japan.kantei.go.jp/policy/it/2017/20170530_full.pdf
2. IMI.https://imi.go.jp/goi/imi-about-en
3. IMI Core Vocabulary (2.4.1). https://imi.go.jp/ns/core/Core241.html
4. NIEM. https://www.niem.gov
5. Biron, P.V., Malhotra, A.: XML Schema Part 2: Datatypes Second Edition. W3C Recommendation (2004)
6. Dublin Core Metadata Initiative: Dublin Core Metadata Element Set, Version 1.1. DCMI Recommendation (2012)
7. Clark, J., DeRose, S.: XML Path Language (XPath) Version 1.0. W3C Recommendation (1999)
8. List of Data Model Description. https://imi.go.jp/dmd/
9. jig.jp: Open Data Platform. https://odp.jig.jp
10. Berners-Lee, T., Fielding, R., Masinter, L.: Uniform Resource Identifier (URI): Generic Syntax. RFC 3986 (2005)
11. Archer, P.: HTTPS and the Semantic Web/Linked Data (2016). https://www.w3.org/blog/2016/05/https-and-the-semantic-weblinked-data/
12. Gillies, S.: GeoJSON-LD (2017). http://geojson.org/geojson-ld/
13. IPA: DMD Editor. https://imi.go.jp/goi/dmd-editor.html
14. Yamamoto, D., et al.: Geographic area representations in statistical linked open data of Japan. In: 5th International Workshops on Semantics Statistics (2017)
15. Cabinet office of Japan and Ministry of Economy Trade and Industry: Corporate Information. https://hojin-info.go.jp
16. Government of Japan Standard Terms of Use. https://www.kantei.go.jp/jp/singi/it2/densi/kettei/gl2_betten_1_en.pdf
17. Vocabulary for Corporate Information, PD2342. https://imi.go.jp/pd/2342/
18. Corporate Analysis Web Application. https://lod4all.net/frontend/
19. Saitama Prefectural Government: Publishing Open Data in the Common Format. https://opendata.pref.saitama.lg.jp/events/news20170119.html
20. City of Osaka Linked Open Data. https://data.city.osaka.lg.jp/api/
21. City of Kyoto Open Data. https://data.city.kyoto.lg.jp/
22. City of Kobe Linked Open Data. https://data.city.kobe.lg.jp/api/
23. B Inc.: opendata.cc. https://sparql.opendata.cc
24. SEMIC: Core Data Model Mapping Directory. http://mapping.semic.eu
25. Object Management Group: UML Profile for NIEM Version 3.0. http://www.omg.org/spec/NIEM-UML/3.0
26. European Commission: Joinup. https://joinup.ec.europa.eu
27. Google, Yahoo, Microsoft and Yandex: Schema.org. http://schema.org
28. W3C: Schema.org Community Group. https://www.w3.org/community/schemaorg/
29. GS1 Web Vocabulary. https://www.gs1.org/voc/

A Conceptual Framework for Linking Open Government Data Based-On Geolocation: A Case of Thailand

Punnawit Budsapawanich[1(⊠)], Chutiporn Anutariya[1],
and Choochart Haruechaiyasak[2]

[1] Asian Institute of Technology, Khlong Luang, Pathum Thani, Thailand
{stll5658, chutiporn}@ait.ac.th
[2] National Electronics and Computer Technology Center, Khlong Luang,
Pathum Thani, Thailand
choochart@nectec.or.th

Abstract. Over the past decade, most governments have steadily progressed towards a policy for more openness, more accountability and more transparency. Such a strategy to publish open data, which are meaningful and valuable, has made available open government data (OGD) that are publicly accessible to everyone. To promote OGD usage, most OGD datasets are published in a tabular form or a CSV spreadsheet format, which can be easily browsed and downloaded by a human user. However, applications of OGD often require data from different datasets to be integrated. This is a challenging and cumbersome task which usually demand huge human effort, especially if metadata as well as data representation and encoding standards are not well defined. With a thorough analysis into Thailand's OGD (ThOGD) having over thousand datasets, we found that OGD datasets often involve data related to geolocation, places or administrative division. Therefore, using such geodata as potential linking nodes is very attractive. However, this is not an easy task due to data heterogeneity issues. For example, a location might be represented using a geographic coordination system (e.g., latitude and longitude) or an administrative division which could be in a different level from highest to lowest division such as regions, provinces, districts, municipalities, etc.). Moreover, in Thailand geographical regions can be divided differently by different division schemes depending on the application domains, e.g., meteorology, tourism and statistics. To tackle this challenge, in this paper, we propose a conceptual framework for mapping and linking OGD datasets using geolocation data which could increase OGD usage and promote the development of new services or applications.

Keywords: Open government data · Linked open government data
Geodata · Data integration

1 Introduction

Open Government Data (OGD) is data produced or commissioned by a government that anyone can freely access, use, modify, and share for any purpose. The benefits of OGD range from improving administrative transparency and accountability, enhancing

© Springer Nature Switzerland AG 2018
R. Ichise et al. (Eds.): JIST 2018, LNCS 11341, pp. 352–366, 2018.
https://doi.org/10.1007/978-3-030-04284-4_24

public service quality and efficiency, promoting citizen participation up to increasing economic opportunities and growth. To make OGD datasets be easily accessible and downloadable by a human user, most datasets are published in a tabular form or a CSV spreadsheet file format. Integrating and linking these various datasets can normally give data consumers a larger perspective and enable a wider range of applications. However, due to a lack of a unified data model, this task requires intense human workload to fully understand the datasets and to manually integrate them especially when dealing with a large number of datasets. Therefore, a framework that can automatically link different datasets is demanded. Existing approaches to addressing this need mostly rely on similarity matching techniques based on schema, metadata, data semantics, ontology, etc.

An analysis of Thailand's OGD (ThOGD) high-value datasets in [1] concluded that its quality is weak in two dimensions of the ISO/IEC 25012 standard which are "Understandability" and "Currentness". The former is mainly caused by a lack of dataset metadata and the latter is due to a lack of timely dataset update. One of the reasons is that its government agencies usually rely on documents, spreadsheets or reports from their own legacy systems with no unified schema nor data standard. This implies low data interoperability, when compared to OGD published by developed countries where the data standards have been concretely defined.

Our comprehensive survey of ThOGD, with over 500 datasets available in a spreadsheet format, reveals that 58.44% of the datasets involve data related to geolocation, places or administrative division. Therefore, using such geolocation data as potential linking nodes is promising. However, several important challenges remain, which include naming ambiguity, naming heterogeneity, different data format and granularity, change of administrative division and different regional division schemes.

To overcome the challenges, in this paper, we propose a conceptual framework for mapping and linking OGD datasets using geolocation data. We also illustrate a few examples of ThOGD datasets and show how the proposed framework can integrate them.

Section 2 reviews related works. Section 3 analyses ThOGD datasets with respect to geolocation data aspect and discusses important challenges. Section 4 proposes the conceptual framework. Section 5 illustrates an example of applying the framework to integrate ThOGD datasets. Section 6 draws conclusions and future work.

2   Related Works

Existing works on integrating or linking datasets mostly employ similarity matching techniques. However, simply matching two geolocation names from two different datasets may cause an error due to naming ambiguity and naming heterogeneity problem, not to mention other issues.

The papers [2] and [3] review schema integration techniques in general which could cover most cases when the datasets have structural similarity to a certain level. However, such techniques could not directly and fully apply to link geo-related datasets because the geo-information in non-similarity schema structured datasets could also be linked.

The paper [4] develops a migration/integration framework for Singapore's OGD by following the best practice guideline for publishing linked data which is presented in [5]. The linking result could guarantee for a highly precision, but it requires intense human workload in many processes especially in data integration to achieve the best result. Thus, it does not suitable for large number of datasets.

Geodata could be stored in a specific Geographic Information System (GIS) format where it treats the geolocation data as point, line and polygon. Therefore, the papers [6–8] aims at integrating spatial databases and geographical datasets by focusing on solving platform heterogeneity issues and geographically integrating the data. Their objectives are different from our work that aims at linking geolocation data in OGD datasets which are usually represented in a human friendly format.

In addition, the works in [9] and [10] propose approaches to adding geo-semantic labels to OGD datasets. The paper [9] relies on Name Entity Recognition (NER) approach instead of an external knowledge base as the data which is represented in Thai language in Wikipedia is insufficient as compared to Latin-base languages. The case study used Thailand OGD datasets, and its result shows a significant improvement of recall rate as compared to the approach that used Wikipedia APIs. Although its precision slight dropped, it is still considerably high. The approach, presented in the paper [10], created a knowledge graph using the datasets from open government data and GeoNames as well as OpenStreetMap APIs. Its case study employed Latin-based languages datasets and could achieve a high precision rate at about 0.83. Both approaches could be applied in our framework.

3   ThOGD: Dataset Analysis Concerning Geolocation Data

3.1   Dataset Survey and Analysis

In order to provide as an official and central data catalog of its open government data, Thailand's national data portal (data.go.th) has been setup and launched since 2013 by Digital Government Agency of Thailand. The portal currently hosts over 1,000 datasets, provided by a hundred government offices.

Our comprehensive survey of Thailand's OGD (ThOGD) focused on over 500 datasets available in a spreadsheet format and excluded unstructured file format e.g. HTML and PDF documents. Table 1 summarizes the survey result by depicting the number of datasets that involved data related to geolocation, which was further classified into country-, regional-, provincial-level and so on. Note that each number in a cell illustrates that for each dataset category how many datasets having geolocation data at the finest granularity level, while a blank in the table means zero. Moreover, a dataset which was split into multiple data files was counted as one.

Consider from the table, for instance, the Agricultural & Irrigation category. There were 4 datasets with country-specific data, 6 datasets with province-specific data, 2 datasets with sub-district-specific data, 5 datasets with an address, 1 dataset with specific place names, 2 datasets with position-specific data (latitude/longitude), and 2 datasets with other kind of geolocation data. Thus, for the Agricultural & Irrigation category, there were the total of 30 datasets, 22 of which contained geolocation data, while 8 of which did not.

Table 1. Thailand's open government dataset survey (as of August 2018)

Dataset Categories	Number of Datasets with Geolocation Data													
	Country	Region	Province	District	Sub-district	Address	Place Name	Geo Coordinate	Capital	Capital District	Custom/Other	All-Geo	Non-Geo	All
Agricultural & Irrigation	4		6		2	5	1	2			2	22	8	30
Education	2		2		1	5	1			3	1	15	2	17
Logistic & Transportation	2		3	3	2	17			5	4	9	45	37	82
Cultural & Religion	3		2			2	3				3	13	15	28
Public Health			6			2		4	8	2	1	23	6	29
Economy & Industry	17	2	1		1	4					1	26	53	79
Law & Jurisdiction			2				2				1	5	28	33
Tourism & Sport			14	1								15		15
Technology			2			1	1	2				6	5	11
Meteorology								1			1	2		2
Social Welfare		1	3	1	2	2					1	10		10
Resources & Environment	1					1		1				3	2	5
Political & Administration	3	2	22	2	6	8	19	1	10	22	8	103	24	127
ICT	1		1									2	19	21
Budget & Spending			2			1		2				5	7	12
Employment	4	3	9			1					3	20	18	38
Total	37	8	75	6	12	30	48	14	23	31	31	315	224	539
Percentage	6.86%	1.48%	13.91%	1.11%	2.23%	5.57%	8.91%	2.60%	4.27%	5.75%	5.75%	58.44%	41.56%	100.00%

In summary, around 58.44% of all datasets contained geolocation data, while 5.75% had a custom regional model. In addition, it is interesting to see that there were 13.91% of the datasets involving information on provincial level, and 17.08% (5.57% + 8.91% + 2.60%) with specific location data (addresses, place names and geo coordinates).

3.2 Challenges

Although integrating multiple ThOGD datasets using geolocation data seems promising, the following important challenges remain and should be handled effectively:

- *Naming ambiguity*: The same place name might refer to different areas. For instance:
  - The name "Ladprao" might refer to a road, a sub-district or a district.
  - Every province in Thailand has a "Mueang" district and every district has a "Nai Mueang" sub-district, which refer to the main area of each province and the district in the next lower-level administrative division, respectively.
- *Naming heterogeneity*: An area could be referred to by several names such as a full name, an abbreviated name, a code, or names in different languages.
- *Different data format and granularity*: Geolocation data in different datasets might be represented in different format such as a geographic coordination system (e.g., latitude and longitude) or an administrative division, which could also be in a different granularity level from highest to lowest division such as regions, provinces, districts, etc.
- *Change of administrative division*: An administrative division may have the following possible changes including name change, an administrative division being created, merged or split, such as Bueng Kan Province, which was split off from Nong Khai Province in 2011.
- *Different regional division scheme*: In Thailand geographical regions can be divided differently by different division schemes depending on the application domains. Figure 1 illustrates three important ones: (a) official administrative division, defined by the National Geo-informatics Board, (b) meteorology-based, defined by Thai Meteorological Department, and (c) tourism-based, defined by the Tourism Authority of Thailand. Furthermore, there exist other custom models, such as 4-region model used in some administrative and statistical contexts, Buddhist monastery regional model, which separates Thailand's provinces into 18 Buddhist monastery regions, agricultural model which separates an area based on soil properties, and electoral districts which are defined by the Election Commission of Thailand, etc.

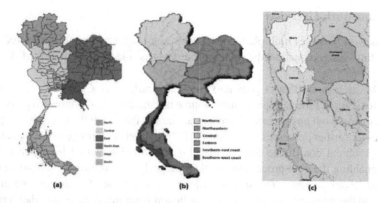

Fig. 1. Thailand's different regional division model: (a) official administrative division, (b) meteorology-based model, (c) tourism-based model

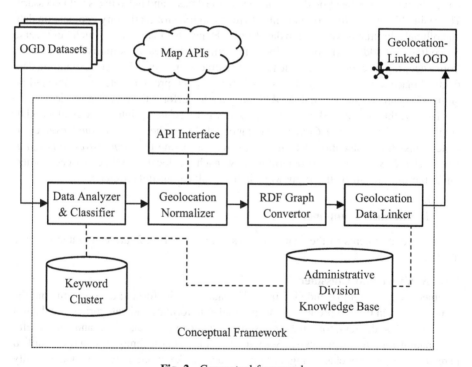

Fig. 2. Conceptual framework

4 Conceptual Framework

Our proposed framework focuses on automatically generating links among data in OGD datasets using geolocation data. Figure 2 depicts the conceptual framework with its main components.

4.1   Framework Overview

The framework receives multiple OGD datasets as an input and performs the following tasks to link the geolocation data within the datasets and constructs linked data as a result.

Firstly, each input dataset goes into the *Data Analyzer & Classifier* component to analyze for its data format, data domain, source organization and possessed geolocation datatype to prune out unsupported formats and classify the rest of the datasets into proper categories for further processes. For example, if the dataset contains geolocation data only in a geographical coordinate format, then this information would be attached to the dataset, enabling the next process to handle it properly. The information from *Keyword Cluster* and *Administrative Division Knowledge Base* are used for recognizing the data domain and the geolocation data type by prediction from field names and data values.

Secondly, the *Data Analyzer & Classifier* component passes its result dataset with the classified geolocation data to the *Geolocation Normalizer* component. Here, it determines the type of geolocation data contained in the dataset and normalizes it if necessary. The main objective of this component is to map and transform arbitrary geolocation data into official administrative division data format. Hence, the main process includes reverse geocoding and address decomposition. The former retrieves an administrative address from a geographic coordinate, while the latter extracts an address into corresponding data fields of place name, street number, sub-district, district, province, etc. Available public *Maps APIs* can be used through an *API interface* to perform the mention services.

Thirdly, the normalized geolocation-dataset is transformed into its equivalent RDF graph by the *RDF Graph Convertor* component. Next, the *Geolocation Linker* component links the geolocation data among the datasets using the *Administrative Division Knowledge Base* in order to determine how each geolocation relates to each other. Thus, the final result of the framework is the geolocation-linked OGD.

4.2   Framework Components

Important components of the framework, as outlined in Fig. 2, are elaborated in more details:

Data Analyzer and Classifier
Its objective is to analyze and classify OGD dataset for its format, data domain and the geolocation data type to prune out unsupported data formats and categorizes the dataset based on data domain, organization source, geolocation data type and any useful information for further processes. Various data analyzing techniques could be applied here to improve the classifying accuracy, such as keyword detection, name entity recognition, word embedding, pattern recognition, etc.

Geolocation Normalizer
Geolocation data in the OGD dataset comes in various forms. It needs to be normalized and transformed into separated administrative division fields for further matching process. For example, geographic coordinates could come in several different formats and require reverse geocoding process for their administrative locations; place names also implicitly refer to specific locations; address strings could be extracted into separate division fields. The framework could use existing geographical Map APIs to deal

with these issues. However, there remain certain challenges. For instance, reverse geocoding does not always return an administrative location in case of a remote area, and address querying are likely to return multiple results. Thus, an additional approach to handling such cases is demanded in order to improve the accuracy.

RDF Graph Convertor

In order to link multiple OGD datasets, each dataset should first be transformed into an equivalent RDF graph. This process is quite straightforward. To reduce structural heterogeneity and to enhance data integration, two important consideration for the development of this component are: (i) appropriate URI naming strategy, and (ii) employment of open, standard RDF vocabulary or schema.

Geolocation Data Linker

This component mainly deals with linking geolocation data among the input datasets. It employs matching techniques to match the geolocation data in the dataset and the one in the *Administrative Division Knowledge Base*. Simply matching the geolocation name might lead to an error due to naming ambiguity and naming heterogeneity issues. This component then measures the similarity of two geolocation names based on several factors such as field name, data value and their patterns. Thus, by linking geolocation to an *Administrative Division Knowledge Base*, the input datasets are automatically linked to each other through its geolocation data node.

Keyword Cluster

This component contains the information regarding how the semantics of keywords closely relate to each other and most likely belong to the same domain. This information is necessary for dataset analysis and classification to recognize the data domain, geolocation type and may be some useful information. It could be constructed manually by using knowledge from human experts, by applying machine learning techniques to a large dataset, or by connecting to existing services or resources.

Administrative Division Knowledge Base

This knowledge base contains a hierarchical structure of administrative divisions, which is necessary for linking geolocation data with different granularity. In principle, this knowledge should be predefined by human experts to ensure its integrity as it would be used as references and a base model for linking OGD datasets. Other relevant information, which can help improve linking accuracy and features, are also included in the knowledge base, such as abbreviated names, aliases, location codes, location boundary and regional division models.

5   Examples: Linking ThOGD Datasets

This section shows a few examples of linking OGD datasets by employment of the proposed framework using actual Thailand's OGD (ThOGD) datasets[1] with Thai-English language translation.

---

[1] https://data.go.th.

While the framework intends to solve all of the challenges discussed in Sect. 3, due to page limitation, this section demonstrates only how to link geolocation data having different administrative division granularity, and shows how to handle varieties of coordination representation systems. Although such issues are common, they are rarely mentioned in any existing frameworks. To avoid unnecessary complexity and to simplify the results, our examples assume the following:

- The datasets in every example are excerpted from the actual ThOGD datasets, and the symbol "ooo" indicates omitted irrelevant attributes or data.
- The results are represented using object diagram notation. Each object property represents a data predicate and its values. The links among objects denote only geolocation-based relationships among geolocation data nodes, while other kinds of links are omitted.
- A dashed arrow denotes a *geolocation-pointer*, and a solid-line arrow denotes a *belongs-to relation*.
- Dashed objects indicate that there exist other similar objects which are omitted to simplify the diagrams.

Example 0 (An Administrative Division Knowledge Base). This example partially shows the structure of Thailand's administrative division which reflects several challenges discussed earlier. Firstly, Thailand has more than one regional models. Secondly, there is naming ambiguity in district and sub-district level. Hence, the linker could not simply match the district or sub-district names, but it must recognize which branch/node it supposes to match by considering several relevant factors.

The symbol "ooo" in this example indicates that there is other relevant information which could help improve the linking accuracy e.g. alias name, local name, postal code, established date, etc. This knowledge is used as a base for geolocation linking between OGD datasets (Fig. 3).

Example 1 (Linking Multiple OGD Datasets Having Different Administrative Division Level). Tables 2, 3 and 4 shows three sample datasets: Dataset A, B and C, respectively. By analyzing the data, the *Data Analyzer & Classifier* could be able to recognize that Dataset A contains geolocation data in the regional level using the 4-region model, while that in Dataset B and C are in the provincial level, which is one step lower from Dataset A. These datasets are classified to be in the same data domain, but different division level; hence no need for normalization. Then, the datasets are converted into RDF graph format and linked together by the *RDF Graph Converter*.

Table 5 Shows Necessary Information for This Example Regarding Thailand's Regional Models, Which Is Stored in the *Administrative Division Knowledge Base*.

According to Table 5, the only provinces in the sample Datasets B and C which belongs to different regions are Kanchanaburi and Kamphaeng Phet, while the rest belongs to the same region, i.e., Northeast. Figure 4 shows the generated geolocation links.

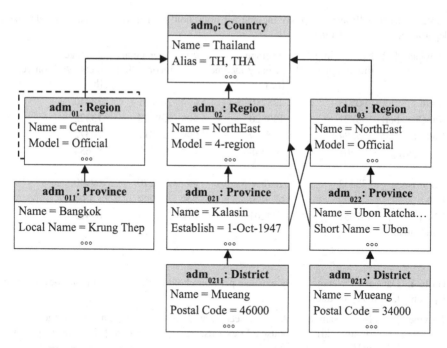

Fig. 3. Example of Thailand's Administrative Division Knowledge Base

Table 2. Dataset A: average monthly income per household (2015) by Thailand's National Statistical Office, Ministry of Information and Communication Technology

Source of income [a1]	Region [a2]	Average monthly income per household 2015 (THB) [a3]
Wage and salary	Central	12898
Wage and salary	North	5813
Wage and salary	Northeast	6900
Wage and salary	South	9820
ooo	ooo	ooo
Interest and dividends	Central	90
Interest and dividends	North	101
Interest and dividends	Northeast	87
Interest and dividends	South	74

This example shows how the dataset with different division level could be linked. In this case, the input data are semantically close to each other, where Datasets B and C could be merged as it was also generated from the same source, but their schemas are almost totally different, except for several key attributes. A framework that relies on schema similarity matching techniques may not be aware of this linking candidate.

Table 3. Dataset B: average yearly income per household (2015) by community development department, Ministry of Interior

Province [b1]	No. of sample (household) [b2]	Average primary income [b3]	ooo	Average all income [b4]	Average income/person/year [b5]
Krabi	90523	228210	ooo	266801	78240
Kanchanaburi	156721	199820	ooo	239648	73322
Kalasin	205284	145769	ooo	255317	70372
Kamphaeng Phet	151561	207548	ooo	272593	87684
Khon Kaen	338432	167898	ooo	252270	69940
ooo	ooo	ooo	ooo	ooo	ooo
Ubon Ratchathani	367651	144201	ooo	246961	69423

Table 4. Dataset C: average yearly expense per household (2015) by community development department, Ministry of Interior

Province [c1]	No. of sample (household) [c2]	Average necessary household expense [c3]	ooo	Average all expense [c4]	Average expense/person/ year [c5]
Krabi	90523	96598	ooo	174746	51245
Kanchanaburi	156721	86416	ooo	159110	48681
Kalasin	205284	59375	ooo	145210	40024
Kamphaeng Phet	151561	61402	ooo	167104	53752
Khon Kaen	338432	67000	ooo	146749	40685
ooo	ooo	ooo	ooo	ooo	ooo
Ubon Ratchathani	367651	48272	ooo	131121	36860

Table 5. Example of Thailand's regional models

Province	Official geographical model (6 regions)	4-region model	ooo
Krabi	South	South	ooo
Kanchanaburi	West	Central	ooo
Kalasin	Northeast	Northeast	ooo
Kamphaeng Phet	Central	North	ooo
Khon Kaen	Northeast	Northeast	ooo
ooo	ooo	ooo	ooo
Ubon Ratchathani	Northeast	Northeast	ooo

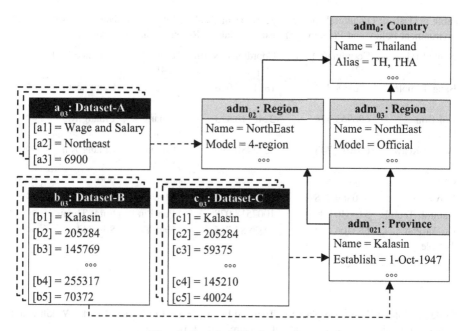

Fig. 4. Partial result of example 1

While Datasets A and B are consider to be similar or close to each other as both of them contain data about an average income per household, they cannot be directly integrated because their data are represented in different time span (monthly vs. yearly) as well as in different administrative division level.

However, these datasets could be linked through their geolocation data using the defined *Administrative Division Knowledge Base*, which could give a broader view of both average income and expense, and thus enabling a wider range of applications to be developed and published.

Example 2 (Linking Datasets with Geographic Coordinates and Administrative Divisions). Consider Datasets D, E, F and their descriptions as shown in Tables 6, 7 and 8, respectively. In this example, the datasets contain a variety of geolocation data patterns:

- Dataset D contains geolocation data in both geographical coordinate (UTM system, zone 47) and administrative division manners;
- Dataset E contains only geographical coordinate in latitude/longitude which is different from Dataset D; and
- Dataset F contains only city names.

The geographical coordinates in Datasets D and E could be normalized and reverse-geocoded to retrieve the administrative addresses. Geolocation data in Dataset F has a small issue as it uses city names which could belongs to different division level. Most of the names in Table 8 are province names except for Hua Hin and Pattaya which are district names. The *Geolocation Data Linker* could also consider this kind of issues.

Table 6. Dataset D: cultural and heritage places in Thailand by Office of Natural Resources and Environment Policy and Planning, Ministry of Natural Resources and Environment

Name [d1]	Coordinate East [d2]	Coordinate North [d3]	District [d4]	Province [d5]	ooo
Bang Temple	556798.873	1821117.026	Mueang	Kampheang Phet	ooo
Doi Don	606963.394	2246110.413	Chiang Sean	Chiang Rai	ooo
Weang Keaw	607013.743	2253480.893	Chiang Sean	Chiang Rai	ooo
ooo	ooo	ooo	ooo	ooo	ooo
Kao Kob	620889.218	1737785.508	Mueang	Nakhon Sawan	ooo
Namrob Temple	513640.890	1002518.078	Pun Pin	Surat Thani	ooo
Ou Ta Pao Temple	663106.464	783984.715	Had Yai	Songkhla	ooo

Table 7. Dataset E: tourism places in Thailand by Department of National Parks, Wildlife and Plant Conservation, Ministry of Natural Resources and Environment

Name [e1]	Coordinate latitude [e2]	Coordinate longitude [e3]	ooo
Wang Nam Yen Botanical Garden	13.497	102.015	ooo
Phu Khae Botanical Garden	14.6712	100.8846	ooo
Ban Phe Botanical Garden	12.6335	101.4586	ooo
Khao Hin Son Botanical Garden	13.7526	101.5064	ooo
ooo	ooo	ooo	ooo
PongSaLee Arboretum	19.835508	99.786769	ooo
Her Majesty The Queen's 80th Birthday Arboretum	6.668518	101.161489	ooo

The partial result is shown in Fig. 5. The result of the reverse geocoding process for "Doi Don" and "PongSaLee Arboretum" coordinates yield that they located in "Pa Sak" and "San Sai" sub-district, respectively. Even if the original datasets lack this information, the links are created at the finest granularity level possible to reduce redundancy. Therefore, those datasets can be linked in the sub-district level.

In this example, the input datasets are service ratings of tourist cities and the tourist locations. Even though, there is no direct link between service ratings and each tourist spots, it might be safely to claim that the ratings for each place in those cities would be roughly around those of the overall city values.

This example indicates that the data in a higher division level could also be roughly estimated to the lower one. Certainly, an estimation would lack the precision. However, it does not harm much for the tasks that do not require such a precision. In this case, the rating score might be gathered from a group of samples, and is not perfectly accurate in

Table 8. Dataset F: rating for Thailand's tourism city by Ministry of Tourism and Sport

City [f1]	Excitement rating [f2]	Service quality [f3]	Security rating [f4]	ooo	Overall rating [f5]
Krungthep	4.03	4.00	4.03	ooo	4.03
Chiang Mai	4.30	4.37	4.36	ooo	4.36
Chiang Rai	4.41	4.43	4.43	ooo	4.44
Pattaya	4.19	4.17	4.16	ooo	4.18
Hua Hin	4.41	4.38	4.40	ooo	4.41
ooo	ooo	ooo	ooo	ooo	ooo
Surat Thani	4.19	4.16	4.08	ooo	4.17

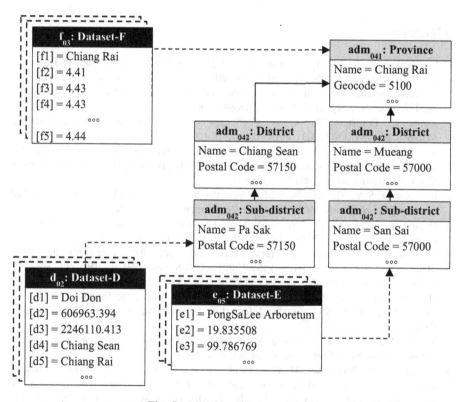

Fig. 5. Partial result of example 2

the first place. Therefore, the work which does not require a high precision and/or has a wide margin of error-tolerable range, such data might be statistically estimated in this manner.

6 Conclusion

In conclusion, the framework generates geolocation-linked OGD from semi-structured and structured OGD datasets. Its benefit is that it could automatically link a number of OGD datasets without intensive human workloads with high precision. Although the framework does not automatically link/integrate non-geolocation fields, it can still provide richer perspectives on the data and enable to discover potential relations to link/integrate the datasets further.

In order to demonstrate the framework's practicability, efficiency and effectiveness, its prototype system implementation and performance evaluation using real ThOGD datasets are underway. In addition, we aim to expand the framework to support other kinds of potential linking nodes such as time. Applications of the framework to visualize linked data and provide insight data analysis in certain selected domains are also envisaged.

References

1. Utamachant, P., Anutariya, C.: An analysis of high-value datasets: a case study of Thailand's open government data. In: Proceedings of 2018 15th International Joint Conference on Computer Science and Software Engineering (JCSSE), Nakhonpathom, Thailand, 2018, pp. 1–6. https://doi.org/10.1109/jcsse.2018.8457350
2. Rahm, E., Bernstein, P.: A survey of approaches to automatic schema matching. VLDB J. **10**, 334–350 (2001). https://doi.org/10.1007/s007780100057
3. Shvaiko, P., Euzenat, J.: A survey of schema-based matching approaches. In: Spaccapietra, S. (ed.) Journal on Data Semantics IV. LNCS, vol. 3730, pp. 146–171. Springer, Heidelberg (2005). https://doi.org/10.1007/11603412_5
4. Raamkumar, S.A., Thangavelu, K.M., Kaleeswaran, S., Khoo, S.G.C.: Designing a linked data migrational framework for Singapore government datasets (2015)
5. Hyland, B., Atemezing, G., Terrazas, V.B.: Best practices for publishing linked data. https://www.w3.org/TR/2014/NOTE-ld-bp-20140109/. Accessed 16 Aug 2018
6. Shvaiko, P., et al.: Trentino government linked open geo-data: a case study. In: Cudré-Mauroux, P., Heflin, J., et al. (eds.) ISWC 2012. LNCS, vol. 7650, pp. 196–211. Springer, Heidelberg (2012). https://doi.org/10.1007/978-3-642-35173-0_13
7. Hakimpour, F., Timpf, S.: A step towards geodata integration using formal ontologies. In: AGILE Conference on Geographic Information Science, Palma, Balearic Islands, Spain (2002)
8. Vaccari, L., Shvaiko, P., Marchese, M.: A geo-service semantic integration in spatial data infrastructures. Int. J. Spat. Data Infrastruct. Res. **4**, 24–51 (2009)
9. Krataithong, P., Buranarach, M., Hongwarittorrn, N., Supnithi, T.: A framework for linking RDF datasets for Thailand open government data based on semantic type detection. In: Morishima, A., Rauber, A., Liew, C.L. (eds.) ICADL 2016. LNCS, vol. 10075, pp. 257–268. Springer, Cham (2016). https://doi.org/10.1007/978-3-319-49304-6_31
10. Neumaier, S., Polleres, A.: Geo-semantic labelling of open data. In: SEMANTiCS 2018-14th International Conference on Semantic Systems. Procedia Computer Science (2018)

Construction and Reuse of Linked Agriculture Data: An Experience of Taiwan Government Open Data

Dongpo Deng[1](✉) (iD), Guan-Shuo Mai[2], and Steven Shiau[3]

[1] Industrial Technology Research Institute, Taipei, Taiwan
dongpo.deng@gmail.com
[2] Biodiversity Research Center, Academia Sinica, Taipei, Taiwan
[3] National Center for High-Performance Computing, Taipei, Taiwan

Abstract. This paper describes our experiences on dealing with the transformation from Traceable Agriculture Product (TAP) records to Linked Open Government Data. By using existing ontologies and vocabularies, TAP Ontology is developed for clarifying the semantics of TAP. To increase the reusability of TAP, the crops and operational processing details of TAP are mapped to Common Agricultural Vocabulary (CAVOC). There are four SPARQL endpoints developed for supporting queries to TAP. To demonstrate the reuse of Linked TAP, we develop a Chrome extension LinkedFood to offer TAP information via reading ingredients in recipe websites.

Keywords: Linked data · Open data · Traceability · Semantics
Traceable agriculture product

1 Introduction

The recent development of open data initiative encourages governments to publish their data on the Web. The openly accessible datasets make a potential benefit for collaborations between citizens and governments. Citizens have an opportunity to obtain the data previously sealed in government applications, and thereby they can do their analyses and investigations for their purposes. Ideally, the analyses and investigations by citizens may provide government agencies specific feedback about how to more efficiently perform their governmental role [4]. However, there are some challenges to achieve the potential benefit. First, the heterogeneous data structures often make the content inconsistent in the distributed datasets from different agencies. To discover new facts and/or figure out problems, citizens need mash up distributed open government data from different agencies for their analyses and investigations. Since the content is often inconsistent, the mashup of open government data meets an obstacle of data integration. Second, it is an important task to make datasets comprehensible to citizens, so that they can obtain right datasets, easily integrate data, and correctly analyze data. The data steward of a large and diverse collection datasets from government agencies requires significant time and effort. It is difficult to use human effort for governing large and diverse datasets from distributed government agencies. This actually leads to a

© Springer Nature Switzerland AG 2018
R. Ichise et al. (Eds.): JIST 2018, LNCS 11341, pp. 367–382, 2018.
https://doi.org/10.1007/978-3-030-04284-4_25

requirement to make datasets automatically machine-processable. Due to the issues of data inconsistency and data stewardship, linked data approach is required to improve the reuse of open government data. Linked data is a paradigm of data integration along with semantic Web technologies. Linked data transfers the scale of data integration from traditionally databases (or data warehouses) to the Web (Ding et al. 2012). That is, data space in Linked data paradigm is not merely local integration of several databases but a global evolution in the entire Web.

The open data initiative flourishes in Taiwan. There are over 36 thousand datasets published on national open data portal (http://data.gov.tw). Such large open datasets encounter the issues of data inconsistency and data stewardship. As abovementioned, linked data is considered to an approach for dealing with the issues. However, the technique of linked data is often a barrier for governmental agencies. There is a need of a practical exhibition to instruct them. To demonstrate the utilizes of linked data for harmonizing data along with its semantics, this study chooses the dataset of Traceable Agricultural Product (TAP) as an illustration. From this illustration, we attempt to point out the problems of current TAP dataset, and then propose approaches to tackle the problems. In addition, TAP is actually suitable for apply to linked data technique. TAP is a collection of records describing the journeys of agricultural products from farms to stores. A journey of an agricultural production has an information flow. The current system of TAP depends on a trace code to record a journey of an agricultural product. The trace code is a primary key for data integration in the way of traditional database management. An information flow of TAP involves several stages that streamline the exchange of data and knowledge. It is challenge that the data and knowledge integration only depends on trace code. There should be more standardized information for data and knowledge integration. Moreover, every piece information of an agricultural production ideally should be able to conserved in the information flow, so that TAP can provide deeper knowledge about the supply chain of agricultural products or food security. The use of trace code only is insufficient to handle the complex data and knowledge integration. Linked data is an excellent candidate approach to make the TAP information interlinkable and sharable.

The release of TAP fits the citizens' demands of being able to track agricultural products. Citizen can easily check the information of an agricultural product, e.g., production place, packing date, and farmer. However, the data quality of TAP cannot reach the level of machine-readable. The ill-defined data semantics of TAP restricts the interoperability, scalability, and usability. For example, a crop can have several names. It often happens that two agricultural products refer to the same crop but they use different crop names. The crop names cannot be consistent in the TAP system, so that the TAP records are difficult to be reused by other agricultural system. For example, the use of a crop name to find the price of a crop in agricultural market information system. In addition, a TAP record provides store information where an agricultural product is sold. But the store information is quite vagueness. For example, a TAP record displays that an agricultural product is sold in the Carrefour stores locating in the northern Taiwan. Two questions are raised in this store information. What is the definition of the northern Taiwan? Which Carrefour stores are located in the northern Taiwan? The entities, e.g., crops and stores, in TAP records are ill-defined and ambiguous. Although the TAP records are valuable dataset, the poor data semantics not only cause problems of data consistency but also restrict them to integrate with other agricultural information systems. In order to overcome the restrictions of interoperability, scalability, and usability in TAP, Linked Data is required to transfer TAP to be interlinked, shared and made available consistently along well-defined data semantics.

The paper is structured as follows. Section 2 discusses related work. Section 3 describes the data process of TAP records. Section 4 presents ontology and how to map to CAVOC. Section 4.3 illustrates a motivating scenario from recipe website. Finally, Sect. 5 presents conclusions and future work.

2 Related Work and Background

In International Organization for Standardization (ISO) 22005:2007 standard, *traceability* is defined as "the ability to follow the movement of a feed or food through specified stage(s) of production, processing and distribution". A *traceability system* is defined as "a system following the movement of a product as it moves through the food chain from farmer to fork", in which "movement" can relate to the origin of materials, their processing history, or the distribution of the feed or food [7]. The process of a traceable agriculture product depends on the coordinating actions and decisions undertaken by the stages of production, processing, and distribution. The sharing of the information of the stages play an important role for the success of the traceable agriculture product system. Solanki and Brewster [8] proposed the concept of 'Linked pedigrees' facilitating to share traceability information of products as they move along the supply chain. Linked pedigrees provides a distributed and decentralised, linked data driven architecture for consuming real time supply chain information. The data in a traceability system can be vast and diverse. On the basis of knowledge organization systems (KOS), Xian et al. [9] utilized linked data to interlink and consume the large amounts of literature and scientific data in agricultural research community.

To enable data interoperability in traceability system, data semantics play a key driver for interlining and consuming data. The development of formalized vocabularies is a critical approach to retrieve data semantics. To enable wheat data interoperability, Kaboré et al. [1] presented a framework fostering the adoption of common standards and vocabularies for wheat data management, and facilitate access, discovery, reuse, and integration of that data. Lawan et al. [3] proposed an approach to use ontology for advance knowledge-sharing on underutilized crops and proposed how to integrate those ontologies with Semantic Web Rule Language (SWRL) rules for added expressiveness. Commonly agreed semantics are essential for making datasets discoverable and re-usable. CIARD RING is a federated and curated metadata registry of agri-food datasets and data service. Pesce et al. [5] described Linked Data layer of CIARD RING for interlinking the catalog of agriculture datasets and publications. L'Abate et al. [2] applied Linked Data technologies to align soil data with existing standards in order to improve the data interoperability. To publish agricultural e-Learning resources on the Web, Rajabi et al. [6] applied Linked Data technologies to interlink content and metadata of organic agriculture data.

3   TAP and Data Processing

The Traceable Agricultural Product (TAP) system was implemented in 2007 by the Council of Agriculture (COA) in accordance with Article 7 of the Agricultural Production and Accreditation Act (COA 2016). The purpose of the system is to provide consumers a transparency information about agriculture products. The TAP contains a certification system which can earn costumers' trusts for agriculture products. With prevail of open data initiative, TAP was often requested to open access by civic communities. Although the TAP information can be accessed, the dataset was incomplete and limited. Due to food safety scandals in several years ago, COA released a more complete TAP dataset to meet the larger and larger requests of food safety information.

The TAP dataset can be openly accessed on Taiwan open data portal (https://data. gov.tw/dataset/7556). The dataset is updated every day except holidays, and it offered by API in three formats: XML, CSV, and JSON. The earliest record in TAP dataset is on January 4, 2015. There are over 1 million TAP records in the dataset. In terms of a TAP record, there are 17 components in a TAP record as shown on Fig. 1. The components are ProductName, OrgID, Producer, Place, FermerName, PackDate, CertificationName, StoreInfo, LandSecNo, ParentTraceCode, TraceCodelist, OperationDetail, ResumeDetail, ProcessDetail, and CertificateDetail.

```
- {
    ProductName: "檸檬-產銷履歷檸檬(產銷履歷檸檬)",
    OrgID: "136947",
    Producer: "原龍合作社",
    Place: "屏東縣竹田鄉新田段",
    FarmerName: "李榮倫",
    PackDate: "2017/03/10",
    CertificationName: "國立屏東科技大學",
    ValidDate: "2019/03/29",
    StoreInfo: "■ 超市：惠康Wellcome超市(全台各分店),■ 量販店：愛買(全台各分店)家樂福(全台各分店)全聯福利中心(全台各分店)好
    市多(Costco)(無提供相關資訊)",
    Tracecode: "1060310104200045",
    LandSecNO: "TC0336,31520000;TC0336,22590000;TC0336,26460000",
    ParentTraceCode: "",
    TraceCodelist: "1060310104200045",
    OperationDetail: "http://data.coa.gov.tw:80/Service/OpenData/Resume/OperationDetail_Plus.aspx?
    Tracecode=1060310104200045",
    ResumeDetail: "http://data.coa.gov.tw:80/Service/OpenData/Resume/ResumeDetail_Plus.aspx?
    Tracecode=1060310104200045",
    ProcessDetail: "http://data.coa.gov.tw:80/Service/OpenData/Resume/ProcessDetail_Plus.aspx?
    Tracecode=1060310104200045",
    CertificateDetail: "http://data.coa.gov.tw:80/Service/OpenData/Resume/CertificateDetail_Plus.aspx?
    Tracecode=1060310104200045"
},
```

Fig. 1. A traceable agricultural product (TAP) record from Taiwan open data portal

The trace code in TraceCodelist is the identifier (ID) of a TAP. This is how consumers can access the TAP information on the Web. Although TAP can be read by human, the data is difficult to be reused and automatically processed by machine. We describe the issues and correspondingly processes as follows.

The Lack of Standard Crop Names for TAP Records

In Fig. 1, it is obviously to see that there no crop name column in the TAP record. The crop name actually appears in the column of 'Product Name'. The words before the hyphen in the product name often present a crop. By using a text mining technique, we obtain 831 crop names. However, there are many crop names represent the same crops. After the clarification of the crop names, we obtain 687 crop names.

A crop name plays an important key to interlink other agricultural information systems. For example, the use of crop names can retrieve the price of crops from agricultural market information system. As a consumer looks up a TAP record, the price of the crop is useful information for she/he to decide to buy or not. Moreover, a user is often used to explore crops and their locations for consuming, but rarely use product name. Although crop name is essential for exchanging agricultural information, there is no a standard vocabulary for crop names using in Taiwan. Every agricultural information system maybe maintains a list of crop names but they are not openly accessible and not mapped each other. The crop names extracted from the TAP records are difficult to mapped to the other Taiwan agricultural information systems. To clarify the semantics of crop names, we map the extracted crop names to Crop Vocabulary (CVO). This mapping work will be introduced in next section.

Ambiguous Store Information in TAP Records

As shown in Fig. 1, the store information exists a long string for store information. In fact, there are many stores described in the string. Although the phrases describing stores can be extracted by using text mining techniques, the phrases are ambiguous and vagueness. For example, the phrase '惠康Wellcome超市(全台分店)' means 226 branches of Wellcome supermarket in entire Taiwan. In addition, the phrase in the bracket '全台分店' actually indicates the region of the supermarkets. It is commonly used in the store information, e.g., 北部分店 is branches in northern Taiwan. To deal with the ambiguous of the words in store information, we develop a rule to extract the phrases and to retrieve store entities. As a result, we collect 7345 stores.

These store entities actually exist in other governmental databases such as Food company registry of Food and Drug Administration (FDA) and Commercial/Corporate Registry of Ministry of Economic Affairs (MOEA). But the store names among TAP, FDA, and MOEA are different. To link these store data, we firstly compare the address between TAP and FDA for matching the store. Since the TAP stores are mapped to FDA food companies, we can get the tax number of the stores from FDA dataset. Through using the tax number of the stores, TAP store can be mapped to MOEA dataset.

Vagueness Place Information

As shown in Fig. 1, there are two components for presenting the place in a TAP record: Place and LandSecNo. The information in the component Place is vagueness and cannot be retrieved to precisely location. The component LanSecNo is actually the cadastre number. We use the cadastre number to retrieve geometry coordinates such as longitude and latitude through using a cadastre map service (http://easymap.land.moi. gov.tw/).

Inconsistent Crop Names Between TAP Restaurants and TAP Records

A TAP restaurant means the restaurants using TAP for their meals. The TAP restaurants are not included in TAP dataset but released in another dataset. Although the two datasets can be linked by trace code, the crop names using in the two datasets are not always consistent. There is required to clean crop names in the dataset of TAP restaurants, and then match the two datasets.

4 The Development of TAP Ontology

4.1 Ontology Engineering

To clarify the semantics of TAP, the TAP Ontology is developed as shown in Fig. 2. The TAP Ontology can be distinguished by three parts: agriculture product, production place, and marketing/production.

In terms of agricultural product, the class 'Traceable Agricultural Product' represents to an agricultural product, which is the same as the concept of agricultural product in AGROVOC. The class 'Traceable Agricultural Product' is the core class of TAP Ontology. Each traceable agricultural product can be referred to a crop, produced at a production place, made by a farmer, produced by a producer, certified by a certification agency, sold at several stores, and processed by several operations. The class 'Crop' is used to describe the crop in traceable agricultural product, which is the same as the concept of crop in AGROVOC. The class 'Operation' is used to describe operational processing during the cultivation of a crop. To formalize the concept of crops and operational processing, the vocabularies of crop and operation in TAP ontology is respectively mapped to Crop Vocabulary (CVO) and Agriculture Activity Ontology (AAO). The mapping process will be discussed in next section. Since the names of traceable agricultural products are often used more than once, the class 'Product Name' is used to describe the names of agricultural products. Also, the product name can be a group of agricultural products.

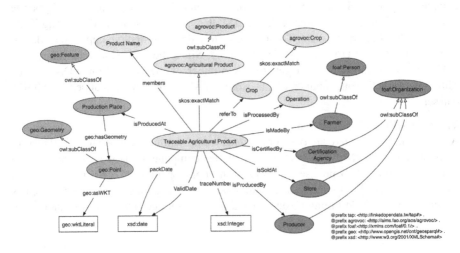

Fig. 2. TAP ontology

In terms of production place, the class 'Production Place' represents the geospatial relations for agriculture production. It is a subclass of geo:Feature that is a vocabulary of OGC GeoSPARQL. Since the class 'Production Place' inherits geo:Feature, so that it can have a geometry property geo:Point for describing geospatial characteristics. Geo:Point uses geo:WKTLiteral to present longitude and latitude. The use of GeoSPARQL vocabulary benefits to perform geospatial queries via SPARQL.

In terms of marketing/production, there are the classes 'Farmer', 'Certification', 'Store' and 'Producer' in TAP Ontology. The class 'Farmer' is the subclass of foaf: Person, and the classes Certification', 'Store' and 'Producer' are the subclass of foaf: Organization.

巨峰

Resource URI: http://tap.linkedopendata.tw/resource/Crop/%E5%B7%A8%E5%B3%B0

Home | All Crop

Property	Value
skos:altLabel	Kyoho
skos:altLabel	Vitis vinifera × labrusca
skos:altLabel	巨峰
skos:broader	<http://tap.linkedopendata.tw/resource/Crop/%E8%91%A1%E8%90%84>
skos:exactMatch	<http://cavoc.org/cvo/ns/1/巨峰>
skos:prefLabel	巨峰
is tap:referTo of	<http://tap.linkedopendata.tw/resource/TraceableAgriculturalProduct/1060105923>
is tap:referTo of	<http://tap.linkedopendata.tw/resource/TraceableAgriculturalProduct/1060105924>
is tap:referTo of	<http://tap.linkedopendata.tw/resource/TraceableAgriculturalProduct/10601220321>
rdf:type	skos:Concept

The server is configured to display only a limited number of values (limit per property bridge: 50).

Fig. 3. The TAP cop 'Kyoho' mapped to CVO

青江白菜-青江白菜(青江白菜)

Resource URI: http://tap.linkedopendata.tw/resource/TraceableAgriculturalProduct/10601020074

Home | All TraceableAgriculturalProduct

Property	Value
tap:certificateDetail	<http://data.coa.gov.tw:80/Service/OpenData/Resume/CertificateDetail_Plus.aspx?Tracecode=10601020074>
skos:exactMatch	agrovoc:xl_en_a3b58d92
tap:hasATracecode	10601020074
tap:isCertifiedBy	環球國際驗證股份有限公司
tap:isMadeBy	廖秀娃
tap:isProducedAt	雲林縣西螺鎮新社段
tap:isProducedBy	雲林西螺蔬菜108班
tap:isSoldAt	<http://store.linkedopendata.tw/resource/Store/7284>
rdfs:label	青江白菜-青江白菜(青江白菜)
is tap:make of	<http://tap.linkedopendata.tw/resource/Farmer/%E5%BB%96%E7%A7%80%E5%A8%83>
is tap:member of	<http://tap.linkedopendata.tw/resource/ProductName/%E9%9D%92%E6%B1%9F%E7%99%BD%E8%8F%9C-%E9%9D%92%E6%B1%9F%
tap:operationDetail	<http://data.coa.gov.tw:80/Service/OpenData/Resume/OperationDetail_Plus.aspx?Tracecode=10601020074>
tap:plantAt	<http://tap.linkedopendata.tw/resource/Place/PC0309%2C11810000>
tap:processDetail	<http://data.coa.gov.tw:80/Service/OpenData/Resume/ProcessDetail_Plus.aspx?Tracecode=10601020074>
is tap:produce of	<http://tap.linkedopendata.tw/resource/Producer/%E9%9B%B2%E6%9E%97%E8%A5%BF%E8%9E%BA%E8%94%AC%E8%9C108%E
tap:referTo	<http://tap.linkedopendata.tw/resource/Crop/%E9%9D%92%E6%A2%97%E7%99%BD%E8%8F%9C>
tap:resumeDetail	<http://data.coa.gov.tw:80/Service/OpenData/Resume/ResumeDetail_Plus.aspx?Tracecode=10601020074>
rdf:type	tap:TraceableAgriculturalProduct

The server is configured to display only a limited number of values (limit per property bridge: 50).

Fig. 4. The triples of TAP record '10601020580' displayed by D2R

4.2   Mapping TAP to Common Agricultural Vocabulary (CAVOC)

There are two mapping process from TAP to Common Agricultural Vocabulary (CAVOC) (http://www.cavoc.org). One is mapping TAP crop to Crop Vocabulary (CVO) for extending the reusability of TAP. The benefit of the mapping will be discussed in the next section for explicating the use of TAP. The matching processing between TAP crop and CVO is based on scientific names. As a result, 268 TAP crops are mapping to CVO. In Fig. 3, Kyoho, a kind of grapes, in TAP is mapped to CVO.

Another mapping process is to match TAP operations to Agriculture Activity Ontology (AAO). The TAP operations are the processes for agriculture products. The

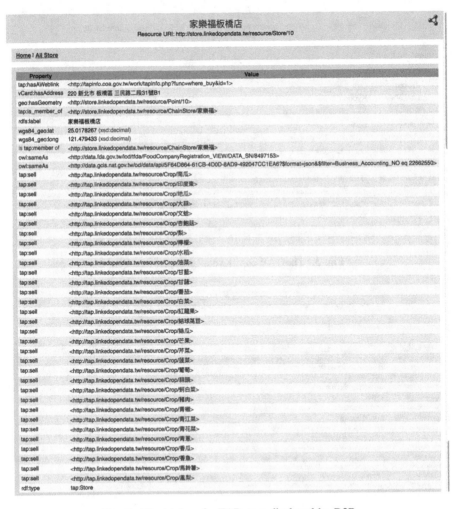

Fig. 5. The triples of a TAP store displayed by D2R

dataset is available on the component 'OperationDetail' of a TAP record. Not every TAP has operation records. In our investigation of the entire TAP dataset, operational processes are often logged in rice productions. Also, the operational processes of rice productions are more complete. Table 1 demonstrates the mapping between TAP operations of rice productions and AAO vocabulary (Fig. 4).

TAP Store (http://store.linkedopendata.tw)

This SPARQL endpoint is developed for TAP stores. By processing the link between stores and crops from TAP records, each store can display the crops selling in the store. As mentioned previously, a store can be linked to a registered company in Food Company Registry of Food and Drug Administration or/and Commercial/ Corporate Registry of Ministry of Economic Affairs. Once a TAP store is matched to the two registries, the store is linked to the company in the two registries via using owl: sameAs, as shown in Fig. 5.

TAP Restaurants (http://rest.linkedopendata.tw)

This SPARQL endpoint serves the triples of TAP restaurants. Like stores, some restaurants also can be mapped to the registries of FDA and MEOA. Basically, triples of a TAP restaurant provide the dishes using TAP and their information such as address and telephone number (Fig. 6).

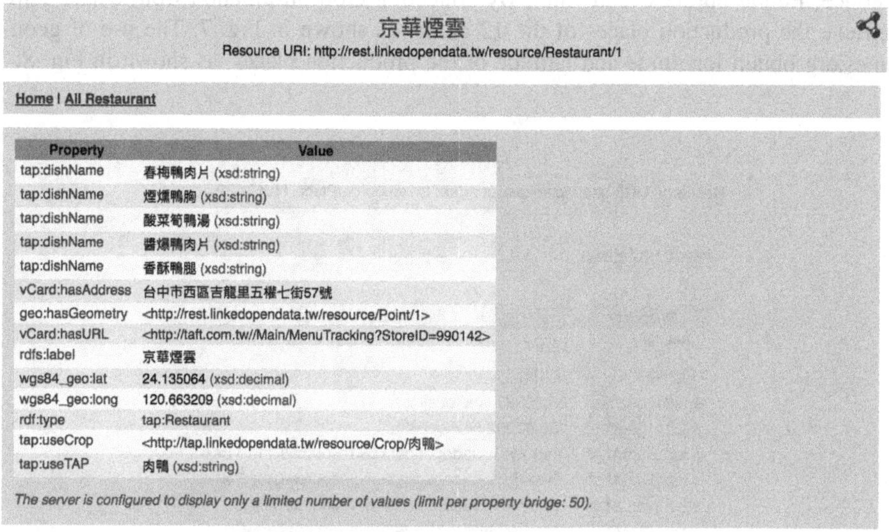

| 京華煙雲 |
| Resource URI: http://rest.linkedopendata.tw/resource/Restaurant/1 |

Home | All Restaurant

Property	Value
tap:dishName	春拘鴨肉片 (xsd:string)
tap:dishName	煙燻鴨胸 (xsd:string)
tap:dishName	酸菜筍鴨湯 (xsd:string)
tap:dishName	醬爆鴨肉片 (xsd:string)
tap:dishName	香酥鴨腿 (xsd:string)
vCard:hasAddress	台中市西區吉龍里五權七街57號
geo:hasGeometry	<http://rest.linkedopendata.tw/resource/Point/1>
vCard:hasURL	<http://taft.com.tw//Main/MenuTracking?StoreID=990142>
rdfs:label	京華煙雲
wgs84_geo:lat	24.135064 (xsd:decimal)
wgs84_geo:long	120.663209 (xsd:decimal)
rdf:type	tap:Restaurant
tap:useCrop	<http://tap.linkedopendata.tw/resource/Crop/肉鴨>
tap:useTAP	肉鴨 (xsd:string)

The server is configured to display only a limited number of values (limit per property bridge: 50).

Fig. 6. The triples of a TAP restaurant displayed by D2R

Japan Crops and Production Places (http://jp.linkedopendata.tw)

To demonstrate the interoperability of the interlinked crops, we select 12 crops to develop a SPARQL endpoint. The 12 crops are Chinese chive, Lady's finger, Pea, Sweet pepper, Wax gourd, Bitter gourd, Chinese mustard, Radish, Welsh onion,

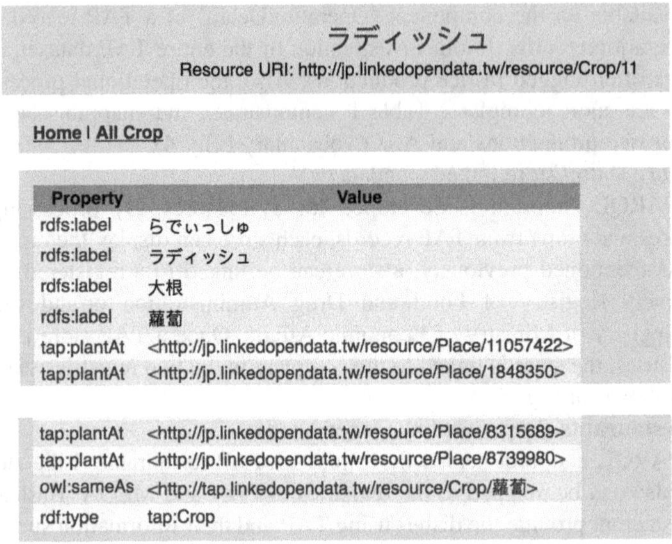

ラディッシュ

Resource URI: http://jp.linkedopendata.tw/resource/Crop/11

Home | All Crop

Property	Value
rdfs:label	らでぃっしゅ
rdfs:label	ラディッシュ
rdfs:label	大根
rdfs:label	蘿蔔
tap:plantAt	<http://jp.linkedopendata.tw/resource/Place/11057422>
tap:plantAt	<http://jp.linkedopendata.tw/resource/Place/1848350>
tap:plantAt	<http://jp.linkedopendata.tw/resource/Place/8315689>
tap:plantAt	<http://jp.linkedopendata.tw/resource/Place/8739980>
owl:sameAs	<http://tap.linkedopendata.tw/resource/Crop/蘿蔔>
rdf:type	tap:Crop

Fig. 7. The triples of radish displayed by D2R

Lettuce, Edible burdock, and Chili. By collecting crop information from e-stats[1], we retrieve the production places of the 12 crops, as shown in Fig. 7. The use of geonames.org obtain longitude and latitude of the production places, as shown in Fig. 8.

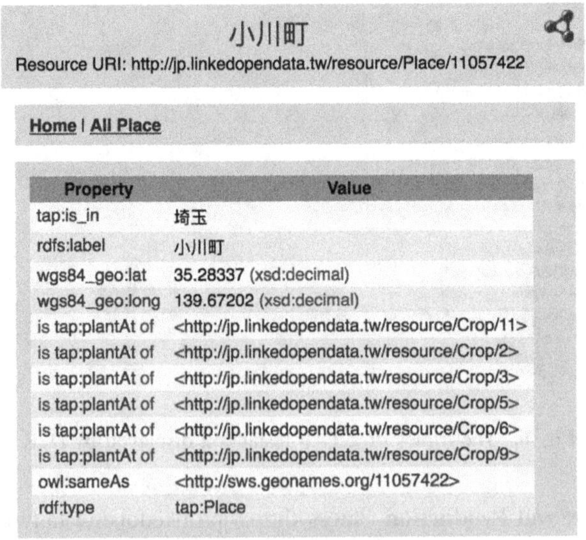

小川町

Resource URI: http://jp.linkedopendata.tw/resource/Place/11057422

Home | All Place

Property	Value
tap:is_in	埼玉
rdfs:label	小川町
wgs84_geo:lat	35.28337 (xsd:decimal)
wgs84_geo:long	139.67202 (xsd:decimal)
is tap:plantAt of	<http://jp.linkedopendata.tw/resource/Crop/11>
is tap:plantAt of	<http://jp.linkedopendata.tw/resource/Crop/2>
is tap:plantAt of	<http://jp.linkedopendata.tw/resource/Crop/3>
is tap:plantAt of	<http://jp.linkedopendata.tw/resource/Crop/5>
is tap:plantAt of	<http://jp.linkedopendata.tw/resource/Crop/6>
is tap:plantAt of	<http://jp.linkedopendata.tw/resource/Crop/9>
owl:sameAs	<http://sws.geonames.org/11057422>
rdf:type	tap:Place

Fig. 8. The triples of 小川町 displayed by D2R

[1] http://www.e-stat.go.jp/SG1/estat/List.do?lid=000001155203.

4.3 Development of an Application for Reusing Linked TAP

To demonstrate the linked data of TAP, we develop a Chrome extension 'LinkedFood' for automatically displaying the TAP information via reading the ingredients on recipe website. The development of 'LinkedFood' is based on RDFLib, which is a package for parsing RDF triples and RDFa and processing owl:sameAs in linked data. LinkedFood is available on Github[2]. The architecture of LinkedFood is shown in Fig. 9. Since the recipe websites are prevailingly using schema.org vocabulary for structuring their content, the structured content provides an opportunity to connect linked TAP. iCook and Cookpad are the recipe websites using schema.org vocabulary for their ingredients in the recipes, as shown in Fig. 10. Thus, LinkedFood is not necessary to parse entire website for obtaining ingredients. As the ingredients are obtained, the SPARQL queries in LinkedFood are triggered to get information from the four SPARQL endpoints mentioned in previous section. Figure 11 displays the TAP stores selling radish that is an ingredient in the recipe. Figure 12 displays the TAP restaurants selling radish that is an ingredient in the recipe. Figure 13 demonstrates the radish price and the amount of radish production. The relationship of price and the amount of production can reveal whether a crop is a seasonal food or not. If a crop is a seasonal

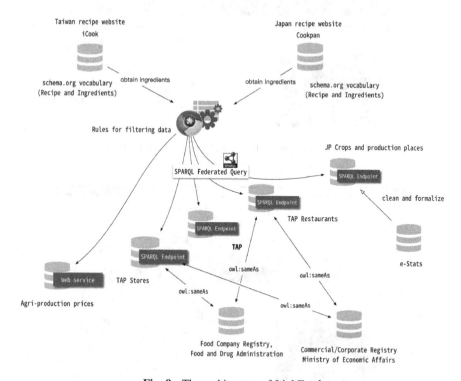

Fig. 9. The architecture of LinkFood

---

[2] https://github.com/trashmai/LinkedFood.

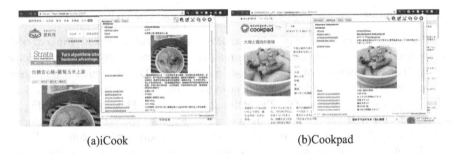

(a)iCook   (b)Cookpad

Fig. 10. The recipe websites, iCook (a) and Cookpad (b), using schema.org vocabulary for structuring their content

Fig. 11. A browse of TAP stores via using LinkedFood

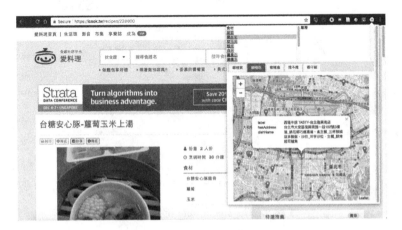

Fig. 12. A browse of TAP restaurants via using LinkedFood

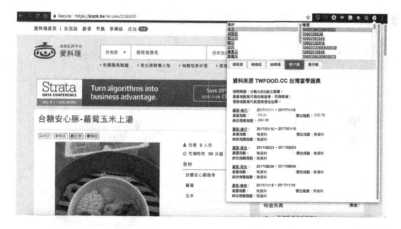

Fig. 13. The price of crops displayed in LinkedFood

Fig. 14. Exploration of radish in Japan by reading Taiwanese recipe website

food, it is usually cheap and has a large amount of production. Once the crops of Taiwan and Japan are interlinked, the linked TAP can support the queries crossing language. Figure 14 displays the use of Taiwanese recipe website can explore the Japanese crop. Moreover, Japanese ingredients can trigger LinkedFood to query TAP information. Figure 15 demonstrates that LinkedFood is used for Japanese recipe website Cookpad.

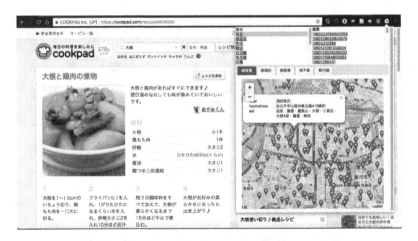

Fig. 15. Japanese recipe website Cookpad using LinkedFood to display TAP stores

Table 1. Mapping TAP operations to AAO vocabulary

TAP operations	AAO vocabulary	
耕地管理	作物生産環境制御作業	Environmental control for crop production
整地	圃場調整	Farm preparation
育苗插秧	種子繁殖作業	Treatment for seed propagation
育苗	苗箱播種	Seeding in nursery box
插秧	湛水直播	Direct seeding in flooded paddy field
田間栽培管理	作物生産環境制御作業	Environmental control for crop production
除草	雑草抑制作業	Treatment for weeding
灌漑/澆水	かん水	Watering
排水	落水	Drainage of ponded water
曬田	太陽熱消毒	Solar heat disinfection
施肥作業	土壌成分制御作業	Treatment for soil fertility arrangement
施肥	施肥	Fertilization
病蟲害防治	害虫抑制作業	Insect pest suppression
施用農藥	殺虫剤散布	Applying the insecticides
栽培防治	誘殺バンド取り付け	Installing tree band
物理防治	物理的害虫抑制作業	Insect pest suppression by physical means
生物防治	生物的害虫抑制作業	Insect pest suppression by biological means
忌避作物	誘殺バンド取り付け	Installing tree band
天然資材	生物農薬散布	Applying biopesticide

(*continued*)

Table 1. (*continued*)

TAP operations	AAO vocabulary	
採收作業	收穫作業	Practice for harvesting
產季結束		
收割	稲刈り	Rice reaping
廢耕		
雜草防治	雑草抑制作業	Weeding
人工除草	手取除草	Manual weeding
稻米(育苗場)作業	繁殖制御作業	Regulation of plant propagation
育苗盤及消毒容器清潔	苗床消毒	Nursery bed disinfection
浸種	浸種	Seed soaking
育苗	採種	Seed production
灌溉	灌漑	Irrigation
施用肥料	施肥	Fertilization
施用防治資材	殺虫剤散布	Applying the incecticides
添加生長促進資材	種子コーティング	Seed coating
秧苗搬運機械清潔		
稻米(育苗場)作業		
進倉	収納作業	Practice for barning
乾燥		
烘乾	子実乾燥	Drying grains or beans
碾製	精米	Rice milling
稻米(貯藏及加工廠)作業		
貯藏倉溫濕度紀錄		
貯藏階段蟲鼠害防治紀錄		
加工階段機器之清理紀錄		
出貨	出荷作業	Shipment

5 Conclusions and Feature Work

The process of developing linked data is a construction of data infrastructure. To interlink dataset, there is a requirement to develop common vocabulary to ensure the data semantics consistent. In this paper, we report our efforts in dealing with vocabulary of TAP for increasing interoperability. Our experience reveals the value of common vocabulary.

While we strongly believe that linked data can make a significant difference to agriculture information, much work still needs to be done. As part of our future work we are investigating the use of rule based reasoning to enable real-time checking of linked data and identify problems of data consistency.

References

1. Kaboré, E., Yeumo, D., Madalli, D., Keizer, J.: Opening and linking agricultural research data. D-Lib Mag. **20**(1–2), 1 (2014)
2. L'Abate, G., Caracciolo, C., Pesce, V., Geser, G., Protonotarios, V., Costantini, E.A.C.: Exposing vocabularies for soil as linked open data. Inf. Process. Agric. **2**(3), 208–216 (2015)
3. Lawan, A., Rakib, A., Alechina, N., Karunaratne, A.: Advancing underutilized crops knowledge using SWRL-enabled ontologies - a survey and early experiment. In: Workshop and Poster Proceedings of the 4th Joint International Semantic Technology Conference Co-located with the 4th Joint International Semantic Technology Conference (JIST 2014). LNCS, vol. 1312 (2014)
4. Lebo, T., et al.: Producing and using linked open government data in the TWC LOGD portal. In: Wood, D. (ed.) Linking Government Data, pp. 51–72. Springer, New York (2011). https://doi.org/10.1007/978-1-4614-1767-5_3
5. Pesce, V., Maru, A., Archer, P., Malapela, T., Keizer, J.: Setting up a global linked data catalog of datasets for agriculture. In: Garoufallou, E., Hartley, R.J., Gaitanou, P. (eds.) MTSR 2015. CCIS, vol. 544, pp. 357–368. Springer, Cham (2015). https://doi.org/10.1007/978-3-319-24129-6_31
6. Rajabi, E., Sanchez-Alonso, S., Sicilia, M.A., Manouselis, N.: A linked and open dataset from a network of learning repositories on organic agriculture. Br. J. Educ. Technol. **48**(1), 71–82 (2017)
7. Setboonsarng, S., Sakai, J., Vancura, L.: Food Safety and ICT traceability systems: lessons from Japan for developing countries. ADBI Working Paper, No. 139. Asian Development Bank, Tokyo (2009)
8. Solanki, M., Brewster, C.: Consuming linked data in supply chains: enabling data visibility via linked pedigrees. In: Fourth International Workshop on Consuming Linked Data (COLD) (2013)
9. Xian, G., Zhao, R., Meng, X., Kou, Y., Zhu, L.: Linking and consuming agricultural big data with linked data and KOS. In: Li, D., Chen, Y. (eds.) CCTA 2014. IAICT, vol. 452, pp. 546–555. Springer, Cham (2015). https://doi.org/10.1007/978-3-319-19620-6_61

Semantic Web for Life Sciences
(Special Session Track)

Inference of Functions, Roles, and Applications of Chemicals Using Linked Open Data and Ontologies

Tatsuya Kushida[1]([⊠]) , Kouji Kozaki[2], Takahiro Kawamura[3],
Yuka Tateisi[1], Yasunori Yamamoto[4] , and Toshihisa Takagi[1,5]

[1] National Bioscience Database Center, Japan Science and Technology Agency,
Kawaguchi, Tokyo, Japan
{kushida,tateisi}@bisciencedbc.jp,
tt@bs.s.u-tokyo.ac.jp
[2] The Institute of Scientific and Industrial Research, Osaka University,
Suita, Japan
kozaki@ei.sanken.osaka-u.ac.jp
[3] Japan Science and Technology Agency, Kawaguchi, Tokyo, Japan
takahiro.kawamura@jst.go.jp
[4] Database Center for Life Science, Research Organization of Information
and Systems, Kashiwa, Japan
yy@dbcls.rois.ac.jp
[5] Department of Biological Sciences, Graduate School of Science,
The University of Tokyo, Bunkyō, Japan

Abstract. A simple method to efficiently collect reliable chemical information was studied for developing an ontological foundation. Even ChEBI, a major chemical ontology, which consists of approximately 90,000 chemicals and information about 1,000 biological and chemical roles, and applications, lacks information regarding the roles of most of the chemicals. NikkajiRDF, linked open data which provide information of approximately 3.5 million chemicals and 694 application examples, is also being developed. NikkajiRDF was integrated with Interlinking Ontology for Biological Concepts (IOBC), which includes 80,000 concepts, including information on a number of diseases and drugs. As a result, it was possible to infer new information on at least one of the 432 biological and chemical functions, applications and involvements with biological phenomena, including diseases to 5,038 chemicals using IOBC's ontological structure. Furthermore, seven chemicals and drugs, which would be involved in 16 diseases, were discovered using knowledge graphs that were developed from IOBC.

Keywords: Chemical · Disease · Drug · Inference · Knowledge graph
LOD · Ontology · RDF · SPARQL

1 Introduction

Chemical information is important for elucidating and recognizing biological phenomena. Information regarding chemical functions and physicochemical qualities are also necessary for the development of various products *e.g.*, drugs, foods, and

© Springer Nature Switzerland AG 2018
R. Ichise et al. (Eds.): JIST 2018, LNCS 11341, pp. 385–397, 2018.
https://doi.org/10.1007/978-3-030-04284-4_26

materials. A simple method to efficiently collect and retrieve reliable chemical information was studied for providing an ontological foundation for researchers, developers, and engineers.

NBDC NikkajiRDF is developed using the Recourse Description Framework (RDF) from the Japan Chemical Substance Dictionary (Nikkaji) [1], which is one of the largest chemicals databases in Japan [2, 3]. It contains 3.5 million chemicals, of which 6,454 chemicals possess at least one of the 694 application examples (*e.g.*, "hypotensive drug," "artificial colorant"). In Nikkaji, InChI and InChIKey are used as unique chemical identifiers, and InChI, which was developed by International Union of Pure and Applied Chemistry and National Institute of Standards and Technology, is a non-proprietary identifier for chemicals [4]. InChIKey is a hashed version of the full InChI. The use of InChI/InChIKey enables us to simplify the process of mapping between chemical database IDs since InChI/InChIKey makes it easier to precisely collect the corresponding chemicals of other databases.

NikkajiRDF uses standard ontologies, which are used in PubChem [5] and ChEMBL [6]. These standard ontologies include Chemical Information Ontology (CHEMINF) [7] and Semanticscience Integrated Ontology (SIO) [8]. As a result, users can perform SPARQL search using these common ontologies (Fig. 1). Moreover, NikkajiRDF has links to chemicals of approximately 30 other databases, which share the same InChIKey. The RDF triples to link them are developed based on a work of UniChem [9] and are described using skos[1]:closeMatch. The RDF data is downloadable from the web sites of both the Life Science Database Archive [2] and NBDC RDF Portal [3]. SPARQL search can be performed using the endpoint [10].

Interlinking Ontology for Biological Concepts (IOBC), which has previously been referred to as "Refined JST thesaurus" [11], contains approximately 80,000 biological concepts, such as various biological phenomena, diseases, molecular functions, gene products, chemicals, drugs, and medical procedures, as well as approximately 20,000 related concepts, such as basic chemistry and environmental science [12]. The concepts are structured by not only "subclass of" but also by 35 additional relations, *e.g.*, "has function," "has role," "has quality," and "is participant in." Each concept is labeled in both English and Japanese. This ontology is visible and downloadable on the homepage [12] through BioPortal [13]. The SPARQL endpoint is prepared [14].

Information on biological and chemical functions/roles/applications is necessary for developing pharmaceutical products and discovering new materials for medical treatment. NikkajiRDF includes a significant number of chemicals with InChI/InChIKey, but it lacks information based on the functions/roles/applications. On the contrary, IOBC contains various biological phenomena including disease in addition to the chemical properties, but it lacks InChI/InChIKey, which is used for easy mapping between chemicals of other data resources. These data sources should be combined for collecting chemicals' functions/roles/applications efficiently and precisely.

Therefore, this study aims to propose a method for finding chemical information efficiently and precisely by combining NikkajiRDF, IOBC, and other open-source

---

[1] sio: <http://semanticscience.org/resource/>.

knowledge-bases regarding chemical information. Using ontological structures and InChI/InChIKey enabled us to infer the functions/roles/applications to more chemicals.

Section 2 describes some representative open-source knowledge-bases and ontologies, as well as how to use them to collect information on chemical functions/roles/applications. In Sect. 3, the attempts to infer the chemical properties through combinations of NikkajiRDF, ChEBI, and IOBC, with knowledge graphs (KGs) developed from IOBC, are described. In Sect. 4, the conclusions are summarized, and future work is discussed.

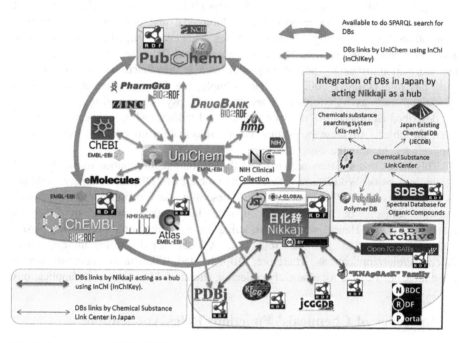

Fig. 1. Integration of NikkajiRDF with major databases of chemicals using InChI/InChIKey.

2 Related Works

In this section, related works regarding the chemical information integration are discussed. ChEBI is a major chemical database and ontology [15]. It includes approximately 90,000 chemicals, which have InChI and InChIKey, and 1,000 roles and applications. Therefore, ChEBI is frequently utilized for annotating and classifying chemicals in various databases of chemicals, including PubChem and ChEMBL using the roles and application terms through InChI/InChIKey. However, the number of chemicals in ChEBI is lacking even in comparison with that of other chemical databases such as Nikkaji, which contains information on approximately 3.5 million chemicals. It is necessary to prepare the knowledge-bases and establish a method that can infer the functions/roles/applications of as many chemicals as possible.

DBpedia is a project that extracts structure information from Wikipedia [16] using RDF [17]. Wikidata is a knowledgebase, which allows every user to extend and edit the stored information [18]. Although DBpedia and Wikidata are wildly used as cross-domain knowledge bases, they have been recently attempted to be utilized for integrating chemical information [17, 19]. They contain information on approximately 18,000 and 150,000 chemicals respectively. However, these numbers are fewer than those of NikkajiRDF, PubChem, or ChEMBL.

The public SPARQL endpoints of DBpedia [20] and Wikidata [21] are prepared, and the users can collect information on biological and chemical functions/roles/applications by performing SPARQL queries. However, DBpedia uses only some annotation properties, such as "dcterms[2]:subject" and "rdfs[3]:seeAlso" for describing the information instead of specific properties, such as "has function (sio:SIO_000225)" and "has role (sio:SIO_000228)." For example, the functions/roles/applications of "Caffeine," such as "Anxiogenics," and "Effect_of_psychoactive_drugs_on_animals" are described as objects of "dcterms:subject" and "rdfs:seeAlso," respectively. Moreover, the objects of these properties include information outside of functions/roles/applications, such as the categories.

This means that the users need to select the appropriate information manually, which is laborious work. Wikidata also faces same problems as DBpedia, namely, Wikidata uses a property "wdt[4]:P31 (instance of)" for describing the functions/roles/applications, and the objects of the property include information outside of functions/roles/applications. Hence, we are considering incorporating some specific properties, such as "has function" and "has role," into Wikidata for describing information on functions/roles/applications. Therefore, DBpedia and Wikidata are currently neither reasonable nor suitable for efficiently collecting chemicals' functions/roles/applications.

3   Inference of Chemicals' Functions/Roles/Applications

3.1   Inference Using ChEBI and NikkajiRDF

In this section, our activities of inferring chemicals' functions/roles/applications using chemical linked open data and ontologies are discussed. NikkajiRDF contains 3.5 million chemicals, however most of them lack application examples such as drugs. We were attempting to integrate NikkajiRDF with ChEBI using InChIKey for adding information on ChEBI's chemical roles and applications to NikkajiRDF chemicals. Prior to that, the ChEBI [22] and NikkajiRDF data [23] were stored into a triple store and the execution environment for SPARQL was prepared. As a result, it was possible to assign 280 ChEBI role and application terms to 2,926 NikkajiRDF chemicals.

---

[2] dcterms: <http://purl.org/dc/terms/>.

[3] rdfs: <http://www.w3.org/2000/01/rdf-schema#>.

[4] wdt: <http://www.wikidata.org/prop/direct/>.

Next, ChEBI's roles/applications were inferred to NikkajiRDF's chemicals using ChEBI's ontological structure. The following SPARQL query was performed.

```
prefix obo: <http://purl.obolibrary.org/obo/>
prefix owl: <http://www.w3.org/2002/07/owl#>
prefix rdfs: <http://www.w3.org/2000/01/rdf-schema#>
prefix skos: <http://www.w3.org/2004/02/skos/core#>
prefix nikkaji: <http://nikkaji.biosciencedbc.jp/>
SELECT distinct ?nikkaji ?chebi ?role
WHERE
{
# NikkajiRDF.ttl
graph nikkaji:link2OtherDBs_basedOnUniChem20180515 {
        ?nikkaji skos:closeMatch ?chebi .
    }
# ChEBI.owl
graph nikkaji:ChEBI2018001.owl.gz {
        ?upperchebi rdfs:subClassOf
            [owl:someValuesFrom ?role ;
             owl:onProperty obo:RO_0000087] .
        ?chebi rdfs:subClassOf* ?upperchebi .
    }
}
```

Figure 2 shows that inference of roles and applications of a NikkajiRDF's chemical "Aspirin" using ChEBI. The inference process is described as follows, (1) it was found that ChEBI's chemicals had the same InChIKey as NikkajiRDF's chemicals using the property skos:closeMatch (*e.g.*, ChEBI's "acetylsalicylic acid" and NikkajiRDF's "Aspirin") in NikkajiRDF structure. (2) The upper chemicals were found using the property rdfs:subClassOf (*e.g.*, oxoacid) in ChEBI's structure. (3) Finally, we collected the roles/applications information of the upper chemicals and assigned the information to the lower chemicals (*e.g.*, "Brønsted acid" to "Aspirin") in ChEBI structure. This indicated that chemicals inherited the ontological upper chemicals' roles/applications through ChEBI's structure.

Consequently, at least one of the 1,062 ChEBI's role and application terms were assigned to each of the 18,386 NikkajiRDF's chemicals through inference using ChEBI's ontological structure, indicating that the number of NikkajiRDF's chemicals with roles/applications information increased by approximately three times after inference, since in NikkajiRDF, 6,454 chemicals originally had at least one of the 694 kinds of applications, which corresponded to ChEBI's roles/applications. This result is downloadable here [24].

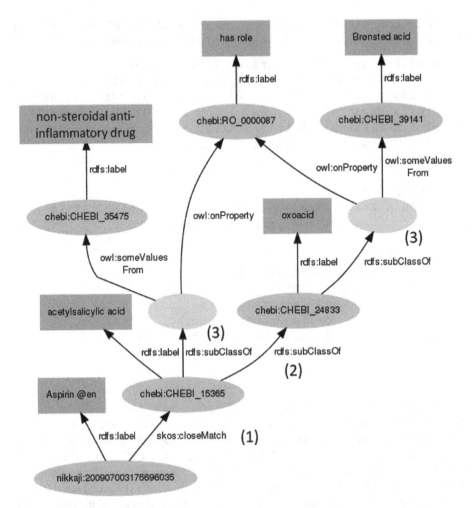

Fig. 2. Inference of the roles and applications of NikkajiRDF's chemicals using ChEBI. It is inferred that "Aspirin" had not only "non-steroidal anti-inflammatory drug" as an application but also "Brønsted acid" as a chemical role. This diagram is visualized by a web service: https://www.kanzaki.com/works/2009/pub/graph-draw.

3.2   Inference Using IOBC and NikkajiRDF

As mentioned before, NikkajiRDF has approximately 3.5 million chemicals with InChI/InChIKey and at least one of the 694 kinds of application examples are assigned to 6,454 chemicals. On the other hand, IOBC has 17,180 organic chemicals, inorganic chemicals, and drugs, which do not contain InChI/InChIKey; for 5,781 of these chemicals, it also has the information on biological and chemical functions (*e.g.* Apoptosis [iobc[5]:2009060391439284621]), roles (*e.g.*, antirheumatic drug [iobc:

---

[5] iobc: <http://purl.jp/bio/4/id/>.

200906008284879667]), and chemical involvements in biological phenomena, including diseases (*e.g.*, hepatitis B [iobc:200906000547096041]). In particular, information regarding the involvement of chemicals in biological phenomena is unique to IOBC.

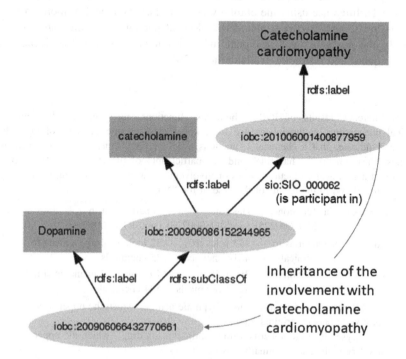

Fig. 3. Inference of the biological and chemical functions, roles, and chemical involvements with the biological phenomena of IOBC's chemicals derived from NikkajiRDF. It is inferred that "Dopamine" would be involved with "Catecholamine cardiomyopathy" with which the upper class "catecholamine" is involved. This diagram is visualized by a web service: https://www. kanzaki.com/works/2009/pub/graph-draw.

We implemented Lexical OWL Ontology Matcher (LOOM) algorithm [25] for matching the labels of between the NikkajiRDF and IOBC chemicals with a SPARQL search. The label-comparison function firstly removed delimiters such as spaces, and underscores. In total, 10,576 NikkajiRDF's chemicals were incorporated into IOBC. Experts confirmed the results, and manually removed 68 false positive data. For example, NikkajiRDF contained two entries whose labels were "HMDP", namely http://stirdf.jst. go.jp/id/200907088719956119   and   http://stirdf.jst.go.jp/id/200907015329956587, while IOBC contained an entry whose label was "HMDP", iobc:200906046710073151. In this case, the experts confirmed that iobc:200906046710073151 corresponded to http://stirdf.jst.go.jp/id/200907015329956587 from descriptions in the database such as their structure information.

Thus, by using the IOBC ontological structure, it was possible to infer information on at least one of the 432 kinds of biological and chemical functions, roles, and chemical involvements in biological phenomena for 5,038 extended chemicals (Fig. 3 and Table 1). Inference using the ontology enabled the assignment of more chemicals functions, roles, and involvements with biological phenomena, which are unique to IOBC. In the cases of "is participant in" and inference is "yes" in Table 1, the SPARQL query and result are available here [26].

Table 1. Inference results of IOBC chemicals' functions, roles and involvements with biological phenomena by the inheritance from upper class chemicals. "No" of the column "Inference" indicates that a chemical's functions, roles or involvements were assigned using properties, "has function," "has role" and "in participant" of the chemicals. "Yes" of that indicates that a chemical's functions, roles or involvements were inferred using them of upper chemicals in addition to the results of the case of the "No."

Inference	Has function (sio:SIO_000225)	Has role (sio:SIO_000228)	Is participant in (sio:SIO_000062)
No	9 functions to 15 chemicals	343 roles to 4814 chemicals	32 biological phenomena to 33 chemicals
Yes	15 functions to 187 chemicals[a]	368 roles to 4839 chemicals[b]	49 biological phenomena to 594 chemicals[c]

[a]*e.g.,* "Barbital" inherits a function "hypnotic action," which the upper class "sedative hypnotic" originally possessed.
[b]*e.g.,* "Lysergic Acid" inherits a role "antiparkinson drug," which the upper class "ergot alkaloid" originally possessed.
[c]cf. Fig. 3.

3.3   Inference Using Knowledge Graphs (KGs)

In previous works, KGs from IOBC were developed by performing SPARQL search [27], and disease-related gene products were discovered from the KG [28]. The primary focus was on the relationships between a preceding biological phenomenon (*e.g.,* platelet aggregation) and the succeeding disease (*e.g.,* thromboembolism), and the relationships were described using a property "precedes [xkos[6]:precedes]" in the KGs. It was claimed that gene products, which regulate or promote a biological phenomenon and precede a disease, were potential candidates for disease-related gene products. IOBC has 35 kinds of properties, such as "has function," "precedes," and "is participant

---

[6] xkos: <http://rdf-vocabulary.ddialliance.org/xkos#>.

in," to strictly describe the relationships between the concepts [11, 26], and it is possible to efficiently and precisely discover potential candidate genes by performing a SPARQL search.

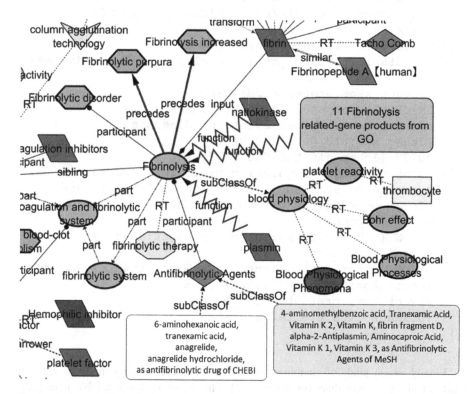

Fig. 4. A part of Fibrinolysis network. This graph is visualized using Cytoscape (http://www. cytoscape.org/).

In this study, the inference of chemicals' involvements with diseases from KGs "Fibrinolysis network" (Fig. 4), and "Bone metabolic turnover network (BMT network)" was attempted. It was assumed that it is possible to infer the involvement of diseases with any chemicals by using the information on the involvement of the diseases with preceding biological phenomena.

At first, a SPARQL query was performed to create KGs: Fibrinolysis network and BMT network. Each of the KGs were constructed as collections of concepts connected with "Fibrinolysis [iobc:200906057747871335]" and "BMT [iobc: 200906094913122330]" within three steps, respectively. Next, these KGs were stored in a triple store. Then, in the Fibrinolysis network and BMT network, we performed the following SPARQL search to infer chemicals' involvements with diseases.

```
prefix dcterms: <http://purl.org/dc/terms/>
prefix sio: <http://semanticscience.org/resource/>
prefix skos: <http://www.w3.org/2004/02/skos/core#>
prefix subject: <http://purl.jp/bio/4/subject/>
prefix xkos: <http://rdf-
vocabulary.ddialliance.org/xkos#>
SELECT distinct ?label_chem ?label_event ?label_disease
{
    {?event xkos:precedes ?disease .}
    UNION {?event sio:SIO_000062 ?disease .}
#finding pre-biological events of diseases
    {?chem sio:SIO_000062 ?event .}
    UNION {?chem sio:SIO_000225 ?event .}
#finding chemicals regulating biological events
    ?disease dcterms:subject subject:LS51 . #diseases
    {?chem dcterms:subject subject:CA06 .}
#organic compounds
    UNION {?chem dcterms:subject subject:CA05 .}
#inorganic compounds
    UNION {?chem dcterms:subject subject:LS44 .} #drugs
    ?chem skos:prefLabel ?label_chem.
    ?event skos:prefLabel ?label_event.
    ?disease skos:prefLabel ?label_disease.
}
```

Finally, seven kinds of chemicals and drugs that were strongly involved with 16 kinds of diseases were discovered (Table 2). This result is downloadable here [29]. Furthermore, ChEBI and MeSH [30], which is a medical controlled vocabulary thesaurus, were utilized. Consequently, 13 kinds of chemicals/drugs (*e.g.*, "6-aminohexanoic acid [iobc:200906077611232267]," "tranexamic acid [iobc: 200906016175942637]," and "Vitamin K [iobc:200906052607096496]") as chemicals/drugs of "antifibrinolytic drug [chebi:CHEBI_48675] and "Antifibrinolytic Agents [mesh[7]:D000933]" were found. Moreover, 38 kinds of chemicals/drugs (*e.g.*, "vitamin D2 [iobc:20090704551560403]," "Raloxifene [iobc:200907039651233937]" and "toremifene [iobc:2009070095994908403]") as chemicals/drugs of "bone density conservation agent [chebi:CHEBI_50646]" were found (Fig. 4). These inferred results are needed to be biologically and clinically validated by further studies.

---

[7] mesh: <http://id.nlm.nih.gov/mesh/>.

Table 2. Results of the inferring chemicals' involvements with diseases using two KGs: "Fibrinolysis network" and "BMT network."

KGs	Chemicals or drugs	Pre-biological events of diseases	Diseases
Fibrinolysis network	Antifibrinolytic agents	Fibrinolysis	Fibrinolysis increased Fibrinolytic disorder Fibrinolytic purpura
BMT network	Bone density conservation agents Nano hydroxyapatite Osteogenesis promoter Teriparatide	Osteogenesis	Abnormal bone metabolism Bony cataract Enostosis Hyper-ALP-emia Lipoma ossificans Osteoplastic sarcoma Osteoplastica Tuberculous dactylitis
	Bone resorption inhibitor Denosumab	Bone resorption	Alveolar Bone Loss Osteitis Fibrosa Cystica Osteolysis Osteolysis, Essential Osteolytic lesion

4   Conclusions

The work of the framework of Semantic Automated Discovery and Integration (SADI) is widely known as an activity of the extraction and inference of chemical information using SPARQL [31]. On the other hand, finding drug targets and predicting side effects by applying machine learning to RDF and KGs has been conducted [32]; the results, issues, and possibilities are being actively discussed. However, it is still difficult for researchers who do not have a highly specialized knowledge and skillset to prepare their execution environments and handle them efficiently.

This study developed a method of collecting reliable chemical information and constructed knowledge bases, such as NikkajiRDF and IOBC to enable many researchers, developers, and engineers to easily collect chemical information on the internet, particularly information regarding chemicals' functions and roles, as well as involvements with biological processes, including diseases. Data sources that are currently dispersed all over the world should become more findable, accessible, interoperable, and reusable based on the FAIR principle [33] to utilize valuable chemical data. Furthermore, the preparation of InChI/InChIKey as a chemical identifier based on the steric structure is necessary for integrating chemicals among different data sources. Enabling the federated search on SPARQL endpoints is also important. For example, the federated search from the public DBpedia SPARQL endpoint [20] to other SPARQL endpoints is currently unavailable.

In the future, the utilization of information on the interactions between chemicals and gene products and metabolic and signal transduction pathways will enable more extensive, and precise collection and prediction of information regarding chemicals' associations with biological phenomena, along with the corresponding side effects. This is expected to make contributions to drug discovery research, to the selection of effective medical treatments, and to the appropriate use and application of materials.

Acknowledgments. This study was supported by an operating grant from the Japan Science and Technology Agency and JSPS KAKENHI Grant Number JP17H01789. A part of this study was progressed and discussed in Japan BioHackathon 2016 (BH16.12), which served as a research and development meeting. We are grateful to all participants who gave us their valuable advice and constructive comments.

References

1. Kimura, T., Kushida, T.: Openness of Nikkaji RDF data and integration of chemical information by Nikkaji acting as a hub. J. Inf. Process. Manag. **58**(3), 204–212 (2015)
2. NikkajiRDF Homepage in Life Science Database Archive. http://doi.org/10.18908/lsdba. nbdc01530–02-000. Accessed 8 Aug 2018
3. NikkajiRDF Homepage in NBDC RDF Portal. https://integbio.jp/rdf/?view=detail&id= nikkaji. Accessed 8 Aug 2018
4. Heller, S., McNaught, A., Stein, S., Tchekhovskoi, D., Pletnev, I.: InChI-the worldwide chemical structure identifier standard. J. Cheminform. **5**(1), 7 (2013)
5. Fu, G., Batchelor, C., Dumontier, M., Hastings, J., Willighagen, E., Bolton, E.: PubChemRDF: towards the semantic annotation of PubChem compound and substance databases. J. Cheminform. **7**(1), 34 (2015)
6. Willighagen, E.L., et al.: The ChEMBL database as linked open data. J. Cheminform. **5**(1), 23 (2013)
7. Hastings, J., Chepelev, L., Willighagen, E., Adams, N., Steinbeck, C., Dumontier, M.: The chemical information ontology: provenance and disambiguation for chemical data on the biological semantic web. PloS **6**(10), e25513 (2011)
8. Dumontier, M., et al.: The Semanticscience Integrated Ontology (SIO) for biomedical research and knowledge discovery. J. Biomed. Semant. **5**(1), 14 (2014)
9. Chambers, J., et al.: UniChem: a unified chemical structure cross-referencing and identifier tracking system. J. Cheminform. **5**(1), 3 (2013)
10. NBDC RDF Portal SPARQL Endpoint. https://integbio.jp/rdf/sparql. Accessed 8 Aug 2018
11. Kushida, T., et al.: Efficient construction of a new ontology for life sciences by sub-classifying related terms in the Japan Science and Technology Agency Thesaurus. In: Proceedings of the 8th International Conference on Biomedical Ontology (ICBO 2017), vol. 2137, pp. 1–6. CEUR-WS.org, Newcastle (2017)
12. IOBC Homepage in BioPortal. http://purl.bioontology.org/ontology/IOBC. Accessed 8 Aug 2018
13. Noy, N.F., et al.: BioPortal: ontologies and integrated data resources at the click of a mouse. Nucleic Acids Res. **37**(suppl_2), W170–W173 (2009)
14. IOBC SPARQL endpoint, http://lod.hozo.jp/repositories/IOBC. Accessed 8 Aug 2018

15. Hastings, J., et al.: The ChEBI reference database and ontology for biologically relevant chemistry: enhancements for 2013. Nucleic Acids Res. **41**(D1), D456–D463 (2013)

16. Wikipedia. https://www.wikipedia.org/. Accessed 8 Aug 2018

17. Bizer, C., et al.: DBpedia-A crystallization point for the Web of Data. Web Semant.: Sci. Serv. Agents World Wide Web **7**(3), 154–165 (2009)

18. Vrandečić, D., Krötzsch, M.: Wikidata: a free collaborative knowledgebase. Commun. ACM **57**(10), 78–85 (2014)

19. Ertl, P., Patiny, L., Sander, T., Rufener, C., Zasso, M.: Wikipedia chemical structure explorer: substructure and similarity searching of molecules from Wikipedia. J. Cheminform. **7**(1), 10 (2015)

20. DBpedia public SPARQL endpoint. https://dbpedia.org/sparql. Accessed 8 Aug 2018

21. Wikidata public SPARQL endpoint. https://query.wikidata.org/. Accessed 8 Aug 2018

22. ChEBI ontology files. ftp://ftp.ebi.ac.uk/pub/databases/chebi/ontology/. Accessed 8 Aug 2018

23. link2OtherDBs_basedOnUniChem   of   NikkajiRDF.   http://doi.org/10.18908/lsdba.nbdc01530–02-006. Accessed 8 Aug 2018

24. SPARQL query result in Section 3.1. http://nikkaji-rdf.biosciencedbc.jp/download/quary24/chebi2nikkajiRDF/0,5000.html. Accessed 8 Aug 2018

25. Ghazvinian, A., Noy, N.F., Musen, M.A.: Creating mappings for ontologies in biomedicine: simple methods work. In: AMIA Annual Symposium Proceedings. American Medical Informatics Association, pp. 198–202 (2009)

26. SPARQL query result in Section 3.2. http://nikkaji-rdf.biosciencedbc.jp/download/quary25/reasoning_Inheritance/.html. Accessed 8 Aug 2018

27. Kushida, T., et al.: Refined JST thesaurus extended with data from other open life science data sources. In: Wang, Z., Turhan, A.-Y., Wang, K., Zhang, X. (eds.) JIST 2017. LNCS, vol. 10675, pp. 35–48. Springer, Cham (2017). https://doi.org/10.1007/978-3-319-70682-5_3

28. Kushida, T., et al.: Refining JST thesaurus and discussing the effectiveness in life science research. In: Proceedings of 5th Intelligent Exploration of Semantic Data Workshop (IESD 2016, Co-located with ISWC 2016), pp. 1–14, Kobe (2016)

29. SPARQL query result in Section 3.3. http://nikkaji-rdf.biosciencedbc.jp/download/quary26/reasoning_knowledgeGraph/.html. Accessed 8 Aug 2018

30. Bodenreider, O., Nelson, S.J., Hole, W.T., Chang, H.F.: Beyond synonymy: exploiting the UMLS semantics in mapping vocabularies. In: Proceedings of AMIA Symposium, pp. 815–819 (1998)

31. Chepelev, L.L., Dumontier, M.: Semantic web integration of cheminformatics resources with the SADI framework. J. Cheminform. **3**(1), 16 (2011)

32. Alshahrani, M., Khan, M.A., Maddouri, O., Kinjo, A.R., Queralt-Rosinach, N., Hoehndorf, R.: Neuro-symbolic representation learning on biological knowledge graphs. Bioinformatics **33**(17), 2723–2730 (2017)

33. Wilkinson, M.D., et al.: The FAIR guiding principles for scientific data management and stewardship. Sci. Data **3**, 160018 (2016)

Semantic Navigation of Disease-Specific Pathways: The Case of Non-small Cell Lung Cancer (NSCLC)

Sung Min Yang and Hong-Gee Kim[✉]

Biomedical Knowledge Engineering Laboratory, Seoul National University, Seoul, Korea
{syang90, hgkim}@snu.ac.kr

Abstract. By studying the cancer genome, scientists can discover what base changes are causing a cell to become a cancer cell. In addition, cancers and diseases are affected by a series of complex interactions between a multitude of entities such as genes and proteins. Biological pathway analysis became necessary to understand these entities within diverse contexts. In this paper, we propose a framework for researchers to navigate disease-specific pathways. The basic structure of analysis data is BioPAX which is described in RDF and is produced by the Reactome database (biological pathway database). For this framework, we utilize a large scale of biological sources such as Pathway Commons, clinical data, dbSNP, and ClinVar. Especially, we choose non-small cell lung cancer (NSCLC) for case study to demonstrate components of semantic navigation. Furthermore, we generate and analyze non-small cell lung cancer (NSCLC) specific pathways. Our proposed system will help researchers find a point at which they begin their interests. For instance, it can help discover which protein or gene most affect a specific disease or it can aid in integrating different sources of biological information. Moreover, plenty of biological data extended by our system suggests a new perspective for scientists to find a direction of research.

Keywords: Pathway analysis · Biomedical semantics · Network analysis

1 Introduction

We live in a world where large amounts of data come from a wide range of fields. This phenomenon is actively researched to efficiently store and share large amounts of data. With this time demand, a way to express data in RDF/OWL has developed. In the field of biology, a vast amount of biologic data is emerging as technology advances. For example, advances in computer technology have made it possible to rapidly obtain DNA sequence (6 billion) and easily manipulate data preprocessing. In addition, the size of individual data, as well as the types of data, has also increased significantly. For instance, protein data, gene data, protein-protein interaction (PPI) database, biological pathway database, drug database etc.

One major challenge of the post-genomic era is to find the genes at risk, identify their functions and develop new techniques for testing, diagnosis, and treatments [1].

© Springer Nature Switzerland AG 2018
R. Ichise et al. (Eds.): JIST 2018, LNCS 11341, pp. 398–409, 2018.
https://doi.org/10.1007/978-3-030-04284-4_27

Diseases are known to be caused by mutations in one or more genes or by genetic or environmental factors [2]. Furthermore, diseases can have a variety of symptoms, and complex diseases can occur at once. Hence, it is important to consider a series of complex interactions between such genes and proteins. Moreover, their pathogenesis should be interpreted with the effects of genetic and environmental factors together. Our research has started with this demand. We will use biological data such as biological pathways, mRNA expression level, and single nucleotide polymorphism (SNP) to understand the disease and to identify biomarkers or risk factors.

Lung cancer is the leading cause of cancer-related mortalities worldwide, accounting for 29% of male and 26% of female cancer deaths [3]. The causes of lung cancer are numerous. however, smoking is unquestionably the leading cause [4]. Moreover, until recently, males had a higher incidence of lung cancer and a higher mortality rate than females [3]. Primary pulmonary neoplasms are classified into two large histological subgroups with different prognoses and therapeutic approaches: non-small cell lung cancer (NSCLC) and small cell lung cancer (SCLC), with NSCLC contributing to about 80% of all cases.

A number of studies have been conducted to generate a pathway or to extract and visualize the data of a pathway according to the desired purpose [5, 6]. Pathway analysis using biological data such as transcript data and SNP data is also active [5, 7, 8]. However, the disadvantage of these studies is that they explain the diseases in a fragmentary way. In addition, the pathway was analyzed using one clinical data related to the disease. In this study, we investigated the complex relationship of various pathways to a disease. We also tried to provide a broad and in-depth understanding of the disease by using transcript levels and mutation data together.

In our paper, there are three chapters without instruction. Chapter 2 describes the five databases used in our system. For examples. biological pathway database, clinical database, and other biological information. The next chapter describes the components of semantic navigation. In addition, NSCLC disease is selected as a case study and the system is verified against previous studies. Finally, the conclusion chapter presents future research directions, limitations of the current system, and expected effects.

2 Data Materials for Semantic Query and Analysis

2.1 Reactome

Reactome is a free, open-source, curated and peer-reviewed biological pathway database [9]. A biological pathway is a series of interactions among molecules in a cell that leads to products or changes. Entities in pathways play an important role in previous studies of genomics. The underlying data is easily downloadable in a number of standard formats including SBML, pdf, and BioPAX (level 2 or level3). In our framework, we use biological pathway data as BioPAX. BioPAX (Biological Pathway Exchange) is an RDF/OWL-based standard language to represent biological pathways at the molecular and cellular level (see Fig. 1) [10]. BioPax level3 can represent metabolic and signaling pathways, molecular and genetic interactions and gene regulation networks.

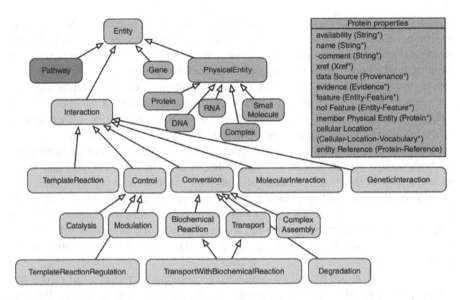

Fig. 1. A high-level view of the BioPAX ontology. Classes, shown as boxes and arrows, represent inheritance relationships. The three main types of classes in BioPAX are Pathway (red), Interaction (green) and PhysicalEntity and Gene (blue). For brevity, the properties of the Protein class only are shown as an example at the top right. Asterisks indicate that multiple values for the property are allowed [10]. (Color figure online)

2.2   Pathway Commons

A goal of Pathway Commons is to collect and disseminate biological pathway and interaction data. Data is collected from several databases and is represented in the BioPAX standard [11]. There is not only biological pathway databases but also protein, drug information, miRNA-target gene relationship database, chemical compounds, and protein-protein interaction databases.

Simple Interaction Format (SIF). Many network analysis algorithms require pair-wise interaction networks as an input. A biological pathway often contains more complex relationships with multiple participants, such as biochemical reactions. To make it easier to use all of the pathway information in Pathway Commons with typical network analysis tools, they developed a set of rules to reduce interactions in pathway to pairwise relationships [6]. Because of SIF interactions are always binary it is not possible to fully represent all of biological pathway, thus adapting this rules to pathway data is lossy in general. Nonetheless, the SIF network is useful for those applications that require pairwise interaction input.

2.3   Genomic Data Commons (GDC)

The National Cancer Institute's (NCI's) Genomic Data Commons (GDC) is a data sharing platform that supports studies to oncology. It is not just a database or a tool; it is an expandable knowledge network supporting the import and standardization of genomic and clinical data from cancer research programs. In our paper, we select a TCGA project for lung adenocarcinoma as well as a non-small cell lung cancer or NSCLC cancer type as a case study. Moreover, we also put to use the participant's clinical data of transcriptome profiling (n = 571) and SNP (n = 561) in the GDC data portal. For more detail analyzing, we utilize participant's metadata to distinguish each cancer type which annotated TNM method.

Transcriptome Profiling. Transcriptome indicates a set of all RNA or just messenger RNA in a cell or population of cells. The study of transcriptomics which includes expression profiling examines the expression level of RNAs in a given cell population. In our research, we make an experiment to compare the expression level of mRNA between normal and tumor cells. Through this experiment, we could get knowledge that some genes are up-regulated or down-regulated when participant got an NSCLC.

SNV Calling from NGS Data. SNV calling refers to a range of methods for identifying the existence of single nucleotide variants (SNVs) from the results of next-generation sequencing (NGS) experiments. These are computational techniques and are in contrast to special experimental methods based on known population-wide single nucleotide polymorphisms.

2.4   dbSNP

The Single Nucleotide Polymorphism database (dbSNP) is a public-domain archive for a broad collection of simple genetic polymorphisms [12]. Our system extracts disease-specific variants from clinical data. And if this variant is registered in dbSNP, the system provides information related variant to the researcher. However, variants that are not registered but have a high frequency in certain diseases can be considered novel. In addition, we can observe changes in amino acid sequence and changes in amino acid properties through base changes.

2.5   ClinVar

ClinVar is a freely accessible, public archive of reports of the relationships among human variations and phenotypes, with supporting evidence [13]. ClinVar thus facilitates access to and communication about the relationships asserted between human variation and observed health status, and the history of that interpretation. ClinVar processes submissions reporting variants found in patient samples, assertions made regarding their clinical significance, information about the submitter, and other supporting data.

Therefore, ClinVar facilitates access to the relationship between human variants and observed health status, and provides a history of studies. ClinVar handles reporting variants, claims of clinical significance, information about submitters, and other support data found in patient samples. In our system, we only focus on variants and claims of clinical significance about NSCLC.

3   Semantic Navigation for NSCLC Related Pathways

The workflow of our system can be seen in Fig. 2. Semantic navigation is composed of two processes, each of which includes several sub-processes. The first is the process of creating a disease-specific pathway, and the second is the step of adding the value of the clinical data supporting the analysis to the generated pathways. The goal of semantic navigation is to understand the disease by analyzing the final network which includes various data.

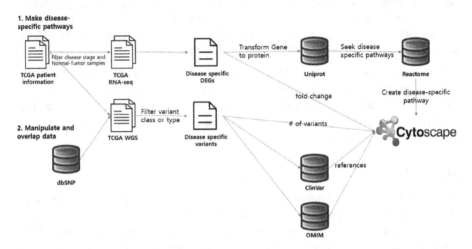

Fig. 2. This figure describes the full system's workflow. Fist process of workflow is making disease-specific pathways. The next is overlapping RNA-seq and variants in merged pathways.

3.1   Selection of Clinically Significant Genes Related to NSCLC

First of all, we collected patients' RNA-seq data and SNVs of whole genome sequencing (WGS) in the GDC data portal to find statistically significant genes related to NSCLC. The RNA-seq results are used to generate DEG (differentially expressed gene) expression levels by calculating FPKM (Fragments Per Kilobase Million) or RPKM (Reads Per Kilobase Million) based on the number of reads attached to each gene. The differences between the two groups of genes are calculated with the discriminated normal samples (n = 59) and disease samples (n = 512). We divided the samples into cancer types (see Table 1) and selected Stage IIA disease group (n = 50). A reason to choose stage IIA of NSCLC is similar to the number of normal samples. Balancing the number of samples between case and control is quite important when we execute statistic methods.

Next, we calculate fold change (FC) at population of separated stage IIA tumor samples (n = 50) and normal samples (n = 59). FC is a relative value that is less or more expressed in the disease group compared to the normal group. This value can be used as a reference for selecting up-regulated or down-regulated genes. Here, the term "up-regulated gene" means that the expression of a transcript of the gene in a specific tissue of a diseased patient is expressed more than in a normal person. On the other hand, down-regulated genes are expressed less than normal human transcript levels. Third, the false discovery rate (FDR) values were calculated using the expression levels of normal group and disease group samples.

Finally, 20 genes with the largest absolute fold change among the genes satisfying the cut-off p-value <0.001 and | fold change | > 1.5 criteria were selected (see Table 2).

Table 1. Distribution of cancer stage and the number of samples

Stage type	# of samples
Stage I	277
Stage IIA	50
Stage IIB	74
Stage III	84
Stage IV	27

Table 2. Top10 Peaked up/down-regulated genes

GeneSymbol	fc	-log10(FDR)
SFTPC | 6440	-8.91691	15.09793
SLC6A4 | 6532	-7.97384	30.13662
CLDN18 | 51208	-7.40251	19.04978
LGI3 | 203190	-7.10363	17.9762
AGER | 177	-6.89014	24.57701
ITLN2 | 142683	-6.63294	16.27671
C13orf36 | 400120	-6.58271	22.41837
HBA1 | 3039	-6.54921	17.11439
SCGB1A1 | 7356	-6.34641	11.25273
UPK3B | 80761	-6.30252	23.07116
COL11A1 | 1301	6.315587	17.51322
FAM83A | 84985	6.189051	31.51814
CST1 | 1469	5.608471	14.30392
PRAME | 23532	5.50382	11.53788
CYP24A1 | 1591	5.418711	17.63465
LOC84740 | 84740	5.39805	17.02415
XAGE1D | 9503	5.360254	11.47636
MMP11 | 4320	5.261746	23.37366
MMP13 | 4322	5.2164	12.30809
SPP1 | 6696	5.107309	22.68295

Twenty genes selected through the NCBI gene database were evaluated for validation. For example, the fold change of −8.9 in the gene SFTPC means that the disease was 512 times less in the patient population when the transcript level of the gene was compared to normal (see Fig. 3). The surfactant is secreted by the alveolar cells of the lung and maintains the stability of pulmonary tissue by reducing the surface tension of fluids that coat the lung. Another example is the FAM83A also known as the BJ-TSA-9 up-regulated gene in NSCLC. BJ-TSA-9 mRNA was expressed in 52.5% (21 of 40) of human lung cancer tissues and was especially higher in lung adenocarcinoma (68.8%) [14].

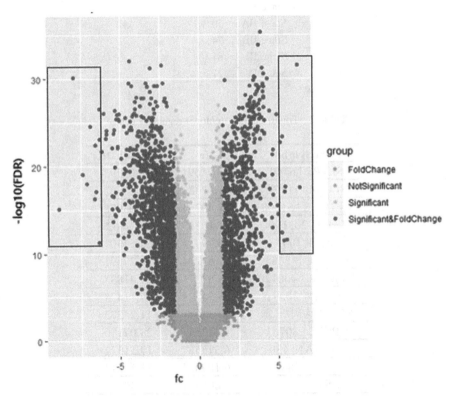

Fig. 3. A figure shows four groups for volcano plot. Yellow color means genes in this group is over cut-off about | fold change | > 1.5. The red group explains that genes are significantly and clinically valid to distinguish between a population of normal and tumor. (Color figure online)

3.2   Extracting Disease-Specific Pathways

First, we should adjust the level of entities. It means that data of transcriptome profiling and pathways have a different level of data. The result of transcriptome profiling consists of genes. On the other hand, pathways made of proteins. So, we converted

GeneSymbol to protein id using UniProtKB included in Pathway Commons. Because of the biological pathways such as Reactome, KEGG present basic entities as proteins. Next, we analyzed the BioPAX structure to extract biological pathways containing selected genes and found two rules. When a specific gene is included in the pathway, it is used as a controller entity or as a controlled entity. We obtained pathways by dynamically generating SPARQL queries with genes associated with NSCLC (see Fig. 4).

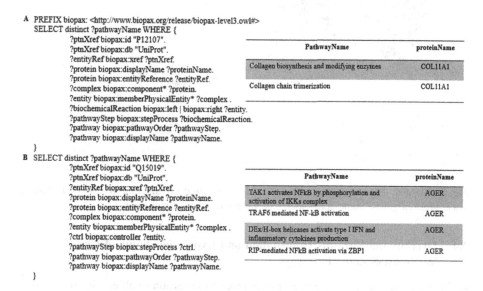

Fig. 4. (a) Figure of left presents that protein 'P12107' is used for the controlled entity in a pathway. (b) It indicates a SPARQL query which contains protein used controller entity in a pathway. The Tables describe results of SPARQL queries.

3.3   Merging Disease-Specific Pathways

There are fourteen types of binary relations in SIF. In our system, we use two types of relations which are controls-state-change-of and controls-expression-of. Because some types of binary relations consist of small molecules which are not considered in our research. In this step, we apply this rules to our disease-specific pathways. Consequentially, we collect not only several inferred binary relations including disease-specific proteins but also relations in the same pathway. In Fig. 5, thirteen pathways including genes related to NSCLC are expressed. Each node represents a gene with a GeneSymbol. Some genes are common to several pathways and serve as hubs between pathways. This is called crosstalk between pathways.

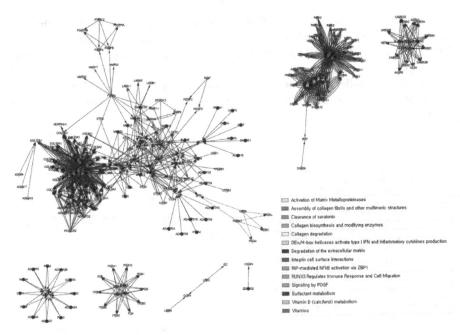

Fig. 5. Merged disease-specific pathways. There are thirteen different pathways including disease-related genes. Some genes locate between two or more pathways.

3.4   Overlapping Variants Information and Expression Value of Genes in Disease-Specific Pathways

In this step, we add the amount of transcriptomic expression to all entities of disease-specific pathways generated through various processes (see Fig. 6). The down-regulated gene is blue and the up-regulated gene is red. The color step by step changes from blue to red depending on the expression. In addition, genes with a large number of variants have gradually increased the size of the nodes. According to previous studies, the upregulation of SPP1 and downregulation of AGER suggested that these were risk factors for NSCLC [15]. These results are not only the same in our study, but also provide information that can be used to predict changes in the expression level of transcripts. It is the relationship between the target gene and the surrounding genes. In addition, variant information can be used to predict the expression level. In our network, the expression level of SPP1 is stimulated by CBFB and RUNX3 genes, and the state is changed by MMP7 and MMP3.

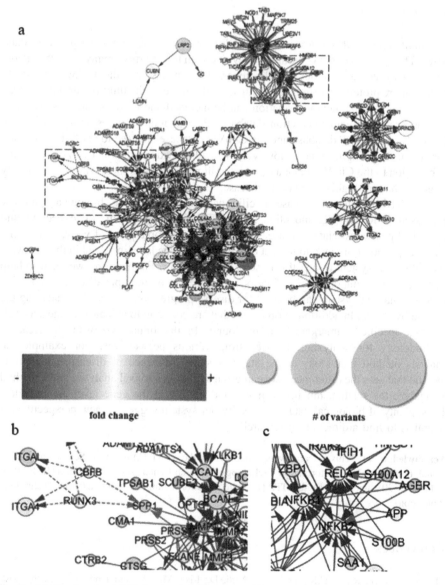

Fig. 6. (a) Overlapping NGS data to the disease-specific network. A result of adding variants and fold change to the disease-specific network. Size property of the node in the network. SNP count '1' means that the gene contains only one variant. The size of a node is gradually increasing by the number of gene's variants. It means that some gene which has more variants comparing to other genes can get a higher probability of risk to make trouble. There is a legend that indicates the value of the gene's transcriptomic expression. The blue means a gene is downregulated. On the other hand, the red is presented as up-regulated genes. (b) relations among SPP1 gene. (c) associations with AGER gene. (Color figure online)

4 Conclusion

The limitations of this study include the limitations of the biological pathway databases. The curation of data continues to evolve with the efforts of many researchers, but the pathway contains about 10,000 genes. This means that the pathway needs to include more protein-protein relationships. Furthermore, if the limit of current BioPAX version is overcome, new information can be included and used for analysis. We may use the protein-protein interaction database (PPI) in future studies as an alternative. Currently, the dbSNP database and the ClinVar database are used to verify that they are variants in meaningful genes. However, we will provide mutational-clinical outcome information to the ClinVar database, which will provide researchers with the credibility of genes that are highly relevant to disease.

We have created a disease-specific network by utilizing biological pathway expressed in RDF/OWL and clinical data. Through our system, we expect to find biological pathways related to diseases from a macroscopic point of view, and from a microscopic point of view, to look at diseases at the gene level involved in the pathway. We called our system as a pathway semantic navigator. Furthermore, we want to help researchers find important risk factors for a disease or multiple diseases. It is also expected that our system can be used for disease progression analysis by analyzing the disease by stages. In addition, biomarkers that are common to all cancer stages, as well as stage-specific biomarkers, can be found. In the future, we want to create a methodology for analyzing diseases from various perspectives. For example, an analysis method that looks at the stage-by-stage difference of disease, an analysis method that sees the difference between groups through survival analysis, and a method to analyze the relationship between sex and disease at the gene level are included. Thus, plenty of biological data extended by our system suggests a new perspective for scientists to find a direction of research.

Acknowledgment. This research was supported by the MSIT (Ministry of Science and ICT), Korea, under the ITRC (Information Technology Research Center) support program (IITP-2018-2017-0-01630) supervised by the IITP (Institute for Information & communications Technology Promotion).

References

1. Mocellin, S., Rossi, C.R., Traldi, P., Nitti, D., Lise, M.: Molecular oncology in the post-genomic era: the challenge of proteomics. Trends Mol. Med. **10**(1), 24–32 (2004)
2. Piñero, J., et al.: DisGeNET: a comprehensive platform integrating information on human disease-associated genes and variants. Nucleic Acids Res. **45**(D1), D833–D839 (2017)
3. Siegel, R., Naishadham, D., Jemal, A.: Cancer statistics, 2012. CA Cancer J. Clin. **62**, 10–29 (2012)
4. Alberg, A.J., Ford, J.G., Samet, J.M.: Epidemiology of lung cancer: ACCP evidence-based clinical practice guidelines (2nd edition). Chest **132**(3 Suppl.), 29S–55S (2007)
5. Chen, L., et al.: Prioritizing risk pathways: a novel association approach to searching for disease pathways fusing SNPs and pathways. Bioinformatics **25**(2), 237–242 (2009)

6. Cho, A., et al.: Using biological pathway data with paxtools. BMC Bioinform. **39**(Database issue), D685–D690 (2010)

7. Bauer-Mehren, A., Furlong, L.I., Rautschka, M., Sanz, F.: From SNPs to pathways: integration of functional effect of sequence variations on models of cell signalling pathways. BMC Bioinform. **10**(Suppl 8), S6 (2009)

8. Çakir, T.: Reporter pathway analysis from transcriptome data: metabolite-centric versus reaction-centric approach. Sci. Rep. **5**(May), 1–10 (2015)

9. David, C., et al.: The reactome pathway knowledgebase. Nucleic Acids Res. **42**(D1), D472–D477 (2014)

10. Demir, E., et al.: The BioPAX community standard for pathway data sharing. Nat. Biotechnol. **28**(9), 935–942 (2010)

11. Cerami, E.G., et al.: Pathway commons, a web resource for biological pathway data. Nucleic Acids Res. **39**(Database issue), D685–D690 (2011)

12. Sherry, S.T.: dbSNP: the NCBI database of genetic variation. Nucleic Acids Res. **29**(1), 308–311 (2001)

13. Landrum, M.J., et al.: ClinVar: public archive of interpretations of clinically relevant variants. Nucleic Acids Res. **44**(D1), D862–D868 (2016)

14. Li, Y., et al.: BJ-TSA-9, a novel human tumor-specific gene, has potential as a biomarker of lung cancer. Neoplasia **7**(12), 1073–1080 (2005)

15. Zhang, W., Fan, J., Chen, Q., Lei, C., Qiao, B., Liu, Q.: SPP1 and AGER as potential prognostic biomarkers for lung adenocarcinoma. Oncol. Lett. **15**(5), 7028–7036 (2018)

Integrated Semantic Model for Complex Disease Network

Junho Park, Sungkwon Yang, and Hong-Gee Kim[(✉)]

Biomedical Knowledge Engineering Laboratory, Seoul National University,
Seoul, Korea
{naon, sungkwon.yang, hgkim}@snu.ac.kr

Abstract. To understand biological phenomena, biologists have identified the interactions between biological molecules in vivo. Until recently, all of the unique and interactive information of such molecules has been built into a database and made available online. Among them, there was an effort to understand the relationship of molecules based on biological pathways, and a standard model called BioPAX was made to enable interchange and operation of data. In particular, Pathway Commons integrates other biological data besides biological pathways using BioPAX. We are interested in identifying the molecular mechanisms of disease and recommending drugs for treatment. In addition to data provided by Pathway Commons, additional disease and drug data was added to be used in various analysis. We extended the model to express the data that BioPAX could not cover and converted all the data to RDF based on the model. We integrate and present diverse biological data using semantic technologies from the perspective of representing disease networks. We hope that this information will aid in a deeper understanding of disease and drug recommendations.

Keywords: Schema modelling · Knowledge representation
Heterogeneous data integration

1 Introduction

Recently, as technologies for obtaining omics data of various kinds of organisms including genomes have been rapidly developed, the infrastructure of biomedical informatics has been developed along with the analysis capability for analysis. Algorithm development and statistical analysis are very important in this area, but interpreting the biological significance of phenomena is also becoming increasingly important. Previously, the work was done by biologists' knowledge and insights, but we now expect the machine to draw automated hypotheses and conclusions based on the data we have accumulated. Because of the emergence of informatics research methodologies in biology, each group of researchers is choosing a strategy to digitize various biological data that can be used as the basis for the research, and to establish and share an open database. A typical example of a database in which unique information such as genes and proteins corresponding to biological entities are stored is NCBI gene [1], which shares genetic information with genetic information, and

© Springer Nature Switzerland AG 2018
R. Ichise et al. (Eds.): JIST 2018, LNCS 11341, pp. 410–417, 2018.
https://doi.org/10.1007/978-3-030-04284-4_28

UniProt [2], which provides comprehensive information on proteins. There are also many databases of biological entities.

Biological phenomena are believed to be fundamentally based on interactions between molecules in vivo, and biologists have sought to elucidate their interactions to understand this phenomenon. An example is the steady increase in Protein-Protein Interaction (PPI) data, which is the interaction of proteins that actually take on various functions. There has also been an effort to understand the relationship of molecules through a biological pathway, which refers to a sequence of activities of molecules that produce specific changes or materials within a cell. These biological pathway data have been built into KEGG [3], Reactome [4], and WikiPathways [5] databases and have been used in several research methodologies. In this way, not only the unique information of biological entities but also the interaction information is constructed and released as a database, so that we can access it.

Although data is growing rapidly, heterogeneous data have been created and stored independently of each other. The semantic web technology is contributing to securing the connection between these data. Gene ontology [6] is one of the most utilized for the connection in bioinformatics. Semantic Web technology is also used to create standard data formats for each various data and generate and store data. A standard format such as PSI-MI [7] for representing PPI is representative.

We noted here a standard model for expressing a biological pathway called Bio-PAX [8]. This is because, in order to link information between biomolecules, it is most likely that each information can be linked when a biological pathway is the center. BioPAX is a standard format created through a consortium, built to enable interchange and operation of pathway data originally built into other databases. In addition to this, Pathway Commons [9] provides an integrated approach to biological pathways and other related biological data.

Personalized medicine is an important issue in the medical and biotechnological fields. This is because a technical environment for acquiring various omics data including each individual's genome can be obtained more easily. We are also interested in identifying the causes of disease in individual patients, studying molecular mechanisms of disease, and recommending drugs for treatment. In order to study these phenomena, we will add data related to diseases and drugs in addition to the data provided by Pathway Commons. But for our research, the data on which Pathway Commons is based is not enough. We extended that model to represent the necessary data that BioPAX could not cover, and we actually converted and integrated the data into RDF based on the model. We try to integrate and present diverse biological data using semantic technologies from the perspective of representing disease networks.

2   Problem Setting

Here we describe our research objectives and the data we need.

First, we want to help understanding by giving the context of disease to the network between biological entities. The interactions of molecules in vivo are fairly diverse, complex, and extensible. These networks are merely empty datasets that are hardly biologically meaningful without a specific context. We want to construct a network between the individuals that cause the disease or those that are caused to interact from the disease by putting the view 'disease' here.

Second, in recent years, whole genome sequencing and exome sequencing research methodologies have been emerging that identify single nucleotide polymorphisms (SNPs) that differ in genome compared to the reference for each patient group. We therefore provide information on the interaction of SNP units of data, rather than disease related gene units, with more detailed information, and thus provide a basis for future patient-specific network analysis.

Third, one of the ultimate goals of our research is to suggest candidates for regulators that can restore normally in vivo intermolecular networks related to disease. This is expected to help develop new drugs or design new uses for existing drugs. Therefore, in addition to the interactions between drugs and genes, it is necessary to collectively understand the relationship between drug interactions, drugs and side effects.

In addition to the integrated data of the biological entities currently provided by Pathway Commons, the data we need for the above purposes are the following additional data (see Table 1). Disease-gene Association, Disease-SNP association, Drug-Drug Interaction, and Drug-side effects are related information about disease and drug. Obviously, the BioPAX model has limitations in expressing other data beyond the biological pathway and its constituent elements.

Table 1. Data provided by pathway commons and data we need in addition.

Data type	Included in pathway commons	Source database
Gene (as reference data)	**No**	**NCBI gene**
Protein (as reference data)	Yes	UniProt
Biological Pathway	Yes	KEGG, Reactome, Wikipathways
microRNA-Gene Interaction	Yes	miRTarBase
Drug-Gene Interaction	Yes	Drugbank
Protein-Protein Interaction	Yes	IntAct
Disease-Gene Association	**No**	**DisGeNET**
Disease-SNP Association	**No**	**DisGeNET**
Drug-Drug Association	**No**	**Drugbank**
Drug-side effects Association	**No**	**SIDER**

3   Expanded Model: BioPAX+

We modified the latest version of the BioPAX level 3 model to include the above information. It is named BioPAX+. The newly added representative classes and their rationale are described below (Fig. 1).

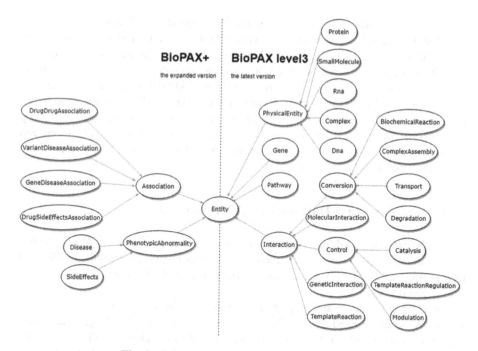

Fig. 1. Scheme of entity classes from BioPAX+.

Phenotypic Abnormality: A subclass of Entity, a superclass of Disease and Side-Effects. Each Disease and SideEffects data comes from their source databases, Dis-GeNET [10] and SIDER [11], and each database uses UMLS [12] and MedDRA [13] terms independently to distinguish these data. Because these phenomena are abstract relative to other classes handled within BioPAX, they cannot belong to such classes and are created as direct subclasses of Entity. Although the dictionary definitions of Disease and Side effects are distinct, the hierarchical relationship between these concepts is not clear. Therefore, the concept of phenotypic abnormality, which is derived from Human Phenotype Ontology (HPO) [14], is set as a superclass. We clarify the terminology confusion here in advance. The phenotype by property for expressing GeneticInteraction in BioPAX and its object is PhenotypeVocabulary but this phenotype are the terms for expressing such as growth rate and viability of a cell in the experimental situation. Therefore, it is different from the phenotype of the living body that we want to express.

Association: The intrinsic goal of BioPAX is to represent the relationship between biomolecules, and therefore, in this model's view, an atomic class is Interaction. Interaction has several subclasses to represent various chemical reactions. However, the entities we add this time, the disease and side effects, are not directly related to the layer for representing the molecular activity involved in the event in BioPAX. We have added the Association class instead of the term Interaction, which is used in BioPAX, since we are meant to indicate that there is a relationship in the layers above them. There are subclasses in the Association class according to the information of the newly added database. Information on the relationship between the disease and the genes considered to be related to the disease corresponds to the GeneDisease Association class and has assigned to the VariantDisease Association information on the relationship between the disease and the DNA Variant, including the SNPs considered to be related to the disease. Information on the relationship between the drug and its side effects was added to the Drug-Side Effects Association. Finally, a relationship, commonly referred to as Drug-Drug Interaction, refers to an increase or decrease in efficacy when two or more drugs are used and not to a direct chemical interaction between drugs. So we decided to replace the Interaction with the expression "Association" and added the Drug-Drug Association class.

4 Converting Raw Data to BioPAX+ Format

Under the extended model above, the raw data in the source database has been converted into RDF instances through class and property mapping, respectively. We will look at some of the notable points in this process here and illustrate an example of the conversion process.

First, we used classes and properties that existed in the original model but were not in use. We actually used the DnaReference to implement the NCBI gene data as a reference. Genes involved in various interactions and associations are all implemented as individual instances. These genes now have a common reference link that makes it much easier to track how many relationships they are involved in when selecting a gene. The link between the DnaReference and ProteinReference is also possible, allowing the flow of information to be understood without being limited to the molecular forms of nucleic acids and proteins.

Second, we need to think deeply about the problem of assigning the DNA variant information to which class. There are Dna, DnaReference, DnaRegion, and DnaRegionReference classes for representing DNA information in BioPAX model. Since DNA variant information, such as SNPs, was never attempted to be translated into BioPAX, we actually tried various modeling, including adding SNP classes. Finally, we reiterated our intention to develop BioPAX to prevent information collision or unnecessary additions, assign SNP information to the Dna class, and express the information using various properties.

Third, there is a problem with Drug. In Pathway Commons, the Drug has already been converted to the Smallmolecule class. However, when considering the unique function of regulating the biological response, there is room for doubt as to whether the transformation that made the drug concept loss was the best while converting the drug information to Smallmolecule. In addition, drug information provided by Drugbank [15] includes about 10% of macromolecule called biologic (biotech), but all of them are converted to Smallmolecule. In order to avoid duplication, the study followed the work transformed by the existing Pathway Commons on drugs. However, we think that we should at least clarify the distinction between drug information in the conversion process and do not draw a single class of Smallmolecule. From the perspective of drug recommendations that present some macromolecule as a new drug, it is necessary to further modify the model of this conversion part at present.

The following is an example of the data conversion process (Fig. 2).

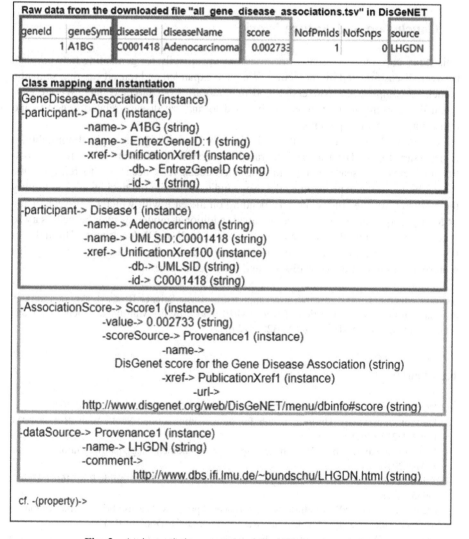

Raw data from the downloaded file "all_gene_disease_associations.tsv" in DisGeNET

geneId	geneSymb	diseaseId	diseaseName	score	NofPmIds	NofSnps	source
1	A1BG	C0001418	Adenocarcinoma	0.002733	1	0	LHGDN

Class mapping and Instantiation

```
GeneDiseaseAssociation1 (instance)
-participant-> Dna1 (instance)
            -name-> A1BG (string)
            -name-> EntrezGeneID:1 (string)
            -xref-> UnificationXref1 (instance)
                    -db-> EntrezGeneID (string)
                    -id-> 1 (string)
```

```
-participant-> Disease1 (instance)
            -name-> Adenocarcinoma (string)
            -name-> UMLSID:C0001418 (string)
            -xref-> UnificationXref100 (instance)
                    -db-> UMLSID (string)
                    -id-> C0001418 (string)
```

```
-AssociationScore-> Score1 (instance)
                -value-> 0.002733 (string)
                -scoreSource-> Provenance1 (instance)
                        -name->
                DisGenet score for the Gene Disease Association (string)
                        -xref-> PublicationXref1 (instance)
                        -url->
        http://www.disgenet.org/web/DisGeNET/menu/dbinfo#score (string)
```

```
-dataSource-> Provenance1 (instance)
        -name-> LHGDN (string)
        -comment->
                http://www.dbs.ifi.lmu.de/~bundschu/LHGDN.html (string)
```

```
cf. -(property)->
```

Fig. 2. An instantiation example of GeneDiseaseAssociation.

The amount of data actually transformed through the above process is as follows. Added 1,988,050 triples for the DnaReference transformation of the NCBI gene, and 11,222,400 and 2,982,980 triples for the conversion of GeneDiseaseAssociation and VariantDiseaseAssociation in DisGeNET, respectively. There are 22,554 triples added with respect to the DrugDrugAssociation of Drugbank, and 6,196,680 triples added with respect to Drug-Side Effects Association in SIDER. So, the total number of triple data we added in our work is 22,257,664.

5   Conclusion and Future Work

This study introduces a research methodology specifically for generating network data between disease-related biomolecules. We have expanded and reused existing semantic models to complete the conversion and integration of our targeted data. We are confident that current network data can be used to analyze disease-related genomic and transcriptomic data in patients.

Future work needs are as follows. In the sub-concept of phenotypic abnormality, it is necessary to use HPO as an integrated expression to eliminate the confusing distinction between disease, symptom and side-effects. It is necessary to reinforce the logical basis for the expression of the drug, and to reconcile the data level or to modify the modeling for the consistency. Depending on the ease with which ChIP-sequencing or Methyl-sequencing data can be obtained, additional modeling may be necessary to account for the individual epigenomic factors as well as DNA variants. Through our research, we hope to develop into an integrated data model and data repository that represents biological data for disease and drug development.

Acknowledgement. This research was supported by Basic Science Research Program through the National Research Foundation of Korea(NRF) funded by the Ministry of Science, ICT and future Planning (No. NRF-2017R1A2B2008729).

References

1. NCBI gene Homepage. https://www.ncbi.nlm.nih.gov/gene. Accessed 8 Aug 2018
2. UniProt Consortium: UniProt: a hub for protein information. Nucl. Acids Res. **43**(D1), D204–D212 (2015)
3. KEGG Pathway Database Homepage. https://www.genome.jp/kegg/pathway.html. Accessed 8 Aug 2018
4. Fabregat, A., et al.: The reactome pathway knowledgebase. Nucl. Acids Res. **46**(4), D649–D655 (2018)
5. Slenter, D.N., et al.: WikiPathways: a multifaceted pathway database bridging metabolomics to other omics research. Nucl. Acids Res. **46**(D1), D661–D667 (2017)
6. The Gene Ontology Consortium: Expansion of the gene ontology knowledgebase and resources. Nucl. Acids Res. **45**(D1), D331–D338 (2017)
7. HUPO Proteomics Standard Initiative, Molecular Interactions. http://www.psidev.info/groups/molecular-interactions. Accessed 8 Aug 2018
8. Emek, D., et al.: BioPAX – a community standard for pathway data sharing. Nat. Biotechnol. **28**(9), 935–942 (2010)
9. Ethan, G.C., et al.: Pathway commons, a web resource for biological pathway data. Nucl. Acids Res. **39**(D1), D685–D690 (2011)
10. Piñero, J., et al.: DisGeNET: a comprehensive platform integrating information on human disease-associated genes and variants. Nucl. Acids Res. **45**(D1), D833–D839 (2017)

11. Kuhn, M., et al.: The SIDER database of drugs and side effects. Nucl. Acids Res. **44**(D1), D1075–D1079 (2016)
12. Bodenreider, O.: The unified medical language system (UMLS): integrating biomedical terminology. Nucl. Acids Res. **32**(D1), D267–D270 (2004)
13. MedDRA Homepage. https://www.meddra.org. Accessed 8 Aug 2018
14. Robinson, P.N., et al.: The human phenotype ontology: a tool for annotating and analyzing human hereditary disease. Am. J. Hum. Genet. **83**(5), 610–615 (2008)
15. Wishart, D.S., et al.: DrugBank 5.0: a major update to the DrugBank database for 2018. Nucl. Acids Res. **46**(D1), D1074–D1082 (2018)

Implementing LOD Surfer as a Search System for the Annotation of Multiple Protein Sequence Alignment

Atsuko Yamaguchi[1(✉)] and Hiroyuki Toh[2]

[1] Database Center for Life Science (DBCLS),
Research Organization of Information and Systems (ROIS),
178-4-4 Wakashiba, Kashiwa, Chiba 277-0871, Japan
atsuko@dbcls.rois.ac.jp

[2] Department of Biomedical Chemistry, School of Science and Technology,
Kwansei Gakuin University,
2-1 Gakuen, Sanda, Hyogo 669-1337, Japan

Abstract. Many life science databases have been provided as Linked Open Data (LOD). To promote the utilization of these databases, we had developed a method that can be referred to as LOD Surfer, that employed federated query search along a path of class–class relationships. In this study, we developed a specified version of the LOD Surfer for the annotation of multiple protein sequence alignment. The system comprised a web application programming interface (API) and a client system for the API. The web API provides a list of classes, and a list of paths between the classes that are specified by a user. The client presents the list of classes and the list of paths obtained from the API and assists a user in selecting classes and paths to acquire the required annotation of proteins. Additionally, the client system generates SPARQL queries to execute a federated query search for a selected path. During the development of the system, we can observe that (1) the client system should display some instances with human readable information because class selection is not an easy task for biological researchers, and (2) it is preferable that the client system stores paths that are selected by a user for reuse by other users because path selection may be time consuming at times and because the selected paths may be valuable for other researchers.

Keywords: Linked Open Data · Class-class relationships
Multiple protein sequence alignment
Database integration in life sciences

1 Introduction

In recent advances of experimental technology, enormous amount of life science data has been accumulated rapidly from a variety of biological fields. Under the situation, knowledge extraction through the integration of such data has

© Springer Nature Switzerland AG 2018
R. Ichise et al. (Eds.): JIST 2018, LNCS 11341, pp. 418–426, 2018.
https://doi.org/10.1007/978-3-030-04284-4_29

become an urgent task in the life sciences. However, not only the size but also the heterogeneity of the biological data have inhibited the integration. Linked Open Data (LOD) is currently utilized to integrate various types of data. In such trend, many life science databases are also published as LOD. An important feature of LOD is to provide an efficient mechanism for linking different datasets one another. It enables the users to mash-up different data, and new innovations are expected through the integration of various datasets [1]. However, users of databases including experimental biologists are not always familiar with the semantic web technologies, and it would be difficult for them to obtain required data from LOD by writing a SPARQL query. Therefore, to utilize information from LOD for study in life sciences effectively, a method to extract data from multiple SPARQL endpoints according to user requirements is strongly needed.

Semantics can be translated based on a sequence of links across different classes of data. Therefore, semantics can be obtained by traversing the paths of the class–class relationships in the LOD. While some studies have investigated methods, such as RelFinder [2], to find the paths between resources in LOD, such methods face difficulties in obtaining paths from among large numbers of instances in classes that are often obtained from experimental results in the life sciences research. Therefore, our approach focuses on the paths of class–class relationships. Such relationships can provide a foundation for semantics in resource description framework (RDF) databases.

Based on this approach, a search system called LOD Surfer has been proposed in a previous study [3] for extracting data by traversing LOD based on class-class relationships over various life science SPARQL endpoints. In this study, we developed a specialized version of LOD Surfer as a search system for the annotation of proteins from LOD for a viewer of multiple protein sequence alignment (MPSA) in case of a large number of proteins. By focusing on a specific type of data, the search method could be improved to be more effective and more efficient. During the implementation and the application, we discovered some problems which should be solved to make the system usable for biological researchers. The possible solutions of the problems are discussed in Sect. 3.

2 ASHViewer

Comparison of homologous sequences is a basic step for computational analysis of proteins. For a set of amino acid sequences derived from common ancestry, the residue-to-residue correspondence is made for all the sequences under consideration. The operation or the product of the operation is called MPSA, which can be used for structure modeling, prediction of active sites, similarity search, construction of phylogenetic tree, etc. Therefore, various tools for MPSA have been developed [4,5]. Enormous amount of sequences have been rapidly accumulated by recent development of sequencing technologies. The increase of sequences has made it difficult to analyze the alignment with the user-interactive manner. One of the problems is the difficulty in visual inspection of the sequences due to the large number. The other is the difficulty in annotation. To solve the problems, we have worked on developing an alignment viewer that can be referred to as ASHViewer. To solve the first problem, the alignment is coarse-grained based on the phylogenetic tree. The tree is divided into a small number of subtrees based on the tree topology. A coarse-grained tree and consensus alignments corresponding to the deployed nodes in the tree are shown in the upper left and upper right subpanels in the main panel of the ASHViewer (see Fig. 1). The resolution of the coarse-grained alignment can be changed by clicking a node of a coarse-grained tree. By clicking a node, the corresponding subtree is deployed or collapsed. Then, the alignment is expanded or compressed linked with the operation. By repeating the operation, a user can identify the level of the resolution that is convenient for the user's object.

The second problem is caused by the necessity of various information for annotation associated with the proteins, such as gene product properties like Gene Ontology (GO) terms, active sites, and chemical compounds that interact with the proteins. The required information is expected to

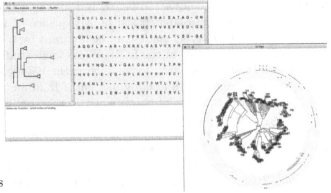

Fig. 1. The main panel of ASHViewer (upper left) and a panel to show annotations obtained from LOD (lower right).

be different among users because of the difference in their objectives for the comparative analyses. To obtain the related data of proteins from multiple datasets in the form of annotation to proteins in a flexible manner, we decided to extract the required information from the LOD datasets. As the first prototype version of ASHViewer, we prepared a text area to input a SPARQL query to extract data from LOD. However, in practice, it is very difficult for biologists to write a SPARQL query based on their interests. Additionally, it is also difficult to find appropriate SPARQL endpoints for a SPARQL query because a relation between the protein and required data may be distributed over the web. Therefore, we introduced a search system that can be referred to as LOD Surfer into ASHViewer, as described in Sect. 3, to support data extraction from LOD for users who are unfamiliar with various semantic web technologies such as RDF and SPARQL.

3 Implementation of LOD Surfer to ASHViewer

A class-class relationship from class c_1 to class c_2 with respect to property p indicates that there is a triple (s, p, o) such that s and o are the instances of

c_1 and c_2, respectively. The LOD Surfer is a search system that discovers data along the paths of class-class relationships over the LOD provided by different SPARQL endpoints. A user can interactively obtain the required data from SPARQL endpoints without writing a SPARQL query by selecting the input and output classes and a path between the two classes. To make this possible, we use two existing semantic web technologies for LOD Surfer. One of the technologies is SPARQL Builder Metadata (SBM) that describes a data schema for each SPARQL endpoint [6]. We collected SBM for 73 datasets and constructed a merged class graph using the collected SBM. A merged class graph is a directed labeled multigraph whose nodes and edges correspond to classes that appear in datasets and class-class relationships, respectively. Using the graph, our system can efficiently compute the paths between classes across two or more datasets. The other technology is YummyData [7] that provides the reliability measures for SPARQL endpoints in the life sciences domain, such as service stability, frequency of update, metadata richness, conformity with Linked Data principles, and response time for a query. By filtering unreliable SPARQL endpoints using information from the YummyData API, LOD Surfer can stably obtain the required data from LOD.

We initially implemented a web API for LOD Surfer as a preliminary trial using the two aforementioned technologies. This enabled flexible data acquisition using a federated SPARQL query from multiple SPARQL endpoints for a user by selecting two classes and paths between the classes. Further, we implemented functions of the web API on ASHViewer. However, we observed that it was still difficult for biologists to select two classes and a path between the classes because it was not easy for them to determine (1) the class to which an ID of some database belonged, and (2) the path with which a user can obtain the required data. To address these issues, we improved our system by adding a specified client system to the architecture of ASHViewer to enable biologists to easily select appropriate classes and paths. In this section, we explain the web API called LOD Surfer API and the client system called PSurfer, which are implemented on ASHViewer, as a specified version of LOD Surfer for the annotation of MPSA.

3.1 LOD Surfer API

The LOD Surfer API is a web API designed to easily develop a search system that can be generally used in the life sciences domain. Using this API, a list of SPARQL endpoints, a list of classes, a list of classes reachable using paths from a given class, and paths between two given classes can be obtained in JSON format using a simple HTTP GET request. We designed the LOD Surfer API to provide the following functions:

- /eplist
  outputs a list of SPARQL endpoints as a JSON array.
- /clist?class1 = class URI
  outputs a list of classes reachable from class1 as a JSON array. If the parameter class1 is omitted, all classes can be listed.

– /path/?class1 = class1&class2 = class2

    outputs a list of paths from class1 to class2 as a JSON array. Each path in the list can be expressed as a JSON object.

From the SBM collected by a crawler, a merged class graph with 14147 nodes can be constructed. Further, the connected components, that are maximal sets of nodes such that each pair of nodes in the same set is connected by a path, are computed for the merged class graph in advance. Our system can efficiently compute the results of this web API using the merged class graph and connected components. For example, a list of classes reachable from a certain class c can be instantly obtained as a set of nodes in the connected component including c, because a path of class-class relationships exists if and only if two classes are in the same connected component. The LOD Surfer API is available for trial at http://lodsurfer.dbcls.jp/api/. For example, a user can obtain a list of classes at http://lodsurfer.dbcls.jp/api/clist. The code for this web API is available at https://github.com/LODSurfer/lodsurfer-api.

3.2   PSurfer: Client System for Protein Annotation

We observe that it is not easy for ordinary biologists to select an input class including IDs of proteins in MPSA, an output class with the required information related to the proteins in MPSA, and a path from an input class to an output class so that a SPARQL query automatically generated from the path can retrieve the required data. To assist a user in selecting the input and output classes and a path for the annotation of MPSA results, we developed a system that can be referred to as PSurfer. PSurfer comprises a client system of LOD Surfer API, a storage system of selected paths, and a federated search system for LOD. While the LOD Surfer API is designed for general use in life sciences, PSurfer is basically designed for MPSA annotation tools such as ASHViewer. Therefore, the variety of possible input classed can be limited because the input classes are restricted to those related to proteins. We limited the input class candidate to two classes. One is a class `<http://purl.uniprot.org/core/Protein>` whose instances are entities of UniProt, which is the largest protein sequence database. The other is a class `<https://rdf.wwpdb.org/schema/pdbx-v50.owl#datablock>` whose instances are entities of wwPDB, which is an information repository related to the three-dimensional structures of proteins. Further, it is easy to determine whether an ID is a UniProt ID or wwPDB ID because UniProt IDs comprise six or 10 alphanumerical characters and wwPDB IDs comprise four characters, such that the first character is a numerical character and the remaining three are alphanumerical characters.

To support biologists in selecting an output class, we adopted a method that displayed some examples of instances for a candidate of output classes. Further, we denote `http://purl.uniprot.org/core` by `up:`. For example, instances such as `<http://purl.uniprot.org/taxonomy/108931>` and `<http://purl.uniprot.org/taxonomy/10090>` for the class `up:Taxon` are displayed Additionally, some literals related to various instances are depicted for enhancing human-readability. For the instance <http://purl.uniprot.org/taxonomy/10090> of the class up:Taxon, by using links with the properties up:scientificName and up:commonName, "Mus musculus" and "Mouse" are displayed. To do so, PSurfer should know a set of properties linked to human readable literals, such as up:scientificName and up:commonName for each candidate class of the output class. However, SBM does not include such information. Therefore, a set of properties to exhibit the human-readable information for each class should be given to PSurfer. We manually prepared sets of properties for some major classes and used rdfs:label and its subproperties for other classes.

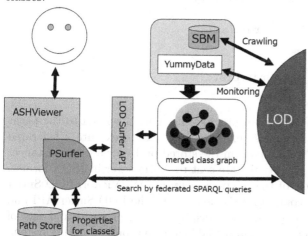

Similarly, PSurfer exhibits the examples of the output of the SPARQL query that is generated from the path to assist a user in selecting a path from an input class to an output class. To denote examples, some instances of the input class are required. Therefore, PSurfer samples some proteins from MPSA, executes a SPARQL

Fig. 2. An overview of the specified version of LOD Surfer for MPSA.

query for the samples, and exhibits the output for the query as examples. Using the sets of properties for classes, PSurfer can show human-readable information for each resulting URL of the output. This is a very effective manner for a user who is unfamiliar with semantic web technologies to semantically capture a path. This is because a user can imagine the output obtained from the path. However, it sometimes requires a large amount of time to execute federated SPARQL query search to show human readable information for each path. Therefore, path selection incurs a relatively high cost. Further, we abandoned the path selection function from ASHViewer GUI. We adopted a method to prepare the function in PSurfer GUI separately from ASHViewer instead. By using the PSurfer GUI, a user can select a path and accumulate the selected paths. The accumulated paths are represented in RDF as follows:

```
@base <http://sparqlbuilder.org/lodsurfer/core/>.
@prefix ldpath:<http://sparqlbuilder.org/lodsurfer/path/>.

ldpath:{id} rdfs:label path name?;
            rdf:type <Path>;
            <description> description for this path?;
            <inputClass> <classURI of input class>;
            <outputClass> <classURI of output class>;
            <classList> ldpath:{id}/class/0;
            <propList> idpath:{id}/prop/0.

ldpath:{id}/class/0 rdf:type rdf:List;
...

ldpath:{id}/prop/0 rdf:type rdf:List;
...
```

For the stored paths, PSurfer can provide information related to the paths in Turtle or JSON-LD. PSurfer also exhibits functions to execute a federated SPARQL query generated from a path in the stored paths for a set of instances of the input class. Further, the results are sent to ASHViewer in JSON format. Figure 2 depicts an overview of the relations between ASHViewer, LOD Surfer API and PSurfer. PSurfer connects ASHViewer with the LOD Surfer API and supports a user with supplemental data such as a store of paths and sets of properties for classes to provide human readable information. Using this system, a user of ASHViewer can obtain various type of annotations from LOD for the large number of aligned proteins to extract novel knowledge from the alignment.

4   Discussion

Currently living organisms are considered to have derived from a common ancestral organisms. In other words, the organisms and the genetic materials are evolutionary related. Therefore, comparative studies of the objects sharing a common ancestry to discuss the similarity and the difference has been used as an effective way to extract knowledge from existing data. Comparison of proteins based on a multiple sequence alignment is a representative method of such studies. Annotations of the objects under comparison are important for the discussion about the similarity and the difference among the objects. Different type of annotations are available at different databases. When the databases provides the annotation information as LOD, the data can be integrated with the semantic web technologies. In the case of proteins, various types of annotations such as gene ontology, source organisms, interacting compounds, are available. ASHViewer has been developed as a comparative tool to analyze proteins with multiple alignment. In this study, we introduced the PSurfer into the ASHViewer to accelerate the analysis with the annotation information.

However, while applying semantic web technologies to ASHViewer that is designed for biologists, we are confronted with difficulties related to human readability in case of classes and class-class relationships. To solve this problem, we built a set of properties for each class to display human-readable information. Although rdfs:label is defined as a property that is used to provide a human-readable version of the name of a resource, it exhibits several subproperties of rdfs:label at time. Further, the most suitable property to provide human-readable label is dependent on the datasets. Therefore, we manually prepared a set of properties for each class. However, we belive that the process to select properties can be automated if the set is considerable larger.

We stored selected paths for reuse. If the number of paths increases, we may be able to analyze the paths and propose a method for ranking the paths that can be used to support a user for selecting a path to obtain the required data.

5   Conclusion

In this study, we developed LOD Surfer API and PSurfer which is a specialized version of LOD Surfer for MPSA. These systems are implemented into ASHViewer, which is a viewer of MPSA for a large number of proteins. The LOD Surfer API provides a list of classes and paths between two classes using the SBM collected from SPARQL endpoints of the life sciences databases. PSurfer connects LOD Surfer API with ASHViewer. PSurfer obtains the information of classes and paths from the LOD Surfer API, and provides human-readable information. Additionally, PSurfer stores the paths selected by a user for a SPARQL query so that the result can be used for the annotation of proteins of MPSA.

Although PSurfer is a specified system of an MPSA viewer, some points such as a store of paths are applicable to general life science tools. Therefore, we would like to apply these points to improve LOD Surfer so as to enhance its usability for biological researchers.

Acknowledgments. The authors would thank members of LOD Surfer project including Kouji Kozaki, Osaka University, Norio Kobayashi and Hiroshi Masuya, RIKEN, and Yasunori Yamamoto, DBCLS, for valuable discussion. This work was supported by JSPS KAKENHI grant numbers 17K00434 and by the National Bioscience Database Center (NBDC) of the Japan Science and Technology Agency (JST).

References

1. Heath, T., Bizer, C.: Linked Data: Evolving the Web into a Global Data Space. Synthesis Lectures on the Semantic Web: Theory and Technology, 1st edn., vol. 1, no. 1, pp. 1–136. Morgan & Claypool (2011)
2. Heim, P., Hellmann, S., Lehmann, J., Lohmann, S., Stegemann, T.: RelFinder: revealing relationships in RDF knowledge bases. In: Chua, T.-S., Kompatsiaris, Y., Mérialdo, B., Haas, W., Thallinger, G., Bailer, W. (eds.) SAMT 2009. LNCS, vol. 5887, pp. 182–187. Springer, Heidelberg (2009). https://doi.org/10.1007/978-3-642-10543-2_21

3. Yamaguchi, A., Kozaki, K., Yamamoto, Y., Masuya, H., Kobayashi, N.: Semantic graph analysis for federated LOD surfing in life sciences. In: Wang, Z., Turhan, A.-Y., Wang, K., Zhang, X. (eds.) JIST 2017. LNCS, vol. 10675, pp. 268–276. Springer, Cham (2017). https://doi.org/10.1007/978-3-319-70682-5_18

4. Larkin, M.A., et al.: Clustal W and Clustal X version 2.0. Bioinformatics **23**(21), 2947–2948 (2007)

5. Nakamura, T., Yamada, K.D., Tomii, K., Katoh, K.: Parallelization of MAFFT for large-scale multiple sequence alignments. Bioinformatics **34**(14), 2490–2492 (2018)

6. Yamaguchi, A., Kozaki, K., Lenz, K., Yamamoto, Y., Masuya, H., Kobayashi, N.: Semantic data acquisition by traversing class–class relationships over linked open data. In: Li, Y.-F., et al. (eds.) JIST 2016. LNCS, vol. 10055, pp. 136–151. Springer, Cham (2016). https://doi.org/10.1007/978-3-319-50112-3_11

7. Yamamoto, Y., Yamaguchi, A., Splendiani, A.: YummyData: providing high-quality open life science data. Database, **2018** (2018). https://doi.org/10.1093/database/bay022

Author Index

Printed in the United States
By Bookmasters